STATE COLLAPSE IN
SOUTH-EASTERN EUROPE

CENTRAL EUROPEAN STUDIES

Charles W. Ingrao, senior editor
Gary B. Cohen, editor

State Collapse in South-Eastern Europe:
New Perspectives on Yugoslavia's Disintegration

Edited by Lenard J. Cohen and
Jasna Dragović-Soso

Purdue University Press
West Lafayette, Indiana

Printed in the United States of America.

ISBN 978-1-55753-460-6

Library of Congress Cataloging-in-Publication Data
State collapse in South-eastern Europe : new perspectives on Yugoslavia's
disintegration / edited by Lenard J. Cohen and Jasna Dragović-Soso.
    p. cm. -- (Central European studies)
  Includes bibliographical references and index.
  ISBN 978-1-55753-460-6 (alk. paper)
  1. Yugoslavia--History--1918-1945. 2. Yugoslavia--History--1945-1980. 3. Nationalism--Yugoslavia.
  4. Europe--Politics and government--1989- I. Cohen, Lenard J. II.
Dragović-Soso, Jasna.
  DR1298.S75 2007
  949.702--dc22
                                      2007004052

To Dennison Rusinow (1930–2004)
A fine man, wonderful colleague,
and distinguished scholar.

Contents

ACKNOWLEDGMENTS

As a project involving fifteen scholars based in several countries of Europe and North America, this book greatly benefited from the ability of most participants to meet and discuss their contributions in London in June 2004. The conference that was held on this occasion, "Rethinking the Dissolution of Yugoslavia," was hosted by the School of Slavonic and East European Studies and received generous funding from the British Academy, the Elisabeth Barker Fund, the British Association for Central and Eastern Europe, the Foreign and Commonwealth Office and the Politics Department of Goldsmiths College, University of London. We thank all these institutions for their support. It certainly made our work on this volume more productive and more fun.

We would also like to thank a number of individuals who helped us in various ways in the course of this project: Wendy Bracewell, Nevenka Martin, Vesna Popovski and Peter Siani-Davies at the School of Slavonic and East European Studies for all their help with the London conference; John Allcock, Sumantra Bose, Richard Clogg, Dejan Djokić, Ger Duijzings, James Gow, Zoran Milutinović, David Norris, Raju Thomas and Robert Thomas for serving as chairs and discussants of the chapters that were presented at the conference; Dame Pauline Neville-Jones, Chairman of QuinetiQ Group Plc., former Political Director in the Foreign and Commonwealth Office and leader of the British delegation to the Dayton Peace Conference on Bosnia in 1995, for her keynote speech on this occasion; Carl Levy, Head of the Politics Department at Goldsmiths, for his support for a brand new colleague and his interest in her project; Charles Ingrao and Tom Emmert from the Scholars' Initiative for providing the context in which the co-editors were able to meet and develop the idea for the book; and Andrea Balogh and Dragan Pucar for their help with the final editing of the volume.

Finally, we must also express our gratitude to Tito Marzio Soso and Terri Cohen, who have been a great source of support and encouragement to us over the course of this project. Without their help and the indulgence of Mina and Alessia Soso, and Benjamin and Mark Nudel while we were spending time away from them, this book would not have been possible.

Jasna Dragović-Soso and Lenard J. Cohen
London and Victoria, August 2006

SERIES EDITOR'S FOREWORD

AT the beginning of June 2002, I received a telephone call from Lenard Cohen. At the time, Lenny and our colleague Jasna Dragović-Soso were co-directing a research team for the Scholars' Initiative[1] that was dedicated to examining the dissolution of Yugoslavia. In a model of understatement, he observed that "We could publish a whole book on the subject!"—rather than the mere sixty pages allotted to them—and offered to assemble a consortium of scholars for a collection devoted solely to the dissolution. As the accomplished authors of three authoritative studies[2], there was little doubt that they could do so. The only question in my mind was whether we could find a publisher for such an ambitious undertaking. After all, scholarly collections tend to have a limited audience and, all too frequently, end up as an incoherent collection of disparate chapters of uneven quality. Hence my delight when Tom Bacher, the director of Purdue University Press, readily authorized an advanced contract for the collection.

In the end, this would be no ordinary collection and certainly not an auxiliary product of a larger project. Rather, this collection stands by itself as the most definitive analysis of this catastrophic event to appear in any language. For this, we owe a debt to the editors. In their quest for the most comprehensive coverage possible, they approached well over twenty leading scholars, including many from the successor states, and several who were not associated with the Scholars' Initiative. All told, the fifteen contributors to this collection have authored more than sixty books on the subject of contemporary Yugoslavia. Nonetheless, the editors closely monitored the process by staying in continuous touch with the contributors to ensure both quality control and thematic cohesiveness, a process that generated many hundred e-mails. Indeed, by the beginning of 2004, both editors left the Scholars' Initiative to devote themselves fully to producing this collection.

Admittedly, the "turbulent process" of Yugoslavia's dissolution continues to this day. The volume preface takes note of the abortive attempt to preserve the union

---

[1] http://www.salzburgseminar.org/ihjr/index3.cfm
[2] Cohen, Lenard, *Broken Bonds: Yugoslavia's Disintegration And Balkan Politics In Transition*, Second Edition (Boulder: Westview, 1995); *Serpent in the Bosom: The Rise and Fall of Slobodan Milosevic* (Boulder: Westview, 2001); Dragović-Soso, Jasna, *Saviours of the Nation: Serbia's Intellectual Opposition and the Revival of Nationalism* (Montreal: McGill-Queen's University Press, 2003).

between Serbia and Montenegro, which formally separated in 2006. As the book goes to press, Kosovo seems poised to secede from Serbia in a process that could take years and spur new tensions in the region. A majority in Bosnia's *Republika Srpska* yearns to secede and merge with Serbia. Some Muslim Bosniaks in Sandjak, Albanians in western Macedonia, and Magyars in northern Vojvodina continue to entertain somewhat more fanciful notions of secession. Nonetheless, the immense amount of new literature will find its way into the historiography of the climactic dissolution process that preceded the outbreak of armed conflict in Slovenia, Croatia, and Bosnia.

Readers will note that the editors and contributors have dedicated this book to the memory of Dennison Rusinow. I first met Denny in 1997, shortly after assuming the editorship of the *Austrian History Yearbook*. Although I was most familiar with his work on central Europe's Habsburg legacy, it was Denny's expertise on Yugoslavia that led me to invite him to co-direct one of the Scholars' Initiative's ten research teams. Although this septuagenarian had just "retired," he readily threw himself into the project, flying to plenary meetings in Sarajevo and Edmonton and even driving on Alpine roads for ten hours straight to convene a special satellite meeting of his research team. Denny contributed not only his expertise to this joint effort, but unfailing conscientiousness and congeniality. Indeed, it was his uncommon gift for diplomacy that led me to seek his advice on several occasions as we contended with a formidable mix of competing agendas and contentious personalities, including one last telephone call to his home on the afternoon of 20 January 2004, just minutes after he had been killed by an inattentive driver. Hence our gratitude to the editors, for Denny would surely be proud of this book that we publish in his honor.

PREFACE

Socialist Yugoslavia's tumultuous dissolution during the 1990s was a quintessential case of the state failure and meltdown of communism that occurred in Eastern Europe near the end of the Cold War. Interest in the causes and features of the Yugoslav case, and its important lessons with regard to the problems of nation-building in failing states, has not abated. Granted, the fragmentation of the Yugoslav Federation into several successor states did not occur on the large territorial and demographic canvas that served as the backdrop for the disintegration of the Soviet Union. But the importance and repercussions of the Yugoslav case were accentuated by its extremely violent character, its horrific human cost, and the international community's evident confusion and helplessness in dealing with its effects. Preoccupied with a new array of post-Cold War imperatives and regional crises, observers were perplexed and to some extent politically paralyzed as they watched the relatively rapid and chaotic collapse of a state that had at least seemed, under Josip Broz Tito, to have elaborated a rather novel and admired formula for worker participation in a single-party system, multi-ethnic coexistence, and independence from the major world power blocs.[1]

Indeed, the turbulent process of Yugoslavia's dissolution would continue throughout the decade following the initial "wars of the Yugoslav succession" in Slovenia, Croatia, and Bosnia. This extended phase of state dissolution would also include substantial military conflict and violent episodes of ethnic tension in Kosovo (1999 and 2004) and in Macedonia (2001), as well as ongoing tensions from unresolved issues of state formation, such as the issue of Kosovo's "final status" (the subject of international negotiations that began in the fall of 2005 and were scheduled to resume in the fall of 2007), and the "latent dissolution" of the still-born "union" of Serbia and Montenegro (formed in 2003 with the assistance of the European Union after the termination of the Milošević-inspired rump two-republic Yugoslav Federation). In early June 2006, not long after a majority vote in a peaceful referendum, Montenegro became an independent state. Only the prospect of eventual accession to the European Union (by mid-2004 Slovenia enjoyed EU membership, but in mid-2007 Croatia was still on the cusp of admission, and talks were just beginning with the other aspirant Yugoslav successor states) seemed to portend the belated end of Titoist Yugoslavia's prolonged and agonizing process of state disintegration.

This book constitutes an effort by a group of academic specialists on South-Eastern Europe to explore the historical antecedents and the dynamic process of Yugoslavia's violent dissolution drawing upon the most recent available evidence. The volume examines both pertinent issues that can assist in broadening our understanding of the Yugoslav case, and also tries to shed light on the challenges of addressing future episodes of state fragility and failure. There are a number of important reasons for continued systematic analysis of Yugoslavia's break-up during the 1990s; some of which fall into the realm of "pure" research priorities, and others that relate to the "applied" significance of research by historians and social scientists.

For example, it remains critical to update, enhance and, when necessary, revise explanations that have already been provided for Yugoslavia's collapse. Moreover, whenever possible, only some fifteen years after the Yugoslav crisis, it is also important to fill in the "blank spots" in the historical record. In that respect, this volume supplements a rapidly evolving and highly disparate literature, which emerged as the process of state breakdown in the Balkans unfolded and will likely continue as a genre for some time to come. This volume also adds to the growing comparative body of historical scholarship which focuses on the saga of collapsed federations and failed states.

A surfeit of new evidence has become available in recent years; material that demands and supports fresh analyses and interpretations of Yugoslavia's dissolution. This relatively new evidentiary base includes—in addition to recent scholarship outside of the former Yugoslavia—the record of the still unfolding testimony and documentation provided by the judicial proceedings of the International Criminal Tribunal on the former Yugoslavia (ICTY) at The Hague, memoir literature by key actors and other participants in the Yugoslav break-up (including indicted war criminals and the children of former leaders), and studies contributed by scholars in each of the Yugoslav successor states. Indeed, one consequence of Yugoslavia's disintegration has been a battle of interpretations; a lively and at times highly acrimonious discourse regarding the facts and underlying motives for the drift toward warfare and eventual state failure that occurred in the Balkans during the late 1980s and 1990s. Both participants in the events, and current actors searching for a "usable past," have endeavored to shape the historical record and memory of what occurred. Because of the emotion stirred by the violent breakup of Yugoslavia, and also the fact that historiography, and other presentations of the recent past in school textbooks and the media, remain highly politicized in the Balkans, professional scholars from outside the region can play a useful complementary role in efforts to set the record straight.[2]

Moreover, because the role of the "memory-power nexus" has been so important in stimulating political mobilization and conflict in the Balkan region—especially by state decision-makers who utilized and manipulated inter-group antagonisms—it is especially critical to reassess the historical record in a professional and fair-minded manner. The ICTY has clearly been a crucial forum for gathering evidence relating to war crime indictments and for establishing justice on an individual case-by-case, rather than collective, basis (the important trial of Slobodan Milošević, which ended with his death in March 2006, received the most attention, but many other cases have also been adjudicated and are pending). Indeed, without the tribunal's resources and momentum, evidence this is critical to evaluating important dimensions of Yugoslavia's demise would have remained buried for many years. But judicial proceedings at The Hague are distinct from the dispassionate scholarly task of sorting and assessing historical evidence; a methodology best conducted without the selective adversarial and inquisitorial methodology utilized in a court setting. And judges and prosecutors are not historians or social scientists. Thus, although the ICTY is an invaluable source for historical analysis, scholars must decipher its evidence and consider the rules and context under which the tribunal's evidence was collected, prepared, and presented, not to mention the blank spots that remain in the judicial record (which is not concluded and still not entirely accessible for analysis).[3]

Clearly, no single method of analysis can offer a final "verdict" on complex historical events. Nor can one author, or group of academic authors—and who are prone to their own values and biases—provide conclusive answers about the complex facets of Yugoslavia's dissolution. But the goal of this volume is to encourage scholarship that can carefully scrutinize our knowledge of events, enhance consensus on established patterns and facts, and endeavor to draw useful general conclusions and implications from the exercise. It is only through such a patient analytical enterprise that elites and citizens within the successor states can hope to find a basis, a knowledge platform, for dealing with the bitter legacy of recent conflicts, and make real progress in achieving inter-state and intra-state reconciliation. To a very substantial extent, issues pertaining to Yugoslavia's disintegration in the 1990s still remain the content of daily politics throughout the Balkans (as illustrated by the recent controversies in different countries about whether and how to apologize for past crimes against citizens of currently neighboring states). Only by thoughtful and unemotional dialogue about contemporary history can the next generation in Southeastern Europe avoid being trapped by its region's controversial past, and help shape more tolerant political cultures.

Re-evaluation of Yugoslavia's dissolution can, hopefully, also assist policy makers and officials who are routinely faced with the challenge of forging or rebuilding coherent, stable, and democratic state institutions in deeply divided societies. Yugoslavia's disintegration vividly, albeit tragically, provides lessons, or a negative model, regarding the pitfalls in developing constitutional and political mechanisms for the accommodation of diverse sub-national or regionally-based groups. The record of state failure in the Balkans offers an illustration of the warning signals and pathways that, if unchecked, can trigger dangerous forms of ultra-nationalism and extremist violence. Of course, a familiarity with the "disintegrative synergies" which befall states such as Yugoslavia cannot provide a template or recipe for successful conflict management in every context. But careful consideration of the various dimensions involved in the Yugoslav case can be, and indeed have already been, useful in developing international norms and methodologies that may help forestall future episodes of inter-ethnic violence, ethnic cleansing, and crimes against humanity.

Insights from Yugoslavia's dissolution can also reveal at what points and how international intervention and cooperation can best shore up or assertively repair the deficiencies of a failing state. For example, looking back at the Balkans in the 1990s, Chris Patten, in an address to the German Bundestag, aptly observed that those who criticize Europe's common foreign and security policy "should study recent history. Europe completely failed to get its act together in the 1990s on the policy for the Balkans. As Yugoslavia broke into bits, Europe was largely impotent because it was not united. Some member states wanted to keep Yugoslavia together at all costs, some wanted to manage its breakup, and others felt we should stay out of the whole mess...We had to do better. A lot better."[4]

It is hardly surprising that foreign policy analysts and officials of the EU, the UN, as well as other multinational and state organizations involved in nation-building (including the Coalition Political Authority in Iraq today and advisors to different Iraqi regional communities) should routinely invoke the Yugoslav dissolution scenario, and its ostensible lessons for multi-confessional and multi-ethnic states, when rationalizing their preferred strategies and suggestions for institution-building.[5] Thus, accurately establishing the various factors that contributed to Yugoslavia's break-up, and what might have productively forestalled or moderated that process, can help provide a more substantial foundation for comparative generalizations with regard to addressing state collapse.

This volume represents a fresh reflection on the causes of Yugoslavia's demise, in light of the existing literature and debates, along with the new sources that are now available. Jasna Dragović-Soso's introductory chapter provides an overview of the scholarly literature on Yugoslavia's disintegration, organized around five groups of explanations: 1) *longue durée* explanations including the "ancient hatreds" and "clash of civilizations" arguments and the legacy of imperial rule in the Balkans; 2) historical explanations based on the incompatibility of the South Slavs' national ideologies and the failure of the first Yugoslav state; 3) explanations focused on the evolution and crisis of Yugoslavia's socialist system; 4) explanations emphasizing the role of political and intellectual agency; and 5) explanations focused on the impact of international factors. She argues that the academic scholarship on Yugoslavia's disintegration generally did not fall into the trap of endorsing the "ancient hatreds" explanation so popular with much of the western media and some policymakers in the 1990s, but that it still often reflected the divisions and convictions typical of the emotionally laden and politically charged atmosphere of the period and privileged certain types of explanations while leaving significant lacunae.

The book is then divided into three parts. The first is focused on "The Historical Legacy," specifically the experience of the first, interwar, Yugoslav state and the effects of the two World Wars. The second part on "The Socialist Legacy" examines constitutional factors and interpretations, the reopening of the "national question" in the 1960s, the legacy of the 1971 "Croatian Spring," and the role of intellectual elites as vectors of national ideology in Tito's Yugoslavia. The third and final part on "The Breakdown of the 1980s" analyzes the failure of "Yugoslavism" in the educational sphere, the role of economic factors and the the inter-regional struggle for resources, the Slovenian-Croatian proposal for a confederation, Slobodan Milošević's policy, the actions of the Yugoslav People's Army, and the role of Western foreign policy prior to the descent into violence.

In the first part, Mark Biondich analyzes the politics of the first Yugoslav state, framing his disscussion in an overview of both the nationalist and the communist historiographies of the period. He notes, first of all, that the Serbian political dominance in the interwar Kingdom of Yugoslavia resulted in the "delegitimation" of the Yugoslav idea among the non-Serbs precisely at the time when their mass national consciousness was being formed. Secondly, he argues that the subsequent partial and biased communist and nationalist accounts of the interwar period further conditioned Yugoslavs to treat the only non-communist Yugoslav state-building experiment as an abject failure. These two factors together left a legacy which worked against attempts to envisage democratic Yugoslav alternative as the communist project failed.

In his chapter, Stevan K. Pavlowitch reflects on the legacy of the First and the Second World Wars, highlighting the importance of previous conflict for subsequent nationalist mobilization, albeit not in the simplistic manner that it has so often been done in order to justify policies of the 1980s and 1990s. Instead, he provides a nuanced overview of the variety of experiences of those previous conflicts among the Yugoslav peoples, noting the ways in which they cut across ethno-national boundaries. He argues that the Yugoslav populations "had been divided by the vagaries of warfare, occupation, resistance and revolution even more than by ethnic feeling, historical memory, religious adherence and ideology" and that "all these differences, perceived as they were with the distance of time, could only be magnified when the disintegration process began," providing a repository of grievances and unhealed wounds that were seized upon and misused to ignite the conflicts leading to the country's violent break-up.

Audrey Budding begins Part II with an essay which traces "the ominous process by which the regime made 'the right to self-determination' a keystone of political legitimacy without specifying who held that right or how it was to be exercised." By examining the relationship between "nation" and "republic" in three distinct periods of socialist Yugoslavia's constitutional evolution—the period of the state's founding, the period of radical constitutional change from 1968 to 1974 and the period of the Yugoslav crisis of the end of the 1980s—she highlights the ambiguities of Yugoslavia's constitutional language on self-determination and the unresolved tensions between competing conceptions of this right. Along the way, she also provides an insightful reflection on the weakness of civic nationalism in Yugoslavia and its successor states, examining the ways in which the socialist regime undermined the conceptual framework that could have supported civic rather than ethno-national identities.

In his chapter, Dennison Rusinow argues that the roots of the revival of the "national question" in the 1960s were primarily economic in nature. He focuses on the ways in which the "liberal" and "conservative" economic agendas during that decade were linked to specific national grievances and interests, and examines the implications of the purge of the Party "liberals" in 1971–72 for the subsequent capacity of the Yugoslav state to reform and overcome its crisis. Unfortunately, Rusinow's analysis was never completed, as its author was tragically killed in a road accident in January 2004. In general agreement with all the contributors to this volume and in consideration of the fact that this chapter represents his last work of scholarship, we have decided to leave it as is, in his own words, and with only minor editorial assistance from his widow, Mary Rusinow.

Jill Irvine's examination of the legacy of the 1971 "Croatian spring"—the most important instance of popular mobilization in socialist Yugoslavia until the 1980s—fills an important gap in the literature on Yugoslavia's disintegration. Irvine argues that the "Croatian spring" represented both a preview and a harbinger of the state dissolution of 1991. Not only did it bring to the fore political figures who later became Croatia's political opposition and eventually the victors of the first multi-party elections in 1990, but its suppression created a political vacuum which allowed the Croatian Catholic Church to undertake programs of ethno-religious mobilization in the republic. The "Croatian spring" also highlighted the tensions within the republic between the Croats' desire for greater political autonomy from the rest of the federation and the Serbian minority's desire for closer links with Serbia, and demonstrated the inability of the undemocratic one-party system, as well as its liberal republican leaderships, to defuse national tensions and contain escalating nationalist demands. Finally, as Irvine points out, the events of 1971 contributed to discrediting the Partisan legacy which underpinned the entire federal structure.

Nicholas Miller concludes the section on Yugoslavia's socialist legacy by focusing on the role of intellectuals as the agents of nationalist mobilization. Noting that intellectuals occupied a "unique, important, but insecure position" in Yugoslavia, Miller compares the rise of nationalism among Serbian, Slovenian, Croatian and Albanian intellectuals during the socialist period. He argues that the nationalist movements that emerged within those intellectual groups did not merely mark the return of prewar nationalisms, but were conditioned by Yugoslav socialism and represented a response to the regime's proposed "solutions" to the national "question." In most cases, they were framed within the discourse and the ideology of "Titoism," creating images of their national communities that were useful to political elites.

Part III begins with Predrag Marković's and Andrew Wachtel's examination of the failure of the final attempts to forge a common educational policy in the early 1980s, exposing the weakness of "Yugoslavism" as a nation-building project and as the cultural "glue" of the common state. From their examination of the debates and disagreements engendered by the proposal for "common cores" in the Yugoslav national curriculum, Marković and Wachtel draw several important conclusions. First, they note that Slovene writers spearheaded the process of national mobilizations in the 1980s, well before the Serbian Academy's 1986 "Memorandum" and the

Belgrade intelligentsia's embracing of the Kosovo Serbs' cause. Second, they high-light that the most unequivocal support for a core curriculum came from Croatia, with tacit backing from Serbia, while the staunchest opposition was to be found in Slovenia and Kosovo—thus showing a somewhat surprising "pro-Yugoslav" align-ment within those republics often held to be the most responsible for the country's ultimate disintegration. Finally, they argue that the failure of this last attempt at the integration of Yugoslav culture represented not merely an omen for the fate of the Yugoslav state, but showed the limitations of "any bureaucratic attempts at cultural integration in multinational systems."

Michael Palairet then examines the economic causes of Yugoslavia's dissolu-tion, particularly the role of the inter-regional struggle for resources in a situation of economic crisis. Palairet notes that after 1979 Yugoslavia was de facto bankrupt and no longer able to rely on foreign sources of funding (now increasingly tied to "structural adjustment" requirements), and that the main problem for regional leader-ships became how to continue to finance corrupt and inefficient enterprises, main-tain employment and stave off total economic collapse. Within this general context, Palairet argues that Milošević's Serbia obstructed the federal government's attempts at economic reform while trying to maintain the Yugoslav federation as such, pri-marily in order to tap the resources of the breakaway republics to continue financing Serbia's unviable industrial enterprises. By 1990, however, the Serbian leadership's policy backfired, reinforcing the already prevailing tendency of the breakaway repub-lics not to seek "Yugoslav" solutions to their economic problems any longer and to go for full independence.

Dejan Jović's chapter provides a careful analysis of the Slovenian and Croatian confederation proposal of 1990, which has often been hailed as a missed opportunity for preserving some kind of Yugoslavia and preventing the descent into war. Jović shows that, in fact, the Slovenian and Croatian leaderships did not view confedera-tion as an ultimate objective, but rather saw it as a tactical resource for the achieve-ment of their real aim: the recognition of their full state independence. He also notes, however, that the proposal did represent a genuine attempt to do so peacefully, as a kind of interim compromise solution. According to Jović, other factors also con-tributed to the failure of the confederal solution: no other Yugoslav republic (nor the two autonomous provinces) supported it when it was first presented; there were important disagreements across the political spectrum in both Slovenia and Croatia and between the two leaderships in regard to their proposal; and finally, all the main international actors at the time still backed "a democratic and united Yugoslavia." When, in 1991, some of Yugoslavia's other republics came round to the idea of a confederation, and when this solution gained international backing, it had already been overtaken by events.

Eric Gordy analyzes the evolution of Milošević's policy, asking whether by 1991 Milošević had abandoned his initial goal of maintaining (and dominating) the Yugoslav federation and shifted to the goal of creating a new "Greater Serbian" state, which would include parts of Croatia and Bosnia-Herzegovina. He argues that—rather than following a long-term political vision or nationalist plan—Milošević was in fact "an immobile Trojan horse," whose policy was predominantly reactive after his attempts at forcing the preservation of the Yugoslav federation backfired. In this situation, having provoked a course of events he was unable to control, Milošević appears to have vacillated between a solution that aimed at creating a third Yugoslavia including Serbia, Montenegro, Bosnia-Hercegovina and whatever parts of Croatia could be conquered, and a "Greater Serbia" solution which involved the partition of Bosnia. Noting that on this point the available evidence remains contradictory, Gordy assesses different explanations that have been given both by scholars and by various actors in the Yugoslav drama and concludes that, "while there is no room for doubt that [Milošević] acted from 1991 onward in ways which appeared altogether consistent with this second goal, there is little definitive evidence to suggest that the goal was ever articulated or that the steps along the way were planned." Whatever its ultimate motivation, however, the Serbian leadership became increasingly reliant on the use of force to achieve its goals.

In his chapter, Florian Bieber examines the role of the Yugoslav People's Army in the dissolution process, particularly focusing on the forging of the army's alliance with the Serbian leadership in the last years of Yugoslavia's existence. In Bieber's view, this alliance was not the result of "ethnic" ties or the disproportionate share of Serbs within its ranks, but had more to do with the army's institutional interests and its loss of ideological orientation. In contrast to commonly held views about the army's power and influence in the Yugoslav state, Bieber argues that it was its ideological and structural weakness that facilitated its support for Serbia during the conflict. Indeed, as Bieber shows, the alliance between Milošević and the army leadership was never complete and often motivated by different priorities. Internally divided, socially isolated, ideologically superseded, suffering severe problems of recruitment, and victim of its own myth concerning Yugoslavia's external enemies, the army not only failed to prevent Yugoslavia's dissolution but became a disintegrative factor itself.

Paul Shoup's examination of the role of Western foreign policy in the process of Yugoslavia's dissolution completes Part III of the book. Shoup challenges the oft voiced critique that the West, and particularly the United States, suffered from disinterest and a frozen image of the Balkans as steeped in "ancient hatreds," which stopped it from engaging in preventive diplomacy to help resolve Yugoslavia's crisis and above all to stave off the outbreak of violence. Exploring alternative Western policy options, Shoup highlights the considerable disagreement in the literature as to when exactly Yugoslavia's violent dissolution became inevitable and active Western involvement should have begun. He argues that decisive Western intervention was unrealistic, however, in the absence of both clear interests and emotional involvement in the region at the time. In Shoup's view, the real choice was not between enforcing Yugoslavia's unity or guiding the process of dissolution at an early stage. Rather, intervention should have been aimed at the more immediate problem of the

Serb-Croat war, in the form of "resolute (but limited) action by the West in defense of Croatia and her borders" accompanied by credible guarantees to Croatia's Serb minority.

In his concluding comparative chapter, Lenard Cohen surveys the various analytical approaches and narratives that have sought to account for the collapse of three federal socialist states at the outset of the 1990s: Yugoslavia, the USSR and Czechoslovakia. He identifies four broad dimensions which explain the dissolution of all the former socialist federations: 1) political-institutional legacies; 2) ethnicized politics and nationalist mobilization; 3) international economic and political factors, and; 4) the politics of reform and democratic transition. He suggests that it is the interaction among those factors, or what might be termed "disintegrative synergies," that best explain the nearly simultaneous break-up of the three communist federations. Explaining the reasons that Yugoslavia experienced such a violent and prolonged course of disintegration in comparison to the relatively peaceful break-up of the USSR and Czechoslovakia's "velvet divorce," Cohen emphasizes four additional factors that should be taken into consideration: 1) distinct political-cultural values; 2) the role of political leadership; 3) the role of military and paramilitary forces, and; 4) the duration and nature of liberalization and emergent pluralism in socialist Yugoslavia. He concludes by pointing out the manner in which the disparate factors that influenced the disintegration of Yugoslavia and the other communist states have been an influence on the cohesion of the successor states to each federation during the last fifteen years.

Lenard J. Cohen
Jasna Dragović-Soso
September 2007

Notes

1. Jared Diamond reminds us that a major lesson learned from the collapse of past societies is that their "steep decline may begin only a decade or two after the society reaches its peak numbers, wealth, and power." Jared Diamond, *Collapse: How Societies Choose to Fail or Succeed* (New York: Viking, 2005), p. 509.
2. Dubravka Stojanović, surveying the portrayal of history in Serbia's textbooks, has observed that "if history was presented from different angles, school children could learn that historical events were not determined, that different solutions were possible so that individuals, the elites, groups, or even the whole society would feel responsible for their historical choices and actions… As a closed system, history becomes a reliable base of an undemocratic society." Dubravka Stojanović, "Construction of Historical Consciousness: The Case of Serbian History Textbooks," in Maria Todorova (ed.), *Balkan Identities: Nation and Memory* (London: Hurst and Company, 2004), p. 338.
3. Ksenija Turković, "Historians in Search for Truth about Conflicts in the Territory of Former Yugoslavia as Expert Witnesses in Front of the ICTY," *Časopis za suvremenu povijest*, 2004, pp. 41-67.

4. RAPID, Commission of the European Communities, April 28, 2004.

5. The former Yugoslavia has also been viewed as a positive model to apply to current state-building projects, usually by those who only superficially or erroneously probe its dynamics. For example, Peter Galbraith, a former U.S. ambassador to Croatia and advisor to the current Kurdistan regional government, has suggested that former Yugoslavia is a model for constitution-making in Iraq. Peter Galbraith, "What Went Wrong," in Brendan O'Leary, John McGarry, and Khaled Salih (eds.), *The Future of Kurdistan in Iraq* (Philadelphia: University of Pennsylvania Press, 2005), pp. 247-248. See also Leslie Gelb, *International Herald Tribune*, June 26, 2003, p. 8; Gelb and Senator Joseph R. Biden, Jr., "Unity Through Autonomy in Iraq," *New York Times*, May 1, 2006, p. 19, and "Bipartisan Redeployment," *Wall Street Journal*, October 24, 2006, p. A18.

WHY DID YUGOSLAVIA DISINTEGRATE? AN OVERVIEW OF CONTENDING EXPLANATIONS

❖ Jasna Dragović-Soso[1] ❖

In January 1992, the Socialist Federal Republic of Yugoslavia formally ceased to exist with the international recognition of several of its republics as sovereign states. But when did the country actually disintegrate and what were the causes of its breakup? Why was it so violent? And, who, if anyone, was to blame? These questions have given rise to a tremendous outpouring of literature of both a scholarly and a journalistic nature, while the causes of Yugoslavia's disintegration and the roots of the violence have remained subjects of considerable disagreement. During the 1990s, as the wars of the Yugoslav succession were going on, passions ran high in response to the immense suffering, destruction, and war crimes, giving rise to some of the most heated scholarly debates not only within Yugoslavia's successor states but also in the Western academic community. Dueling explanations for these events were also generally linked to rival policies, polarizing scholarly opinion further and often giving it a highly politicized character.[2] Even now, years after the country disintegrated and emotions have subsided, new histories of the "rise and fall" of Yugoslavia and studies of different aspects of the breakdown continue to appear, testifying to the continuing interest in the subject and the undiminished relevance of the debates to which it gave rise.

This chapter will present a critical overview of the main lines of explanation that have emerged in the scholarship since the early 1990s, along with an examination of the most important debates that they have engendered.[3] Overall, studies of the disintegration of Yugoslavia have tended to reflect frameworks of analysis more generally found in the social sciences and in history: some authors have placed a greater emphasis on long- and medium-term structural factors, others on the role played by agency or historical contingency.[4] This review will thus follow a chronological time frame, which will serve to highlight the causal factors emphasized by various authors in their accounts of Yugoslavia's breakup. The five categories of explanation examined here are:

1. Explanations focused on the *longue durée*, emphasizing "ancient hatreds," a "clash of civilizations," or the legacy of imperial rule in the Balkans

2. Explanations focused on the historical legacy of the nineteenth-century South Slav national ideologies and the first Yugoslav state-building experiment from 1918 to 1941

3. Explanations focused on the legacy of Yugoslavia's socialist system, its constitutional development and federal structure, its ideological delegitimation, and its economic failure

4. Explanations focused on the period of Yugoslavia's breakdown in the second half of the 1980s and the role of political and intellectual agency

5. Explanations focused on the impact of external factors

As I consider each of these categories of explanation, I will highlight the existing scholarly challenges or complements to them and indicate where I believe gaps in our knowledge continue to exist.[5]

The *Longue Durée:* Ancient Hatreds, Civilizations, Empires

The *longue durée* explanations were generally the first to appear in the early 1990s (alongside explanations centered on the role of political agency discussed below). Initially, there were two main variants of these types of explanations: one that has since become known as the ancient ethnic hatreds argument and the other as the clash of civilizations argument. What such explanations had in common was their vision of conflict's being the result of Yugoslavia's multinational and multiconfessional character—a character that in the view of these authors was forged in the distant past, giving rise to immutable and conflicting primordial identities among the country's different national groups. A third, more nuanced explanation, emerged later on and highlighted Yugoslavia's historical geography of being located in the frontier regions of large multinational empires. Unlike the first two variants, this explanation did not represent an essentialist vision of Yugoslavia's peoples and did not fall into the trap of historical determinism.

The first, ancient hatreds, variant of the *longue durée* approach portrays the Yugoslavs as intrinsically predisposed to violence and mired in their deep-seated hatred of each other. Among scholars, the best-known exponent of this vision was the veteran American diplomat and historian George Kennan. In his preface to the 1993 reprint of the Carnegie Endowment's 1913 inquiry into the Balkan Wars, Kennan argued that the "aggressive nationalism" motivating the wars of the Yugoslav succession of the early 1990s "drew on deeper traits of character inherited, presumably, from a distant tribal past: a tendency to view the outsider, generally, with dark suspicion, and to see the political-military opponent, in particular, as a fearful and implacable enemy to be rendered harmless only by total and unpitying destruction."[6] Kennan's vision of "tribal ancient hatreds" was replicated by some Western journalists and politicians, but scholars of Yugoslavia overwhelmingly rejected this explanation from the start, pointing out that peaceful coexistence and even cooperation between the Yugoslav peoples was just as much a characteristic of the region as periods of conflict.[7] Indeed, the effort to counter the "ancient hatreds" thesis gave rise to a whole new body of literature that applied Edward Said's Orientalist paradigm to the Balkans and focused not so much on the Balkans *per se* but on lingering Western images of the region.[8]

The second variant of the *longue durée* approach is the clash of civilizations thesis, first proposed by political scientist Samuel Huntington in 1993.[9] Although this view was also not widely adopted by scholars of Yugoslavia, it attracted considerable scholarly and public attention and debate.[10] The clash of civilizations approach emphasizes Yugoslavia's historical geography of being situated at the centuries-old fault line between Islam, Orthodox Christianity, and Catholicism, arguing that Yugoslavia's disintegration and wars typify the new "cultural" or "civilizational" type of conflict that affects the post-Cold War world. In Huntington's own words, "countries that bestride civilizational fault lines tend to come apart."[11] He also noted that although there were many ingredients to "civilizational" identity (such as history, language, tradition, culture), religion was the most important, "perhaps *the* central force that motivates and mobilizes people."[12] Finally, in Huntington's view, the Yugoslav conflict of the 1990s demonstrated not only an internal clash of civilizations but broader patterns of "civilizational kinship," explaining why Orthodox Greeks and Russians generally sympathized with the Serbs, Muslim countries backed the Bosnian Muslims, and the West favored Roman Catholic Croats and Slovenes.

While appealing by virtue of its simplicity, this argument suffers from some of the same flaws as the ancient hatreds one. I will not dwell here on the internal contradictions of Huntington's thesis or his tenuous definition of civilizations but merely on how these arguments apply to the Yugoslav case.[13] First of all, what needs to be highlighted is that although Yugoslavia clearly was a diverse, multinational state, the more salient differences within it were regional variations rather than civilizational ones. Some scholars have thus noted that inhabitants of any particular locality or region had more in common with each other whatever their ethnic or religious background than they did with other Yugoslavs—including their own ethnic or religious brethren—in other parts of the country.[14] Indeed, the cleavage used more often to explain the Yugoslav wars of the 1990s has been the rural-urban divide, which has in some accounts even led to the characterization of these wars as "the revenge of the countryside."[15] Ideological differences have also represented a more important source of conflict in the past (such as those between communist Partisans and royalist Chetniks, or the fascist-inspired Ustasha during the Second World War), cutting across ethno-national identities. And, in contrast to the current literature focused on Yugoslavia's internal divergences, scholars have in the past also noted the many cultural, linguistic, and other similarities between the Yugoslav peoples that once gave rise to the very notion of "Yugoslavism" as a unifying idea and have posited that the Yugoslavs' national disputes were essentially a case of "narcissism of minor differences."[16] Huntington's differentiation between intercivilizational fault lines and those that have existed within the entities he defines as civilizations is also difficult to sustain. His vision of a "Western" civilization ignores the much more violent historical and religious fault lines, such as the Protestant-Catholic watershed that affected Europe for centuries or the intra-Islamic divisions that have been a feature of Middle Eastern relations.[17] Finally, the civilizations paradigm fares no better when accounting for foreign policy decisions during Yugoslavia's dissolution and wars: it cannot explain why the United States and the European Community governments initially opposed the German policy of recognizing the breakaway republics in 1991 or why the "West" eventually did intervene on behalf of Muslim Bosniaks in 1995 and Albanians in 1999. It also does not account for the Greek government's participation in the NATO bombing of Orthodox Serbs and Montenegrins in 1999.

Indeed, as many scholars have pointed out, the clash of civilizations approach is essentially ahistorical and static. Because it views civilizations as constants, it makes no effort to explain why cultural, historical, or other differences become highlighted *at a particular time,* nor does it view identity-formation as a fluid and continuous historical process.[18] This is especially clear when it comes to its treatment of religion (according to Huntington the most basic and fundamental ingredient of civilizational identity and thus an "unchangeable" given). As the many studies of the role of religion in the Yugoslav wars of the 1990s have shown, rather than a preexisting incompatibility of different religions in the multinational and multiconfessional Yugoslav state, it is the instrumentalization of religion by the various national elites and the conflict itself that reinforced religious cleavages and antagonistic identities.[19] In other words, rather than focusing on culture as Huntington does, these studies examine the role of agency.

The ubiquity of the ancient hatreds and clash of civilizations explanations in parts of the media and the statements of some Western politicians—often used by the latter to justify inaction during the wars of the Yugoslav succession—produced a situation in which scholars generally felt compelled to emphatically reject all *longue durée* explanations for Yugoslavia's dissolution and wars. Yet the essentialist visions of ancient hatreds and civilizations aside, the question remains whether there *are* any legacies of the *longue durée* that could contribute to our understanding of why Yugoslavia disintegrated—judiciously placed within a multifactorial approach and without falling into the trap of historical determinism. While such factors alone do not explain Yugoslavia's dissolution, they could arguably present one as yet underexplored aspect of it. In this respect, it might be useful to highlight Yugoslavia's historical geography of having been located at the periphery of two large, multinational empires—the Ottoman and the Habsburg.[20]

In a rare work of scholarship on the impact of the Ottoman legacy on Yugoslavia's disintegration, Dennison Rusinow notes that the structure of the Ottoman imperial system—defined as it was on a confessional rather than a territorial basis and granting considerable local autonomy to its constituent peoples—inhibited the homogenization and assimilation that was concurrently shaping the development of states in other parts of Europe. This legacy, Rusinow argues, continued to defy all subsequent attempts at establishing homogenous national states in the region, with control over all of their territory—particularly in border areas, which have seen periods of ethnic strife and rebellion in the era of nation-building since the nineteenth century and where most of the fighting of the 1990s also took place (Bosnia-Herzegovina, the former Military Frontier in Croatia and Kosovo).[21]

The utility of a *longue durée* approach has also been noted by Maria Todorova, who highlights the importance of subjective understandings of the imperial legacy in addition to the "objective" impacts of empire on demography, state structures, and social and economic patterns. She notes that competing perceptions of the imperial legacy in the region have dominated the scholarship, with many authors exhibiting a tendency toward implicitly presupposing monolithic entities that either stand in opposition to such a legacy (particularly regarding the Ottoman heritage) or form an organic part of it (as within the "Central Europe" paradigm).[22] An important aspect of such interpretations of empire has been the way in which historical visions of empire have shaped over time the various Yugoslav local, regional, and national identities.[23] In addition, as she argues, the variable and multifaceted regional legacies of empire in the Balkans need to be understood in the context of their interaction with the nineteenth-century West European ideal of the homogenous nation-state.[24]

Finally, a number of scholars have argued that the dissolution of multinational Yugoslavia represents a quintessentially European process dating from the unraveling of the large multiethnic nineteenth-century empires and experiencing a high point in the radical racial ideologies and civil strife of the Second World War. From this perspective, the breakdown of Yugoslavia in the late 1980s and the wars of the 1990s represent a continuation of this trend. In the words of historian Gale Stokes, the process of "redrawing of state borders onto ethnic lines" was "not an aberrant Balkan phenomenon or the striking out of backward peoples involved in tribal warfare" but "the final working out of a long European tradition of violent ethnic homogenization."[25] In Stokes's view, the sources of this process are to be found in the continuing relevance of the political ideology of nineteenth-century nationalism, which emerged in reaction against the multinational empires and provided the inspiration of Balkan national uprisings and state-building projects until today.

The Weight of History: National Ideologies and the Legacy of the First Yugoslav State

Historical explanations rooted in Yugoslavia's twentieth-century experience have tended to focus on the national ideologies of its constituent peoples and the failure of the integrative ideology of "Yugoslavism." In the English-language scholarship, the historian Ivo Banac is probably the earliest exponent of the argument that the "real reason" for the country's disintegration lies in Yugoslavia's twentieth-century history and in the national ideologies of its main national groups rather than in explanations based on ancient hatreds, problems of modernization, or social structures.[26] Already in his 1984 history, *The National Question in Yugoslavia*, Banac argued that "these ideologies assumed their all but definite contours well before the unification and could not be significantly altered by any combination of cajolery or coercion."[27] Other scholars have since made a similar point in their studies of Yugoslavia's dissolution (although not necessarily adopting Banac's view of these ideologies).[28] There are two main schools of thought concerning the role of national ideologies in Yugoslavia's ultimate failure as a state.

The first focuses on the inherent incompatibility between Serbian national ideology and those of the other two "state-building nations"—the Croats and the Slovenes. One variant of this argument is championed by Banac himself, who argues that Serbian national ideology was shaped from the start by a desire for assimilation and territorial expansion and that it was thus incompatible with the desire of the Croats and Slovenes to be recognized as different and equal nations.[29] Noting that by the time of Yugoslavia's unification in 1918 the national goal of uniting all Serbs into a single state was omnipresent among Serbian intellectual and political elites, he highlights the instrumental role of Serbia's political and military dominance and its victor status at the end of the First World War in imposing the Serbian national vision for the new Yugoslav state—a state that effectively became a "Greater Serbia" despite Croatian opposition.[30] Banac emphasizes the continuity of these nineteenth-century national ideologies throughout the first Yugoslavia's existence and into the socialist period when "in the context of Communist thinking, all of Yugoslavia's six territorial parties came to resemble, even duplicate, the national ideologies that have evolved and prevailed in the given party-state before the [Second World] war."[31] According to him, Serbia's communists after Tito's death in 1980—particularly with Slobodan Milošević's rise to power in 1987—"had more in common with the prewar Radical Party, the party of Serbian supremacy, than with Slovene or Croat communists."[32] For Banac, the Slovenes' and Croats' drive for independence at the end of the post-Tito decade were thus essentially a "defensive mechanism" against the renewed threat of Serbian hegemony.[33]

The second variant of the national ideologies explanation can be found in the writings of some Serbian historians. In contrast to Banac, they portray Serbian national ideology as the main integrative and pro-Yugoslav force and blame what they see as an inherently obstructionist Croatian national ideology (shaped by a virulently anti-Serb Catholicism and the influence of Austro-Hungarian rule) for Yugoslavia's problems and ultimate dissolution.[34] For them, all Croatian appeals for Yugoslav unity in the nineteenth century merely represented a tool to win over the Habsburg Serbs to the project of securing a separate Croatian unit within the Empire and ultimately an independent Croatian state.[35] They argue that Serbian political and intellectual elites were not simply pursuing the expansion of the Kingdom of Serbia but were genuinely (and, from these authors' perspective, mistakenly) committed to a common Yugoslav state and willing to sacrifice Serbian national interests to this project. As proof for this claim they cite the Serbian government's rejection in 1915 of the "Greater Serbia" option offered by the Allies in the secret Treaty of London in favor of a Yugoslav state.[36] In the words of historian Ljubodrag Dimić:

> For the sake of the new [Yugoslav] state, Serbia sacrificed its sovereignty and its tradition, as well as more than a quarter of its population [in the First World War]. It defined and diplomatically secured the Yugoslav programme, and with its army preserved the integrity of that state. At the end of the war, Serbia was among the victors and, by including the other Yugoslav nations (the Croats and the Slovenes) in the newly created Yugoslav state, it enabled the latter to leave the defeated powers and—virtually without any war losses of their own—side with the victors.[37]

Indeed, while these authors acknowledge Serb political dominance in the first Yugoslavia, they note that this political preponderance did not result in the oppression of Slovenes or Croats, who themselves dominated the economy, enjoyed considerable cultural autonomy, and generally prospered—using the common state as a stepping stone toward their main goal of national integration and ultimately independence on those territories they claimed as their own. From this perspective, the decentralization and eventual dissolution of socialist Yugoslavia merely confirmed the victory of long-standing and inherently "separatist" Croatian and Slovenian aspirations for their own national states.[38]

Both sides in this controversy date back at least to the Yugoslav historical debates of the early 1970s, and are thus not unique or particularly new to the scholarship on Yugoslavia's dissolution.[39] Despite their differences, however, the implication of these rival explanations is essentially the same: Yugoslavia was an essentially "impossible" country from the start, whether because of inherent Serbian "hegemonism" or Croatian and Slovenian "separatism." In this respect, such explanations are no less deterministic than the longue durée approaches.[40] Rather than examining the various alternatives that did exist at every stage both in Serbian and Croatian national thought and seeking to understand what in the particular circumstances of the time conditioned the choice of some alternatives over others, they generally ascribe the worst possible motives to the "other side" and assume that bad outcomes are necessarily the result of premeditation and plan.[41]

Another school of thought on national ideologies focuses not on the differences between Serbs and Croats but, rather, on the incompatibility of all "particularist" nationalist visions (Serb, Croat, Slovene) with an overarching, supranational "Yugoslavism" acting as the cultural and ideological foundation of the common state. As Andrew Wachtel puts it, Yugoslavia was "the quintessential battleground between collectivistic national visions based on ideals of synthesis versus those based on particularity."[42] This is echoed by Aleksandar Pavković, who highlights the fundamental similarity of aims of Serbian and Croatian national ideology: the achievement of national statehood on a particular and, to a large degree, overlapping territory.[43]

As both these authors argue, the only way of uniting the country's diverse national groups and overcoming such competing claims to territory was by means of the overarching national ideology of Yugoslavism. In their view—as in that of most authors writing in the 1990s—however, Yugoslavism was ultimately incapable of keeping particularist nationalisms at bay. Pavković argues that it essentially came too late (he refers to it as a "belated national idea"), whereas Wachtel argues that it was abandoned as a cultural nation-building project by Yugoslavia's political and intellectual elites in the 1960s.[44] Without the previous dismantling of Yugoslav cultural unity and revival of separate national cultures, he argues, the political and economic malaise of the 1980s would not have led to the disintegration of the state.

Although these approaches add valuable insight into the importance of cultural nation-building and the powerful role played by national ideology as opposed to material factors, there are a number of problems with their characterization of a quintessential conflict between an overarching, supranational Yugoslavism and particularist nationalisms. The first of these concerns the problem of identity. As has been argued by a number of authors, Yugoslavism and other particularist identities were not mutually exclusive but often coexisted with each other—sometimes even within the same person, as illustrated by the self-definition of a former Yugoslav diplomat as "a Dalmatian from Dubrovnik, a Belgrader, a Croat—and therefore a Yugoslav."[45] Sociological research undertaken in Yugoslavia in the 1970s and 1980s confirms this ambivalence in questions of national identity, and it appears that the more educated social strata generally tended to identify with notions of Yugoslavism.[46] Indeed, even recent studies of popular culture have indicated the continued existence of a shared identity despite the country's collapse.[47] On a political level, Yugoslavism was adapted to specific national circumstances and blended with various particularist national goals at different times.[48] Dejan Jović's work on the Yugoslav communist elite also indicates that—far from abandoning ideas of national unity in the 1960s—they in fact adapted Yugoslavism to their evolving ideological and political needs. Jović also argues that even those political leaderships that brought the country to its collapse in the 1980s often acted under the assumption that they were doing what they could to save it.[49] All of this research raises the question of whether the very malleability of Yugoslavism as a national ideology—which had been its greatest strength over time and had contributed to the Yugoslav state's being created not once but twice[50]—perhaps ultimately led to its undoing, as different factions in the debate over the common state proposed their own ultimately irreconcilable understandings of it.[51]

Secondly, what is often missing from accounts of Yugoslav national ideologies is the fact that their evolution over time was significantly shaped by their dynamic interaction with each other. There has been a tendency to view these ideologies as somehow separate from each other—built on the basis of religious, cultural, and ideological tendencies internal to each national group. Yet, in many instances already in the nineteenth century there was evidence that the adoption of particular ideological stances—whether over issues such as language or in regard to the political agendas of the different actors—decisions were made in reaction to and anticipation of processes and actions that were taking place among political and intellectual elites of other national groups. Once a common state of Yugoslavia was established, such dynamic interaction became even more apparent, shaping political and cultural agendas and standpoints.[52]

Thirdly, the existing historical explanations also highlight the continuing need for analyses of the legacy of the interwar state for the subsequent evolution of Yugoslavia.[53] In this respect, it seems that too much emphasis has been put on national ideologies; perhaps it was ultimately the practical reality of life in the interwar state that was instrumental for its internal legitimacy problem rather than the intentions underlying different political strategies and state-building concepts. New research could thus focus on the everyday experience of state centralism and Serb political, military, and administrative dominance in interwar Yugoslavia for the non-Serbs *and* on the effects of the apparently permanent crisis of this state on the Serbs, many of whom identified with Yugoslavia and saw themselves as its guardians.[54] In this respect, much would be gained by shifting the focus from the study of elites to social history.

Despite their various problems and lacunae, however, these explanations do raise the important question of historical continuity. If we accept that separate Serbian and Croatian national ideologies were defined well before 1918, then—even without ascribing the worst possible motives to them—the question of Yugoslavia's viability as a state inevitably arises. Was any common state possible that would have accommodated the Serbs' and the Croats' (and, later on, also the other Yugoslav nations') desire for national statehood on at least partially the same, nationally mixed, territory? Could "Yugoslavism" as a political or a state-building project alone (rather than as a synthesizing national ideology) have satisfied these various particularist national aspirations, replacing their ideals of independent statehood with loyalty to the common state? In other words, the dilemma of satisfying desires for national statehood and of defining the principles governing the notion of self-determination, as well as the issue of how to divide sovereignty and power within a single political entity, were present in 1918, 1945, and throughout Yugoslavia's existence until 1991. In this respect, our understanding of Yugoslavia's historical legacy would be enhanced by new diachronic comparative analyses linking the interwar experience with that of postwar socialist Yugoslavia.[55] Finally, more synchronous comparative work is also necessary. Are Serbian and Croatian national ideologies different from other European ideologies? How does the integrative ideology of Yugoslavism compare to other overarching notions of identity and political nation-building, such as *Deutschtum, Italianità,* or even Britishness? Clearly, there is much to be gained from examining the Yugoslav experience alongside wider European trends, as some scholars have argued throughout the 1990s.[56]

Yugoslavia's Socialist Experience: Institutions, Ideology, Modernization, and Legitimacy

The third body of scholarship traces the causes of dissolution specifically to the country's socialist experience. Most of these scholars clearly differentiate between the fact of Yugoslavia's disintegration and its violent nature, and generally their analyses seek to explain the former rather than the latter. Most of them also highlight the transformation of Yugoslavia in the late 1960s and early 1970s into a semiconfederation as the major turning point in the country's evolution.

The first, institutionalist, approach focuses on the evolution of Yugoslavia's federal structure. It emphasizes the "confederalization" of Yugoslavia since the early 1970s—embodied by the Constitution of 1974—as the main factor that eventually led to state collapse. The legal scholar Vojin Dimitrijević thus argues that the constitution, among other things, "weakened the [Yugoslav] federation by paralyzing the decision-making process and removing real federal competences, [and] promoted the federal units into sovereign states and the only real centres of power, making decision-making in the federation subject to consensus."[57] Other scholars have noted that the powers of the federal units were such that, by the time of Tito's death in 1980, Yugoslavia had "disappeared de facto from the constitutional order of the country in that 'Yugoslavia' was now only what the federal units decided, by consensus, it would be."[58] Valerie Bunce, who takes on much of this analysis in her comparative study of the collapse of socialism and the state in the Soviet Union, Czechoslovakia, and Yugoslavia, also argues that "the very institutions that had defined these systems and that were, presumably, to defend them as well, ended up functioning over time to subvert both the regime and the state."[59] These scholars all argue that the republics effectively "constructed" nations and gave them (to quote Bunce) "the institutions, elites, boundaries, and, ultimately, incentives and opportunities they needed to mount nationalist movements, to liberate themselves from regimes and states, and to construct new regimes and sovereign states in their place."[60] Indeed, Bunce explains the violent nature of Yugoslavia's dissolution (in contrast to the other two cases) partly as a function of Yugoslavia's having gone the farthest on this road—by the late 1970s it was, in her view, essentially confederal, thus pitting the (strong) republics against each other, not against a weakened centre.[61]

These institutionalist arguments highlight the structural importance of Yugoslavia's system, which provided the fault lines along which state dissolution was ultimately to take place. Certainly the evolution of Yugoslavia's system made republican competition and disagreement a more important feature in the absence of Tito as the ultimate arbiter during the political debates of the 1980s. However—although there can be no doubt about the progressive weakening of the centre—the institutionalists' characterization of the strength of the republics is more questionable. Indeed, Bunce's assessment of Serbia's institutional power does not really correspond to the reality of Serbia's situation in the 1970s and 1980s. In fact, Serbia's constitutional particularity of being the only republic with two autonomous provinces (which had been raised to the status of republics in all but name) was noted by Serbian commentators at the time and created the most important impetus for Serbia's revisionist stance toward the 1974 Constitution, as well as the rise of nationalism among its intellectual opposition.[62] The limits to large-scale nation-building were also demonstrated by the suppression of the Croatian "spring" in 1971; whereas the 1974 Constitution eventually fulfilled most of the Croatian constitutional demands, the mass resurgence of traditional Croatian nationalism was met by large-scale repression in the republic.[63] It would thus be more accurate to say that while the *tendency* in Yugoslavia was toward the creation of a more confederal structure with units acting as *de facto* national states—the *reality* of the individual federal units and the level of attainment of this status was extremely variable (with Yugoslavia's smaller republics having gone farther on this path than Serbia and Croatia).[64] Finally, these institutionalist analyses do not account for the *causes* of Yugoslavia's constitutional development. As Dejan Jović notes, "a constitution is not a factor in and of itself, but above all it is the outcome of politics, which is the interaction of different subjective positions in the context in which it happens."[65]

Jović's own study of the dissolution of Yugoslavia focuses on ideology and makes the case that it was ideological innovation rather than nationalism or economic rationale that lay behind the decentralization of the late 1960s and 1970s. For him, these changes were "the expression of the ideological position of the Yugoslav political elite, which wanted to use advantageous economic, political and international trends in order to promote the socialist project as it had formulated it in its own vision."[66] Based on his analysis of the writings of Edvard Kardelj, the principal architect of Yugoslavia's constitutional and ideological evolution, Jović concludes that "the main aim of Kardelj's concept was to increase the difference between socialist Yugoslavia and the pre-war, 'bourgeois' one, and between the Yugoslav self-management model of socialism and the model of state socialism developed in the Soviet Union," as well as to preserve this system after the passing of Tito and the Partisan generation.[67] Jović also argues that in the last fifteen years of its existence Yugoslavia acted more as an "ideological community" than a state, so that—when the political elite's consensus on this ideological project broke down in the 1980s—no other foundation was left for the continuation of the Yugoslav state.

A somewhat different perspective on the argument that the Yugoslav system contained within itself the seeds of its own destruction is given by scholars who have placed economic factors at the forefront of their explanations. These scholars note that Yugoslavia, despite all its institutional peculiarities, suffered from exactly the same systemic weaknesses as all the other socialist economies, such as low efficiency, lack of technological dynamism, and low adaptability. These weaknesses became increasingly obvious against the background of the wider processes of change characterized by increasing interdependence and globalization, which intensified from the late 1970s.[68] Self-management only exacerbated these problems by further politicizing all aspects of Yugoslavia's economic life, eliminating other political alternatives, and thwarting the application of market-driven economic rationale. John Allcock notes that by the time the federal commissions trying to tackle the economic crisis concluded that the reform of the economy required a complete revision of the political system, the republics' interests were too divergent and the legitimacy of the federal centre was too tied to the ideology of self-management to allow the necessary reforms to take place.[69] In his view it was this combination of Yugoslavia's failed modernization and the lure of Western levels of prosperity that ultimately sealed the fate of the country.

What these approaches have in common is their emphasis on the crisis of the Yugoslav system—a crisis that manifested itself in the 1980s but whose roots ran much deeper, sometimes even to the very core of the Yugoslav system itself.[70] In this respect, there are two questions that arise: a first that concerns the alternatives to this particular evolution and a second that focuses on the interconnectedness between the Yugoslav state and the Yugoslav system. The explanations analyzed in this section make a convincing argument that the viability of the Yugoslav state was intrinsically tied to the viability of its system based on its twin claims of providing a different and unique road to socialism and of having resolved Yugoslavia's national question (by virtue of its federal structure, which gave equality to each of its nations). However, when did this system actually become unviable, and—specifically—were there roads not taken in the course of Yugoslavia's evolution that could have prevented the full-scale crisis and breakdown of the 1980s?

Here, a number of scholars have pointed to the watershed of 1971, marked by the suppression of the Croatian "spring" and the purge of the party "liberals" in Serbia and Croatia (and, perhaps somewhat less importantly, in Slovenia and Macedonia). Had the liberals remained in power, could their policies of economic modernization and constitutional decentralization have guaranteed Yugoslavia's survival in the longer term? Would they have been able to steer Kardelj's ideologically inspired system toward a more realistic process of political and economic modernization and possibly ensured the system's legitimacy—albeit on grounds other than those of the Partisan generation—and thus prevented its ultimate collapse? While all this remains in the realm of speculation, it would nevertheless be fruitful to explore the period of liberal rule in the late 1960s and early 1970s in greater depth than has been done so far.

Secondly, it would be worthwhile examining the interconnectedness between Yugoslavia's system and the state in more detail. By the 1980s, both the economic and political pillars of Yugoslavia's *system*—as well as its ideological foundation—were clearly in crisis. Yet, while most scholars were predicting that some sort of change was inevitable, the complete disintegration of the state, and particularly the kind of violence it was to engender, were not yet being envisaged.[71] Indeed, one could make the case that the final disintegration of the Yugoslav state in 1991 came as a surprise not just to most scholars but also to most of Yugoslavia's citizens.[72] Even in Slovenia, which was arguably set on the course to independence after its referendum at the end of 1990, polls indicated ambivalence about whether independence would actually be achieved.[73] So the question remains: if the state had effectively already "withered away," why did nobody notice?

Finally, there is also the question of why Yugoslavia's disintegration was violent, which most of these explanations do not seek to answer.[74] Indeed, there is a general acknowledgment among scholars that while longer-term structural factors may contribute to explaining why violence is more likely to occur in certain regions, the timing of such violence is highly contingent on the events and the context in which it takes place. Some scholars have thus attributed the outbreak of conflict to what is known in international relations theory as the "security dilemma." The argument is that in a situation of state dissolution marked by the absence of an overarching "sovereign," various groups (ethnic, religious, etc.) find themselves having to resort to "self-help" in order to protect their own security—a function that is normally the preserve of the state. In such circumstances, individual actions to reinforce their own group's security—even if undertaken for purely defensive purposes—will undermine the security of other groups, producing a spiral akin to that of an arms race between countries. In conditions of heightened uncertainty and fear and a particular military balance—the argument goes—preemptive action and the possibility of escalation leading to war become more likely.[75] A number of scholars have pointed out, however, that the security dilemma represents a symptom of conflict rather than a cause of it, and that what needs to be explained is the construction (and subsequent instrumentalization) of the security dilemma itself, along with the fear and hatred that fueled it. In this respect, they highlight the role played by political and intellectual elites and the importance of human agency.[76]

The Twilight of Yugoslavia: The Role of Political and Intellectual Agency

The fourth cluster of explanations for Yugoslavia's demise focuses on the last years of the country's existence and the role of political and intellectual agency. In the view of these authors, although Yugoslavia was experiencing a general systemic crisis in the 1980s, there was nothing foreordained about its dissolution as a state; rather—they argue—state collapse was the outcome of the policies and strategies of specific domestic (or, according to some authors, international) actors taking place within the particular context of the end of the Cold War. As Dennison Rusinow put it:

> Yugoslavia's second disintegration actually became "inevitable" only shortly before it occurred, and primarily because the calculations and/or ineptitude of post-Tito politicians from several regions and nations, superimposed on a decade of mounting economic, political and social crisis that had "de-legitimized" the regime and system *but not yet the state,* transformed endemic tensions and conflicts among its diverse nationalities into collective existential fears for their communal survival that progressively infected them all.[77]

In Rusinow's view, as in that of most other authors in this group, Yugoslavia did not "dissolve" of its own accord, as a result of structural and historical forces, or the delegitimation of its socialist system. The country could have effected a peaceful transformation as communism collapsed, but it was violently destroyed by certain republican leaderships, who used the state-controlled media and other levers of power to produce a veritable "industry of hate" and launch wars aimed at the creation of new states.[78]

The question of agency will be examined by focusing on three main debates characteristic of the scholarship belonging to this last group of explanations: the first debate concerns the motivations, goals, and strategies of the political leaderships, particularly of Serbia's leader Slobodan Milošević, who has been singled out as the most responsible for the country's violent breakup; the second debate concerns the role and responsibility of intellectuals, and specifically of the Serbian Academy's 1986 draft Memorandum; and the third debate concerns the extent to which disintegration was an elite-led, as opposed to a grassroots, phenomenon. After considering these three debates surrounding these internal factors, I will finally turn to the role of external factors in Yugoslavia's breakup, examining the work of authors who have placed their emphasis on the importance of Western policies toward the Yugoslav crisis.

In the scholarship—as well as in the writings of journalists and Western policy makers involved in the Yugoslav crisis—there is a near consensus concerning the centrality of the role played by Serbia's leader Slobodan Milošević in the disintegration process. The general perception of his importance is mirrored in the fact that (at the time of writing this chapter) there are at least twelve English-language books specifically devoted to analyzing Milošević—compared to the scant interest in any of his contemporaries among the Yugoslav leaders.[79] Indeed, many accounts of Yugoslavia's disintegration and wars begin in 1987 with Milošević's rise to power and his first speech in Kosovo Polje, where he famously declared to the local Serbs that "nobody [would] be allowed to beat [them]."[80] But the exact nature of Milošević's role and strategy, as well as the importance and strategies of other actors, remain matters of considerable dispute.

One side of the debate on Milošević's role takes a broadly intentionalist approach in the sense that it derives motives from actions and ascribes a level of coherence to these actions indicating a premeditated strategy. In his 2002 biography, Louis Sell thus states that "Yugoslavia did not die a natural death; it was murdered, and Milošević, more than any other single leader, is responsible."[81] In Sell's view, until January 1990 Milošević pursued "a careful and well-planned strategy, aimed first at winning supreme power for himself in Serbia proper and then at dominating all of Yugoslavia."[82] This hegemonic strategy, as well as his harnessing of Serbian nationalism and the repression unleashed by him against the Kosovo Albanians convinced the leaders of the other republics that "there was no place for them in a country that also included Milošević," effectively leaving them no other choice but to opt for independence.[83] At this point, Sell argues, Milošević adopted a new strategy of using armed force to carve out a "Greater Serbian" state "with the full knowledge that this would cause the disintegration of Yugoslavia and war."[84]

Other scholars do not share this intentionalist view of Milošević. According to Lenard Cohen, "it would be wrong to assume that the blueprint for the entire course of events connected with the disintegration of Yugoslavia, the subsequent wars in Croatia and Bosnia, and various policies such as 'ethnic cleansing' were all part of some master plan or conspiracy hatched by Milošević and a coterie of Serbian intellectuals during the 1987–1988 period."[85] Instead, Cohen presents Milošević as a ruthless, intelligent, and tactically astute but ultimately reactive and unstrategic political gambler who was far too much of a pragmatist to have followed any preset plan for a Greater Serbia and whose only overarching cause was to ensure his own political survival. In his 1993 book *Broken Bonds*, Cohen distributed blame for the country's disintegration more evenly among the republican leaderships, viewing it a result of their failure in the second half of the 1980s "to agree upon a revised model of political and economic coexistence that could have preserved some form of state unity"—a failure he attributes to both inter-elite mistrust and elite-led ethnic nationalism.[86] In his political biography of Milošević, Cohen explicitly rejects what he calls "the paradise lost/loathsome leaders perspective" that came to replace the "ancient hatreds" paradigm in American policy circles in the mid-1990s, as placing too great an emphasis on the instrumentalization of ethnic divisions, fears, and grievances by leaders and assuming that once those leaders were out of power such differences would be overcome.[87]

Finally, some scholars have argued that while political elites were indeed important in bringing about Yugoslavia's demise, they did not actually aim to destroy the country. They also believe that far too much emphasis has been placed on Milošević and Serbia's policy. Susan Woodward thus argues that it was the Slovenian leadership of Milan Kučan that first "attacked the stabilizing political mechanisms of the socialist period" and first began using "popular Slovene national sentiment and protest activity to serve the republic's objectives in foreign policy and reform" (although Serbia was not far behind).[88] In her opinion, however, neither Kučan nor Milošević were following a coherent plan; instead, she argues, they were both responding to specific events and "choosing tactics of consequence, but not necessarily thinking out the chain of those consequences or the logic of their daily steps."[89] Dejan Jović also argues that "the sources available . . . do not provide sufficient grounds for the conclusion that the members of the Yugoslav political elite in this period (including, therefore, Slobodan Milošević and Milan Kučan) intended to break up Yugoslavia." He believes that, in fact, "many of those whose actions in the end brought about the disintegration had a completely opposite motive: to save Yugoslavia, not to destroy it."[90]

Despite the wealth and variety of sources available to scholars studying Yugoslavia's dissolution (which include memoirs, interviews, and speeches by the actors themselves, transcripts of discussions within government bodies, accounts by various international negotiators, and testimonies and evidence presented to the International Criminal Tribunal for the former Yugoslavia), the problem concerning the role of Milošević is that so far no official government document or transcript of a meeting has been discovered that would incontrovertibly implicate Milošević in a coherent, premeditated strategy of breaking up Yugoslavia in order to create a Greater Serbia.[91] The evidence used by advocates of all the scholarly interpretations discussed above is based on witness accounts and memoirs, media reports, and Milošević's public pronouncements made during the period. But this evidence is in many cases contradictory and hardly impartial, leaving a variety of interpretations possible. The main stumbling block remains the fact that Milošević's policy style was extremely secretive, leaving very little documentary trace. Strategic decisions were usually made in the privacy of his home, with his wife, Mira Marković (who is alleged to have had a significant influence on him), and a small group of select advisors (who were often changed and only privy to limited discussions).[92] As has been noted, his public pronouncements do not represent a clear statement of purpose. Until 1991 and even after the onset of the war, he never openly rejected Yugoslavism; to the contrary, he usually professed his actions were aimed to preserve the common state.[93] While the sincerity of such statements may be doubted—as, indeed, it most often has been—it has been difficult to extrapolate a clear strategy from his speeches and interviews. Rather, such a strategy has been pieced together by scholars from specific actions (such as the creation of Serb "autonomous units" in Croatia and Bosnia in 1990), eyewitness accounts (such as that of Milošević's 1991 meeting with Croatia's President Tudjman in Karadjordjevo, where they allegedly agreed on the carving up of Bosnia) and the conduct of war in the 1990s (notably the pattern of "ethnic cleansing" campaigns).[94]

Also, Milošević's policy went through several different stages in the 1980s and 1990s, often leaving former mentors and advisors surprised and puzzled at his chameleon-like permutations. Beginning his career as an economic reformer but a political conservative committed to keeping alive Tito's "image and legacy," in 1988–89 Milošević turned to nationalist populism. Having backed the Serbs' war effort in Croatia and Bosnia-Herzegovina in the early 1990s, by 1994 he recast himself as an advocate of peace, accepted the fall of the Serb "republic" in Croatia, and played an instrumental role in ensuring the success of the Dayton peace accords in 1995, giving up many important Bosnian Serb territorial claims. In 1998, as the situation in Kosovo deteriorated, Milošević once again adopted an indiscriminately belligerent and repressive policy in the province and a more directly authoritarian form of rule in Serbia. When he was expected to be recalcitrant and a tough negotiator (as in Dayton), he ended up being more than accommodating; when he was viewed as a political pragmatist who was only concerned with his own power and would give in quickly to superior U.S. and NATO pressure (as in Rambouillet and its aftermath in 1999), he did nothing of the kind—even at the risk of war against the world's most powerful alliance. Although many ex post facto explanations for

Milošević's behavior have been given, during the period of his rule, scholars, pundits, and international negotiators found it virtually impossible to predict his actions or the course of his policy.

The overwhelming focus on Milošević and Serbia's policy has left some crucial gaps in our understanding of the role played by political agency. Only a few scholars have examined the dynamics of the road to Slovenian independence dating from the initial debates over the shape of Yugoslavia in the early 1960s to the post-Tito constitutional debates, as well as the personal and political transformation of Milan Kučan and of Slovenia's process of "national homogenization" at the end of the 1980s. The connection between the "Croatian Spring" of 1971 and the revival of nationalism in 1989, along with the return of many of the leading personalities from 1971 onto the Croatian political scene, have not been explored.[95] Neither have the post-1971 Croatian leadership's chronic lack of popular legitimacy and its own internal divisions, which facilitated the rise of Franjo Tudjman and his Croatian Democratic Union at the end of the 1980s. The Slovenian and Croatian proposal for a Yugoslav "confederation" in October 1990, which has often been hailed as a missed opportunity to save Yugoslavia in some form and thus forestall the descent into violence, has also not been adequately analyzed.[96] Furthermore, while the impact of Milošević's reckless and belligerent actions on the electoral results and proindependence policies in other Yugoslav republics have been highlighted, the same kind of approach is often missing from analyses of Serbia's evolution; in other words, to what extent did Milošević's actions, as well as his electoral successes, represent a response to the policies and standpoints taken by other Yugoslav actors?

Finally, existing analyses of Yugoslavia's dissolution have not paid adequate attention to the pro-Yugoslav alternatives that existed in the political sphere of all the republics, as well as on the federal level. Considering that sociological data point to the existence of considerable grassroots support for some kind of Yugoslavia, why were the pro-Yugoslav forces so unsuccessful at politically mobilizing that support in the late 1980s? The existing literature provides some answers to this question: Juan Linz and Alfred Stepan have highlighted the role of electoral sequencing (the fact that the first multiparty elections in 1990 were held on the republican instead of the federal level), whereas institutionalist accounts have emphasized the decentralization of Yugoslavia, which meant that, by the 1980s, republican leaderships had control of the key levers of power, including the media.[97] What is missing, however, is a more thorough analysis of the forging and the internal dynamics of the Yugoslav alternative itself, made up as it was of a myriad of intellectuals and civic groups and, from 1989, political parties. A reflection about the implications of the official abandoning of Yugoslavism in the mid-1960s for the ultimate failure of the Yugoslav political option and of the cooptation of a Yugoslav rhetoric by Milošević in the late 1980s would also be a welcome addition to such an analysis. Within this general examination of Yugoslav alternatives, the role of the Yugoslav People's Army (JNA) as an authoritarian Yugoslav option represents another important case study. Considering the army's commitment to upholding Tito's legacy and the Yugoslav state and the fact that military coups at a time of deep national crisis are certainly not uncommon, why did the JNA not intervene at crucial moments when it could have done so (as, for example, in March 1991 when the Serbian-led resignation of several members of the collective federal presidency deliberately created an opportunity for a JNA take-over)? How unified was the army leadership at this stage, and in what ways did its own evolution mirror the disintegration of Yugoslavia's political and cultural institutions? Would a military coup have been a realistic way of preventing the violent disintegration of the country, as has at times been argued?[98]

The second debate in the scholarship concerns the role and responsibility of intellectual elites in the process of Yugoslavia's dissolution, and once again the overwhelming focus has been on Serbian intellectuals. This debate has most often crystallized around the draft Memorandum of the Serbian Academy of Sciences and Arts, an eclectic and contradictory document drafted by a commission of sixteen academicians charged with analyzing the causes of Yugoslavia's post-Tito crisis. The text, which is divided into two parts—one on the causes and manifestations of the crisis and one specifically concerned with "the status of Serbia and the Serbian nation"—was leaked unfinished to the press in September 1986 and vehemently criticized by the Serbian political establishment. In 1989, with Milošević's resorting to a more nationalist discourse and populist tactics to help him force through constitutional changes that aimed at the recentralization of Serbia and Yugoslavia, the document was revived—in Croatia and Slovenia as the "master plan" of Milošević's policy and in Serbia as a prescient analysis of Yugoslavia's woes and Croatian and Slovenian secessionism.[99] Since then, the Memorandum has become the most-cited text in accounts of Yugoslavia's disintegration and remains unavoidable in any discussion of the causes of the breakdown.

There are several opposed positions on the nature and the significance of the Memorandum. Some analysts view the document as the intellectual foundation of Milošević's "Greater Serbia" policy and even as a "blueprint for war."[100] As Branimir Anzulović puts it, the Memorandum "formed the ideological platform for the pan-Serbian policy of Slobodan Milošević" and "became a program for action when the disintegration of the communist order made many Serbs believe that they had a unique opportunity to transform federal Yugoslavia into Greater Serbia with the help of the Serb-dominated Yugoslav armed forces."[101] Other scholars, such as Aleksandar Pavković, argue—to the contrary—that many Serbian intellectuals remained Yugoslav in their orientation, in some cases even after the end of the common state in 1991. Although Pavković notes the contradictions inherent in the document (unfinished as it was and with different parts written by different authors) and states that the Memorandum contained an expression of an "unspecified and rather rudimentary Serbism—the conception of an independent state of the Serbs"—he argues that the Memorandum advocated above all a "reformed Yugoslav federation" of the kind that prevailed prior to the decentralizing reforms of the 1960s and 1970s.[102] In his view, the Memorandum's significance lies not so much in the solutions it proposes but in the very fact of its "re-opening" of the "national question" in the 1980s, triggering a new debate on Serbian national goals. Finally, a somewhat different point of view is taken by Audrey Budding. Like Pavković, she rejects the view that the Memorandum represented "an explicit post-Yugoslav Serbian national program," but for her the document had a more ominous significance, acting as an "indicator" of a particular belief system and a change of attitude toward the common state—increasingly viewing Yugoslavia as expendable but without acknowledging the destruction that its breakup would entail.[103]

My own view is closest to this third interpretation. The Memorandum does not advocate the dissolution of Yugoslavia, let alone the creation of a Greater Serbia or ethnic cleansing. Of course, this does not mean that some intellectuals associated with the Memorandum did not eventually come to embrace such policies, but at the time when it was written (between the summer of 1985 and September 1986) mentioning anything of the kind would have led to instant imprisonment.[104] There is also no proven connection between the authors of the Memorandum and Milošević at the time, nor was Milošević's own position significantly different from that of the rest of the Serbian leadership, which unequivocally condemned the text. This said, however, the Memorandum is important in a different way: it represents above all a repository of Serbian nationalist grievances against Yugoslavia and an embodiment of the kind of discourse that was becoming dominant in Serbia's intellectual circles—a discourse that was based on an extreme vision of victimization, used terms such as *genocide* to depict the situation of the Serbs in Yugoslavia (particularly in Kosovo), and created links between it and the greatest Serbian trauma of the twentieth century—the mass extermination of Serbs in the wartime Independent State of Croatia. In a situation where public discourse about both the historical memory of the war and the present situation of the Kosovo Serbs was ideologically predetermined and certain themes represented official taboos, these types of images were extremely potent, providing a sense of existential crisis that could be harnessed for a more belligerent and uncompromising policy and could later be used to justify repugnant wartime practices such as ethnic cleansing.[105]

The debate on the nature and significance of the Memorandum raises a wider question about the role and responsibility of intellectuals, not just as the articulators of a nationalist worldview but also as the carriers of a political alternative. In view of Yugoslavia's single-party system and the historical legacy of intellectual engagement in East-Central Europe where the cultural sphere often had to act as a surrogate for politics, intellectuals should have been the natural vectors of a democratic opposition to what was essentially an undemocratic regime. And, indeed, this was the case from the late 1970s, particularly in the two least repressive republics, Serbia and Slovenia, where intellectual oppositions coalesced around the defense of freedom of expression and civil rights. In the end, however, the language of democracy became subsumed in the language of nationalism, and the struggle for democratic change was inherently tied to the struggle for national rights and entitlements to territory. In this respect, one of Yugoslavia's main problems was that in the 1980s, when opportunities for a different outcome still existed, the divided and bickering republican intellectual oppositions did not present any genuine alternative to the undemocratic and unproductive practices of the regime. The voices of those individuals who advocated dialogue and compromise on all sides were drowned out by the increasingly radical and ubiquitous nationalist rhetoric. It is this failure to present a peaceful political alternative and to set an example of tolerance and compromise that represents Yugoslavia's intellectual elites' most devastating contribution to their country's violent dissolution. Indeed, the first common Yugoslav institution to disintegrate at the end of the 1980s was a cultural one—the Yugoslav Writers' Union—representing an important precursor of the political breakdown of the common state.[106]

Finally, as in the case of political agency, existing analyses of the role of intellectuals in Yugoslavia's dissolution process call for more comparative work.[107] The activities and discourse of Serbian intellectuals have been analyzed in great detail, but what of parallel streamings in other Yugoslav republics? Slovenian intellectuals (particularly contributors to the journal *Nova revija*) have played as important a role as their Serbian counterparts in the revival of nationalism in their own republic, but their trajectory has not received nearly as much attention in the literature. The development of the Croatian dissidence since the suppression of the 1971 "spring" would also merit more sustained examination, as would the evolution of the intellectual sphere in Bosnia-Herzegovina, Kosovo, Macedonia, and Montenegro. Sociological analyses of the transmission of the ideas and "products" of intellectuals to the mass level, particularly in the course of the 1980s, are also missing. For example, it would be interesting to know who actually read the Memorandum in the 1980s and how the ideas contained in it reached the wider public. Who were the "consumers" of the nationalist histories and literary works that began to appear in the 1970s and 1980s throughout Yugoslavia? It is only when we are able to answer questions like these that we will gain a better understanding of the impact intellectuals had on Yugoslavia's process of dissolution.

The third scholarly debate covering the proximate causes of Yugoslavia's breakdown concerns the extent to which dissolution was an elite-led, as opposed to a grassroots-driven, phenomenon. The strongest statement of the former position is provided by V. P. Gagnon, who has argued that the Yugoslav wars of the 1990s were imposed from outside on peaceful multiethnic communities (such as in Bosnia-Herzegovina), in particular from Milošević's Serbia and Tudjman's Croatia. The violence that accompanied Yugoslavia's dissolution was, in Gagnon's view, "a strategic policy chosen by elites who were confronted with political pluralism and popular mobilization" in an attempt to demobilize domestic challengers and impose political homogeneity within their own republics.[108] Affirming that ethnicity is a fluid and malleable identity, Gagnon argues that the Serbian and Croatian political elites did not simply play the "ethnic card" by appealing to preexisting identities and fears but "constructed" ethnicity as "a hard category" and ethnic groups as "clearly bounded, monolithic, unambiguous units"; as he puts it, "it is the very inability of elites to 'play the ethnic card' as a means to mobilize the population that leads them to rely on violence."[109]

Other scholars, such as Rogers Brubaker, have, in contrast, argued that it would be wrong to treat the mobilization of national minorities (such as the Croatian Serbs) as a simple story of outside manipulation. While he acknowledges the important role played by nationalist elites from Serbia in the process of Croatian Serb mobilization, he notes:

> Although representations of wartime atrocities—often greatly exaggerated—were indeed widely propagated from Belgrade, memories of and stories about the murderous wartime Independent State of Croatia and especially about the gruesome fate of many Croat and Bosnian Serbs (Bosnia having been incorporated into the wartime Croatian state), were not imports. They were locally rooted, sustained within family and village circles, and transmitted to the postwar generations, especially in the ethnically mixed and partly Serb-majority borderland regions.[110]

In this respect, Brubaker argues, national minorities should be recognized as active participants in the conflict and as political subjects in their own right, not just as pawns of hostile outside forces.

This debate raises some important questions, the first being the nature of historical memory of past conflict and its role in national mobilization. Most existing studies indicate that ignoring historical memory is impossible when trying to account for Yugoslavia's violent breakup. This is particularly true of those parts of the country—the multiethnic border regions of Croatia and Bosnia-Herzegovina—that saw the worst of the civil and national strife during the Second World War and that were again the main theaters of war in the 1990s.[111] As Jan-Werner Müller correctly notes, however, "while very few would doubt that memory mattered and exercised power in the Yugoslav wars, even fewer would be able to explain precisely how it mattered."[112] Understanding the role played by historical memory inevitably entails an examination of both "official memory"—sponsored and propagated by the political authorities and intellectual elites under the communist regime, as well as by their various successors in the post-Yugoslav states—and "private" memory, generally transmitted across generations through family oral history.[113] The problem is, however, that all such memory (both official and private) is inevitably partial, multiple, and conflicting; most commentators of Yugoslavia's wars have noted the impossibility of reconciling the diametrically opposed historical narratives presented not only by the various national groups but also by supporters of different ideologies (communist, liberal, or nationalist) and members of different social strata. Even more importantly, as the anthropologist Ger Duijzings notes in his study of history and memory in eastern Bosnia, "views even conflict within the self-same individuals in their attempts to resolve all these contradictions and construct coherent stories for themselves."[114]

This type of evidence corroborates Gagnon's argument that memory and identity were—within certain parameters—fluid categories that were shaped largely by their particular context. Much valuable work already exists on the construction and instrumentalization of memory by political and intellectual elites in the Yugoslav republics.[115] Yet, in order to understand better why certain images and stereotypes resonated with parts of the population in such a potent way (while others, notably of periods of peaceful coexistence, were suppressed), more research is needed into the way that everyday social interaction, rumor and hearsay, economic crisis, and local power relations shaped identity and memory. In other words, it is the *interaction* between existing private memories, the changing official memory—shaped as it was by accounts of the victimization of one's own nation—and the evolving patterns and relations of everyday life that needs further study. A fruitful way of tackling this complex task might be to move away from national or even republican categories and focus instead on local or family histories.[116]

The second, related, question concerns the nature of national mobilization in the period leading up to Yugoslavia's breakdown and the outbreak of war. To what extent was this mobilization orchestrated and controlled from above, and to what extent did it come about as a local, grassroots phenomenon in response to the particular community's fears and grievances, as well as specific political opportunity structures of the time? As Nebojša Vladisavljević notes, the overwhelming focus on elites has resulted in comparatively few studies' being devoted specifically to the grassroots aspects of national mobilization.[117] His own work on the Kosovo Serb mobilization in the 1980s indicates that this was a genuine grassroots social movement that predated Milošević's rise to power and remained an autonomous political force, despite at times cooperating with the Serbian regime.[118] Indeed, grassroots national mobilization was recurrent in the country even before the late 1980s, as shown by the mass demonstrations of Kosovo Albanians in 1968 and 1981 and the 1971 Croatian spring.[119] Analyses of the 1989 mobilization of Kosovo Albanians in response to Serbia's constitutional changes have also indicated the essentially grassroots nature of this political protest.[120] The rise of the Slovenian youth and social movements in the early 1980s, as well as the 1988 "national mobilization" that coalesced against the trial of three Slovenian journalists and an army officer before a military court (known as the *Mladina* trial), were also largely grassroots-driven forms of political protest.[121]

In their different ways (and despite their various exaggerations), all these grassroots movements did represent expressions of genuine popular discontent with aspects of the Yugoslav system and reactions to real discrimination combined with an acute sense of fear—emotions that could be harnessed by political elites for policies that were sometimes far removed from the desires of those they allegedly represented. They also show that despite Yugoslavia's comparatively liberal and "Westernized" veneer, it remained an essentially undemocratic state where breaches of human and civil rights were endemic and where citizens did not have recourse to legitimate institutions to voice their grievances. Minimizing grassroots discontent and writing off such mobilization as simply manipulated from above means ignoring the conditions that not only enabled the rise of nationalism but also made particular leaders possible and popular. As some scholars have noted, the inauguration of democratization with the 1990 multiparty republican elections did not resolve this fundamental problem but only exacerbated it by further empowering nationalist leaderships.[122] Finally, the overwhelming focus on political elites does not enable us to understand the continuing problems in the region even after the political removal (or death) of former leaders, such as the persistence of nationalism and the challenge of defining states and constructing democratic institutions.

The Impact of International Factors

The great majority of the scholarship on Yugoslavia's dissolution has tended to emphasize internal causes rather than external ones. Although there has been a tremendous amount of debate on the international *reaction* to the Yugoslav crisis, scholars have seen the international context and the policies of the major Western institutional and state actors as a contributing factor at best. Generally, they mention the end of the Cold War in relation to both the erosion of Yugoslavia's internal legitimacy and its loss of strategic importance to the West, which conditioned Western ambivalence and "lack of will" to act decisively in the Yugoslav crisis.[123] Since the mid-1990s, however, this has begun to change as more and more studies have appeared arguing that Western policies were a crucial cause of the country's disintegration. Two main explanations have emerged in regard to the role of external factors in Yugoslavia's breakdown: a first focused on international financial institutions and American neoliberal economic policies in the 1980s, and a second focused on the support of certain Western states, particularly Germany, for Slovenia's and Croatia's independence.

The role of external economic factors in the process of Yugoslavia's disintegration was first highlighted in the English-language scholarship by Susan Woodward in her 1995 book *Balkan Tragedy*. Woodward argues that the breakdown of Yugoslavia's political and civil order was exacerbated by Western insistence on economic austerity policies, which upset the delicate checks and balances that governed state authority, turning normal political conflicts over economic resources and reforms into constitutional conflicts and a crisis of the state.[124] She notes that, in a situation of harsh austerity, budgetary conflicts, and economic policy aimed at reducing trade deficits and foreign debt, republican governments effectively abandoned the systemic guarantees of national equality, defied tax obligations to the federation, and began increasingly to question the very foundations of state legitimacy.[125]

Woodward's analysis has since informed the work of a number of other scholars, particularly in Great Britain. Kate Hudson thus argues that in the 1980s Yugoslavia's external debt made it particularly vulnerable to the liberal macroeconomic reform advocated by Western financial institutions, which fueled the resistance of the wealthier republics against subsidizing the poorer parts of the federation and encouraged their perception that without the ballast of the rest of the country they would more easily gain admission to the German economic zone and the European Community.[126] This situation was exacerbated following the fall of communism in Eastern Europe in 1989, when Yugoslavia lost its strategic importance to the United States and the reintroduction of capitalism and the institutionalization of liberal democracy in the region became the only remaining superpower's prime objectives. David Chandler notes that after 1989, although the United States still nominally supported the Yugoslav federal government of Prime Minister Ante Marković, it perceived the weakness of the federal government as a liability and undermined the federation's legitimacy by asserting that unity could not be preserved by force. Instead, new American officials (notably the U.S. Ambassador to Yugoslavia, Warren Zimmermann), who were "keen to reshape their links in the region," increasingly began to argue in favour of "democracy" over "unity."[127] This change in U.S. policy was immediately seized upon by separatist forces in Slovenia and Croatia, which portrayed their own cause as one of human rights, self-determination, and democracy against the "communist national-authoritarianism" of Milošević's Serbia and the Yugoslav army. In this, they received support from leading politicians in Germany and Austria, as well as from leading German-language newspaper editors and journalists sympathetic to their cause. Thus emboldened, the Slovene and Croat leaderships refused to compromise either in the negotiations on reforming the federation or—in the case of Croatia—in their talks with the Serb minority in the republic. Instead of unequivocally backing the federal government, Western policy-makers attempted to "mediate" between the state and the separatist republics, thus effectively legitimating separatist claims and eventually imposing a settlement on the separatists' terms.[128] Chandler concludes: "Far from contributing to peace and stability, the policy and actions of Western powers undermined the federal institutions that held Yugoslavia together and then prevented compromise solutions, between and within republics, that could have minimized the conflict."[129]

Scholars emphasizing the role of external factors in Yugoslavia's disintegration have been particularly critical of the Western powers' recognition policy in 1991–92. Raju Thomas thus argues that Yugoslavia did not disintegrate or collapse, but rather that it was "*dismembered* through a selective and prejudicial international recognition policy of its internal 'republics.'"[130] According to Thomas, Yugoslavia's crisis of the 1980s was not unique; it was a "domestic constitutional crisis" of the kind that represented a "perennial Yugoslav situation." The implication is that without external meddling and "promises of support for secession followed by formal recognition" this crisis would not have led to the disintegration of the state.[131] Other scholars have viewed the European Community (EC) Arbitration Commission (also known as the Badinter Commission) as deeply flawed. The Commission's Opinions of November 1991 that Yugoslavia was "in the process of dissolution" but that its internal (i.e., republican) borders were inviolable have been singled out for particular criticism. Leslie Benson thus argues that "the combined effect [of these two opinions] was to deny the legal existence of Yugoslavia, so cutting the ground from under the feet of the Serbs, and to make lines on maps the object of diplomacy."[132]

Finally, scholars have noted that even those guidelines that were provided by the Arbitration Commission were ultimately disregarded, as the EC, headed by Germany, proceeded to grant recognition to the seceding republics prior to the achievement of an overall settlement and without regard to the Arbitration Commission's recommendations, which—when they came out in January 1992—were contrary to some of the decisions made by the EC member governments.[133] Above all, it has often been argued that Germany's preemptive recognition of Slovenia and Croatia on December 23, 1991, effectively sabotaged international efforts to negotiate an overall settlement for Yugoslavia by creating a diplomatic fait accompli and removing the one tool that the international community could have credibly used to get the parties to compromise.[134] As Susan Woodward put it:

> The precedent set by the German maneuver was that the principle of self-determination could legitimately break up multinational states, that EC application of this principle was arbitrary, and that the surest way for politicians bent on independence to succeed was to instigate a defensive war and win international sympathy and then recognition.[135]

Similarly, the American drive for the recognition of Bosnia-Herzegovina in April 1992 has at times been blamed for being the spark that set that republic on fire.[136]

In contrast to these views, some scholars have argued that the Western powers' main mistake was not the recognition of the seceding republics but the continuing adherence to the fiction of a "united" Yugoslavia, which only encouraged the army-backed Serbian military onslaught. Citing the visit of U.S. Secretary of State James Baker to Belgrade on the eve of the Slovenian and Croatian declarations of independence in June 1991, Sabrina Ramet thus argues that America's commitment to Yugoslavia's unity must have been read by Milošević as "an open invitation to ignite hostilities."[137] In a similar vein, Daniele Conversi has defended Germany's drive for immediate and unconditional recognition of the two breakaway republics, arguing that such a policy could have acted as a deterrent against Serbia's territorial designs and that internationalizing the conflict would have enabled more effective international (military) intervention to protect the borders of the newly recognized states.[138] Ramet details the approach she believes would have been advisable at the time:

> What could the West have done? First, the West could have granted de facto recognition to Slovenia and Croatia at the end of June 1991, and begun talks about arms supplies to these two republics. Second, the economic embargo against Serbia and Montenegro could have been imposed earlier (at the latest in August 1991). Third, Slovenia and Macedonia could have been granted full diplomatic recognition (de

jure and de facto) in December 1991, after the EC study commission commended these two republics on their respect for human rights. Croatia could have been given a solemn pledge of full recognition upon the fulfilment of certain tasks. Fourth, the West could have conducted aerial bombardment of Serbian transport infrastructure, fuel tanks, arms factories, hydroelectric plants, radar stations, and farmlands (the last of these to impact food supplies) as a demonstration of seriousness of purpose and in order to complicate the Serbian war effort. . . . Fifth, the West could have provided guarantees of the borders of Slovenia, Croatia, and Macedonia, arranged for the peaceful partition of Bosnia into three roughly equal sections, and assisted the sides in conducting population exchanges to eliminate minority problems in Croatia, Serbia and the truncated Muslim Bosnia. And, sixth, the West could have proposed an international conference to settle the Kosovo question . . . (that is, . . . the transfer of all or most of the province to Albania).[139]

In other words, rather than seeing Western policy as favouring the secessionist republics and undermining Yugoslavia's unity, these scholars argue that it in fact contributed to the pursuit of the Greater Serbian project and the onset and escalation of the conflict.[140] The European Community's recognition policy was thus the right course of action, but effectively came too late and was not accompanied by more robust forms of intervention, which it made possible by internationalizing the conflict.[141]

This debate on the role of Western policy in Yugoslavia's breakup is based on very different answers to two related questions: first, the question of the continuing viability and desirability of Yugoslavia as a state; and second, the question of the intentions and policies of the main domestic actors in the Yugoslav drama. One side in the debate has generally viewed Yugoslavia as a greatly weakened and crisis-ridden state but as an essentially viable and desirable one. Although they generally did not endorse Milošević's policy, these scholars saw Serbian concerns over the breakup of the common state as legitimate and the outbreak of war as the result of policies of all the sides involved. From this point of view, their preferred course of action would have been an unequivocal commitment to Yugoslavia's unity and a stronger international economic and political backing for the federal government of Prime Minister Ante Marković and other democratic pro-Yugoslav forces in the country. The other side in the debate has tended to emphasize the legitimacy of Croatian and Slovenian desires for independence over that of Yugoslavia as a state. Scholars belonging to this group argue that Yugoslavia's federal institutions were neither representative nor legitimate and believe that the internal breakdown of the federal state had gone past the point of no return by spring 1991. They generally have little sympathy for Serbian concerns, viewing them as a mere pretext for what they argue was essentially a war of aggression and territorial conquest. From this perspective, they would have preferred immediate recognition of the Yugoslav federal units (including Kosovo) and a strong military commitment to protecting their borders.[142]

This controversy over the role of external factors raises further questions that have to date not received conclusive answers. As many scholars have noted, there was no such thing as a single Western policy in the spring of 1991—rather there were many mixed messages, based primarily on interests and calculations that had less to do with Yugoslavia than with other geopolitical concerns linked to the end of the Cold War and the implosion of the Soviet Union.[143] Yet, if we are to understand how Western policies affected the calculations of the main Yugoslav actors, more information is needed on the actual contacts that took place between them and on any eventual promises made by Western interlocutors to their Serbian, Slovene, or Croat counterparts in the last few years of Yugoslavia's existence. Secondly, a better understanding is needed of how the various Yugoslav leaderships *interpreted* Western leaders' statements and how their interests and policies were shaped by their *perceptions* of the changing geopolitical context. Such information is now accessible from the many memoirs and eyewitness accounts that have appeared since the early 1990s, as well as testimonies before the International Criminal Tribunal for the Former Yugoslavia and the publication of certain government documents and transcripts. A close examination of these types of sources may help us understand, for example, the nature of Slovenian and Croatian contacts with politicians and opinion-makers in Germany (and other Western countries), and how such contacts may have affected their calculations and strategies in the drive for independence in 1990–91. It would also contribute to an assessment of whether Serbian policy was driven by the perception that the Western powers would allow it to use force with impunity or whether—to the contrary—it was based on the conviction that the international environment was no longer genuinely committed to Yugoslav unity and that, in the process of redefining Yugoslavia's political space, control over territory could present a position of strength. Another question that has not received enough attention due to the overwhelming focus on Western policy is the "Russian factor," particularly in regard to the policies and calculations of the Serbian leadership and the Yugoslav army high command. What was the nature of contacts between Serbian politicians and Yugoslav army generals with members of the conservative Russian political and military establishment, and how did such contacts affect the Yugoslavs' decisions in the run-up to war? As Yugoslavia's breakup recedes farther into history, it is such analyses of the interaction between external and internal factors that represent the most fruitful way forward.

Conclusion

In his analysis of official U.S. approaches to Yugoslavia, Lenard Cohen highlights the paradigm shift that occurred in the mid-1990s from the "ancient hatreds" theory to an explanation focused on the role of "loathsome leaders" in the country's violent breakup.[144] It would be fair to say that most European politicians, as well as many journalists writing on the Yugoslav wars, also adhered to one of these two paradigms. In this respect, the academic scholarship on Yugoslavia's disintegration has, on the whole, been more nuanced—overwhelmingly rejecting the ancient hatreds paradigm and showing greater sensitivity to the multiple causal factors that brought about Yugoslavia's violent demise. As I have shown in this chapter, explanations in academic accounts of the breakup have ranged from those emphasizing historical legacies and the failings of the Yugoslav communist system to those focused on the various domestic and international factors that shaped the last years of Yugoslavia before its breakdown in 1991. This said, however, scholarship does not exist in a vacuum but tends to be influenced by the dominant cognitive frameworks of its time and often seeks to respond to prevailing public perceptions and political debates. From this point of view, the scholarship on Yugoslavia's disintegration has been no different.

Throughout the wars of the 1990s, academics have not remained above the fray. More often than not, they felt compelled both to dispel public perceptions of specific Yugoslav national groups (particularly when such perceptions were derogatory and prejudicial) and to position themselves in regard to policy debates on the ethics and instruments of international intervention. Writing at a time when the human toll of the wars was rising and when international responses were often confused, inadequate, or—in the view of some authors—too partial toward one or the other side in the conflict, in the early 1990s academics were generally critical of their governments' policies toward Yugoslavia. As the United States, followed by its NATO allies, adopted a more directly interventionist approach in the mid-1990s and again at the end of that decade, academic opinion became more polarized—with some enthusiastically endorsing the use of military force first against the Bosnian Serbs (in 1994–95) and then against Milošević's Serbia itself (in 1999), and others vehemently opposing such action. Throughout the decade, therefore, scholars generally found it very difficult to maintain an academic distance from their subject, and their analyses often reflected their political positions and convictions. In the heated atmosphere surrounding the disclosures of war crimes and inhumane practices not seen in Europe since 1945, academic conferences and communications often became arenas of acerbic, emotionally tinged, and at times openly aggressive exchanges.

In view of these circumstances, it is perhaps unsurprising that—despite the sheer quantity of studies—certain types of explanation have generally been privileged over others, leaving significant lacunae that call for further research and reflection. While there are, of course, exceptions to the rule, the academic literature on Yugoslavia's breakup has been focused on elites rather than on local, social, and family histories and on grassroots forms of mobilization. It has also been overly concentrated on Serbia, and—once war began—on Bosnia and later Kosovo, leaving significant gaps in our understanding notably of the evolution of Slovenia and Croatia in the 1970s and 1980s. In addition, there has been a tendency to "read history backwards," ignoring alternatives that did exist to the dominant nationalist discourses and policies throughout Yugoslavia's history. At times Yugoslavia's national groups have been treated in an overly "homogenous" way (as the Serbs, the Croats, the Slovenes, etc.) at the expense of highlighting the diversity of experiences and attitudes existing within each of them. Whether on an elite or a grassroots level, accounts of the process of Yugoslavia's dissolution have often neglected the *interactive* nature of the various particularist nationalisms or of the policies and decisions of the different federal, republic, and province leaderships. The policies of outside powers also need further elucidation, both in terms of their motivation and their impact on the Yugoslav actors' strategies and decisions. Finally, studies of Yugoslavia have historically tended to emphasize the country's exceptionalism at the expense of more comparative approaches that would have integrated events and processes in Yugoslavia into wider European and international frameworks. By highlighting the different historical precedents and legacies, the "congenital birth defects" contained in Yugoslavia's two state-building experiments of the twentieth century, and the processes and policies that informed the country's final breakdown in the late 1980s, this book seeks to fill some of these gaps and shed new light on the debates that have characterized both academic and non-academic reflections on this event.

Notes

1. I thank Audrey Budding, Lenard Cohen, Dejan Jović, and Veljko Vujačić for their helpful suggestions for this chapter.
2. A thoughtful treatment of these divisions can be found in Dušan J. Djordjevich, "Clio amid the Ruins: Yugoslavia and Its Predecessors in Recent Historiography," in Norman M. Naimark and Holly Case (eds.), *Yugoslavia and Its Historians: Understanding the Balkan Wars of the 1990s* (Stanford: Stanford University Press, 2003), pp. 3–7.
3. This chapter deals with scholarly approaches to Yugoslavia's dissolution. Most book-length accounts provided by journalists (with one notable exception, cf. footnote 4) have focused overwhelmingly on the period immediately preceding state collapse and the outbreak of war. The most important of these (and adopting a variety of perspectives) are: Laura Silber and Allan Little, *The Death of Yugoslavia* (London: Penguin, 1996); Misha Glenny, *The Fall of Yugoslavia: The Third Balkan War* (London: Penguin, 1992); Christopher Bennett, *Yugoslavia's Bloody Collapse: Causes, Course, and Consequences* (London: Hurst, 1995); Branka Magaš, *The Destruction of Yugoslavia: Tracking the Break-Up* (London: Verso, 1993); and Viktor Meier, *Yugoslavia: A History of its Demise* (London: Routledge, 1999). A useful collection of essays mainly by journalists is Jasminka Udovički and James Ridgeway (eds.), *Burn This House: The Making and Unmaking of Yugoslavia* (Durham, NC: Duke University Press, 1997).
4. Other comprehensive literature reviews can be found in: Sabrina Petra Ramet, "'For a Charm of Pow'rful Trouble, Like a Hell-Broth Boil and Bubble': Theories of the Roots of the Yugoslav Troubles," *Nationalities Papers,* Vol. 32, No. 4 (Dec. 2004), pp. 731–763; Dejan Jović, "The Disintegration of Yugoslavia: A Critical Review of Explanatory Approaches," *European Journal of Social Theory,* Vol. 4, No. 1 (2001), pp. 101–120; James Gow, "After the Flood: Literature on the Context, Causes, and Course of the Yugoslav War-Reflections and Refractions," *Slavonic and East European Review,* Vol. 75, No. 3 (July 1997), pp. 446–484; Gale Stokes, John Lampe, and Dennison Rusinow with Julie Mostov, "Instant History: Understanding the Wars of Yugoslav Succession," *Slavic Review,* Vol. 55, No. 1 (Spring 1996), pp. 136–150; and Sarah A. Kent, "Writing the Yugoslav Wars: English Language Books on Bosnia (1992–1996) and the Challenges of Analyzing Contemporary History," *American Historical Review,* Oct. 1997, pp. 1085–1114.

5. This is not to say, of course, that authors necessarily adopted monocausal explanations for Yugoslavia's dissolution. However, it would be fair to say that some authors have been identified as leading proponents of particular types of explanation and will be identified as such.

6. *The Other Balkan Wars: A 1913 Carnegie Endowment Inquiry in Retrospect with a New Introduction and Reflections on the Present Conflict by George F. Kennan* (Washington, DC: Carnegie Endowment for International Peace, 1993), p. 11.

7. The best-known journalist's account based on the "ancient hatreds" approach was Robert Kaplan's *Balkan Ghosts: A Journey through History* (New York: St. Martin's Press, 1993). For a knowledgeable refutation of this vision (though possibly overemphasizing harmony) see Robert J. Donia and John V. A. Fine, *Bosnia and Hercegovina: A Tradition Betrayed* (London: Hurst, 1994).

8. See particularly Maria Todorova's critique of Kennan in "The Balkans: From Discovery to Invention," *Slavic Review,* Vol. 53, No. 2 (Summer 1994), pp. 453–482, and her *Imagining the Balkans* (Oxford and New York: Oxford University Press, 1997), as well as Vesna Goldsworthy, *Inventing Ruritania: Imperialism of the Imagination* (New Haven: Yale University Press, 1998).

9. Samuel Huntington, "The Clash of Civilizations?" *Foreign Affairs,* Summer 1993, pp. 22–49, and his *The Clash of Civilizations and the Remaking of World Order* (New York: Simon & Schuster, 1996).

10. It has also been evoked by some nationalist politicians and intellectuals in the former Yugoslavia, as well as by their Western sympathizers, to legitimize their policies and claim a greater degree of "Europeanness" for their nation. This has been the case particularly with Franjo Tudjman, the first president of independent Croatia, and Radovan Karadžić, the leader of the Serbian Democratic Party in Bosnia, and can also be found in the "Central Europe" rhetoric against "the Balkans" in Slovenia from the mid-1980s. For a well-known Western intellectual's endorsement of such an Orientalist vision, see Alain Finkielkraut, *Comment peut-on être croate?* Paris: Gallimard, 1992. Finkielkraut presents "the aggression" against Croatia as "directed against its very Europeanness" (p. 26). For a critique of all such discourses, see Milica Bakić Hayden and Robert Hayden, "Orientalist Variations on the Theme 'Balkans': Symbolic Geography in Recent Yugoslav Cultural Politics," *Slavic Review,* Vol. 51, No. 1 (Spring 1992), pp. 141–174, and Milica Bakić Hayden, "Nesting Orientalisms: The Case of Former Yugoslavia," *Slavic Review,* Vol. 54, No. 4 (Winter 1995), pp. 917–931. For a good overview of all such myths, see Pål Kolstø, "Introduction: Assessing the Role of Historical Myths in Modern Society," in Pål Kolstø, *Myths and Boundaries in South-Eastern Europe* (London: Hurst, 2005), pp. 1–34.

11. Huntington, op. cit., pp. 22–49 passim.

12. Ibid.

13. For example, Huntington cannot decide between the novelty of the clash of civilizations and its ancient nature. First he argues that conflicts of the past (between princes, nation-state, and ideologies) were primarily conflicts "within the Western" civilization, only to then emphasize that civilizational differences are "the product of centuries" and that "over the centuries . . . differences among civilizations have generated the most prolonged and the most violent conflict" (ibid., pp. 23–25).

14. Aleksa Djilas, "Fear Thy Neighbor: The Break-Up of Yugoslavia," in Charles A. Kupchan (ed.), *Nations and Nationalism in the New Europe* (Ithaca: Cornell University Press, 1995), pp. 86–88. See also John Allcock, "Huntington, 'Civilizations,' and Bosnia and Hercegovina: A Sociological Critique," *Sociological Imagination,* Vol. 36, No. 2–3 (1999), p. 138.

15. See, for example, Bogdan Bogdanović, *Grad i smrt* (Belgrade: Beogradski krug, 1994). For a critique of the revenge of the countryside approach, see Xavier Bougarel, "Yugoslav Wars: The 'Revenge of the Countryside' between Sociological Reality and Nationalist Myth," *East European Quarterly,* Vol. 33, No. 2 (June 1999), pp. 157–175.

16. Djilas, op. cit., p. 87, and see also his "Funeral Oration for Yugoslavia: An Imaginary Dialogue with Western Friends," in Dejan Djokić (ed.), *Yugoslavism: Histories of a Failed Idea, 1918–1992* (London: Hurst, 2003), pp. 321–323.

17. Ivo Banac, foreword to Sabrina Ramet, *Balkan Babel,* 2nd ed. (Boulder: Westview, 1996), p. xiv, and Stevan K. Pavlowitch, "Who Is Balkanizing Whom? The Misunderstandings between the Debris of Yugoslavia and an Unprepared West," *Daedalus,* Vol. 123, No. 2 (Spring 1994), pp. 203–204.

18. This is also argued by Allcock, "Huntington, 'Civilizations,' and Bosnia and Herce-govina," op. cit., p. 139. It is particularly highlighted by the social constructivist school, notably by V. P. Gagnon, *The Myth of Ethnic War: Serbia and Croatia in the 1990s* (Ithaca: Cornell University Press, 2004).

19. On the role of religion in Yugoslavia's dissolution and wars see notably Vjekoslav Perica, *Balkan Idols: Religion and Nationalism in Yugoslav States* (Oxford: Oxford University Press, 2002); Xavier Bougarel, "L'Islam bosniaque, entre identité culturelle et idéologie politique," in Xavier Bougarel and Nathalie Clayer (eds.), *Le Nouvel Islam balkanique* (Paris: Maisonneuve & Larose, 2001), pp. 79–132; Paul Mojzes, *Yugoslav Inferno: Ethnoreligious Warfare in the Balkans* (New York: Continuum, 1994); Lenard J. Cohen, "Prelates and Politicians in Bosnia: The Role of Religion in Nationalist Mobilization," *Nationalities Papers,* Vol. 25, No. 3 (Autumn, 1997), pp. 481–499; Radmila Radić, "The Church and the 'Serbian Question'" in Nebojša Popov (ed.), *The Road to War in Serbia* (Budapest: CEU Press, 2000), pp. 247–273; Sabrina Ramet, *Balkan Babel: The Disintegration of Yugoslavia from the Death of Tito to Ethnic War,* 2nd ed. (Boulder: Westview, 1996); Milorad Tomanić, *Crkva u ratu i ratovi u njoj* (Belgrade: Krug, 2001); Michael Sells, *The Bridge Betrayed: Religion and Genocide in Bosnia* (Berkeley: University of California Press, 1996); Bojan Aleksov, "Adamant and Treacherous: Serbian Historians on Religious Conversions," in Kolstø, op. cit., pp. 158–190; and Maja Brkljačić, "'Velebit je hrvatski Sinaj': O hrvatskoj katoličkoj imaginaciji," *Reč,* Vol. 70, No. 16 (June 2003), pp. 147–170.

20. I am grateful to Audrey Budding for this point.

21. Dennison Rusinow, "The Ottoman Legacy in Yugoslavia's Disintegration and Civil War," in L. Carl Brown (ed.), *Imperial Legacy: The Ottoman Imprint on the Balkans and the Middle East* (New York: Columbia University Press, 1996), p. 81.

22. Todorova, *Imagining the Balkans,* op. cit., p. 166. It should be noted that Todorova focuses on the Ottoman legacy, but a similar point could be made about the legacy of the imperial experience in the Balkans more generally.

23. Ibid. See also her "The Ottoman Legacy in the Balkans," in Brown, *Imperial Legacy,* op. cit., pp. 45–77. In this regard it is necessary to mention the work of two scholars. Veljko Vujačić explores the impact of the very different imperial legacies—among other factors—on Serbian and Russian national mobilization in his "Historical Legacies, Nationalist Mobilization, and Political Outcomes in Russia and Serbia: A Weberian View," *Theory and Society,* Vol. 25 (1996), pp. 763–801, and "Perceptions of the State in Russia and Serbia: The Role of Ideas in the Soviet and Yugoslav Collapse," *Post-Soviet Affairs,* 20/2, 2004, pp. 164–194. John Allcock provides a thoughtful *longue durée* analysis of violence in the region (*Explaining Yugoslavia,* London: Hurst, 2000, Ch. 13).

24. Ibid., p. 175.

25. Gale Stokes, "Solving the Wars of Yugoslav Succession," in Norman Naimark and Holly Case (eds.), *Yugoslavia and its Historians* (Palo Alto: Stanford, 2003), pp. 204 and 194.

26. Ivo Banac, "The Fearful Asymmetry of War: The Causes and Consequences of Yugoslavia's Demise," *Daedalus,* Vol. 121, No. 2 (Spring 1992), p. 143. This view is restated in his *Raspad Jugoslavije* (Zagreb: Durieux, 2001), p. 116.

27. Ivo Banac, *The National Question in Yugoslavia* (Ithaca: Cornell University Press, 1984), p. 406.

28. Aleksandar Pavković, *The Fragmentation of Yugoslavia* (London: Macmillan, 1997), p. ix; Gale Stokes, *Three Eras of Political Change in Eastern Europe* (New York: Oxford University Press, 1997), p. 109; Andrew Wachtel, *Making a Nation, Breaking a Nation: Literature and Cultural Politics in Yugoslavia* (Palo Alto: Stanford University Press, 1998), p. 4; Paul Lendvai, "Yugoslavia without Yugoslavs: The Roots of the Crisis," *International Affairs,* Vol. 48, No. 2 (1991), pp. 251–261. See also Charles Ingrao, "Understanding Ethnic Conflict in Central Europe: An Historical Perspective," and the responses by Istvan Deak, John Lampe, and Gale Stokes, *Nationalities Papers,* Vol. 27, No. 2 (1999), pp. 291–333.

29. Ivo Banac, "Nationalism in Southeastern Europe," in Charles Kupchan (ed.), *Nationalism and Nationalities in the New Europe* (Ithaca: Cornell UP, 1995), p. 113. According to Banac, this Serbian hegemonic tendency was expressed by the merger of Vuk Karadžić's linguistic definition of all South Slav *štokavian* speakers as Serbs (which included most Croats and Bosnian Muslims) and Serbia's nineteenth-century program of state expansion, as expressed in a secret 1844 government document known as the *Načertanije*. Similar views can be found in Mirko Grmek, Marc Gjidara, and Neven Šimac, *Le nettoyage ethnique* (Paris: Fayard, 1993); Jasna Adler, *L'Union forcée: La Croatie et la création de l'État yougoslave (1918)* (Geneva: Georg editeur, 1997); Sabrina Petra Ramet, *Balkan Babel: The Disintegration of Yugoslavia from the Death of Tito to Ethnic War* (Boulder: Westview, 1996), p. 1; and Mojmir Križan, "New Serbian Nationalism and the Third Balkan War," *Studies in East European Thought,* Vol. 46, No. 1–2 (June 1994), pp. 47–68. Branimir Anzulović, *Heavenly Serbia: From Myth to Genocide* (London: Hurst, 1999), presents a variation on the same theme.

30. As Banac puts it, the first Yugoslav state was "centralized, with Serbs holding all the levers of power—the army, dynasty and state institutions—and it was basically irrelevant whether it was called Greater Serbia or Yugoslavia" (*Raspad Jugoslavije,* op. cit., p. 117).

31. Banac's foreword to Ramet, *Balkan Babel,* op. cit., p. xvi.

32. Ibid.

33. "Separating History from Myth: An Interview with Ivo Banac," in Rabia Ali and Lawrence Lifschultz (eds.), *Why Bosnia?* (1994), p. 161.

34. Milorad Ekmečić, *Srbija između Evrope i Srednje Evrope* (Belgrade: Politika, 1992), p. 11. Whereas for Banac "religion played virtually no part" in the construction of Croatian national ideology, for Ekmečić, it "without a doubt inspired all separatist movements which rejected the Yugoslav idea and later the Yugoslav state, and without a doubt was also the principal cause of that state's historic collapse" (Banac, "Nationalism in Southeastern Europe," op. cit., p. 112 and Ekmečić, op. cit., p. 16)

35. This is notably the claim of historian Vasilije Krestić. See, for example, *Un peuple en hôtage: Les Serbes de Croatie et l'État croate,* (Lausanne: L'Age d'homme, 1993).

36. See, for example, Ljubodrag Dimić, *Srbi i Jugoslavija* (Belgrade: Stubovi kulture, 1998) or Đorđe Đ. Stanković, *Nikola Pašić i Hrvati* (Belgrade: BIGZ, 1995).

37. Dimić, *Srbi i Jugoslavija*, op. cit., p. 33.

38. See, for example, the chapters by Vasilije Krestić and Slavenko Terzić in *Velika Srbija: istine, zablude, zloupotrebe* (Belgrade: Srpska književna zadruga, 2003), pp. 243–260 and 315–328.

39. They are also unlikely to be laid to rest in the near future. On these earlier polemics, see Michael Boro Petrovich, "Continuing Nationalism in Yugoslav Historiography," *Nationalities Papers,* Vol. 6, No. 2 (1978), pp. 161–177.

40. John Lampe makes a similar point in his *Yugoslavia as History: Twice There Was a Country,* 2nd ed. (Cambridge: Cambridge University Press, 2000), p. 4.

41. Some scholars have challenged these assumptions by highlighting the diversity of approaches to the "national question" that coexisted with each other within each national group, as well as within the various political movements in interwar and wartime Yugoslavia. See Jill Irvine, *The Croat Question* (Boulder: Westview, 1993); Mark Biondich, Stjepan Radić, *The Croat Peasant Party, and the Politics of Mass Mobilization, 1904–1928 (Toronto: University of Toronto Press, 2000)* and his "'We Were Defending the State': Nationalism, Myth, and Memory in Twentieth-Century Croatia" in John Lampe and Mark Mazower (eds.), *Ideologies and National Identities: The Case of Twentieth-Century Southeastern Europe* (Budapest: CEU Press, 2003), pp. 54–81; Marko Bulatović, "Struggling with Yugoslavism: Dilemmas of Interwar Serb Political Thought," in ibid., pp. 254–90; Dejan Djokić (ed.), *Yugoslavism: Histories of a Failed Idea, 1918–1992* (London: Hurst, 2002) and his *Elusive Compromise: A History of Interwar Yugoslavia* (London: Hurst, 2007); and Jasna Dragović-Soso, "Rethinking Yugoslavia: Serbian Intellectuals and the 'National Question' in Historical Perspective," *Contemporary European History,* Vol. 13, No. 2 (May 2004), pp. 170–184.

42. Andrew Wachtel, *Making a Nation, Breaking a Nation: Literature and Cultural Politics in Yugoslavia* (Palo Alto: Stanford University Press, 1998), p. 17.

43. "The ideology of Croat state rights claimed, on the basis of the historic rights and the continuity of the Croat medieval state, the whole of Croatia, Slavonia, Dalmatia and Bosnia-Hercegovina as Croat lands which were to form the future independent Croatia. The Serb national liberation ideologies proclaimed (a rather non-historic) right of the Serbs living in the very same regions to be freed from foreign rule and unified with Serbs in Serbia. Although the boundaries of this latter claim had never been clearly demarcated, substantial portions of Croatia, Slavonia and Dalmatia and the whole of Bosnia-Hercegovina were often included in the territories to be liberated by each side" (Pavković, *The Fragmentation of Yugoslavia,* op. cit., pp. 10–11).

44. Ibid., and Wachtel, op. cit., p. 229. Wachtel does not provide an explanation as to why it was abandoned, however.

45. Cvijeto Job, *Yugoslavia's Ruin: The Bloody Lessons of Nationalism. A Patriot's Warning* (Oxford: Rowman & Littlefield, 2002), p. 5.

46. See, for example, Steven L. Burg and Michael L. Berbaum, "Community, Integration, and Stability in Multinational Yugoslavia," *American Political Science Review,* Vol. 83, No. 2 (1989), pp. 536–551, or V.P. Gagnon, *The Myth of Ethnic War: Serbia and Croatia in the 1990s* (Ithaca: Cornell University Press, 2004, chapter 2).

47. See, for example, Eric Gordy, *The Culture of Power in Serbia* (University Park: Penn State Press, 1999), or Catherine Baker "The Politics of Performance: Transnationalism and its Limits in Former Yugoslav Popular Music, 1999–2004," *Ethnopolitics,* Vol. 5, No. 3 (2006), pp. 275–293.

48. See the various contributions to Djokić, *Yugoslavism*, op. cit., and Audrey Helfant Budding, "Yugoslavs into Serbs: Serbian National Identity, 1961–1971," *Nationalities Papers*, Vol. 25, No. 3 (1997), pp. 407–426.

49. Dejan Jović, *Jugoslavija—država koja je odumrla* (Zagreb: Prometej, 2003).

50. As highlighted by the title of John Lampe's history of Yugoslavia, *Yugoslavia as History: Twice There Was a Country* (Cambridge: Cambridge University Press, 2000).

51. This is particularly highlighted in Audrey Budding's contribution to this volume.

52. On such interaction between Serbian and Slovenian national ideologies in the period leading up to Yugoslavia's dissolution see Jasna Dragović-Soso, *"Saviours of the Nation": Serbia's Intellectual Opposition and the Revival of Nationalism* (London: Hurst, 2002), chapter 4.

53. This is the subject of Mark Biondich's contribution to this volume.

54. This latter point is examined by Marko Bulatović, "Struggling with Yugoslavism," op. cit.

55. Such as comparisons of the perceptions of the Yugoslav state and ideology among the Croatian and Slovenian communist elites in the late 1950s and early 1960s with those of the 1920s, or of Franjo Tudjman's vision of a Croatian state in the 1990s with the Croatian unit incorporating parts of Bosnia created within the Kingdom of Yugoslavia by the 1939 *Sporazum* (Agreement). A striking parallel exists also in regard to Serb elite responses to the decentralization of socialist Yugoslavia after 1971 with those articulated in response to the 1939 *Sporazum*. This latter comparison is effectively made by Veljko Vujačić, "Perceptions of the State in Russia and Serbia: The Role of Ideas in the Soviet and Yugoslav Collapse," *Post-Soviet Affairs*, Vol. 20, No. 2 (2004), pp. 181–186.

56. Stevan Pavlowitch, "Who is 'Balkanizing' Whom? The Misunderstandings between the Debris of Yugoslavia and an Unprepared West," *Daedalus*, Vol. 123, No. 2 (Spring 1994), pp. 203–223. See also Maria Todorova, "The Trap of Backwardness: Modernity, Temporality, and the Study of East European Nationalism," *Slavic Review*, Vol. 64, No. 1 (Spring 2005), pp. 140–164. Lenard Cohen's contribution to this volume examines the existing comparative analyses of Yugoslavia's dissolution.

57. Vojin Dimitrijević, "Sukobi oko ustava iz 1974," in Nebojša Popov (ed.), *Srpska strana rata* (Belgrade: Republika, 1996), pp. 466–67. See also Robert Hayden, *Blueprints for a House Divided: The Constitutional Logic of the Yugoslav Conflicts* (Ann Arbor: University of Michigan Press, 2000), chapter 2.

58. Ivan Vejvoda, "Yugoslavia 1945–91: From Decentralization without Democracy to Dissolution," in David Dyker and Ivan Vejvoda (eds.), *Yugoslavia and After: A Study in Fragmentation, Despair, and Rebirth* (London: Longman, 1996), pp. 15–16. The different interpretations of the 1974 Constitution, particularly in regard to the issue of self-determination, are analyzed by Audrey Budding in her chapter.

59. Valerie Bunce, *Subversive Institutions: The Design and Destruction of Socialism and the State* (Cambridge: Cambridge University Press, 1999), p. 2.

60. Ibid., p. 147.

61. Ibid., p. 112.

62. This issue is particularly well-treated in Veljko Vujačić, "Institutional Origins of Contemporary Serbian Nationalism," *East European Constitutional Review*, Vol. 5, No. 4 (Fall 1996), pp. 51–61, and Jović, op. cit.

63. On the Croatian spring, see Jill Irvine's contribution to this volume.

64. The ability of some republics to scupper federal attempts at educational integration is analyzed in Andrew Wachtel's and Predrag Marković's chapter in this volume.

65. Jović, op. cit., p. 86.

66. Jović, op. cit., pp. 132–33.

67. Ibid., p. 136.

68. Vesna Bojičić, "The Disintegration of Yugoslavia: Causes and Consequences of Dynamic Inefficiency in Semi-Command Economies," in Dyker and Vejvoda, op. cit., p. 28. See also, John Lampe, *Yugoslavia as History*, 2nd ed. (Cambridge: Cambridge University Press, 2000), pp. 315–321, and Susan Woodward, *Socialist Unemployment: The Political Economy of Yugoslavia* (Princeton: Princeton University Press, 1995). Economic factors in Yugoslavia's demise are explored in Michael Palairet's chapter in this volume. The revival of nationalism in the 1960s, which is analyzed in Dennison Rusinow's chapter, was also largely shaped by economic factors.

69. Allcock, *Explaining Yugoslavia*, op. cit., p. 97.

70. Sabrina Ramet has also emphasized the illegitimacy of the socialist system as the "root cause" of Yugoslavia's disintegration, for example, in her *Thinking about Yugoslavia: Scholarly Debates about the Yugoslav Breakup and the Wars in Bosnia and Kosovo* (chapter 3) (Cambridge: Cambridge University Press, 2005).

71. An exception to this rule is Steven Burg's prescient article, "Elite Conflict in Post-Tito Yugoslavia," *Soviet Studies*, Vol. 38, No. 2 (1986), pp. 170–193. Burg states that "it might not be long before the country simply disintegrated—peacefully if true 'confederation' were achieved, or violently, if nationalist programs were to escalate" (p. 189).

72. See, for example, the opinion polls cited by Dejan Jović in this volume.

73. Ibid.

74. The exception here is Bunce, discussed above.

75. See, for example, Barry Posen, "The Security Dilemma and Ethnic Conflict," *Survival*, Vol. 35, No. 1 (Spring 1993), pp. 27–47.

76. See notably Gagnon, *The Myth of Ethnic War*, op. cit. A critique of the security dilemma can also be found in Stuart J. Kaufman, *Modern Hatreds: The Symbolic Politics of Ethnic War* (Ithaca: Cornell University Press, 2001), pp. 9–10, and Veljko Vujačić, "Perceptions of the State in Russia and Serbia," op. cit., pp. 168–171.

77. Dennison Rusinow, "The Avoidable Catastrophe," in Sabrina Petra Ramet and Ljubiša S. Adamovich (eds.), *Beyond Yugoslavia* (Boulder: Westview, 1995), p. 14 (author's emphasis).

78. Ibid. The role of the media has received a lot of attention in the literature. See notably Mark Thompson, *Forging War: The Media in Serbia, Croatia, and Bosnia-Hercegovina* (London: Article 19/International Centre Against Censorship, 1994) and Aljoša Mimica and Radina Vučetić's thorough analysis of the Serbian daily *Politika* from 1988 to 1991, *"Vreme kada je narod govorio"* (Belgrade: Fond za humanitarno pravo, 2001).

79. The nine biographies are Lenard J. Cohen, *Serpent in the Bosom: The Rise and Fall of Slobodan Milošević* (Boulder: Westview, two eds., 2001 and 2002); Slavoljub Djukić, *Milošević and Marković: A Lust for Power* (Montreal: McGill-Queen's University Press, 2001); Duško Doder and Louise Branson, *Milošević: Portrait of a Tyrant* (New York: Free Press, 1999); Vidosav Stevanović, *Milošević: The People's Tyrant* (London: IB Tauris, 2002); Adam LeBor, *Milošević: A Biography* (London: Bloomsbury, 2002); and Louis Sell, *Slobodan Milošević and the Destruction of Yugoslavia* (Durham: Duke University Press, 2002). There are also several books specifically devoted to Milošević's trial in The Hague: Norman Cigar and Paul Williams, *Indictment in The Hague: The Milošević Regime and Crimes of the Balkan Wars* (New York: New York University Press, 2002); William Schabas and William Scharf, *Slobodan Milošević on Trial: A Companion* (New York: Continuum, 2002); and Chris Stephen, *Judgement Day: The Trial of Slobodan Milošević* (London: Atlantic, 2003).

80. There is also disagreement over the extent to which Milošević's famous statement was prepared in advance and to which it represented a spontaneous response to the Kosovo

Serbs' claims of being mistreated by the Kosovar police. (For the former view, see Silber and Little, op. cit., pp. 37–47, and for the latter, Cohen, op. cit., pp. 106–110.)

81. Louis Sell, *Slobodan Milošević and the Destruction of Yugoslavia* (Durham: Duke University Press, 2002), p. 4.
82. Ibid., p. 5.
83. Ibid., p. 4.
84. Ibid., p. 5.
85. Cohen, *Serpent in the Bosom,* op. cit., p. 130.
86. Lenard J. Cohen, *Broken Bonds: The Disintegration of Yugoslavia* (Boulder: Westview, 1993), p. 265.
87. Cohen, *Serpent in the Bosom,* op. cit., p. 465.
88. Woodward, op. cit., p. 80.
89. Ibid., p. 94.
90. Jović, op. cit., pp. 491–492.
91. As is argued by Eric Gordy in his contribution to this volume.
92. Marković's role is particularly highlighted by Slavoljub Djukić in *Milošević and Marković: A Lust for Power* (Montreal: McGill-Queen's University Press, 2001).
93. This is well-argued by Jović, *Jugoslavija—država koja je odumrla,* op. cit.
94. This last approach can notably be found in James Gow, *The Serbian Project and Its Adversaries* (London: Hurst, 2003).
95. They are the subject of Jill Irvine's contribution to this volume.
96. This is the subject of Dejan Jović's contribution to this volume.
97. Juan Linz and Alfred Stepan, "Political Identities and Electoral Sequences: Spain, the Soviet Union, and Yugoslavia," *Daedalus,* Spring 1992, pp. 123–139. The institutionalist approaches are discussed above.
98. This position is notably taken by the historian John Fine, "Heretical Thoughts about the Postcommunist Transition in the Once and Future Yugoslavia," in Naimark and Case (eds.), *Yugoslavia and Its Historians,* op. cit., pp. 183, 259–261. The role of the JNA in Yugoslavia's dissolution is discussed in Florian Bieber's contribution to this volume.
99. On the events surrounding the Memorandum's publication and its revival in 1989, see Jasna Dragovic-Soso, *Saviours of the Nation,* op. cit., pp. 182–189 and 220–221.
100. Sell, p. 46. See also Gjidara, Grmek, and Simac, *Le nettoyage ethnique,* op. cit. Križan, "New Serbian Nationalism and the Third Balkan War," op. cit.; Magaš, op. cit., p. 4; and Philip J. Cohen, "The Complicity of Serbian Intellectuals in Genocide in the 1990s," in Thomas Cushman and Stjepan G. Meštrović (eds.), *This Time We Knew: Western Responses to Genocide in Bosnia* (New York: New York University Press, 1996), p. 39.
101. Anzulović, op. cit., p. 114.
102. Aleksandar Pavković, "Yugoslavism's Last Stand: A Utopia of Serb Intellectuals," in Djokić, op. cit., pp. 254–257.
103. Audrey Budding, "Serbian Nationalism in the Twentieth Century: Historical Background and Context," Expert Report for the International Criminal Tribunal for the Former Yugoslavia, p. 57. See also her "Systemic Crisis and National Mobilization: The Case of the 'Memorandum of the Serbian Academy,'" *Cultures and Nations of Central and Eastern Europe: Essays in Honor of Roman Szporluk,* Harvard Ukrainian Studies Special Volume, 22, 1998, pp. 49–69.
104. As it did in the case of Vojislav Šešelj in 1984. (See Dragović-Soso, *Saviours of the Nation,* op. cit., pp. 57–59.)
105. All these arguments are elaborated in ibid., chapter 4.
106. See Jasna Dragović-Soso, "Intellectuals and the Collapse of Yugoslavia: The End of the Yugoslav Writers' Union," in Djokić, *Yugoslavism,* op. cit., pp. 268–285.

107. This is done by Nicholas Miller in his chapter in this volume.
108. Gagnon, *The Myth of Ethnic War*, op. cit., p. 7. See also his "Ethnic Nationalism and International Conflict: The Case of Serbia," *International Security,* Vol. 19, No. 3 (1994–95), pp. 130–166.
109. Ibid., p. 8.
110. Rogers Brubaker, *Nationalism Reframed: Nationhood and the National Question in the New Europe* (Cambridge: Cambridge University Press, 1996), p. 72.
111. An analysis of the legacy of the two world wars in Yugoslavia's dissolution is presented by Stevan K. Pavlowitch's contribution to this volume.
112. Jan-Werner Müller, "Introduction: The Power of Memory, the Memory of Power, and the Power over Memory," in Jan-Werner Müller (ed.), *Memory and Power in Post-War Europe* (Cambridge: Cambridge University Press, 2002), p. 2.
113. For an illuminating treatment of the two types of memory, see Dejan Jović, "'Official Memories' in Post-Authoritarianism: An Analytical Framework," *Journal of Southern Europe and the Balkans,* Vol. 6, No. 2 (2004), pp. 97–108.
114. Ger Duijzings, "History and Reminders in East Bosnia," Appendix 4 of *Srebrenica: Reconstruction, Background, Consequences, and Analyses of the Fall of the Safe Area,* Special Report of the Netherlands Institute of War Documentation, Amsterdam, 2002–2003, available on the World Wide Web at http://213.222.3.5/srebrenica (Appendix 4), accessed 08/07/2005.
115. See, for example, Wolfgang Höpken, "War, Memory, and Education in a Fragmented Society: The Case of Yugoslavia," *East European Politics and Societies,* Vol. 13, No. 1 (Winter 1999), pp. 190–227; Bette Denich, "Dismembering Yugoslavia: Nationalist Ideologies and the Symbolic Revival of Genocide," *American Ethnologist,* Vol. 21, No. 2 (1994), pp. 367–390; Ivo Goldstein, "The Use of History: Croatian Historiography and Politics," *Helsinki Monitor,* 1994, pp. 85–97; Robert M. Hayden, "Recounting the Dead: The Rediscovery and Redefinition of Wartime Massacres in Late- and Post-Communist Yugoslavia," in Rubie S. Watson (ed.), *Memory, History, and Opposition Under State Socialism* (Santa Fe: School of American Research Press, 1994), pp. 167–201; and Dragović-Soso, *Saviours of the Nation,* op. cit., chapter 2.
116. As do Duijzings, op. cit., or Tone Bringa, *Being Muslim the Bosnian Way: Identity and Community in a Central Bosnian Village* (Princeton: Princeton University Press, 1995). The journalist Chuck Sudetic's *Blood and Vengeance: One Family's Story of the War in Bosnia* (New York: Penguin, 1998) is another good example of such an approach.
117. Nebojša Vladisavljević, "Nationalism, Social Movement Theory, and the Grass Roots Movement of Kosovo Serbs, 1985–1988," *Europe-Asia Studies,* Vol. 54, No. 5 (2002), pp. 771–790. Roger Petersen also emphasizes the grassroots nature of ethnic mobilization in Yugoslavia in his *Understanding Ethnic Violence: Fear, Hatred, and Resentment in Twentieth Century Eastern Europe* (Cambridge: Cambridge University Press, 2002), chapter 10.
118. Ibid. See also his "Grassroots Groups, Milosevic, or Dissident Intellectuals? A Controversy over the Origins and Dynamics of Mobilization of Kosovo Serbs in the 1980s," *Nationalities Papers,* Vol. 32, No. 4 (2004), pp. 781–796.
119. An excellent analysis of the Albanian protests of 1968 and 1981 can be found in Branko Horvat, *Kosovsko pitanje* (Zagreb: Globus, 1989). On the Croatian "spring," see notably Sabrina Ramet, *Nationalism and Federalism in Yugoslavia, 1962–1991,* 2nd ed. (Bloomington: Indiana University Press, 1992), chapter 7; Dennison Rusinow, *Crisis in Croatia,* Fieldstaff Reports (IR-72), Southeast Europe Series, 19/4, 1972; and Stephen Burg, *Conflict and Cohesion in Socialist Yugoslavia* (Princeton: Princeton University Press, 1983).

120. See notably Shkelzen Maliqi, "The Albanian Movement in Kosova," in Dyker and Vejvoda (eds.), *Yugoslavia and After*, op. cit.

121. On the Slovenian social movements, see Danica Fink-Hafner, *Nova družbena gibanja—subjekti politične inovacije* (Ljubljana: Fakultet za družbene vede, 1992); Tomaž Mastnak, "From Social Movements to National Sovereignty," in Jill Benderly and Evan Kraft (eds.), *Independent Slovenia: Origins, Movements, Prospects* (Basingstoke: Macmillan, 1994), pp. 95–108, and his "Civil Society in Slovenia: From Opposition to Power," in Jim Seroka and Vukašin Pavlović (eds.), *The Tragedy of Yugoslavia: The Failure of Democratic Transformation* (London: M. E. Sharpe, 1992), pp. 49–66; and Jozef Figa, "Socializing the State: Civil Society and Democratization from Below in Slovenia," in Irvine et al. (eds.), *State-Society Relations in Yugoslavia*, op. cit., pp. 163–182.

122. See notably Jack Snyder, *From Voting to Violence: Democratization and Nationalist Conflict* (New York: Norton, 2000).

123. See, for example, James Gow, *Triumph of the Lack of Will: International Diplomacy and the Yugoslav War* (London: Hurst, 1997).

124. Susan Woodward, *Balkan Tragedy* (Washington, DC: Brookings, 1995), p. 15.

125. Ibid., pp. 79–80. John Lampe, on the other hand, argues that in the 1980s both Western governments and private initiatives (such as that of the American-led independent consortium, the Friends of Yugoslavia, assembled by former U.S. Ambassador and Deputy Secretary of State Lawrence Eagleburger) made important efforts to alleviate the burdens of Yugoslavia's international debt crisis. Such initiatives were misguided, however, because they appeared to sanction the existing system and its resistance to reform, and it was the postponement of reform rather than its rigid implementation that exacerbated Yugoslavia's crisis (Lampe, op. cit., p. 325).

126. Kate Hudson, *Breaking the South Slav Dream: The Rise and Fall of Yugoslavia* (London: Pluto Press, 2003), pp. 56–57.

127. David Chandler, "Western Intervention and the Disintegration of Yugoslavia, 1989–1999," in Philip Hammond and Edward S. Herman (eds.), *Degraded Capability: The Media and the Kosovo Crisis* (London: Pluto Press, 2000), p. 21.

128. Ibid., pp. 20–23.

129. Ibid., p. 20.

130. Raju G. C. Thomas, "Sovereignty, Self-Determination, and Secession: Principles and Practice," in Raju G. C. Thomas (ed.), *Yugoslavia Unraveled: Sovereignty, Self-Determination, Intervention* (Lanham: Lexington Books, 2003), p. 3 (author's emphasis). In another contribution to the debate over terminology, Aleksandar Pavković argues that Yugoslavia was experiencing "recursive secessions" rather than "dissolution" (Aleksandar Pavković, "Recursive Secessions in Former Yugoslavia: Too Hard a Case for Theories of Secession?" *Political Studies*, Vol. 48 [2000], pp. 485–502).

131. Thomas, op. cit., p. 5.

132. Leslie Benson, *Yugoslavia: A Concise History* (Basingstoke: Palgrave, 2001), p. 164. The argument for the inviolability of internal borders was based on the principle of *uti possidetis*, originally applied in international law to settling decolonization issues in Latin America and Africa with a purpose to "prevent the independence and stability of new states being endangered by fratricidal struggles" ("Opinion No. 3 of the Arbitration Committee," *European Journal of International Law*, 3/1992, p. 185). The appropriateness of this principle for Yugoslavia's situation has been contested in parts of the scholarship. See notably Peter Radan, "The Badinter Arbitration Commission and the Partition of Yugoslavia," *Nationalities Papers*, Vol. 25, No. 3 (1997), pp. 549–552, and his *The Break-Up of Yugoslavia and International Law* (London: Routledge, 2002), pp. 228–233.

133. Notably, the Commission opposed recognition for Croatia until it had satisfied the provisions concerning treatment of minority populations, while recommending the recognition of Macedonia, which was, however, opposed by Greece. See Richard Caplan, *Europe and the Recognition of New States in Yugoslavia* (Cambridge: Cambridge University Press, 2005), pp. 37–38.

134. See, for example, Woodward, op. cit., p. 189; Steven Burg, "The International Community and the Yugoslav Crisis," in Milton J. Esman and Shibley Telhami (eds.), *International Organizations and Ethnic Conflict* (Ithaca: Cornell University Press, 1995), p. 249. The two main international negotiators, Lord Carrington and Cyrus Vance were also deeply critical of Germany's recognition policy (see Cohen, *Broken Bonds,* op. cit., p. 235).

135. Woodward, op. cit., p. 189.

136. Hudson, op. cit., p. 102, Woodward, op. cit., pp. 197–198, Cohen, *Broken Bonds,* op. cit., p. 238.

137. Sabrina Petra Ramet, "The Yugoslav Crisis and the West: Avoiding 'Vietnam' and Blundering into 'Abyssinia,'" *East European Politics and Societies,* Vol. 8, No. 1 (Winter 1994), p. 197. In fact, Baker's visit was nowhere near as clear an expression of support for Yugoslav unity. Rather, Baker gave different messages to the different parties: to Croatia and Slovenia that the United States would not recognize any "unilateral" acts on their part, while concurrently warning Milošević that the United States would not endorse any use of force and that if it had to choose between unity and democracy it would choose the latter. A detailed account of Baker's visit is provided by the last U.S. ambassador to Yugoslavia, Warren Zimmermann, in *Origins of a Catastrophe* (New York: Random House, 1999), pp. 133–138.

138. Daniele Conversi, *German-Bashing and the Breakup of Yugoslavia,* The Donald W. Treadgold Papers, Jackson School of International Studies, University of Washington, 1998.

139. Ramet, "The Yugoslav Crisis and the West," op. cit., p. 202.

140. This argument is also made by James Gow particularly in regard to Bosnia, which in his view should have been internationally recognized in January 1992, along with a credible commitment to defend it against the "Serbian project" of carving out parts of its territory (Gow, *Triumph,* op. cit., pp. 84, 89).

141. For an elaboration of this argument, see Caplan, op. cit., particularly chapter 4.

142. Paul Shoup explores the implications of Western policy-makers' visions of Yugoslavia's crisis and different policy alternatives in his chapter in this volume.

143. Most authors argue that the turning point in Western policy in favour of recognition was not the result so much of the evolution of events within Yugoslavia but of the failed military coup in the Soviet Union in August 1991, which announced the impending dissolution of the Soviet state. After that, the only discrepancy between Germany and some of her partners in the EC concerned the *modalities* of recognition (i.e., the timing and conditions for recognition) but not the principle of recognition itself. See Caplan, op. cit., p. 18. For a contrasting view, see Dejan Jović's contribution to this volume.

144. Cohen, *Serpent in the Bosom,* op. cit., pp. 451–455. A similar point was also made by Susan Woodward, *Balkan Tragedy,* op. cit., pp. 7–8.

THE HISTORICAL LEGACY

The Historical Legacy: The Evolution of Interwar Yugoslav Politics, 1918–1941

❖ Mark Biondich ❖

Scholars interested in the dissolution of Yugoslavia will undoubtedly continue to look back to the "first" Yugoslavia to determine how this formative period of Yugoslav history affected the country's development and eventual demise. They will unquestionably want to know how the experience of the interwar period and the political evolution in the kingdom affected Yugoslavia's viability as a state. They will also try to determine the nature of interethnic relations in this state, particularly the relationship of Serbs to non-Serbs in Yugoslavia's political, economic, military, and cultural spheres. Did the experience of the interwar kingdom alienate the various national groups, reducing their commitment toward a common state? They may also ask why the South Slav peoples of Yugoslavia failed to assimilate to a single identity. In short, why did the interwar Yugoslavist project fail?

These are difficult questions to answer, which is why they will no doubt continue to be hotly debated for years to come. This chapter will try to address these questions without necessarily answering them. The reader should be cautioned at the outset that the chapter is not a comprehensive political history of interwar Yugoslavia. Nor does it provide a detailed account of interwar political parties, their luminaries, or the emergence of modern Serb, Slovene, and Croat nationalist ideologies and nationalism. The reader will be referred to the works of scholars who have already treated these subjects.[1] The chapter is organized into two general sections. The first deals with communist and nationalist historiographies of interwar Yugoslavia. The second is a survey of the interwar era, using the following periodization of interwar politics: (a) the period of parliamentary democracy, 1918–28; (b) the period of the royal dictatorship, 1929–35, that is, the period from the proclamation of the royal dictatorship on January 6, 1929, to the 1935 elections, which followed the assassination of King Aleksandar on October 9, 1934; and, (c) the 1935–41 period, that is, from the 1935 elections to the Axis invasion and partition of Yugoslavia.

The central issue throughout was the national question, which was at the crux of Yugoslavia's political problems. The national question was essentially a question of how the state was to be organized, and it became acute because of the inability of the two largest nationalities (Serbs and Croats), and their respective parties, to resolve the issue. Although it is certainly not this author's intention to trivialize or belittle the importance of the other peoples of Yugoslavia, this chapter acknowledges the centrality of the Serb-Croat conflict in the history of interwar Yugoslavia. It is a matter of the historical record that interwar Yugoslavia's many issues were all overshadowed by the troubled Serb-Croat relationship.

Historiographies of the Interwar Experience

One way of addressing the legacy of the troubled interwar era is to navigate official historiographies and how they have portrayed the era. In the former Yugoslavia, whether in the communist era or after, "national memories" have been based in no small part on historical narratives of collective guilt and collective victimization. Historians have often been willing soldiers in the communist and nationalist struggles and in forging these narratives.[2] The historiographies in question have more often than not merely reflected received wisdom as dictated by official state policy; as such, they provide some sense of what the general population was told about the interwar period.[3]

Historians from the former Yugoslavia have often depicted the history of the interwar era (and the country, generally) in relatively conventional, simplistic, and narrow terms. They were less interested in the underlying factors that shaped the historical process in this period than in the supposed victimization of their respective national groups. It is fair to say that two perspectives have dominated historical writing and historiography in former Yugoslavia and its successor states: communist and nationalist. Both perspectives were deeply flawed, which of the two the more so being a matter of debate. But it is this author's contention that communist historiography, despite all its flaws, was at least in its "mature" phase often less doctrinaire than its nationalist counterpart and generally produced works that were intellectually more rigorous and sound. Having said that, both communist and nationalist historiographies contend that the interwar political experiment was a failure.

In the first two decades of communist rule, the authorities did not encourage objective research into the history of interwar Yugoslavia. Following the Second World War, the Yugoslav communist authorities faced the task of governing a multinational society torn by complex divisions that had been exacerbated by horrifying wartime atrocities. The regime of Josip Broz Tito had its own official version of the interwar and wartime periods, which was reinforced by state authority. Discordant memories of the past were suppressed, as were manifestations of Serb, Croat, and other nationalisms.

The official communist party line held that the Great Serbian bourgeoisie dominated the interwar regime and that a militarist clique around the Karađorđević Court
stood at its core. The first "democratic" decade was but an elaborate façade, merely
a prelude to a formal dictatorship after January 1929. Josip Broz Tito set the tone.
Interwar Yugoslavia was "the most typical case of national oppression in Europe. . . .
A numerically insignificant minority of Great Serb hegemonists, headed by the King
and insatiable in its greed for riches, ruled Yugoslavia for twenty-two years by creating a regime of gendarmes, of dungeons, of racial and national injustice."[4] According
to communist historiography, non-Serbs (and, to be sure, Serb peasants and workers) lived in the clutches of dictatorial "Great Serbian hegemony."[5] The communist
authorities would argue that the failed interwar era led directly to the fratricide of
the Second World War. What is more, they would contend that an abandonment of
communism and a return to the interwar era would be disastrous. The historiography
largely mirrored this attitude. Over time and as Yugoslavia decentralized, historians
more and more served the interests of their constituent republics and a common
historiography was increasingly undermined. The official Yugoslav historiography
would first come under assault during the cautious political liberalization of the late
1960s, particularly in Croatia during the Croatian Spring (1966–71). Following the
purge of reformist elements in both Croatia and Serbia in 1971–72, however, the
official historiography was again placed under firmer party controls. But far more
important fissures appeared in official historiography following Tito's death in May
1980, at which point nationalist interpretations of interwar Yugoslavia, particularly
in Serbia, increasingly came to the forefront.[6]

Outside the country, Serb and Croat political émigrés had since 1945 cultivated
very different interpretations and memories of the interwar era.[7] When the official
communist historiography began to crumble, many dissident and formerly Marxist
scholars in Yugoslavia simply adopted or borrowed from the views of the émigrés.
Nationalist historiographies largely agreed with the communists that the interwar
era had been a failure. They differed only as to the causes of that failure. In Serbian
nationalist historiography, virtually all Serb actions of the interwar era are seen as
defensive and an attempt to save the Yugoslav state from Croat secessionist intrigues,
which were ultimately to blame for the country's dysfunctional parliamentary system.[8] According to this interpretation, the Kingdom of Serbs, Croats, and Slovenes
stood a good chance of evolving into a liberal democratic society had it not been
for Croat recalcitrance. The nascent state found itself under constant attack by disaffected Croat intellectuals and politicians who, working in conjunction with the
Catholic Church, Vatican, and revisionist powers like Italy and Hungary, worked to
sabotage the state.[9] The democratic Yugoslav state failed in 1929, but it was Croats
who provoked the failure.[10]

According to one prominent émigré Serb scholar, King Aleksandar had little choice but to suspend the constitution and National Parliament; he was forced
to impose a dictatorship because the very concept of Yugoslavism and Yugoslavia

itself were threatened. The various political parties had placed their specific interests above those of state and people. But the people of all nationalities had welcomed Aleksandar's decision.[11] His decision to impose a dictatorship was made reluctantly and was not motivated by a desire for power. Because the Croat leader Vladko Maček and his Croatian Serb ally, Svetozar Pribićević, were no longer prepared to work with the Serbian parties, the king had no alternative but dictatorship. In short, "It is wrong, and factually incorrect, to regard the first January 6 government (1929) as some kind of expressly Serb even Great Serbian government."[12] Thus, the dictatorship of King Aleksandar is seen in Serbian nationalist historiography as temporary; his intention was eventually to affect a return to liberal democracy. Serb historians for the most part continue to reject the term *dictatorship* in favor of *personal regime* and maintain that the major institutions sponsored by King Aleksandar's regime were innately liberal. The failure of King Aleksandar's project was due largely to the inability of the old party personnel to realize his "new" vision.[13]

In short, these scholars deny the existence of Serb hegemony. They may admit to a disproportionately large number of Serbs in the bureaucracy and military during the first decade of Yugoslavia's existence but portray this as a result more of Croat abstention than of Serb obstruction. What is more, because Serbs sacrificed the most in blood, thereby liberating Croats and Slovenes from the Habsburgs, they were entitled to play the leading role. As one Serb scholar recently observed, the interwar Kingdom "was the state of the Serb nation in which it lived together with Croats and Slovenes. The new state was the result of international circumstances but also of the decision of the Serb political elite, which presupposed Yugoslav unification as the enlargement of the Serbian state." But it was also "a state of reconciliation" that brought together "victor" (Serbs) and "vanquished" (Croats, Slovenes).[14] Unification contributed to the national, cultural, and economic emancipation of all South Slavs.[15] Only Croat recalcitrance and collusion with revisionist powers ultimately doomed the Yugoslav state. In effect, Croats and Slovenes were equal before the law and not disadvantaged. Serbs sacrificed everything for Yugoslavia, tried to guard and maintain its existence, but were in the end treated with disdain by non-Serbs. Not long ago, two noted Serb scholars claimed that "in the interwar era the Serb people objectively exploited no one, but was itself exploited by its own bourgeoisie and its Yugoslav allies." In the event, the Serb political elite was not a compact group; as the interwar years passed, it became ever more deeply divided between the bearers of a conservative political ideology that saw Yugoslavia merely as Great Serbia and liberal thinkers who saw Serbia's emancipation through Yugoslavism and in an agreement with the Croats.[16] Rather than arrogant rulers, Serb nationalist historians contend, Serbs were victims of Croat, Macedonian, and Albanian irredentists during the interwar period. In the end, therefore, the failure of interwar Yugoslavia has to be assessed in relation both to the dangers posed by a difficult international climate (e.g., Nazism, Communism, Depression, and Revisionism) and internal circumstances. These circumstances proved too great for the Serbian establishment.[17]

Croatian nationalist historiography has tended to see the interwar period as a struggle against "Serbian hegemony" on all fronts, although *hegemony* is a term that is seldom well defined and thus open to abuse.[18] The ideological foundation of the interwar Kingdom was unitarist, and as a result, the state system was centralist. Consequently, after 1918 Croatia lost its state continuity, which it had supposedly preserved for centuries, and its political autonomy; it was exposed to a harsh regime of political "terror."[19] By 1941 Croat public opinion was supposedly decidedly in favor of independence and separation from Serbia. This attitude was the result of two historical facts: the murder of the Croat politicians in Belgrade in 1928 and the dictatorship of King Aleksandar. Prior to 1928, Croat leaders still believed that it might be possible to solve the Croat Question within Yugoslavia. After that point, all Croat parties favored independence, a sentiment that was only intensified during the period of the dictatorship.[20]

All in all, the failure of interwar parliamentary democracy is seen by Croatian historiography as inevitable. Parliamentarism had to fail because from the outset it conflicted with the Serbian concept of Yugoslavia, which was ideologically unitarist and politically centralist. Conversely, Croat conceptions of Yugoslavia are held to have been "healthy" in that they were ideologically pluralist and politically federalist. Although Serbs formed the largest nation in Yugoslavia, they could not dominate the country based purely on demographics. And because Serbia was economically and culturally relatively more backward than the former Habsburg lands, Belgrade lacked all the means necessary for democratic rule. Hegemonic methods were needed to preserve the dominance of the Serb people: "Dictatorship was, therefore, Yugoslavia's fate."[21] In this sense, the dictatorship of King Aleksandar is viewed as just another, albeit harsher, attempt at enforcing Serb hegemony. It attempted to paralyze the Croat national front under the leadership of the Croat Peasant Party, employing the ideological chimera of unitarist Yugoslavism and state centralism. In reality, however, the dictatorship was "above all anti-Croat, although it also struck at the other separatist forces among all non-Serb peoples."[22]

This interpretation of the inevitability of democracy's demise is significant because it inured Croat nationalist historians' views of Croat political behavior. More specifically, Croatian historiography views almost all forms of Croat political conduct as defensive and hence intrinsically legitimate; whether and how Croat actions may have exacerbated political problems is a question seldom explored.[23] The role of the Croat Peasant Party is viewed as positive in that it contributed to the democratization of Croatian society and the defense of Croat national rights, but seldom has Croatian historiography looked at the increasingly undemocratic nature of the party's internal organization, its leadership cult, or how its policies may have harmed or undermined democracy in Yugoslavia, at least in the 1930s. Studies of Croat Peasant Party founder and leader Stjepan Radić still tend to be hagiographical portraits, although this is less true of his successor Vladko Maček.[24] Even the fascist Ustaša movement, which was formed after the imposition of the royal dictatorship, is seen as an understandable reaction to Belgrade's "tyranni-cal" rule.[25]

Much like Croat historians, Bosnian Muslim (or Bosniak) historians have adopted a negative view of the entire history of interwar Yugoslavia.[26] To begin with, the official nomenclature of the new state denied the existence of a distinct Bosnian Muslim identity. With the creation of the Kingdom of Serbs, Croats, and Slovenes, the Bosnian Muslims were allegedly exposed to a genocidal policy; this policy origi-nated in the pre-1918 era but was now supposedly intensified on the part of Belgrade and directed against Bosnian Muslims because they were Muslims, both in Sandžak and in Bosnia-Herzegovina. The first years of the new state were catastrophic for the Muslim population; many were murdered, and others lost their property. In eastern Herzegovina alone, in the first years of the new state the Serbian army, Serb and Montenegrin irregulars allegedly murdered more than 3,000 Bosnian Muslims.[27] The state authorities did little or nothing to put a stop to these killings or to punish those responsible, which was proof of its complicity in these crimes.

Although conditions normalized in the 1920s, the advent of the royal dictator-ship proved extremely difficult for Muslims. Bosnian Muslim historians regard the January 6 dictatorship as a harsher manifestation of Great Serbian nationalism. To support their case, they cite the dictatorship's elimination of the historical boundaries of Bosnia-Herzegovina and the high number of Serb nationalists, drawn from the ranks of the National Radical Party, the most Serbian of Serb parties, in government administration. They also criticize the assumption made at the time that Muslims were either Serbs or Croats.[28] Thus far, Bosnian Muslim historiography has not delved into the role of the Yugoslav Muslim Organization, which was the leading interwar Bosnian Muslim political party, or that of Bosnian Muslims generally in interwar Yugoslavia; it sees Muslims merely as victims of the wider Serb-Croat conflict in interwar Yugoslavia. But as the foregoing short summary has tried to demonstrate, all three nationalist historiographies (Serb, Croat, Bosnian Muslim) see their respec-tive peoples as victims of the others and the interwar political experiment as a failure. When the Yugoslav communist system began to unravel after Tito's death, there was already a generalized sense in the country that the interwar Yugoslav project too had been a failure. Both communist and nationalist writings suggested that a democratic Yugoslav alternative to communism was historically unviable. In other words, both communist and nationalist presentations of the interwar project contributed to the widespread sense that no positive lessons could be drawn from the interwar experi-ence, to whit: a democratic Yugoslavia was virtually impossible.

The National Question: Political Parties and National Ideologies

The Yugoslav state, formed on December 1, 1918, and known officially until 1929 as the Kingdom of Serbs, Croats, and Slovenes, was composed of historically distinct lands. These included the Slovene lands (Carniola, parts of Styria, and Carinthia), Croatia-Slavonia, Dalmatia, Bosnia-Herzegovina, what later became known as Vojvodina (i.e., Bačka, Syrmia, Banat), Montenegro, and Serbia, which included Kosovo (or Old Serbia) and Vardar Macedonia (or Southern Serbia). These lands were also ethnically very heterogeneous. The two interwar censuses (1921, 1931) used language as their primary criterion of enumeration and thus counted all speakers of Serbo-Croatian as Serbo-Croats. Because the interwar Yugoslav authorities did not recognize the existence of distinct Bosnian Muslim, Macedonian, and Montenegrin nationalities, all three groups were subsumed within the Serbo-Croat category. This problem can be partially overcome by associating the linguistic data with census information on religion. This enables one to determine the approximate number of Croats, who were overwhelmingly Catholic, and Serbo-Croatian speaking Bosnian Muslims. Determining the precise number of Macedonians or Montenegrins is more problematical, however. The following estimates, made by Joseph Rothschild (see Table 1), may be regarded as reasonable percentages for the interwar

Table 1: Ethnolinguistic-national composition of Yugoslavia (1931)[1]

Nationality	Number	Percentage
"Serbo-Croatians"[2]	10,731,000	77.0
Serbs (with Montenegrins)		43.0
Croats		23.0
Bosnian Muslims		6.0
Macedonians		5.0
Slovenes	1,135,000	8.1
Albanians	505,000	3.6
Germans	500,000	3.6
Magyars	468,000	3.3
Romanians (and Vlachs)	138,000	1.0
Turks	133,000	0.9
Slovaks	76,000	0.5
Gypsies	70,000	0.5
Czechs	53,000	0.4
Russians	36,000	0.3
Ukrainians	28,000	0.2
Jews	18,000	0.1
Italians	9,000	0.1
Others/Unknown	34,000	0.3
Total	13,934,000	100

[1]Paul Robert Magocsi, *Historical Atlas of East Central Europe* (Toronto: University of Toronto Press, 1993), 141.

[2]The breakdown of "Serbo-Croatians" is taken from Joseph Rothschild, *East Central Europe Between the Two World Wars* (Seattle: University of Washington Press, 1974), 202f.

period: Serbs (with Montenegrins), 43 percent; Croats, 23 percent; Slovenes 8.5 percent; Macedonians, 5 percent; Bosnian Muslims, 6 percent; and non-Southern Slavs (including Albanian and Turkish Muslims, Germans, Magyars, Romanians, and Jews), 14.5 percent.[29]

The two leading Serbian political parties of the interwar era were the National Radical Party (NRS, *Narodna radikalna stranka*) of Nikola Pašić and the Democratic Party (DS, *Demokratska stranka*) of Ljubomir (Ljuba) Davidović, although the Democrats attracted many non-Serb unitarists. The NRS was essentially the party of the Serbian establishment (middle class, bureaucracy, army) and pursued a policy that can legitimately be characterized as Great Serbian: it wished to maintain Serbia's preeminence and to expunge non-Serb identities through a policy of cultural assimilation.[30] State centralism was seen as the most effective way of doing this and of preserving the recently obtained unity of all Serbs. Although the Radicals' base was prewar Serbia, they had substantial support in Syrmia and Vojvodina, where the Serb Radical Party of prewar Hungary and Croatia-Slavonia merged with the Serbian Radicals and established a solid base of support among Bosnia-Herzegovina's Serbs.

In their national ideology the Radicals clung to Vuk Karadžić's notion of linguistic Serbianism, although they also assumed that in Bosnia-Herzegovina and Croatia all Orthodox were Serbs. Most of their leaders, like Pašić, Stojan Protić, Ljubomir (Ljuba) Jovanović, and Lazar Marković, believed that the Štokavian dialect was Serbian alone. In the minds of many Radicals, the Croats were confined to the Kajkavian-speaking regions of Zagreb and its environs, but once they too adopted Štokavian as their literary language, they would hopefully be assimilated to a Serb identity. In this respect there was a powerful assimilationist strain in radical national ideology, for they believed that state centralism would eventually result in the cultural Serbianization of the non-Serbs, particularly the Bosnian Muslims and Croats. It is therefore not surprising that the Radicals, with few exceptions, rejected as artificial the historical provinces of Yugoslavia.

The ethnic component in radical nationalism was complemented by an equally important statist component. The NRS idolized the state as an entity unto itself and saw the need to protect it virtually at any cost. It saw state centralism as being a national interest of the Serb people. The Serbs were, quite simply, "centralists from conviction, centralists from experience." The Serbian state's evolution was instructive, the NRS claimed, for before 1918 centralism gave Serbia "that which is most important: one will and one strength." The non-Serbs who contested centralism were pursuing a path of "individualist regional wishes and individualist tribal demands [that] do not lead to the true aim," namely, the state's consolidation. By opposing centralism the non-Serbs were also rejecting "a modern organization of our state." The NRS would protect a strong centralized state because the state was "dearer than everything else. It is the idol which we served, which we serve, and which we will serve to the last breath." These remarks obviously begged the question of whether the NRS regarded the new state merely as an extension of Serbia or as a new state requiring a markedly different system of governance. On this matter the NRS left no doubt. The foes of state centralism were cautioned that "they cannot force us to forget our obligations to the state, in whose foundations are included mostly Serb blood, Serb bones and Serb sweat." Under a centralized state system Croats and Slovenes would be perfectly equal to the Serbs before the law. Anything more than that would be "unjustified." The confederalist program of the Croat parties was rejected as "regressive" and as hindering "the organization of our new state." What is more, the "separatism" of the Croats was providing the country's enemies with an opportunity to weaken it and only "creates bad blood in the country."[31]

The DS, on the other hand, was a party of *narodno jedinstvo* (national oneness), but it too pursued a policy of state centralism. A heterogeneous party, the DS was composed of radical dissidents and others from Serbia, the Serb wing of the prewar Croato-Serb Coalition (from Croatia) and some Slovene and Croat unitarists. It believed that there was only one, trinomial Yugoslav nation composed of the Serb, Croat, and Slovene "tribes." Whereas the Radicals believed centralism would lead to the assimilation of the non-Serbs, the democrats were convinced that the end result would be a hybrid Yugoslav nationality. Like the Radicals, they rejected Yugoslavia's historical provinces as artificial but for different reasons. For the Radicals these provinces not only limited Serbia's borders but also might hinder the assimilationist march of Serb national identity. The democrats, conversely, believed these provinces only heightened the tribal divisions within the new Yugoslav nationality instead of nurturing its oneness. Consequently, they opposed all political movements that aspired to preserve these political-historical divisions. Federalism was rejected as dangerous, for it would only weaken state unity and foment anarchy, thus opening the door to foreign intervention on the part of Yugoslavia's rapaciously revisionist neighbors.

In the immediate postwar period (1919–22), the democrats' two luminaries, Davidović and Svetozar Pribićević, shared virtually identical views on the issue of state organization. Eventually Davidović's Serbian-based wing of the party indicated a willingness to consider some reform of the political system. Increasingly it saw the need for some reform, and it also hoped to displace the NRS in Serbia. Pribićević's predominantly Croatian Serb wing resisted any change to the centralized state system, to whit: it was prepared to cooperate with the NRS in order to preserve that system.[32] Whatever the differences in principle between the NRS and DS in the early postwar period, in practice both sought a centralized state order, which is why they formed a coalition government in the state's critical early years from January 1921 to December 1922.

The Communist Party of Yugoslavia (KPJ, *Komunistička partija Jugoslavije*) also supported a centralized state system in the immediate postwar years.[33] The Yugoslav socialists supported *narodno jedinstvo*, and in practice their variant differed little, if at all, from the one espoused by the "bourgeois" DS; its common denominator was a disavowal of all national and historic individualities among the South Slavs.

However, after the KPJ was outlawed in August 1921, it began to reexamine its position on the national question and state organization. This process engendered a series of factional disputes, with the left faction associated with federalism and the right with antifederalism. The internal party debate on the national question culminated in the KPJ's Resolution on the National Question, issued at its Third Landed Conference (January 1924) in Belgrade. The document was an important victory for the left faction. Although it asserted that the 1918 unification was in "the interests of the class struggle of the proletariat," it directed the KPJ formally to adopt a federalist platform. What is more, the resolution acknowledged the right of each nation to secession and the creation of its own state. In order for unification to fulfill its historical mission, the Yugoslav state had to be organized "on the basis of a voluntary union and on the total equality of all of its parts, which hitherto was not the case." Because unification had been carried out by the bourgeoisie in a monarchist form and for its own class interests and then usurped by the Serbian bourgeoisie, the process of the formation of one Yugoslav nation was halted and national differences intensified.[34] Throughout the interwar era, the KPJ would continue to debate the national question as it moved from centralism to federalism to separatism and then back to an advocacy of federalism.

The main non-Serb party was the Croat People's Peasant Party, which in December 1920 formally became the Croat Republican Peasant Party (henceforth referred to as HRSS, *Hrvatska republikanska seljačka stranka*).[35] This party emerged after 1918 as both a peasant social and Croat national movement. The HRSS and its leader Stjepan Radić were committed to Croatian independence in 1918–20; they believed the creation of the Kingdom of Serbs, Croats, and Slovenes amounted to an unconstitutional and undemocratic act. It was unconstitutional because it was never ratified by the Croatian *Sabor* (Diet) and undemocratic because it was never authorized or subsequently approved by the Croat people. They were prepared to accept unification only after Croats had been allowed to express their wishes in a Croatian constituent assembly that would determine the terms of Croatia's status within any new Yugoslav state. But because they believed that this constituent assembly would proclaim a Croatian republic, this fact would have made unification with the Serbian Kingdom exceedingly difficult and probably impossible. In the months following unification, as the Serbian state and military apparatus were extended to Croatia, Radić's thinking only radicalized, especially following his imprisonment.[36]

Only in 1919–20, when Radić realized that the Paris Peace Conference would not act on behalf of the Croats, did the party adopt a (con)federalist Yugoslav platform. By that point, the HRSS had already adopted a policy of abstention from Belgrade. It refused to participate in the Temporary National Representation (or PNP),[37] which was to lay the groundwork for the Constituent Assembly of the new Yugoslav state. To participate in the PNP (1919–20), the Constituent Assembly (1920–21), or the National Parliament (after 1921) that followed would have meant legitimizing the unification act. This the HRSS would not countenance; the policy of abstention was abandoned only in 1924, but the tactic would be used repeatedly throughout the interwar era. The other major Croat parties, the Croat Union (HZ, *Hrvatska zajednica*) and Croat Party of Right (HSP, *Hrvatska stranka prava*), were forced to defer to the HRSS's leadership.[38] The introduction of universal male suffrage showed all too well that they lacked mass support in Croatia's socially dominant countryside. In 1921 both parties joined the HRSS to form the Croat Bloc, a united Croat national front against Belgrade that stood on the principles of Croat national individuality and Croatian state sovereignty. Thus, the other Croat parties were grudgingly forced to recognize the HRSS's leadership. This was based on their realization that Radić's party was the only political force of significance in Croatia. Even his many Croat critics recognized that Radić had come to represent the Croat people's resistance to Belgrade's state centralism.[39] By the early 1920s Radić's name had become synonymous with Croatdom and the preservation of Croat national individuality, and the HRSS would remain the only significant political party in Croatia until the Second World War.

The leading interwar Slovene political party was the Catholic clericalist Slovene People's Party (SLS, *Slovenska ljudska stranka*) of Anton Korošec. Already well established in the Slovene lands before 1918, the SLS was not especially enthusiastic about Yugoslav unification; it was concerned lest unification jeopardize Slovene autonomy. What is more, roughly 30 percent of Slovenes remained outside Yugoslavia's borders. In the November 1920 elections to the Constituent Assembly, the SLS confirmed its domination by securing a relative majority; in subsequent elections it would handily win absolute majorities in the Slovene lands. In 1920–21 it opposed a centralized state system and voted against the Vidovdan Constitution. From that point until 1927 it pursued, with minor exceptions, an autonomist platform. But in 1927 the party adopted the so-called Bled Agreement, abandoned its autonomist platform, and together with the NRS, defended the existing system. The SLS participated in various NRS-led governments in 1927–28, and its leader, Korošec, served as premier from July to December 1928. After the imposition of the royal dictatorship, the SLS would participate for a time in government. After briefly courting the opposition, in 1935 it again entered the government, where it would remain until 1941.

The leading (and really the only) interwar Bosnian Muslim political party was Mehmed Spaho's Yugoslav Muslim Organization (JMO, *Jugoslavenska muslimanska organizacija*).[40] The JMO sought to preserve Muslim religious autonomy, the socio-economic privileges of the Muslim elite, and the autonomy of Bosnia-Herzegovina. During the period of the Austro-Hungarian occupation (1878–1908) and annexation (1909–18), the Muslim autonomist movement was political but not overtly anti-Habsburg; it emphasized Muslim religious freedoms and Bosnian territorial integrity, but its political edge was tempered by the fact that the Habsburgs never threatened Muslim socioeconomic privileges. During the last stages of the First World War, Bosnian Muslim autonomist leaders made no effort to link their movement to the Yugoslav cause. That is because the Austro-Hungarian administration and the

Muslim elite tolerated one another; peaceful coexistence had been established long ago; and Muslim leaders satisfied themselves largely with religious autonomy and their socioeconomic privileges.

The formation of the Kingdom of Serbs, Croats, and Slovenes changed matters radically. The new state was highly centralized, a fact that threatened the Bosnian Muslim elite. The JMO was formed in this context. On the one hand, the JMO was autonomist in character, and yet it was prepared to strike compromises and pacts with the authorities, just as the Bosnian elite had done in the Habsburg era. It participated in Belgrade governments and in opposition coalitions; from the mid-1930s it became, in effect, a "regime party" because of its participation in Milan Stojadinović's government. At times the JMO compromised its own autonomist program, but at the same time it clung firmly to religious autonomy and retained its dominant position among Muslims. The JMO returned to its autonomist platform after the 1939 *Sporazum* (Agreement), which partitioned Bosnia-Herzegovina between Belgrade and the Croat Peasant Party. The JMO wanted Bosnian autonomy but was increasingly ignored by both Belgrade and Zagreb.

The Political System and Experiment, 1918–41

The significant anomalies in nationalist ideologies and political programs between the dominant Serb (NRS, DS) and Croat (HRSS/Croat Bloc) parties meant that a negotiated solution to the national question repeatedly eluded the new Kingdom's political leaders. The elections to the Constituent Assembly (see Table 2), which

Table 2: Elections to Constituent Assembly, 28 November 1920, Major Parties, 419 seats

Party	Votes	Percentage	Seats
Democratic Party (DS)	319,448	19.8	92
NRS	284,575	17.7	91
Communist Party (KPJ)	198,736	12.3	58
HPSS	230,590	14.3	50
Serbian Agrarians	151,603	9.4	39
Slovenes (SLS)*	111,274	6.9	27
Bosnian Muslims (JMO)	110,895	6.8	24
Social Democrats	46,792	2.9	10
Džemijet	30,029	1.8	8
Croat Husbandmen	38,400	2.3	7
Croat Union	25,867	1.6	4
Other	–	4.2	9

* The SLS's (Slovene People's Party) total numbers also include the votes of the Clericalist Croat People's Party.
Sources: Branislav Gligorijević, *Parlament i političke stranke u Jugoslaviji 1919-1929*, 86, 89; Ferdo Čulinović, *Jugoslavija između dva rata* (Zagreb, 1961), vol. 1, 312–313.

determined the form of government and drafted a constitution, did not occur until November 1920. In the interim, the prewar Serbian state and military apparatus were extended to the former Habsburg territories and rigorously enforced. A popular conviction soon arose among most non-Serbs that the new bureaucracy and the state it served were markedly worse than their predecessors and merely facilitated the political interests of Belgrade. The centralization of all political authority in Belgrade necessarily meant the diminution of other political individualities. In the first two years of the state's existence, a veritable dictatorial regime was established in Croatia and Bosnia-Herzegovina but less so in Slovenia and Dalmatia, where support for the new state was considerably stronger because of fears of Italian imperialism. Because the Serbian army had a well-organized command and had been untouched by the revolutionary disturbances that had convulsed Croatia in 1918, it was increasingly relied upon by Belgrade to preserve order in the former Habsburg lands. What is more, the Serbian elite felt entitled to rule in the former Habsburg lands in part because of Serbia's heavy wartime losses and in part because it had fought on the winning side.

The suppression of the KPJ and abstention of the HRSS from Belgrade (the third and fourth largest parties in the Constituent Assembly, respectively) enabled the centralist parties (NRS, DS) to enact a centralist constitution in 1921. The ideological basis of the constitution was unitarist: Article 3 designated the official language of the new state as "Serbo-Croato-Slovenian," while Article 19 referred to the "Serbo-Croato-Slovene nationality."[41] The proclamation of the Vidovdan Constitution, so-called after the date of its promulgation (St. Vitus's Day, or Vidovdan, June 28), by a small majority (223 for, 35 against, 161 boycotted), proved deleterious to the country's political evolution. A popular belief arose among most non-Serbs that the constitution was a Serbian document and represented a victory for Serb interests, for it was a product of centralist principles. It was adopted without the approval and against the will of most of the non-Serb parties.

In addition to confirming state centralism and Serbian dominance, the Vidovdan Constitution gave far-reaching powers to the Monarch. Theoretically the constitution recognized the national parliament (*Skupština*) as a sovereign organ of authority and thus established the new kingdom as a parliamentary monarchy.[42] But the constitution did not obligate King Aleksandar Karadjordjević to name ministers from the national parliament or even to respect the will of parliamentary majorities. Because the form of parliamentarism enshrined in the 1921 Constitution was derived from the 1903 Serbian Constitution, both king and national parliament shared legislative authority. The king was the highest symbol of the state, which is why he was accorded the role of constitutional actor equal to the national parliament.[43] In actual fact, the king was the more important factor who stood above the national parliament, possessing the right to sanction or reject parliamentary bills and to call to session or dissolve the national parliament at any time. Moreover, the king controlled the army and conducted foreign policy. He could also make administrative appointments and wielded considerable authority over the judiciary. In short, King Aleksandar was answerable to no one. These facts seriously threatened parliamentarism and its institutions from the very outset. Between 1921 and 1928 governments were formed not in the national parliament but at Aleksandar's court; he brought down governments with majorities and sustained those lacking them. His right to call to session or dissolve the national parliament at any time made him the ultimate arbiter of the Yugoslav political system.[44]

Despite the chasm separating centralists and federalists, Serbs and non-Serbs, there were attempts at dialogue and negotiation by the major Serb and Croat parties. In late 1922 the DS and HRSS held a series of unsuccessful discussions on a political alliance. In the spring of 1923, following the March elections of that year (see Table 3), the HRSS and its new allies, the SLS and JMO, held talks with the ruling NRS. But these negotiations were undertaken on both occasions largely for short-term, tactical reasons by all sides.[45] All parties found it difficult to reach a negotiated solution because they were often internally deeply divided between moderates and Radicals and mutually at odds over nationalist ideologies and political programs. In spring 1923 negotiations between the HRSS and NRS finally collapsed; in July 1923 Radić left the country to internationalize the Croat Question. He would return in August 1924, but not before enrolling the HRSS in the Soviet-sponsored Krestintern (Peasant International),[46] which endorsed Radić's policy of Croat national self-determination. The Belgrade authorities would use Radić's decision to join the Krestintern to suppress the HRSS. In December 1924 the Pašić-Pribićević (NRS-SDS) minority coalition government adopted the Law for the Protection of the State against the HRSS. The party was placed outside the law and its leadership jailed. Radić was arrested on January 5, 1925, as were the most prominent leaders of the party. In late March, informal negotiations began between the imprisoned Radić and emissaries of the king; that same month, the HRSS finally recognized the existing state system, that is, the Karadorđević dynasty and Vidovdan Constitution.[47] On July 16, 1925, a new government coalition was formed between the NRS and HSS (*Hrvatska seljačka stranka*, Croat Peasant Party), as the party was now called.[48]

Radić's political defeat of 1925 was a major victory for the defenders of centralism and the Vidovdan order. It was a Pyrrhic victory, however. In the event the constitutional crisis of the pre-1925 period, and with it the vexing Croat Question, was set aside only temporarily. What is more, the NRS, hitherto the strongest Serbian party and the main defender of the Vidovdan order, began to implode. If there was one political factor that seemed to have emerged unscathed—indeed, strengthened—by the events of 1925, it was King Aleksandar. And if there is one salient trait that characterized Yugoslav political life after 1925, it is the growing and ever palpable influence exerted by the Yugoslav monarch over the country's political life.

Both the DS and NRS were deeply divided after 1925 over leadership disputes and on matters of principle.[49] Certain elements were committed to genuine

Table 3: National Elections in the Kingdom of Serbs, Croats, and Slovenes

Party	1923			1925			1927		
	Votes	%	Seats	Votes	%	Seats	Votes	%	Seats
NRS	562,213	25.8	108	702,573	28.8	122**	742,111	31.9	112
H(R)SS	473,333	21.8	70	545,466	22.3	67	367,570	15.8	61
DS	400,342	18.4	51	279,686	11.8	37	381,784	16.4	59****
SLS	139,171	6.4	24*	105,304	4.3	20	139,611	6.0	21
JMO	112,228	5.2	18	132,296	5.4	15	58,623	2.5	9****
SDS	–	–	–	117,953	5.0	8**	199,040	8.6	22
National Bloc	–	–	–	210,843	9.6	33**	–	–	–
Democratic Union	–	–	–	–	–	–	73,703	3.2	11****
Serbian Agrarians	164,602	7.6	11***	130,254	5.3	5***	136,076	5.9	11
Others	–	14.8	30	–	7.5	8	–	9.7	11

*SLS: in 1923, includes votes of the Croat People's Party and Croats from Vojvodina.

**National Bloc (NRS-SDS joint candidates in 1925): of its 33 seats, 19 went to the NRS (giving it 141) and 14 to the SDS (giving it 22).

***Serbian Agrarians: in 1923 and 1925, includes one seat from Slovene Independent Peasant Party and the votes cast for that party.

****In 1927, the Democratic Party (DS) and Bosnian Muslims (JMO) ran jointly as the "Democratic Union." Of the 11 seats won, 9 went to the JMO (giving it 18) and 2 to the DS (giving it 61).

Sources: Branislav Gligorijević, *Parlament i političke stranke u Jugoslaviji*, 145–149, 192–195, 239–242; Ferdo Čulinović, *Jugoslavija između dva rata*, 406–411, 454–457, 500–501.

parliamentary government and opposed the court's growing influence in political life but were repeatedly obstructed by more conservative and nationalist elements. In practice these elements assisted the weakening of parliamentarism and strengthening of the court's influence in political life.[50] But in spite of the internal fissures and mutual differences of these groups, they nevertheless generally demonstrated a great deal of uniformity with respect to what they perceived to be the state's interests. When the NRS and DS clashed, it was usually only for Serbian votes in parliamentary and local elections. Because most Radicals and democrats still regarded Radić and his party as a threat to the state's stability, cooperation with him was exceedingly difficult. The fear of some Serbian politicians of the king's growing influence in political life notwithstanding, the Serbian parties generally tended to view the king as a natural ally against Croat demands for greater autonomy.

The increasingly bitter factional struggles within the two major Serbian parties were closely tied to the king's growing political assertiveness and had fateful consequences for interwar Yugoslavia's political evolution. The king possessed an antipathy toward strong parties and political personalities. Throughout the 1920s he and his inner political circle waged a subtle campaign first to discredit and then to remove all prominent political personalities, with the purpose of gradually facilitating the king's sway over the country's political life. In April 1925 King Aleksandar acknowledged that of all the party political leaders Pašić alone knew what was best for the state and thus that he had to work with him. He observed that "besides Pašić, there is not a single man in the Radical party who could successfully develop a political policy to the benefit of the state." If one adds to this his conviction that the liberal Davidović was naïve and that none of the other parties had a leader "who could bring order to the state," then his growing concern that he personally had to exert greater influence over political life becomes comprehensible.[51] Pašić, the first victim of this campaign, was certainly cognizant of the wider political significance of the attempt to oust him from the NRS leadership. Two months before his death, he remarked that "there is no longer a true Radical party." He had nothing positive to say about the current radical leaders and was now attempting to form a new radical bloc that would complete "the consolidation of the state." When this bloc was formed, he promised to go to the king and "energetically to warn him about this intolerable [political] situation, and to caution him not to toy either with the state or his position."[52] In the event, he did see the king but died shortly thereafter, his plans to reconstruct the NRS dying with him.

It is not coincidental that the king's influence over political life became more palpable after 1925. Prior to that point he had been committed to a working relationship with the NRS, the strongest Serbian party, because of the threat posed by Radić's republican movement. With Radić seemingly neutralized in 1925, the King moved against the NRS. Though it had its dissidents in the early 1920s (e.g., Stojan Protić, Momčilo Ivanić, Nastas Petrović), the NRS remained cohesive because of its commitment to the protection of the Vidovdan order. After 1925 these weaknesses came to the fore and became significant fissures. Because both the NRS and DS had weak party organizations, their leaders were the parties' main cohesive forces. To discredit these leaders naturally meant weakening their parties. Pašić was ousted in a carefully orchestrated campaign originating with one faction of the party, which in turn also was eventually ousted from the party. By the time his faction, which was eventually headed by Velimir (Velja) Vukićević, was readmitted to the NRS in February 1927, the party was factionalized beyond repair. By promoting and exploiting these differences, and thereby weakening the Serbian parties, the king emerged as the arbiter of the country's political fate.[53]

Under the circumstances, the political situation in the country became more fluid, and politics were in a greater state of flux. From July 1925 to January 1927, the NRS and HSS formed a government coalition, popularly referred to as the R-R (Radical-Radićist) government. Neither side was particularly enthusiastic about the arrangement. This was no agreement between equals. Radić's capitulation formed the basis of the NRS-HSS government. Thus, the key ministerial portfolios (e.g., internal and foreign affairs, et al.) remained in the NRS's hands, and with them the NRS's hegemony. The NRS-HSS government was an unworkable association from its inception. The troubled and unproductive eighteen-month HSS-NRS relationship ended following the January 1927 district elections.

One of the main characteristics of the country's political life in the late 1920s was the ever-increasing political polarity between the two Serbian parties (NRS, DS) and the opposition, notably the HSS. Throughout 1927–28, the factionalized NRS formed each government, first under Nikola Uzunović (February to April 1927) and then under Vukićević, the leader of a competing NRS faction (April 1927 to July 1928). These cabinets were constituted with Anton Korošec's Slovenes (SLS), DS factions, and occasionally, the Bosnian Muslims (JMO). In opposition stood a new political alliance, formed in November 1927 by Radić (HSS) and Pribićević (SDS), known as the Peasant-Democratic Coalition (SDK, *Seljačko-demokratska koalicija*), a political front of Croats and Croatian Serbs. After February 1928, when its plans for a national democratic front collapsed, the SDK launched a concerted struggle for equality for the non-Serbian regions. The political debates in 1928 became so bitter that parliamentary sessions often degenerated into chaos. It was during these debates that Radić and Pribićević, undeniably two of the most gifted rhetoricians on the Yugoslav political scene, excelled in exposing the inequalities of the country's political system and at the same time raising political tensions through their acerbic diatribes against the Serbian parties. By early June, parliamentary sessions had degenerated to a level of bitter recrimination. At the June 20 session of parliament, the Montenegrin Serb NRS deputy Puniša Račić drew his pistol and shot five HSS deputies. Djuro Basariček and Pavle Radić were killed instantly. Ivan Pernar and Ivan Grandja would survive. Stjepan Radić was hit in the abdomen and seriously wounded; he died more than six weeks later on August 8.

With this crime the country's acute political crisis reached a crossroads. The SDK's deputies withdrew to Zagreb, which now formed their political center. From this point onward the SDK demanded sweeping changes to the Vidovdan state system. According to its June 21 resolutions, the SDK refused to further participate in the Belgrade parliament or conduct any business with the existing government. "We have experienced a terrible scandal," the HSS paper *Dom* declared, "at which distant future generations will shudder."[54] Pribićević was even more categorical. At the funerals of Basariček and Pavle Radić, he alleged that the assassin's bullets had "fatally wounded the present [state] system which always seeks its final arguments in the gun-butt and in terror, instead of searching for them in an agreement of all national forces."[55] The entire state system was now called into question and its fundamental reform demanded. Given the SDK's perception that the assassinations were organized, it refused even to consider dialogue with the authorities. It is hardly surprising, therefore, that the SDK's resolution of August 1 denied the legitimacy of the existing system; the bloodshed of June 20 had completely destroyed the existing state order.[56] Radić's position had now radicalized. According to one of his deputies, who met with Radić shortly before his death, Radić had concluded that "we have nothing more to look for in Belgrade."[57] That is hardly surprising, particularly in light of Radić's and Pribićević's threats, even before the assassinations, to withdraw from Belgrade. Returning to Belgrade was simply not a credible alternative in the immediate aftermath of June 20, 1928.

Although the SDK's resolution of August 1 did not explicitly call for a federal state system, undoubtedly because some elements of Pribićević's SDS opposed such a move, the HSS saw federalism as the only solution to the state crisis. Pribićević himself noted, writing from his Parisian exile in 1934, that "these resolutions demanded a new organization of the Kingdom of Serbs, Croats and Slovenes, in the form of federalism of the historic and national individualities in the country." He added that perhaps the Southern Slavs "would today be much closer to true unitarism, had they begun with a federal organization of the state that would correspond to their different historical pasts, instead of beginning with unitarism which the leading factors in Belgrade understood and realized as the hegemony of Serbia, which with the number of its citizens and its territory comprises hardly more than one fifth of the entire state."[58]

After the events of June 20 there was clearly little willingness for compromise either in Belgrade or Zagreb. There was a feeling among the HSS leaders and Croats generally that the shots fired at Radić and his colleagues were fired at the entire Croat people. This sentiment only intensified after Radić's death. His funeral on August 13 turned into a political manifestation of massive proportions.[59] Following his death, and with the abstention of the SDK's deputies from Belgrade, there were renewed calls in the Belgrade press for an "amputation."[60] Talk of amputation was not new, for this notion had been raised at different times throughout the 1920s. Basically, amputation meant that Croatia proper, including Slovenia, but not Slavonia and

Dalmatia, should be severed from the state. This would ostensibly solve the Croat Question. There was no common ground between the regime parties and court in Belgrade and the SDK in Zagreb. Throughout late 1928 the political situation deteriorated. On January 6, 1929, King Aleksandar proclaimed the imposition of a royal dictatorship. The Vidovdan Constitution was suspended; the national parliament and all political parties were dissolved; and press censorship was imposed. A new government was formed under the leadership of General Petar Živković, the commander of the Royal Guard. And thus the shots fired in the national parliament in June 1928 eventually killed not only Radić but also the democratic experience in the Kingdom of Serbs, Croats, and Slovenes, for the two were intimately tied. The Yugoslav state now stood at a crossroads, a fact that was not lost on contemporaries. The existing political system had broken down completely. In January 1929 Yugoslavia's first and only ostensibly democratic decade ended in political failure.

The attempt at parliamentary government failed not only because a strong monarchical authority handicapped it but also because substantial segments of the population did not accept the constitutional basis on which the Yugoslav state had been founded. Positions hardened after 1929. The Serb parties refused to consider any decentralization of power while the Croatian front refused to return to Belgrade. After the death of Radić and his colleagues, a turning point in the development of the Yugoslav state was reached; the Yugoslav experiment in democracy and parliamentary government came to an end. Whether or not the court was connected to this crime, King Aleksandar certainly used the crisis to establish the January 6 dictatorship.[61] He evidently concluded that he had no alternative but to govern by decree. At this point, the interwar Yugoslav Kingdom lost whatever legitimacy it may have possessed among Croats. What is more, with Radić's death Croats gained a martyr.

After January 1929, the dictatorial regime of King Aleksandar systematically labored to indoctrinate the populace into an abandonment of their old tribal identities in favor of a new Yugoslav national identity. The ideology of integral Yugoslavism was now promoted with new vigor. A reorganization of the local administration abolished the old system of thirty-three departments (*oblasti*) in favor of nine large provinces (*banovine*) that took the names of geographical features rather than historic and cultural entities.[62] The borders of the new banovine cut across the historic prewar frontiers of provinces like Bosnia-Herzegovina, Croatia, and Montenegro. The governors of these provinces were appointed by royal decree and were directly responsible to the king. The state's name was officially changed to Kingdom of Yugoslavia. On September 3, 1931, the king issued his Octroyed Constitution. Although it guaranteed personal liberties, it simultaneously forbade most forms of political activity. The executive was given extensive powers, as was the king; elections to the national parliament were no longer by secret ballot, and half the members of the senate were nominated by the king. The state apparatus, army, and judiciary remained firmly in Serb hands, and the new government party, the Yugoslav National Party (JNS,

Jugoslovenska narodna stranka), was a predominantly Serb affair. In the same period, many of the moderate leaders of the Croat, Slovene, and Bosnian Muslim parties spent time in prison and were otherwise harassed by the authorities.[63] The radical opponents, like Ante Pavelić, the leader of the Croat fascist Ustaša, fled abroad to enlist the support of Fascist Italy and other revisionist states and to work for the destruction of Yugoslavia.

King Aleksandar's Yugoslavist project began to unravel even before his October 1934 assassination in Marseilles by a Macedonian terrorist working for the Ustaša movement.[64] His political experiment in dictatorship resulted in the construction of an elaborate police state and undermined the project of establishing a widely shared unitary Yugoslav identity, which was one of his stated objectives. To what degree Aleksandar's regime was "monarcho-fascist" is still debated, but that it was antiliberal, anticommunist, and oppressive is beyond dispute. Although the regime seemingly attempted to reduce interethnic distrust and hatred, its methods resulted in further alienation. There was a nearly universal shift to the political right among all the Yugoslav peoples, although this shift also reflected the spirit of the times in Europe. As such, the royal dictatorship undoubtedly contributed to an increase in interethnic tensions.[65]

After October 1934, a Regency Council was established, headed by Prince Pavle Karađorđević, the late king's cousin. Much of Aleksandar's system, like the 1931 Constitution, was retained, although the reins of dictatorship were definitely loosened.[66] Prince Pavle combined a reactionary attitude toward parliamentary pluralism and socioeconomic reform with a desire to reach a political compromise with the HSS.[67] Attempts under Bogoljub Jevtić (1934–35) and then Milan Stojadinović (1935–39) to consolidate the political situation in the country failed. A significant change came only in early 1939, when Dragiša Cvetković replaced Stojadinović as premier. In August 1939, Cvetković and the HSS leader Vladko Maček negotiated the *Sporazum* (Agreement), which created an autonomous Croatian banovina. This autonomous Croatian unit included prewar Croatia-Slavonia (minus most of Syrmia), Dalmatia, and those parts of Bosnia-Herzegovina with a Croat plurality. Croatia had its own elected diet, the Sabor, and autonomy in most internal administrative matters; foreign policy, defense, and taxation remained in the hands of Belgrade.

What prompted the conclusion of the Sporazum between Belgrade and the HSS was the international climate that seemed ominously threatening to the future of the Kingdom of Yugoslavia. For Croat nationalists around Ante Pavelić and much of the HSS's right wing, the Sporazum was too little, too late. They objected to the exclusion from the banovina of those lands that were supposedly historically Croatian, that is, Syrmia and Bosnia-Herzegovina. In the event these groups were already committed to independence. Conversely, among the Serbs who opposed it were the Serbian parties, the Serbian Orthodox Church, and the army. These groups were generally politically conservative and believed the Sporazum was too generous to Croats; it supposedly weakened the Yugoslav state while simultaneously jeopardizing the status of Croatia's large Serb minority. It should be said, however, that many Serb democrats opposed the Sporazum because they saw it as a Croat betrayal of democracy in Yugoslavia; the HSS had abandoned its allies of the Serbian opposition, and as a consequence the 1931 constitution remained in place. Furthermore, because the Sporazum did not establish federalism, Slovene and Bosnian Muslim leaders also opposed it. For Bosnian Muslim leaders, who had hoped to preserve Bosnia-Herzegovina's territorial integrity, the Sporazum offered no advantages.[68] In the event, when war came to Yugoslavia in April 1941, the Nazis had no difficulty in breaking asunder the politically fragile structure of royal Yugoslavia.

Conclusion: The Legacy of Interwar Yugoslavia

The attempt to foster a common identity from among the different groups that came together in 1918 to form the Kingdom of Serbs, Croats, and Slovenes would have been extremely difficult for any regime, even one that was well intentioned and faced no external obstacles to its existence. The failure of the Yugoslavist project should not surprise anyone, therefore. Although the interwar state was the joint creation of the Serb, Croat, and Slovene political elites, it was not the Yugoslavia desired by two of the three cofounding peoples, namely, Croats and Slovenes. Serb predominance and Croat resistance, and the concomitant growth of Serb-Croat tensions, became the principal theme of interwar Yugoslavia.[69] One consequence of this disenchantment was the delegitimation of the Yugoslav idea among most non-Serbs. One of the lessons of the interwar political experiment was that the South Slavs' political individualities and historical identities could not be sacrificed for the sake of or subsumed within the greater Yugoslav community. The nationalist antagonism between Serb and Croat over the issue of state organization, which was at the core of the national question in Yugoslavia, could only be resolved if each side respected the political individuality and rights of the other. As long as the rights of any one of its constituent peoples went unrecognized, the Yugoslav state would be unable to secure political stability and legitimacy or to evolve along democratic lines.

The reality is that interwar Yugoslavia was a Serb-dominated state, where the Serb political elite was generally insensitive to the rights of non-Serbs. Through the two decades of its existence the Yugoslav Kingdom never effectively came to grips with the problem of relations between the nationalities. Neither of the two leading Serbian parties (NRS, DS) was firmly committed to state reform, although the state and parliamentary system of the 1920s was in dire need of reform. The powerful role of King Aleksandar was part of that problem. This is not to suggest that Croat political leaders were faultless. Croat abstention from 1919 to 1924 also undermined the political system, giving it a more pronounced Serb character than it otherwise might have possessed. The policy may also have hurt more than helped the Croat cause. In the event, after 1925 the parliamentary system saw the growing influence of the court. The king's role was paramount and ultimately jeopardized parliamentarism.

What is the legacy of King Aleksandar and the royal dictatorship? King Aleksandar undoubtedly wanted to strengthen the country he ruled, and one way of doing this, at least to his mind, was to promote an ideology of integral Yugoslavism. It is this author's contention that Aleksandar genuinely hoped to promote a Yugoslav identity among all his subjects but that his political and ideological project ultimately failed for at least two reasons: (a) the regime's personnel were drawn mainly from the NRS and to a lesser extent from the Democrats, which meant that the royal dictatorship was staffed by the old political elite, which seriously undermined its status among non-Serbs. In short, the dictatorship did not represent a sufficient break with the past to instill any confidence among the broader populace; and (b) the regime's methods, which were coercive and undemocratic to the end, could hardly be expected to win a broad following, either among Serbs or non-Serbs. Even if one accepts that King Aleksandar genuinely believed that he could nurture a Yugoslav identity and loyalty, many in Serbia and elsewhere saw him as a symbol of Serbian hegemony just as they saw Yugoslavia as Great Serbia. This is not meant to suggest that many Croats and Slovenes did not feel a genuine sense of grief following his assassination in 1934, which undoubtedly came as a shock. But this grief was momentary and soon punctured by the painful political realities of the day.[70]

The Serbian political character of the interwar state was so pronounced that national consciousness among many non-Serbs, for example, among Croats, Bosnian Muslims, and Macedonians, became a mass phenomenon only after the First World War. By 1918 a Croat national identity had already been established among the Catholic peasantry of Croatia-Slavonia. But only in the postwar circumstances was a Croat mass consciousness firmly established among the Catholic peasants of Dalmatia, Bosnia-Herzegovina, and Vojvodina (i.e., the *Bunjevci* and *Šokci*), in large part thanks to the activism of the HSS. The policies of the Yugoslav authorities, who were seen after 1918 to be serving Serbian (Orthodox) state interests, only helped to strengthen this new consciousness. Much the same may be said for Bosnian Muslims and Macedonians, although in these two cases the process of forming a mass national consciousness took much longer and was not completed until after 1945.

All this had significant implications for the interwar and later history of Yugoslavia. This mass national consciousness was formed in the context of bitter political struggles against the Serb "other"; in particular, it was formed in opposition to Belgrade and the Serbian political establishment, and this formative experience naturally had ramifications for the evolution of Serb-dominated interwar Yugoslavia and also for future Yugoslavist projects. As Branko Petranović and Momčilo Zečević have noted, "The weak, uncultured and corrupt apparatus of the new state administration, in actual fact the adopted former bureaucratic apparatus, functioned as anti-propaganda for Serbian policy outside Serbia and in Yugoslavia." The rampant corruption and often brutal methods of the police and gendarmerie only further inflamed anti-Serbian sentiment in Croatia, Bosnia-Herzegovina, and elsewhere.[71] These heavy-handed Serbian policies outside Serbia gradually fomented resentment of Serbs generally, who were collectively identified with the oppressive new Yugoslav state and the political parties that supported centralism, just as many Serbs began to nurture a distrust of Croats and others for undermining the unity of the new state, which was viewed by Serbs as the culmination of the nineteenth-century struggle for Serb unification. The only common symbols of national unity were the Vidovdan Constitution, the monarch, and a vague feeling of common cultural identity. In reality, however, the Constitution and monarch were symbols of Serbian hegemony to the non-Serb majority, and Yugoslavist sentiment was confined largely to a segment of the intelligentsia, while the socially dominant countryside held on to its Serb, Croat, Slovene, or other identities. The constitution and the apparatus of state provided a framework that was imposed from above.

In the final analysis, what is the legacy of interwar Yugoslavia? Whether or not one believes that the interwar state was a political failure, what is perhaps far more significant is the widespread *perception* of failure. I have tried to show that communist and nationalist historiographies alike agreed that the interwar political experiment was an abysmal failure. As such, communist and nationalist presentations of the interwar period were responsible for the widespread sense that no positive lessons could be drawn from the interwar experience. Thus, when the communist experiment failed in Yugoslavia, everyone in the former country had already been conditioned to treat the interwar, noncommunist experiment as an abject failure, whether politically, socially, economically, or culturally. The alternate view, nurtured by dissidents at home and émigrés abroad, was equally disparaging and pessimistic. No one drew inspiration from the interwar experiment; it was virtually impossible to look on that era with confidence or for inspiration. The lesson appeared to be, and here there was almost universal agreement, that the noncommunist experiment had failed and that there was no viable democratic alternative.

Why were ideological positions seemingly nonnegotiable and political leaders so intractable in Yugoslavia's interwar period? If light can be shed on this question, then perhaps the more difficult question of why the Yugoslavist project failed can be properly addressed. The answer undoubtedly has much to do with national ideologies and prevailing conceptions among Serb and Croat leaders of the proper place and status of their peoples in Yugoslavia. State centralism was a key component in Serb national ideologies, rooted in the fact that Serbs had long been scattered across so many different lands, for example, Serbia proper, Kosovo, Bosnia-Herzegovina, Croatia, and Vojvodina. Because Serb leaders viewed the creation of the new state in 1918 primarily in terms of the completion of Serb unification, a protracted process that had been started a century earlier, they were loath to abandon their centralist convictions. Conversely, Croat leaders, who had struggled long and hard to affirm their nationality in the Austro-Hungarian Empire and had been recognized in 1868 by the Magyar ruling oligarchy and Habsburg Crown as a "political nation" entitled to autonomy in Croatia-Slavonia (1868–1918), were unprepared to abandon this individuality in a politically centralist and ideologically unitarist state.

What is more, the Great War undoubtedly contributed to a hardening of attitudes on the part of both Serb and Croat leaders. On the one hand, for Serbs the Great War had been a painful and costly victory, and their leaders felt entitled to make the decisions in the new state, especially as Croats and Slovenes were, to their minds, liberated parties. On the other hand, the Great War had radicalized much of Croatia's rural population, as the 1918 disturbances demonstrated. As a result, the HSS leadership was equally reluctant to compromise, for it had to contend with its own politically and socially radical constituency. In other words, nationalist ideologies and the postwar conditions were not necessarily conducive to compromise, which made a political agreement between Serb and Croat all the more elusive. As time passed, bitterness grew on both sides and compromise became even more difficult.

The way in which unification had been achieved was also part of the problem. There is little doubt that Serb support for unification was universal and virtually unqualified. In Croatia, unification had a far narrower social and political base. Although much of Croatia's middle class and intelligentsia supported unification, her socially dominant countryside did not. Thus, support for unification was limited to Croatian Serbs and a segment of the Croat intelligentsia; in the event, the latter group was politically marginalized after the 1920 elections, increasingly disenchanted with the new state, and eventually joined the HSS in opposing centralism. In Bosnia-Herzegovina, support for unification was limited largely to Serbs and some Croat intellectuals of Yugoslavist persuasion. But for Bosnian Muslim leaders, the Muslim masses, and the majority of the Croat population, unification did not necessarily mean liberation or emancipation. In Slovenia and Dalmatia, where fears of Italian imperialism were palpable, support for unification was far stronger. But if one keeps in mind the relatively narrow ethnic, social, and political base of support for unification, it is not difficult to understand why many non-Serbs saw unification as a Serbian fait accompli and why they believed that the Yugoslav state was a Serbian project. This conviction was fueled by the fact that unification was never sanctioned by popularly elected regional assemblies or in referenda in the constituent regions of the country. It is no wonder then that national identities were forged in opposition to Serbian domination, a fact that had deleterious consequences not only for interwar but also communist and post-communist Yugoslavist projects.

All this in turn helps explain why a negotiated political solution or compromise was so elusive in interwar Yugoslavia. Only the threat of war and the possibility of invasion in 1939 compelled the political elites (i.e., the regency and the HSS) to compromise, but even then agreement was contested on all sides by broad sections of political and intellectual opinion. One might be tempted to blame many of the political problems of interwar Yugoslavia on the failure of leadership. To be sure, there clearly were such failures. But even different leaders would have been saddled with the same burdens. This may sound overly fatalistic, which is why it is important to keep in mind the wider European context. In the interwar era, every state in east-central and southeastern Europe, with the exception of Czechoslovakia, witnessed a disintegration of parliamentary democracy and the concomitant rise of authoritarianism. This trend occurred in the context of similar tendencies throughout Europe. Yugoslavia was hardly an exception, therefore, and its political failure needs to be properly contextualized. Even Czechoslovakia, which remained a democracy practically to its demise in 1938–39,[72] failed to solve its national question. That having been said, the failure of democracy in interwar Yugoslavia was decidedly linked to the national question, and it was this issue that ultimately had an equally deleterious impact on the both the "first" and "second" Yugoslavias and the fates of all their peoples.

Notes

1. For works on the interwar kingdom, nationalist ideologies, and the kingdom's major political groups, see Ivo Banac, *The National Question in Yugoslavia: Origins, History, Politics* (Ithaca: Cornell University Press, 1984); John R. Lampe, *Yugoslavia as History: Twice There Was a Country* (Cambridge, New York: Cambridge University Press, 1996); Dennison Rusinow, "The Yugoslav Peoples," in *Eastern European Nationalism in the Twentieth Century*, ed. Peter F. Sugar (Lanham: American University Press, 1995), 305–411; Aleksa Djilas, *The Contested Country: Yugoslav Unity and Communist Revolution, 1919–1953* (Cambridge: Harvard University Press, 1991); Jill A. Irvine, *The Croat Question: Partisan Politics in the Formation of the Yugoslav Socialist State* (Boulder, CO: Westview Press, 1993); and Wayne S. Vucinich, "Interwar Yugoslavia," in *Contemporary Yugoslavia: Twenty Years of Socialist Experiment,* ed. W. S. Vucinich (Berkeley: University of California Press, 1969). Although now half a century old, Jozo Tomasevich's *Peasants, Politics, and Economic Change in Yugoslavia* (Palo Alto: Stanford University Press, 1955), is still well worth the read. On the cultural aspects of Yugoslavism, see Andrew Baruch Wachtel, *Making a Nation, Breaking a Nation: Literature and Cultural Politics in Yugoslavia* (Palo Alto: Stanford University Press, 1998). For more recent works, see Leslie Benson, *Yugoslavia: A Concise History* (New York: Palgrave Macmillan, 2001), and the collection of essays in Dejan Djokić (ed.), *Yugoslavism: Histories of a Failed Idea, 1918–1992* (Madison: The University of Wisconsin Press, 2003). A brief clarification of my usage of Croat/Croatian, Serb/Serbian, and Slovene/Slovenian seems to be in order. Throughout this article, Croat, Serb, and Slovene will refer to peoples, regardless of the territory they inhabit, while Croatian, Serbian, and Slovenian will refer to land, language, institutions, and the like. Thus, Serbian state, Croatian language, Slovenian history, etc. In a few cases, however, Serbian refers to the Serbs of Serbia, as reflected in the native language's distinction between *srbijanci* (i.e., Serbs from Serbia) and *srbi* (Serbs, regardless of the territory they inhabit).
2. See Peter Fritzsche, "The Case of Modern Memory," *The Journal of Modern History*, Vol. 73 (March 2001), pp. 87–117.
3. The Western literature on interwar Yugoslavia, although improving, is still wanting. As Dušan Djordjevich has recently observed, the "first" Yugoslavia "has long suffered from historiographical neglect." See Dušan Djordjevich, "Clio amid the Ruins: Yugoslavia and Its Predecessors in Recent Historiography," in Norman M. Naimark and Holly

Case (eds.), *Yugoslavia and Its Historians: Understanding the Balkan Wars of the 1990s* (Palo Alto: Stanford University Press, 2002), p. 18.

4. Josip Broz Tito, "Nacionalno pitanje u Jugoslaviji u svetlu narodnooslobodilačke borbe," (December 1942), in Josip Broz Tito, *Sabrana djela,* vol. 13 (Belgrade: Komunist, 1982), pp. 95–96. It should be pointed out, however, that communist historiography did refer to the collaboration of the Croat and Slovene bourgeoisies with the Serbian bourgeoisie.

5. This interpretation can be found in Ferdo Čulinović, *Jugoslavija između dva rata,* 2 vols. (Zagreb: Izdavacki zavod JAZU, 1961); the two works of Branislav Gligorijević, *Parlament i političke stranke u Jugoslaviji 1919–1929* (Belgrade: Institut za Savremenu Istoriju, 1979), and "Parlamentarni sistem u Kraljevini SHS (1919–1929)," in *Politički život Jugoslavije, 1914–1945: Zbornik radova,* ed.Aleksandar Acković (Belgrade: **Radio-Beograd,** 1973), 365–88; the relevant sections of Branko Petranović, *Istorija Jugoslavije 1918–1978* (Belgrade: Nolit, 1978); and Vladimir Dedijer et al., *Istorija Jugoslavije,* 2nd ed. (Belgrade: Prosveta, 1973).

6. In both Serbia and Croatia, historical revisionism broached similar subjects and taboos, e.g., the question of republican borders, the alleged unequal treatment of Serbs and Croats by the Communist Party of Yugoslavia, and the rehabilitation of important noncommunist political figures like Slobodan Jovanović in Serbia and Stjepan Radić in Croatia. On the "outburst" of history in Serbia, see Jasna Dragović-Soso, *"Saviours of the Nation": Serbia's Intellectual Opposition and the Revival of Nationalism* (Montreal: McGill-Queen's University Press, 2002), pp. 64–114. On historical revisionism during the Croatian Spring, and particularly on the role of the historian and later president of independent Croatia, Franjo Tudjman, see Marinko Čulić, *Tudjman: Anatomija neprosvijećenog absolutizma* (Split: Feral Tribune, 1999), pp. 55–78.

7. On the politics and historical memory of the Serb and Croat émigré communities, see Paul Hockenos, *Homeland Calling: Exile Patriotism and the Balkan Wars* (Ithaca: Cornell University Press, 2003).

8. Generally speaking, Serb émigré writers and their sympathizers defended the behavior of the interwar Serb ruling establishment, including the monarchy and the two leading Serb parties (i.e., NRS, DS). In their view the demise of interwar Yugoslavia had less to do with the short-sightedness of Serb political leaders than with Croat intransigence and the hostility of foreign powers. In other words, the failure of interwar Yugoslavia was blamed on others primarily as a way of justifying Serb political behavior. The memoir literature recounting the interwar period includes the works of Konstantin Fotić, *The War We Lost* (New York: Viking Press, 1948), and Milan Stojadinović, *Ni rat ni pakt: Jugoslavija između dva rata* (Buenos Aires: El Economista, 1963). The former Serb Radical politician Branko Miljuš penned a number of works, two representative tracts of which are *Sporazum 1939. godine* (Windsor: Avala, 1957) and (under the pseudonym Hervé Laurière) *Assassins au nom de Dieu* (1951; reprint, Lausanne, Switzerland: Editions l'Age d'Homme, 1991). An extreme nationalist position is articulated by Lazo M. Kostich in *Sporni predeli Srba i Hrvata* (Chicago: **Američki institut za balkanska pitanja,** 1957) and *Sve su to laži i obmane: Fraze i parole komunističke Jugoslavije* (Munich: **Iskra,** 1975). One of the more thoroughly researched and better works is Đoko Slijepčević, *Jugoslavija uoči i za vreme Drugog svetskog rata* (Munich: Iskra, 1978). Finally, a sympathetic academic account of the Serb nationalist position may be found in Alex Dragnich, *Tito's Promised Land, Yugoslavia* (New Brunswick: Rutgers University Press, 1954), *Serbia, Nikola Pašić, and Yugoslavia* (New Brunswick: Rutgers University Press, 1974), and *The First Yugoslavia: Search for a Viable Political System* (Stanford: Hoover Institution Press, 1983).

9. See the two works of Nikola Žutić, *Kraljevina Jugoslavija i Vatikan: Odnos jugoslovenske države i rimske crkve, 1918–1935* (Belgrade: Arhiv Jugoslavije, 1994), and *Rimokatolička crkva i Hrvatstvo od ilirske ideje do velikohrvatske realizacije,* 1453–1941 (Belgrade: Institut za Noviju Istoriju, 1997). See also Milan Čubrić, *Između noža i križa* (Belgrade: Knjizevne Novine 1990); and Sima Simić, *Vatikan protiv Jugoslavije* (1958; reprint, Belgrade: Kultura, 1990).

10. Branislav Gligorijević, *Kralj Aleksandar Karađorđević, sv. 1: Ujedinjenje srpskih zemalja* (Belgrade: Zavod za Udžbenike i Nastavna Sredstva, 2003 & 1996), p. 148. Gligorijević is a good example of a noted Serb historian who, although formerly a Marxist, adopted nationalist reasoning in his scholarship. In the communist period, Gligorijević's works were critical of Aleksandar's role in the demise of democracy, but his cited biography of Aleksandar is a hagiographic portrait.

11. Slijepčević, *Jugoslavija,* pp. 53–54.

12. Ibid., pp. 55–56.

13. Ibid., pp. 58–59. It must be noted that the quality of much of this scholarship often compares unfavorably with the earlier, pre-1991, production of these same scholars. For a recent and very helpful overview of the historiography of the interwar era generally and the royal dictatorship specifically, see Christian Axboe Nielsen, "One State, One Nation, One King: The Dictatorship of King Aleksandar and His Yugoslav Project, 1929–1935" (Ph.D. dissertation, Columbia University, 2002). For a recent treatment of Aleksandar's Yugoslavism, see Dejan Djokić, "(Dis)Integrating Yugoslavia: King Alexander and Interwar Yugoslavism," in *Yugoslavism: Histories of a Failed Idea,* 1918–1992, (London: C. Hurst, 2002), pp. 136–56.

14. Ljubodrag Dimić, *Srbi i Jugoslavija: Prostor, Društvo, Politika (Pogled s kraja veka)* (Belgrade: VINC, 1998), pp. 37 and 29.

15. Branko Petranović and Momčilo Zečević, *Agonija dve Jugoslavije* (Belgrade: Zaslon, 1991), p. 50.

16. Ibid., pp. 253, 259–61.

17. Ibid., p. 51.

18. The Croat émigré literature may be grouped into two broad categories. To the first belong the works of the "democratic" emigration, the older generation of which generally tended to belong to or sympathize with the Croat Peasant Party, whereas the younger generation consisted of émigrés of the post-Croatian Spring era. The second category included Ustaša and pro-Ustaša writers. The line separating these two groups was not always very clear, and generally their views were consistent vis-à-vis the interwar period; they saw interwar Yugoslavia as a Great Serbian state in all but name. In the first category I would include Vladko Maček, *In the Struggle for Freedom,* trans. Elizabeth and Stjepan Gaži (Philadelphia: Pennsylvania State University Press, 1957); Jere Jareb, *Pola stoljeća hrvatske politike, 1895–1945: Povodom Mačekove autobiografije* (1960; reprint, Zagreb: Institut za Suvremenu Povijest, 1995); Stjepan Hefer, *Croatian Struggle for Freedom and Statehood* (Buenos Aires: Croatian Information Service, 1959); Ilija Jukić, *The Fall of Yugoslavia* (New York: Harcourt Brace Jovanovich, 1974); and Bruno Bušić, *Jedino Hrvatska! Sabrani spisi,* comp. Vinko Lasić (Toronto: Ziral, 1983). In the second group I would include Matija Kovačić, *Od Radića do Pavelića: Hrvatska u borbi za svoju samostalnost* (Munich: Knjižnica Hrvatske Revije, 1970); Ivan Oršanić, *Vizija slobode,* comp. Kazimir Katalinić (Buenos Aires: **Hrvatski informativni centar,** 1979); and Eugen Dido Kvaternik, *Sjećanja i zapažanja, 1929–1945: Prilozi za hrvatsku povijest,* comp. Jere Jareb (Zagreb: **Hrvatski institut za povijest,** 1995). Although Kvaternik's book appeared posthumously and following the dissolution of Yugosla-

via, much of it had already been published in émigré periodicals in the 1950s and early 1960s.

19. For example, see Bosiljka Janjatović, *Politički teror u Hrvatskoj, 1918–1935* (Zagreb: Hrvatski Institut za Povijest, 2002). As in the case of Gligorijević in Serbian historiography, Janjatović represents a similar circumstance in the Croatian case. A noted Marxist historian of the interwar period, her postcommunist writings have tended to be far more nationalist in tone. Admittedly, in some respects the leap for Croat (and other non-Serb) historians is not as great as it is for their Serb colleagues, insofar as they already accepted the Great Serbian nature of interwar Yugoslavia as a matter of the historical record. For an example of her earlier work, see Bosiljka Janjatović, *Politika Hrvatske seljačke stranke prema radničkoj klasi: Hrvaski radnički savez, 1921–1941* (Zagreb: Centar za Kulturnu Djelatnost, 1983).

20. Jere Jareb, "Hrvatski narod u Drugom svjetskom ratu 1941.–1945.," *Časopis za suvremenu povijest,* Vol. 27, No. 3 (1995), pp. 403–6.

21. Dušan Bilandžić, *Hrvatska moderna povijest* (Zagreb: Golden Marketing, 1999), p. 86.

22. Ibid., p. 88.

23. The relatively poor state of Croatian historiography of the interwar era is reflected in the number of reprints from that period and the fact that the works of Rudolf Horvat and Ivo Pilar are still regarded as legitimate. See Rudolf Horvat, *Hrvatska na mučilištu* (1942; reprint, Zagreb: Školska Knjiga, 1992), and Ivo Pilar, *Južnoslavensko pitanje: Prikaz cjelokupnog pitanja,* trans. Fedor Pucek (1943; reprint Zagreb, Varaždin: Hrvatska Demokratska Stranka; Podružnica Varaždin, 1990), which was originally published as L. von Südland, *Die Südslawische Frage und der Weltkrieg* (Vienna: Manz, 1918).

24. Among the first communist-era works of Radić to fit this description and to go beyond the standard communist characterization of him merely as a petty bourgeois politician are those of Zvonimir Kulundžić. See his *Živi Radić: Uoči stote obljetnice rodjenja hrvatskog velikana,* 2nd ed. (Zagreb: Nezavisno Autorsko Izdanje, 1971), and Stjepan Radić, *Politički spisi: Autobiografija, članci, govori, rasprave,* comp. Z. Kulundžić (Zagreb: Znanje, 1971). In the same vein, see Ivan Mužić, *Stjepan Radić u Kraljevini Srba, Hrvata i Slovenaca* (Zagreb: Nakladni Zavod Matice Hrvatske, 1987). Kulundžić was a former HSS activist who joined Tito's Partisans and became prominent during the Croatian Spring. He would author several books on Radić and interwar Yugoslavia, including *Atentat na Stjepana Radića* (Zagreb: Stvarnost, 1967), *Politika i korupcija u kraljevskoj Jugoslaviji* (Zagreb: Stvarnost, 1968), and *Tragedija hrvatske historiografije: O falsifikatorima, birokratima, negotorima hrvatske povijesti,* 2nd ed. (Zagreb: Nezavisno Autorsko Izdanje, 1970).

25. The Ustaša movement still awaits its historian. In October 1995, the Croatian Institute of History in Zagreb commemorated the fiftieth anniversary of the end of the Second World War by hosting a symposium on Croats in the Second World War. The symposium lent the unfortunate impression that the NDH and Ustaše were a legitimate option for Croats in 1941, a view conditioned, at least in part, by nationalist historiography's interpretation of the Croat experience in interwar Yugoslavia. Few truly controversial themes were addressed at the symposium. The conference proceedings may be found in *Časopis za suvremenu* povijest, Vol. 27, No. 3 (1995).

26. For the major works of Bosniak historiography, see Atif Purivatra, Mustafa Imamović, and Rusmir Mahmutćehajić, *Muslimani i bošnjaštvo* (Sarajevo: Izdavačko-Trgovinsko Preduzeće Biblioteka Ključanin, 1991); Mustafa Imamović, *Historija Bošnjaka* (Sarajevo: BZK "Preporod," 1997); and Šaćir Filandra, *Bošnjačka politika u XX. stoljeću* (Sarajevo: Sejtarija, 1998).

27. Imamović, *Historija Bošnjaka,* pp. 489–91. According to Imamović, the Bosnian Muslims have endured no fewer than ten genocides in the last three hundred years.

28. Although focusing most of their attention on the regime and Great Serbian parties, they are also highly critical of Vladko Maček and the HSS, which consistently sought to include Bosnia-Herzegovina in an autonomous Croatia and regarded Muslims as Croats.

29. Joseph Rothschild, *East Central Europe between the Two World Wars* (Seattle: University of Washington Press, 1974), p. 202f.

30. Petranović and Zečević. *Agonija dve Jugoslavije,* p. 248 (Belgrade: Zaslon, 1991).

31. See "Ustavno pitanje i zagrebački kongres," *Zastava,* September 22, 1922, 1; "Novi blok," *Samouprava,* April 1, 1923, p. 1; "Da se zna," *Samouprava,* June 27, 1923, p. 1; "Srpski 'imperijalizam' i srpski 'balkanizam'," *Samouprava,* June 13, 1923, p. 1; "Na prekretnici," *Samouprava,* September 13, 1923, p. 1, and "Radić i lojalnost," *Straža,* November 2, 1921, p. 1, cited in Djordje Dj. Stanković, *Nikola Pašić i Hrvati, 1918–1923* (Belgrade: BIGZ, 1995), pp. 425–26, 452, 463, 465, 476, 478–80, 488–89.

32. For the DS, see Branislav Gligorijević, *Demokratska stranka i politički odnosi u Kraljevini Srba, Hrvata i Slovenaca* (Belgrade: Institut za Savremenu Istoriju, 1970); Hrvoje Matković, *Svetozar Pribićević i Samostalna demokratska stranka do šestojanuarske diktature* (Zagreb: Institut za Hrvatsku Povijest, 1972); and Ljubo Boban, *Svetozar Pribićević u opoziciji, 1928–1936* (Zagreb: Institut za Hrvatsku Povijest, 1973), pp. 1–13.

33. For studies of the interwar KPJ, see Ivo Banac, *With Stalin against Tito: Cominformist Splits in Yugoslav Communism* (Ithaca: Cornell University Press, 1988), pp. 45–116; Rodoljub Čolaković *et al.* (eds.), *Pregled istorije Saveza komunista Jugoslavije* (Belgrade: Institut za Izucavanje Radnickog Pokreta, 1963); Ivan Avakumovic, *History of the Communist Party of Yugoslavia,* vol. 1 (Aberdeen: Aberdeen University Press, 1964); and Aleksa Djilas, *The Contested Country: Yugoslav Unity and Communist Revolution, 1919–1953* (Cambridge: Harvard University Press, 1991), pp. 49–102. On the KPJ's position on the national question, see Banac, *The National Question in Yugoslavia,* 328–39; Dušan Lukač, *Radnički pokret u Jugoslaviji i nacionalno pitanje 1918–1941* (Belgrade: Institut za Savremenu Istoriju, 1972); and Gordana Vlajičić, *KPJ i nacionalno pitanje u Jugoslaviji* (Zagreb: Institut za hrvatsku povijest, 1974).

34. "Rezolucija o Nacionalnom pitanju," in Moša Pijade (ed.), *Istorijski arhiv Komunističke partije Jugoslavije* (Belgrade, 1951), pp. 68, 70–71.

35. On the HRSS, see Mark Biondich, *Stjepan Radić, the Croat Peasant Party and the Politics of Mass Mobilization, 1904–1928* (Toronto: University of Toronto Press, 2000); and Ljubo Boban, *Maček i politika HSS, 1928–1941: Iz povijesti hrvatskog pitanja,* 2 vols. (Zagreb: Liber, 1974).

36. Radić remained in detention from March 25, 1919, until February, 27, 1920. See Radić, *Politički spisi,* 92.

37. For a study of the PNP, see Neda Engelsfeld, *Prvi parlament Kraljevstva Srba, Hrvata i Slovenaca. Privremeno Narodno Predstavništvo* (Zagreb: Globus, 1989). The regional distribution of seats in the PNP was as follows: Serbia (with Kosovo and Macedonia) 108, Croatia (with Medimurje, Rijeka, and Istria) 66, Bosnia-Herzegovina 42, Slovenia 32, Vojvodina 24, Dalmatia and Montenegro 12 each. Its deputies were representatives of the prewar regional parliaments. The PNP began its deliberations on March 1, 1919, and was dissolved on November 28, 1920; its task was to prepare the groundwork for the Constituent Assembly and draft an electoral law.

38. The Croat Union was the party of Croatia's middle classes and a significant segment of the liberal intelligentsia, while the Croat Party of Right's social base was the petite bourgeoisie and the nationalist intelligentsia. For the Croat Union, see Hrvoje Matković,

"Hrvatska zajednica: prilog proučavanju političkih stranaka u staroj Jugoslaviji," *Istorija XX veka: zbornik radova 5* (Belgrade: Institut za Savremenu Istoriju, 1963), pp. 5–136. There is no good study of the Croat Party of Right in the 1920s. See Banac, *The National Question in Yugoslavia,* pp. 260–70.

39. Mate Drinković, *Hrvatska i državna politika* (Zagreb: Vlastita Naklada, 1928), p. 72.

40. For the SLS and JMO, see Banac, *The National Question in Yugoslavia,* pp. 340–51, 359–77; Atif Purivatra, *Jugoslavenska muslimanska organizacija u političkom životu Srba, Hrvata i Slovenaca* (Sarajevo: Svjetlost, 1974); and the relevant sections of Enver Redžić, *Muslimansko autonomaštvo i 13. SS divizija: Autonomija Bosne i Hercegovine i Hitlerov Treći Rajh* (Sarajevo: Svjetlost, 1987).

41. *Nova istorija srpskog naroda,* comp. by Dušan Bataković (Belgrade: Naš Dom, 2000), p. 283.

42. For elections in the 1920s (i.e., 1920, 1923, 1925, 1927), see Čulinović, *Jugoslavija između dva rata,* vol. 1, pp. 308–13, 405–12, 453–57.

43. *Nova istorija srpskog naroda,* p. 284.

44. Petranović, *Istorija Jugoslavije,* pp. 54 and 76; and Gligorijević, *Parlament i političke stranke u Jugoslaviji,* pp. 278–79.

45. For an analysis of the DS-HRSS talks, see Branislav Gligorijević, "Politička previranja u Demokratskoj stranci na pitanju taktike prema Hrvatskom bloku u drugoj polovini 1922," *Istorija XX veka: zbornik radova* 8 (Belgrade: Institut Društvenih Nauka, Odeljenje za Istorijske Nauke, 1966), pp. 165–269.

46. For Radić's trip to Moscow, see Mužić, *Stjepan Radić,* pp. 152–65. This led Pribićević to secede from the DS and constitute his own party, the Independent Democratic Party (SDS, *Samostalna demokratska stranka*), which joined Pašić's government. On Pribićević, see Hrvoje Matković, *Svetozar Pribićević i Samostalna demokratska stranka do šestojanuarske diktature* (Zagreb: **Institut za hrvatsku povijest,** 1972).

47. Mužić, *Stjepan Radić u Kraljevini Srba, Hrvata i Slovenaca,* p. 199.

48. On Radić's negotiations with the authorities, see Mita Dimitrijević, *Mi i Hrvati: Hrvatsko pitanje, 1914–1939. Sporazum sa Hrvatima* (Belgrade: Stamparija "Privednik," 1939), pp. 162–86; Bogdan Krizman, "Izaslanik kralja Aleksandra kod Stjepana Radića u zatvoru 1925 godine," *Mogućnosti*, Vol. 18, No. 9 (1971): 1087–1109; and Hrvoje Matković, "Stjepan Radić pod Obznanom 1925. godine," *Mogućnosti*, Vol. 18, Nos. 7–9 (1971), pp. 844--913, 987–1052, 1109–46.

49. The HSS too suffered from factionalism. Eleven dissidents broke ranks in 1925, including five former members of the Croat Union who had been elected on the HRSS ticket. In January 1926 they formed the Croat Federalist Peasant Party (HFSS, *Hrvatska federalistička seljačka stranka*), which wanted constitutional reform and a federal Yugoslav state. On the HFSS, see Ljubomir Antić, "Hrvatska federalistička seljačka stranka," *Radovi Instituta za hrvatsku povijest* 15 (1982), pp. 163–222.

50. For a discussion of the factionalism in the NRS and DS and the king's role, see Gligorijević, *Parlament i političke stranke u Jugoslaviji,* pp. 204–10, 245–47; Petranović, *Istorija Jugoslavije,* pp. 76–78; and Nadežda Jovanović, *Politički sukobi u Jugoslaviji* (Belgrade: Institut za Istoriju Radničkog Pokreta Srbije, 1974), pp. 121–31, 142–55, 171–80.

51. Hrvatski državni arhiv (HDA), Rukopisna ostavština Đure Šurmina, Box 5: Političke bilješke, April 25, 1925, King Aleksandar's comments to Šurmin.

52. Ibid., Box 5: Političke bilješke, October 18, 1926, Pašić's comments to Šurmin. After being forced from office in April 1926, Pašić managed in turn to force Jovanović and his followers out of the NRS. According to Gligorijević, by ousting Jovanović,

Pašić believed he was counteracting the king's growing influence within the NRS. Gligorijević, *Parlament i političke stranke,* pp. 207–8.

53. Jovanović, *Politički sukobi u Jugoslaviji,* 206.
54. M. Bartulica, "Veličanstveno hrvatsko jedinstvo," *Dom,* July 11, 1928, p. 3.
55. "Veličanstveni sprovod hrvatskih mučenika," *Narodni val,* June 24, 1928, p. 3.
56. The resolution is reprinted in Vladko Maček, *Memoari* (Zagreb: Hrvatska Seljačka Stranka, 1992), p. 79, and Svetozar Pribićević, *Diktatura kralja Aleksandra* (Zagreb: Globus, 1990), pp. 78–79.
57. Ivan Krajač, "Dvije političke sinteze," *Hrvatska revija* Vol. 11, No. 11 (1938), p. 566.
58. Pribićević, *Diktatura kralja Aleksandra,* p. 80.
59. Maček, *Memoari,* p. 81.
60. Čulinović, *Jugoslavija između dva rata,* pp. 544–47.
61. Some Croat scholars have suggested that the court had a role in the events of June 20, 1928, but this contention has never been proven. See Zvonimir Kulundžić, *Atentat na Stjepana Radića* (Zagreb: Stvarnost, 1967).
62. The banovine were Drava (the Slovene lands), Sava (Croatia-Slavonia without Syrmia), Littoral (Dalmatia, western Herzegovina), Vrbas (northwestern Bosnia), Drina (south-eastern Bosnia, western parts of Serbia, parts of eastern Slavonia), Vardar (Macedonia and part of Kosovo), Zeta (Montenegro, with parts of eastern Herzegovina and southern Dalmatia), Morava (Serbia proper, part of Kosovo), and Danube (Vojvodina, Baranja), with the city of Belgrade as a separate prefecture.
63. On the political opposition at the time of the dictatorship, see Todor Stojkov, *Opozicija u vreme šestojanuarske diktature, 1929–1935* (Belgrade: Prosveta, 1969). On the leading opposition party (i.e., the HSS) and Svetozar Pribićević during this period, see the two works by Ljubo Boban, *Maček i politika HSS, 1928–1941: Iz povijesti hrvatskog pitanja,* 2 vols. (Zagreb: Liber, 1974), and *Svetozar Pribićević u opoziciji, 1928–1936* (Zagreb: Institut za Hrvatsku Povijest, 1973). According to Slijepčević, the Octroyed Constitution of September 1931 and the elections of November 1931 represented the tentative rehabilitation of the old, pre-1929 system rather than being steps in the direction of creating a new system (see Slijepčević, *Jugoslavija,* pp. 59–60).
64. For studies of the Ustaša movement, see the relevant sections of Jozo Tomasevich, *War and Revolution in Yugoslavia, 1941–1945: Occupation and Collaboration* (Palo Alto: Stanford University Press, 2001); Martin Broszat and L. Hory, *Die kroatische Ustascha-Staat, 1941–1945* (Stuttgart: Deutsche Verlags-Anstalt, 1964); Holm Sundhaussen, "Der Ustascha-Staat: Anatomie eines Herrschaftssystem," *Österreichische Osthefte,* Vol. 37, No. 2 (1995), pp. 497–533; Bogdan Krizman's books, *Ante Pavelić i ustaše* (Zagreb: Globus, 1978), *Pavelić između Hitlera i Mussolinija* (Zagreb: Globus, 1980), and *Ustaše i Treći Reich,* 2 vols. (Zagreb: Globus, 1982); and Fikreta Jelić-Butić, *Ustaše i Nezavisna Država Hrvatska* (Zagreb: Globus, 1977).
65. See the unpublished Ph.D. thesis of Christian Axboe Nielsen, "One State, One Nation, One King: The Dictatorship of King Aleksandar and His Yugoslav Project, 1929–1935," Columbia University, 2002. The Croatian Serb politician Svetozar Pribićević was the first to write a book on King Aleksandar's dictatorship, which was published in 1933 while he was an émigré in France. The remaining works on Aleksandar in Serbian and Croatian are of dubious value; they tend to be tendentious, either hagiographies or demonizations. See Pribićević, *Diktatura kralja Aleksandra* (Zagreb: Globus, 1990); Jacques Augarde and Emile Sicard, *Alexandre Ier, le roi chevalier* (Paris; Baudinière, 1935); and Stephen Graham, *Alexander of Yugoslavia: Strong Man of the Balkans* (London: Cassell and Company, Ltd., 1938).

66. For example, during the May 1935 elections voting was conducted in the open. The regime party, the JNS of Bogoljub Jeftić, won 60.6 percent of the vote, whereas the United Opposition (UO) of Vladko Maček won 37.4 percent; the UO consisted of the HSS, the SDS (Pribićević's party), the DS, the Serbian Agrarians, and the JMO. See Dušan Bilandžić, *Hrvatska moderna povijest* (Zagreb: Golden Marketing, 1999), p. 100.

67. Djilas, *The Contested Country,* p. 131.

68. See the discussion in ibid., pp. 130–35.

69. Rusinow, "The Yugoslav Peoples," pp. 373–74.

70. By the same token, many ordinary Serbs and other non-Croats undoubtedly felt a genuine sense of loss following the death of Stjepan Radić, but that certainly did not mean that they sympathized with Radić or the HSS's political ideology.

71. Petranović and Zečević, *Agonija dve Jugoslavije,* pp. 251–52.

72. One should remember, however, that the Czechoslovak Constituent Assembly excluded German, Hungarian, and Ruthenian delegates, thus creating a system designed to suit the interests of the Czech and Slovak, or rather the unitary "Czechoslovak" people. Following the Munich Agreement in September 1938, the Czechoslovak government issued anti-Semitic decrees as it desperately attempted to accommodate its policies to the interests of the Third Reich. Czechoslovakia was thus a democracy, at least to the end of 1938. See Victor S. Mamatey and Radomir Luža (eds.), *History of the Czechoslovak Republic, 1918–1948* (Princeton: Princeton University Press, 1973). For a discussion of rump Czechoslovakia's anti-Semitic laws and post-Munich accommodation, see Telford Taylor, *Munich: The Price of Peace* (New York: Vintage, 1979).

The Legacy of Two World Wars: A Historical Essay

❖ Stevan K. Pavlowitch ❖

The founding fathers of the first Yugoslav state in 1918 could not foresee the events of 1941. The founding fathers of the second Yugoslav state in 1943–46 had hindsight but no foresight. They knew what had happened between 1914 and 1941, but they could not imagine what would happen in 1991. Both the founders of the Kingdom of the Serbs, Croats, and Slovenes (later Kingdom of Yugoslavia) and those of the Federal Peoples' (later Socialist Federal) Republic of Yugoslavia believed that they were building something new for the future. However, the destroyers of Yugoslavia, of the first and of the second, did indeed look to the past; they were allegedly correcting history. To that extent, they were inspired by past experiences. In the 1990s, some wanted to go back to 1914, others to 1941, others still to what they imagined could and should have been done at the end of the First or the Second World Wars.

*

In 1914 it was not obvious that the Great War was about to break out. Very few people were plotting the downfall of Austria-Hungary, without which there could be no political unification of the Southern Slavs or Yugoslavs. The Yugoslav idea received at least tacit support from an increasing section of the Southern Slav population of the Habsburg Monarchy, but its vocal proponents formed only a small proportion of educated and semieducated opinion, and they hardly considered how a unified Yugoslavia would come about. There were revolutionaries among its younger adherents. In the one-time Ottoman provinces of Bosnia and Herzegovina, administered by Austria-Hungary under a mandate of the Great Powers since 1878 and annexed as recently as 1908, there were small and secretive groups loosely defined as Young Bosnia, whom the authorities called Young Slavs, and who sought radical solutions to all problems. They mistrusted politicians, intellectuals, and peasants alike. The elected politicians, who claimed to speak for their national groups, came from an equally small segment of the population and entertained hopes of legal reform after the death of the old Emperor Francis Joseph. However, the general staff, who saw

Belgrade as the font of Southern Slav nationalism, did think in terms of a preventive war against Serbia.

Serbia—along with the rest of the Balkans—was recovering from the two successive Balkan wars. Opinion there moved between the dream of an extended Serbia and the concept of Serbia as unifier of all Yugoslavs—without understanding the difference between the two, although there were people among the higher intelligentsia beginning to entertain a genuine Yugoslav idea. The government, however, went no further than to consider some form of union with Montenegro. Contrary to enduring assumptions, it was the Young Bosnian revolutionaries who initiated the "Sarajevo conspiracy," and who sought the cover of agents of Belgrade-based nationalist groups. The Austro-Hungarian reaction to the assassination of Archduke Francis Ferdinand was one of fear—of following the Ottoman Empire on the road to decline and of other national groups' aspiring to the same status as the Austro-Germans and the Hungarians. The military option suddenly came to the forefront. Hence an ultimatum designed to be rejected, followed by a declaration of war, the clarion call "Serbia must die," and an attack at the end of July, a month after the assassination.

The majority Croato-Serb coalition of parties controlling the Sabor (diet) of Croatia-Slavonia was not subversive. Croatian and Slovenian conservative and clerical parties supported the war against Serbia. The mobilization went smoothly. Some of the divisions that launched the attack were more than 50 percent Croat and 20–25 percent Serb. Yet the authorities, apprehending pro-Serbian feelings, organized and encouraged anti-Serb repression and mob action. In Bosnia-Herzegovina, Catholic and Muslim volunteers were recruited into "special battalions" to carry out arrests, deportations, and executions of civilians accused of supporting Serb rebels, thus pushing the Serbs of the provinces into Serbia's arms.

The Belgrade government understood that the outcome of the war would bring great changes, for better or worse, to the country's position. If defeated, the Serbian state risked being turned into a protectorate of, or even integrated into, the Habsburg Monarchy. The government decided to pose publicly the Yugoslav question—the creation of a state of all Serbs, Croats, and Slovenes—albeit within the parameters of liberating kith and kin from foreign rule. This was a way of weakening the enemy, perhaps even of guaranteeing the future.

Serbia's entente allies were quite oblivious to the Yugoslav question; the war in the Balkans was to them a sideshow to the main conflicts. Serbia anyhow just about held its own until a new combined offensive of Germany, Austria-Hungary, and Bulgaria overran the country in October 1915. Faced with the choice of either capitulating or retreating in midwinter through the mountains of Albania to the Adriatic coast and Allied shipping, the Serbian government decided for the latter. It went on to survive in exile, in the most precarious situation, on Greek territory, by courtesy of the Allies. Montenegro was in an even worse situation, with its exiled monarch sidelined not only by his own people but also by the Serbs and the Allies.

In the following two years (1916–17), neither Serbia's exiled political leadership nor the parliamentary leadership of the Habsburg Southern Slavs knew what the outcome of the war would be or what would happen to Austria-Hungary. The Allies made territorial offers to attract neutrals; they explored possibilities of a separate peace with Austria-Hungary, while the Central Powers dominated most of the Balkan Peninsula. Austria's South Slav parliamentarians increasingly bargained over their loyalty in exchange for partial unification within a reformed Habsburg Monarchy. Serbia and Montenegro were under harsh enemy occupation, with active and passive resistance, internment, deportation, maltreatment, hunger, and disease. Having concentrated at first on union with Montenegro to counter Austrian and Italian plans for the smaller kingdom, the exiled Serbian government went on to talks with exiled politicians from Austria-Hungary for full union around Serbia under the Karadjordjević Dynasty in order to oppose projects for partial unification around Croatia under the Habsburgs.

The war ended suddenly in the Balkans—almost as suddenly as it had begun. At the beginning of 1918, the Allies were still inclined to preserve Austria-Hungary. Its refusal to face the facts and make concessions precipitated events. Once the Allied offensive into Macedonia (with a restored Serbian army) had started to liberate Serbia; once the military defeat of Austria-Hungary appeared as evident and the rule of Vienna and Budapest crumbled, the unification process presented itself as a fact that could no longer be delayed. As the Serbian army hurried to Belgrade, the Yugoslavs of Austria-Hungary began liberating themselves by default. All over the empire, ad hoc regional councils appeared, set up on ethnic lines, to take over from the disintegrating regular authorities. There was disagreement among the Southern Slav politicians of the dissolving empire over the pace and the extent of Yugoslav unification until fears of a breakdown of law and order, Italy's insistence on redeeming the Allies' territorial promises, and the Allies' equivocal attitude got them all together.

Unification just occurred, unplanned, with no liberation by anyone but with pressure from below and from the periphery threatened by Italy. The newly set-up National Council in Zagreb, of elected national and provincial parliamentary representatives of Slovenes, Croats, and Serbs of Austria-Hungary, broke off all links with Vienna, Budapest, and the Habsburgs, and on October 28 proclaimed a sovereign State of Slovenes, Croats, and Serbs over the whole territory inhabited by their nation. That state was in a critical situation, unrecognized and challenged. For many it seemed that the Serbian army was the only force that could restore order in the countryside—particularly in Bosnia-Herzegovina, where Serb peasants were taking revenge against Muslims who had formed the bulk of the special battalions—and turn back the Italian army advancing under cover of the armistice terms. New local authorities of lands nearest to Serbia entered into direct negotiations with Belgrade, where the government was reorganizing itself.

Montenegro had expressed from the very beginning its solidarity in defence of "our Serbian nation." Negotiations over union had been under way and envisaged preserving some form of identity along with its dynasty. Once in exile, the autocratic King Nicholas was marginalized by the setting up, in Paris, of a Montenegrin Committee for National Unification, supported by the Serbian government. It was this committee that returned to liberated Montenegro, to organize elections to an assembly that deposed the dynasty and proclaimed union with Serbia. The generally urban, better educated, and younger elements, along with representatives from the newer northern territory, were in favour of unconditional and total unification. They left the rest, and the core of historic Montenegro, to nurse its wounded pride. There was an attempted rebellion, supported by Italy, in favour of preserving its dynasty and autonomy.

The final proclamation of unification as the full Kingdom of the Serbs, Croats, and Slovenes on December 1, 1918, in Belgrade by the regent of Serbia, Crown Prince Alexander, and in the presence of his Serbian ministers and of delegates of the Zagreb National Council, consecrated a process that had already taken place in a haphazard and messy manner over the preceding weeks. In the final analysis, there was perhaps no alternative to the way in which it was achieved. The option facing the National Council in Zagreb was either that of a Yugoslav union at any price or partition of the formerly Habsburg Slovenes, Croats, and Serbs among Italy, Serbia, Austria, and Hungary, with a residual Croatia not unlike Albania. For Serbia, any solution but a Yugoslav one would have left ethnic Serbs outside Serbia, and any addition of territory would have taken in more non-Serbs, for whom Serbia would have been more difficult to accept than Yugoslavia. On the eve of the First World War, Serbia was thus already facing the problem of integrating new territories and new populations.

It is almost impossible to gauge how much the population at large supported the idea of unification during the war. Pressured, drafted into embattled armies, living under harsh occupation regimes or a state of emergency, with constrained loyalties, harassed, interned, deported, isolated from the political actors abroad, they waited for the outcome of the Great War. By the end of the war, a majority of the population was probably in favour of unification, but the Yugoslav idea had not penetrated in depth except perhaps in Dalmatia. The Muslims and a vocal minority of Croats (republicans or nostalgic Habsburg reactionaries) were clearly opposed.[1]

Contrary to an idea that is often encountered, Yugoslavia was no creation of the Paris peace settlement—mistakenly called the Versailles settlement after the treaty with Germany signed at Versailles, which was just one of the peace treaties signed between the one-time belligerents. There had been little international support for the idea of a Yugoslav state. The United States had been the first Great Power to encourage it from the summer of 1918 but did not recognize it until February 1919—after Greece and Norway had. France and Great Britain reluctantly followed more than six months after its creation because the peace treaty with Germany was ready to be signed and needed the signature of the Belgrade government. Nobody had plans to deal with the problems of dissolving empires and of unification across existing international borders. The final borders of all the new states in the peace settlements were based on vague ideas of "anthropo-geography" and "ethno-linguistics" applied in a subjective manner so as to reinforce the structure of the winning states.[2]

The new Kingdom of the Serbs, Croats, and Slovenes was definitely on the winners' side by virtue of being the successor in international law to the old Kingdom of Serbia. However, it was exhausted by warfare that, for its southern parts, had been a veritable Seven Years' War. Its combined human losses for the whole period have been assessed at 1.9 million, of which 0.9 million were military losses, with Serbia and Montenegro bearing the brunt of about 0.75 million.[3] In the pressure and haste of the last months of 1918, its various sections had had no time to work out how the union was to be implemented. Whereas the newly promoted Croatian Peasant Party representing the now enfranchised mass of the Croat population thought of Yugoslavia as an improved version of Austria-Hungary where Croatia would be Serbia's Hungary, the government, relying on the two largest and Serb-based parties, acted as if Yugoslavia were just an extended Serbia that took in Croatia and Slovenia as well. No imagination was forthcoming to cope with the novelty of the Yugoslav state.

The constitution adopted in 1921 by a majority of the full total membership of the Constituent Assembly and in spite of the boycott of many Croat and other deputies kept the essentials of Serbia's prewar centralist constitution. Parliamentary government survived until 1929, when King Alexander abrogated the constitution and then went on to grant a new one that kept most powers for the crown. His system survived his assassination in 1934 by an agent of the Croatian terrorist separatist organization Ustaša until the eve of the Second World War, in spite of a regency for the boy King Peter II. Then, barely a week before the Second World War began with the invasion and partition of Poland, a veiled process of constitutional revision was started under the crown's reserved emergency powers, granting a measure of autonomy to a Province of Croatia extending over Croatia, Slavonia, Dalmatia, and additional districts of Bosnia and Herzegovina. This partial solution to the Croatian question, inspired by the Austro-Hungarian compromise of 1867, satisfied the leadership of the Croatian Peasant Party and even a minority of the Serb opposition. However, it left most of the Serb opposition frustrated. Many Croats thought that what had been agreed was too little, too late. Prince Paul's regency did not command the loyalty of substantial portions of public opinion. Extremist Ustaša and Communists were waiting in the wings to appear with one or the other of Nazi Germany and Soviet Russia.

*

Whereas the First World War had started with an attack on Belgrade, the Second World War came to Belgrade some nineteen months after Germany had invaded Poland. In March 1941 the Yugoslav government gave in to Hitler's firm demand that it should adhere to the Tripartite Pact. No sooner done than an officers' conspiracy proclaimed King Peter II of age, thus ending the regency, and ushered in an all-party government. Hitler attacked on April 6, without a declaration of war but not before he had launched a violent campaign against Yugoslavia, inciting Croats against Serbs. It was 1914 all over again with a vengeance, the Nazi Reich taking the place of the Habsburg Monarchy. Hitler's Austrian prejudices reinforced his anti-Slav racism. He saw the Serbs as disturbers of the European order. He was out to correct history, to forever destroy Yugoslavia, the state that had come out of the defeat of Austria-Hungary and Germany in 1918. Mercilessly bombed, invaded from all sides except Greece, the country was overrun within twelve days.[4]

The King and government once again went into exile—by air to London via Athens and Jerusalem—but the armed forces had capitulated. The conquerors considered that Yugoslavia had been destroyed as a state along with its army. Italy, Germany, Hungary, Bulgaria, and Albania helped themselves to territory. Montenegro was formally restored under Italian control. Serbs were singled out as the defeated enemy to be punished collectively. Slovenes were to be Germanized, Italianized, or dispersed; Croats to be brought over as pseudo-Aryans.

Almost 40 percent of the Yugoslav territory was set up as the Independent State of Croatia—NDH for short (*Nezavisna Država Hrvatska*) under the rule of the Ustaša and of their leader, Ante Pavelić, who had returned from exile. Extending across Bosnia and Herzegovina to the gates of Belgrade, the new state contained almost as many "alien" Orthodox Serbs (1.9 million), Muslims, Gypsies, Jews, and Germans, as it did "pure" Croats. Ethnic Germans were given privileged status. The Muslims were said to be Croats. Their elected political representation had usually sided with the government in Belgrade. It was now broken up, and its factions would look to the Ustaša government, the Italians, the Germans, and different resistance organizations.

It was stated that the Serbs would be converted, expelled, or eliminated. "Greater Croatia" the NDH might have been, but it was shorn of most of the coast in favour of Italy and divided between a German and an Italian zone. It was independent only insofar as its leadership, which had spearheaded the secession in the wake of the defeat, was able to exploit the rivalry of its protectors. Set up and run by the Fascist-inspired extreme fringe of Croatian nationalism, it was accepted initially by a majority of Croats with the feeling that the worst had been avoided. Most of the Croatian Peasant Party leadership withdrew into passivity, its right wing having rallied the new regime, and a small part gone with the government in exile.

The Ustaša's savage fury was vented on Serbs, Jews, and Gypsies. Immediate measures were taken against them. Alongside a state-sponsored conversion campaign, mass killings were started and concentration camps set up. Those fortunate or near enough fled to German-occupied rump Serbia or to Italian-occupied coastal areas. The rest took to woods and uplands. What began as a panicked flight to avoid horrible death soon turned to disjointed revolt. A mix of ferocious racialism and farcical inefficiency, Ustaša rule could not extend to the mountainous areas of Bosnia and Herzegovina, where more than half of the NDH Serbs lived.

Not surprisingly, resistance was, on the whole, Serb-based, but the reactions of the different Serb communities were fragmented and diverse. Unrelated rebellions in the summer of 1941 followed in the wake of the German invasion of the USSR. The Serbs in the NDH rose in self-defence. In Montenegro there was a general revolt led by Communists and officers against the Italian attempt to set up a separate client state. In German-occupied Serbia, there was an upsurge of rekindled hope. Colonel (later General) Mihailović had gone into hiding to build a clandestine military organization with officers who did not accept the capitulation. He was pushed into premature action by the Communists' zeal to advance the cause of revolution in expectation of the arrival of a victorious Red Army. Having set up a collaborationist government subservient to their commanding general, the Germans responded to insurgency with punitive expeditions, internment, concentration camps, and the execution of hostages. Their ruthless retaliation turned the popular mood against further confrontations with occupation forces. The ensuing ups and downs of the various insurgencies turned into civil war between Communists and anti-Communists, especially in Serbia between the two movements who alone had some pan-Yugoslav vocation—Mihailović's officer-led secret army and Tito's Communist Party organization.

The Allies wanted risings to occur when and where it suited their grand strategy, and their interest in Yugoslavia came and went accordingly, but the Balkans were again in the shadow of other fronts. It seemed that there were two rival resistance groups—Mihailović's Četnik units, loyal to the exiled government, and Tito's Communist-led Partisans. However, Mihailović had no political agenda beyond maintaining a symbolic continuity of the Yugoslav kingdom, initially reacting against the mood of defeatism and preparing the ground for a rising when the tide had turned. The few civilians who joined him in 1941 were nationalist Serb intellectuals who were pro-Western but stood outside the main political parties, who blamed Croats and the state establishment for the collapse and who feared the threat posed by their Communist rivals. They thought of restoring Serbia within the framework of a new Yugoslavia to be set up after the war, of ensuring links between Serb-inhabited territories, and of punishing those responsible for the collapse and ensuing massacres.

Initially and wherever they were formed, Serb armed bands called themselves Četnik, from a word used originally by marauders in the Dinaric mountains and eventually by all armed bands of the central Balkans at the beginning of the twentieth century. They were called Partisans if and when taken over or organized by Communists, after which Četniks became synonymous with Serb anti-Communist fighters. The conquerors had not only destroyed the Yugoslav state, they had also set its components against each other in an unprecedented way. An infernal cycle of large-scale massacres had been started by the Ustaša. The Serbs of the NDH had risen in self-defence, as Četniks and Partisans, who went on to do their best, there and elsewhere, to eliminate each other and their supporters in the hope or fear of the arrival of the Red Army or the Western Allies. They also had to face brutal periodic anti-insurgency operations organized by the German army.

All those who had aligned themselves with the conquerors promoted a national-tribal pastoral ideology, a return to narrow native roots under German overlordship. Like Hitler's, theirs was a wish to correct history. It was the expression of opposition to the cosmopolitanism associated with liberalism, democracy, communism, the West, and the mistaken experiment that pan- or supranational Yugoslavia had been.

Hitler had left the Italians to occupy (and pacify) most of the conquered lands of the Balkans, a task made harder by the Germans' own policies. Italians blamed Germans for stimulating resistance, whereas Germans blamed Italians for failing to repress it. Italian territory was, more often than not, a relative haven for Serbs and Jews. It was certainly a base and a source of support for anti-Ustaša and anti-Communist Četnik bands. Insurgents moved about, were double-faced, changed sides, and fought each other in a complex and ever-changing pattern. In the NDH, they responded with their own terror to the terror of Ustaša fanatics. In Bosnia, the Ustaša authorities also enlisted Muslims, as Austria-Hungary had done during the First World War, exploiting the bitterness felt by landowners reduced to poverty by the interwar land reform. In the mixed Serb and Muslim areas of Herzegovina and of the old Sandžak of Novi Pazar, there was ethnic settling of scores. Italian-armed Muslims took their revenge on Serbs who had paid old scores in earlier wars; Serb Četniks then did their best to clear the region of Muslim militiamen and villages. In the territory annexed to Albania, the Italian occupation was welcomed by the Albanian population, who turned against Serbs, particularly the new settlers of the agrarian reform. Where there were no such accounts to settle, there was ideological civil war between Communists and anti-Communists. Because Mihailović was based in German-occupied Serbia, even when German pursuits made it too hot for him to remain there, he could not do much. He was obsessed with Serb losses through massacres and repression following on the bloodletting of the First World War. He did not control the proliferation of Serb and anti-Communist groups elsewhere who intermittently acknowledged him. The various Četniks were a traditional Balkan guerrilla, local and seasonal. Mihailović was no more than a symbolic authority who followed events more than he could coordinate them. Although he always stressed the legitimist Yugoslav nature of his endeavour, he was in fact almost entirely Serb-based, drawing support from Serbs who viewed change as a threat. Whatever his intentions, he held little or no attraction for non-Serbs.

It was from this complexity that Tito's movement arose once it had found its way to the Serbs of the NDH. It was there that he built the basis from which to liberate, conquer, and restore Yugoslavia on totally new foundations, with the support of Serbs outside Serbia, and the ability to attract non-Serbs. The Communists throve on the anarchy of the NDH. Mostly Serbs themselves, the Partisans penetrated the leaderless and desperate struggle of the Bosnian Serbs while defending Croats and Muslims from retaliation, thus enabling them to adhere eventually.

The Communist leaders were internationalists who knew how to adapt their discourse to audience and circumstances. They fought a revolutionary war in a constantly shifting pattern with clear aims. They were interested in power over the whole territory of prewar Yugoslavia and more if possible. Only at the head of a patriotic resistance movement could they hope to acquire and retain the support of non-Communist followers, but their object was to destroy all who opposed the transformation of their war of liberation into one for the establishment of Communist rule. Tito was able to coordinate strategy and keep overall control, to manage his public relations, and to find his way in the bloody entanglement of antagonisms and arrangements between the different sides of occupation, collaboration, and resistance. As the balance of war tipped against the Axis, the main reason for Tito's success was the failure of sectional nationalism, which was associated with the Powers that were now losing the war. In the mixed regions that had suffered so much, the Communists' new order, with its slogan of "brotherhood and unity" of communities, was especially attractive.

With the acknowledged failure of unitarist Yugoslavism, a federal reconstruction of Yugoslavia was generally accepted by both Mihailović and Tito. The Communist leadership had clarified its own idea in November 1943 at its movement's congress held at Jajce in free Bosnian territory. This was to be a community of equal nations within a number of units set up to fit in with the Communists' concept of an ethnic equilibrium. To Serbia, Croatia, and Slovenia, they had added a separate Macedonia, as well as a separate Montenegro. Bosnia and Herzegovina were kept as a single territory within their old Ottoman and Austro-Hungarian borders to prevent the impossible division of this mixed region in which no ethnic group had an absolute majority, to give the Muslims a territorial base, and to enhance it as a miniature model of Yugoslavia.

The Communists had turned their attention to Macedonia, where they saw the opportunity to benefit from the local population's alienation from both prewar Serbian and wartime Bulgarian rule. They had, from Macedonia, established their patronage over Albanian Communists and Partisans, hoping initially to achieve in common the reunion of Kosovo with Albania in Yugoslavia or in a Yugoslav-led Balkan federation once communism had prevailed in both countries and all over the Balkans.

The Communists' project countered fears of too large a Serbian unit; it attracted Macedonian aspirations from all over the central Balkans; and it dealt with Montenegrin frustrations. Every nation was given a home unit, but Serbs were acknowledged to be a constituent element in Croatia and in Bosnia-Herzegovina as well. Tito's was also a Serb-based movement, but it was not based in Serbia, and all those who wanted to get out of the enemy's camp or out of the past were turning to it. As a power vacuum appeared and expanded, the Communists filled it.

Most of that was anathema to Serb nationalists and royalists. They too were thinking of a Yugoslavia restored on a federal basis, but one that still needed a strong Serbia. Separating Macedonia and Montenegro was unthinkable to them. Mihailović's belated answer to Jajce was his own congress held in January 1944 at Ba in free Serbian territory. By now he had the support of a broader spectrum of Socialist-led political advisers. Delegates from Slovenia and some Croats attended the Ba meeting, which adopted a resolution for a reorganization of Yugoslavia as a federation of just three units—Serbia, Croatia, and Slovenia.

Mihailović's own base remained in Serbia. The Partisans had, for all practical purposes, had to withdraw from Serbia at the end of 1941. They fought their way back into it with both Western and Soviet support as the Germans carried out their evacuation of the Balkans through that territory. Although Tito was installed in Belgrade by October 1944, the liberation of Serbia turned out to be a difficult conquest. Tito had obtained the support of a significant part of the population of Yugoslavia, yet whole regions resisted the Partisans as they completed the country's liberation. The Communists used the opportunities offered by the war to take revenge on opponents, all branded as collaborators and traitors. They resorted to mass conscription in Serbia to strengthen their army, but also to remove the Mihailovićist youth.

As the anarchic NDH was being rolled up by Tito's People's Liberation Army, the Ustaša fought with suicidal fury with various Četniks caught in between as they tried to head west. Civil war was pitiless in Montenegro. The establishment of control over Kosovo turned into full-scale reconquest. The Partisans completed the cycle of massacres by doing away in the last days of the war with more opponents, who had retreated into Austria from where they had been returned by the British. These were native units armed by the occupiers, the numerous and lukewarm regular soldiers of the NDH, Slovene anti-Communist paramilitaries, soldiers of the collaborationist Serbian State Guard, Serbian fascist volunteers, and various Četniks.

The Axis Powers had destroyed the Yugoslav state and then shared control with increasing mutual distrust until Italy dropped out of the war. The occupiers had attempted to impose a brutal peace without the strength to enforce it, which was an ideal situation for the propagation of a revolutionary war. Naïve expectations of a Soviet arrival in 1941, real expectations of the Soviet arrival in 1944, and induced expectations of an Anglo-American landing in the meanwhile had aroused resistance and rivalries within it. The exiled government, although recognized by the Allied Powers (and by neutrals as well), was based on the tenuous legitimacy of a royal power formalized in a constitution granted by, and inherited from, King Alexander's authoritarian rule. Paralyzed by divisions among the party leaders who had been brought together into the cabinet on the eve of the German attack, it provided no leadership and no really viable alternative to the Communist-led resistance. The Communist Party of Yugoslavia under Tito was the ultimate liberator, reunifier, and overall winner.

*

The outcome of the Second World War led again to a united Yugoslavia. The victorious Powers supported it from the start. In terms of international law, the second Yugoslavia was the successor to the first as the first had been successor to Serbia. In their different ways, those in the occupied and partitioned country who had refused to accept the Nazi New Order (which anyhow had been but a brutal disorder), were also in favour of Yugoslavia. The defeat of the Axis destroyed the chances of the native movements that had thought a solution to Yugoslavia's problems was to withdraw into the confines of sectional nationalism and to return to an imagined pre-Yugoslav past under the aegis of Hitler's Reich.

Taking full advantage of the old regime's failure to weld together Yugoslavia's separate identities into a single national consciousness, the Communists had restored the country as a community of related nations. Regional units had been set up pragmatically according to the needs of the Communist Party in the later stages of the war, and the borders between them aroused only minimal disagreement between the decision makers at the time. Even though they generally conformed to historic realities, they were considered as no more than administrative borders. Federalism was capped with unitarism of power, and ideological integration substituted for ethnic integration. The Constitution of 1946, which followed the Stalinist model, finalized the Jajce project by setting up six federated republics with two autonomous provinces in Serbia.

The Communist Party of Yugoslavia had inserted itself into the resistance of Serbs during the Second World War, particularly in the mixed regions of Croatia and Bosnia. Those western Serb fighters and the ones from Montenegro had been the nucleus of the revolutionary army with which the Communist Party had come to power. It had also used the notion of greater-Serbian hegemony to win support among other groups. Communist federalism was a tool. The nationalism of the core groups of Serbs and Croats was repressed as being respectively hegemonistic and separatist, whereas that of smaller or peripheral groups was accepted, favoured, or even fostered to keep Serbs and Croats in check, to resolve nationalist competition over territory, and to help Tito's Communist federation to expand.

Disorganized bands still operated in the late 1940s. Mihailović's capture, his trial on charges of collaboration with the enemy and war crimes, and his execution in July 1946 marked the final defeat of the losers in the complex war that had been fought over the partitioned and occupied territory of Yugoslavia. The disposal of his body has not been revealed to this day, thus enhancing his myth and posthumous stature. The trial did not discredit him in Serbia any more than the trial in October 1946 of Archbishop (later Cardinal) Stepinac of Zagreb, sentenced to sixteen years of imprisonment for collaboration with the enemy and complicity with Ustaša crimes, discredited him in Croatia. Stepinac's imprisonment and his subsequent death in supervised residence in 1960 turned him into a martyr. What the two show trials did was effectively to confirm most Croats in their belief that Mihailović and the Serbian monarchy had been planning revenge and renewed hegemony and to provide most Serbs with proof that the Croats had betrayed the state in 1941 and that the Catholic Church had been instrumental in devising conversions and massacres.

Party propaganda stressed the joint struggle of all nationalities against the occupation forces and their native auxiliaries. It attributed to that joint "anti-fascist" struggle the greater part of the Communists' success in solving the "national question." One should not underestimate the legitimizing power of the slogan of brotherhood and unity, which contained a large dose of optimism and self-interest. It was needed to hold the party together and to deal with all the problems of reconstruction, for the scale of losses was once again huge. The real total loss of population for the whole territory was about 1 million, of whom more than half were Serbs. They had died in concentration camps; in Ustaša massacres; in action against occupiers and their supporters; in fighting between Partisans, Četniks, and Ustašas; in retaliations and other punishments. As if the real figures were not big enough, they were inflated both at the official level (to obtain reparations) and at the popular level (to make up for the suffering and to achieve greater glory in greater martyrdom).[5]

The questions of the civil wars within the war were frozen behind a façade of slogans. People did not speak of them. It was forbidden to do so. They evoked wartime memories that many preferred not to pass on to their children. There were more immediate worries. Wartime animosities between Serbs and others, between Serbs and Serbs, Croats and Croats, thus went largely unnoticed in the flush of revolution and reconstruction. Yet the feelings remained to feed the differences, destined in time to be sharpened by the impossibility of fostering anything common to all Yugoslavs other than communism. Disintegrating tendencies would later feed on them.

History was made to serve the revolution and the construction of socialism. It began with the Communist Party. The legitimacy of Communist rule needed a simplified and static memory of its foundation in what came to be known as the People's Liberation Struggle, fixed exclusively on the Partisans. The attempted final solutions in the NDH, the "anticollaborationist" and "anti-insurgent" killings between Serbs, Albanians, and Muslims, the reconquest of Serbia or that of Kosovo, the indiscriminate lumping together of victims of fascism not otherwise specified, the murkier aspects of Communist survival tactics, the eleventh-hour massacres of defeated opponents, and all the other gaps and inconsistencies that lurked under the veil of the official version were partly filled by secret stories.

They all began to emerge as the Communist Party lost its monopoly of public discourse and its control over memory. Throughout the twilight of Tito's long reign, feelings of instability and fears for the future led to ever-increasing interest in the 1940s. People wanted to know what had really happened in those years that had given birth to the Communist regime; they were afraid that they might be on the threshold of a similar period. The professional historians had, on the whole, been too shy, unscholarly, or unimaginative to tackle such hot issues. Initially, they had generally left it to writers outside their ranks who broke out into print after Tito's death. The revelations by all sides of the horrors committed during the Second World War by *them* against *us* went hand in hand with the disintegration of the ruling party into its republican components.

The historiography of the two world wars, especially the second, flowed from Belgrade and from Zagreb in two ever more different directions, stressing the suffering of Serbs and Croats respectively at the hands of the others and of the others' international protectors. Serb-centred interpretations stressed how Croats had fought in the Austro-Hungarian army that had invaded and occupied Serbia during the First World War, and even more so how the greater-Croatian, Ustaša-ruled NDH had massacred Serbs during the Second World War under overall Axis protection before turncoat Ustaša Croats joined the Partisans led by the Croat Tito. Croat-centred interpretations dwelt on the role played by the Serbian army in setting up a Serb-dominated Yugoslavia at the end of the First World War with the support of France and Britain and on the massacre of Croat soldiers by Serb Partisans at the time of the revolution that established a Serb-dominated Communist Yugoslavia.

The experience of the First World War and that of the Second had not been, and could not have been, common experiences for the Yugoslav populations from the Alps to Macedonia, from the Danube to the Adriatic. These populations had been divided by the vagaries of warfare, occupation, resistance, and revolution even more than by ethnic feeling, historical memory, religious adherence, and ideology. All these differences, perceived as they were with the distance of time, could only be magnified when the disintegration process began. As the unofficial and private memories emerged from the ruins of ideological interpretation, they were seized upon and misused to ignite the Serbo-Croatian controversies of the 1980s. All possible simmering resentments added fuel to the fire.

The inter-Yugoslav wars, the Balkanization into ever-smaller former Yugoslav republican states, the Milošević regime in Serbia, the Tudjman regime in Croatia, the violence of the 1990s, and the aftermath of these two regimes have left many open questions with unhealed wounds going back to the Second World War and even before. The unification of Yugoslavia at the end of the First World War is rejected along with the Communist Party that reunited Yugoslavia at the end of the Second World War. Post-Yugoslav "former-Yugoslav" historiography of the Second World War, and even of the First World War, has mostly gone into two opposite and equally distorted directions, with a dangerous loss of scholarly bearings. On the one hand, the belief in a romanticized and ethnocentric past is associated with a tendency both to rehabilitate and to lump together right-wing anti-Communist resistance and fascist movements as being victims of respectively anti-Serb or anti-Croat Communism, linked to strange international bedfellows (the so-called Versailles settlement, the Communist International, the Roman Catholic Church, Eastern Orthodoxy, Freemasonry). On the other hand, and in reaction to the previous direction, the belief in an idealized Titoist past surfaces again among those who had benefited from it, those who expected better after Titoism, those who regret the prestige that Yugoslavia enjoyed under Tito, and those who yearn for stability and order.

Bogus pasts confront each other and reject one another. It seems that the time has not yet come for the legacy of the two world wars, and in particular that of the

Second World War, to be left to the unimpeded study and discussion of critical historians from Ljubljana to Skopje. It is still being manipulated by inspired interpreters of the past, aided and abetted by those who think that a degree in history and a file of selected documents are sufficient to set up the past as a model for the future. Andrej Mitrović for one, Serbia's historian of the First World War, calls for a historiography that questions and analyses and an end to the sort of history that "people want to believe in."[6]

Notes

1. See Kosta St. Pavlowitch, "The First World War and the Unification of Yugoslavia," in Dejan Djokić (ed.), *Yugoslavia: Histories of a Failed Idea, 1918–1992* (London: Hurst and Co., 2003), pp. 39–41.
2. The description is taken from Taline Ter Minassian, "Les géographes français et la délimitation des frontières de la Bulgarie à la Conférence de la Paix en 1919," *Balkanologie*, No. 1–2 (2002), who borrows the typology presented by Stephen B. Jones in his *Boundary-Making: A Handbook for Statesmen, Treaty Editors, and Boundary Commissioners* (Washington, D.C.: Carnegie Endowment for International Peace, 1945).
3. Serbia's military losses alone were relatively 2.5 times higher than those of France. See Ivo Lederer, *Yugoslavia at the Paris Peace Conference: A Study in Frontiermaking* (New Haven, CT, and London: Yale University Press, 1963), pp. 221–225.
4. Nevertheless, the Yugoslav army had been able to score a local success against the Italians by pushing across Albanian territory to Shköder before being turned back. Since Albania had been set up as an independent state in 1912, the Serbs had made five attempts to get to the sea through its northern part, and atrocities had been committed by both Montenegrin and Serbian troops. The successful push to the sea in June 1915 had also been an intervention in support of an Albanian faction that in return assisted the Serbs during their epic retreat later that year, pursued by the Austro-Hungarians and by a generally hostile local Albanian population.
5. For a scholarly approach, see Bogoljub Kočović, *Žrtve drugog svetskog rata u Jugoslaviji* [The victims of the Second World War in Yugoslavia] (London: Naše delo, 1985); 2nd ed. (Sarajevo: Svjetlost, 1990); and Vladimir Žerjavić, *Gubici stanovništva Jugoslavije u drugom svjetskom ratu* [Yugoslavia's Population Losses in the Second World War] (Zagreb: Jugoslavensko viktimološko društvo, 1989). For a summary in English based on an often indirect reading of secondary sources, see David Bruce MacDonald, *Balkan Holocausts? Serbian and Croatian Victim-Centered Propaganda and the War in Yugoslavia* (Manchester: Manchester University Press, 2002), chapter 6.
6. Interview in *NIN*, February 20, 2003.

THE SOCIALIST LEGACY

Nation/People/Republic: Self-Determination in Socialist Yugoslavia[1]

❖ Audrey Helfant Budding ❖

The clash of two concepts of self-determination, one based on the nation and the other on the republic, was crucial to the dynamic of the post-Yugoslav wars. The wars were shortest and least destructive in Slovenia (where the two concepts were most congruent), longest and bloodiest in Bosnia (where they were least so). Understanding the struggle over self-determination, therefore, is vital to understanding the course of Yugoslavia's dissolution. This chapter will show how competing concepts of self-determination were built into the conceptual framework of Yugoslav politics during the socialist period and how the unresolved tension between them shaped both the state's dissolution and its aftermath.[2]

Highlighting the struggle over self-determination does not, of course, mean accepting claims that it alone explains the motivations of major actors. Particularly after the wars began, politicians facing conflicting imperatives could and did cite different rationales to suit different needs.[3] Nevertheless, during Yugoslavia's dissolution the battle over self-determination took center stage, and its lines were clearly drawn. In confronting each other and in appealing to their bases, politicians were unanimous in invoking self-determination as a sacrosanct principle but bitterly divided over what political subject could exercise that right. A meeting of the six republican presidents held in Split on March 28, 1991, offers a striking example of this clash of concepts. This meeting was the first in a series of interrepublican summits held as Yugoslavia's long crisis reached its final stages. Federal political institutions were increasingly deadlocked or marginalized, and negotiations over the future organization of the Yugoslav state had reached an impasse (with Slovenia and Croatia adamant in their commitment to a confederation of sovereign republics and Serbia equally so in its call for a strengthened federation). By the end of 1990, Slovenia was taking open steps toward independence: in the Slovenian referendum held on December 23, 1990, 88 percent of those voting supported independence.[4] The situation in Croatia was even more volatile because assertions of republican sovereignty were contested at each stage by the Belgrade-backed claims to national self-determination put forward by some of Croatia's Serbs, notably the inhabitants of the Krajina. Though Slovenia and Croatia would not formally declare independence until June 25, the first clashes of the post-Yugoslav wars had occurred before the Split summit convened.[5]

At the meeting, Slovenia's Milan Kučan was the main spokesman for a republican right to self-determination including secession, and Serbia's Slobodan Milošević for a national right. Whereas Kučan insisted that Slovenia could act unilaterally to leave Yugoslavia (and indeed was obligated to do so by the results of the December 1990 referendum), Milošević maintained that Yugoslavia's dissolution could take place "only on the basis of the freely expressed will of each of its nations individually in a referendum."[6] In one direct exchange, Kučan and Milošević went to the heart of their differences:

> Milan Kučan: Here in this document [a proposed joint statement] it doesn't say anywhere, this is a presumption, but it must be clearly written, that first so that we can resolve the political crisis we recognize to every nation, that is [*odnosno*] to the republic in which it lives together with other citizens, not of its nationality, the right to realize its right to self-determination.
>
> Slobodan Milošević: Well, do you put an equal sign between nation and republic?
>
> Milan Kučan: Yes.
>
> Slobodan Milošević: I do not.
>
> Milan Kučan: That's where the problem lies now.[7]

This meeting was one of many occasions during Yugoslavia's protracted dissolution when Slovenian leaders claimed the right of self-determination for republics, whereas Serbian leaders claimed it for nations. On one level (as many observers have noted), their opposing stances reflected differences in the ethnodemographic fit between nation and republic. Only 1 percent of Yugoslavia's Slovenes lived outside Slovenia, whereas 26 percent of Yugoslavia's Serbs lived outside Serbia (and about 20 percent of Croats outside Croatia).[8] Serbian perspectives were also influenced by memories of the Independent State of Croatia's genocidal campaign against its Serb inhabitants during the Second World War.

This chapter (while fully acknowledging the importance of such structural and historical factors in shaping politicians' stances on self-determination) will approach the issue from a different point of view. It will seek to elucidate the ideological and constitutional concepts that structured the exchange between Milošević and Kučan and furnished the language they used. Its point of departure is a particular phrase used by Kučan in the passage cited above: the phrase *narod, odnosno republika* (the nation, that is the republic). This phrase presents some difficulties of translation. (Perhaps only the rendering of *republika* as "republic" can be considered wholly unproblematic!) Depending upon the context, the word *narod* (like its equivalents in many other Slavic languages) can be translated into English either as "nation" (people in the national sense, e.g., *hrvatski narod*, the Croat people), or as "people" with no national content (e.g., *radni narod Hrvatske*, the working people of Croatia).[9] The word *odnosno* has even more potential meanings. It is sometimes used to correct a misstatement, in which sense it might best be translated as "or rather." In other contexts, it can mean and/or: for example, *odnosno* was frequently used to indicate that various constitutional provisions applied to both republics and provinces.[10] The primary usage of *odnosno*, however, is to make the speaker's meaning more precise; thus, one dictionary suggests "that is," "in other words," or "more exactly" as possible English translations.[11] In general, then, using *odnosno* to link two objects suggests that they are (in the given context) equivalent.

Kučan's acceptance of Milošević's contention that he was placing "an equal sign between nation and republic" is a clear indication that he was using *odnosno* in this sense rather than to correct a misstatement. In what sense did Kučan consider nation and republic to be equivalent? One possible interpretation would be that the formula simply reflected Slovene realities: the exceptional fit between nation and republic alluded to earlier. Yet even for Slovenia, "the [members of the] nation" and "the [citizens of the] republic" represented two different groups. Kučan showed himself fully aware of this fact in the passage cited above (with its reference to "other citizens not of its nationality"), and later in the same exchange he explicitly disavowed any claim to represent Slovenes outside Slovenia.[12]

In fact, the ambiguous phrase *narod, odnosno republika* (and other formulas that similarly conflated nation and republic) was neither an accident nor a Slovene specificity but, rather, a central feature of Yugoslavia's ideological and constitutional development from the foundation of socialist Yugoslavia to its dissolution. Through this formula the regime consistently and fatefully blurred the distinction between two concepts of nationhood. One—variously called the "ethnic" or "cultural" or "personal" concept—is conceived of as linking an individual to other members of a (generally linguistic) "imagined community," in Benedict Anderson's much-used but still evocative phrase, regardless of where they are to be found.[13] The other— the "territorial" or "political" or "civic" concept—is conceived of as constituting a political community and linking each individual in it to the institutions of a state. In practice, of course, the two aspects of nationhood have tended to converge. Very broadly speaking, in one pattern (generally associated with Eastern Europe), elites have pursued statehood in the name of a community defined by culture, and in another (generally associated with Western Europe), states have used their control of territory to achieve a more-or-less culturally homogeneous citizenry. In either case, the outcome is one in which, as George Schöpflin has put it, "Nationhood . . . should be conceptualized as simultaneously having a political (civic) and a cultural (ethnic) dimension."[14]

This chapter will examine the interplay between nation and republic in three critical eras: the founding of socialist Yugoslavia, when federal units were set up in the name of (ethnic) nations' self-determination but with a far-from-perfect correspondence between personal and territorial nationality; the period of radical constitutional change between 1968 and 1974, when decentralization was justified in the name of the nation but implemented on an exclusively territorial basis; and the shift from crisis to dissolution in 1989–91, when competing concepts of self-determination became the stuff of daily politics. Throughout, the essay will trace the ominous process by which the regime made "the right to self-determination" a keystone of political legitimacy without specifying who held that right or how it was to be exercised.

Designing a Federal Yugoslavia

During and just after the Second World War, the Partisans reconstituted Yugoslavia as a federal and officially multinational state and so began the process of institutionalizing both territorial and personal nationality. As the discussion above indicated, these are different but not necessarily opposing concepts. Within a federal state, a tension arises between them when territorial units are understood to have an ethnonational content—to "belong" in some sense to a given nation. Was this how Yugoslavia's federal units were conceptualized? Answering this question requires a brief examination of both the national policies of the Communist Party of Yugoslavia (CPY) in the interwar period and the decisions made by the Partisans during and immediately after the Second World War.

In its essentials, the Yugoslav Communists' approach to their country's national problems followed the Soviet model. Like their Soviet mentors, the Yugoslav Communists proclaimed the right of nations to self-determination and defined self-determination in territorial terms. Both Soviets and Yugoslavs, in other words, rejected the Austro-Marxist idea that personal nationality should trump territorial, with members of a nation constituting a self-governing body regardless of where they lived.[15] In Bolshevik practice, of course, the right to self-determination was strictly bounded by the needs of the revolution. (In Walker Connor's pithy formulation, Lenin "made a distinction between the abstract right to self-determination, which is enjoyed by all nations, and the right to exercise that right, which evidently is not."[16]) For the CPY also, the revolution came first. The party's approach to Yugoslavia's national questions was essentially tactical and reflected the Comintern's changing priorities as well as its own factional struggles. The interwar CPY thus adopted very different positions at different times, including (from the late 1920s to the mid-1930s) advocating the breakup of the Yugoslav state.[17]

In the mid-1930s, in keeping with the Comintern's new policy of building a broad coalition against fascism, the CPY stopped advocating Yugoslavia's dissolution. It still, however, maintained its support for self-determination and the rights of the "nationally oppressed" peoples (which for the CPY meant all of Yugoslavia's inhabitants except the Serbs). To reconcile the two concepts, it put forward the idea that self-determination could be realized through territorial autonomy within the

Yugoslav state.[18] Thus, after the CC CPY's June 1935 Plenum—a defining moment in the Party's change of course—the Politburo issued a statement saying:

> We continue with all our strength the struggle against the regime of great Serbian oppression, for freedom and the rights of the oppressed peoples. We are not changing our position which is expressed in our basic demand: the right of self-determination including the right to secession. But we must not place the emphasis on secession but rather underline that every people has the right and should decide itself about its fate. The emphasis, therefore, is placed on the process of self-determination. Precisely because of this we are putting forward the demand for popular assemblies or *sabors*, which will be chosen in free elections, in Zagreb, Ljubljana, Skoplje, Cetinje and Sarajevo.[19]

If we assume that the existing Yugoslav parliament was seen by the Party as a Serbian one, the "popular assemblies" envisioned in this statement foreshadow the six republics established after the war.[20] Some other CPY documents of the time envisioned Vojvodina as a seventh unit whose people should have the right to some form of self-determination.[21] The CPY's inclusion of Bosnia-Herzegovina and (often) Vojvodina—two regions with heavily mixed populations and no national majority—in its programmatic statements was especially significant. It indicated that in the Party's view the "people" entitled to self-determination could be defined by historic factors as well as ethnonational ones.[22]

In most respects, the Party's internal organization corresponded to its programmatic statements. On the eve of the Second World War, Slovenia and Croatia had their own communist parties, and the CPY had formed provincial *(pokrajinski)* or regional *(oblasni)* committees for Bosnia-Herzegovina; Macedonia; Montenegro, Boka [Kotorska] and the Sandžak; Serbia; Vojvodina; and Kosovo-Metohija.[23] This organizational structure reflected several relatively recent developments. The Communist Parties of Slovenia and Croatia had been formed in 1937. (No Communist Party for Serbia was formed then on the grounds that for Serbs "the class struggle does not take the form of a national liberation struggle."[24]) The Regional Committee for Dalmatia had been subsumed within the Croatian Party when the latter was formed. (Dalmatian leaders nevertheless maintained considerable independence of action in the late 1930s and, indeed, through the war years.) Finally, in October 1940 the CPY leadership had granted a request from the regional party organization for Kosovo-Metohija, formerly subordinate to the Montenegrin Provincial Committee, to come directly under the CPY.[25] Although the Party's organization just before the war offers a rough preview of the future federal units, the correspondence is not perfect. Most important, the CPY's interwar structure did not foretell Vojvodina's future position within the republic of Serbia. The Vojvodina party organization was never part of the Serbian one during the interwar period and, as noted above, the party's programmatic statements suggested that it viewed both Vojvodina and Bosnia-Herzegovina as territories with a claim to self-determination based on a specific historic identity.

The outlines of a federal settlement in which territorial status was understood as expressing national self-determination emerged more clearly in the course of the war. The new Yugoslavia's founding document—the "Decision about Building Yugoslavia on the Federal Principle" promulgated in November 1943—cited "the right of every people to self-determination, including the right to secession or to unification with other peoples." Here, "people" should certainly be understood in the ethnonational sense. Furthermore, Article 2 of the decision stated that "Yugoslavia is being built and will be built on the federal principle, which will ensure the full equality of Serbs, Croats, Slovenes, Macedonians and Montenegrins, that is to say [*odnosno*] the peoples of Serbia, Croatia, Slovenia, Macedonia, Montenegro and Bosnia-Herzegovina."[26] As in many later formulations, the difference between ethnic and territorial peoples (e.g., "Croats" vs. "people of Croatia") was glossed over through the use of *odnosno*.

The Partisans' basic concept was simple: giving each nation its "own" federal unit would satisfy the claims of self-determination and distance the new Yugoslavia from the old. Realities on the ground, however, were more complex. Much of Yugoslavia's territory was nationally mixed, and important areas of Serb settlement (in particular) were noncontiguous. Thus, even if the Partisans had taken a *tabula rasa* approach to organizing the new Yugoslavia—ignoring all previous political borders and constructing their federal units on the basis of an ethnonational census—they could not have produced a perfect correspondence between territorial and personal nationality. In the event, they made no such attempt. Although their new federation was justified with the rhetoric of national self-determination, it was constructed on a far more complex basis.

Any discussion of the process by which the federation was created must begin by acknowledging the limits of historical knowledge on this subject. Key decisions about which regions would become federal units and where their borders would be were made within a narrow circle of top Party leaders.[27] Only in a few instances do we have direct evidence as to how members of that circle weighed competing criteria—ethnonational, historic, political, or economic. More commonly, we must deduce the criteria they used from the results. Taken together, these results indicate that the Partisans (following on from the interwar CPY) took historic borders as a starting point but modified them in some instances according to ethnic, political, and other criteria.[28] Examining some specific cases will clarify this assertion.

Arguably the most important application of the historic criterion was the creation of the republic of Bosnia-Herzegovina within borders very close to those established in 1878 by the Congress of Berlin (borders that were themselves based in part on a long-standing frontier between the Ottoman and Habsburg empires). Bosnia-Herzegovina—with a population that was 44 percent Serb, 31 percent Muslim, and 24 percent Croat in the 1948 census—thus became the only republic with no national majority. (At this time, the Party regarded Slavic Muslims as a religious rather than a national group, expecting them to define themselves as either Serbs or Croats "of the Muslim faith."[29])

In a decision that would later arouse much controversy, the Partisans took the territory of the Kingdom of Serbia before the Balkan Wars of 1912–13 (as opposed to that with which Serbia entered the Yugoslav state in 1918) as their starting-point in creating the republic of Serbia. Thus Vardar Macedonia ("Southern Serbia" in earlier Serbian parlance) became the Republic of Macedonia, and Kosovo-Metohija became an Autonomous Region within Serbia—a separate administrative status that was more formal than real when it was instituted but crucial later.[30] Only in the case of the Sandžak (which the Ottomans had retained after losing Bosnia-Herzegovina in 1878 but then lost to Serbia and Montenegro in the Balkan Wars) did the Republic of Serbia keep without reservation the territorial gains made by the Kingdom of Serbia in the years before the First World War.

The disposition of the Sandžak offers a rare record of open debate over the competing criteria for establishing federal units. Although the Sandžak had entered the war under the jurisdiction of the CPY Provincial Committee for Montenegro, organizational developments during the war gave grounds for supposing that it would become a federal unit in its own right.[31] Sandžak party leaders supported this option, citing the region's historic distinctiveness and the sentiments of its large Slavic Muslim minority (about 40 percent of the population in the 1931 census). Nevertheless, the Partisans' top leaders decided to reaffirm the Balkan Wars' division of the Sandžak between Serbia and Montenegro. Overriding unusually open resistance from Sandžak leaders, they cited mainly economic and logistical arguments for their decision.[32] Some statements, however, suggested that political reliability was a paramount consideration: "For the Muslims themselves this [i.e., the division of the Sandžak] will be more useful and they will thus be less liable to become the booty of reactionaries and regressive forces who so alienated them from the national-liberation struggle."[33]

Some of the most complex and contested issues involved in creating the republic of Serbia concerned the Vojvodina region north of Belgrade. Under Hungarian rule until 1918, Vojvodina had been a center of the nineteenth-century Serb national movement.[34] As noted above, the interwar CPY had sometimes included Vojvodina— with its very heterogeneous population of Serbs, Hungarians, Germans, Croats, and others—in the list of regions entitled to self-determination. During the Second World War there were bitter disagreements within the CPY itself about what territory Vojvodina included and how it should fit into the federation.[35] The ultimate decision to include it within Serbia (as an "Autonomous Province," which denoted a higher administrative status than Kosovo's "Autonomous Region" title) followed ethnic more than historic principles. Vojvodina had belonged to pre-Yugoslav Serbia for only a few days, but Serbs and Montenegrins (37 percent of the region's population in the 1931 census) became a majority (52 percent) after the Second World War with the expulsion of the ethnic Germans and settlement of some Partisan veterans.[36] The Partisans also attempted to follow the ethnic principle in drawing the border between Vojvodina and Croatia, a task complicated by the existence of substantial Serb and Croat enclaves.[37]

The other borders of the Republic of Croatia reflected a mixed application of historic and ethnic principles.[38] Undoing the territorial gains of the Axis-sponsored Independent State of Croatia (as well as the more modest ones of the 1939 Croatian Banovina), the Partisans reestablished the historical border with Bosnia-Herzegovina. The disposition of Dalmatia, with its distinctive identity based on centuries of political separation from Croatia-Slavonia, was controversial. Dalmatian Party leaders (having spent the war years in constant friction with the Communist Party of Croatia) sought autonomous status within Croatia but were overruled. Within Dalmatia itself, an ethnic rather than historical criterion was applied in assigning the Bay of Kotor to Montenegro rather than to Croatia.[39] Finally, Croatia's border with Slovenia generally followed the administrative divisions of 1931 (the *banovine*), with an ethnically based demarcation in the Istrian peninsula newly acquired from Italy. The resulting border traced the ethnic line quite closely, leaving only 16,000 Croats and 39,000 Slovenes in the "other" republic.[40]

As even this brief discussion demonstrates, no single criterion guided the Partisans' decisions either in creating federal units or in drawing their borders. Considerations of historical precedent, ethnonational demarcation, economic development, and political reliability all played their parts. If the end result is evaluated according to the simple yardstick of "a political principle, which holds that the political and the national unit should be congruent" (Ernest Gellner's famous definition of nationalism), it will immediately be clear that some of Yugoslavia's nations achieved a much closer congruence with "their" republics than others.[41] Most important for the future were the distributions of Yugoslavia's two largest nations: the federal borders left about 30 percent of Serbs and 20 percent of Croats outside of Serbia and Croatia, respectively. At the other end of the spectrum, 96 percent of Yugoslavia's Slovenes were included within the Republic of Slovenia (and this republic had a population that was 97 percent Slovene, making it the only territorial unit that approached national homogeneity).[42]

During Yugoslavia's crisis and dissolution, critiques of the federation's post-1945 internal borders became especially prominent in Serbian national discourse: assertions that the postwar settlement was deliberately designed to divide and weaken Serbs and Serbia became a commonplace.[43] On this point, each observer's conclusions will depend on the point of comparison adopted. If the Yugoslav Communists' 1945 decisions are compared with their interwar platforms and organization, then the inclusions of Kosovo, Vojvodina, and part of the Sandžak within the Serbian republic might reasonably be interpreted as concessions to Serbian national feeling. (The reason for the Party's change of course must be sought during the war itself, not only in each region's specific wartime history but also in the broader dynamic that made support from Serbs outside Serbia crucial to the Partisans' success.) If these same decisions are compared with earlier conceptions of "Serbian lands"—including Macedonia, Montenegro, Bosnia-Herzegovina, Vojvodina, and parts of Slavonia and Dalmatia—or with some of the frontiers of the post-Balkan Wars Kingdom of Serbia, they will be seen as deliberate affronts.[44]

In addressing these issues, one should avoid anachronistic interpretations of the Partisan leaders' motives in drawing borders where they did. Borders between republics did not have in 1945 the importance they would acquire with Yugoslavia's decentralization (let alone with its dissolution), and there is no reason to believe that Tito and his associates anticipated these developments. A well-known passage from Tito's May 1945 statement to the Founding Congress of the Communist Party of Serbia illustrates the leadership's initial conception of the republican borders: "Serbia is in Yugoslavia, and we do not intend to create within Yugoslavia states that will make war with each other. If Bosnia-Herzegovina is equal, if they have their federal unit, then we have not divided Serbia, but we have made Serbs in Bosnia happy, just as much as Croats and Muslims. It is a question only of administrative division."[45]

Similarly, an AVNOJ Presidium directive on the Sandžak emphasized that there was no need to keep the Sandžak autonomous in order to avoid dividing Muslims: "They will have the same rights in Montenegro as in Serbia."[46]

Even more striking is another passage from Tito's speech to the Serbian Party Congress: "loving one's own federal unit—means loving a monolithic [*monolitnu*] Yugoslavia."[47] Tito's new Yugoslavia was indeed monolithic because it was founded on the rule of a centralized party: its federalism did not at first involve any true division of powers.[48] The Party's unquestioned primacy allowed the regime to gloss over a paradoxical aspect of the federal structure. On the one hand, the new Yugoslavia's legitimating language emphasized the republics' national content. For example, Article 10 of the 1946 Constitution stated: "Any act directed against the sovereignty, equality and national freedom of the peoples of the Federal Peoples Republic of Yugoslavia and *their* people's republics is contrary to the constitution" (author's emphasis).[49] On the other hand, as noted above, Party leaders emphasized that because the new order would prevent national discrimination there was no need for members of any nation to live in their "own" unit. In theory the correspondence between nations and republics was crucial to national equality, but in practice its implications were undefined.

An early episode of Yugoslavia's long-running debate over secession rights illustrates the founders' unthinking confidence that the Party's supremacy made it unnecessary to distinguish between the rights of nations and those of republics. Article 1 of the 1946 Constitution defined Yugoslavia as a state founded upon each people's "right to self-determination, including the right of separation."[50] Within a few years of the constitution's promulgation, a controversy arose over whether this language meant that the constitution allowed for republican secession. Moša Pijade, one of the constitution's drafters, responded that there was no such right. Drawing an explicit contrast with the Soviet Constitution and its Article 17 (which specified that each Union Republic had the right to secede), he said: "Insofar as the Constitution has mentioned the right to secession, it is only in connection with the origin of the FNRY and not in order to ensure that our republics still have today the right of separation." (This theory of the "consummation" of the right to secession—that the Yugoslav peoples and/or republics had exercised their right to self-determination once and for all in forming the new Yugoslavia—would reappear at various points in the Yugoslav constitutional debate.) Pijade went on to say: "It is theoretically possible that some people or people's republic would bring up the matter of its secession. But that would be a thing to be solved in concreto, either as a revolutionary or as a counterrevolutionary case, according to the situation, the social causes and so forth."[51]

In this thoroughly Leninist passage, it is Pijade's unthinking assumption that a unified party would rule on any proposed secession that lets him refer to "some people or people's republic" wishing to secede, without bothering to distinguish between the two cases. The language of the 1946 Constitution might give grounds for asserting both that nations were sovereign and that republics were sovereign, but in fact the party was sovereign.[52] As long as this remained the case, there was no need to consider any of the political issues concealed in the phrase "the nations and their republics."

"Two Dimensions of Federalism": Personal and Territorial Nationality in the Era of Constitutional Decentralization

As Zoran Đinđić put it from the vantage-point of 1987: "[Yugoslav] Federalism was unproblematic until it was expected to regulate socio-political relations. As an emotional symbol it performed its role."[53] Only in the immediate postwar years, however, could Yugoslavia's federalism be considered "unproblematic." The economic and political de-Stalinization that began as an improvised reaction to Yugoslavia's 1948 excommunication from the Soviet bloc and became "Yugoslav self-managing socialism" soon allowed national and political conflicts to reemerge. Indeed, economic decentralization welded new economic grievances to older ones. The stage was set for a protracted conflict over the locus of decision making, in which the proponents of decentralization were ultimately victorious.[54] The following section will explore one phase of the process of decentralization—the era of constitutional change between 1968 and 1974—focusing on how constitutional change affected the relation between territorial and personal nationality. As a preliminary, it will set out a few specificities of the way personal nationality was conceived in socialist Yugoslavia.

First, in spite of its *ideological* importance to a state legitimated in large part by the proclaimed sovereignty and equality of its nations, personal nationality in socialist Yugoslavia had a relatively weak *institutional* basis. This is clearest by contrast with the Soviet Union, where personal nationality (once it was codified in the early 1930s) took on an enduring and pervasive institutional reality. In Yuri Slezkine's words, "Every Soviet citizen was born into a certain nationality, took it to day care and through high school, had it officially confirmed at the age of sixteen and then carried it to the grave through thousands of application forms, certificates, questionnaires and reception desks."[55] Nationality—especially as it affected educational and employment opportunities—was a legal attribute of considerable importance.

The Yugoslav situation was very different. In socialist Yugoslavia, as in the Soviet Union, personal nationality was recorded on a multitude of official forms. But whereas the Soviet concept of nationality was "objective" (i.e., determined by birth, not choice, except that the child of a mixed marriage could choose the nationality of either parent), in Yugoslavia a subjective concept was dominant.[56] Indeed, Article 41 of the 1963 Constitution included language stating not only that an individual was not obliged to *declare* his or her nationality but also that an individual was not obliged to *have* a nationality: "The citizen shall be guaranteed the freedom to express his nationality [*narodnost*] and culture, as well as the freedom to speak his language. No one shall have to declare himself as to nationality or determine himself for one of the nationalities."[57]

The contrast with Soviet practice is striking: a constitutional provision allowing the individual to stand outside the whole system of personal nationality would have been inconceivable in the USSR. As Yugoslavia unraveled, the fact that personal nationality was not a legally required component of identity (and so was not listed on Yugoslav identity cards as it was on Soviet internal passports) meant that national affiliation could be uncertain even as it became a matter of life and death. (Hence the many tragic or tragicomic wartime anecdotes in which individuals attempted to "prove" their national heritage.[58])

A second specificity of the Yugoslav case was the contested significance of the "Yugoslav" identity. The regime very consistently defined its "socialist Yugoslavism" in *non-national* terms as "a socialist Yugoslav consciousness, a Yugoslav socialist patriotism, which is not the opposite of but rather a necessary internationalist supplement to democratic national consciousness in the conditions of a socialist community of nations. It is not a question of creating some new 'Yugoslav nation' instead of the existing nations . . ."[59]

It followed logically from this definition that (as a constitutional textbook published in Serbia in 1971 put it) "In the conditions of self-managing socialism, Yugoslavism cannot mean any kind of national category."[60] According to the politically dominant view, a person who declared himself/herself a "Yugoslav" on the census or elsewhere was not stating a national identity but rather exercising the right not to declare one.[61] (Actually, many "Yugoslavs" did see their identity as a national one: in refusing to recognize their choice the regime was violating its own principle of subjective nationality.[62]) Moreover, even after the 1963 Constitution affirmed the individual's freedom to declare any (or no) national identity, bureaucrats did not always accept Yugoslav under the nationality rubric on official forms. For example, the League of Youth regularly fielded complaints from members who had been told that they could not call themselves Yugoslavs on school documents.[63] Thus, the concept of an emerging Yugoslav nation survived only on the margins of socialist Yugoslavia's official discourse.

The framework within which socialist Yugoslavia understood personal nationality was well established by the time that constitutional change gathered momentum in the late 1960s. Between 1967 and 1971, three sets of constitutional amendments inaugurated the radically decentralized constitutional order that was then repackaged in the Constitution of 1974.[64] The most important effect of the first two amendment packages (Amendments 1–6, passed on April 18, 1967; and 7–19, passed on December 26, 1968) was a restructuring of the federal parliament to give the republics and provinces effective control over the legislative process. The Chamber of Nations (the *Veće naroda*, made up of twenty delegates from each republic and ten from each province) gained a new independence of action and was particularly charged with considering matters that concerned equality between the republics or between the nations and nationalities or the constitutional rights of the republics and autonomous provinces.[65]

The package of constitutional amendments passed in 1968 also changed the positions of Serbia's autonomous provinces in vital ways.[66] (Kosovo had been upgraded from Autonomous Region to Autonomous Province in 1963.) Whereas the 1963 Constitution had stated that the six republics made up the SFRJ, Amendment 7 of December 1968 also listed the two "Socialist Autonomous Provinces" as elements of the federal state. The provinces' changed status was confirmed by a new description of their origins included in Amendment 18: they had been created "through the common struggle of the peoples and nationalities of Yugoslavia during the National Liberation War and Socialist Revolution" and had joined Serbia "on the basis of the freely expressed will of the population—the peoples and national minorities of the Provinces and of Federal Serbia."[67] This language suggested that the autonomous provinces, like the republics, were to be seen as the territorial vessels of ethnonational self-determination.[68] Furthermore, Amendment 19—while not explicitly addressing the status of the provinces—strengthened the position of Albanians and Hungarians by specifically asserting that the constitution's basic provisions on the rights of Yugoslavia's nations also applied to its "nationalities." The use of *"nationality"* [*narodnost*] in place of *"national minority"* to designate those citizens of Yugoslavia who were ethnically affiliated with a neighboring state—Albanians, Hungarians, Romanians, and others—was introduced in the Constitution of 1963 and further developed in the 1968 amendments.[69]

Amendment 18 also greatly increased the provinces' independence of Serbia, stressing their direct relation with the federation. Among other provisions, this amendment granted the provinces their own supreme courts, specified that the territory of an autonomous province could not be changed without the consent of its assembly, and affirmed that the federation "shall safeguard the constitutional rights and duties of the Autonomous Provinces."[70] Organizational changes in the Party paralleled those in the state. In November 1968, what had been sections of the League of Communists of Serbia for Vojvodina and for Kosovo became the independent Leagues of Vojvodina and of Kosovo.[71]

The amendments of 1967 and 1968 had altered the balance between the federation and its units, as well as that between the republics and the provinces. The amendments of 1971 (Amendments 20–42, passed on June 30, 1971) went even further in both regards.[72] The first article of Amendment 20 asserted: "The working people, nations and nationalities realize their sovereign rights in the Socialist Republics, and in the Socialist Autonomous Provinces in accordance with their constitutional rights, and in the Socialist Federative Republic of Yugoslavia when that is in the common interest established by the Constitution of the SFRY."[73] In contrast to earlier formulations that had mentioned only the republics, this language indicated that certain "sovereign rights" could be exercised through the autonomous provinces.

Two further amendments increased the republics' and provinces' control over decision making at the center. Amendment 33 instituted a requirement that federal decisions involving a range of economic matters be reached through harmonization (*usaglašavanje*) of the positions of the republics and provinces.[74] This introduction of what amounted in practice to a republican and provincial veto was arguably the most important of the 1971 measures. Amendment 36 established a twenty-three member collective state presidency consisting of three representatives from each republic and two from each province, as well as Tito. (The presidency assumed its full political importance after Tito's death, by which time it had been restructured to include one member from each republic and province and the LCY president ex officio.)

As the content of all these amendments makes clear, Yugoslavia's constitutional decentralization occurred on the *territorial* level. Republics and provinces, not nations, gained greater independence in their own actions and greater control over decisions taken at the federal center. The process was legitimated, however, with reference to *national* rights and *national* equality. Kardelj, the ideological architect of Yugoslavia's decentralization, very consistently equated the interests of nations with those of republics.[75] For example, at the LCY's pivotal Eighth Congress in 1964, Kardelj supported decentralization by arguing that under self-management nations should have the same right to control the fruits of their own labor that individual workers did.[76] (This argument is notable for its reification of "the nation" as well its equation of nations with republics.)

Even more striking is a sentence from the speech with which Kardelj presented the 1971 amendments (which introduced the republican "veto") to the LCY Presidency: "We must take account of the fact that in the relations between the nations, that is to say [*odnosno*] the republics, of Yugoslavia there exist not only different but also certain *objectively* contradictory interests."[77] Here Kardelj—like Milan Kučan twenty years later—used the word *odnosno* to suggest that nations and republics were for political purposes the same thing or, to put it another way, that the republic was the (only) framework through which nations expressed their interests. It should be emphasized that this interpretation of Yugoslavia's constitutional doctrine was not limited to Slovenes. Serbia's leading constitutional lawyer, Jovan Đorđević (who played an important role in the drafting of both the 1971 amendments and the 1974 Constitution), expressed a variation on the same idea when he stated in 1983, "[Yugoslavia's] form of federalism is decentralized, with its sovereign basis in the nation, that is, in the republics as the nearest expression of that sovereignty…"[78]

In one sense, the equation of nations and republics simply expressed the logic of federal Yugoslavia's founding doctrine: the idea that each republic (with the perennial Bosnian exception) was the vehicle of a particular nation's political self-determination. As the discussion above indicated, this doctrine can be traced back at least to the mid-1930s. The fact that the 1946 Constitution's phrase, "the nations and their republics," recurred in Amendment 20 of 1971 and also in the 1974 Constitution underscores this continuity.[79] Although the Constitution of 1963 does not contain this particular phrase, it reveals the same guiding assumption in Article 42: "Members of the peoples of Yugoslavia on the territories of republics other than their own [*na teritoriji druge republike*] shall have the right to school instruction in their own languages, in conformity with republican law." As F. W. Hondius points out in his classic study of Yugoslavia's constitutional development, this phrasing "presumed another rule, apparently too obvious to be put in writing, viz. that the members of each people could point to one 'home' Republic."[80]

The claims of territorial and personal nationality clashed more openly during the years of constitutional decentralization than at any other time before the period of Yugoslavia's dissolution. In the late 1960s, as in the late 1980s, constitutional decentralization was particularly controversial in Serbia. This is not to say that Serbian opinion in either era was uniformly opposed to decentralization. In fact, the figures who led the Serbian party between 1968 and 1972—later known as the Serbian liberals—threw their full support behind decentralization, seeing it as a means to their end of a "modern Serbia." Many prominent intellectuals, however, held different views.[81] During the period of officially mandated "public discussion" that preceded the passage of each set of amendments, the law faculty of the University of Belgrade was a leading forum for opposition to the ruling constitutional trend and specifically for attacks on the assumption that nations and republics were politically interchangeable. As early as October 1968, one law faculty speaker pointed out that, because the delegations in the Chamber of Nations (Veće naroda) in fact represented the federal units, it would more accurately be called the Chamber of Republics and Provinces.[82] (A few years later, the 1974 Constitution made precisely this change.)

At the better-known law faculty debate of March 1971, a young scholar named Budimir Košutić offered a more developed critique of the amendments' equation of national and republican interests.[83] In a scarcely veiled attack on Kardelj's claim that republican economic autonomy guaranteed national equality, Košutić asserted that "the idea of a national economy on which the Draft of the constitutional amendments is based represents in itself an invitation to discrimination against national minorities." (By "national minorities" Košutić here meant all groups in the minority in a given republic.) In the amendments, Košutić went on to say, "the existence of two dimensions of federalism was completely overlooked. One is politico-territorial and the other multinational." If nations required the protection of a political unit, as the logic of decentralization implied, then this principle should be honored *within* republics (through the creation of more autonomous provinces) as well as between them.[84] Speaking at the same session, philosopher Mihailo Đurić drew a more radical conclusion. Constitutional decentralization, he said, had established "several independent and even opposing national states" on Yugoslavia's territory. In these circumstances it was imperative to reconsider the relation between republican borders—above all, those of Serbia—and national ones.[85]

Đurić represents an important strand of Serbian thought: one that responded to decentralization by attempting to redefine the relation between the republic of Serbia and the nation of Serbs. (In the late 1960s this was an opposition view: the Serbian liberals explicitly rejected the idea that Serbia could or should be the protector of Serbs elsewhere.[86]) At the same time, some voices within the Croatian national movement known variously as the Croatian Spring or the Maspok (short for Mass Movement) were approaching the nation-republic nexus from a different but equally controversial angle. The Croatian movement—or more accurately movements, given the diversity of the currents within it—focused mainly on the republic's relation to the federation, putting forward demands that ranged from greater control over foreign exchange earnings to a Croatian seat at the U.N.[87] As regards the relation between nation and republic, the position of Serbs in Croatia was most controversial (though the status of Croats in Bosnia-Herzegovina and Vojvodina was an issue for some in Croatia). Some Croats resented the fact that Serbs were overrepresented in the republic's political structures.[88] Some Serbs saw in the Croatian national movement a threatened revival of the extremist Croatian nationalism of the Second World War.[89]

In both Serbia and Croatia, the broader issue looming behind the specific controversies that accompanied constitutional decentralization was the relation between nation and republic. Should the Republic of Serbia be the patron of Serbs elsewhere (or even, as Đurić implied, stretch its borders to encompass them)? To what extent should the Republic of Croatia represent the interests of the Croat nation? In 1971–72, when the Yugoslav regime reimposed ideological orthodoxy, such debates were silenced in both republics. The parameters of public speech contracted dramatically as the Party reasserted its monopoly over the discussion of contentious questions. (Mihailo Đurić's own story illustrates this process: he was arrested for his law faculty remarks in June 1972, sixteen months after making them.[90]) The political crackdown of the 1970s did not bring a renewed centralization of government powers, still less a blanket suppression of national identities or claims. Rather it combined decentralization with repression to produce a model of government that has aptly been dubbed "consociational authoritarianism."[91]

As the regime moved to suppress unacceptable forms of nationalism, it had to set limits on how the concept of "the nations and their republics" could be interpreted. Drawing this line was a delicate matter, for the link between nation and republic—already prominent in federal Yugoslavia's founding documents—had been further highlighted during the period of constitutional decentralization. A comparison between the republican constitutions of 1963 and those of 1974 illustrates this increased emphasis on the republics' role as national homelands and not simply socialist communities. Article 1 of each 1963 republican constitution contained identical language defining the republic as "a state [*državna*] socialist democratic community of the people of [the republic] founded on the power of the working people and on self-management."[92] In this formulation, *"people"* was understood in territorial, not national, terms. (The Slovenian Constitution is conclusive in this regard because Slovenian—unlike Serbian or Croatian—has separate words for *narod,* the nation, and *ljudstvo,* the people.[93] Article 1 of the 1963 Constitution uses *ljudstvo.*) In the 1974 republican constitutions, the first articles were longer, and their symbolically charged phrases were no longer identical. Mixed in with language defining the republics' socialist and self-managing foundations came variations on more nationally tinged formulas. The Socialist Republic of Croatia was now "the national state of the Croatian nation, the state of the Serbian nation in Croatia and the state of the nationalities that live in it."[94] The Socialist Republic of Slovenia was "a state that is founded on the sovereignty of the Slovene nation and the people of Slovenia [and] . . . a socialist self-managing democratic community of working people and citizens, of the Slovene nation and the Italian and Hungarian nationalities."[95] The Socialist Republic of Serbia was "the state of the Serbian nation and of the parts of other nations and nationalities that live and realize their sovereign rights in it."[96]

As Novi Sad legal scholar Tibor Varady has put it: "'Minority' and 'majority' are interlocking concepts strongly influenced by the extent of devolution [of government powers]."[97] It is hardly surprising, therefore, that in the era of constitutional decentralization the status of groups in the minority in a given republic assumed a new prominence. In very many ways (including the arguments put forward and even some of the individuals involved) the controversies of Yugoslavia's decentralization prefigured those of its dissolution. Viewed from this perspective, the Yugoslav regime's "success" in the first period provides an ominous portent of its failure in the second. Its response to the issues posed by decentralization was an increased reliance on the Party's leading role. On the ideological level, the 1970s' renewed insistence on class issues and the primacy of "the working people" meant a decreased emphasis on peoples (nations).[98] On the political and organizational level, Yugoslavia's famous "key" system (i.e., rotating offices to ensure the representation of all groups) reached its fullest development, taking the form it would keep until the state's collapse. At the federal level, the key's operation was territorially defined and constitutionally guaranteed. For example, Article 321 of the 1974 Constitution stipulated that each republic and province would send a representative to the collective presidency.[99] Within each federal unit, however, the key's operation depended primarily upon the Party, working within its own largely extraconstitutional sphere. The republican and provincial constitutions all contained language asserting national equality, but it was the Party's task to translate these phrases into the stuff of daily politics.[100] As political scientist Vladimir Goati has put it (with particular reference to Bosnia-Herzegovina), the national key meant that "politocracy members of diverse ethnic origin succeeded each other in strategic places on the political pyramid according to an order strictly determined in advance."[101] Within each republic, in other words, the institutions of national equality were simultaneously institutions of one-party rule.

The consequence was that Yugoslavia's balancing act between personal and territorial nationality was as dependent upon the Party's organization in practice as it was upon the ideology of self-managing socialism in theory. The regime's overall premise remained (as Kardelj had put it in 1953): "Discrimination is impossible according to the very foundations of the socialist system."[102] It followed that the task of preventing discrimination was understood as one aspect of building socialism. The idea of protecting the rights of minorities through laws and institutions that could function independently of the one-party system was marginal at best; indeed, the very concept of the minority was illegitimate.[103] Explaining why the term *nationality* had replaced *national minority*, a leading Party ideologist asserted that the word *minority* was "unsuited to a self-managing community, in which a person should not feel that he belongs to some sort of national majority or national minority."[104] (This conviction led on occasion to elaborate circumlocutions, as when Slobodan Milošević said of Kosovo's Serbs and Montenegrins, "We cannot say that they are a minority, but it's a fact that there are many fewer of them."[105]) As long as Yugoslav socialism endured, excluding the word *minority* from political life seemed to be merely one more idiosyncrasy of the self-management vocabulary. When first the socialist system and then the state collapsed, however, the dubious status accorded to concepts of minorities and minority rights served to strengthen the chimerical ideal of redrawing borders to make every minority a majority.[106]

Conclusion: Crisis and Collapse

With the economic prosperity and political repression of the 1970s, many of the controversies that had accompanied constitutional decentralization faded into the background. In the next decade, however, the situation changed. Tito's death in 1980 ushered in a period of political stalemate and increasing economic hardship. As the situation worsened, even Party leaders were forced to acknowledge the existence of a crisis. The competing political programs put forward in Serbia, Slovenia, and elsewhere from the mid-1980s on must be understood against this background. They represented competing responses to Yugoslavia's systemic crisis (and not simply "traditional" national grievances reemerging as the regime's grip on public discussion loosened).[107] As the Yugoslav crisis deepened, self-determination took on a new significance: it meant the right to choose one's own way out of an increasingly unendurable situation. Its importance was further heightened by the end of one-party rule in 1989–90. Introducing democracy, the rule of the people, required deciding who "the people" were—who, in other words, belonged to the political community.[108]

As Yugoslavia staggered from crisis to dissolution in 1989–91, the idea of self-determination was omnipresent in political speech. It was a vital part of the mental framework through which politicians formulated their goals, argued with each other, and appealed to their constituents. At this juncture, the unresolved tensions between competing concepts of self-determination that this chapter has analyzed shaped the course of events in three ways. First, the ambiguities of the Yugoslav Constitution's language on self-determination meant that constitutional authority offered little help in adjudicating competing claims. Second, an uncritical acceptance of national self-determination as a sacrosanct value proved a fateful legacy as the multinational Yugoslav state collapsed. Third, the ill-defined concept of "the nations and their republics" survived the socialist system that had regulated its political application, becoming an obstacle (one of many, of course) to the development of civic nationalisms in the postsocialist republics. The remainder of the essay will set out grounds for each of these conclusions.

Questions of self-determination were posed most directly in controversies over secession rights. Debates over secession had flared up intermittently throughout the postwar era, but they gained a new urgency as Yugoslavia's dissolution entered the realm of the thinkable. Did the Yugoslav Constitution guarantee a right to secede, and if so what political subject held that right? Most Western treatments of Yugoslavia's dissolution have dealt with this question only in passing, and (not surprisingly, given basic dissension among former Yugoslavia's constitutional experts) even specialists offer contradictory assertions on whether the Yugoslav Constitution of 1974 conferred a right to republican secession.[109] A more detailed examination of the constitutional debate is thus appropriate here.

Yugoslav debates over secession rights hinged on the interpretation of language (included in every constitution except the 1953 Constitutional Law) referring to "the right of every nation [or people, depending upon the translation of *narod*] to self-determination, including the right to secession." In the context of Yugoslavia's dissolution, proponents of a national (as opposed to republican) right of self-determination identified the nation with Yugoslavia's six officially recognized *narodi* (Croats, Macedonians, Montenegrins, Muslims, Serbs, and Slovenes), apparently taking it for granted that the distinction between *narod* (nation) and *narodnost* (nationality) would survive the socialist regime that had introduced it. This contested premise was central to the Serbian leadership's espousal of national self-determination: most of the non-Serbs living on Serbia's territory in 1990–91 (notably the Albanians) belonged to Yugoslavia's nationalities rather than to its nations.[110]

In the 1974 Constitution the language on self-determination was part of Basic Principle I, which stated:

> The nations of Yugoslavia, proceeding from the right of every nation to self-determination, including the right to secession, on the basis of their will freely expressed in the common struggle of all nations and nationalities in the National Liberation War and Socialist Revolution, and in conformity with their historic aspirations, aware that further consolidation of their brotherhood and unity is in the common interest, have, together with the nationalities with which they live, united in a federal republic of free and equal nations and nationalities and founded

a socialist federal community of working people—the Socialist Federal Republic of Yugoslavia . . .[111]

This language was open to widely divergent interpretations. Its generality is particularly striking because the 1974 Yugoslav Constitution (one of the longest in the world) was notorious for its detailed regulation of matters that in most states are left to legislation.[112] Thus, it seems reasonable to suppose that if the constitution's framers had wished to include an unambiguous provision for the secession of any group (however defined) they would not have been deterred by considerations of space. The constitution's language on self-determination, however, was intended to legitimate the state's creation rather than to facilitate its peaceful dissolution: it offers one more indication that the leaders who created socialist Yugoslavia did not envision the possibility of the state's outliving the Party.[113]

Earlier debates over secession rights had hinged mainly on whether the constitution's language on self-determination described an *existing* right or one that had been used once and for all in the act of joining federal Yugoslavia.[114] The 1989–91 debates took a different course. Official actors on all sides affirmed the existence of a continuing right to self-determination including secession, effectively removing this issue from the agenda.[115] The debate focused instead on two interrelated issues. The first was who could exercise the right to self-determination—the (citizens of a) republic or the (members of a) nation. The second was who could establish a procedure for realizing that right. Could a republic act unilaterally to leave Yugoslavia, or was some form of all-Yugoslav agreement required?

Opposing stances on these issues crystallized in September 1989, when the Slovenian legislature adopted a set of amendments to the republic's constitution.[116] Amendment 10 stated that Slovenia was part of Yugoslavia "on the basis of the lasting, integral and inalienable right of the Slovene nation to self-determination, which also includes the right to secession and to association [with other nations]." Amendment 72 asserted that the Slovenian legislature could determine the procedures through which the republic could exercise the right to secession.[117] The Yugoslav Constitutional Court was asked by the Federal Parliament to assess whether these amendments were contrary to the federal constitution. In an opinion published on February 23, 1990, the court asserted that "the peoples of Yugoslavia and their socialist republics have the right to self-determination, which includes in itself the right to secession." The court went on to say, however, that establishing procedures for realizing the right to self-determination was a matter for the federal constitution, not the republican ones, and that it could be decided only "with the agreement of all socialist republics and autonomous provinces." The court's conclusion (one it had no means of enforcing, however) was that some portions of Amendment 72 to the Slovenian Constitution were contrary to the federal constitution. To support its opinion the court cited, inter alia, the Constitution's Basic Principles and also Article 5, one clause of which stated that the borders of the SFRY "may not be altered without the consent of all Republics and Autonomous Provinces."[118]

In the spring of 1991—with Slovenia's "disassociation" from the Yugoslav state planned for June—members of an interrepublican working group attempted to reach agreement on a procedure for realizing the "right to self-determination."[119] Their deliberations were overtaken by events, and the course of Yugoslavia's dissolution was determined by political and military actions rather than by the outcome of constitutional debates. Indeed, the most influential legal opinions connected with Yugoslavia's dissolution—those issued by the Badinter Commission at the request of the European Community—did not attempt to determine whether the Yugoslav Constitution granted republics the right to secede. Rather, the commission asserted that the Yugoslav state was "in the process of dissolution." In this context, its endorsement of the inviolability of republican borders was based primarily on the international law principle *uti possidetis* (previously applied to postcolonial territorial disputes).[120]

If constitutional debates did not decide political outcomes, what was their significance in Yugoslavia's endgame? Would it have played out differently—perhaps with less bloodshed—if the constitution *had* contained unambiguous language on secession? A comparison with the Soviet Union at least suggests this possibility. In the Soviet case, as Edward Walker has persuasively argued, the fact that the constitution contained an explicit assertion of the Union Republics' right to secede (Article 72 in the "Brezhnev" Constitution of 1977) empowered pro-independence forces at the republican level and constrained the actions of pro-Union ones. This is not to say that the Soviet Union's dissolution followed a defined constitutional procedure. Soviet constitutional drafters not having intended secession to be a real possibility any more than Yugoslav ones did, no such procedure was in place at the end of the 1980s—and events quickly outstripped attempts to create one.[121] Nevertheless, at a time of state crisis, the Soviet Constitution—unlike the Yugoslav one—provided a clear standard to which political actors could and did appeal. It is difficult to imagine the March 1991 exchange between Kučan and Milošević cited at the beginning of this chapter taking place at a summit meeting of Soviet republican leaders.

The second legacy of socialist Yugoslavia's treatment of self-determination emerges most clearly if one contrasts Yugoslavia's path through the twentieth century with a general pattern seen with variations throughout much of Central and Eastern Europe. In this region, the First World War and the associated collapse of multinational empires ushered in an era marked by often-brutal efforts to make national and political lines congruent.[122] This process culminated in the massive eliminations and transfers of populations that took place during and after the Second World War.

In the second half of the twentieth century, the geopolitical context changed in ways that generally privileged the maintenance of existing borders over the implementation of the principles of nationalism. Both Soviet control and the larger constraints of the Cold War made the pursuit of irredentist goals unrealistic during the communist era. Since the collapse of communism, different factors—largely connected with aspirations to "join Europe"—have had a similar effect. Thus, in much of Central and Eastern Europe, irredentist claims that were at the center of political life between the First and Second World Wars have moved to its margins in the postcommunist era. Mainstream politicians and their publics appear to have internalized (if not fully legitimized) the borders fixed after the First or Second World Wars.

Bulgarian politics offer the most striking illustration of this pattern.[123] From the late nineteenth century through the Second World War, Bulgaria's foreign policy and often its domestic politics were driven by the conviction that Bulgaria's "rightful" borders were those of San Stefano (the 1878 treaty reversed at the Congress of Berlin). Yet irredentism has been marginal to postcommunist Bulgarian politics; indeed, in 1992 Bulgaria signaled the final abandonment of its long-standing claims to Vardar Macedonia when it became the first state to recognize an independent Macedonia.[124] The contrast between interwar and present-day Hungary, though less dramatic, reflects a similar evolution. Conceptions of rightful borders (in this case, pre-Trianon borders) have been more prominent in the political discourse of postcommunist Hungary than in Bulgaria, and Diaspora issues—especially those concerning Hungarians in Transylvania—have sometimes sparked irredentist rhetoric. Nevertheless, no major party has endorsed border revisions.[125] In general, although nationalism has been prominent in the region's postcommunist political life, issues concerning the status and rights of minorities have loomed larger than lost lands.[126]

During the postwar decades, when existing international borders were gradually gaining acceptance as facts of political life throughout most of the region, the lands and peoples of Yugoslavia followed a different path. Yugoslavia's rebirth as a multi-national state after the Second World War meant that the war and its aftermath did not produce the large-scale unmixings of peoples seen elsewhere in the region (with the important exception of the expulsion of the ethnic Germans).[127] Moreover, the continued existence of a Yugoslav state allowed competing Serbian and Croatian maximalist national programs to pass through the twentieth century without confronting the political and institutional reality of international borders. For those so inclined, it remained possible (certainly more possible than it was in Bulgaria or Hungary) to view them as deferred rather than defeated ideals. It is unsurprising, then, that variants of these programs reemerged at the moment of Yugoslavia's dissolution.[128] They proved most powerful where they could plausibly be coupled with the claim to "self-determination," which was invoked as a matter of self-evident justice regardless of how destructive its implementation might be in areas of mixed population.[129]

My third and final conclusion concerns the ways that the political legacy of "the nations and their republics" operated in the postsocialist context. I have argued throughout that this concept was one of socialist Yugoslavia's foundation-stones.[130] As a result Yugoslavia's political discourse frequently merged territorial and personal nationality, casting republics as the political representatives of nations. During the socialist era, this principle's political application was strictly regulated by the Party, which had primary responsibility for balancing the competing claims of territorial and personal nationality within each republic. Under the Party's tutelage, each socialist republic functioned (even if imperfectly) as a multinational polity. In the postsocialist and post-Yugoslav context, however, the idea that each republic belonged to a particular nation took on a new significance, becoming a significant obstacle to the development of civic nationalisms.

Making this argument does not mean denying the importance of other reasons for the weakness of civic nationalisms in the post-Yugoslav states. In fact, this outcome was strongly overdetermined. To begin with, the idea that each state belongs primarily to a certain ethnic nation has enjoyed broad acceptance in Central and Eastern Europe, although its political application has varied greatly from state to state.[131] Moreover, the historical experience of many regions of former Yugoslavia was one in which each change of rulers meant increased status and power for one religious or ethnonational group and decline or even disaster for others. This process, which sociologist Veljko Vujačić has aptly called the "never-ending cycle of status-reversal," inevitably strengthened ethnic concepts of group identity at the expense of the territorial ones that could have laid the basis for civic nationalisms.[132] The events of the Second World War, which remained in living memory during Yugoslavia's dissolution, provided a potent basis for the production of a sense of endangerment among some of the former Yugoslavia's "new minorities"—above all among Serbs outside Serbia.[133] Finally, leading politicians in Serbia and Croatia sought to bolster their own positions by deepening ethnonational divisions and undercutting civic options both in their own republics and in Bosnia-Herzegovina.[134]

Clearly, then, the Yugoslav socialist regime does not bear sole responsibility for the postsocialist weakness of civic nationalism. Yet it remains fair to note that even given forty-five years in power and two generations of European peace, the regime failed to overcome the obstacles it had inherited. In this era, urbanization, secularization, and associated modernizing processes led to an unprecedented degree of social integration among Yugoslavia's peoples, but the regime failed to promote a corresponding political integration. On the Yugoslav level, it defined civic identity exclusively in terms of loyalty to the precepts of "socialist self-management"—a decision that chained the fate of the Yugoslav state to the fate of the socialist project.[135] At the same time, by constructing a federal system in which territorial institutions were legitimated by ethnonational ideologies, the regime weakened the conceptual framework for civic identities at the republican level.[136] In the circumstances of Yugoslavia's dissolution—when this problematic legacy was reinforced by political and later military intervention across republican borders—it is not surprising that republics could more easily marshal the institutional resources to assert themselves as independent states against the collapsing center than the political resources to achieve equal legitimacy in the eyes of all their citizens.

Notes

1. I would like to thank Professor Veljko Vujačić of Oberlin College, Professor Peter Vodopivec of the University of Ljubljana, and Dr. Predrag J. Marković of the Institute for Contemporary History, Belgrade, for their insightful reactions to earlier versions

of this essay. My thanks are also due to both of this volume's coeditors, Jasna Dragović-Soso and Lenard J. Cohen, for their helpful critiques, and to Dr. Dragović-Soso especially for organizing the June 2004 conference on Rethinking Yugoslavia's Dissolution, at which I received many useful comments. Finally, I gratefully acknowledge the opportunity to present an earlier version of the project when the Institute of Slavic, East European, and Eurasian Studies at UC Berkeley invited me to give the Third Annual Peter N. Kujachich Lecture in November of 2003.

2. On a conceptual level, this essay owes its major intellectual debt to Rogers Brubaker's "Nationhood and the National Question in the Soviet Union and Its Successor States: An Institutionalist Account," in Rogers Brubaker (ed.), *Nationalism Reframed: Nationhood and the National Question in the New Europe* (Cambridge: Cambridge University Press, 1996), pp. 23–54. Although my analysis of socialist Yugoslavia naturally differs from Brubaker's of the USSR, I share his focus on the interplay between personal and territorial nationality and his basic premise that "Institutional definitions of nationhood did not so much constrain action as constitute basic categories of political understanding. . . . As political space expanded, they made specific types of political action conceivable, plausible, even compelling, transforming the collapse of a regime into the disintegration of the state" (p. 24).

More specifically, my emphasis on the socialist regime's role in structuring the conflicts of Yugoslavia's dissolution has been influenced by several works. The most important are Vojin Dimitrijević's "Sukobi oko Ustava iz 1974.," in Nebojša Popov (ed.), *Srpska strana rata: Trauma i katarza u istorijskom pamćenju* (Belgrade: Republika, 1996), pp. 447–71; Zoran Đinđić's *Jugoslavija kao nedovršena država* (Novi Sad: Književna zajednica Novog Sada, 1988); Mitja Žagar's "Nekaj hipotez o kvadraturi kroga: Ustava SFRJ in proces osamosvajanja Republike Slovenije," *Razprave in gradivo* 29–30 (1994–95), pp. 231–59; and the works of Dejan Jović, particularly his *Jugoslavija—država koja je odumrla: Uspon, kriza i pad Četvrte Jugoslavije (1974.–1990.)* (Zagreb: Prometej and Belgrade: Samizdat B92, 2003), and "Fear of Becoming *Minority* as a Motivator of Conflict in the Former Yugoslavia," *Balkanologie*, Vol. 5, Nos. 1–2 (2001), pp. 21–37. While their arguments differ in important respects, all of these authors emphasize that the failure of the Yugoslav state cannot be understood apart from the socialist experience. Of course, neither they nor I would place sole responsibility for the Yugoslav catastrophe on the events and political choices of the socialist period. Inherited concepts and institutions certainly shaped the options available to individual politicians during Yugoslavia's dissolution, but they did not predetermine their choices.

3. The government of Croatia invoked the doctrine of republican self-determination to justify its own independence but followed the logic of national self-determination when it backed forces fighting for a Croat state in Bosnia, whereas the government of Serbia supported a right of self-determination for Serbs in other republics but not for non-Serbs in Serbia. (The latter issue is complicated by the fact that most of Serbia's non-Serb inhabitants—including Albanians and Hungarians, though not the Slavic Muslims of the Sandžak region—belonged to "nationalities," defined as groups ethnically linked with a state outside Yugoslavia. As the discussion below indicates, those who claimed a right of self-determination for nations generally denied it to nationalities.)

4. See Lenard J. Cohen, *Broken Bonds: Yugoslavia's Disintegration and Balkan Politics in Transition* (Boulder: Westview Press, 1995), p. 176.

5. Croatia's Serbs, who made up approximately 12 percent of the republic's population, held diverse political views. In particular, their attitudes varied along regional and urban-rural lines. The Belgrade-backed movement for territorial autonomy or

independence came primarily from the Serb-majority districts where approximately one-quarter of Croatia's Serbs lived. The beginning of March had seen fighting between Serbs and Croatian police units in Pakrac (Western Slavonia), and clashes took place at Croatia's Plitvice Lakes during the Split meeting itself. See Cohen, *Broken Bonds,* pp. 126–35 for Serbs in Croatia and chapter 7 for the political context of the inter-republican summits. For events in Croatia see also Ivo Goldstein, *Croatia: A History* (London: C. Hurst & Co., 1999), pp. 218–22, and Slobodanka Kovačević and Putnik Dajić, *Hronologija jugoslovenske krize 1942–1993* (Belgrade: Institut za evropske studije, 1994).

6. All quotations from this meeting are taken from a transcript cited in Audrey Budding, "Serbian Nationalism in the Twentieth Century: Historical Background and Context" (expert report prepared for the Prosecution in the Trial of Slobodan Milošević, 2002), pp. 68–71. The report is available online at http://hague.bard.edu/icty_info.html. For this citation, see note 318.

7. Budding, "Serbian Nationalism," note 329.

8. These figures are taken from Dennison Rusinow, "Yugoslavia's Disintegration and the Ottoman Past," in L. Carl Brown (ed.), *Imperial Legacy: The Ottoman Imprint on the Balkans and the Middle East* (New York: Columbia University Press, 1996), p. 80.

9. For the dual meaning of *narod* as *etnos* or *demos* see especially Vojin Dimitrijević, "The Absolute Nation State: Post-Communist Constitutions," *Jugoslovenska revija za međunarodno pravo* #2–3 (1992), pp. 167–77. Cf. the discussion in Geneviève Zubrzycki, "'We, the Polish Nation': Ethnic and Civic Visions of Nationhood in Post-Communist Constitutional Debates," *Theory and Society*, Vol. 30 (2001), pp. 635–36.

10. To give one of many possible examples, Article 171 of the 1974 Yugoslav Constitution states: "Members of the nations and nationalities of Yugoslavia shall, on the territory of each Republic and/or Autonomous Province, have the right to instruction in their own language in conformity with statute" (*The Constitution of the Socialist Federal Republic of Yugoslavia,* trans. Marko Pavičić for the Secretariat of the Federal Assembly Information Service [Ljubljana: Delo, 1974]. This volume is the source for all English translations of the 1974 Constitution cited in this chapter).

11. Morton Benson, *Srpskohrvatsko-engleski rečnik,* 2nd ed. revised (Belgrade: Prosveta, 1979).

12. Budding, "Serbian Nationalism," note 329.

13. Benedict Anderson, *Imagined Communities: Reflections on the Origin and Spread of Nationalism* (London: Verso, 1991).

14. George Schöpflin, "Nationalism and Ethnicity in Europe, East and West," in Charles Kupchan (ed.), *Nationalism and Nationalities in the New Europe* (Ithaca: Cornell University Press, 1995), p. 39. I follow Schöpflin in emphasizing the simultaneous existence of both dimensions rather than classifying nationalisms as wholly civic or ethnic as some other scholars have done. For thoughtful critiques of such classifications, see Tim Nieguth, "Beyond Dichotomy: Concepts of the Nation and the Distribution of Membership," *Nations and Nationalism*, Vol. 5, No. 2 (1999), pp. 155–73, and Zubrzycki, "We, the Polish Nation," pp. 629–30 and *passim.*

15. For the Austro-Marxists, see especially Leszek Kolakowski, *Main Currents of Marxism: Its Origins, Growth, and Dissolution* (Oxford: Oxford University Press, 1978), pp. 2:285–90. Two excellent discussions of Leninist and Stalinist doctrine are Terry Martin, "An Affirmative Action Empire: The Soviet Union as the Highest Form of Imperialism," in Ronald Grigor Suny and Terry Martin (eds.), *A State of Nations: Empire and Nation-Making in the Age of Lenin and Stalin* (Oxford: Oxford University

Press, 2001), pp. 67–90, and Yuri Slezkine, "The USSR as a Communal Apartment, or How a Socialist State Promoted Ethnic Particularism," *Slavic Review*, Vol. 53, No. 2 (1994), pp. 414–52.

16. Walker Connor, *The National Question in Marxist-Leninist Theory and Strategy* (Princeton: Princeton University Press, 1984), p. 35.

17. For overviews in English of the CPY's interwar policies, see chapter 1 of Paul Shoup, *Communism and the Yugoslav National Question* (New York: Columbia University Press, 1968), and chapters 2–3 of Aleksa Djilas, *The Contested Country: Yugoslav Unity and Communist Revolution, 1919–1953* (Cambridge: Harvard University Press, 1991). Djilas offers (pp. 74–76) an interesting analysis of differences between the Comintern and CPY approaches to Yugoslavia.

18. The new policy took shape between the CPY's Fourth Land Conference of December 1934 and the CC CPY's Plenum of June 1935 (held in Split and generally known as the Split Plenum). See Dušan Lukač, *Radnički pokret u Jugoslaviji i nacionalno pitanje 1918–1941* (Belgrade: Institut za savremenu istoriju, 1972), pp. 271–303; Dragoljub S. Petrović, *Konstituisanje federalne Srbije* (Belgrade: Nova knjiga, 1988), pp. 19–33; and Dragan Subotić, "Komunistička Partija Jugoslavije o federalizmu, 1918–1941," *Gledišta*, Nos. 3–4 (1991), pp. 96–100.

19. Cited in Lukač, *Radnički pokret*, p. 292. In this passage, I have translated *samoopredeljenje* as "self-determination" and *samoopredeljivanje* as "the process of self-determination."

20. For the Serbian parliament question, see Lukač, *Radnički pokret*, pp. 292–93, n. 47.

21. See Subotić, "Komunistička Partija," p. 98; Lukač, *Radnički pokret*, pp. 358–59; and Josip Broz Tito, "Pismo za Srbiju" (November 1936) in *Nacionalno pitanje u djelima klasika Marksizma i u dokumentima i praksi KPJ/SKJ* (Zagreb: Naklada CDD, 1978), p. 259.

22. Petrović, *Konstituisanje*, pp. 29–30; Lukač, *Radnički pokret*, pp. 292 and 348–49.

23. For more detail on Party organization, see Lukač, *Radnički pokret*, and Edib Hasanagić (ed.), *Komunistička Partija Jugoslavije 1919–1941, Izabrani dokumenti* (Zagreb: Školska knjiga, 1959). For Bosnia-Herzegovina's changing status in the CPY, see also Drago Borovčanin, "Bosna i Hercegovina u odlukama Drugog Zasjedanja AVNOJ-a," in *AVNOJ i Narodnooslobodilačka borba u Bosni i Hercegovini (1943–1943), Materijali sa naučnog skupa održanog u Sarajevu 22. i 23. novembra 1973. godine* (Belgrade: RAD, 1974), pp. 587–88.

24. From "O stvaranju KP Hrvatske i KP Slovenije" (July–August 1935) in *Nacionalno pitanje*, p. 255. Cf. Djilas, *Contested Country*, pp. 100–101.

25. Petrović, *Konstituisanje*, p. 28.

26. The full text is given in Slobodan Nešović and Branko Petranović (eds.), *AVNOJ i revolucija: Tematska zbirka dokumenata 1941–1945* (Belgrade: Narodna knjiga, 1983), pp. 452–53.

27. For the documentation question see Miodrag Zečević and Bogdan Lekić, *Državne granice i unutrašnja teritorijalna podela Jugoslavije* (Belgrade: Građevinska knjiga, 1991), especially pp. 19–23. There is generally more documentation for relatively minor postwar border adjustments than for the basic decisions involved in creating the federal units. For the former, see Bogdan Lekić, "Administrativne granice u Jugoslaviji posle Drugog svetskog rata," *Istorija 20. veka*, Vol. 10, Nos. 1–2 (1992), pp. 145–62.

   An overview covering many of the postwar border issues appears in Ivo Banac, *With Stalin against Tito: Cominformist Splits in Yugoslav Communism* (Ithaca: Cornell University Press, 1988), pp. 103–11; also useful though less detailed is John Lampe, *Yugoslavia as History: Twice There Was a Country*, 2nd ed. (Cambridge: Cambridge University

Press, 2000), pp. 231–32. Many works on this subject have appeared in former Yugoslavia. Of these I have used mainly Dušan Bilandžić, *Hrvatska moderna povijest* (Zagreb: Golden Marketing, 1999), pp. 224–26; Ljubo Boban, *Hrvatske granice od 1918. do 1993. godine* (Zagreb: Školska knjiga and HAZU, 1993), chapter 8; *The Creation and Changes of the Internal Borders of Yugoslavia* (Belgrade: Ministry of Information of the Republic of Serbia, 1991); articles in *Istorija 20. veka* Vol. 10, Nos. 1–2 (1992) [special issue on Yugoslavia's borders]; and Zečević and Lekić, *Državne granice.*

28. Many authors have noted the general primacy given to historic borders. See, e.g., Aleksandar Pavković, *The Fragmentation of Yugoslavia: Nationalism and War in the Balkans,* 2nd ed. (New York: St. Martin's Press, LLC, 2000), pp. 48–49; Boban, *Hrvatske granice,* p. 51; and Zečević and Lekić, *Državne granice,* p. 20.

   The Partisans' use of prior borders (from various historical periods) as a basis was explicit at the February 24, 1945, session of the AVNOJ Presidium, when a speaker referred to "the population of the federal units in the current borders" in discussing how many AVNOJ representatives each federal unit (i.e., future republic) should have. In this context, the units were defined as follows: "SLOVENIA in the borders of the former Drava banovina; CROATIA in the borders of the former Savska banovina with thirteen counties of the former Primorje banovina and the county of Dubrovnik from the former Zeta banovina; BOSNIA-HERZEGOVINA in the borders determined by the Congress of Berlin; SERBIA in the borders before the Balkan Wars with the counties taken from Bulgaria by the Peace of Versailles; MACEDONIA—Yugoslav territory south of Kačanik and Ristovac; MONTENEGRO in the borders before the Balkan Wars with the counties of Berane and Kostor and with Plav and Gusinje" (*Zakonodavni rad Predsedništva Antifašističkog veća narodnog oslobođenja Jugoslavije i Predsedništva privremene narodne skupštine DFJ [19 novembra 1944–27 oktobra 1945] po stenografskim beleškama i drugim izvorima* [Belgrade: Prezidijum Narodne skupštine FNRJ, 1951, p. 58). As Ivo Banac has noted, the final republican borders incorporated a number of changes from those referred to in this document (above and beyond the changes produced by designating the boundaries of Kosovo and Vojvodina and dividing the Sandžak). See Banac, *With Stalin against Tito,* pp. 103–4.

29. Top Partisan leaders were initially uncomfortable with Bosnia's anomalous position and reluctant to grant it the same status as the other future republics. According to participant accounts, they yielded to the arguments of Bosnian representatives just before AVNOJ's second session convened. See Borovčanin, "Bosna i Hercegovina," pp. 589–90, and Nešović and Petranović, eds., *AVNOJ i revolucija,* pp. 432–45.

   Unlike the Soviets, the Partisans did not set out explicit standards for republican status. In the Soviet case, a "Union Republic" had to meet three criteria: a population majority belonging to a single nation, at least a million inhabitants, and a location on the USSR's external border (to allow it to use its right of secession). Yugoslav constitutional theorists explicitly rejected these criteria, which would have disqualified both Bosnia-Herzegovina and Montenegro from republican status (Frits W. Hondius, *The Yugoslav Community of Nations* [The Hague: Mouton, 1968], p. 145).

30. It is unclear exactly when the Partisan leaders decided what Kosovo's status would be. The first organizational decision that placed Kosovo within Serbia was the subordination of the Kosovo-Metohija military command to the Serbian one in September 1944, but this decision was itself superseded in February 1945 when martial law was introduced in Kosovo in the face of a major revolt by Albanian groups (Petrović, *Konstituisanje,* pp. 80–81 and 124).

31. For the Sandžak's status during and after the war see Petrović, *Konstituisanje,* pp. 81–87 and 100–9. Petrović provides abundant archival support for his contention

(p. 102) "that until February 1945 the Sandžak, albeit incompletely and inconsistently, was being built as a separate political unit *[posebna politička jedinica]* in the new Yugoslavia." Cf. Zoran Lakić, "Zemaljsko antifašističko vijeće narodnog oslobođenja Sandžaka," in *AVNOJ i Narodnooslobodilačka borba*, pp. 678–94, and Banac, *With Stalin against Tito*, pp. 100–2.

32. For the Sandžak Party leaders' stance, see their February 6, 1945, letter to the CC LCY (Petrović, *Konstituisanje*, pp. 102–3). For the census figures see Banac, *With Stalin against Tito*, p. 100, n. 121. The Sandžak's status was the subject of an unusually open debate at an AVNOJ Presidium session held on February 24, 1945 (see *Zakonodavni rad Pretsedništva*, pp. 51–59). Even after the Presidium approved the decision, some Sandžak leaders refused to sign the document endorsing it. Nešović and Petranović (eds.), *AVNOJ i revolucija*, p. 730 n. 4, emphasize that such open opposition was extremely unusual.

33. See Petrović, *Konstituisanje*, pp. 102–5; the quotation is from p. 105. Cf. Lampe's conclusion that "Historically and ethnically, the Sandžak was closer to Bosnia-Herzegovina, but the disproportionate role of the Montenegrin Partisans in the Second World War made their republic the safer custodian of this volatile region for the Communist regime" (Lampe, *Yugoslavia as History*, p. 232).

34. While the term *Vojvodina* had a long history under the Habsburgs, it did not always designate the same territory. For its development, see Stevan K. Pavlowitch, *Serbia: The History of an Idea* (New York: New York University Press, 2002), pp. 20 and 46–47.

35. In the CPY's internal wartime rivalries over Vojvodina, the main bone of contention was Srem/Srijem between the Sava and Danube Rivers (historically part of Slavonia but with a Serb majority). See Banac, *With Stalin against Tito*, pp. 101–2, and for more detail Ranko Končar, "Problem autonomije Vojvodine u kontekstu odluka Drugog zasedanja AVNOJ-a," in *AVNOJ i Narodnooslobodilačka borba*, pp. 622–31, and Petrović, *Konstituisanje*, pp. 60–70. Also useful is the detailed discussion of wartime territorial divisions, including those affecting Vojvodina, in Slobodan D. Milošević, "Okupatorska podela Jugoslavije 1941–1945," *Istorija 20. veka*, Vol. 10, Nos. 1–2, pp. 125–44.

36. For the (relatively minor) differences between "Autonomous Region" and "Autonomous Province" status, see Hondius, *Yugoslav Community*, pp. 158–60. Kosovo was upgraded to "Autonomous Province" status in the 1963 Constitution (Hondius, *Yugoslav Community*, pp. 306–7).
   A Vojvodina assembly (elected by Slavs only) proclaimed union with Serbia on November 25, 1918. Lazar Rakić, "Vojvodina u vreme stvaranja jugoslovenske države 1918. godine," in *Srbija 1918. godine i stvaranje jugoslovenske države* (Belgrade: Istorijski institut, 1989), pp. 223–32, offers a useful analysis of these events.
   For the 1931 and 1948 census figures see table 60a in Bogoljub Kočović, *Etnički i demografski razvoj u Jugoslaviji od 1921. do 1991. godine* (Paris: Bibliothèque Dialogue, 1998).

37. A Party commission headed by Milovan Djilas drew up the border between Vojvodina and Croatia. See Ljubodrag Dimić, "Nekoliko dokumenata o privremenoj administrativnoj granici između jugoslovenskih republika Srbije i Hrvatske," *Istorija 20. veka*, Vol. 10, Nos. 1–2 (1992), pp. 231–46, and Boban, *Hrvatske granice*, pp. 52–57.

38. For a point-by-point discussion of Croatia's borders see Boban, *Hrvatske granice*, pp. 52–60.

39. For the Venetian and Habsburg history of Dalmatia see Goldstein, *Croatia*, pp. 29–32 and 58. For Dalmatia's wartime history and the postwar decisions, including the intense rivalries between Dalmatian and Croatian party leaders, see Jill A. Irvine, *The Croat*

Question: Partisan Politics in the Formation of the Yugoslav Socialist State (Boulder: West-view Press, 1993), pp. 167–70 and 224–25.

40. For the border between Croatia and Slovenia, which included several controversial aspects, see Boban, *Hrvatske granice*, pp. 58–60, and Zečević and Lekić, *Državne granice,* pp. 34–36. For the census figures see Kočović, *Etnički i demografski razvoj,* tables 55b and 56b.

41. Ernest Gellner, *Nations and Nationalism* (Ithaca: Cornell University Press, 1983), p. 1.

42. See Pavković, *Fragmentation of Yugoslavia,* p. 51, for the Serb and Croat percentages. For more detail on the distribution of Serbs and Croats and for Slovenia, see the 1948 census figures given in Kočović, *Etnički i demografski razvoj,* tables 54a through 64b.

43. See, for example, Kosta Čavoški, "The Formation of Borders and the Serbian Question," in *The Creation and Changes of the Internal Borders of Yugoslavia,* pp. 33–56. Čavoški had published a similar evaluation of Serbia's borders as early as 1986; see Jasna Dragović-Soso, *"Saviours of the Nation": Serbia's Intellectual Opposition and the Revival of Nationalism* (London: Hurst & Company, 2002), pp. 84–86.

    It should be stressed that the border decisions cannot be considered in isolation. Veljko Vujačić's insightful "Institutional Origins of Contemporary Serbian National-ism," *East European Constitutional Review,* Vol. 5, No. 4 (1996), pp. 51–61, takes account of both Serbian national grievances over the construction of federal units and Serbs' political overrepresentation in Bosnia-Herzegovina and Croatia to argue (p. 60) that "the fatal combination of an institutional grievance and institutional overrepresen-tation provided Serbian nationalism both with a cause and a constituency."

44. For the conception of "Serbian lands" see Milan Vesović and Kosta Nikolić *Ujedinjene srpske zemlje: Ravnogorski nacionalni program* (Belgrade: Vreme knjige, 1996).

45. Milan Borković and Venceslav Glišić (eds.), *Osnivački kongres KP Srbije* (Belgrade: Institut za istoriju radničkog pokreta Srbije, 1972), p. 213. For Tito's view of borders in the immediate postwar period see also Jović, *Jugoslavija,* pp. 147–48.

46. Cited in Petrović, *Konstituisanje,* p. 105.

47. *Osnivački kongres KP Srbije,* p. 210.

48. Zoran Đinđić's essay "Jugoslavija kao nedovršena država" (in his book of the same name), pp. 25–27, offers a perceptive discussion of this point.

49. *Constitution of the Federal Peoples Republic of Yugoslavia* (Washington: Embassy of the Federal Peoples Republic of Yugoslavia, 1946). All English translations of the 1946 Constitution cited in this chapter are taken from this version. For more on this point—especially the concept of Yugoslavia's peoples as founders of the republics—see Hondius, *Yugoslav Community,* pp. 137–40.

50. In the original, "[na osnovu] prava na samoopredeljenje, uključujući pravo na otce-pljenje." The 1946 translation cited here renders *otcepljenje* as "separation"; official translations of a similar phrase in the 1974 Constitution's Basic Principle 1 (cited below) use "secession."

51. Hondius, *Yugoslav Community,* pp. 141–43, cites Pijade's letter (published in *Vojno-politički glasnik* No. 10 of 1950) extensively; the translation given here is his. Hondius also cites (p. 141) Yugoslav debates on the consummation of the right to secession. For Lenin's similarly equivocal response to a query about the possibility of secession, see Connor, *National Question,* p. 35.

    Some leading Western specialists have asserted that the 1946 constitution contained a republican right to secession. See, for example, Lampe, *Yugoslavia as History,* p. 234. It should be noted that the language in regard to self-determination was virtually identical in the constitutions of 1946, 1963, and 1974. (It was omitted only in the Constitutional Law of 1953.) Any argument for a different significance in 1946 must rest on the location of the relevant language: it was in Article 1 of the 1946 Constitution but in the Basic Principles in those of 1963 and 1974. For this point, see Monika Beckmann-Petey, *Der jugoslawische Föderalismus* (Munich: R. Oldenbourg Verlag, 1984), p. 128. By contrast, every Soviet constitution endowed Union Republics with an explicit right to secession. See chapter 2 of Edward W. Walker, *Dissolution: Sovereignty and the Breakup of the Soviet Union* (Lanham: Rowman & Littlefield Publishers, Inc., 2003).

52. See Hondius, *Yugoslav Community*, pp. 145–48, for an analysis of national and republican sovereignty in the 1946 Constitution.

53. Đinđić, *Jugoslavija kao nedovršena država*, 28. Cf. Slobodan Samardžić, "Federalizam u Švajcarskoj i Jugoslaviji—ustavni koncepti i političke institucije," in Tomas Flajner and Slobodan Samardžić (eds.), *Federalizam i problem manjina u višeetničkim zajednicama: uporedna analiza Švajcarske i Jugoslavije* (Belgrade: Institut za evropske studije, 1995), pp. 95–98.

54. For the struggles over decentralization in the late 1950s and early 1960s (and especially the crucial March 1962 Executive Committee Meeting of the CC LCY), two excellent sources are Božo Repe, "Utrinki iz bližnjega leta 1962," *Teorija in praksa*, Vol. 26, Nos. 11–12 (1989), pp. 1498–511 and Vol. 27, Nos. 1–2 (1990), pp. 224–31, and Mile Bjelajac, "Karakter jugoslovenskog centralizma u svetlu analize tajne sednice Izvršnog komiteta CK SKJ marta 1962. godine," paper delivered at the "Dijalog istoričara/povijesničara" on September 19–22, 2002. I am grateful to Dr. Bjelajac for a helpful discussion of the issues and for sharing the text of his paper with me. For the structure and functioning of the mature Yugoslav system, Steven L. Burg's *Conflict and Cohesion in Socialist Yugoslavia* (Princeton: Princeton University Press, 1983) remains an outstanding analysis.

55. Slezkine, "The USSR as a Communal Apartment," p. 450. See also Walker, *Dissolution*, p. 30.

56. See Hondius, *Yugoslav Community*, pp. 182–85.

57. English translations of this and other passages from the 1963 Constitution are taken from *The Constitution of the Socialist Federal Republic of Yugoslavia*, trans. Petar Mijušković (Belgrade: Secretariat for Information of the Federal Executive Council, 1963). In the original, this part of Article 41 runs: "Građaninu je zajemčena sloboda izražavanje svoje narodnosti i kulture, kao i sloboda upotrebe svog jezika. Građanin nije dužan da se izjašnjava kojoj narodnosti pripada niti da se opredeljuje za jednu od narodnosti." Article 170 of the 1974 Constitution asserts the citizen's right not to declare and not to choose a nationality, using very similar language.

58. See Dušan Kecmanović, "His Father Saved Him," in his *Ethnic Times: Exploring Ethnonationalism in the Former Yugoslavia* (Westport, CT: Praeger, 2002). Another telling anecdote is "Prove You Are a Serb" in the same volume. The first-person accounts collected in Svetlana Broz's *Good People in an Evil Time: Portraits of Complicity and Resistance in the Bosnian War*, ed. Laurie Kain Hart, trans. Ellen Elias-Bursać (New York: Other Press, 2004) provide several examples of "mistaken" national identities. See, for example, pp. 161–65.

59. From the 1958 LCY Program, *Program Saveza komunista Jugoslavije*, pp. 147–48.

60. Milivoje Kovačević, *Ustavni amandmani XX do XLII sa objašnjenjima tekstova i pojmova* (Belgrade: Zavod za izdavanje uđbenika Socijalističke Republike Srbije, 1971), p. 26. Similarly, a Croatian textbook explained that "Yugoslavism can only be a sign of belonging to the Yugoslav socialist community of equal nations." Josip Sruk, *Ustavno*

uredenje Socijalističke Federativne Republike Jugoslavije (Zagreb: Informator, 1976), p. 229.

I discuss the development of the regime's stance on Yugoslavism in "Yugoslavs into Serbs: Serbian National Identity, 1961–1971," *Nationalities Papers* 25/3 (1997), pp. 407–26. See also Dejan Jović's illuminating "Yugoslavism and Yugoslav Communism: From Tito to Kardelj" in Dejan Djokić (ed.), *Yugoslavism: Histories of a Failed Idea, 1918–1992* (London: Hurst & Company, 2003), pp. 157–181. Jović traces the triumph of Kardelj's exclusively non-national concept of Yugoslavism over Tito's more nationally tinged idea and makes the important point that "Kardelj's concept marginalised Tito. . . . Tito was still allowed to defend 'Yugoslavism', but no other politicians would escape the 'unitarist' label if they attempted the same" (p. 176).

61. See, e.g., Stipe Šuvar, "Unitarizam i nacionalizam u suvremenoj jugoslavenskoj stvarnosti," p. 175, in his *Nacionalno i nacionalističko: eseji i polemički prilozi* (Split: Marksistički centar, 1974), pp. 159–90. Šuvar, a leading Croatian Communist, was among the regime's most prominent spokesmen on the national question from the mid-1960s on.

The 1953 census introduced the category: "Yugoslav [nationally] undetermined *(Jugosloven—neopredeljen)*." In this census, as opposed to later ones, the Yugoslav category retained a South Slav ethnic connotation. According to the census form, a person of Yugoslav (i.e., non-Bulgarian South Slav) background who did not have a more specific national identity *(lice jugoslovenskog porekla koje nije bliže nacionalno opredeljeno)* was to use this designation. Others who did not declare a national identity were to use the designation "nationally undetermined" *(nacionalno-neopredeljen).* See "Popisnica," in *Popis stanovništva 1953* (Belgrade: Savezni zavod za statistiku, 1959), p. ix.

For the shifting use of the Yugoslav category in postwar censuses, see Dušan Ičević, *Jugoslovenstvo i jugoslovenska nacija* (Belgrade: Naučna knjiga, 1989), pp. 123–32, and Dušan Đošić, "'Jugosloveni' u popisu 1981," *Naše teme*, Vol. 28 (1984), pp. 1979–96.

62. Some of those who protested the designation of "Yugoslav" as a non-national category made precisely this argument. See Milan Bulajić, "Problemi samoopredeljenja nacija i čovjeka i jugoslovenski federalizam," in *Federalizam i nacionalno pitanje: zbirka radova* (Belgrade: Savez udruženja za političke nauke Jugoslavije, 1971), pp. 264–68.

63. At a May 9, 1967, meeting of the League of Youth Central Committee Presidency, several presidency members reported such complaints ("Aktuelna pitanja međunacionalnih odnosa i jugoslovenstva" [Minutes of CK SOJ Presidency May 9, 1967], unpublished document held at the Inštitut za narodnostna vprašanja, Ljubljana).

64. Portions of this discussion are adapted from Budding, "Serbian Nationalism," pp. 21–23. Burg, *Conflict and Cohesion,* chapters 2 and 4, offers a valuable analysis of the amendment process.

65. For the chamber's changing role and composition from 1946 to 1967, see Burg, *Conflict and Cohesion,* pp. 64–67. The relevant amendments are Amendment 1 of 1967 and Amendments 8–9 and 12–14 of 1968.

66. For some interpretations of the constitutional changes affecting the provinces, see Sami Repishti, "The Evolution of Kosova's Autonomy within the Yugoslav Constitutional Framework," in Arshi Pipa and Sami Repishti (eds.), *Studies on Kosova* (Boulder: East European Monographs, 1984), pp. 195–232; Paul Shoup's "The Government and Constitutional Status of Kosova: Some Brief Remarks" (pp. 233–38 in the same volume); Beckmann-Petey, *Der jugoslawische Föderalismus*, pp. 106–117; and Đukić-Veljović, "Ustavnopravni razvoj autonomije."

67. Amendment 18, Article 1, in *The Constitution of the Socialist Federal Republic of Yugoslavia: Constitutional Amendments,* trans. Marko Pavičić (Belgrade: Secretariat of the Federal Assembly Information Service, 1969). This translation is the source for all passages cited in English from Amendments 1–19 to the 1963 Constitution.
68. This is an important contrast with Kosovo's and Vojvodina's original status as reflected in the language of the 1946 Constitution. As Hondius says (*Yugoslav Community,* p. 159), in that Constitution "The autonomous areas have been made from above . . . there is neither in fact nor in law any indication that the autonomous units were the result of the self-determination of their populations."
69. The first of the 1963 Constitution's Basic Principles referred to Yugoslavia as "a federal republic of free and equal nations and nationalities [*narodi i narodnosti*]," and Article 43 asserted the linguistic and cultural rights of "every nationality—national minority." This Constitution, however, still sometimes used *narodnost* in the older sense of national identification: Article 41 (cited above) used it in this sense.
70. Amendment 18 to the 1963 Constitution, Article 2.
71. Othmar Haberl, *Parteiorganisation und Nationale Frage in Jugoslawien* (Wiesbaden: Otto Harassowitz, 1976), pp. 85–86.
72. See, for example, Burg, *Conflict and Cohesion,* pp. 204–14, and Dušan Bilandžić, *Historija Socijalističke federativne Republike Jugoslavije, Glavni procesi 1918–1985* (Zagreb: Školska knjiga, 1985), pp. 373–81.
73. Amendment 20 to the 1963 Constitution (my translation). The significance of the new language on the provinces was played down at the time especially because the amendment defined the republics but not the provinces as states. In later years, however, the 1971 amendments were seen as marking a crucial change in the provinces' status. Compare Kovačević's 1971 textbook *Ustavni amandmani XX do XLII,* 22, with Đukić-Veljović's 1990 article "Ustavnopravni razvoj autonomije," p. 90.
74. Burg, *Conflict and Cohesion,* pp. 205–10, reviews the provisions of Amendment 33 and examines the practice of *usaglašavanje.*
75. Kardelj shared this stance with many other prominent Slovenes. For an earlier example see Slovene literary critic Dušan Pirjevec's reference to the republics as "clearly formed national organisms" in his 1961–62 polemic with Serbian novelist Dobrica Ćosić (Budding, "Yugoslavs into Serbs," p. 409).
76. ". . . u odnosima među narodima treba da bude primenjen, uz određene modifikacije, isti princip koji važi za socijalističke ekonomske odnose među ljudima, to jest da svaki narod ima pravo i realnu mogučnost da živi i da se razvija u skladu sa rezultatima svoga rada. . . ." *Osmi kongres SKJ* (Belgrade: Kultura, 1964), p. 98. Cf. Samardžić, "Federalizam u Švajcarskoj i Jugoslaviji," p. 97; and more generally on Kardelj's conception of the relation between nationalism and socialism Jović, *Jugoslavija,* pp. 134–50.
77. *Ustavne promene: šestnaesta sednica Predsedništva SKJ* (Belgrade: Komunist, 1971), p. 29. Cf. my discussion in "Yugoslavs into Serbs," p. 417.
78. Jovan Đorđević, "The Creation of the 1974 Constitution of the Socialist Federal Republic of Yugoslavia," in Robert A. Goldwin and Art Kaufman (eds.), *Constitution Makers on Constitution Making: The Experience of Eight Nations* (Washington: American Enterprise Institute for Public Policy Research, 1988), p. 193. Although Đorđević's text (based on a paper delivered at a conference held in Washington in 1983) is in English, this phrase certainly appears to be a variation of the *"narod, odnosno republika"* formula.
    For the sovereignty debate in relation to the 1946, 1953, and 1963 Constitutions, see Hondius, *Yugoslav Community,* pp. 145–47, 195–98, and 252–54. For the 1974 Constitution, see Beckmann-Petey, *Der jugoslawische Föderalismus,* pp. 124–26.

79. See Article 10 of the Constitution of 1946, Paragraph 2 of Amendment 20 to the Constitution of 1963, and Article 1 of the Constitution of 1974 (which refers to Yugoslavia as "a federal state having the form of a state community of voluntarily united nations and their Socialist Republics, and of the Socialist Autonomous Provinces of Vojvodina and Kosovo, which are constituent parts of the Socialist Republic of Serbia").

80. More broadly, Hondius argues that "The general tendency which transpired from the new [1963] federal and republican constitutions was to make a definite link between ethnic peoples and Republics" (Hondius, *Yugoslav Community,* p. 276).

    The translation of Article 42 given here is taken from *The Constitution of the Socialist Federal Republic of Yugoslavia* (Belgrade: Secretariat for Information of the Federal Executive Council, 1963).

81. For the Serbian liberals and their opponents, see Budding, "Yugoslavs into Serbs," pp. 412–18; Jasna Dragović-Soso, *"Saviours of the Nation,"* pp. 28–46; and Jović, *Jugoslavija,* chapter 3.

82. *Anali Pravnog fakulteta u Beogradu* 16/4 (1968), p. 493.

83. The law faculty discussion was printed in *Anali Pravnog fakulteta u Beogradu* 19/3 (1971), pp. 207–359. (This issue was banned but later reissued in facsimile.) Jasna Dragović-Soso, *"Saviours of the Nation,"* pp. 42–46, offers an insightful analysis of the various strands of Serbian intellectual opposition expressed in the law faculty's discussion.

84. *Anali,* Vol. 19, No. 3, pp. 301–2.

85. Đurić argued, "The existing borders are not adequate for any republic in Yugoslavia—except perhaps Slovenia—and especially not for Serbia" (*Anali,* No. 19, No. 3, p. 232).

86. For more on this point see Budding, "Yugoslavs into Serbs," pp. 412–13.

87. Dušan Bilandžić emphasizes the existence of multiple centers within the movement (*Hrvatska moderna povijest*, chapter 12). Ivo Goldstein argues that "although the publicly avowed goal was a more independent Croatia within Yugoslavia, between the lines of some writing and in some incidents the wish for complete Croatian independence could be discerned" (*Croatia,* p. 179).

88. For controversies over Croatia's Serbs in 1970–71 see Bilandžić, *Hrvatska moderna povijest*, pp. 621–23.

89. See, for example, Goldstein, *Croatia,* pp. 179–80.

90. Charged with "undermining the brotherhood and unity of the peoples of Yugoslavia" and misrepresenting conditions in the country, Đurić was sentenced to two years in prison (a sentence reduced upon appeal to nine months). See Rajko Danilović, *Upotreba neprijatelja: politička suđenja 1945–1991 u Jugoslaviji* (Valjevo: Anecija Valjevac, 1993), pp. 182–84.

91. William Zimmerman, *Open Borders, Nonalignment, and the Political Evolution of Yugoslavia* (Princeton: Princeton University Press, 1987), pp. 61–63. For more on the 1970s see Burg, *Conflict and Cohesion*, chapters 5 and 6.

92. See *Ustav Socijalističke Federativne Republike Jugoslavije sa Ustavima Socijalističkih Republika i Statutima Autonomnih Pokrajina* (Belgrade: Službeni list SFRJ, 1963).

93. My thanks to Professor Peter Vodopivec for bringing the linguistic point to my attention.

94. *Ustav SFRJ; Ustav SRH* (Zagreb: Narodne novine, 1975).

95. *Ustava Socialistične Republike Slovenije* (Ljubljana: Uradni list SRS, 1974). The first part of this formulation, "ki temelji na suverenosti slovenskega naroda in ljudstva Slovenije," incorporates both nation (*narod*) and territorial people (*ljudstvo*).

96. *Ustav SR Srbije, Ustav SAP Vojvodine, Ustav SAP Kosova sa ustavnim zakonima za sprovođenje ustava* (Belgrade: Službeni list SFRJ, 1974).

The idea of the republic as "national state" was applied, with variations, to Bosnia-Herzegovina as well. In his speech introducing the 1974 constitution, Hamdija Pozderac (then president of the Assembly of Bosnia-Herzegovina), explained that "although Bosnia-Herzegovina is not defined as a national state in the classic sense, it really is a national state for Serbs, and for Croats, and for Muslims and for the members of other nations and nationalities who live on its soil" (*Ustav Socijalističke Republike Bosne i Hercegovine* [Belgrade: Savremena administracija, 1974], p. 13). Article 1 of the new constitution defined the republic as "a socialist democratic state and a socialist self-managing democratic community of working people and citizens, of the nations of Bosnia-Herzegovina—Muslims, Serbs, and Croats, and of the members of other nations and nationalities who live in it."

97. See Tibor Varady's illuminating "Minorities, Majorities, Law, and Ethnicity in Yugoslavia," in Dušan Janjić (ed.), *Ethnic Conflict Management: The Case of Yugoslavia* (Ravenna: A. Longo, 1997), pp. 132–33. Varady served as Yugoslavia's minister of justice in the government of Milan Panić.

98. In theory, the Yugoslav system was one where nations and the working class enjoyed "dual sovereignty." See for the 1963 Constitution Hondius, *Yugoslav Community*, p. 253, and for the 1974 Constitution, Slobodan Samardžić, *Jugoslavija pred iskušenjem federalizma* (Belgrade: Stručna knjiga, 1990), pp. 30–33.

99. For more general provisions relating to national equality, see especially Articles 170–171 and 244–249 in the 1974 Constitution. These constitutional provisions are discussed in Robert M. Hayden, *Blueprints for a House Divided: The Constitutional Logic of the Yugoslav Conflicts* (Ann Arbor: University of Michigan Press, 1999), p. 76; Varady, "Minorities," pp. 138–39; and Samardžić, "Federalizam u Švajcarskoj i Jugoslaviji," pp. 95–96. For the regime's attempts to implement constitutional provisions for proportional representation in the officer corps see Mile Bjelajac, *Jugoslovensko iskustvo sa multietničkom armijom 1918–1991* (Belgrade: Udruženje za društvenu istoriju, 1999), pp. 49–53. For language provisions, see the articles collected in Ranko Bugarski and Celia Hawkesworth (eds.), *Language Planning in Yugoslavia* (Columbus, OH: Slavica Publishers, 1992).

100. Although every republican constitution included a general statement affirming the equality of the members of all nations and nationalities, more specific constitutional provisions generally dealt only with linguistic equality. The 1974 Constitution of Bosnia-Herzegovina, however, did include an article (Article 3) calling for the republic's nations and nationalities to enjoy proportional representation in the assemblies of its social-political organizations.

101. Vladimir Goati, "Politički život Bosne i Hercegovine 1989–1992," in *Bosna i Hercegovina između rata i mira* (Belgrade: Institut društvenih nauka, 1992), p. 49. The key's application was not limited to politics. As Tibor Varady puts it ("Minorities, Majorities, Law, and Ethnicity," p. 140): "If a Yugoslav movie had a scene in which a Serb was mistreating a Croat, it had to have another scene in which a Croat was mistreating a Serb (or at least a scene in which a Serb helped a Croat). If a Serb was punished for what was classified as a 'nationalist excess,' the Party tried hard to find a candidate for similar punishment among Croats or Hungarians living in the same region."

102. Cited in Đinđić, *Jugoslavija kao nedovršena država*, p. 27, author's translation. Cf. Jović's point (*Jugoslavija*, p. 152) that "The idea of creating socialist republics as national states was not an abstract political idea that could have been imagined in the framework of another political and ideological concept. Socialism was the precondition for the existence of national states of the type that Kardelj wanted."

See also the more general arguments concerning Yugoslav federalism's dependence on the party in the title essay (pp. 19–37) of Đinđić's *Jugoslavija kao nedovršena država,* Dimitrijević, "Sukobi oko Ustava iz 1974." Jović; "Fear of Becoming Minority"; Samardžić, "Federalizam u Švajcarskoj i Jugoslaviji"; and Lidija Basta-Posavec, "Federalizam bez demokratije, politička prava bez građanina," in Radmila Nakaradav (ed.), *Evropa i raspad Jugoslavije* (Belgrade: Institut za evropske studije, 1995).

103. As Dejan Jović has pointed out in an insightful analysis, official ideology held that under self-management the process of reaching agreement *(dogovaranje)* would eliminate the majority/minority distinction in the political and economic spheres as well as the national one (Jović, "Fear of Becoming Minority," pp. 23–25).

104. Stipe Šuvar, *Nacije i međunacionalni odnosi u socijalističkoj Jugoslaviji* (Zagreb: Naše teme, 1970), p. 120.

105. Milošević on April 25, 1987, in Slobodan Milošević, *Godine raspleta* (Belgrade: BIGZ, 1989), p. 147. In the original, "Ne možemo da kažemo da su manjina, ali je činjenica da ih ima mnogo manje."

106. Cf. Sabrina Ramet, "Introduction: The Roots of Discord and the Language of War," in Ramet and Ljubiša Adamovich (eds.), *Beyond Yugoslavia: Politics, Economics, and Culture in a Shattered Community* (Boulder: Westview Press, 1995), pp. 5–6, and Jović, "Fear of Becoming Minority," pp. 34–35.

107. I develop this argument further in "Systemic Crisis and National Mobilization: The Case of the 'Memorandum of the Serbian Academy,'" in Zvi Gitelman et al. (eds.), *Cultures and Nations of Central and Eastern Europe: Essays in Honor of Roman Szporluk* (Cambridge: Harvard Ukrainian Research Institute, 2000), pp. 49–69.

108. For further discussion of this point, see Juan J. Linz and Alfred Stepan, "Political Identities and Electoral Sequences: Spain, the Soviet Union, and Yugoslavia," *Daedalus,* Vol. 121 (1992), pp. 123–39, and Đinđić, "Ustav i 'nacionalno pitanje,'" in his *Jugoslavija kao nedovršena država,* pp. 38–51.

109. For example: Sabrina P. Ramet asserts that "All [postwar Yugoslav constitutions] but the second (1953) have guaranteed the republics the right of secession" (Ramet, *Nationalism and Federalism in Yugoslavia, 1962–1991,* 2nd ed. [Bloomington: Indiana University Press, 1992], p. 72). Leslie Benson states: "The Titoist constitutions made peoples, not territorial entities, the bearers of sovereignty in Yugoslavia" (Benson, *Yugoslavia: A Concise History* [Houndmills: Palgrave, 2001], p. 164). For Susan Woodward, "It was a matter of unresolved constitutional interpretation whether republics had the right to secede and, if so, whether individuals who identified with another constituent nation within these republics had to give their consent" (Susan L. Woodward, *Balkan Tragedy: Chaos and Dissolution after the Cold War* [Washington: Brookings Institution, 1995], p. 210). Robert M. Hayden argues, "The right to secession was mentioned only in the introductory part of the constitution, while the stipulation that the external boundaries of Yugoslavia could be changed only with the consent of all republics was in the operative part (art. 5)" (Hayden, *Blueprints,* p. 183 [n. 8]).

For a more detailed discussion of the Yugoslav constitutional debate over sovereignty in the 1974 Constitution and the related question of secession rights, see Beckmann-Petey, *Der jugoslawische Föderalismus,* pp. 124–31. For the period around the dissolution, opposing viewpoints can be seen in Ivan Kristan, "Koncepcija jugoslovenske federacije po Ustavu od 1974. godine," *Arhiv za pravne i društvene nauke* 44/1–3 (1988), pp. 145–60, and the same author's "Odnosti v federaciji v luči ustavnih sprememb," *Pravnik: revija za pravno teorijo in prakso,* Vol. 46, Nos. 3–5 (1991), pp. 93–107; Gavro Perazić, "O dvojnosti republike kao države" *Arhiv za pravne i društvene nauke,* Vol. 44, Nos. 1–3

(1988), pp. 185–92; Omer Ibrahimagić, *Politički sistem Bosne i Hercegovine* (Sarajevo: Magistrat, 1999), pp. 67–69; and Momir Milojević, "Ustavna kriza i ustavnost u Jugoslaviji," *Gledišta*, Nos. 3–4 (1991), pp. 65–78.

110. See Vladimir-Đuro Degan, "Samoodređenje naroda i teritorijalna cjelovitost država u uvjetima raspada Jugoslavije," *Zakonitost: časopis za pravnu teoriju i praksu* 46/4 (April 1992), pp. 556–57.

Tibor Varady argues that those who excluded nationalities from the right to self-determination were exploiting a "terminological coincidence" to place international concepts of the "right of people to self-determination" within the framework of the Yugoslav distinction between nation/people *(narod)* and nationality *(narodnost)*. Varady, "Minorities, majorities," pp. 132–33.

111. Very similar language was contained in the 1963 Constitution's Basic Principles and in the 1946 Constitution's Article 1, which describes Yugoslavia as "a community of peoples equal in rights who, on the basis of the right to self-determination, including the right of separation, have expressed their will to live together in a federative state." Translations are taken from the official versions cited earlier.

112. As one legal scholar puts it, "this extraordinarily vague phrase [i.e., the language of Basic Principle I] in a constitution that is known for its attention to minute details leaves wide room for controversy on a right of secession held by member republics" (Ben Bagwell, "Yugoslavian Constitutional Questions: Self-Determination and Secession of Member Republics," *Georgia Journal of International and Comparative Law*, Vol. 21, No. 3 [1991], pp. 515–16).

113. As Vojin Dimitrijević emphasizes, the 1974 Constitution was written at a time of general communist self-confidence (Dimitrijević, "Sukobi," pp. 448–49).

114. See Hondius, *Yugoslav Community,* pp. 141–42 and 250–51.

115. A report on talks held in September of 1990 between the federal presidency and the leaderships of all republics and of Vojvodina (with no representatives from Kosovo owing to the suspension of the assembly there) stated: "The leaderships of all the republics and of the province of Vojvodina are agreed that every people in Yugoslavia, exercising its sovereignty rights, has a right to self-determination including secession. This right, which had frequently been questioned or denied in various quarters as obsolete, was thus confirmed as still valid" (*Focus,* No. 19, October 2, 1990, p. 2).

116. The initial impetus for amendments in Slovenia and elsewhere was the passage of federal constitutional amendments in 1988. As Robert Hayden notes, "The republics and provinces had in the past amended their own constitutions to reflect changes in the federal constitution, and this pattern was continued immediately following the 1988 federal amendments." In Slovenia, however, this seemingly routine process soon took a different turn. See Hayden, *Blueprints,* chapter 2 (p. 33 for the citation).

117. See *Uradni list Socialistične republike Slovenije*, Vol. 46, No. 32 (October 2, 1989), p. 1762. The quotation—in the original, "na temelju trajne, celovite in neodtujljive pravice slovenskega naroda do samoodločbe, ki vključuje tudi pravico do odcepitve in združitve"—is from Amendment X. The procedure for secession is covered in Amendment LXXII.

118. For the text of the Constitutional Court's decision, see *Službeni list SRFJ*, Vol. 46, No. 10 (February 23, 1990), pp. 593–95 (author's translation). Analyses of the Slovenian amendments and the Constitutional Court's response include Milojević, "Ustavna kriza i ustavnost"; Kristan, "Odnosti v federaciji"; and Hayden, *Blueprints,* pp. 38–46.

119. See the draft proposal, "Concept of the Contents of the Essential Relations in the Yugoslav State Community," printed (in English) in *Focus* #6 (March 19, 1991),

pp. 26–34. Under the heading, "Proposed Procedure for Disassociation from Yugoslavia," this proposal stated (p. 32): "The right of peoples to self-determination, as one of the universal rights of modern law, is set out in the basic principles of the SFRJ Constitution. However, the realization of the right of peoples to secession, which includes the possibility of certain republics withdrawing from the SFRY, is not regulated by the SFRY Constitution. It is therefore necessary to amend the SFRY Constitution in order to create a basis for exercising this right."

The same proposal included (p. 33) a proposed procedure for *national* referendums within republics and possible border changes. ("If one nation votes against, all settlements in which this nation is predominant and which border on the remaining territory of Yugoslavia and can constitute its territorial compactness will remain part of the SFRY.")

Focus's note on the document states (p. 25): "The concept of the future organisation, however, has not been verified in the Assembly of the SFRY, the stumbling block being Serbia's refusal to recognise Yugoslavia's internal border."

120. For the text of the Badinter Commission's Opinions, see *European Journal of International Law*, Vol. 3, No. 1 (1992), pp. 182–85, and Vol. 4, No. 1 (1993), pp. 74–91. Opinion Number 3, which supports the application of the principle *uti possidetis*, also cites Article 5's provision that the borders of republics cannot be altered without their consent (but does not address Article 5's clause regarding the external borders of Yugoslavia).

There is now a large literature on the Badinter Commission. To cite only a few pieces, Marc Weller's "The International Response to the Dissolution of the Socialist Federal Republic of Yugoslavia," *The American Journal of International Law*, Vol. 86, No. 3 (1992), pp. 569–607, explains the Commission's role in the EC recognition process (pp. 589–96). Peter Radan's *The Break-Up of Yugoslavia and International Law* (New York: Routledge, 2002) includes a very critical assessment of the Commission's role in a broader analysis of the legal issues raised by Yugoslavia's dissolution.

121. See Edward W. Walker, *Dissolution: Sovereignty and the Breakup of the Soviet Union* (Lanham: Rowman & Littlefield Publishers, Inc., 2003). Article 72 stated: "Every union republic shall retain the right of free secession from the USSR." (The translation is taken from Walker, *Dissolution,* p. 38.)

Of course, many factors besides constitutional provisions must be taken into account in explaining the differences between Yugoslavia's dissolution and the Soviet Union's. Two illuminating comparisons are Veljko Vujačić, "Historical Legacies, Nationalist Mobilization, and Political Outcomes in Russia and Serbia: A Weberian View," *Theory and Society*, Vol. 25 (1996), pp. 763–801, and Valerie Bunce, *Subversive Institutions: The Design and the Destruction of Socialism and the State* (Cambridge: Cambridge University Press, 1999).

122. The essays collected in Karen Barkey and Mark Von Hagen (eds.), *After Empire: Multiethnic Societies and Nation-Building: The Soviet Union and Russian, Ottoman, and Habsburg Empires* (Boulder, CO: Westview Press, 1997) offer sophisticated perspectives on the earlier part of the process. For a more general discussion of the post-Yugoslav wars as the "continuation of a long-term trend" of "violent national homogenization" in Europe, see Gale Stokes *et al.,* "Instant History: Understanding the Wars of Yugoslav Succession," *Slavic Review*, Vol. 55, No. 1 (1996), p. 160.

123. Luan Troxel, "Bulgaria and the Balkans," in Constantine P. Danopoulos and Kostas G. Messas (eds.), *Crises in the Balkans: Views from the Participants* (Boulder: Westview Press, 1997), pp. 195–210 provides an excellent analysis of how the larger context

shaped Bulgaria's foreign-policy aims in the twentieth century (with most attention to the postcommunist era). See also James Pettifer, "The New Macedonian Question," *International Affairs*, Vol. 68, No. 3 (1992), pp. 475–85. Contrasting contemporary and late-nineteenth-century incarnations of the Macedonian question, Pettifer notes that today "the area of decision already extends to a wider Europe" and "the single great power of the European Community has replaced the competing northern European powers of the late nineteenth century."

124. See Troxel, "Bulgaria and the Balkans." For current relations between Bulgaria and Macedonia see, e.g., *RFE/RL Newsline* for February 15, 1999.

125. Richard Andrew Hall, "Nationalism in Late Communist Eastern Europe: Comparing the Role of Diaspora Politics in Hungary and Serbia," parts 1–5, *RFE/RL East European Perspectives*, Vol. 5, No. 5 (March 5, 2003) through Vol. 5, No. 11 (May 28, 2003), offers a detailed examination of the emergence of diaspora politics in communist Hungary. In *Return to Diversity: A Political History of East Central Europe since World War II* (New York, Oxford: Oxford University Press, 2000), Joseph Rothschild and Nancy M. Wingfield note that "After 1989, much right-wing rhetoric focused on the Hungarian territories lost at Trianon" but also that "no mainstream politician publicly advocated revisionism" (p. 279).

The broader European context has clearly shaped Hungarian positions on Transylvania. See, for example, the issues of *RFE/RL Newsline* for December 22, 2003; March 5, 2004; and March 31, 2004.

126. Again, Bulgaria—where national mobilization has centered on the status of the Turkish minority—is an especially clear case. See Michael Shafir, "Radical Politics in East-Central Europe, part 7: Bulgaria's Radical Transfigurations," *RFE/RL East European Perspectives*, Vol. 2, No. 15 (August 2, 2000), at http://www.rferl.org/reports/, and Peter Stamatov, "The Making of a 'Bad' Public: Ethnonational Mobilization in Post-Communist Bulgaria," *Theory and Society* 29 (2000), pp. 549–72.

Zubrzycki, "We, the Polish Nation," shows how the competition between ethnic and civic concepts of nationhood can shape politics even in a country without numerically significant minorities.

127. Instead, these unmixings happened in the post-Yugoslav wars. Cf. "Instant History: Understanding the Wars of Yugoslav Succession," *Slavic Review*, Vol. 55, No. 1 (1996), where Gale Stokes et al. present the post-Yugoslav wars as (among other things) the "continuation of a long-term trend" of "violent national homogenization" in Europe (p. 160), and Robert M. Hayden, "Schindler's Fate: Genocide, Ethnic Cleansing, and Population Transfers," *Slavic Review*, Vol. 55, No. 4 (1996), pp. 727–48.

128. In 1990–91, most Serbian political parties (inside and outside Serbia) opposed the transformation of the existing republican borders into international ones. See, inter alia, Dubravka Stojanović, "Traumatični krug srpske opozicije," in Nebojša Popov (ed.), *Srpska strana rata* (Belgrade: Republika, 1996), pp. 501–30; Aleksandar Pavković, "From Yugoslavism to Serbism: the Serb national idea, 1986–1996," *Nations and Nationalism*, Vol. 4, No. 4 (1998), 511–28; and Audrey H. Budding, "From Dissidents to Presidents: Dobrica Ćosić and Vojislav Koštunica Compared," *Contemporary European History*, Vol. 4, No. 2 (2004), pp. 185–201. Tuđman's own adventurism notwithstanding, support for republican borders was stronger in Croatia, where many were aware that seeking self-determination for Croats in Bosnia-Herzegovina weakened the premises underlying Croatia's own claims to inviolable borders. See Marko Prelec, "Franjo Tuđman's Croatia and the Balkans," in Constantine P. Danopoulos and Kostas

G. Messas, *Crises in the Balkans: Views from the Participants* (Boulder, CO: Westview Press, 1997), and Goldstein, *Croatia*, pp. 244–48.

129. On the propagandistic use of the right to self-determination see Vesna Pešić, "Zdravora-zumsko i 'naučno' prikrivanje stvarnih ratnih ciljeva," *Republika*, No. 123 (September 1–15, 1995), pp. 13–14. Cf. Vojin Dimitrijević's insightful point that "One of the rules of the emerging communitarian order is that no ethnic group is willing to submit to any numerical majority of citizens" (Dimitrijević, "The Construction of States: Nation-alism and the Definition of Nation-States in Post-Communist European Countries," in Brigitte Stern [ed.], *Dissolution, Continuation and Succession in Eastern Europe* [The Hague: Martinus Nijhoff Publishers, 1998], p. 151).

130. In emphasizing this concept's continuity across the socialist and postsocialist eras, I dif-fer from the American scholar who has written most extensively on Yugoslavia's consti-tutional issues, Robert M. Hayden. In *Blueprints for a House Divided: The Constitutional Logic of the Yugoslav Conflicts,* Hayden states (pp. 16–17): "The argument of this book is that the collapse of the former Yugoslavia and the structures of the resulting conflicts can all be explained as the logical consequences of the adoption of certain constitutional concepts, beginning in the late 1980s. In mid-1989, the ruling elite of Slovenia adopted the structures of constitutional nationalism, viewing Slovenia as the state of the sover-eign Slovene nation, and denying legitimacy to any central authority as an infringement on this nation [*sic*] sovereignty." Cf. the arguments put forward in Robert M. Hayden, "Constitutional Nationalism in the Formerly Yugoslav Republics," *Slavic Review*, Vol. 51, No. 4 (1992), pp. 654–73.

　　While I accept several aspects of Hayden's analysis, and of course recognize that political *practice* changed greatly in the postsocialist era, I would contend that some of the *principles* he cites (e.g., the conception of "Slovenia as the state of the sovereign Slo-vene nation") date to the founding of socialist Yugoslavia rather than to its dissolution.

131. For a discussion that places postcommunist Yugoslavia in a broader regional context, see Vojin Dimitrijević, "Stečena prava starih i novih manjina u postkomunističkim nacionalnim državama," *Jugoslovenska revija za međunarodno pravo,* Nos. 1–2 (1993), pp. 119–33. Cf. Hayden, "Constitutional Nationalism," pp. 670–73. Zubrzycki, "We, the Polish Nation" offers a particularly interesting analysis of the interplay of ethnic and civic concepts of nationhood in contemporary Poland.

132. Vujačić, "Historical Legacies," p. 769. The passage cited refers specifically to Serb-Albanian relations in Kosovo, but the argument has a broader application. I thank Professor Vujačić for his comments on an earlier draft, which helped me to refine this part of the argument.

133. For "new minorities" in former Yugoslavia, see Dimitrijević, "The Construction of States," pp. 158–60. Jovan Mirić, *Demokracija u postkomunističkim društvima: primjer Hrvatske* (Zagreb: Prosvjeta, 1996), pp. 239–92, analyzes the position of Serbs in post-communist Croatia.

134. For the interplay of top-down and bottom-up factors in creating the perception of endangerment among Serbs outside Serbia see Bette Denich, "Dismembering Yugosla-via: Nationalist Ideologies and the Symbolic Revival of Genocide," *American Ethnolo-gist*, Vol. 21 (1994), pp. 367–90, and Anthony Oberschall, "The Manipulation of Ethnicity: From Ethnic Cooperation to Violence and War in Yugoslavia," *Ethnic and Racial Studies*, Vol. 23, No. 6 (2000), pp. 982–1001. See also Prelec, "Franjo Tuđman's Croatia and the Balkans," pp. 82–89, for Tuđman's varying policies in Bosnia.

135. I make this argument in "Yugoslavs into Serbs" (p. 418); cf. Jović's "Yugoslavism and Yugoslav Communism."

136. Thus, Belgrade legal scholar Vladimir Đerić has said: "Although the criteria applied for determining the *self* was 'territorial' (federal unit in a federal state), self-determination as such was *understood* by everyone as the self-determination of the dominant ethnic group" (Vladimir Đerić, "Right to Self-Determination: Criteria for Determining 'Self,'" *Jugoslovenska revija za međunarodno pravo*, Vol. 42, Nos. 1–3 (1995), p. 233. Though this statement should be qualified to acknowledge the struggle between proponents of ethnic and civic politics in each republic, it captures an important aspect of the political dynamic.

Reopening of the "National Question" in the 1960s

◈ Dennison Rusinow ◈

For two decades after the founding of the second Yugoslavia, the regime proudly claimed that the "national question" had been solved in principle and was well on its way to being solved in practice. Friendly foreign observers were inclined to go along with this claim until (and sometimes after) it became increasingly apparent in the early 1960s that it was not true.[1]

In the first postwar years, to be sure, these claims seemed to have a degree of plausibility. There were several reasons, of varying importance but cumulatively significant. The Partisan slogan of "brotherhood and unity" (*bratstvo i jedinstvo*), more effective than largely suppressed social-revolutionary slogans in mobilizing members of all nationalities (in varying numbers) to the Partisans, was manifest in careful if not proportionate representation of all of the South Slav nations, but not non-Slavic minorities, in leading bodies of the Communist Party of Yugoslavia (CPY), and in the composition of the Anti-Fascist Council of National Liberation of Yugoslavia (AVNOJ) that declared itself a provisional government for a new Yugoslavia at its second congress in Jajce in November 1943. It was further manifest in AVNOJ's formal commitment at Jajce to a federal Yugoslavia with a federal republic for each South Slav nation—a list now expanded to include Macedonians and Montenegrins, unrecognized in prewar Yugoslavia, with Slavic Muslims as a vaguely recognized sixth quasi nation.

Federalism as the CPY's basic solution to the national question was formally proclaimed in the Constitution of the Federal People's Republic of Yugoslavia adopted by a Constituent Assembly in January 1946, which institutionalized the six people's republics promised at Jajce plus an autonomous province (*pokrajina*) of Vojvodina and an autonomous region (*oblast*) of Kosovo-Metohija within Serbia, the largest republic.[2] In one of this constitution's few departures from its Soviet model, the six republics were endowed with slightly greater fiscal powers than were republics in the Soviet Union—the thin end of a wedge that would one day lead toward confederation. By 1948 each republic, and thus nation, had a Communist Party and apparatus of its own—a process foreshadowed by the formation of autonomous Slovenian and Croatian Communist Parties in 1937 and of provincial or regional Party committees for Serbia, Kosovo, and other districts in subsequent years.

Although in practice both state and Party were highly centralized and hierarchical, the modest real effects and (perhaps more importantly) the psychological impact of even formal creation of republics that were defined (except for officially tri-national Bosnia-Herzegovina) as national quasi states of their eponymous nations, added to popular revulsion against ethnic nationalism after the horrors of interethnic civil war (arguably the most important factor), acted to pacify interethnic tensions. Where this was not enough, most spectacularly in the case of a Kosovar Albanian insurgency that lasted three years, the regime ruthlessly suppressed any display of what it chose to define as "nationalist" rather than acceptable "national" sentiment.[3]

For a time the national question was indeed quiescent, which seemed to support the claim that it was at least on its way to being solved. It was not unnoticed, and a source of private grumbling among non-Serbs about renewed "Greater Serbian" domination, that Montenegrins and Serbs were overrepresented (in proportion to their share in total population) at all levels in both Party and state apparatuses, including the security police (both OZNa and its later reincarnation as UDBa), and in the officer corps of the Yugoslav People's Army.[4] Another issue of discontent among non-Serb minorities was that Belgrade, the Serbian capital associated in popular consciousness with Serbian domination in the first Yugoslavia, was again also the capital of the new federation and the locus of highly centralized power. On the other hand it was equally true, and a public issue, that postwar economic development, although ostensibly favoring the underdeveloped and far poorer regions south of the Sava-Danube line with the lion's share of investment and new factories, was still leaving Slovenia and Croatia (along with Vojvodina and the Belgrade region, which was usually overlooked) progressively richer than the south.[5] Meanwhile, however, the behavior of the (multinational) Communist regime in its early years—generalized and for the most part[6] ethnically nondiscriminatory harassment, arrests, nationalization, forced labor, forced collectivization of agriculture (from 1949 until abandoned in 1952–53), and other oppressive acts—gave those who suffered a set of basically non-national grievances which at least temporarily took precedence over national ones in their consciousness.

In the Beginning, the Economy

The roots of the increasingly obvious revival of the national question in the 1960s were primarily, but not exclusively, economic in nature. Its first manifestations took the form of interregional and intersectoral competition for centrally controlled investment funds and disputes over development priorities that came to be regarded as between corresponding national communities and interests. Meanwhile, serious economic problems that proved impervious to the usual governmental remedies and liberalizing minireforms in 1961–62, which were quickly reversed, led to a major debate over basic changes in the economic system, initially among economists and then in Party and state organs and the media. Most of the participants tended to align along regional lines again regarded as reflecting divergent national interests.

Economic reforms of the 1950s, theoretically derived from the principles of "workers' self-management," had created a distorted quasi-market economy for goods and services (a "socialist market economy"). In addition to ubiquitous but constantly changing rules and controls, most prices were still administratively set, to the disadvantage of both processing industries concentrated in Slovenia and Croatia (too high to encourage demand and expanded production) and raw material producers in the south (too low to encourage expanded production). Of equal or greater importance, almost all investment funds were centrally allocated to economic sectors and to banks that were supposed to distribute them to enterprises and other final users as interest-bearing credits on the basis of economic criteria. Because the banks were in effect only disbursement agents for (central) state investment funds, political rather than economic criteria usually prevailed. Meanwhile, a significant degree of political decentralization, also in the name of "social" as well as workers' self-management, had endowed Yugoslavia's local (communal) governments with both incentives and the capability to take investment initiatives, the essential ingredient of the later condemned vice of "economic localism."[7] The consequences included a multitude of political factories (so called because of the "political" decision that a commune should have a factory and because of later political decisions that a factory, once there, could not be allowed to close—or even to merge with a stronger enterprise located somewhere else, therefore under the control of another communal government and tax regime) that Tito once said were capable of producing nothing except losses. More to the point for the present argument, they created and nurtured a symbiotic relationship between local and republican Party-state elites whose patronage in competing for centrally allocated investment and other funds was essential for profitable as well as unprofitable enterprises, and both socially and politically increasingly important socialist enterprises and entrepreneurs—a symbiosis of interests that would survive and even become more important despite and because of subsequent changes in the economic system. This was the core element in communal and republican "localism," increasingly significant and effective with further decentralization in subsequent years, that became ever more "national" as local and republican interests were increasingly equated with national interests in republics that had been defined as national (quasi) states.

What seems to have been the earliest public suggestion of concern over "republican economic particularism" came in March 1956, when Tito convened a plenum of the Central Committee of the League of Communists of Yugoslavia (LCY, the Party's name since 1952) to discuss "various negative phenomena" that he blamed on a "decline in Party discipline and responsibility." The list of problems on the agenda included hints that the national question, reemerging in the guise of republican economic interests, was involved. "Negative phenomena," the plenum agreed,

> were particularly found in the economy, in which they were assuming the proportions of an outbreak of negative localistic and technocratic tendencies. Instances of . . . passivity towards localism and *republican particularism,* alleged to be "in the interest of the economy," were among the deformations. . . . This had a destructive effect on Communists as socio-political workers and converted them into economic "managers" who closed themselves up within *local or republican contexts* and "swam down the stream of spontaneity."[8]

Two years later the LCY Executive Committee, in a circular letter to all Party organizations in February 1958, again cited ethnic particularism in a litany of "abuses" that had to be remedied. "Very often," the letter said, "members of leading bodies of the League of Communists fall under the influence of the petty-bourgeois intelligentsia and . . . are guilty of nationalist and chauvinist influences."[9]

Examples of interrepublican competition for centrally controlled investment funds and disputes over development priorities already abounded when this author came to live in Yugoslavia in early 1963. Seaports as competitive symbols of Slovenian, Croatian, Bosnian, or Serbo-Montenegrin national pride and interests provided a revealing case. In interviews during an October 1963 research visit along the coast from Slovene Koper to Serbo-Montenegrin Bar, I found a universal, sometimes happy and sometimes bitter but almost always open recognition that the national sentiments of the appropriate political authorities were more important than economic and geographic considerations in determining which ports would grow and hold or expand their hinterlands and which would not.[10]

Analogous considerations underlay a lively debate that same year that attracted the attention of Yugoslav media as well as economists and implicated Cold War foreign policy as well as domestic issues. The debate concerned the relative advantages of a "Danubian concept" or an "Adriatic concept" of the future prime focus of economic development, the first based on river and the second on maritime transport. The Adriatic coast is largely Croatian, and beyond it lies the west; the Danube and its navigable tributaries flow through Serbia toward the east. Croats argued that this was a false dilemma and that their coast linked east and west and was nonaligned, as proved by growing East European transit traffic through their ports. Serbs replied that this was not the issue, but rather that population, arable land, industry, and the future lay along the broad river valleys, not on the rocky coast.[11]

Similar perceptions, also manifest in debates over the share of investment in national income, surfaced in media as well as private discussion of the allegedly disproportionate number of major infrastructure projects requiring massive federal financing that were being built or planned in Serbia and that now supplied an important practical reason for continuing Serbian support of (and Croato-Slovenian opposition to) the disputed federal role in investment. The list included the huge

Yugoslav-Romanian dam at the Iron Gates on the Danube, on which engineering work began in 1963; long-delayed completion of a Danube-Tisza-Danube canal in Vojvodina; and (most contentious of all) the Belgrade-Bar railroad, the Serbian outlet to the sea that Serbian and Montenegrin politicians had dreamed of since 1879.

These and other strands of the smoldering national question came together when serious economic problems beginning in 1961 and characterized by an unsettling (and unsocialist) "double-dip" boom-to-recession business cycle inaugurated an agonizing reappraisal of the entire economic system. By the time it was over the political as well as the economic compromises of the 1950s were in tatters.

The Road to "Reform" and the National Question

The decentralizing and marketizing reforms ultimately adopted in 1964–65, in principle intended to "de-etatize" the economy, represented a victory by proreform and sometimes also political "liberals" concentrated in Croatia and Slovenia but having allies in Macedonia and Serbia over "conservative" antireformers under primarily Serbian leadership.[12] The latter, which included Tito, initially appeared to hold the winning hand. Supported by many Party cadres (especially from middle ranks) and government bureaucrats, they claimed to represent and sought to recruit the less-developed republics/regions and political factories (most frequently in the same regions) that also had the most to lose. The liberals meanwhile won the support of successful "socialist entrepreneurs" chafing under the existing system; of widening circles (reflecting changes in social and economic stratification and demographic patterns) of people and groups who were sharing in the dividends of their entrepreneurship or had other (including national) reasons to favor further decentralization and marketization; and eventually of leaderships in Macedonia and elsewhere who decided that they feared Serbian domination and potential Serbianization under recentralization or the status quo more than the loss of redistributions from central funds.

The road to the Reform of 1965 (at the time always with a capital *R* to emphasize its fundamental nature, which Tito himself called "revolutionary") was long and tortuous, its outcome for two years uncertain. It began with a grand debate among the initially unserried ranks of the country's economists, pitting mostly Croatian advocates of decentralization, who were not always as enthusiastic about genuine full marketization, against mostly Serbian advocates of either the status quo or a return to more central planning, less market.[13] In early 1964 the debate passed out of the domain of meetings of economists and, in their limited circulation, that of professional journals into that of political forums and mass media.[14] Both phases made extensive and bewildering use of contradictory statistics and their interpretation to "prove" that one's own region or nation had been "exploited" under the existing system and would continue to suffer exploitation if reform proposals were accepted/rejected. Croatian Party leader Vladimir Bakarić, himself an initiator of Croatian reform proposals and chief architect of an eventually victorious proreform coalition, was driven to cry in despair: "Who *does* receive something in Yugoslavia if we are all plundered?"[15]

In the course of the debate, the liberal argument came to focus on three major target areas: existing proportions in the distribution of national income between investment and consumption, favoring the former; centralized and political control of the investment system; and the existing (controlled and distorted) price system, with the first and third treated as primarily functions of the second and now most important target. In the style of their attack they had also shifted their ground slightly but significantly. The key word was no longer *decentralization* (*decentralizacija*) but *de-etatization* (*de-etatizacija*). In part this was a canny tactical move to counter accusations that through decentralization they were advocating local and national (specifically Croatian and Slovene) interests against all-Yugoslav ones. But it also had wider and more profound implications, again involving the national question. These would be identified only later, when it was realized that the incompleteness of the reform, alongside the success of subsequent further decentralization (confederalization) of state and Party, had indeed decentralized control of the economy, primarily to the republics, but without effective de-etatization.[16] The result was six still almost totally "politicized" republican economies sponsored and promoted by their respective national state-Party apparatuses.

Meanwhile, the reform, already endorsed by a number of other "socio-political" organizations (including the Federation of Yugoslav Trade Unions, which had played a critical role in promoting its principles), won formal approval in principle first by the Federal Assembly and then by the LCY at its Seventh Congress in December 1964—a startling reversal of the usual order in such matters and another reflection of the growing importance of Yugoslavia's parliaments under new federal and republican constitutions adopted in 1963, which also constituted a liberal victory curiously uncontested by conservatives.

Endorsement of the reform by the Seventh Congress, by then almost a formality, was nevertheless significant. Under the rules of "democratic centralism," it formally ended the period of legitimate debate and opposition inaugurated in 1962–63. All Party members would now be expected to loyally support reforms that many of them still opposed. Failure to do so could henceforth be considered grounds for disciplinary action, including dismissal from office or the Party.

A cascade of implementing legislation and decrees began with abolition at the end of 1964 of the General Investment Fund (GIF), which had managed between a third and a quarter of primary investment financing under the old system. Its assets were transferred, possibly for lack of a better idea, to three federal banks in Belgrade that had been its principal disbursement agencies—a fateful decision that would become a centerpiece of Croatian grievances and demands later in the decade. In March 1965, the Federal and Economic Chambers of the Federal Assembly passed a new banking law that sought to de-etatize the country's banks by making them responsible to all of their institutional depositors (as "shareholders") rather than to state agencies alone. The rest of the reform package, a dozen laws (often drafted in haste, later regretted, in order not to miss the tide of a proreform political constellation that some feared might prove temporary), was approved at a Party plenum on June 17 and submitted to a joint session of the Federal and Economic Chambers on July 24, 1965. All were passed, signed by President Tito, and promulgated that same day.[17]

Aftermath and "Liberal Ascendancy"

It was evident within months that the reform was in serious trouble—and because of missing links, inherent flaws, and early signs of undesirable effects (some anticipated, others not) more than because of widespread opposition and even sabotage. By midwinter prominent liberal politicians and economists were at least privately deeply discouraged. "It's like punching a rubber wall," one of these said in December: "You seem to make an impression, but then it's just like it was." By the following month another said despondently, "The Reform is dead!"[18]

It was also increasingly clear, even before Tito and others began to say so openly, that initially unspecified persons and Party and state apparatuses that had opposed the new course before it was adopted and were unreconciled to their defeat constituted the most effective core of such "underground" resistance. A series of closed-door meetings of the Party Executive Committee between November 1965 and February 1966, summoned to discuss failure to implement the Reform and the national question, narrowed the focus still further: in describing the last of these meetings in its February 3 issue, *Komunist* (the Party's official and authoritative publication) referred specifically to Serbia as the center of anti-Reform resistance. It was also announced that a special Party commission, including members of Executive and Central Committees, was being formed to look further into "inter-nationality relations in the field of the economy."[19]

Such warnings, repeated at an extended plenum of the Party Central Committee in late February and early March, and increasingly strident appeals for a return to discipline of "democratic centralism" (with its requirement that all Party members support an adopted Party position) all failed to have any noticeable effect. Yugoslavia might still be ruled by a single Communist party, but that Party was clearly no longer united in action or in purpose.

In an interview published in *Borba* on March 6, between the February and March sessions of the Central Committee's extended plenum, Croatia's Vladimir Bakarić was unusually blunt and also prophetic. A correspondent commented that "in spite of everything, it seems to me that at the present nationalism is not even a number two question for our socio-political and economic development," to which Bakarić replied:

> . . . at the present moment I should say that it is at least question number two. The question is whether we will be able, by carrying out our reform, to win our struggle

against nationalism as well. If we do not win it, our progress in the reform will be much slower, and then it may indeed happen that the question of nationalism will from a question number two become question number one.

The dramatic denouement came on July 1, 1966, when the Central Committee met for its Fourth Plenum at Tito's favorite retreat on the Brioni islands—as it had for the fall of Milovan Djilas, also at a Fourth Plenum, twelve years earlier.[20] This time it was the turn of the country's leading Serb, Aleksandar Ranković—Yugoslavia's vice president and Tito's presumptive heir, the Party's organizational secretary (in charge of "cadre policy"), founder and still de facto head of the Security Police (recently renamed but still universally called UDBa), and long considered the leader of conservative opposition to the liberal coalition and reform.

While the meeting was still in progress the island's teleprompters broadcast the news of Ranković's resignation and denunciation of UDBa and elements of the Party leadership alleged by Tito himself to have been part of a "factional group" engaged in a "struggle for power." The plenum also promised a purge of Communists opposed to the reform, a reorganization of the Party, and publication of a report by a special Party-state commission (headed by Krsto Crvenkovski, now the leading Macedonian liberal) that had been investigating responsibility in high places for insubordination, illegal wire-tapping of top Party and state leaders—allegedly including Tito—and UDBa crimes and corruption.[21]

The Fourth Plenum and its aftermath, affirming the ascendancy of the liberal coalition assembled during the struggle for reform and the power of the increasingly autonomous republican "Party barons" who had been its principal architects, opened the doors to further liberalizing, decentralizing, and perchance democratizing reforms. But two risks were also inherent in the events of summer 1966.

The first risk was a Serb nationalist backlash that might unite all or most Serbs on a neoconservative platform understood or disguised as a defense of Serb national interests and revenge for a Serb national humiliation. All precautions taken after Brioni—replacement of every purged Serb by another Serb; the use of Serbs to make almost all speeches denouncing UDBa and the Ranković "factional group"; rumors of quid pro quo purges on the other side, of "pseudo-liberal" and "anarcho-liberal" elements in Zagreb and elsewhere—could do little to dissuade those, including most Serbs and more Croats, who were inclined to view Ranković's fall, the reform, and the purge of UDBa (however also feared and hated by most Serbs) as a Serb defeat and humiliation.

There was an equal danger that some of Yugoslavia's other "constituent peoples," intoxicated by what they viewed as their own national triumph and either incompetently or irresponsibly led, might indulge in displays of national sentiment and demands that could also bring about a conservative backlash or even invoke a coup de main (by Tito?) to restore strong central control as a defense against disintegrative nationalisms and the specter of separatism. For observers living in Zagreb in the summer of 1966 (as I was) and experiencing the euphoria over the fall of Ranković and almost universal tendency to interpret it as a victory for Croatian interests, it was clear that it would take a team of extraordinarily level-headed and able leaders to forestall such developments and to channel enthusiasm in the officially desired direction of mobilization for further reforms.[22]

The first of these risks did not materialize, despite the efforts of groups that came to be called the political underground and were said to consist of former Ranković men, ex-Cominform supporters, ex-Četniks, and others, all with a common platform of "Serbian chauvinism."[23] The primary reasons were the political convictions and skill of Serbia's liberal and antinationalist post-Ranković Party leadership, headed after November 1968 by Central Committee President Marko Nikezić and Executive Committee Secretary Latinka Perović. Serb resentment over Ranković's fall as a Serb disempowerment and humiliation persisted, even among many non- and anti-Communists, but impotently until the 1980s.

The second risk did materialize in all of its dimensions, as described below. Party and other political and constitutional reforms in the years after Brioni resulted from and implemented the program of the "liberal ascendancy" at the federal center and in most republics that the reform and Brioni had heralded. They also represented a major effort to contain the national question by killing it with kindness—by devolving so much additional power to republics (and Serbia's two autonomous provinces) that their political elites, and perhaps their masses, should be content.

The liberal coalition that authored these reforms—with Tito's blessing, despite growing reservations[24]—included Serbian (and other) antinationalist political liberals alongside Croatian, Slovene, and other leaders better described as national-liberals. Its most prominent republican exponents included Nikezić and Perović in Serbia, Stane Kavčič in Slovenia, Bakarić and his protégés in Croatia (in particular Miko Tripalo and Savka Dabčević-Kučar), and Crvenkovski in Macedonia. Some of its members now embarked on earnest efforts to find a way further to democratize Yugoslavia or their own republic, usually still within a one-party system. But the primary result was that republican leaderships were increasingly regarded, and regarded themselves, as national (but not necessarily nationalist) leaders. Meanwhile, the dynamics of political developments and associated constitutional amendments, adopted or proposed, were converting federal Yugoslavia into a quasi confederation.

The most important aspects for the future evolution of the national question were Party and constitutional reforms that furthered republican and provincial autonomy.[25]

To and after the Croatian "Maspok" of 1970–71

The net result of these and other developments—and the incompleteness and partial nonfulfillment of economic reforms, which left more economic power to republics as states than to enterprises and the market, and the social as well as economic consequences of rising unemployment, stagnation, and inflation ("stagflation"), enterprise illiquidity and withheld wages, and the further growth of personal, sectoral, and interregional income disparities[26]—was a resurgence almost everywhere of particularist nationalisms that culminated in the Croatian Mass Movement of 1971.

The first dramatic premonitory public signal of this resurgence came in March 1967, when Zagreb's leading literary weekly published a "Declaration on the Name and Position of the Croatian Literary Language" signed in the name of 19 Croatian literary groups by 130 prominent Croatian intellectuals. Eighty of them were Communists. The declaration denounced the Novi Sad agreement of 1954, which had proclaimed "Serbo-Croatian or Croato-Serbian" to be one language with two scripts (Latin and Cyrillic) and two variants (*ijekavski* and *ekavski*). It called for official recognition of two separate languages, an end to alleged discrimination against the Croatian variant, and its exclusive use in Croatian schools, press, and official documents. Forty-five Serbian writers, half of them again Party members, promptly drafted a reply in the same terms, namely "A Proposal for Reflection." Its demands included the use of Cyrillic by Belgrade television and that the 700,000 Serbs of Croatia should be educated in their own language. A political and media uproar ensued. The signatories of both documents were anathematized, and some Communists among them who refused to recant lost their Party memberships.

Other warning signs followed.

Slovenes and Macedonians pressed vigorously and successfully for greater recognition of their languages at the federal level.

Then, at a May 1968 meeting of the Serbian Central Committee, two members—writer Dobrica Ćosić and historian Jovan Marjanović—prematurely dared to criticize alleged manifestations of Albanian and Magyar nationalism in Kosovo and Vojvodina. Albanian "nationalism and irredentism" were being openly promoted in Kosovo, they said, and Kosovar Serbs and Montenegrins were suffering systematic discrimination in employment, forcing growing numbers of them to emigrate. Although both Ćosić and Marjanović also criticized manifestations of Serbian nationalism, they were condemned by their colleagues for being "nationalistic" and "opposed to self-management." Both were dropped from the Central Committee at the Serbian Party's Congress the following November and soon thereafter resigned from the Party.[27]

In the summer of 1969 the Slovenes precipitated that year's major political crisis and almost brought down the federal government, then headed by a Slovene prime minister. The subject was a World Bank loan for the construction of Yugoslavia's first motorways, in the distribution of which the federal government ignored Slovenia's clearly high-priority need for an improved Nova Gorica-Ljubljana artery in favor of less urgent Serbian and Croatian projects. Although they ultimately failed to achieve a share of the loan,[28] Slovenian Prime Minister Kavčić and his cabinet accomplished what Cvijeto Job describes as "a historic first": "They publicly opposed the federal allocation of the World Bank highway loans. Not only that. They invited public, open patriotic, demonstrations of support. The issue of the 'economic sovereignty' of the republics versus the federation entered the public political arena. . . . The affair rankled and it fed a growing Slovenian challenge to the existing federal setup."[29]

More ominous events that autumn again shook what passed for peace in Kosovo: widespread, apparently well-organized, and sometimes violent demonstrations by Kosovar Albanians, significantly timed to coincide with neighboring Albania's National Day, November 27. Instead of being satisfied with the considerable increase in equality and personal security they had enjoyed since the taming of the province's UDBa after July 1966, the demonstrators were demanding more of the same and transformation of their autonomous province into a seventh Yugoslav republic in which Albanians, now the overwhelming majority of Kosovo's population, would become politically dominant.

However, in Job's accurate retrospective judgment and characterization of the Croatian *Maspok*, "the most serious event, when the simmering cauldron really boiled over, was the so-called Croatian Spring or Maspok (from *Masovni pokret*—Mass Movement) of 1970–71. It mixed anti-centralist, nationalist, extreme nationalist, pro-Ustaše, anti-communist, reformist, democratic, democratic socialist, liberal, and libertarian elements."[30]

By late 1969 the Croatian Party leadership was deeply frustrated by deadlock at the federal center, where each republic now had an effective veto but consensus on anything was proving difficult or impossible, and by consequent economic and political stagnation[31] that was fueling both nationalism and neocentralism. Under Bakarić's guidance they effectively abandoned, for the moment, their pursuit of further liberalizing as well as decentralizing pan-Yugoslav reforms (although decentralization in fact continued, with Croats playing the key role, in further constitutional amendments in 1971). As Bakarić seems to have read it,[32] the center was disabled by interrepublican stalemates. A republican Party and state were not so hampered but needed adequate economic instruments with which to act, a legitimating constituency, and firm unity of cadres and conviction. Croatia, so armed and under progressive Bakarić-trained leaders, could set an example for the rest of Yugoslavia of a successful, modern, democratic socialism. Modern socialism could be built in one republic.

Bakarić then reluctantly went to Belgrade, which he had always resisted but whence he was now summoned by Tito—a Louis IV[33] who now ordered rebellious regional barons to his capital as members of a new LCY Executive Bureau, unexpectedly created at the end of the LCY's Ninth Congress in March 1969 and another (ineffectual) attempt by Tito to create an authoritative supraregional Party center. Croatia was left in the charge of Bakarić's anointed disciples: Tripalo (the second member of the two-member Croatian representation on the LCY executive bureau but who continued to spend most of his time in Zagreb), Croatian LC President Savka Dabčević-Kučar (Europe's first woman prime minister as head of the Croatian government since 1967), and executive committee secretary Pero Pirker. Croatia thus came under the spell of a triumvirate of Bakarić disciples who lacked the skills and balance of their tutor.

The road to Karadjordjevo, like that to the reforms of 1965, would be tortuous, characterized by shifting balances of forces and intents and subject to other possible outcomes. For Bakarić's former protégés, the principal actors until the final phase, it would also be a road of good intentions that led to hell for them and their initial intentions.

After Karadjordjevo . . .

Croatia, under Party and government leaders that Tito had in effect imposed, entered a period that came to be known as "silent Croatia"—it might equally be called sullen Croatia—that would continue for almost two decades.

Meanwhile, the second chapter of the denouement of the crisis in Croatia, extending the purge to other republics, was postponed to the autumn of 1972. In part this was because the LCY presidency and other relevant bodies were still largely packed with supporters of these republican leaders, and realignment of the balance of political forces took time and was still not complete even then. In part it was also because some of these leaders, Nikezić and Perović in particular, had made themselves additionally difficult to attack through their consistent antinationalism and generally effective demonstration of "modern" Party tactics, exerting "influence" through activity, manipulation, and a stern approach to *organized* political activity outside Party and Party-controlled frameworks. When the attack finally came, the core accusation was therefore "rotten liberalism" or "anarcho-liberalism," not nationalism. But such liberalism, with its insistence that the Party could warn and advise but must not otherwise interfere in "self-management" and that the Party center was no longer entitled to dictate to subordinate Party organs, was also said to be threatening the unity of Yugoslavia by seeking to render the LCY and its central organs as impotent as federal state organs already were.

When the attack did come in September–October 1972—spearheaded by Tito, Kardelj, and Stane Dolanc, the latter a new star in the central Party firmament who had impressed Tito by his role in the December crisis in Croatia and was now secretary of the LCY's executive bureau—the removal of "erring" Serbian leaders proved momentarily more difficult than its prolegomenon, the removal of Croatia's leaders ten months earlier.

Preparations for a showdown with the Serbian leaders included a "talk" by Dolanc with regional party leaders in Split on September 19, a Tito interview in *Vjesnik* (Zagreb) on October 7, and a subsequently famous letter presented to and signed by Tito and Dolanc on behalf of the executive committee on September 18, sent to all Party organizations on October 2 but published only on October 18, two days after the showdown at an interrupted plenum of the Serbian Central Committee had ended.[34]

Tito was forced to confront the Serbian leadership from an unprecedented weak position, without the backing of the Party presidency that he had invoked against the Croats at Karadjordjevo and with no formal authority except his own and that of the still unpublished executive bureau letter of September 18. The latter, moreover, was arguably a technical violation of the Party Statute, under which the bureau was responsible to the LCY presidency in policy matters of such importance.

The plenum did not go as Tito had clearly expected. It began on October 9, lasted four days, and was then suspended after a majority of those present and declaring themselves had supported their own leaders against Tito, an event unprecedented in postwar Yugoslav history. Tito himself referred to what had happened in shocked, resentful, and threatening words when the plenum reconvened on October 16:

> I wish to say here that when a Party's line, results, and weaknesses are being discussed, then the number of speakers for or against a certain view is not the decisive factor in revolutionary choice and assessment of which path to take and what is to be done. . . .
>
> I saw at the very start that the discussion was taking a quite different direction from what I wished and which I thought it should take in response to my criticism both before this meeting and in my introductory remarks. . . . It became clear that not a small number of comrades to whom I listened, I am thinking primarily of leaders, lack virtues such as self-criticism. . . .
>
> And now, here, I have gained the impression that it is not a question of how to remove what is hampering the unity of ideas and action in implementing the general line, but of who will remove whom. Even before we have finished our work, the story began to circulate around Belgrade that those who were criticized had won, . . . I think that the majority of members of the LCY and the LCS [League of Communists of Serbia] expect something quite different of us . . . [35]

Publication of this speech and of the Tito-Dolanc letter of September 18 one day later marked Tito's now unavoidable escalation of the crisis. He had in effect issued public orders to Nikezić, Perović, and their central committee, telling them clearly what he expected them to do. With this simple act he had won. It was still literally unthinkable that anyone should openly oppose him on such a clear-cut issue once it had been openly stated in this way. Besides, it did not take a long memory to recall his threat to use the army in the Croatian crisis.

The Serbian Central Committee duly met on October 21, but in closed session, to receive and approve Nikezić's and Perović's resignations. It reconvened on October 26, again in closed session, to elect new leaders, almost entirely a collection of new or resuscitated (pre-1968) nonentities.

Further resignations followed in Serbia and in Slovenia and Macedonia. These included Kavčič in Slovenia, the Party secretary in Macedonia (a protégé of Crvenkovski, who served out his 1972 rotational one-year term as chair of Yugoslavia's collective state presidency before vanishing from the scene), Mirko Tepavac (a Nikezić protégé) as foreign minister, his successors and colleagues in the Vojvodina Party, and others. Before it was all over, only Bosnia-Herzegovina and Montenegro were largely untouched by the cleansing that had begun in Croatia.

Yugoslavia's "liberal coalition," already gravely weakened by elimination of its important Croatian segment, was history. What would replace it was still unclear, despite Tito's and others' declared intention and corresponding action to return to "Leninist principles" of a monolithic and strictly hierarchical Communist party in firm if partly indirect control.

Epilogue

In the following months and years Yugoslavia's putative return to Leninism would be crippled by failure to eliminate continued republican Party control of their own cadre policies, including their members of LCY bodies. At the same time, and more surprisingly, "confederalizing" amendments to the constitution adopted in 1967–68 and 1971 were taken over almost intact and sometimes even expanded in a new constitution in 1974. Furthermore, adoption after their fall of the substance of the deposed Croatian leaders' proposals for further changes in banking and foreign trade foreign currency laws and regulations—stubborn pursuit of which had contributed to their fall—sustained and expanded the republican economic autonomy and tendency to "closed republican economies" they had fought for. Nor was there any diminution of the etatization of the economy, now almost exclusively at republican and local levels, which had been the ostensible goal of "de-etatizing" reforms in the 1960s.

The consequences were only briefly abated and then renewed devolution of the LCY into a loose federation of republican/provincial LCs, emasculated central Party and state organs that attracted ever fewer ambitious and talented persons, and reinforcement of that old symbiotic relationship between local and republican (national) political elites and "their" enterprises and managers. But all happened now without the often very talented and genuinely "reform-Communists" and social-democratic leaders whom the purges of 1971–72 had banished from the scene.

All of this together further weakened the Yugoslav state and Party and their potential for further democratization while strengthening national-regional elites and ambitions and nationalist tendencies throughout Yugoslavia. In this sense the purges of 1971–72 and their consequences can be regarded as the beginning of the (then still far from inevitable) end of Yugoslavia.

Notes

Editors' note: Dennison Rusinow's tragic accident in January 2003 prevented him from ever updating and finishing this chapter. Considering that this text represents his last written work, it has been left as is, with only minimal editing, and should be read in this light.

1. See, for example, the largely optimistic judgments (alongside some evidence to the contrary) in George W. Hoffman and Fred Warner Neal's then seminal work, *Yugoslavia and the New Communism* (New York: Twentieth Century Fund, 1962).
2. See the chapter by Audrey Helfant Budding, "Nation/People/Republic: Self-Determination in Socialist Yugoslavia," for sometimes portentous issues raised in the drawing of postwar internal borders and over other potential autonomous provinces.

3. Paul Shoup, *Communism and the Yugoslav National Question* (New York: Columbia University Press, 1968), chapter 3, is still the most thorough survey in English of early postwar nationalist disturbances, their suppression, and other aspects of the national question in this period.

4. This was almost inevitable (however much non-Serbs might regard it as deliberate) because the regime and army were based on a Partisan movement in which Montenegrins and Bosnian and Croatian Serbs had been similarly "overrepresented." In part this was because those Serbs had nowhere else to go if they preferred fighting to passively awaiting massacre and in part because Partisan operations and, hence, recruitment were until late in the war centered in the Dinaric highlands, where most of the inhabitants were Serbs, Montenegrins, and Slavic Muslims. That these ethnic disproportions continued in later years was partly a function of "old boy networks," favoring friends, relatives, and home-town youngsters, and partly because in Yugoslavia, as in other societies, economically backward regions with fewer jobs or promotional opportunities tend to send a higher proportion of their sons and daughters into government or the army (as argued in my book *The Yugoslav Experiment*, 1948–1974 [London & Berkeley: University of California Press, 1977], p. 18).

5. In 1953 Social Product per head of population in the northern regions was 110 percent (and in Slovenia 182 percent) of the Yugoslav average; that of the republics south of the Sava-Danube line (therefore including Serbia south of Vojvodina and the Belgrade area) was 71 percent and in Kosovo, the poorest region, only 53 percent. By 1957 Social Product per head in the more developed north had increased to 116 percent and that of the south had fallen to 67 percent (and in Kosovo to 42 percent) of the Yugoslav average. These trends continued with only a few local exceptions through the following decade (ibid., pp. 99f).

6. That is, with local exceptions in some ethnically mixed areas and one major one: Albanians, especially in Kosovo.

7. It was obviously a good thing for a commune to have a factory, paying taxes and creating employment, on its territory. With a blueprint for a nice, cheap little factory and the support of local and preferably also republican Party-state politicians, a credit could be obtained. And once the plant was started it could be discovered that costs had been drastically underestimated, so that additional credits were needed. As the commitment by commune and bank grew, so did the difficulty of calling a halt, especially when it was not them but the federal or republican government that must provide the means to keep an unprofitable enterprise in business (Rusinow, "Yugoslavia's Problems with 'Market Socialism,'" in *AUFS Reports*, DIR-4-'64 [May 1964]).

8. From the plenum's "Conclusions" as quoted in Rodoljub Čolaković, et al. (eds.), *Pregled istorije Saveza komunista Jugoslavije* (Belgrade: Institut za izučavanje radničkog pokreta, 1963), p. 540 (author's emphasis).

9. *Komunist*, February 28, 1958, as quoted at length by Hoffman and Neal, op. cit., pp. 196–99.

10. Rusinow, "Ports and Politics in Yugoslavia," in *AUFS Reports, Southeast Europe Series*, Vol. 11, No. 5 (DIR-5–64) (June 1964).

11. The clearest statement of the Danubian concept was by Serbian economist Kosta Mihajlović, "Regional Aspects of Economic Development," in Radmila Stojanović (ed.), *Yugoslav Economists on Problems of a Socialist Economy* (New York: International Arts and Sciences Press, 1964); of the "Adriatic concept" by Croatian economist Rudolf Bičanić in the Croatian periodical *Pomorstvo*, Nos. 9–10 (1964). See also Rusinow, *The Yugoslav Experiment*, op. cit., p. 133.

12. My use of the terms *conservative(s)* and *liberal(s)* requires explanation. Conservatives in this struggle were those who sought to conserve (if also to improve upon) the partly decentralized quasi-market economic system and partly de-Stalinized but still monopolistic and basically centralized Party control. The other side, pace their own dislike of the term, can with definitional and also historical accuracy be called liberals because they sought an expansion of entrepreneurial and also civil liberties, a diminishing role for the state, and a (usually limited) extension of the effective franchise. Some of the latter, to complete the historical analogy implicit in my use of the term, were in the course of a decade to pass like ghosts out of nineteenth-century Central Europe from liberalism through national-liberalism to nationalism.

13. Deborah Milenkovitch, in *Plan and Market in Yugoslav Economic Thought* (New Haven: Yale University Press, 1971), pp. 125ff., makes the important point that there were "decentralizers" for whom "decentralization was used to express an opposition not to planning as such, but to planning done at the [federal] center instead of at the republican or local level," as well as two kinds of "centralizers": those advocating more central planning and control over enterprises and those who accepted the existing limits of the market economy but did not want them enlarged.

14. Both phases are discussed and documented in detail in a number of 1960s books by "Western" economists and in my book *The Yugoslav Experiment*, chapter 4, "The Great Debate Resumed."

15. Quoted by Paul Lendvai (who interviewed leaders on both sides at the time, noting that "figures, figures, figures dominate the conversation wherever one travels"), *Eagles in Cobwebs: Nationalism and Communism in the Balkans* (New York: Doubleday, 1969), p. 143.

16. Except in the first two years, when the role of economic organizations in distribution of national income grew (according to one calculation) from control over 45 percent in 1961 to 49 percent in 1964 and nearly 58 percent in 1967. Their share in the financing of investments in the economy peaked at 39.4 percent in 1966. In 1967 and subsequent years these trends were reversed.

17. Details can again be found, inter alia, in *The Yugoslav Experiment*, chapter 5, "Laissez-faire Socialism."

18. Rusinow, "Yugoslavia, 1966: The Titoist Revolution Enters a New Phase," in *AUFS Reports*, Vol. 13, No. 6 (DIR-4-'66), p. 5.

19. Edvard Kardelj's description at the Central Committee's follow-up Third Plenum in February–March, as quoted in *Borba*, March 13, 1966.

20. Central Committee plenums were numbered serially, beginning anew after each LCY or republican Party congress.

21. Early "eyewitness" accounts of the Fourth Plenum and the final political maneuvering that led to Brioni include a series of well-informed reports by Belgrade correspondent David Binder in *The New York Times*, summer 1966, passim, Lendvai, op. cit., chapter 3, and my AUFS report cited above.

22. As described in *The Yugoslav Experiment*, p. 194.

23. The alleged political underground enjoyed some minor successes in communal, republican, and federal assembly elections in 1967 and 1969 (the freest and most open in Communist Yugoslav history). This may have been one reason why Kardelj and other liberals soon devised a new and largely indirect electoral system (of "delegations and delegates") that precluded a repetition of such "anomalies" (see my three-part analysis, "Yugoslav Elections, 1969" in *AUFS Reports*, Vol. 16, Nos. 4–6 (July 1969).

24. Hints of these can be found in his speeches and interviews after 1967, but clearer statements of them came—ominously including repeated references to the Party Congress of 1952 as a Congress he "had never liked"—only after the 1970–71 crisis in Croatia.

25. For a discussion of these reforms see the chapters by Audrey Budding and Jill Irvine in this volume.

26. See Rusinow, *The Yugoslav Experiment*, pp. 202–9, for summary statistics and analysis, and Susan Woodward, *Socialist Unemployment: The Political Economy of Yugoslavia, 1945–1990* (New Jersey: Princeton University Press, 1995), for a more detailed treatment.

27. Plenum speeches in 14 sednica CK SK Srbije (Belgrade, 1968). Marjanović was the outstanding historian of recent Yugoslav history belonging to the Serbian Partisan generation; Ćosić was/is generally considered the best living Serbian writer and would play a major role in the later development of Serb nationalism and as president of the (rump) Federal Republic of Yugoslavia in the Milošević era.

28. The Nova Gorica end of the motorway was finally under construction in 2003.

29. Cvijeto Job, *Yugoslavia's Ruin: The Bloody Lessons of Nationalism* (Lanham: Rowman and Littlefield, 2002), p. 74. Cf. Dušan Bilandžić, *Ideje i praksa društvenog razvoja Jugoslavije 1945–73* (Belgrade, 1973), where he refers to the crisis as "threatening the fall of the Federal Government" and thereby "strengthening the practice of republican pressures for the realization of their interests."

30. Job, op. cit., p. 75. My own early (and controversial) account and interpretation is in a four-part series, "Crisis in Croatia," in Fieldstaff Reports, Vol. 19, Nos. 4–7 (June–Sept. 1972).

31. The term *stagnation*, taking on the aura of a slogan, was significantly gaining in popularity. It and others with similar import appear with growing frequency from 1968 in the speeches and writings of leaders at all levels, including Tito, but were seldom used before that year.

32. Although in his case difficult to prove, there was no informed observer of the Yugoslav and Croatian scene at the time who was not convinced that the shift was not on Bakarić's initiative and meant to be part of a new strategic plan concocted in his fertile but impenetrable mind.

33. King Louis IV of France reigned from 936 to 954. Although he effectively enjoyed sovereignty only over the town of Laon and parts of northern France, he was particularly astute in obtaining the recognition of his authority by his feuding local nobles. [editors' note]

34. All published, along with Tito's October 16 speech, in Stane Dolanc et al., *Ideological and Political Offensive of the League of Communists of Yugoslavia* (Belgrade: The Secretariat for Information of the Federal Executive Council, 1972).

35. In ibid., pp. 91–95.

THE CROATIAN SPRING AND THE DISSOLUTION OF YUGOSLAVIA

❖ Jill Irvine ❖

On December 3, 1971, Tito called the "triumvirate" of Croatian liberal leaders to his hunting-lodge retreat in Karadjordjevo, where he delivered an ultimatum that brought an abrupt and dramatic end to a period of liberalization and popular mobilization in Croatia (known variously as the Croatian Spring or the mass movement). Within weeks the proreform Party leaders tendered their resignations, ushering in a period of repression during which many of their prominent supporters were expelled from the Party, fired from their jobs, or given prison terms. Twenty years later, in December 1991, as the war raging in Croatia was halted by a tenuous cease-fire, many of these reformers occupied positions of power in the new Croatian state. On December 23, Germany recognized the Republic of Croatia, and over the next weeks and months the world's other major powers followed suit. The government of this newly independent state was dominated, as it had been since the first multiparty elections in the spring of 1990, by a generation of leaders who had experienced the Croatian Spring firsthand and had suffered the consequences of its aftermath. Indeed, the president of Croatia, Franjo Tudjman, had himself been imprisoned after the crackdown at the end of 1971. Thus the period of reform, popular mobilization, and political turmoil during the Croatian Spring shaped the political perceptions and actions of both the leaders and the public in Croatia during the dissolution of Yugoslavia twenty years later. But what exactly was the legacy of the Croatian Spring for later developments in Croatia and Yugoslavia?

This chapter considers the causes and consequences of the popular movement in Croatia in 1971 by focusing on three main sets of questions. The first question has to do with the origins of the reforms of the 1960s that culminated in the Croatian Spring. Was the Croatian Spring, as many have argued, an outgrowth of various situational factors at the time, in particular, the need for economic reform? Or was it triggered primarily by national sentiments that were exacerbated but certainly not created by the economic situation in Croatia in the 1960s? In other words, was the Croatian Spring the result of more enduring

149

tensions that may have contributed, ultimately, to the disintegration of the state? The second question concerns the vision (or possible lack thereof) among liberal Communists in Croatia who spearheaded economic and political reforms, particularly reform of the federal system. Did they champion a viable alternative to the Yugoslav federal system put into place in 1945, an alternative that Tito and other Party leaders cast aside with ultimately tragic consequences? Or was it the inability of Croatian liberal Communists to put forth such an alternative in 1971 that allowed them to be manipulated by ethnonationalists bent on Croatian separatism? Finally, what were the implications of the Croatian Spring for subsequent political developments in Yugoslavia? Did the events at Karadjordjevo and their political aftermath signal the beginning of the end of the Yugoslav state, as some have claimed? Should the political unrest of 1971 be viewed as a preview of what was to come?

The answer to many of these questions lies, I argue, in the founding period of the Yugoslav socialist state. The entire state order, including the federal system and the solution to the national question it symbolized, was embedded in the structures that emerged at this time. But the character of this federal system through which the various nations of Yugoslavia were said to have exercised their right of self-determination was, in fact, highly contested during the war. When the question of relations among Yugoslavia's nations and republics was reopened during the constitutional reforms of the 1960s and the 1980s, it quickly became the subject of fierce political struggle once again.

There were two main and related problems concerning the right of self-determination and the character of the federal system that the regime failed to resolve during the wartime period. The first had to do with the nature of the federal units and how to define the political communities embodied by them. Were they primarily territorial communities encompassing all the citizens of a particular republic or province, or were they primarily ethnic communities, the titular nations of "their" particular republics? The second had to do with the relationship between these units and the central political authority, of how to define the competencies of the republics and provinces. Did political authority emanate from the central institutions of the party-state (thus rendering the very validity of federalism suspect) or from the republic institutions? The first problem of defining political communities was simply glossed over or obscured, as Audrey Helfant Budding has aptly demonstrated in her contribution to this book. The second problem, which I will focus on in this chapter, was less glossed over than repeatedly fought over. At least two competing concepts of one-party federalism emerged during the founding period of the Yugoslav socialist state: a loose or decentralized model implemented by Croatian Communists in 1943 and 1944 and a tight, or centralized, model imposed in 1945. Although the republic institutions created during this period were ultimately subordinated to central control, the legacy of this period of loose federalism in Croatia was never officially repudiated by the Communist Party of

Yugoslavia, and it provided both the inspiration for and the legitimization of the federal reforms championed during the Croatian Spring.

Yugoslavia, then, suffered from what might be called a congenital birth defect, for while the regime based its legitimacy and its claim to have resolved the national question in large part on the institutions that emerged during the National Liberation Struggle, the character of these institutions was not clear. Given the importance of the wartime period for legitimizing federal institutions, it is no accident that both rounds of major reforms in Yugoslavia in the late 1960s and in the mid-1980s began by attempting to reappropriate the "forgotten" legacy of the Partisan period (in the case of the Croatian reformers in 1970–71) or to repudiate the legacy of this period (in the case of Serb reformers in the 1980s). Contention over loose and tight federal concepts, which were tied to the traditional goals of the national movements of Yugoslavia's two largest ethnic groups, became an enduring feature of the Yugoslav socialist state and a point of sharp disagreement during periods of major constitutional reforms (with the exception of the introduction of self-management in the early 1950s). Although the introduction of the loose federal system alarmed the Serb community in Croatia and elsewhere in the country, even during the war but certainly during 1971 and 1990, the tighter model of federalism did not fulfill the statehood aspirations of the majority of Croats. Moreover, the problems raised in implementing the loose federal model remained the same from 1943 to 1971 to 1991; Croatian Communist proponents of this model faced difficulties in their relations with Serbs in Croatia (who began to talk of autonomy or separation from Croatia) but also with other forces of Croatian nationalism (which they could not easily control) and with the leaders of other republics (who objected to possible claims on their territory). In this sense, the dynamics of Croatian Spring not only harkened back to the founding period of the Yugoslav socialist state but also provided a preview and a harbinger of the dissolution of the second Yugoslavia in 1991.

The Roots of the Croatian Spring

One enduring question in Yugoslav historiography has been the relationship between economic and political reforms in the 1960s and its impact on developments in Croatia leading to the Croatian Spring. The usual interpretation offered in the several fine studies of these reforms published in the 1970s and 1980s is that they were a response, first to the break with Stalin in 1948 and subsequent reformulation of Yugoslav political doctrine and practice, and then to the economic difficulties that beset the regime in the early 1960s. According to this explanation of Yugoslav political developments, the decentralization of the Party and state, spearheaded by Communists in Croatia in the mid-1960s, was a response to immediate economic problems that only gradually took on more political overtones.[1] These economic problems were created in part by the introduction of self-management in 1953 and the economic distortions that its reliance on some market mechanisms created. Moreover, though self-management itself did not mean a significant revision of the federal formula adopted at the end of the war, it did leave the door open for such a change.[2] In short, the federal reform of the party-state beginning in the mid-1960s, representing a sharp break with previous practice in Yugoslavia and other Communist countries, had its roots in the situation and character of Yugoslavia at this time.

A second interpretation of the relationship between political and economic reforms that led up to the Croatian Spring has been offered by some of the many works published since the outbreak of violent conflict in Yugoslavia in 1991. These works, focusing on the causes of the violence there, have tended to interpret all major political developments in socialist Yugoslavia as arising from ethnic grievances and animosities. As the ever-present backdrop and driving force of Yugoslav politics, the nationalism that simmered just beneath the surface could only be contained through continued political repression. According to this view of Yugoslav history, the Croatian Spring was an expression of festering national resentments that burst forth at the first possible opportunity. When the repression of the Party weakened, first through the introduction of self-management in the early 1950s and then after the fall of Ranković in 1966, an outbreak of long-standing tensions between national groups and expressions of mutually contradictory national goals was the inevitable and dramatic result.[3]

Although these interpretations highlight some important dynamics of the reforms leading up to the Croatian Spring, they disregard the roots of these reforms in the struggle over federalism during the founding of the Yugoslav socialist state. As Dennison Rusinow's chapter in this book demonstrates, pressing economic issues and grievances concerning developmental priorities, the disposition of republican assets, and a downturn in economic performance all raised the need for substantive economic and political reform. Nevertheless, although it is true that support for reform among some LCC leaders (and leaders in other republics) was at least partially a response to pressing economic needs, the contours of this reform were not new. Proponents of confederal reforms in the 1960s appealed to the origin of this federal model in the policies adopted by Croatian Communists in 1943–44. According to Croatian Party liberals, the reforms were simply a return to the "true principles" of the revolution abandoned after the war. Opponents of reform countered in a similar fashion by referring to the centralizing federal strategy adopted in 1945. In advocating reform of the federal system and in opposing it, both sides could point to competing concepts of federalism institutionalized during the formation of the Yugoslav socialist state. Thus Croatian Communists' promotion of political reforms in the late 1960s was neither merely a response to short-term developments nor an outburst of pent-up national resentment. It was, rather, also a resumption of a struggle over different visions of the federal order (and the distribution of power among the national groups it signified) that was an integral part of the "founding moment" of the Yugoslav socialist state. The clash over competing concepts of the federal order, inherited from the Partisan period, was a defining feature of the Croatian Spring and the period of reform leading up to it.

The Partisan Legacy: Competing Concepts of One-Party Federalism

In advocating reform of the federal system in the 1960s, LCC liberals—led by President of the LCC Central Committee Pero Pirker, member of the Presidency of the LCY Executive Bureau Miko Tripalo, and LCC Secretary Savka Dabčević-Kučar—attempted to reappropriate the loose federal model that had been adopted in Croatia during 1943 and 1944. This model, associated with then Communist Party of Croatia (CPC) leader Andrija Hebrang, sought to carve out maximum autonomy for Croatian Party and governmental organizations in relation to central political (Communist Party) authorities. As Hebrang and his supporters established the political structures they believed would provide the framework for the postwar socialist state, authority in the federation would emanate from the republic upward, not the other way around. Thus, central political institutions, such as the main antifascist council (AVNOJ) established in the fall of 1942, would derive their authority from the regional antifascist councils, (abbreviated as ZAVNOH in Croatia), whose decisions would be shaped by republic Party leaders. Hebrang repeatedly asserted that the institutions the Communists were creating during the war, such as ZAVNOH (renamed the Sabor in 1944), would have full authority over matters pertaining to Croatia and its interests. As the true expression of Croatian sovereignty, ZAVNOH would be responsible for making decisions on all matters pertaining to the Croatian republic. "And this means," Hebrang wrote, "that Croats alone, through their Sabor as the vessel of sovereignty, independently decide their fate." In other words, only the Croatian Sabor as an expression of the democratic will of Croats and Serbs in Croatia can make authoritative decisions about the internal order of Croatia and her relations with other peoples and states.[4] By the end of 1943, ZAVNOH ministries were turning out a stream of directives on all aspects of social and political life in Croatia, including peasant debt and landholdings, currency, banking, health care, education including religious instruction, marriage, and divorce, without consulting Tito or referring to any higher authority.[5]

By asserting the autonomy of Croatian institutions, Hebrang cast himself in the role of leader of the Croatian national movement. According to him, the goals and activities of the Croatian Communist Party were responding to the centuries-long aspirations of Croats for their own state. Indeed, the CPC, he argued, was the only force capable of realizing these goals within the context of the civil war and the struggle against the Axis occupying forces. As he stated at the third session of ZAVNOH in 1944, "We fellow members of ZAVNOH are not only realizing the aspirations of the current generation; we are realizing the aspirations of the best Croats sons and the best ideas of the Croatian past."[6] As leader of the Croatian national movement,

Hebrang argued that he and other CPC leaders should determine the best position toward the Allies when it affected Croatia and, perhaps more importantly, to determine relations with other popular forces in the Croatian national movement, particularly the Croatian Peasant Party.[7]

The central Party leadership under Tito increasingly opposed this concept of loose one-party federalism in which Croatian Party and state institutions would have full control over matters pertaining to Croatia. Although Tito was prepared to tolerate a degree of decentralization during the early period of the war, the second meeting of the central antifascist council (AVNOJ) in the fall of 1943 signaled a period of greater centralization as Tito sought to bring the various regional councils and Party leaders under firmer control. The tight concept of federalism laid out at this meeting and put into place during the ensuing months required a clear subordination of republic and regional councils, Party leaders, and military forces to the control of central Party organizations and the state council (AVNOJ). Thus, Tito entirely rejected Hebrang's understanding of federalism, calling Hebrang to task on many occasions for failing to refer to the higher authority of AVNOJ and to submit to central Party organs. He also objected to other aspects of the CPC policies that sought to address Croat grievances and concerns, including its emphasis on the unity of Croatian lands, its relations with the Croatian Peasant Party, and its efforts to reduce the dominance of Serbs in the Partisan movement in Croatia. Charging that Hebrang "was entering with all [his] might into separatism"[8] and that this was having a negative effect on the Serb population in Croatia, Tito further admonished him for the inappropriate "tone" of his communications with higher party authorities.[9]

By the fall of 1944, Hebrang's pursuit of a system of loose federalism and his resistance to the imposition of a centralized model of federalism were becoming intolerable to Tito and other central Party leaders. When ZAVNOH announced in mid-September the formation of an independent telegraph agency for Croatia, Tito saw it as a direct challenge to the centralization of the movement. He issued a sharp reprimand to Hebrang. "Why don't you see that a federal state order has one official telegraph agency?" he wrote. "If no one else will do, let your example be the Soviet Union."[10] This last sentence was extremely revealing, for Tito made it clear that the greater degree of autonomy regional Party leaders had possessed during the war was not permissible in the centralized order the CPY was now establishing. After receiving negative reports from other central Party leaders, who objected to Hebrang's "false" understanding of federalism and his "nationalist proclivities," Tito removed Hebrang in the fall of 1944 and replaced him with Vladimir Bakarić.[11] The domineering personality of postwar political life in Croatia, Bakarić lost little time in implementing the tight concept of federalism laid out at the second meeting of AVNOJ and subordinating developments in Croatia to central Party control. The federal system established by the end of the war and enshrined in the 1946 Constitution closely resembled the Soviet model, instituting a unitary system in which republic borders and institutions were, in

Tito's words, "a question only of administrative division."[12] And that was where matters stood for the next two decades.

Legitimizing the Liberals' Vision

During the years and months of reform leading up to the Croatian Spring, the most persistent aim of the LCC reformers regarding the federal system was, like Hebrang's in 1943, to maximize the decision-making authority of republic institutions within the Party and the state. The turning point in LCC's role in redefining the Yugoslav federal system came at the LCC Tenth Plenum held in January 1970, which signaled that discussion of national issues and grievances would no longer be prohibited or even discouraged.[13] This apparent invitation to express national sentiments unleashed a mass movement (abbreviated *maspok* by the Communists), demanding fundamental revision of the tight federal model imposed at the end of the war. The series of amendments to the federal constitution adopted in the summer of 1971 and the revision of Croatia's constitution in the fall provided the backdrop for the discussion of these issues. As popular agitation for expanding Croatian autonomy increased, the struggle among LCC leaders over the aims and control of the popular movement grew. Although Tito initially appeared to support (or at least acquiesce to) the activities of LCC liberals, he became increasingly alarmed by the implications of these activities for the political authority of the LCY. When students went on strike at Zagreb University in November 1971, Tito supported LCC conservatives who demanded the removal of LCC liberals and the suppression of the mass movement.

In attempting to redefine Croatian sovereignty during the spring and summer of 1971, liberal Party leaders drew upon the model of federalism institutionalized through ZAVNOH during the war, and they emphasized that the roots of this vision were to be found in the Partisan struggle. Indeed, though according to Dabčević-Kučar they did not dare associate themselves explicitly with Hebrang's policies, it was no coincidence that there was an effort to rehabilitate him at this time.[14] LCC liberals declared that the Croatian question had not been resolved in the way that had been promised by ZAVNOH and that the federation must be reorganized to more fully realize that promise.[15] They put forth three important ideas, all of which they linked to the Partisan legacy: first, that national (Croatian) sentiments were a legitimate expression of popular interests; second, that Communists should defend these interests; and third, that the Yugoslav state must be organized so that the republic, which was the political unit in which the national sovereignty was embodied, had the most power.

In justifying popular expression of national sentiments and in responding to them, LCC leaders pointed out that the National Liberation Struggle, as its name suggested, had been a struggle for national as well as social liberation. According to them, this fundamental aspect of the Yugoslav revolution had been negated during the period of centralism after the war; LCC reformers were attempting to return it to its rightful place in Yugoslav theory and practice. "Self-management reforms," Tripalo wrote, "also mean a reaffirmation of some principles concerning national relations which were established during the National Liberation Struggle and which were called into question during the period of administrative socialism."[16] LCC liberal leaders increasingly cast themselves as leaders of a mass movement like the one that had emerged during the Second World War, and Tito appeared to concur with this analysis when he remarked on a trip to Croatia in the fall of 1971 that the enthusiasm he encountered among the populace there reminded him of the National Liberation Struggle.[17] At a rally held in Bogomilje to celebrate the thirtieth anniversary of the Partisan uprising of 1941, Tripalo stressed that the LCC had drawn the "broadest segment of our nation" into the reform movement in 1971. "Because of that," he went on, "one can claim with certainty that our movement is a direct successor and continuation of the mass movement of the National Liberation Struggle and of the post war reconstruction and socialist construction of our country."[18]

As leaders of a popularly based Croatian national movement, LCC reformers were particularly vociferous in their claims that the organization of the federation after 1945 had hurt Croatia economically and in demanding that Croatia acquire greater control over the dispensation of its revenues. They further emphasized their essential role in defending the particular national interests of the Croatian population. Since 1945, official rhetoric had stressed the LCY's role in creating "brotherhood and unity" among the nations of Yugoslavia, especially among Serbs and Croats; its role in realizing the more particular national aspirations of these nations was seldom mentioned. LCC liberals returned, however, to the Croatian national themes emphasized by the CPC during 1943 and 1944, including the unity of Croatian lands, the promotion of Croatian culture, language and history, the important role of the Catholic Church and, perhaps most controversially, the reduction of Serb dominance of public institutions in Croatia, including the police, Party organizations, and certain economic enterprises.

The unity of Croatian lands as a precondition to achieving full Croatian sovereignty was a historic theme of the Croatian National Movement. The division of what Croats referred to as the historic Croatian lands and the large numbers of Serbs residing within these historic borders had made the unity of Croatia a sensitive issue. Convinced that the Partisan movement could never succeed in Croatia unless it responded to popular aspirations for Croatian statehood, the CPC had emphasized its role in preserving the unity of Croatian lands by reuniting Dalmatia and Istria to the Croatian state. In 1943, ZAVNOH formally declared Istria to be part of Croatia, a decision that Tito later charged had usurped the rightful powers of AVNOJ.[19] Hebrang was also determined to firmly link Dalmatia to the emerging state structures in Croatia and to curb the "autonomist" tendencies of Communists and non-Communists in this area.[20] Though he promoted greater autonomy for Croatia, Hebrang had no intention of allowing regional autonomy within Croatia, and he in turn faulted Tito for failing to subordinate the Dalmatian regional leadership to the CPC's authority.[21]

In promoting Croatian interests in 1970 and 1971, LCC liberals echoed many of these themes about the unity of Croatian lands. In language and tone remarkably like CPC pronouncements during 1943 and 1944, Tripalo argued that the Communists were the true defenders of Croatian national interests because the Independent State of Croatia had abandoned Dalmatia, Istria, and Medjumurje, whereas the Communists had won the unity of Croatian lands.[22] At an event commemorating the anniversary of ZAVNOH's decision to attach Istria to Croatia, Savka Dabčević-Kučar described it as one of "historic, legal and state-building significance."[23] But just as the CPC had struggled with "autonomists" and "unitarists" in Dalmatia, LCC liberals worried that their support for greater autonomy in Croatia would lead to fragmentation within Croatia itself. Like the CPC in 1943 and 1944, the liberal leadership adamantly rejected any application of the federal principle within Croatia itself. Indeed, they reacted with fury to the attempt to have regional identity included in the census then underway. Allowing citizens to designate Dalmatia, Istria, or Slavonia on the census, Dabčević-Kučar argued, was confusing the two concepts of regional and ethnic identity, which were not the same.[24] Mindful of the CPC's experience, LCC liberals were particularly concerned about the possibility of autonomist sentiments in Dalmatia, though these fears proved unfounded.[25] As Dabčević-Kučar later wrote, "[o]ur main goal was, and we succeeded in achieving it for the first time: the homogenization of Croatia."[26]

In addition to promoting Croatian territorial unity, LCC liberals attempted to promote Croatian language, history, and culture, which they believed had been repressed during the past twenty-five years. This issue had first been raised in a dramatic fashion in 1967 when over one hundred prominent Croatian intellectuals, the majority of them Communists, signed a declaration calling for the (re)establishment of Croatian as an official language and an end to what they alleged was the preference given to the Serbian form of Serbo-Croatian. During the months after the tenth LCC plenum, LCC liberals repeatedly expressed their dissatisfaction with the "incorrect" information about Croatian history being taught in the schools.[27] In response to what they claimed was a biased and discriminatory program of study, LCC liberals proposed an educational plan for elementary and middle school aimed at the "Croatinization" of instruction. Under this plan, 75 percent of instruction in history and literature would be required to treat Croatian topics. For many supporters of the Croatian Spring, increasing instruction in Croatian history and culture was essential to the success of the Croatian national movement. As Franjo Tudjman wrote in his "Outline of Theses for the Congress of Croatian Culture," "today when it's a question of building Croatian statehood . . . pedagogical, educational, political and cultural-scientific efforts [must be directed] so that the Croatian people as quickly as possible develop active, state-building, political thought."[28] In other words, education was to be used for consciousness-raising and to help achieve the goal of Croatian statehood. To this end, the cultural organization Matica Hrvatska, with the support of LCC liberals, sponsored numerous celebrations of historical events and figures, many of which, like Ban Jelačić, had been condemned as traitors in Communist historiography.[29]

Another area in which the LCC liberals attempted to promote Croatian national interests was in their policy toward the Catholic Church. Here, too, they justified their position by pointing to the Partisan legacy in Croatia. According to Dabčević-Kučar, LCC liberals were aware of the importance of the Catholic Church not just for Croatian culture but also for Croatian political identity. In attempting to mitigate what they saw as systematic hostility toward the Catholic Church, despite the regime's official policy of religious tolerance, they referred to the legacy of ZAVNOH. In the fall of 1944, ZAVNOH had passed a decision instituting Catholic religious instruction in Croatian schools, over the strong protests of the central Party leadership.[30] This decision, which according to Dabčević-Kučar reflected "a more correct stance" toward the role of the church, had been forgotten after 1945. "Some basics were forgotten from the time of ZAVNOH," she wrote, such as the "more democratic and freer relations toward religious faiths and believers."[31] Convinced that they "could not build anything against believers nor without them," LCC liberals initiated a series of measures designed to remove police pressure from Catholic Church officials and members and to include them in the popular mobilization occurring at that time.[32] Dabčević-Kučar makes clear in her memoirs that they also understood this policy as an essential counterbalance to the "catastrophically dangerous role of the Orthodox Church as a disseminator of Greater Serbian chauvinism."[33] Politicizing the Catholic Church, then, was intended to help achieve a central goal of the mass movement, diminishing the role of Serbs in Croatian political life.

While promoting these traditional themes of the Croatian national movement and using the legacy of ZAVNOH to legitimize their efforts, the LCC liberals also tackled a far more sensitive issue—predominance of Serbs in Croatian political life. This issue had also preoccupied Hebrang and other CPC leaders in 1943 and 1944. Hebrang had attempted to modify the image of a Serb-dominated Partisan movement that developed during the first two years of the war when Serbs joined the Partisans in large numbers in order to defend themselves against Ustasa massacres.[34] His efforts to increase the visibility of Croats in the movement and to emphasize the CPC's role in achieving Croatian statehood, however, appear to have made many Serbs uneasy. By the spring of 1944, this uneasiness had grown to outright unhappiness and complaints about the lack of Serb representation in ZAVNOH and the CPC Central Committee, pressure to use Latin script in ZAVNOH publications and the CPC's "sectarian" propaganda toward Serbs.[35] As morale plunged among Serbs, resulting in defections from some units in Kordun, members of the CPY Politboro became increasingly concerned about the effect of Hebrang's policies on Serbian support for the Partisan movement, a concern that contributed to Hebrang's removal in the fall of 1944.

This issue of Serb predominance in political bodies and some economic organizations in Croatia continued after the war. As a result of their active participation in the crucial early stages in the Partisan struggle in Croatia, Serbs had retained a disproportionate influence—by virtue of their relatively higher numbers—in the LCC and in the police and security apparatus. At the beginning of 1971, LCC Secretary Savka Dabčević-Kučar emphasized that this "sensitive" problem must be addressed "openly, publicly and ethically," and she called for "adequate proportional representation" in all social and political organizations.[36] On a number of occasions, Tripalo also expressed his concern about this problem to Tito, who warned him to be "very cautious and patient [in his approach] because it involve[d] a very sensitive question."[37] What this effort to reduce Serb predominance amounted to, in effect, was a great deal of head counting as Communists and non-Communists alike began to catalogue the number of Serbs in various military, political, and economic institutions and to call for their replacement by Croats.[38]

In addition to reducing the predominance of Serbs in positions of authority in Croatia, LCC reformers sought to fashion their own policy toward popular forces within the mass movement, including the increasingly visible and vocal non-Communist portion of this movement. LCC leaders insisted that the activities of non-Communist individuals and organizations such as Matica Hrvatska must be permitted, emphasizing the ostensible pluralist heritage of Croatian political culture and, in particular, of the Partisan legacy in Croatia under Hebrang's leadership. They defended their willingness to permit pluralism, in particular the activities of Matica Hrvatska, by the CPC's similar tolerance of widespread non-Communist political activity during the war. And they perceived themselves to be in an excellent position to control these forces because Matica Hrvatska did not appear to have the political power the Croat Peasant Party had once possessed. Hebrang had keenly appreciated the threat the Croatian Peasant Party had posed to the Communists' political position. Consequently, while wooing its members, he sought to discredit CPP leaders and to undermine the Peasant Party's organizational strength.[39] Believing they had little to fear from Matica Hrvatska, LCC leaders took a less cautious approach. As Dabčević-Kučar later expressed it, "We weren't for a priori throwing out Yugoslavia or socialism because we thought they could be fixed. But when we encountered something we considered unacceptable or nationalist we weren't for forbidding it. We weren't for separatism but we didn't fear it but rather those who by ignoring Croatian interests caused it."[40]

Indeed, LCC liberals appeared to believe that by supporting pluralism and referring to the legacy of ZAVNOH to legitimize it they could solve what Rusinow once called "the two great unsolved problems of contemporary Yugoslavia," namely the national question and socialist democracy.[41] This strategy caused increasing difficulties for the LCC reformers, however, because Matica Hrvatska used its considerable popularity and organizational autonomy to pressure them to adopt more radical positions on federal reforms. Like Hebrang, LCC reformers faced the constant pressure to truly fulfill popular aspirations for statehood or lose support. The thinly veiled threat of the president of the Socialist Alliance, Ivica Vrkić, revealed this danger of being outflanked by non-Communist forces in the national movement who could more directly appeal to these national sentiments. Vrkić stated: "So let everyone know that we are fighting for and will direct our political organization toward the relation of Croatian statehood as a union of equality of Croats, because here is a unique chance for Croatia, for the Croatian people, to create their state which they have sought throughout history, and if they do not get it now, it seems to me that the Croatian people will never again even be for a Communist movement."[42]

While LCC liberals became increasingly intent on leading the reemerging Croatian national movement, the thrust of their efforts remained focused on implementing a loose model of federalism. Indeed, according to LCC liberals, the vehicle for achieving any national goals was a return to the principle of self-determination embraced during the Second World War, which clearly meant the right to form national states. As the decisions of the third meeting of ZAVNOH had made clear, this right to statehood in the Yugoslav context meant states based on the republics. The republics, Tripalo argued, must be regarded as "the purveyors of statehood"; unfounded fears of the disintegration of Yugoslavia should not prevent them from assuming their correct position in the Yugoslav federation. Sovereignty must mean the right of Croatian authorities to have the first and final say on all issues pertaining to the cultural, economic, and political (national) interests of Croatia (though the question of whether this meant Croats or the republic of Croatia was never clearly addressed). Although they embraced the notion of the withering away of the state in principle, LCC reformers believed this process of withering away should apply only to the central organs of the Party and government.

The LCC liberals urged a further reorganization of federal institutions to reflect the resolution adopted by the Yugoslav presidency in April 1970, which recognized "the sovereignty" of the republics and provinces. Discussion concerning the character of this sovereignty and the organization of the state took place as part of the process of amending the 1963 Federal Yugoslav Constitution and, subsequently, the constitutions of the republics and autonomous provinces. Amendments to the federal constitution were drafted by a constitutional commission at the beginning of 1971, approved by the LCY presidium at its sixteenth session in March 1971, and then submitted for public debate. Building on the nineteen amendments adopted in 1967 and 1968, which trimmed the prerogatives of the federal government and central Party organizations, the amendments proposed in the spring of 1971 introduced a collective state presidency and required unanimity among republics and provinces concerning federal policy on a range of economic issues. The reforms were designed, in the words of the drafters, to reaffirm "that the working people, nations and nationalities realize their sovereign rights in the

Socialist Republics, and in the Socialist Autonomous Provinces." After the Federal Assembly promulgated the amendments in June, republics were left to define how this sovereignty should be exercised through republic institutions. At the heart of this issue was economic reform of banking and foreign currency systems; LCC liberals and their supporters insisted upon their right to control the economic instruments necessary to full sovereignty. This matter of defining Croatian sovereignty prompted a heated discussion both about the character of the political community in which sovereignty would be vested and about the institutional manifestation of this political community.

Although the liberal faction of the LCC emphasized the importance of returning to the "correct" approach to national relations embraced during the war, hardliners in the leadership opposed this understanding of the Partisan legacy.[43] They challenged the liberals' attempt to return to the loose model of federalism adopted by ZAVNOH and their renewed emphasis on republic sovereignty. Interestingly, they received increasing support from the powerful Vladimir Bakarić, who had also opposed Hebrang's policies in 1944. Charging that the decisions taken by ZAVNOH had a nationalist character, Bakarić disputed LCC reformers' attempts to legitimize their policies by appealing to the legacy of ZAVNOH under Hebrang's leadership.[44] Bakarić asserted, not entirely consistently, that Communists in Croatia had not been concerned with national issues at the end of the war, and that they, too, were responsible for the imposition of a centralized state order.[45] LCC hardliners further objected that Matica Hrvatska had pressured the liberals into adopting positions on the national questions that were not in line with central Party directives. This question of LCC control over the popular forces led by Matica Hrvatska became the most serious point of contention between the liberal and hard-line factions in the LCC.[46]

LCC Liberals and Matica Hrvatska: Controlling the Popular Movement

As the LCC attempted to formulate and implement a looser form of federal relations in Croatia, it joined forces with a growing popular movement led by the Croatian cultural organization Matica Hrvatska.[47] By 1970, Matica Hrvatska had begun to play a more active political role. At its annual assembly in November 1970, Matica Hrvatska launched a new membership drive and adopted a program that addressed various political and economic questions; its attention to these matters gave it an instantaneous and enthusiastic following. During the next year, its membership increased twentyfold, from 2,323 members in November 1970 to 41,000 members in November 1971.[48] In response to the discussion of the federal system and Croatian national aims opened by the tenth plenum, Matica publications began to tackle themes on Croatian history, culture, and political life that had previously been taboo.[49] They addressed at length the ways in which Croatia was suffering from its current position in the Yugoslav federation—what it considered Croatia's punitively high payment of revenue to the central government, the unusually high rate of emigration from Croatia compared to other republics, the "denigration" of the Croatian language, and the lack of instruction about Croatian history in schools and universities. In a new publication, *Hrvatski tjednik,* launched in the spring of 1971, Matica Hrvatska became the widely accepted voice of the Croatian national movement and a strong advocate of redressing Croats' grievances.

Matica Hrvatska, like the LCC liberals, drew upon the legacy of ZAVNOH to bolster its own increasingly radical stance on Croatian sovereignty. In a series of articles about the proposed reform of Croatia's constitution published in *Hrvatski tjednik*, Matica Hrvatska presented its positions concerning the Yugoslav federal system and Croatia's place in it. Matica Hrvatska strongly embraced the idea endorsed by LCC liberals that the reorganization of the federation meant a return to the original guiding principles of the revolution. "The fact is that the reconstruction of the federation," *Hrvatski tjednik* wrote in September 1971, "is really the renewal of those ideals which were established and realized in the course of the National Liberation Struggle and the socialist revolution."[50] Matica Hrvatska stressed that attaining Croatian sovereignty was the fundamental principle of the Partisan struggle in Croatia and that it remained the most important goal to be achieved in 1971. As Marko Veselica, a frequent contributor to *Hrvatski tjednik* wrote, "The Croatian nation, like the other nations of Yugoslavia, in the National Liberation Struggle for the new Yugoslavia, wanted to completely realize its national essence and to be completely sovereign within the framework of a federal Yugoslavia, not losing one part of its sovereignty and not recognizing any kind of advocate from outside in view of interpreting what is and what is not in its justifiable national interest."[51] Sovereignty meant a Croatian Communist leadership not susceptible to interfering central authorities.

Contributors to *Hrvatski tjednik* argued that ZAVNOH's decisions and method of operation provided the current model for achieving Croatian political independence. In an article by Franjo Tudjman celebrating the anniversary of the 1941 Partisan uprising in Croatia, *Hrvatski tjednik* featured an article glorifying the achievements of ZAVNOH accompanied by a large picture of Andrija Hebrang (though Hebrang was still treated as a traitor and a spy by official Party history).[52] On the front page of the next issue, Vladimir Bakarić and another old Partisan, Jakov Blažević, were charged with working against the decision of the third session of ZAVNOH, which had proclaimed "the unification of all Croatian lands and the renewal of Croatian statehood."[53] The fact that this issue of *Hrvatski tjednik* was banned reflected the sensitivity not only of criticizing top Party leaders like Bakarić and Blažević but also of using their ostensible betrayal of the revolution to do it.[54]

In their attempt to base the current reorganization of the federation on the principles championed during the Communist revolution, members of Matica Hrvatska also insisted that the historical record concerning the Partisan movement in Croatia be set straight. This had been a preoccupation of Franjo Tudjman before and during his tenure as director of the Institute for the History of the Workers' Movement of Croatia, a position from which he was dismissed after he signed the declaration on the Croatian language in 1968.[55] As part of his series of articles in *Hrvatski tjednik* on Croatian historical themes and personalities, Tudjman emphasized the importance of Croatia's contribution to the Partisan movement, arguing that it was essential to clear up misunderstanding about "Croatia's guilt" for the fall of the first Yugoslavia and the misdeeds of Ustasa.[56] His purpose was to refute what many Croats felt was the erroneous assumption (or accusation) that Croats had been primarily passive or under the sway of fascist forces during the war. According to Tudjman, the regime had exaggerated the number of Serbs killed in Croatia during the war for political purposes. Tudjman expressed the views not only of Matica Hrvatska but of the majority of liberals within the LCC leadership, who felt that the Partisan legacy in Croatia had been doubly misappropriated: first by repudiating the federal model introduced by Hebrang and second by (at best) underestimating the contribution of Croatian Partisans and by (at worst) holding Croats collectively responsible for the Ustasa regime. As one author protested in an article on constitutional reform in *Hrvatski tjednik*, "We Croats don't have a 'guilt complex.' We participated massively in the National Liberation Struggle [in which] we were the purveyors of a traditional Croat idealism."[57]

Matica Hrvatska members also argued that there was a greater tendency toward a more democratic, pluralistic understanding of Communism in Croatia than elsewhere in Yugoslavia, a tendency evident in the attempt to include popular forces in ZAVNOH in 1944 and again in the reform movement in Croatia in 1971. In pointing to the democratic character of ZAVNOH, Matica Hrvatska was attempting to legitimize a more prominent political role for non-Communist political organizations in the Croatian Spring. In October 1971, *Hrvatski tjednik* called for the formation of a National Congress of Social Forces in Croatia that would make decisions on all crucial political matters. In an obvious attempt to reduce the power of the LCC and its control over the Sabor, Matica Hrvatska called for the inclusion in this congress of members of the Sabor, as well as the LCC, the Socialist Alliance, economic firms, and cultural, university, and municipal organizations.[58]

Although Matica Hrvatska advocated a return to the "true principles" of the revolution adopted by ZAVNOH, its attitude toward the Partisan legacy was not entirely positive. Matica Hrvatska viewed ZAVNOH as providing a basis for modern Croatian statehood. It emphasized, however, that the National Liberation Struggle was not the defining moment in Croatian history. Rather "it signified the complete renewal and continuation—on a new basis—of the centuries-old Croatian legal continuity."[59] Moreover, certain positions adopted by ZAVNOH had given "an imprecise understanding and . . . inadequate feeling for Croatian sovereignty" that, Matica argued, must be overcome in the new constitution.[60] Thus, while legitimizing its positions by appealing to their roots in the Partisan legacy, Matica attempted to reformulate this legacy in order to diminish the role of the Communist Party.

As part of its effort to diminish the significance of Communist achievements during the wartime period, in its first draft of the proposed constitutional amendments, Matica Hrvatska mentioned the National Liberation Struggle in Article Six instead of Article One of the First Amendment. This amendment stated that in carrying out their right of self-determination in the National Liberation Struggle, the Croatian people had "founded their state as a continuation of the centuries-long legal tradition of the Croatian state."[61] As a result of the LCC's strong negative reaction to this shift in emphasis, mention of the Communist revolution was moved back up to Article One of the First Amendment in the final draft of the constitutional amendments published by Matica Hrvatska in November.[62] Nevertheless, Matica Hrvatska continued to insist that during the Second World War the Croatian nation had simply been "guarding and perpetuating the historical continuity of the Croatian state" and pursuing its "desire for complete national sovereignty."[63]

In discussing the attributes of Croatian statehood in the new Croatian Constitution, Matica Hrvatska stressed two essential and interrelated aspects of sovereignty, both of which, it maintained, derived their legitimacy from the legacy of the Partisan movement; the first was its indivisible nature—that it must reside in the Croatian nation and only in the Croatian nation; the second was the unity of Croatian lands—that sovereignty must extend to all parts of Croatia. Matica's emphasis on these two aspects of sovereignty was troublesome because it raised questions about relations with Serbs in Croatia. CPC leaders had struggled with a similar problem in 1943–44 because their promotion of Croatian concerns and autonomy had raised questions in the minds of Serbs about their status in Croatia and their protection as a minority group. This problem was resolved by the imposition of a highly centralized state in which the borders of the republics had signified very little. Because borders were not meaningful, Serbs did not need to fear the prospect of being separated politically or culturally from their brethren in Serbia. When Matica Hrvatska began to champion more far-reaching sovereignty for Croatia, however, and to insist that sovereignty was based solely upon the Croatian nation, Serb apprehensions about their status in Croatia were raised again.

In the summer of 1971, the LCC put forth its proposed amendments to the Croatian Constitution. In these proposals, Croatia was declared to be the "sovereign national state of the Croatian nation, the state of the Serbian nation in Croatia, and the nationalities that live in it."[64] Matica Hrvatska emphatically rejected this formulation, insisting that meaningful sovereignty could only reside in one nation. According to Matica Hrvatska, the indivisibility of sovereignty was the key to establishing control over Croatian historical lands. Consequently, in its own proposed amendments to the Constitution, Matica Hrvatska stated simply that the Socialist Republic of Croatia was the sovereign state of the Croatian nation. As the September issue of *Hrvatski tjednik* wrote, "We stand firmly on the position that the Socialist Republic of Croatia is a unified, national state of the Croatian nation and that Croatian sovereignty is one, indivisible, and inalienable."[65] Attempting to assuage Serb fears about this understanding of sovereignty, Matica Hrvatska emphasized that "only the most die-hard reactionary" could doubt that Serbs and other nationalities would be completely equal to Croats under the new constitution."[66]

Matica's emphasis on the unity of Croatian lands and its understanding of Croatian sovereignty also began to raise questions about Croatia's borders and the status of Croats living in other republics. As during the Second World War, emphasis on Croatian national aims raised old questions about the shape of the Croatian political unit. In 1945, a commission headed by Milovan Djilas had determined the borders between Croatia and Serbia's Vojvodina.[67] Since that time, Tito had made it abundantly clear that this issue was not to be further negotiated. The discussion of previously taboo themes in 1971, however, inevitably led to talk about this sensitive question. Matica Hrvatska began to voice concerns about the well-being of Croats in Bosnia-Herzegovina and Vojvodina.[68] Claiming that Serbs were repressing Croats in Bosnia, especially under Ranković, and that they were denied their rights in other republics, Matica Hrvatska made aggressive attempts to establish its organizations outside of Croatia. Before long, Matica members began to call for changes in the borders between Croatia and Bosnia-Herzegovina, apparently with the support of some LCC liberals.[69] These territorial claims were vigorously rejected by Communist leaders in Bosnia-Herzegovina, who denied the existence of any serious discrimination against Croats.

At the end of October 1971, Matica Hrvatska completed the final draft of its proposed constitutional amendments and presented them to the Sabor for discussion. In presenting these proposals, Matica maintained that they were based on the principles that had been fought for during the socialist revolution. The concept of Croatian sovereignty presented in the amendments was far-reaching and represented a fundamental change in the distribution of power in the Yugoslav federation. Croatia would have a separate monetary policy and complete control over its tax revenue, and Croatian would be the sole official language. Perhaps the most striking aspect of this proposed constitution was its call for the formation of an independent defense force in Croatia.[70] Matica Hrvatska argued that the Partisan struggle had endorsed the concept of separate national defense forces by having Partisans fight in their own republics and speak their own languages.[71] Consequently, the new constitution should require Croatian troops to speak Croatian and to serve only in Croatia except during exceptional times, and it elaborated the rules for joint command when these troops served elsewhere in the country.[72]

These proposals overlapped with the LCC proposals submitted for discussion during the summer but went considerably further in the prerogatives assigned to the federal units. Perhaps more importantly, however, they went further in their understanding and definition of the political communities of these units; for whereas LCC liberals emphasized the importance of republic autonomy as a means of attaining Croatian statehood, they understood sovereignty primarily to reside in the institutions of the republic.[73] Matica Hrvatska, however, understood sovereignty to reside in a particular ethnic community, in this case, Croats. By defining sovereignty in terms of ethnicity, Matica Hrvatska shifted the terms of the discussion in a way that had important repercussions for Serbs living in Croatia.

LCC Liberals and Serbs in Croatia

Matica Hrvatska's focus on Croatian sovereignty as part of a wider emphasis on Croatian national concerns soon aroused fear and dissatisfaction among Croatia's Serb population. The mouthpiece for these fears, and the counterpart to Matica Hrvatska, was the Serb cultural organization Prosvjeta, which had been formed by Vladimir Bakarić in 1944.[74] Like Matica Hrvatska, Prosvjeta became increasingly politicized during 1971 as it began to champion more specifically political interests. At a meeting in March 1971, the Main Committee of Prosvjeta adopted several decisions aimed at revamping the organization and changing what many members felt was a rather desultory mode of operation.[75] Most importantly, it declared that because the tenth plenum had opened up a discussion of national feelings, "and with this had come an increasing lack of clarity and uncertainty about the position of Serbs in Croatia," Prosvjeta must direct itself foremost to a discussion of this matter.[76]

Prosvjeta complained that in the previous months the status of Serbs in Croatia had been called into question in a number of ways and that "certain actions had created unease among the Serb community."[77] Charging that the recent emphasis on Croatian culture threatened Serb cultural rights, Prosvjeta called for the convocation at the end of the year of an extraordinary congress that would discuss the protection of Serbian culture.[78] Prosvjeta particularly objected to the proposed educational plan aimed at "Croatinization" of instruction. The plan to require that 75 percent of instruction in history and literature treat Croatian topics denied the fact that Serbs in Croatia had a separate language and history. Moreover, Prosvjeta complained that Serbs were never even consulted about this plan.[79] The Serb cultural organization concluded from these actions that Croats intended to exert pressure on Serbs in Croatia to assimilate, which was a violation of their most fundamental political and human rights.

Prosvjeta further objected to the reformers' attempt to reinterpret the legacy of the Partisan struggle as it had been understood for the past two decades. This dissatisfaction with Matica Hrvatska's and LCC liberals' approach to the founding period was particularly evident in veterans' organizations, many of which were dominated by Serbs. Veterans objected to recent attempts to deemphasize the theme of "brotherhood and unity" from the war and even to question the enormous sacrifices Serbs had made for the Partisan cause. During the 1971 celebrations for the anniversary of the uprising in Croatia, there was evidence of unhappiness among Serbs, especially in the Lika region, and there were confrontations between Serb veterans and Croat youths.[80] Dabčević-Kučar also met with hostility from Serbs in Lika when she traveled there to give such a commemorative speech.

In the months after its March meeting, Prosvjeta began to articulate its positions concerning Serbs' cultural and political rights in Croatia. Prosvjeta reiterated that the National Liberation Struggle had resolved the national question, although the changing circumstances of recent months required a renewed examination of it. Rejecting Matica's attempt to adopt the loose federal model embodied by ZAVNOH, Prosvjeta leader Milan Žalžić insisted that, although articulation of the separate national aims of Yugoslavia's national groups during the war may have been necessary at this earlier stage of development, it was no longer necessary because the nations of Yugoslavia had moved from a "provincial to a more national [Yugoslav] consciousness." The Serb cultural organization further emphatically rejected the notion that sovereignty should reside only in the Croatian nation in Croatia. Denouncing the one-nation–one-state message of Matica Hrvatska, it warned that this position would lead to the dangerous conclusion that Serbs in Croatia could only realize their statehood in Serbia.[81] In order to preserve their national identity, they must be certain that republic borders would not stand between them and Serbs in Serbia. "Since the unity of the Serbian nation and its culture without regard to federal borders is indisputable," Prosvjeta wrote, "Serbs in Croatia must look to Serbia to help them in their task of national preservation."[82]

Prosvjeta also argued that Serbs in Croatia must have greater political representation in Croatia, hinting that it might play this more formal political role. The July issue of *Prosvjeta* called for the "formation of a Sabor committee which would follow and consider questions related . . . to the equality of nations and nationalities."[83] This issue was initially banned on the grounds that the organization Prosvjeta was attempting to obstruct Croatian national aims and, by drawing on its wartime role, to operate autonomously of the LCC.[84] Although this issue of *Prosvjeta* was eventually permitted to circulate, its initial banning and the LCC's failure to establish a Sabor committee to represent Serb interests did little to assuage Serbs' fears about their position in Croatia, and Prosvjeta's demands began to escalate.[85] Shortly thereafter Prosvjeta functionary Rade Bulat called for the establishment of an autonomous region of Serbs in Croatia.[86] Calls were also heard from Dalmatia for granting greater autonomy to this area.

LCC leaders and Matica Hrvatska responded vehemently to demands for the establishment of an autonomous region of Serbs. An LCC meeting was convened for the purpose of expelling Bulat from the Party, although Tripalo intervened to prevent this move.[87] Nevertheless, Tripalo himself firmly rejected Serb autonomy in Croatia, as did other Party leaders from both factions. Matica Hrvatska insisted that any call for federalization of Croatia was aimed directly against the positions adopted by the CPY during the war. As the September issue of *Hrvatski tjednik* wrote, "the constitutional concept of Croatia as a federation of nations . . . negates the Croatian revolution, Croatian history and the Croatian right to self-determination."[88] The main aim of the LCC reformers, and to an even greater extent of Matica Hrvatska, was to achieve a greater degree of political autonomy for Croatia, but this did not under any circumstances mean a federal Croatia. While democratic centralism was not appropriate for relations between the central Party organs and republic Party organizations, it was to be strictly adhered to in intrarepublic Party relations. And reformers could point to the legacy of ZAVNOH and the Partisan struggle in Croatia to give weight to this position. The last few years, *Hrvatski tjednik* wrote, had "liquidated the historical speculation of autonomists and returned to Croatia the basis for resolving this question that had been established by the revolution."[89]

Nevertheless, it was just such a specter of serious challenges to the integrity of republic borders that appears to have weighed heavily in Tito's decision to intervene militarily and bring a halt to the Croatian Spring. During the summer and fall of 1971 there was evidence that Serbs and possibly Croats in villages and towns in the Kordun region were arming for the possibility of a violent confrontation.[90] Memories of the violence of the Second World War were perilously close to the surface for many in this area and other areas of Croatia where there had been heavy internecine fighting during this period. This is precisely what Tito had in mind when he called the LCC liberals to task for failing to understand how divisive their course of action could be for relations between Serbs and Croats in Croatia. "Do you want to see 1941 all over again?" he exhorted the liberal LCC leaders.[91] For if there was one legacy of the National Liberation Struggle upon which they could all agree, it was that violent confrontation between Serbs and Coats over the federal system would have devastating consequences for everyone involved. This, as later events proved, was indeed a correct assumption.

Implications of the Croatian Spring

The end of the Croatian Spring ushered in a period of bitter quiescence in which Croatia was often described as "the sullen republic." But the significance of the Croatian Spring was much wider than simply its effect on Croatia. It signified, in important ways, the beginning of the end of Yugoslavia, although that was not readily apparent at the time. It also provided a preview of some major dynamics involved in the dissolution of Yugoslavia in 1990 and 1991.

In what sense was the Croatian Spring the beginning of the end of Yugoslavia? The usual answer to this question has been that the Croatian Spring resulted in the removal of the most energetic, capable, leaders in Yugoslavia. In the case of Serbia, they were also the leaders most resistant to the forces of nationalism. Their removal and replacement by mediocre obedient leaders who lacked legitimacy robbed Yugoslavia of the good leadership it desperately needed to solve the pressing economic and political problems that had contributed to the Croatian Spring in the first place. Good leadership was especially important after Tito's death, when there was no longer an ultimate arbiter to resolve conflicts among national groups and prevent paralysis of the political system. Instead, the second- or third-rate leaders put in place by Tito himself were left to steer the country through the extraordinarily difficult period after his departure from the scene in 1980. Although their dearth of political capital and skill was not immediately apparent as a result of the complicated mechanisms of collective leadership, which ensured their constant rotation and lack of accountability, it was only a matter of time before more charismatic and effective leaders came to the fore. And, the argument goes, these leaders could not be counted on to exercise the restraint or good judgment that the generation removed after 1971 might have demonstrated.[92]

Although the removal of the popular liberal leaders in Croatia, Serbia, and other republics certainly had a negative effect on Yugoslav political developments, the picture is considerably more complicated than this argument suggests. The lack of good leadership may have weakened the Yugoslav state, but it did not destroy it. Rather, at least three additional factors rendered the outcome of 1971 crucial for the subsequent dissolution of the Yugoslav state: the institutional logic of loose federalism, the increased activity and authority of religious leaders, and the weakening of the Partisan legacy that provided legitimacy to the federal order.

First, the theory and practice of the institutions put into place after 1971 and enshrined in the 1974 Constitution ensured that there would be strong forces of dissolution at work. In effect, the disintegration of the state was the most likely result of the institutional logic of the loose federal system that remained after 1971. As we have seen, although Tito squelched the popular forces advocating a loose federalism in Croatia, he adopted this model of federalism in the 1974 constitution. This ensured that power would be concentrated in republic rather than central institutions. At the same time, however, in an attempt to ensure the unity of the Communist Party and, therefore, the centralization of the state, Tito removed the genuinely popular Communist leaders in Croatia and Serbia after 1971 and appointed leaders who were loyal to him. This strategy appears to have offered the worst of both worlds. Croats and Serbs were unhappy because they had leaders who were unresponsive to their most fundamental political aspirations. At the same time, these republic Party leaders began to use the extensive decision-making powers they had acquired through the reforms to pursue particularistic interests, especially relating to the economy.[93] This pattern of decision making soon paralyzed the political system.

Since the collapse of state socialism in 1989 and 1990, a great deal has been written about the way in which federal structures contributed to the subsequent disintegration of multinational states. The institutionalization of national identity in federal state socialist systems reinforced individuals' personal sense of their membership in a particular national group. Moreover, the ethnoterritorial basis of one-party federalism created protonations and protostates. Not only did these systems establish regions with the juridical status upon which to establish independence, but they also provided republic elites with resources to challenge the center. When the Party collapsed, the dual models of territorial-political and ethnocultural nationhood could not be easily reconciled. The simultaneous reinforcement of numerous nations and a more limited number of territorial units associated with a titular nation rendered extremely difficult the task of establishing borders between newly independent political units. Moreover, these regimes' previous nation-building efforts reinforced the claims of a greater number of national groups to sovereignty over a particular territory.[94]

These dynamics had gone furthest in the Yugoslav case because of the loose model of federalism introduced during and after the Croatian Spring. Although the loose model of federalism came closest to achieving the national aspirations of the majority of Croats, it ultimately proved unworkable in the Yugoslav context. In this sense, the LCC liberals' vision did not offer a viable alternative to the federal system introduced in 1945. Not only did it raise questions in the minds of Serbs concerning their position in the Croatian protostate; it also offered opportunities and incentives for republic elites to sponsor popular mobilization along ethnic lines in an effort to achieve their goals at the center, unleashing nationalist and ultranationalist forces that might be difficult to control. Just as LCC liberals used this strategy in 1971 in their struggle with Tito and the central Party leadership, leaders in other republics would turn to it after 1971. Ironically, it was Slobodan Milošević who first grasped the opportunities inherent in the loose model of federalism for sponsoring ethnic mobilization in order to challenge and reform the constitutional order. And although this challenge initially involved an attempt among Serbian Party leaders to return to the tight model of federalism imposed at the end of the war, other popular forces soon repudiated the legitimacy of the wartime solution altogether.

Second, it is not simply that poor leaders had replaced good ones but that the lack of effective popular leadership allowed religious authorities to step into the vacuum and to undertake programs of ethnoreligious mobilization that contributed to the dissolution of the state. It has frequently been pointed out that the Catholic Church was not an important actor in the Croatian Spring and that, in contrast to places like Poland, the German Democratic Republic, and Slovakia, where the church provided the institutional and ideological forces for resistance, the popular movement in Croatia was primarily a secular affair.[95] This is a largely accurate portrayal of the role of the Catholic Church in the Croatian Spring, although it is important not to underestimate the support it lent to Matica Hrvatska and even to the LCC liberals. Catholic clergy organized parallel activities and events throughout 1970 and 1971 aimed at reinforcing the popular national forces.[96] For example, the cult of Mary was reintroduced as a major Croatian symbol; the first native saint was canonized; and Archbishop Alozije Stepinac was commemorated. It was for this reason that the Catholic clergy were also subjected to repressive measures after 1971, and several dozen priests were handed down jail terms.[97] But though individual members of the church hierarchy faced repression after 1971, the Catholic Church as a whole was not targeted, at least not for long. By 1972, the regime resumed its policy of improving relations with the Catholic Church and loosening the bounds on religious practice in Yugoslavia.[98] Thus, the real significance of the Catholic Church's role in the Croatian Spring is its improved position in society after 1971.

In the two decades after the Croatian Spring, the Catholic Church launched a program of ethnoreligious mobilization that ultimately involved hundreds of thousands of people. Vjekoslav Perica convincingly argues that in emphasizing "the tribulations of Croatia and the Virgin Mary" after 1971, the Church was attempting to follow the Polish model of popular mobilization against the state socialist regime.[99] Whereas major strands of the Croatian national movement had previously been anticlerical in orientation, the movement now became intertwined with religious concepts and institutions. When the church launched the Great Novena in 1974, it undertook a nine-year jubilee whose purpose was to underscore "religious history as the hallmark of nationhood."[100] Ultimately, this greater role for the church reinforced the religious component of national identity in Croatia as well as the ethnic component of the political community. Although the violent disintegration of Yugoslavia was not caused by religion, religion proved an increasingly potent force in demarking the national communities and emphasizing their mutually incompatible claims to political control over particular territory.

And finally, perhaps the most far-reaching consequence of the events of 1971 was to discredit the Partisan legacy (albeit a contested legacy), that underpinned the entire federal structure. The proponents of the Croatian Spring had attempted to legitimize their reforms by placing them squarely within the context of the National Liberation Struggle. By the 1980s, the strong legitimizing function of the founding period had weakened, making it more likely that leaders would seek solutions outside the confines of one-party federalism. When Serb intellectuals began to press for reform of the federal system in 1983 and 1984, they began by criticizing the way in which the national question had been resolved during the Second World War.[101] Before long, the activities of Tito himself and other illustrious Partisan leaders became the subject of critical inquiry. This process of de-Titoization, as it was quickly labeled by the Yugoslav press, soon called into question the entirety of Tito's and the Partisans' legacy. At the Thirteenth Party Congress in June 1986, as Serb and Slovene Communists squared off on the question of constitutional reform of the federal system, LCY Head Vikoje Žarković called for an end to this deadlock by returning to the principles of the Partisan movement. In his opening remarks to the Congress, Žarković stated that confusion about the federal system could only be clarified by looking to the National Liberation Struggle. "[The Yugoslav Federation] was created in the fire of the National Liberation Struggle and the Socialist revolution as an expression of the desire of all Yugoslavia's nations and nationalities," Žarković explained, and that "is why it can develop successfully only on the basis from which it sprang."[102] This attempt to appeal to the founding myth of the revolution was a last-ditch effort, however, and it did not succeed. Žarković's words went unheeded.

By 1989, as preparations were being made for the next Party congress, the Partisan legacy as a legitimizing force for the state order had been seriously undermined. The repudiation of the Partisan legacy ultimately challenged the legitimacy not only of the regime but of the entire state. The CPY, later the LCY, had, as we have seen, based its legitimacy on the fact that it had led a popular revolution for national liberation during the Second World War. As the only all-Yugoslav political force, the CPY's success had become associated with the survival of the state. By claiming to be the only force capable of achieving a just solution to the national questions through the implementation of federalism, the CPY made this the key to its own legitimacy and the state's cohesion. The growing perception after 1971, especially among Croats, Serbs, and Slovenes that the LCY had failed to achieve this goal undermined simultaneously both the LCY's legitimacy and the viability of the state.

Serbs had come to feel that the arrangements of borders and republics worked out during the war were tolerable only under the tight model of federalism, which no longer prevailed. Any further weakening of the federation, as Croats and Slovenes soon began to propose, must mean a reexamination of the border question. Fearing that any redrawing of borders would lead to claims on their territory, most Croats opposed this challenge to the wartime settlement. But they were determined to achieve the kind of sovereignty they believed the National Liberation Struggle and ZAVNOH had promised and failed to deliver. As the main players in the Croatian Spring, such as Franjo Tudjman, became the most important figures in Croatian political life, they were determined to avoid the mistakes of 1971; if they could not achieve a loose federation within a more democratic Yugoslavia, then they would go it alone.

If Tudjman was determined to avoid the mistakes of 1971 as far as achieving Croatian statehood was concerned, he nevertheless failed to avoid the tensions that had arisen between Serbs and Croats during this period. On the contrary, there can be no doubt that many of his actions in 1990 and 1991 exacerbated these tensions when the federal system came under fire in 1990. An even cursory examination reveals a great deal of continuity in the struggles over federalism in 1944, 1971, and 1990–1991. In this sense, the dynamics of the Croatian Spring offer a chilling preview of what occurred later when there was no Tito to intervene. To be sure, there were important differences between 1971 and 1991, particularly the fact that in the late 1980s Slobodan Milošević´ had launched an aggressive policy of achieving Serbian national aims that was absent in 1971. Nevertheless, the issues raised in the struggle over the federal order remained the same, as did the problems caused in Croatia by the introduction of a loose model of federalism. Emphasis on Croatian statehood, the sovereignty of republic institutions, and an increasingly ethnic understanding of membership in the political community (which produced a system of what Robert Hayden has called "constitutional nationalism") aroused the fears of Serbs in Croatia and demands for cultural and territorial autonomy. Despite having participated in the National Liberation Struggle and the Croatian Spring, or perhaps because of it, Tudjman was willing to risk the violence inherent in this situation in an effort to achieve Croatian statehood. The legacy of both these periods of history made such a choice likely.

NOTES

1. For example, see Pedro Ramet, *Nationalism and Federalism in Yugoslavia* (Bloomington: Indiana University Press, 1984); Steven L. Burg, *Conflict and Cohesion in Socialist Yugoslavia* (Princeton, NJ: Princeton University Press, 1983); and Dennison Rusinow, *The Yugoslav Experiment: 1948–1974* (Berkeley and Los Angeles: University of California Press), 1977.
2. Self-management provided the theoretical underpinning for the reduction of central power and the articulation of pluralist interests, including national interests. Moreover, it signaled a definite break from the Bolshevik approach to all aspects of social engineering, including the construction of the federal system.
3. Christopher Bennett, *Yugoslavia's Bloody Collapse: Causes, Course, and Consequences* (New York: New York University Press, 1995); Marcus Tanner, *Croatia: A Nation Forged in War* (New Haven and London: Yale University Press, 1997).
4. *Vjesnik*, No. 14 (July 25, 1944), p. 1.
5. Zagreb: Institute za historiju radničkog pokreta Hrvatske, 1970.
6. ZAVNOH, *Zbornik dokumenata*, (Zagreb, 1970), Vol. 2, p. 604. The republic and re-gional Party organizations were instructed to emphasize the particular national concerns of their areas during the first two years of the war. The CPC, however, continued to pursue this line after the shift toward centralization in the fall of 1943.
7. For a complete discussion of these policies see Jill Irvine, *The Croat Question: Partisan Politics in the Formation of the Yugoslav Socialist State* (Boulder, CO: Westview Press, 1995).
8. *Arhiv Instituta za historiju radničkog pokreta Hrvatske* (hereafter *AIHRPH*) NOV-2/162.
9. Josip Broz Tito, *Sabrana djela*, Vol. 19, p. 115.
10. *AIHRPH* NOV-2/162.
11. Kardelj was particularly critical of Hebrang's policies, charging that Hebrang's "whole mentality and outlook [were] such as to minimize Croatia's connection to Yugoslavia" (Naša reč, Vol. 33 [March 1980], p. 313).
12. *Osnivački Kongres KP Srbije* (Belgrade: Institute za istoriju radničkog pokreta Srbije, 1972). Cited in Audrey Helfant Budding, chapter 5 in this volume.
13. For a discussion of this meeting see Savka Dabčević-Kučar, *'71 Hrvatski snovi i stvarnost* (Zagreb: Interpublik, 1997), pp. 127–150; and Latinka Perović, *Zatvaranje krug, ishod političkog rascepa u SKJ 1971/1971* (Sarajevo: Svetlost, 1991), pp. 116–126.
14. Just how much associating themselves with him openly would have had repercussions, Dabčević-Kučar wrote in her memoirs of this period, could be seen from the fact that when

Jure Bilić denounced the LCC liberals after Karadjordjevo, he accused them of being the "direct descendents" of Hebrang's line (Dabčević-Kučar, *Hrvatski snovi i stvarnost,* p. 294).

15. As Franjo Tudjman and others argued during this period, the "real intent" of the National Liberation Struggle "could be found in the documents of this period." See "Pismo glavnim poličkim čelnicima u Republici Hrvatskoj, 20 lipnja 1970," in Franjo Tudjman, *Usudbene Povjestice* (Zagreb: Hrvatska Sveučilišna Naklada, 1995), p. 181.

16. Miko Tripalo, "Aktuelni politički trenutak I reorganizacija federacije," in *Reorganizacija federacije i razvoy političkog sistema* (Zagreb: 1971), p. 26.

17. Rusinow, *The Yugoslav Experiment,* p. 301.

18. Dennison Rusinow, "Crisis in Croatia, Part 4: The Road to Karadjordjevo-The Final Miles," *Southeast Europe Series,* Vol. 19, No. 7, p. 5.

19. ZAVNOH, *Zbornik dokumenata,* Vol. 1, p. 37. In a sharp reprimand to the CPC shortly after this ZAVNOH decision, Tito instructed that henceforth all such decisions would be made by AVNOJ and issued in its name. See Josip Broz Tito, *Sabrana djela* (Belgrade, 1977–1980), Vol. 17, p. 3. Tito to Main Staff of Croatia, October 1, 1943.

20. At the same time that Tito was centralizing military command in Yugoslavia, Hebrang was attempting to subordinate the Dalmatian regional Party leadership to greater CPC control. The process of centralization occurring in the Partisan movement as a whole in 1943 was also occurring in Croatia. See, for example, *AIHRPH* KP-33/2205, minutes from CC CPC meeting, March 24, 1944. For more on this see Irvine, *The Croat Question,* pp. 167–170.

21. In December 1943, Hebrang complained twice about the wording of Tito's speech at the second meeting of AVNOJ in which Tito referred separately to Dalmatia and Croatia. Hebrang argued that distinguishing between Croatia and Dalmatia in this manner made it sound as if Dalmatia were not part of Croatia. See Vladimir Dedijer, *Novi prilozi za biografiju Josipa Broza Tita,* Vol. 2 (Rijeka and Zagreb, 1982), p. 1,050.

22. Rusinow, "Crisis in Croatia, Part 4: The Road to Karadjordjevo—The Final Miles," *Southeast Europe Series,* Vol. 19, No. 7, p. 5.

23. Dabčević-Kučar rejected those who accused her of exhibiting "an exaggerated Croati-anness" on this occasion. "As if it [this decision] wasn't an historical fact," she wrote. Hebrang's words about Croatian statehood were, according to her, wrongly criminalized in 1945 and again in 1972" (Dabčević-Kučar, *'71 Hrvatski snovi i stvarnost,* p. 296).

24. Ibid., pp. 303–304.

25. In fact, Dalmatian party organizations appear to have been firmly in the LCC liberals' camp, agitating for the removal of those whom they considered hardliners from the LCC leadership (Rusinow, "Crisis in Croatia, Part 3: The Road to Karadjordjevo," *Southeast Europe Series,* Vol. 19, No. 6, p. 21).

26. Dabčević-Kučar, *'71 Hrvatski snovi i stvarnost,* p. 704.

27. Ibid., p. 290

28. Franjo Tudjman, "Nacrt teza za kongres hrvatske kulture," in *Usudbene Povjesnice,* pp. 187–195.

29. At a meeting with the LCC leadership in July 1971 during which Tito criticized recent developments in Croatia, Tito denounced the practice of "glorifying" such historical figures as Ban Jelacic, who in 1848-19 "extinguished the Hungarian revolt which was progressive" (Rusinow, "Crisis in Croatia, Part 3: The Road to Karadjordjevo," *Southeast Europe Series,* Vol. 19, No. 6, pp. 18–19).

30. Tito objected to this wide interpretation of ZAVNOH's power and in a sharp reprimand instructed the CPC that Croatia was usurping sovereignty which belonged only to the federation" (Dabčević-Kučar, *'71 Hrvatski snovi i stvarnost,* p. 296).

31. Dabčević-Kučar, '71 Hrvatski snovi i stvarnost, p. 449.

32. Ibid., p. 451.

33. Ibid., p. 455.

34. See Irvine, The Croat Question, chapter 4.

35. For a discussion of these and other complaints and defections of Serbs in the Kordun region, see Djuro Zatežalo, Četvrta konferencija Komunističke partije za okrug Karlovca, 1945 (Karlovac, 1985), pp. 49–51.

36. Though she later wrote that she believed the number of Serbs living in Croatia to be officially higher than it actually was (Dabčević-Kučar, '71 Hrvatski snovi i stvarnost, p. 310).

37. Tripalo, Hrvatsko proljeće, p. 154.

38. Dennison Rusinow, who was living in Zagreb at the time, describes a situation in which everyone possessed "a sudden detailed knowledge about kinds and values of exploitation or about the number of Serbs who are directors of Croatian enterprises, commanders of Croatian regiments or to be found in Croatian factories, on Croatian railroads or on the Zagreb police force." Rusinow describes the change as "atmospheric and difficult to describe: an exponential rise in intensity" (Dennison Rusinow, "Crisis in Croatia, Part 2: Facilis Decensus Averno," Southeast Europe Series, Vol. 19, No. 5, p. 14).

39. Hebrang's alleged toleration of pluralism received the most attention from the CPY Politboro during the war and at the second congress in 1948 when Hebrang was denounced. Hebrang was accused of myriad mistakes in his approach to the Croatian Peasant Party, from seeking to join it in a political coalition to pursuing a dangerously "sectarian" policy toward it. In his speech to the CDPC Second Party Congress in 1948, Bakarić dwelt longest on Hebrang's mistakes in this realm and suggested in the same breath that Hebrang was both too harsh and too conciliatory toward the Peasant party. See Drugi Kongres Komunističke partije Hrvatske (Zagreb, 1949), pp. 71–72. See also Marko Belinić, Put kroz život (Zagreb, 1985), p. 130.

40. Dabčević-Kučar, '71 Hrvatski snovi i stvarnost, p. 310.

41. Dennison Rusinow, "Crisis in Croatia, Part 1: Post-Mortems after Karadjordjevo," Southeast Europe Series, Vol. 19, No. 4, p. 10.

42. Dennison Rusinow, "Crisis in Croatia, Part 3: The Road to Karadjordjevo," Southeast Europe Series, Vol. 19, No. 6, p. 20.

43. The hard-line faction of the LCC consisted roughly of the following leaders: Vladimir Bakarić, Milka Planinc, Josip Vrhovec, Milutin Baltić, Ema Derossi, Dušan Dragosavac, Jure Bilić, and Jakov Blažević. In addition to Pirker, Dabčević-Kučar, and Tripalo, the liberals consisted of Ivan Šibl, Dragutin Haramija, Srecko Bijelić, Marko Koprtla, and Ivica Vrkić.

44. Tripalo, Hrvatsko proljeće, p. 211.

45. Hrvatski tjednik, No. 21 (September 10, 1971), p. 1.

46. Tripalo, Hrvatsko proljeće, p. 165.

47. For a detailed account of the relationship between LCC liberals and Matica Hrvatska, see Dennison Rusinow, "Crisis in Croatia, Parts 1–4," Southeast Europe Series, Vol. 19, Nos. 4-7.

48. Izveštaj o stanju u Savezu komunista Hrvatske, August 3, 1984, as cited in Ramet, Nationalism and Federalism in Yugoslavia, p. 128.

49. For a summary of these publications see Ivan Perić, Suvremeni hrvatski nacionalizam (Zagreb: August Cesarec, 1976).

50. Hrvatski tjednik, No. 21 (September 10, 1971), p. 1.

51. Hrvatski tjednik, No. 17 (August 3, 1971), p. 7.

52. Hrvatski tjednik, No. 15 (July 23, 1971), p. 13.

53. Hrvatski tjednik, No. 20 (August 30, 1971), p. 1.

54. For an explanation of the reasons why the issue was banned, see *Hrvatski tjednik,* No. 19 (August 27, 1972), pp. 4–7.
55. Tudjman later writes that he began the "struggle against the way the National Liberation Struggle was being depicted" from 1958 on. See Tudjman, *Usudbene Povjestice,* p. 181.
56. Franjo Tudjman, "Nacrt teza za Kongres hrvatske kulture," in *Usudbene Povjestice,* p. 194.
57. *Hrvatski tjednik,* No. 31 (November 19, 1971), p. 2.
58. *Hrvatski tjednik,* No. 24 (October 1, 1971), p. 3.
59. *Hrvatski tjednik,* No. 21 (September 10, 1971), p. 2.
60. Ibid., p. 1.
61. *Hrvatski tjednik,* No. 23 (September 24, 1971), p. 1.
62. *Hrvatski tjednik,* No. 29 (November 5, 1971), p. 12.
63. Ibid.
64. *Hrvatski tjednik,* No. 21 (September 10, 1971), p. 2.
65. *Hrvatski tjednik,* No. 21 (September 10, 1971), p. 3.
66. Ibid.
67. See Irvine, *The Croat Question,* pp. 227–231.
68. According to Tudjman, he and other participants in the Croatian Spring believed that Hebrang had called for the inclusion of Bosnia-Herzegovina in Croatian territory during the Second World War. Although they did not refer to him directly nor make such a demand themselves, one might assume that they may have influenced this aspect of the Partisan legacy. See Tudjman, *Usudbene Povjesnice,* p. 341.
69. Although LCC liberals never formally raised the question of revising the wartime borders, they were not entirely unsympathetic to Matica Hrvatska claims. Tripalo relates an incident in mid-October 1971 when the former head of the Communist Party of Bosnia-Herzegovina confronted him. Djuro Pučar demanded to know why the LCC had failed to denounce Matica Hrvatska members such as the president of the Croatian Society of Novelists, Petar Šegedin, who were making claims on Bosnian territory. Tripalo replied that it would "take awhile" to correct some of the "injustices" in borders delineated after the war. And he reminded Pučar that the Bosnian leader himself had offered to exchange Cazinska Krajina for Dubrovnik after the war. Such remarks about the need for revision of the current republic borders could only have increased the hostility of Croatia's neighbors to the escalating rhetoric of the mass movement. Indeed, Communist leaders in Bosnia-Herzegovina, who feared such claims on their territory, appear to have been instrumental in having LCC liberals removed. See Tripalo, *Hrvatsko proljeće,* pp. 163–164.
70. This proposal was building on the territorial militia under republic control that had been created by a new defense law in 1969 and received constitutional sanction under the reforms. See Rusinow, "Crisis in Croatia, Part 2: Facilis Decensus Averno," *Southeast Europe Series,* Vol. 19, No. 5, p. 12.
71. *Hrvatski tjednik,* No. 21 (September 10, 1971), p. 13.
72. *Hrvatski tjednik,* No. 29 (November 5, 1971), p. 12.
73. According to Dabčević-Kučar, the issue of defining the political community was simply not a crucial one, and for the most part LCC liberals sought a compromise position between Serbs such as Srečko Bijelić, who held a position that Serbs were a "constitutive agent of statehood" and those "outside the Party" who felt that Serbs couldn't be considered a "constitutive People" in Croatia. Some outside the republic felt that anything but the first definition carried elements of inequality for Serbs in Croatia, she explained. "We didn't quite agree with this but we did think it unnecessary to insist on the Croat only

formulation and for the most part we defended their 'constitutiveness'" (Dabčević-Kučar, '71 Hrvatski snovi i stvarnost, p. 318).

74. The founding of Prosvjeta was an effort by the CPC leadership under Bakarić to reassure Serbs about their future in Croatia and to respond to Serb complaints that not enough had been done to promote their cultural life in Croatia. In November 1944, the CPC founded a new Serbian cultural organization, Prosvjeta (whose mouthpiece would be a journal of the same name) to further the development of Serbian education and culture. See Srpska riječ, No. 28 (November 28, 1944).

75. Prosvjeta, April 1971, p. 2.

76. Ibid.

77. Ibid.

78. Prosvjeta, July 10, 1971, p. 1.

79. Prosvjeta, September 1971, p. 1.

80. Tripalo, Hrvatsko proleće, p. 159.

81. Prosvjeta, April 1971, p. 3.

82. Prosvjeta, April 1971, p. 16.

83. Prosvjeta, June 1971, p. 2.

84. For the documents relating to the banning of this issue, see Prosvjeta, September 1971, pp. 6–7.

85. Dabčević-Kučar explains why they decided not to establish a separate political body for Serbs. She admits that there was the wartime precedent since Hebrang had established a separate Serb Club under ZAVNOH's auspices. Nevertheless, he says that they decided instead to establish a body that could include other "nationalities," implying that this was felt to be a good way for the LCC to preempt the need to defend the Serbs themselves. See Dabčević-Kučar, '71 Hrvatski snovi i stvarnost, p. 318.

86. Tripalo, Hrvatsko proleće, p. 168.

87. Ibid.

88. Hrvatski tjednik, September 10, 1971, p. 2.

89. Hrvatski tjednik, May 7, 1971, p. 7.

90. Tito referred to the fact that Serbs were arming themselves during his meeting with LCC leaders in July. For a description of this meeting see Tripalo, Hrvatsko proljeće, p. 155.

91. Tripalo, Hrvatsko proljeće, p. 163.

92. For example, see John Lampe, Yugoslavia as History: Twice There Was a Country (Cambridge: Cambridge University Press, 1996), and Leslie Benson, Yugoslavia: A Concise History (New York: Palgrave Macmillan, 2004).

93. Best discussion of this is in Susan L. Woodward, Balkan Tragedy: Chaos and Dissolution after the Cold War (Washington, D.C.: The Brookings Institute, 1995).

94. For a detailed discussion of this subject see Jill Irvine, "State-Society Relations in Yugoslavia, 1945–1992," and Valerie Bunce, "The Yugoslav Experience in Comparative Perspective," in Melissa K. Bokovoy, Jill A. Irvine, and Carol S. Lilly (eds.), State-Society Relations in Yugoslavia, 1945–1992 (New York: St. Martin's Press, 1997).

95. For example see Ante Čuvalo, The Croatian National Movement, 1966–1972 (New York: Columbia University Press, 1990).

96. Vjekoslav Perica, Balkan Idols: Religion and Nationalism in Yugoslav States (New York: Oxford University Press, 2002).

97. Ibid.

98. Stella Alexander, Church and State in Yugoslavia since 1945 (Cambridge, England, and New York: Columbia University Press, 1979), and Perica, Balkan Idols.

99. Perica, Balkan Idols, chapter 3.

100. Perica, *Balkan Idols,* p. 64

101. Serbs complained foremost that the settlement of the national question in the wartime period had resulted in a "parcelization" of Serbia. Many Serbs felt that Tito had wanted to weaken Serbia in the new Yugoslav federation and had so reduced Serbia in size and strength that 40 percent of its population was living in its autonomous provinces or outside its borders. The "parcelization" may have been tolerable when a highly centralized state order was in effect and republic borders were virtually meaningless, but with the decentralization of political power to the republics after 1974, this arrangement had become unacceptable.

102. *Danas,* July 1, 1986, p. 7.

Return Engagement: Intellectuals and Nationalism in Tito's Yugoslavia

❧ Nick Miller ❧

Intellectuals were heroes of the collapse of Communism across Eastern Europe. Adam Michnik, Václav Havel, and many others left an uplifting imprint on an era that witnessed the emergence of their inspiring progeny, including flying universities, the notion of "living in truth," KOR, and Charter 77. In Yugoslavia, intellectuals were as prominent and as influential as their counterparts elsewhere in Eastern Europe, but the results of their engagement were radically different. Whereas the new civil societies of East-Central Europe were built on a foundation of human rights, tolerance, and indifference to ideology,[1] intellectual engagement in Yugoslavia produced nationalisms that ranged from the relatively more civic-minded Slovenian variant to the exclusive and intolerant movements in Serbia and Croatia. The lasting images of the work of Yugoslav intellectuals may well be the sieges of Vukovar and Sarajevo, the flight of a quarter of a million Serbs from Croatia in a couple of weeks in the summer of 1995, and the bone fields of eastern Bosnia, which are far different images than those bequeathed by KOR or Charter 77.

When Yugoslav intellectuals constructed nationalist movements, they did so by continuing the mission of engagement with which the new Communist regime of Josip Broz Tito had first charged them in the aftermath of the Second World War and the Tito-Stalin split of 1948. The Tito regime demonized nationalism after the Second World War. Officially, national identity would retreat following the Communist takeover before a supranational working-class Yugoslav identity.[2] The 1958 program of the League of Communists of Yugoslavia argued that "Yugoslav socialist consciousness" was based on the equality of the Yugoslav peoples, which in turn "is made certain primarily through a material basis, social-economic relations and the socialist system itself."[3] The program explicitly rejected any suggestion that a new nation was in the making: "This is not a question of creating a new 'Yugoslav nation' to replace the existing nationalities but of organic growth and strengthening of the socialist community of producers or working men of all nationalities of Yugoslavia. . . . Such Yugoslavism does not stand in the way of national languages and cultures. It presupposes them."[4] The LC then did not declare national identity dead or even try to kill it; instead, national identity was *presupposed* but would be pushed to the margins. It still existed and it was still officially acknowledged, which meant that it could potentially reemerge as a cultural and political force.

To marginalize national identity, the regime took advantage of its own murky approach to the national question to forestall the reemergence of national resentments. For Serbs, the rhetoric of Yugoslav "brotherhood and unity" and the weak federalism that prevailed in Yugoslavia until the early 1960s allayed fears that they would ever be subject to the horrors that they faced during the Second World War. For Croats and Slovenes, the same federalism, combined with the presupposition of national languages and cultures, left the door open to a more vigorous advocacy of national interests in the future. Albanians were led to believe after 1966 that Yugoslavia would encourage their development as a nation while including them under the broader Yugoslav umbrella. Thus, as Andrew Wachtel has pointed out, the breezy appeal of the Titoist mantra "brotherhood and unity" cloaked the great tension that the situation embodied: Serbs might have hoped all Yugoslavs were truly *brothers*, but Croats and Slovenes (and others) understood that they were no more than friendly but separate relations living in *unity*, which could by definition be impermanent.[5] The regime's unclear rhetoric allowed for one overarching irony to emerge: these national movements were fueled to varying degrees by the belief of their leaders that they were actually remaining true to the original promise of Titoism. The fact that those movements were mutually hostile brings into some relief the ambivalence of Titoism's approach to national identity.

Until the early 1960s, Yugoslavia was governed centrally, albeit with a formal federalist commitment; Serbs were happiest with their situation because they believed that centralism assured the continued health of their community, spread as it was through not only Serbia but also Bosnia, Croatia, Montenegro, and Macedonia.[6] Thereafter, as the regime initiated constitutional reforms that gave substance to the formal federalism of the first two decades, Serbs grew disappointed and fearful, whereas Slovenes, Croats, and Albanians all rejoiced. Serbs, inclined to view themselves as the losers in an extended period of constitutional change lasting from 1963 to 1974, responded by arguing the need to return to the original Titoist model and eventually for national consolidation. Croats, inclined to view constitutional changes as a beginning rather than a process of limited change, argued gleefully and immediately for ever more autonomy for their republic. The conditions of the births of the various national movements (Serbian disappointment and Croatian glee, for instance) left persistent marks on the ways that intellectuals of different national communities articulated their national vision. Where the Croatian Spring movement of 1971 was euphoric, by the 1980s Serbs, clinging to a version of Titoism that had expired in the late 1960s, wallowed in their self-styled degradation.

Why did intellectuals have the moral authority to lead nationalist movements in Yugoslavia? Who charged them, or why did they feel comfortable charging themselves, with such a task? The negative response would be that nobody else would initiate change: politicians either did not question the nature of Tito's Yugoslavia or were pushed out of positions of power if they did, and "the people" did next to nothing in Yugoslavia without cue cards. A more affirmative answer would be that intellectuals occupied a unique, important, but insecure position in Yugoslavia, as they did in all of the Eastern European Communist states. This position was partly the result of conditions peculiar to Communism but also a continuation of a long tradition of intellectual engagement in Europe generally.

The deeper origins of the engaged Yugoslav intellectual can be traced to the nineteenth-century German nationalist and Russian radical intelligentsias, whose roots can in turn be found in the romantic conception of engagement offered by J. G. Herder, for whom "the intelligentsia [was] a sacred order called upon by history to dedicate their lives to the discovery and use of all possible means—intellectual and moral, artistic and technological, scientific and educational—in a single-minded effort to discover the truth, realize it in their lives, and with its aid to rescue the hungry and the naked, and make it possible for them to live in freedom and be men once more."[7] More to the point, the intellectual under Communism simply continued and expanded an earlier role, described by one scholar as "defend[ing] the nation's very right to exist . . . [or] as the voice of conscience in oppressive regimes."[8] As embraced by the Russian radicals, this formulation of the social role of the intellectual fed the understanding of intellectual engagement that was so necessary to Lenin's revision of Marx's ideas. When in Leninism intellectuals could replace social structures as the force behind revolutions, they had arrived; they were *engaged*. This tradition of engagement would spread as the Leninist revolution spread.

Thus, where revolutions begin with ideology, intellectuals matter. For Serbian sociologist Nenad Dimitrijević, it was precisely the Yugoslav regime's ideological basis that pointed to the specific character of the engagement of Yugoslav intellectuals. "Ideology produces reality," he writes. "What makes it possible for intellectuals to act as artificers of reality?"[9] His answer is that Marxists were forced to abandon historical materialism for an ideologically founded version of Communism, given that the revolution was not part of the natural flow that Marx predicted but an intervention, as produced by Lenin. Intellectuals became the framers of the new reality in that reality's absence.[10]

Their social position assured by the need to translate ideology into action, intellectuals are less likely to directly influence the people than they are to interact with power in a Communist state via their special role as revolutionaries. Intellectuals did have some leverage in their relationship with the state. Just as intellectuals depended on the state that empowered them, so the Marxist-Leninist state had come to depend on them. The state seduced and manipulated intellectuals, but only because it needed them. Thus, even in the dark days of the 1970s, when previously empowered intellectuals had been thrust aside by the Tito regime, the regime still worked assiduously to find intellectual support—in the form of lackeys, perhaps, but the impulse to find that support was real.

The Yugoslav case has its idiosyncrasies. Yugoslavia emerged from the Second World War as a Communist country without all that many true Communists. Its various national elites had been heavily compromised by their wartime passivity or by their collaboration. Making Yugoslavia Communist required many compromises and a lot of education, and intellectuals were keys to both processes: they were susceptible to the seductions of a new ideology, and they were integral to any process envisioning the transformation of high culture or the education of the masses. In the new era, the engaged intellectual made the construction of Communism his/her highest duty. Dobrica Ćosić, the Serbian novelist who would almost single-handedly put the Serbian national "question" on the Yugoslav agenda, saw engagement as a goal to which the writer had to devote himself totally in practice: in his writing, in his service to the Party, in his service to the Yugoslav people. Others were less confident in their understanding of the term, but remained dedicated to the general goal.[11]

After the turbulent years of the Communist takeover and the split with Stalin, parameters for intellectual involvement in state and Party affairs were set at the Sixth Congress of the Communist Party of Yugoslavia in Zagreb in November 1952, where Tito pronounced his support for the *borba mišljenja* (struggle of ideas). The struggle of ideas was at that point envisioned as something rather limited: in essence, Party members would be encouraged to question and test the theoretical positions of other Party members.[12] The proclamation of the opening of the era of the struggle of ideas, accompanied by the renaming of the Communist Party of Yugoslavia as the League of Communists of Yugoslavia (Savez komunista Jugoslavije, SKJ), served to change the atmosphere for intellectual discourse. The regime's invitation to intellectual Party members to participate in the building of socialism was taken up with enormous enthusiasm, and the League of Communists, while vigilant where politics was concerned, was generally confused by the profusion of cultural polemics, so it let the intellectuals do their thing.

The opening of the struggle of ideas encouraged the development of divergent convictions among intellectuals who thought their contributions mattered. Serbian and Slovene intellectuals, and to a lesser extent Croats and Albanians, came to believe that their peoples would achieve their primary national aims within the context of Titoism. The best example of (a) how apparently critical thinkers could reach these conclusions, (b) how thin a line there really was between the Serbian and Slovenian orientations, and (c) how engagement could cloak the manipulations of a powerful state, came in 1961–62 via a polemic between Dobrica Ćosić, a Serbian novelist and member of the central committee of the League of Communists of Serbia, and Dušan Pirjevec, a Slovene Communist writer. The occasion for the polemic was a January 1961 interview of Ćosić in the Zagreb newspaper *Telegram*. In that interview and in passing, Ćosić was asked whether Yugoslavs were still "too passive in inter-republican contacts." Ćosić responded that the question would be valid "as long as republics exist." To this formulation, which implied that Ćosić believed that republics would eventually disappear, Pirjevec responded with a sarcastic, biting commentary in the

Return Engagement ◆ 183

Slovene journal *Naša sodobnost*. The sense of this lengthy polemic is fairly simple to encapsulate: Pirjevec argued that nationality is an integral part of human identity, and that any attempt to create a Yugoslav socialism that undermined national identity could not be supported in ideological or human terms. Ćosić argued otherwise, that Yugoslavism would, even when it reached its full development, coexist with national identities as cultural identities, which would be by necessity less important than the higher identification with a Yugoslav socialist society.[13] Pirjevec believed that Ćosić's comment cloaked a desire that Yugoslavia's republics be eliminated in favor of a single, centralized state organization that would assimilate Yugoslavia's nations.

Ćosić's debate with Pirjevec is often cited as the first major public discussion of the nature of the national problem in postwar Yugoslavia.[14] But the Ćosić-Pirjevec polemic was actually a surrogate for intra-Party debate over the Yugoslav future. Ćosić claims that he was prompted to action by Jovan Veselinov, a leading Serbian Communist, and Tito himself.[15] Pirjevec also had higher authority on his side—he was almost certainly guided by Slovenian Communist leader Boris Kraigher.[16] The fact that the polemic was encouraged by leading Serbian and Slovenian Communists illustrates the fact that at that moment the Party was going through a period of rethinking its approach to the national question. Ćosić represented a policy that was on the way out, and Pirjevec an approach that was soon to be adopted by the regime. Thus they were both acting according to the rules of the cultural/political game in Yugoslavia at that time: they were engaged. But something else stands out about the polemic. It is hard not to conclude that they were divided less by substance than by the nature of their mutual fears: Ćosić suspected (in the abstract, at this point) that republican bureaucracies would sponsor division among the peoples of Yugoslavia and perhaps endanger the Serbs of other republics, and Pirjevec believed that Serbs were fundamentally expansionist.

The Ćosić-Pirjevec polemic indicates how the struggle of ideas easily could be manipulated by the Party. Nevertheless, toward the end of the reform period that would culminate with the promulgation of the Constitution of 1974, Tito reined in political and intellectual critics of the Party line, probably thanks to the behavior of the Croats during their Spring of 1971 and the Serbian Praxists through the 1960s and early 1970s.[17] The collaborative role enjoyed by intellectuals now came to an end. The struggle of ideas was over, replaced by the application of the stultifying principle of "moral-political suitability," the new measure of one's worth in public life in Yugoslavia. The situation had changed radically, but intellectuals would remain engaged in their own way; if no longer as insider/collaborators, they could remain engaged as critics.

Serbian Intellectuals and Nationalism

The Serbian nationalism that dominated the 1980s and 1990s was an intellectual construction that first barely emerged in the mid-1960s during the official rethinking that led to reforms decentralizing state administration. Because Serbs were scattered among four republics and the two autonomous provinces of Serbia, such reforms appeared to some Serbian intellectuals to be purposely anti-Serbian. As a result, a growing number of them concluded that Tito and his advisors had reneged on the promise of Titoism, which these Serbs believed was to work assiduously to render national identity irrelevant. Thus, the origins of Serbian nationalism were in the profound fear and even depression that came with the gradual realization (which was confirmed for them by the 1974 Constitution) that Serbs were on their own among empowered and allegedly hostile Croats, Muslims, and Albanians. With more freedom than the intellectuals of any other Yugoslav republic save perhaps Slovenia, the Serbian opponents of Titoism were able to invest enormous time and effort to incrementally build intellectual and then public support for a reunified Serbia. There were Serbian intellectuals who resisted and then rejected the nationalism that came to dominate their milieu, but they were lonely in Serbia.[18] By the late 1980s, the national movement that Serbian intellectuals created proved to be of great use to politicians in Serbia, who searched for new sources of legitimacy as they picked up the pieces of the failed Titoist experiment.

There were few influential Serbian intellectuals in the mid-1960s who shared the fear of Titoism described above, although after Aleksandar Ranković was purged in 1966, that number grew; the most important was Ćosić. But Ćosić was almost alone as an influential protonationalist[19] in the late 1960s or at best found succor with a group of intellectual and political outcasts who offered little for the League of Communists to fear.[20] Two events marked the distant origins of a nationalist opposition among Serbian intellectuals, and both were reactions rather than initiatives. One was the language debate of 1967, which saw the Declaration on the Name and Position of the Croatian Literary Language of March 1967, which was signed by Croatian intellectuals and organizations, quickly followed by the Proposal for Consideration, signed by a group of Serbian writers; the other was Ćosić's speech to the Fourteenth Plenum of the Central Committee of the League of Communists (LC) of Serbia in May 1968.[21] The language controversy saw a small number of Serbian writers respond (perhaps facetiously[22]) to the Croatian assertion that the Croatian variant of Serbo-Croatian should be official on Croatian territory with agreement, so long as Serbian becomes official on territory inhabited by Serbs. In Ćosić's speech a year later, he bemoaned LC policies that he believed encouraged the growth of nationalisms in Yugoslavia. In particular, he argued that in Kosovo and Vojvodina, Albanians and Hungarians, respectively, were being given too much authority. He feared a rise in Serbian nationalism as a response to that of others. The speech has since been described as the opening of the Serbian nationalist movement, but I believe it is more appropriate to view it as a tendentious but credible criticism from a Serbian perspective of then-current LC administrative reforms. As was the case with the Proposal for Consideration, the League of Communists condemned Ćosić's speech. The instigators of these events were lonely voices in the late 1960s.

Only later would the proposal and the fourteenth plenum appear to have been the beginning of a national movement.

Ćosić was a lonely dissenter but not completely alone. On March 18, 19, and 22, 1971, the law faculty of the University of Belgrade hosted discussions of proposed amendments to the 1963 constitution of Yugoslavia. Like the University of Belgrade, other universities in Yugoslavia sponsored such public forums; these events were endorsed by the League of Communists as part of the function of self-management in this Communist society. The most famous, and now even legendary, presentation at the law faculty in March 1971 came from Mihajlo Djurić, who refused even to speak about the amendments themselves. Instead, he argued that Yugoslavia was "virtually a geographical expression, given that on its soil, or more precisely, on its ruins . . . a few independent, autonomous, even mutually opposed nation-states have been established."[23] Over a year later, in July 1972, Djurić was imprisoned for his presentation at the law faculty and one other written piece protesting the erection of a mausoleum for Njegoš that was designed by Ivan Meštrović (in that case, Djurić was one of dozens of Serbian cultural and intellectual figures who protested the destruction of the old mausoleum). It was following these events that the Party silenced its intellectual critics (see above); that silence lasted until the death of Tito.

Their contributions rejected from above, Ćosić and a slowly growing number of Serbian intellectuals began to act as engaged intellectuals *outside* of the Party. The most useful window on this process is to examine the work of four committees that were formed after 1969, and a journal that was proposed but never published. The committees included the governing board of the *Srpska književna zadruga* between 1969 and 1971[24]; the Committee for the Protection of Artistic Freedom, which was formed on May 19, 1982[25]; the more glorious Committee for the Defense of the Freedom of Thought and Expression, which was formed in November 1984[26]; and a committee of the Serbian Academy of Sciences and Arts, formed in May 1985 to produce a document outlining the problems Yugoslavia faced at that point. The journal, titled *Javnost* (the Public), was proposed in 1980.

Under the presidency of Ćosić, the board of the SKZ consisted of a wide range of cultural figures of various political orientations, nearly all of whom would become key actors in the nationalist 1980s. Ćosić and his colleagues emphasized the need to revive the spirit of Serbianness in the face of the forces of fragmentation, which were the League of Communists and its "Bolshevik" ideology. This was a logical continuation of the critique of Titoism in his fourteenth plenum speech. This committee's work ended as part of the series of purges that occurred in 1971 and 1972 in the aftermath of the Croatian Spring.

A tangible Serbian movement that can be called nationalist only emerged in the 1980s, following the death of Tito in May 1980. Immediately upon Tito's death, Ćosić, Ljubomir Tadić (a Praxis philosopher), and others proposed the journal *Javnost* (the Public), which its inspirers suggested would bring Serbian, and more generally Yugoslav, intellectuals back into the fold as critical contributors to the good of the state; in other words, they wished to reinvigorate the old struggle of ideas. *Javnost* was not permitted by the state, which was dominated by those who feared the potential for change in light of Tito's death. But Serbs' attempts to reengage were not only institutional; there were also literary reexaminations of the Tito era, including novels reevaluating the Serbian experience in the First World War, Goli Otok, the Tito-Stalin split, and other events.[27]

The other three committees were formed in the aftermath of Tito's death. They had different immediate tasks and memberships, but all were formed by their leaders as means of concentrating Serbian intellectual energy on finding solutions to the problems that Yugoslavia and Serbia faced. The Committee for the Protection of Artistic Freedom, which was formed on May 19, 1982,[28] and the more glorious "Committee for the Defense of the Freedom of Thought and Expression," which was formed in November 1984,[29] both advocated for freedom of expression and brought together a diverse group of people. The most memorable attempt of Serbian intellectuals to reengage came with the formation of a committee of the Serbian Academy of Sciences and Arts (SANU) in May 1985 to produce a document outlining the problems Yugoslavia faced. The document that this committee produced (the Memorandum of SANU) illustrates how a substantive critique of the way that Yugoslavia was administered could lapse into something bordering on a nationalist manifesto: beginning with the argument that the 1974 Constitution had critically harmed the functioning of the state and its economy, the memorandum concluded that the 1974 Constitution and its negative affects were symptomatic of Titoism's fundamental anti-Serbianism. *Javnost*, the outpouring of novels and plays, and the committees were methods by which the intellectual community of Serbia attempted to return to—or continue—earlier days of engagement.

One can argue that until 1986, the Serbian intellectual movement might have retained the purity of its origins as a return to engagement and advocacy of democratic reform, had the issue of Kosovo not emerged. Nevertheless, and with great force, Kosovo did come to subsume virtually every other principled issue that comprised the platform of the Serbian intellectual elite from about 1985 onward. The "Martinović case," the petition movement of Kosovo Serbs and then the intellectuals themselves, and the memorandum's emphasis on genocide against Serbs in Kosovo all indicated the intellectuals' passionate conviction that (as Ćosić put it), "in Kosovo, Kosovo does not fall; Yugoslavia falls."[30] At the foundation of this hyperbole were some reasonable concerns: Serbs and Montenegrins were emigrating from the province at an increasing rate; two significant Albanian rebellions in 1968 and 1981 certainly frightened Serbs of the region.[31] But, unfortunately, Serbian intellectuals' arguments regarding Serbian suffering became spiritual, and they ultimately focused much more on the alleged desire of Tito and his heirs to crush the Serbian nation as such, with Kosovo as Tito's proving ground, than they did with actual conditions in Kosovo or relatively more banal (and certainly less emotional) issues like respect for intellectual engagement. Kosovo revealed the ways that Serbs had contributed to

their own demise. This phenomenon gave a peculiar quality to the Serbian national-
ist euphoria: it emphasized Serbian degradation under Tito, and the willingness of
Serbs in the past to suffer their own humiliation or, as Ćosić often put it, a sort of
"Serbian masochism."[32]

The Serbian intellectual opposition accomplished one critical task: it painted a
picture of a divided and degraded Serbia, victimized by Bolshevism as it had earlier
been victimized by other foreign notions and demands; it developed what became a
"deeply embedded cognitive blueprint" that framed the actions of politicians, intellectuals, and ordinary Serbs thereafter.[33] They are often accused of having produced a
Great Serbian program, with the memorandum as the centerpiece of the movement.
But in too many ways, Serbia's nationalist intellectuals were divided by ideology
and practical politics. The single point on which they could agree was the general,
almost mystical, conviction that Serbs must commit to work together to throw off
the legacy of division and subordination to foreign ideas. Their movement did not
become political until a political figure emerged who would at least initially and
perhaps only manipulatively embrace the picture that the intellectuals had created;
Slobodan Milošević did this. Early on (1988–90), Milošević satisfied the intellectuals'
demand for a socialist who was: (a) hostile to the entrenched Titoist bureaucracy and
(b) capable of unifying the divided Serbs.[34] Ćosić christened Milošević as both charismatic and populist, the perfect antidote to the hated Serbian Party bureaucracy.

It is important to note at this point that the movement of the intellectuals *preceded* Milošević. The early support that Ćosić and other intellectuals' gave Milošević
was a product of their blind hatred of the bureaucratic Party, whose existence Ćosić
had bemoaned since the early 1960s; Milošević's adoption of Kosovo as a symbol
of the oppression of Serbs in Tito's Yugoslavia; and the intellectuals' own prepared-
ness to welcome any politician who appeared capable of returning to Serbs a sense
of national unity and purpose. Although the intellectuals' influence did help make
Milošević popular through 1990, many of them turned on him almost immediately,
revolted by his authoritarian methods. Milošević himself must be given credit for
forging and maintaining the power he had through political means. Nonetheless,
the vision that made Milošević possible preceded him, thanks to the cultural figures
that created it.

Slovenian Intellectuals and Nationalism

The potential for a Slovenian nationalist movement arose during the tumultuous
1960s, but the Slovenian position never devolved to the level of insoluble grievances
because that position was officially sanctioned by the Party under constitutional
reforms enacted between 1963 and 1974. The Ćosić-Pirjevec debate exemplified
the contention of many Slovenian commentators that Slovenes always understood
Yugoslavia to be a place where different nations could flourish while contributing
to a greater whole. Pirjevec's assertion that "nationality is a constituent element of

human personality, the basis of human existence, and the starting point for human communication with the world" was more or less a consensus position of Slovenian intellectuals.[35] Dimitrij Rupel and others have noted that Edvard Kardelj elaborated a position similar to Pirjevec's as early as 1957 in his work *On the Development of the Slovene National Question.*[36] This notion diametrically opposed that of the most idealistic Serbs, who hoped to see national identity become irrelevant in the face of social progress. One Slovenian historian has written that Slovenes always believed that Yugoslavia should "assure its development while maintaining its diversity" and "accept its variety as a positive quality."[37]

Slovenian intellectuals were relatively quiescent—after all, the 1974 constitution did fairly reflect their interests—until the 1980s, when the death of Tito opened the door to discussions of Yugoslavia's future and economic crisis introduced new tensions into Slovenian relations with their neighbors. Then, resentful of being forced to live with other peoples who allegedly dragged their economy down, who implicated them in oppressive policies elsewhere in Yugoslavia, and who appeared occasionally to wish to turn them into Serbo-Croats, Slovenian intellectuals found their voice anew. The Slovenian Party did not exactly embrace this movement, but it did not distance itself from it either. The movement proceeded relatively smoothly and collaboratively as the 1980s, and Yugoslavia itself, ended. The novelty of the Slovenian movement, and its most contentious point, was its assertion that territory and nationality were contiguous in principle. The Slovenes could make this argument because they were the one Yugoslav constituent nation that inhabited one republic with a small non-national population. Coupled with the republics' arguable constitutional right to secession, this assertion completed an argument for Slovenian statehood.

The Slovene and Serbian movements are often paired and compared because they both developed from the position that they each best encapsulated the Titoist approach to nationality. In fact, they each exemplified a distinct phase in the development of that policy. The parallelism began with the Pirjevec–Ćosić polemic. The similarities are impossible to miss, and each case developed according to the same logic: Serbs and Slovenes both believed that their understanding of Tito's system was accurate. The fact that the Serbian position lost pride of place in the mid-1960s led to the self-pity that characterized the Serbian national movement thereafter; the fact that the Slovenian position became the norm in Yugoslavia was the source of the triumphalism that characterized the Slovene movement in the 1980s.

The parallels between the two movements are easy to find. Just as the Serbian intellectual elite joined to propose the publication of *Javnost* in 1980, so the Slovenian elite requested to be allowed to publish *Nova revija* in the same year. Dimitrij Rupel used words to argue for *Nova revija* that could well have been used by Ćosić and Tadić when proposing *Javnost*: "It was the initiative of a group of Slovenian cultural workers of the younger-middle generation who after several months of discussion and search for the possibility to found a new cultural review in Slovenia, and indeed after long years of disappointment with the Slovenian cultural situation" collected signatures and made the formal request.[38] The actual proposal was also amazingly similar to that for *Javnost*: points included a more open flow of cultural political viewpoints; rejection of the subordination of scientific and artistic creation to ideology; critique of Stalinist, bourgeois, petit bourgeois, techno-bureaucratic and other outmoded tendencies in culture and art.[39] One important difference was that the government allowed *Nova revija* to publish, where it had denied *Javnost*. Another was that *Javnost* was imagined as a Yugoslav journal, whereas *Nova revija* was strictly Slovenian. But the fact remains that in both instances, reengagement, or more substantive engagement, was the goal of the promoters of the journals.

Both the Slovenian and the Serbian milieus were invigorated by the publication of *Goli otok* novels (Branko Hoffman's *Noč do jutra* in Slovenia and Antonije Isaković's *Tren II* in Serbia), and the Slovenian and Serbian writers' associations engaged along similar lines. When Tone Pavček became chair of the Slovene association in 1979, Aleš Gabrič writes, it "began to become involved in more diverse public action and to take an interest in pressing social issues—particularly those which directly affected its members. These included the issue of Slovene nationality, equality of the Slovene language within Yugoslavia and freedom of artistic expression."[40] Both movements also produced committees to defend human rights.[41] And just as the memorandum came to be considered the centerpiece of the Serbian national movement, so volume 57 of the journal *Nova revija*, titled "Contributions for a Slovenian National Program," came to occupy center stage in the Slovenian revival. They addressed similar concerns in similar forms. The major difference was that the authors of the *Nova revija* articles argued for the sovereignty of Yugoslav republics on an ethnic basis, whereas the authors of the memorandum seemed to be arguing for the recentralization of Yugoslavia. Although that is indeed a critical distinction, the two sets of documents were analogous, because they expressed (or in the case of the memorandum, were meant to express), outside official channels, a consensus position on the "state of the state" in the mid-1980s.

In one important way, the Slovenian situation did diverge from the Serbian: whereas the Slovenes who produced *Nova revija*, dominated the writers' association, and demanded to be allowed to contribute to the future of Yugoslavia were from similar generations to those around Ćosić in Serbia, in Slovenia a younger generation of regime critics was also engaged and along a substantively different line than their elders. This generation, according to Tomaš Mastnak, advanced "a plurality of struggles for a number of concrete, everyday, particular, specific issues and concerns."[42] In other words, the older generation defended the interests of "the nation," whereas the younger generation arguably engaged on "civic" rather than "national" lines. The varieties of youth engagement were in fact impressive, beginning with the dissident industrial rock of the music group Laibach, which emerged in the late 1970s, and eventually spawning a peace movement, an environmental movement, and a multifaceted movement for cultural freedom. The Slovenian Communist Youth organization, after a slow initial reaction, embraced most of these initiatives, which helped make the youth movement generally accepted. When two editors of *Mladina*, the youth organization's magazine, and two other Slovenes were charged with espionage in 1988 after the magazine published an article about corruption in the Yugoslav People's Army, the youth movement became a national concern. The trial of the four Slovenes proceeded according to military law, with the official language being Serbo-Croatian, and the Slovenian government even expressed its concern with the violations of Slovenian sovereignty. From that point, "the cause of democracy was linked to the question of national sovereignty."[43] Just as the Kosovo issue had led to the crystallization of a unified Serbian nationalist opposition, so the *Mladina* trial helped bring disparate strands of Slovenian opposition together.

Another major difference between the Serbian and Slovenian cases is the fact that there was much less tension between the Slovenian Party and the Slovenian intellectuals during the critical years from 1988 to 1991. While Milošević answered the yearnings of many Serbian intellectuals for a short time, the Slovenian leader Milan Kučan found common ground with the Slovenian intellectual elite and was able to maintain its support through the constitutional crises of 1988–91; the fact that he was willing to see Communist power diminished after the first elections in Slovenia in 1990 contrasts with the behavior of Milošević, who clearly intended to maintain personal power at any cost.

Croatian Intellectuals and Nationalism

Whereas Serbian and Slovenian intellectuals executed a rather slow and stealthy takeover of opposition discourse among their peoples, Croatian intellectuals took part in a national movement between 1967 and 1971 that exploded onto the scene and had several different catalysts. The pattern of intellectual involvement in the Croatian movement generally followed that outlined above for the Serbian and Slovenian movements, but Croatia's movement was so immediate and so multifaceted (intellectuals were but one of the sets of major actors) that fruitful comparisons are difficult to make.

Croatian discontent with Tito's Yugoslavia crystallized earlier and more strongly than it did among Serbs and Slovenes. As with the Serbs and Slovenes, this discontent was first channeled through Party members (both officials and intellectuals) who believed that they were working within the Titoist paradigm of national development. Without question, the fall of Aleksandar Ranković emboldened Croats as much as it irritated and frightened Serbs because it promised a transition in the regime's administration of the state and implied a new definition of the roles of republics and their national constituencies. The Croatian movement, and the intellectuals' role in it, was complex from the outset: while economists debated the exploitation of Croatia by the federation, cultural figures debated the role of the Croatian language; at the same time, Croatian Party leaders urged that the post-Ranković reforms go further toward establishing a Yugoslav confederation. All of this began within the Party as efforts to reform rather than to overturn Titoism. For instance, when "The Declaration on the Name and Position of the Croatian Literary Language" (see above) was issued on March 15, 1967, signed by 19 Croatian institutions and 130 people, it was not envisioned by its signatories as a revolutionary act; rather, it was seen as an attempt to convince authorities to recognize that Titoism's foundation was being threatened by current practice.[44] All of the institutions that approved the Declaration were "official," and eighty of the individual signatories were Party members.

The Croatian Spring had several foci: within the Party, leaders like Savka Dabčević-Kučar and Miko Tripalo fought vainly to further post-Ranković reforms and to control the movement as a whole; intellectuals made their mark through their work in the *Hrvatski tjednik* and other journals and newspapers and through the revitalization of the Matica Hrvatska; students operated outside the control of the Party, pushing the movement in more radical directions. The intellectuals who emerged as leaders of the Croatian Spring were all members of the Party: Vlado Gotovac, Marko Veselica, Šime Djodan, and Franjo Tudjman all emerged from within the Titoist system. But these Croatian intellectuals framed their movement in the universal language of minority nationalist movements: their stated goals included decentralizing Yugoslav investment decisions, political autonomy for republics, autonomous republic foreign policies, the nurturing of Croatian national pride, and national equality within the republic.[45] These are all standard goals for national movements, but there is no obvious link between them and Titoism in practice. When the Serbs and Slovenes proposed their own reforms to the system, they did so by recalling that Titoism's original intent supported them. It would have been difficult to argue that such a goal included autonomous republican foreign policies. Does this mean that the Croats used Titoism as window dressing whereas the others were more sincere in their loyalty to the original intent of Titoism? Perhaps, to a point, but we are dependent on the words of the participants. Thus, we must take the word of Vlado Gotovac, who once said that he "was never so convinced in the possibility of Yugoslavia as I was then . . ."[46] The government response to the Croatian Spring was fairly brutal by Yugoslav standards. Gotovac, Marko Veselica, Franjo Tudjman, Dražen Budiša, and other leaders of the movement were imprisoned. Thousands were purged from the Party. The result, of course, was that the "Yugoslav" feelings of the participants were replaced by anger and rejection, an alienation so predictable and severe that any thought of future engagement, as defined in the Serbian and Slovenian cases, was out of the question.

The commonalities of the Croatian, Serbian, and Slovenian movements end with the conclusion of the Croatian Spring in late 1971. From that point, the Croatian national leaders suffered the sort of persecution that the Serbs and Slovenes feared and occasionally idealized,[47] but never actually endured. In the late 1980s, as the Serbian and Slovenian movements gained strength, the Croatian leaders turned their attention to the Croatian diaspora, which helped mold a new Croatian nationalism that fed off the fixations of emigrant Croats, especially those in Canada and the United States.

Thus, whereas the Serbs and Slovenes both nurtured the notion that they remained consistent with Titoism's original intent, the Croats (led by Tudjman at this point) nurtured the opposite sort of notion: that the Independent State of Croatia, for instance, reflected the legitimate historical desire of Croats for independence.[48] The Croats, or perhaps it would be better to say the Croatian Democratic Union, which became the face of Croatian nationalism in the 1990s, thus openly harbored hopes of regaining Western Herzegovina and potentially all of Bosnia as well. They are the one Yugoslav nation that can be clearly said to have developed a "Greater" national program—in this case, of course, striving for a "Greater Croatia."

Albanian Intellectuals and Nationalism

Serbian, Slovenian, and Croatian intellectuals developed nationalist movements that operated within the context of and responded to the innovations of Tito's regime. It is impossible, for instance, to imagine Serbian self-pity and Slovenian self-confidence without the conditioning of Titoism. Serbs, Slovenes, and Croats occupied a special status in Yugoslavia, though. They were all South Slavs, they all (along with Monte-negrins, Macedonians, and eventually "Muslims") were part of the eventual nation imagined by the various Yugoslavisms, and they were designated nations in Yugoslav constitutional practice. The torch displayed on various Yugoslav paraphernalia of state had a lick of flame for each of them. Albanians (and Hungarians, and all remaining national groups within Yugoslavia) had the lesser constitutional status of nationalities. The argument for this status was that nationalities were fragments of nations whose homelands were outside of Yugoslavia. Nevertheless, the Albanians and Hungarians were privileged among the nationalities: the autonomous region of Kosovo and the autonomous province of Vojvodina were created within Serbia to satisfy the territorial longings of these two large ethnic groups. This was an inventive solution to a histori-cal and administrative problem, but it would eventually become a key ingredient in nationalist discourses, especially among Serbs and Albanians.

Yugoslavia's Albanian population therefore occupied a position not unfamil-iar to students of national movements. A minority in their state, with a national home-land right across the border in Albania, they resembled the Serbs or Romanians in the Habsburg monarchy, both of whom were asked to embrace an imperial idea in place of a commitment to their nation. In the Albanian case, the imperial idea was Yugoslavism, which did not even have a place for them. Thus, unlike Serbs, Slovenes, or Croats, Albanians existed in a constant state of tension with authority in Yugosla-via, tension that was moderated by concessions from on high but that could never be fully ameliorated. The state treated them as a problem to be dealt with rather than as potential full partners, and the postwar period saw various attempts to address Albanian discontent administratively.

From 1945 to 1966, Kosovo's autonomous status was an illusion because the security forces kept close watch and Serbs and Montenegrins dominated the regional educational, police, and administrative bureaucracies. After 1966, the Tito regime gradually embellished Kosovo's autonomy, until in 1974 the province was granted a status virtually equal to that of the republics in Yugoslavia. On three occasions (1968, 1981, and 1988–89), Albanians rebelled to gain more, ranging from full republican status to (presumably) union with Albania. Because Albanians really never had the protection of an assumed commitment to Yugoslavia or Yugoslavism, and because the existence of Albania right across the border always placed them under the suspicion of separatism, it was, and remains, difficult to determine exactly who stood behind the rebellions and what they truly wished to achieve. The only safe aspiration was republican status, but it defies common sense to believe that at least some Albanians did not desire union with their brethren next door. Still, until the collapse of Yugoslavia, Albanian intellectuals, with one prominent exception, claimed only to want full republican (and thus equal) status in Yugoslavia. Thereafter, with the ultimate composition and nature of the state in flux, the situation changed. Unlike the Serbs, Croats, and Slovenes, the Albanians were not free to act and speak as they wished, especially after 1981. Thus the parameters of the Albanian nationalist movement will not be clear until the dust is cleared from the history of the 1968, 1981, and 1988–89 rebellions. To date, we only know what assorted Kosovar politicians and intellectual leaders have told us, which always includes the argument that although the rebellions were not a surprise, they are not clear who led them or if there was any organizational structure to them.[49]

Albanian intellectual engagement from the 1960s to the 1990s coalesced around one question: whether it was possible for Albanians to find a secure and rewarding place in a Yugoslavia created in the spirit of brotherhood and unity, and if not, was unity with Albania the solution to the problems faced by the Albanians of Kosovo. As in the other cases examined in this paper, there were Albanians who worked within the Titoist framework and believed it to be a feasible solution to Albanian desires. For instance, Mahmut Bakalli was the president of the provincial committee of the League of Communists at the time of the 1981 rebellion and cannot really be described as a part of an Albanian nationalist movement. Rather, he exemplifies the constraints of Titoism on its Albanian loyalists—one of his jobs was to keep tabs on the nationalist movement in Kosovo. Ultimately, though, he became an opponent of Milošević's Serbia and a proponent of a free Kosovo. As a Party leader, he had some insight into the attitudes of moderate nationalists within the Party. He has said that after 1974 there were voices in Kosovo calling for republican status but that the Kosovo Party "checked the idea of separation as unrealistic and unacceptable."[50] But Bakalli also understood that "the struggle for the emancipation of the Albanian people . . . include[d], as expected, the question of their unification. The Albanian people never rejected that vision."[51]

Bakalli's polar opposite was Adem Demaci, who became a symbol of the Albanian nationalist movement by virtue of his long period of incarceration (from 1958 to 1990, with one short break). Because of his long period of imprisonment, he could never have been a leader of a movement; at best, he may have inspired younger Albanians to act. All that we have are interviews he gave after his release from prison, and in those he presents himself as having always understood that Albanians in Yugoslavia were profoundly oppressed. His "only political interest was the preservation, defense, and salvation of the Albanians from ultimate annihilation."[52] In this, he was not really different from any other active nationalist Albanian of his generation. Even in the previous generation, the war and the Partisans had created a bond among many Albanians and the Tito regime, but this appears to have been understood by virtually all to have been artificial. In later interviews, Demaci does provide some insight into the attraction of Enver Hoxha's Albania for young and discontented Albanians. The Hoxha regime, bitterly hostile to Yugoslavia after the Tito-Stalin split in 1948, was for them a natural ally, a source of hope, because it was both an independent Albanian state and an enemy of their enemy: "I cannot say that I did not entertain a 'naive confidence in Comrade Enver,' . . . after all, he was at least doing something for the liberation of subjugated Albanians."[53] Insofar as loyalty to Enver Hoxha implied a desire for the unification of Kosovo and Albania, Demaci could be said to harbor Greater Albanian intentions; however, recent scholarship has cast much doubt upon Hoxha's commitment to such unification.[54] But the fact that Demaci was a dreamer does not render his desires less real.

Midway along the continuum from Bakalli to Demaci, we find prominent Albanian intellectuals who emerged from the same sort of context as Ćosić in Serbia: they believed in the Tito regime, but were ultimately disappointed. Fehmi Agani, who as a child had been involved with the Partisans, first criticized the situation in Kosovo, he said, in the 1960s, "from the standpoint of values that were betrayed," which Ćosić could easily have said for himself.[55] The 1968 demonstrations, according to Agani, led to the development of two lines among Albanians in Kosovo: one legal and institutional (which included Agani and led to the improved status of Kosovo enshrined in the 1974 Constitution) and a second one, which "opted for demonstrations."[56] Among prominent Albanian intellectuals in Kosovo, only Rexhep Qosja (occasionally described—on the basis of his "fatherly" role, rather than his progress as an intellectual—as the Albanian answer to Dobrica Ćosić[57]) has consistently (i.e., since before Yugoslavia's collapse after 1991) argued for union with Albania.[58]

Most Albanian intellectuals would not publicize their real views on the issue of unification until the collapse of the Yugoslav federation in 1991. One recent study of the idea of Greater Albania has concluded that "the evidence suggests that calls for unification of the Albanian nation emanated not from Tirana but from Priština."[59] By the mid-1990s, of course, autonomy or even republican status was no longer possible in the eyes of most Albanians: "the conditions for it no longer exist," Bakalli said.[60] Fehmi Agani would only then acknowledge that "in Kosovo there was always a current that strived for unification with Albania . . . the desire for unification was general . . . at that time [post-1974], nobody could state such a demand publicly."[61]

Since then, however, sentiment has been virtually unanimous that all Albanians should be unified in a single state. Rexhep Qosja stated: "I regard the Albanian question as one embracing all unliberated Albanians living on Albanian territory bordering on Albania, i.e., in regions which are ethnically and geographically continuous with Albania and in which the Albanians constitute either the only inhabitants or the vast majority of the inhabitants. These regions include not only Kosovo, but also Western Macedonia and Albanian land, inhabited by Albanians, in Montenegro."[62] Others now claim to have agreed all along: Agim Vinca has asserted that he is "convinced, and have been convinced since the early days of my youth, that the only just and permanent solution to the Albanian question in the Balkans is the unification of Kosovo and other territories, where the Albanians constitute the only or majority inhabitants, with Albania."[63] And Shkelzen Maliqi said: ". . . the best solution would be unification with Albania . . ."[64] Does such a desire indicate that they are all Great Albanians? Qosja applies his skills as a rhetorician to argue that it does not: "Albania, including Kosovo with its 90% Albanian majority within its borders, should not be called Greater Albania, but simply a real or normal Albania."[65] The hair that he is splitting is that because Kosovo is overwhelmingly Albanian, his unitarism does not fit the usual understanding of "Great" programs, by which maximal goals ignore eventual minority inhabitants of the envisioned state. But to Serbs, for instance, the inclusion of Kosovo, a "Serbian" territory, makes Qosja (and any others who support union with Albania) a Great Albanian.

Conclusions

A number of questions present themselves at this point. For instance, in comparison with other the other endgames in Eastern Europe, the Yugoslavs did not produce any Havels or Michniks—in other words, leaders who embraced universal rather than narrowly national values. The reason for this is that in Yugoslavia, any potential Havels were drowned out by the din created by national grievances. I am not willing to argue that Ćosić or Qosja or Tudjman would have acted as Havel acted had circumstances allowed. These men were nationalists. But there were other intellectuals in Yugoslavia whose values were universal. One thinks of some of the members of the Praxis group, reformists in the League of Communists who were shunted aside by nationalists, human rights activists . . . they were there; the intellectual communities of Yugoslavia were not monolithically nationalist. Alas, in a state where the national question had not been solved, intellectuals would inevitably be called upon to help solve it or to fulfill that nineteenth-century task, the salvation of the nation. In other words, the intellectual elites of the Communist states of Eastern Europe concerned themselves with the issues that dominated their societies. If the Czechs, Poles, and Hungarians did not feel compelled to view their problems through the prism of national identity, it was because their national problems had been largely solved. If in Yugoslavia virtually every problem came to be viewed through the prism of national identity and competition, it was because the national question there had been inflamed rather than solved by the Titoist administration.

These movements are at least as interesting for the light they may shed on the debate over the nature of post-Communist nationalism. Are the nationalisms that we are experiencing throughout Eastern Europe and the former Soviet Union examples of the "return of the repressed," or are they fundamentally new phenomena? In the case of Yugoslavia, the nationalisms that destroyed the country emerged from within rather than alongside or in opposition to Titoism. With the exception of the unique Albanian case, they defined themselves—for a time, as in the Croatian case, or at all times, as in the Serbian and Slovenian cases—as consistent with Titoism. But even the Albanian case, in which the nationalism of the Kosovars was different than the nationalism of Albanians, was clearly a product of the Titoist system. This alone calls into doubt the simple generalization that these movements reflected the return of prewar nationalisms. They obviously did not: they were conditioned by socialism in its Titoist variation in ways that have only begun to be explored.[66]

One way that nationalism was conditioned by Titoism should be apparent: the Tito regime's administration of Yugoslavia made national identities more rather than less relevant. In other words, the maintenance of republics as expressions of nationhood, and the embellishment of their autonomy over time, made it likely that discontents would be expressed in national forms. But even administration cannot account for the startling transition of good Communists into virulent nationalists. I agree with Nenad Dimitrijević, who has suggested that the conceptual and behavioral (collectivist, idealist) similarities between Communism and nationalism made it easy for intellectuals to move between categories and ideologies, but these are questions that still need answers.[67]

Finally, what did the intellectuals actually accomplish? Did they create the politicians who led Yugoslavia to disaster? Did politicians create the intellectuals to serve their needs? Did intellectuals respond to the demands of the masses? Did intellectuals create mass movements, as populist leaders? The only certain conclusions appear to be that intellectual nationalists neither made politicians nor were made by them, and they neither responded to nor guided the masses. Instead, the intellectuals created images of their national communities that were useful to political elites. They drew from their national traditions, they worked from their own (usually) socialist/Titoist premises, and they drew a picture. The picture they drew wasn't an inevitable one, which is about all that gives one hope for the future of intellectual communities so degraded by their recent pasts.

Notes

1. The founders of KOR and Charter 77 wished their organizations to ignore ideology. See Barbara Falk, *The Dilemmas of Dissidence: Citizen Intellectuals and Philosopher Kings* (Budapest and New York: Central European University Press, 2003), pp. 35–36, 89–91.

2. Jasna Dragović-Soso, *"Saviours of the Nation": Serbia's Intellectual Opposition and the Revival of Nationalism* (Montreal: McGill-Queen's University Press, 2002), p. 29; Aleksa Djilas, *The Contested Country: Yugoslav Unity and Communist Revolution* (Cambridge: Harvard University Press, 1991), pp. 164–65.

3. *Yugoslavia's Way: The Program of the League of the Communists of Yugoslavia*, trans. Stoyan Pribichevich (New York: All Nations Press, 1958), p. 192.

4. *Yugoslavia's Way*, p. 193.

5. Andrew Wachtel, *Making a Nation, Breaking a Nation: Literature and Cultural Politics in Yugoslavia* (Stanford: Stanford University Press, 1998), p. 132.

6. See Audrey Helfant Budding, "Yugoslavs into Serbs: Serbian National Identity, 1961–1971," *Nationalities Papers*, Vol. 25, No. 3 (1997), 407–26.

7. Isaiah Berlin, "Herder and the Enlightenment," in Henry Hardy (ed.), *Three Critics of the Enlightenment: Vico, Hamann, Herder* (Princeton: Princeton University Press, 2000), p. 228. On the Germans, see Liah Greenfeld, *Nationalism: Five Roads to Modernity* (Cambridge: Harvard University Press, 1992), pp. 275–395.

8. Andrew Wachtel, "Writers and Society in Eastern Europe, 1989–2000: The End of the Golden Age," *East European Politics and Societies*, Vol. 17, No. 4 (Winter 2003), p. 584.

9. Nenad Dimitrijević, "Words and Death: Serbian Nationalist Intellectuals," in Andras Bozoki (ed.), *Intellectuals and Politics in Central Europe* (Budapest: Central European University Press, 1999), p. 120.

10. Dimitrijević, "Words and Death," pp. 121–22.

11. Miroslav Krleža described his own expectations of engagement circumspectly: "I never had—fortunately—too many illusions about immediate results of my engagement. The number of political disagreements that I see in my past offer in that sense a monumental example to future generations" (Predrag Matvejević, *Razgovori s Miroslavom Krležom*, 4th edition [Zagreb: Liber, 1978], p. 8). Marko Ristić also expressed limited goals for his own engagement: "The truth is that artistic creativity and social action are two different spheres of human activity. Artistic creativity carries within it . . . certain constants which make it only partially reducible to a purely social conditionality" (Marko Ristić, *Za svest, 1971–1977* [Belgrade: Nolit, 1977], p. 93).

12. The notion had been first considered at the third plenum of the KPJ in June 1951, as follows: "The development of new theoretical viewpoints in the KPJ will be accomplished on the basis of discussion and the struggle of ideas . . . Members of the KPJ have the full right to freely express and discuss, whether verbally or in the Party or non-Party press, the theoretical views of individual members of the Party, regardless of the function they fulfill . . . " "(Predlog) Rezolucije o teorijskom radu u KPJ, Treći plenum CK KPJ (Juna 1951)," in Petranović, *Jugoslavija*, p. 830.

13. On this polemic, see Dimitrij Rupel, *Od vojnog do civilnog društva* (Zagreb: Globus, 1990), pp. 96–113. Jelena Milojković-Djurić, "Approaches to National Identities: Ćosić's and Pirjevec's Debate on Ideological and Literary Issues," *East European Quarterly*, Vol. 30, No. 1 (Spring 1996), pp. 63–73, is not all that enlightening. Two of Ćosić's contributions to the polemic are in his collected works: "O savremenom nesavremenon nacionalizmu" and "Nacija, integracija, socijalizam," in Dobrica Ćosić, *Odgovornosti: Akcija II*, Vol. 8 of *Sabrana dela Dobrice Ćosića* (Belgrade: Prosveta, 1966), pp. 18–85. Pirjevec's installments were republished as "Izvinite, kako ste rekli?" *Delo* (Belgrade), Vol. 7, No. 12 (December 1961), pp. 1,396–99; "Slovenstvo, jugoslovenstvo, i socijalizam," *Delo* (Belgrade), Vol. 8, No. 1 (January 1962), pp. 9–30; and "Odgovor Dobrici Ćosiću," *Delo* (Belgrade), Vol. 8, No. 4 (April 1962), pp. 526–51; Ćosić's final word, "Čitaocima," can

be found in *Delo* (Belgrade), Vol. 8, No. 5 (May 1962), pp. 645–48. The quote is from Ćosić, "O savremenom nesavremenom nacionalizmu," p. 48.

14. There had been one other polemic, with similar positions taken, between a Serb, Zoran Mišić, and a Slovene, Drago Šego, in 1956, but that debate did not achieve the same level of notoriety.

15. Slavoljub Djukić, *Lovljenje vetra: Politička ispovest Dobrice Ćosića* (Belgrade: Samizdat B92, 2001), p. 67.

16. Rupel, *Od vojnog do civilnog društva*, p. 101.

17. The key event in this process was the issuance of "The Letter" in September 1972. The letter was composed and signed by Tito and Stane Dolanc, the secretary of the Executive Bureau of the League of Communists. The essence of that letter's message was that the LCY would now reassert control of cadre policy throughout the country; would now determine the Party's line for the entire federation and all republican and regional parties; and would do so to return to its status as a revolutionary party responsible for defending the achievements of Yugoslav socialism, especially self-management (Dennison I. Rusinow, *The Yugoslav Experiment, 1948–1974* (Berkeley: Published for the Royal Institute of International Affairs, London, by the University of California Press, 1977).

18. Inspiring but irrelevant: when political parties were created in Serbia in 1990–91, the nonnationalists found themselves isolated and ignored in organizations like the Civic Alliance, which rarely mattered when elections came around.

19. One would have a hard time demonstrating that Ćosić was a nationalist on the basis of his actions and comments in the 1960s.

20. Maybe Antonije Isaković could be included in this group, which would make two influential Serbs. Others were largely non-Communist or had a foot out the door: Borislav Mihajlović Mihiz, Brana Crnčević, Matija Bećković.

21. Dobrica Ćosić, "Kritika vladajuće ideološke koncepcije u nacionalnoj politici," in Ćosić, *Stvarno i moguće: Članci i ogledi* (Ljubljana and Zagreb: Cankarjeva založba, 1988).

22. See Nick Miller, "Mihiz in the Sixties: Politics and Drama Between Nationalism and Authoritarianism," *Nationalities Papers*, Vol. 30, No. 4 (December, 2002), 327–51.

23. Mihailo Djurić, "Smišljene smutnje," in Mihailo Djurić, *Iskustvo razlike* (Belgrade: Tersit, 1994), pp. 13–14.

24. The board included Mica Popović, Radovan Samardžić, Mihailo Djurić, Kosta Mihajlović, Vojislav Djurić, Pavle Ivić, Dimitrije Bogdanović, Slobodan Selenić, Meša Selimović, Milorad Pavić, Dušan Matić, Ivo Andrić, Erih Koš, Svetlana Velmar-Janković, Skender Kulenović, Mihailo Marković, and others.

25. "Sastanak beogradskih pisaca," *Književne novine* (Belgrade) May 27, 1982, p. 2.

26. The committee's first public declaration was dated November 10, 1984, and can be found in Serbian in *Naša reč* (London) January 1985, 6; a translation is in Oskar Gruenwald and Karen Rosenblum-Cale (eds.), *Human Rights in Yugoslavia* (New York: Irvington Publishers, 1986), pp. 644–48.

27. By the time Tito had died, Ćosić had published *Time of Death*, his endless novel about Serbian suffering and the mendacity of its allies during the First World War, and he had been made a regular member of the Serbian Academy (in 1977). Within years of Tito's death, two committees defending the right to free expression had been founded and were operating on a relatively open basis; a novel had been published on the horrors of Goli Otok (*Tren II*, by Antonije Isaković), plays had been published questioning the official line on the break with Stalin (*Karamazovi*, by Dušan Jovanović) and the Second World War in Croatia (*Golubnjača*, by Jovan Radulović), and another of Ćosić's books, this

one a book of essays, many of which openly challenged the Titoist order in Yugoslavia (*Stvarno i moguće*) was published.

28. "Sastanak beogradskih pisaca," *Književne novine* (Belgrade) May 27, 1982, p. 2.

29. The committee's first public declaration was dated November 10, 1984, and can be found in Serbian in *Naša reč* (London) January 1985, p. 6; a translation is in Oskar Gruenwald and Karen Rosenblum-Cale (eds.), *Human Rights in Yugoslavia* (New York: Irvington Publishers, 1986), pp. 644–48.

30. Dobrica Ćosić, "Koliko smo mi sami krivi," *Književne novine* (June 1, 1987).

31. See testimonies included in Julie Mertus, *Kosovo: How Myths and Truths Started a War* (Berkeley and Los Angeles: University of California Press, 1999), pp. 56–74.

32. This is Dobrica Ćosić speaking, on many occasions.

33. The phrase comes from Greenfeld, *Nationalism*, 390; she uses it to describe intellectual life in Germany in the early nineteenth century.

34. This "dual legitimation" allowed Milošević to bring together otherwise disparate interests in Serbia, including Communists and non-Communist nationalists. Ćosić embodies the unification of the two: a leftist who bemoaned the corruption of the original mission of Marxism, and a nationalist who longed for a national revival.

35. Petar Vodopivec, "Seven Decades of Unconfronted Incongruities: The Slovenes and Yugoslavia," in Jill Benderly and Evan Kraft (eds.), *Independent Slovenia: Origins, Movements, Prospects* (New York: St. Martin's, 1994), p. 37.

36. Rupel, *Od vojnog do civilnog društva*, pp. 182–83. Also, Petar Vodopivec asserts that "Socialist Yugoslavia clearly acknowledged the equal rights and individuality of all its peoples and took a stand against their forcible combination" (Vodopivec, "Seven Decades," p. 37).

37. Vodopivec, "Seven Decades," p. 43. Vodopivec drew on the ideas of Edvard Kocbek, an early Slovene dissident, in making his point about continuity in Slovenian national thought.

38. Rupel, *Od vojnog do civilnog društva* (Zagreb: Globus, 1990), p. 174.

39. Rupel, *Od vojnog do civilnog društva*, pp. 180–81.

40. Aleš Gabrič, "Cultural Activities," in Leopoldina Plut-Pregelj (ed.), *The Repluralization of Slovenia in the 1980s: New Revelations from Archival Records* (Seattle: Henry Jackson School of International Studies, University of Washington, 2000), p. 24.

41. Tomaš Mastnak, "From Social Movements to National Sovereignty," in J. Benderly and E. Kraft (eds.), *Independent Slovenia: Origins, Movements, Prospects* (New York: St. Martin's Press, 1994), p. 102.

42. Mastnak, "From Social Movements," p. 95.

43. Mastnak, "From Social Movements," p. 106.

44. I am using the translation by Christopher Spalatin, "Serbo-Croatian or Serbian and Croatian? Considerations on the Croatian Declaration and Serbian Proposal of March 1967," *Journal of Croatian Studies*, Vols. 7–8 (1966–67), pp. 6–9.

45. "Interview with Dr. Marko Veselica," M. Meštrović (trans.) (London: United Publishers, 1980), pp. 3–12; Vlado Gotovac, *Moj slučaj* (Ljubljana and Zagreb: Cankarjeva založba, 1989), pp. 157–61.

46. Gotovac, *Moj slučaj*, p. 163.

47. Dobrica Ćosić, for instance, repeatedly refers to himself as persecuted throughout the 1970s and 1980s, but in fact he never suffered anything more than searches and bugging.

48. On this topic, see the recent stimulating book by Paul Hockenos, *Homeland Calling: Exile Patriotism and the Balkan Wars* (Ithaca, NY: Cornell University Press, 2003).

49. For instance, Fehmi Agani, a professor at the University of Priština in 1981, revealed that he was not an inspiration to or leader of the movement of that year, but that unnamed students were, and that "they did not tell me anything, wishing to protect me" (Momčilo Petrović, *Pitao sam Albance sta žele, a oni su rekli: republiku . . . ako može* [Belgrade: Radio B92, 1996], p. 164).

50. Petrović, *Pitao sam Albance*, p. 13.

51. Petrović, *Pitao sam Albance*, p. 18.

52. Robert Elsie, *Kosovo: In the Heart of the Powder Keg* (Boulder, CO: East European Monographs, 1997), p. 483.

53. Elsie, *Kosovo*, p. 483.

54. Paulin Kola, *The Myth of Greater Albania* (New York: New York University Press, 2003).

55. Petrović, *Pitao sam Albance*, p. 161.

56. Petrović, *Pitao sam Albance*, p. 169.

57. Qosja: "Ćosić's nationalism is aggressive, conquering nationalism, because Serbian nationalism has been such through history all the way to today, and my nationalism is positive" Elsie, *Kosovo*, p. 498).

58. For an extensive collection of Qosja's articles from the 1980s, see Rexhep Qosja, *Nezastičena sudbina: O Albancima u Jugoslaviji danas* (Zagreb: HSLS, 1990).

59. Kola, *The Myth of Greater Albania*, p. 392.

60. Petrović, *Pitao sam Albance*, p. 28.

61. Petrović, *Pitao sam Albance*, p. 173.

62. Elsie, *Kosovo*, p. 495.

63. Elsie, *Kosovo*, p. 512.

64. Petrović, *Pitao sam Albance*, p. 68.

65. Elsie, *Kosovo*, p. 498.

66. See, for instance, Katherine Verdery, "Nationalism and National Sentiment in Postsocialist Romania," in *What Was Socialism, and What Comes Next?* (Princeton: Princeton University Press, 1996), pp. 83–103.

67. Dimitrijević, "Words and Death," p. 124.

THE BREAKDOWN: THE 1980s

A Last Attempt at Educational Integration: The Failure of Common Educational Cores in Yugoslavia in the early 1980s

◈ Andrew Wachtel and Predrag J. Marković ◈

It is a common belief in most of the contemporary world that a successful national state requires some form of unified educational system, at least in the primary grades. Though nationalists of all stripes tend to insist vociferously that national affiliation is natural and perhaps even hereditary, few are willing to risk losing the opportunity to proselytize to school-age children during their formative years. National curricula are instituted in order to provide citizens with a common body of knowledge and common way of interpreting that knowledge, which are thought to provide life-long cultural glue. The presumed necessity for a common educational system is all the greater in states with heterogeneous populations, and it persists even in today's highly globalized world.

It was an article of faith among the elites whose work led in 1918 to the founding of the new country officially called the Kingdom of Serbs, Croats, and Slovenes (and unofficially Yugoslavia) that the new Yugoslav citizens needed to be convinced of their commonalities. As one observer put it, "The problem of our revolution is not one of destruction, but of building . . . we need to build our new country, to build a new citizen and person. The basic problem of our revolution is not state-building, social or economic development. It is—for on this rests the possibility of a satisfactory answer to the aforementioned questions—to a much greater extent national and cultural."[1] Initiatives to create a feeling of Yugoslav national solidarity took a variety of forms during the lifetime of both the interwar monarchy and the post-World War II Communist state. In the cultural sphere, these included attempts to create a national literary canon, the production of a variety of Yugoslav-oriented works of literature and art, festivals that drew people from all parts of the country together, and so forth. Some received state support, especially in the postwar period, whereas others were carried out by private groups or individuals. In the modern world, however, education, particularly primary education, is a matter of state concern, and at various points in Yugoslavia's seventy-year history the state decided that there was indeed a need to build Yugoslavs from the ground up, as it were. To this end, a number of efforts were made to create some kind of unified educational system whose goal was to provide, at a minimum, a common core of knowledge that all Yugoslav citizens would possess. At a maximum, such a core program would, it was felt, create Yugoslavs where once there had been Croats, Serbs, Slovenes, and so forth. Apparently, these efforts achieved some degree of success, particularly in the 1960s, when a substantial portion of the population reported at least some level of Yugoslav identification to sociologists. For a variety of reasons, however, efforts at creating Yugoslavs lagged in the 1970s and early 1980s. A fear that the national educational glue that had held Yugoslavia together was beginning to disintegrate was, it appears, behind the final attempt in the educational sphere to define a core national curriculum in 1983 and 1984. In this essay, we will focus on the failure of attempts to introduce a common core curriculum in literature in this period. In our view, the fault lines revealed in the discussions that took place around these efforts not only show that the Yugoslav project was already on the verge of collapse at this time but also were harbingers of trends that became far more ominous later in the decade.

Interwar Period

The desire in some quarters for a unified school curriculum dated to the beginning of the Yugoslav state. According to Charles Jelavich,

> [t]he royalist government understood well that a major road to national unity led through education. Hence, one of its first decisions was to call for uniform centralized education. . . . The problems that the government would face surfaced with the report of the first committee appointed by the minister of education to examine the prewar education laws, practices, and curriculums in all the South Slav lands and to submit proposals for education. Acting hastily, the committee called for a single uniform education system and curriculum for elementary schools. Immediately, the report was strongly criticized by teachers, education organizations, and even many politicians. They not only challenged the competence of the committee members, but, more important, they charged that the committee had not taken into consideration the diverse educational experiences of the South Slavs.[2]

In response to these protests, the implementation of a national curriculum was delayed, and students continued to be educated according to prewar approaches, which, as Jelavich points out, were in many cases inimical to the idea of a single Yugoslav nation.

Attempts at a national curriculum were revived in 1929, the year in which King Alexander's dictatorship was introduced. In March 1929, two months after the proclamation of the dictatorship, the minister for education, Božidar Maksimović, outlined a common educational and cultural program. This program would in principle have unified orthography and terminology and above all, enabled common textbooks for all of Yugoslavia.[3] On the whole, the project failed, however, despite the strong advocacy of the king and of the Yugoslav teachers' union. Still, an examination of school readers from the late 1920s and early 1930s indicates that some progress toward providing a Yugoslav-oriented curriculum was made in this period even if full integration was not achieved.

As an example, we might analyze the excellent reader dating from 1928 compiled for the third level of middle schools.[4] It included representative selections from Serbian, Croatian, and Slovenian literature, and its multicultural Yugoslav orientation is clear from the fact that texts were grouped thematically rather than by the author's nationality. Furthermore, authors were identified by their region of origin rather than by their "tribal" affiliation, thereby allowing the compiler to avoid the whole question of whether a given text belonged to Serbian or Croatian literature. Should anyone have wanted to check, however, he would have discovered that the percentage of authors of a given nationality mirrored almost exactly the population percentages of the country as a whole, although there is no overt indication that affirmative-action criteria were applied to the selection process.[5] The texts themselves include a large number of folk songs, riddles, and poems, and although most of them date from the nineteenth century, the compiler also provided excerpts from the work of such major living authors as Krleža, Andrić, and Župančič. There seems to have been no effort made to instill Yugoslav patriotism directly through this anthology (i.e., it does not contain poems thematically devoted to South Slav unity), but the compiler frequently placed texts on the same theme by Serbian, Croatian, and Slovene authors side by side, creating an impression of commonality and difference simultaneously.[6] All texts were presented in the alphabet and language in which they had been originally published. Slovenian-language selections were glossed heavily below, but in theory at least, Serbian and Croatian students would have become familiar with the Slovenian language in this fashion.

Furthermore, though not designed for use in schools, a number of important books were written in the spirit of the common Yugoslav cultural heritage in this period, most notably Antun Barac's *History of Yugoslav Literature,* which was translated into English and reprinted in Yugoslavia after World War II. Also, four historical syntheses were written in the "integral Yugoslav" spirit in the 1930s: Viktor Novak's *Antologija jugoslovenske misli i narodnog jedinstva* (1930), Ćorović's *Istorija Jugoslavije* (1931), Ferdo Šišić's *Istorija ideje jugoslovenskog narodnog ujedinjenja i islobođenja od 1790–1918* (1937), and Vladimir Dvornikovic's monumental *Karakterologija Jugoslovena.* Unlike Barac's history, these books were not republished after World War II.

The Search for a Common Core after World War II

In the federal Yugoslav state created after World War II, responsibility for education was at least in principle devolved to the republics (indeed, after 1948 there was no federal ministry of education at all), each of which promulgated its own educational plan. But as was the case in all other areas, republican freedom was severely circumscribed, particularly in the years surrounding the Tito/Stalin break. The difficult balancing act between central and republican control can be followed most easily by an examination of the program guides that were published periodically by the education ministries in all the Yugoslav republics.

The first published programs (for grades 1–4) appeared in 1947. In each of the plans pride of place was given to instilling in the students general goals such as "love and respect for their homeland and its peoples," as well as "an appreciation for the principles of brotherhood and unity." The latter formulation was the most popular catchphrase in the postwar period, repeated frequently enough to be almost meaningless. Many elements of the curriculum were more or less uniform throughout the country, including the total number of hours in school (20 hours per week in first grade, rising to 26 in fourth), as well as the basic subjects to be taught—language, history, geography, natural science, mathematics, drawing, singing, and physical education. Nevertheless, a careful reading of the plans reveals significant differences of emphasis in the various republics; these are most apparent in the treatment of history, and in particular interwar history.

In Croatia, for example, teachers were given a detailed blueprint and were supposed to teach

> Old Yugoslavia and its founding. Our peoples during the First World War, their struggles for freedom from foreign yokes, their unification as the only path to independence, and the construction of a unified state; the dissatisfaction of the masses with the monarchical and centralizing state order (the Vidovdan constitution); the struggle of the Croatian and other oppressed peoples, the excitation of national and religious hatred by the ruling classes; the murder in the parliament [of Stjepan Radić] and the institution of dictatorship.[7]

The plan from Bosnia and Herzegovina implied that a bit less attention should be paid to the interwar problems of Yugoslavia, or at least it gave teachers wider latitude in their treatment of them: "The founding of the Kingdom of the Serbs, Croats, and Slovenes. The Vidovdan Constitution and the situation in 1921. The situation from 1921 to 1929; the situation from 1929 to 1941."[8] The amazing contrast, however, is between the Croatian plan and its Serbian counterpart. In the latter republic, teachers were left entirely to their own devices regarding the treatment of interwar history. They were directed to deal with "the founding of Yugoslavia. Yugoslavia from 1918 to 1941," and that was all.[9] This does not necessarily mean that in Croatian schools children learned in great detail the fact that Serbian attempts at political unitarism had been a major problem in interwar Yugoslavia. Nor does it necessarily mean that Serbian children did not learn this. But there is good reason to suspect that children educated in various Yugoslav republics would not have had an identical view of the vital question of what their country had been like before the Communist era.

Communist authorities faced a similar problem when it came to providing a unified history of the country at a more advanced level. The regime's plans for the writing of a unified national history were, despite initial ambitions, abandoned quite quickly. In 1949 federal authorities formed a commission to write a History of the Yugoslav Peoples (the recognition of a need for plurality is stressed in the very title). Two volumes, reaching the end of the eighteenth century, were published in 1953 and 1959 respectively. But the nineteenth century, the main period of nation formation, proved too touchy to be written about, nor could the even more vexed twentieth century be broached. In the early 1970s *Istorija Jugoslavije* (History of Yugoslavia)[10] provoked a major confrontation between Croatian historians and the authors (mostly Serbs).[11] Interestingly enough, it proved impossible even to write a common history of the Communist Party. The first such attempt, *Pregled istorije SKJ* in 1963, was severely criticized by a group of Croatian historians gathered around Franjo Tudjman. In this debate Tudjman's group did not get overt support from the Croatian Communist Party, although a recent study has argued that the affair was a "trial balloon" and that at least some Croatian Party leaders tacitly supported Tudjman and his associates.[12]

A final attempt to create a "common historical memory" for school children was undertaken during the 1980s, following the legitimacy crisis that truly began for Communist Yugoslavia after Tito's death in 1980. Tito's personal cult was one of the main "pillars of the common identity" from the regime's point of view.[13] It is not just a coincidence that the first open request for the redefinition of internal borders and constitutional arrangements was made by Kosovo Albanians in March 1981, one year after Tito's death. The creation of common cores in historiography began after the Agreement of Socialist Republics and Autonomous Provinces (*Dogovor socijalističkih republika i pokrajina*) signed on March 6, 1981. These common cores were divided in two parts: the first was for the eight-year elementary school, and the second was for the first two years of secondary school. This agreement envisaged that some 60 percent or more of the history curriculum should be common in all Yugoslavia. A revised common core was agreed upon in July 1983. The implementation of common cores in the history curriculum was planned for the years 1983 and 1984. In the meantime, the need for such a common core was demonstrated by research organized by several Zagreb and Belgrade historians (Drago Roksandić, Nikša Stipčević, Đorđe Stanković, and Marjan Maticka), which revealed that, as concerned the period up to 1918, only six persons were mentioned in all eight history textbooks of the Yugoslav republics and provinces.[14] As for national names, the most ethnocentric textbooks were those of Kosovo Albanians, measured by the frequency of the mention of one's own national name, whereas this frequency was lowest in the textbooks of central Serbia.[15]

Oddly enough, by this period nobody seemed to care about common cores in historiography. In the absence of public disputes and comments, we cannot say much about the implementation of the common core in historiography curricula thereafter.

Similar silence covered the last failed attempt to write a History of the Yugoslav Peoples and Minorities (*naroda i narodnosti*). This final attempt at common historical synthesis failed in spite of the official political support of the Thirteenth Party Congress (1986) and adequate financial support provided by federal and republic authorities.[16] Surprisingly, educational policy did not reflect the fierce conflict in academic historiography and public life (mostly weekly magazines and newspapers) along national lines that raged from the beginning of the 1980s, a decade that witnessed what Jasna Dragović-Soso has called a "breakdown of official historiography."

The most important all-Yugoslav scholarly project, *Encyclopedia of Yugoslavia,* was the focus of particularly fierce disputes along ethnic lines. The most disputed *Encyclopedia* entries concerned the ethnogenesis of some of the Yugoslav peoples (Kosovo Albanians, Montenegrins, and Bosnian Muslims) and one tricky formal problem: should the entries for Serbia's autonomous regions, Kosovo and Vojvodina, be separate entries or subentries within the broader entry "Serbia." A compromise was finally found in 1987, by which time it was becoming obvious that no common Yugoslav scholarly project was viable any longer.

Many silenced historical issues were also (re)opened during the 1980s (World War II victims, the real contribution to the Resistance/collaboration of different Yugoslav nations during the war, Communist repression, the rehabilitation of the pre-Communist Yugoslav state, etc.).[17] Nevertheless, this "outburst of history"[18] did not find a reflection in school history curricula, which remained frozen throughout the decade. Not that the history curricula was unimportant for the regime. On the contrary, it was so important that nobody dared to change it, for this curriculum had been one of the few pillars of common identity as imagined by the state and regime ideologues.[19] Nor was the community of professional historians socially and politically self-confident enough to defy the authorities as writers did.

The issue of common cores in the realm of literature was another story, however. From the very beginning, the common literature curriculum became a battleground for writers entrenched in republic-level literary unions, and their disputes were covered extensively in the Yugoslav press.[20] Common cores in literature had been suggested in the conclusions of the conference *Nastava književnosti u srednjim školima Jugoslavije* (The Teaching of Literature in Yugoslav High Schools) organized in Dojran (Macedonia) as early as October 1977. Following these conclusions, a commission of the Yugoslav writers' union unveiled a *Nacrt minimuma nastave književnosti u srednjim školima* (Draft of a Minimal Common Curriculum in Literature Courses in High Schools) in May 1981. A preliminary version was published in *Književna reč.* The republic-level literary unions, educational institutions, and the Committee of the Savezne konferencije SSRNJ (Federal Conference of the Socialist Alliance of Working People) were then supposed to evaluate the plan.

Before considering the controversy this plan engendered, it would be a good idea to examine what was actually proposed and what the writers of the proposed core curriculum thought they were accomplishing. First of all, the common core in literature was never meant to create a fully unified educational plan for the country. In the original draft, 50 percent of the literary works to be taught would be covered by the core, whereas the other 50 percent would be left to the discretion of republic or province-level authorities.[21] A clear affirmative-action principle was used in selecting writers for inclusion in the core, although this was vehemently denied by some of those who participated in drafting the proposal.[22] Writers were grouped by national origin, and efforts were made to ensure that the overall number of writers from a given "national" tradition corresponded roughly to the size of that nation's population in the country.

In order to provide an idea of what was to be covered by the cores, let us look at the works proposed for two different grades. In the fifth grade of elementary school, the core was to encompass four fields: lyric poetry, epic poetry and stories, drama, and books to be read at home. Lyric texts included one Macedonian author, one Croatian, and one Kordun folk poem from World War II. Epic poetry and stories included a speech of Tito's (!), one story each by Branko Ćopić, Ivan Cankar, Danko Oblak, Mikola Kočiš, Stole Popov, and Stefan Mitrov Ljubiša (Serb, Slovene, Croat, Hungarian, Macedonian, and Montenegrin writers respectively), one epic poem from the folkloric tradition (*The Building of Skadar*), and one humoristic folk story ("Ero from the Other World"). Drama was represented by a text from the Serbian writer Dušan Radović ("Kapetan Džon Piplfoks"). The books proposed for reading at home were the following: a selection of folk literature from all regions of Yugoslavia; an Albanian and a Macedonian novel; and Jules Verne's *20,000 Leagues under the Sea*.

For the final year of high school (twelfth grade), the recommended books for reading at home were: *For Whom the Bell Tolls* (Ernest Hemingway), *The Cursed Yard* (Andrić), and *The Return of Filip Latinović* (Krleža). In this same year, interwar and World War II writers were supposed to be read during the school lessons. As for interwar literature, the books proposed were by the following writers: Bertolt Brecht, Tin Ujević (Croat), Srečko Kosovel (Slovene), Mekuli (Albanian), Kočo Racin (Macedonian), Krleža (Croat), Andrić (usually considered Bosnian in such company), and Miloš Crnjanski (a Serb). War and revolutionary literature was represented by: Oton Župančič (Slovene), Vladimir Nazor (Croat), Mirko Banjević (Montenegrin), Ivan Goran Kovačić (Croat), Skender Kulenović (Bosnian Moslem), Branko Ćopić (Serbian writer from Bosnia), Matej Bor (Slovene), Aco Šopov (Macedonian), Jovan Popović, and Slavko Vukosavljević (Serbs from Central Serbia).[23] The suggested core does not imply cultural hegemony of any group nor the wish to suppress literature in smaller (other than Serbo-Croatian) languages.

A number of overlapping reasons for the creation of cores were noted in the course of the discussion. The first was purely practical: because there was so little correlation between the school programs in various republics, students whose families moved from one part of the country to another were at an enormous disadvantage in a school system that measured progress in terms of the knowledge of a given body of facts. A core curriculum, it was thought, would remove one impediment to increased geographical and social mobility. A second, frequently cited, reason had specifically to do with the need for Yugoslavs of all nationalities to know about "others" who lived in their country and to correct what was perceived as an ever-increasing tendency toward national disintegration. Thus, Radovan Lazarević, one of the authors of the core, insisted that it was planned simply to stop the "drifting apart of the eight separate educational systems and to overcome localism and isolation within republic limits. It is hoped that after the implementation of common cores it would be impossible for a high school student not to know about the most important persons and events from the cultural and historical heritage of the other republics."[24]

From the time the core curriculum proposal was first unveiled it became the subject of vigorous and sometimes acrimonious debate, generally through the institutions of republic- and province-level writers' unions and sometimes with the backing of political leaders as well. In response to a variety of objections, the core curriculum proposal was revised at least five times between 1982 and 1986. Nevertheless, even the final, very watered-down proposal was never implemented, a strong indication that at least on the cultural level the idea of a supranational Yugoslav culture, even one based firmly in the separate national cultures, was a dead letter well before the political breakup of the country. Interestingly enough, the last Party effort to create a common Yugoslav identity also dated from 1986. In that year, at the last regular congress of the LCY (Federal Yugoslav Party), a resolution was passed stressing the need for the education of the new generations in the spirit of "(common) Yugoslav socialist patriotism," especially in Kosovo.[25]

Objections to the core curriculum fell into three basic categories. The first had to do with how writers were chosen for inclusion; this included disputes about how national literatures should be understood in the context of Yugoslavia, what nation a given writer had "really" belonged to, what grounds should be used for including or excluding writers, and so forth. The second concerned linguistic issues, always a problem in a multilingual society. And the final, most contentious and broadest one had to do with whether the Yugoslav state had any business in attempting to create a unified education system in the first place.

Interestingly, the literary quality of the writers chosen for the cores was rarely at issue. To be sure, Branko Ćopić, one of the most popular Yugoslav writers, opined that the core should include only the best writers, not those who had been recommended by national origin and "who were known to be writers only by members of their own family."[26] Such statements were isolated instances, however, an indication that at least in public the basic affirmative-action nature of the federal Yugoslav state was broadly accepted by most members of the cultural elite.

Among the first objections raised to the original core curriculum proposal was that it projected the contemporary political situation into the past and organized writers according to present-day republic and province borders. Jelena Balšić, for example, the daughter of medieval Serbian prince Lazar, was regarded as a representative of Montenegro (because she was married on what eventually became Montenegrin territory), despite the fact that Montenegro did not exist in her day. To compound the problem, some writers were attached to the republic (or province) of their birth and others to the republic where they had lived. A prime example of this sort was, on the one hand, Ivo Andrić. Born in Bosnia, he appeared in the draft core curriculum as a representative of Bosnian literature, despite the fact that at various points in his career he had identified himself as a Croatian, a Yugoslav, and a Serbian writer.[27] On the other hand, Simo Matavulj, born in Šibenik (Croatia), was regarded as a writer from Serbia (where he spent the second part of his life). Veljko Petrović, Isidora Sekulić, and Miloš Crnjanski were all born in Vojvodina and lived in Belgrade, but the core proposal attached the first two to Vojvodina, whereas Crnjanski represented central Serbia.[28] Complaints about classification were among the first objections to the proposal made by the working group of the Serbian writers' union.[29] They concluded that such an organizational approach disintegrated Serbian and, to some degree, Croatian literature as well.[30]

The appropriate national affiliation of writers was not the only subject of controversy. A related problem was the exclusion of certain writers for reasons of political correctness. Political criteria had been commonly applied in the earlier days of the Communist regime when choosing writers for inclusion in school textbooks. Thus, the poet Jovan Dučić, widely viewed as a Serbian chauvinist, had been declared persona non grata in Yugoslav school anthologies immediately after World War II (at that time he had been accompanied into oblivion by other major interwar writers such as Crnjanski, Ujević, and Stanislav Vinaver, whose work was viewed as overly modernist and therefore not in keeping with the needs of socialist nation building). In the core curriculum proposal of the 1980s, the major modernists reappeared, but Dučić remained excluded and was joined now by Radovan Zogović and Dobrica Ćosić, disputed by the Macedonian and Croatian writers' unions.[31] Zogović, ironically enough, had been the Communist culture tsar in the early years of the Tito regime and at that point had been a leading advocate of the cleansing of undesirable elements from the Yugoslav literary pantheon. His star had fallen after the Tito/Stalin split. Ćosić, whose partisan novel *Far Away is the Sun (Daleko je sunce)* had been one of the few books to make it into the postwar Yugoslav school canon, had become increasingly identified with Serbian nationalism in the 1970s.[32]

Some specific authors became a focus of conflict between various writers' unions. Njegoš was a major problem, for example. Thus, Vaso Milinčević, a member of the Serbian working group, expressed the widespread opinion that up to the nineteenth century Serbian and Montenegrin literature were one and the same and that therefore, for the purposes of the core, Njegoš should be identified as a Serbian rather than a Montenegrin writer.[33] An immediate reaction came in several articles of the official Montenegrin newspaper *Pobjeda*. The possibility that Njegoš could belong to two literatures was disregarded as "paternalism" and "hegemonism." The Bosnian writers union supported the Montenegrin side in the dispute.[34]

In 1984, at a later stage in the discussions about the core curriculum, Njegoš became an even more polarizing figure. The opening salvo in this later round of controversy was fired by a school teacher named Mubera Mujagić in 1984 at a public meeting sponsored by the Writers' Organization of Sarajevo to discuss proposed revisions to the nationwide core. Hinting at what had hitherto been a taboo topic, the anti-Ottoman and anti-Muslim messages in Njegoš's *The Mountain Wreath (Gorski vijenac)*, as well as Ivan Mažuranić's *The Death of Smail-Aga Čengić (Smrt Smail age Čengića)*, she suggested that they be excluded from the primary school core because they might "evoke national intolerance."

This led to a series of responses and counter-responses in the Belgrade biweekly *Intervju*.[35] While not disputing Njegoš's position as a great writer and thinker, Mujagić, who publicly identified herself as a Yugoslav, asked: "What kind of spirit can these works offer us? Can they evoke catharsis in the reader, a feeling of unity, Yugoslavism, accord, solidarity, toleration, and cosmopolitanism, or do they create bile, poison, and hatred towards anyone who belongs to another belief or nation." Mujagić's critics responded to her allegations in a couple of ways. Some defended Njegoš as a great thinker and writer whose thought soars above all petty local differences and forms an indelible part of the national legacy that should not be censored just because it might offend someone in the present (Egerić). Others insisted that the characters and times described in Njegoš's work had nothing to do with the nations of contemporary Yugoslavia (Vučelić). All agreed that only poor teaching could possibly allow any student to come away from the text with an incorrect impression. No one responded directly to the claims made by Mujagić and backed up by a teacher named Jakov Ivaštović, who reported having the same experience, namely that students did indeed interpret *The Mountain Wreath* in a nationalist vein.

A second key issue relating to the core curriculum had to do with language. For if some 75 percent of the population spoke Serbo-Croatian (at this point still recognized as a single language with multiple dialects) as their native language, native speakers of Slovene, Macedonian, and Albanian made up almost 22 percent of the population. What to do about texts from languages other than Serbo-Croatian had been a problem for intellectuals of a Yugoslav bent from the beginning. The most radical experiment in creating a multicultural Yugoslav culture was provided by the journal *Književni jug*, which began appearing in January 1918 and continued to publish until the end of 1919. Its contributors included practically every major writer from Serbia, Croatia, and Slovenia. Each issue published literary work in Serbo-Croatian and Slovenian and employed both the Cyrillic and Latin alphabets. Even this journal did not include work from other minority languages, however, and it remained an isolated experiment. To our knowledge, neither during the existence of the first nor the second Yugoslavia was there a literary journal that consistently published work in more than one language. As far as schools went, in the Communist period primary schooling was available in most minority languages. Serbo-Croatian was generally also a required subject in those schools.[36] The converse, however, was not true. That is, children who spoke Serbo-Croatian as their mother tongue were not required to learn any of the other languages spoken in Yugoslavia.

Following what had been accepted practice, the core curriculum proposal envisaged including an appropriate percentage of texts from the various minority languages, but all texts were to be presented in Serbo-Croatian translation. In the context of this debate, however, accepted practice in the linguistic arena came up for discussion. Thus, the president of the Council for Culture of the Slovene SSRN (the Socialist Alliance of Working People—this was the largest political organization in each of the Yugoslav republics; it supplemented the Communist Party, allowing membership of religious and other non-Party people), France Šetinc, insisted that if there was to be a core curriculum, Slovenes would create a version with a special focus on the problem of language. Slovene participants in the debate (Matevž Krivic, for example) stressed the fact that Serbo-Croatian was compulsory in Slovene schools, whereas Slovene was not in the curricula of other republics.[37] Not surprisingly, the Slovenes were backed up in this instance by their colleagues from Macedonia. In February 1984, Macedonian writers demanded several more Macedonian writers in the cores. And the Macedonian writers union refused to participate in the work on cores before the solution of the national language problem.[38]

By far the biggest issue relating to the core curriculum proposal, however, was not which writers should be chosen in which languages and according to which criteria, but rather whether there should be any core curriculum at all. The strongest resistance in this part of the debate came from Slovenia after the *Međurepubličko-pokrajinska komisija za reformu obrazovanja* (Joint Republican and Provincial Commission for Education reform) accepted the more than 600-page fourth version of the "common educational core" in July 1983. In August 1983, the Slovene writer Ciril Zlobec wrote an emotionally loaded critique of the core curriculum in the official Slovene newspaper *Delo*. He claimed that "the proposal offers a state education instead of the conscious knowledge of one's own national and personal essence. . . . It is an anticultural, antipedagogic, antieducational and antiethical document." And he wondered what would happen to the spiritual, cultural, and historic identity of Slovene children after their twelve-year "journey through the desert of spirit" that was embodied in this document.[39] Another Slovene writer, Janez Menart, calculated that according to the core proposal a Serbo-Croatian speaking primary school pupil would read only three Slovene poems, whereas a Slovene-speaking pupil would read more than thirty-five Serbo-Croatian poems. "What a bad trade!" he concluded.[40]

Defenders of the core noted that only half of the literature curriculums were to be covered by it. The rest of the curriculum was to be at the disposal of republics and provinces, thereby allowing ample room to present individual national traditions.[41] Nevertheless, at a public meeting organized in Ljubljana by the Slovene writers union on September 19, leading Slovene writers (Ciril Zlobec, Rudi Šeligo, Janez Rotar, and Bojan Štih) rejected the proposed common core out of hand. By this point they were not so much concerned with the raw numbers of writers or texts included or

214 ❖ ANDREW WACHTEL AND PREDRAG J. MARKOVIĆ

even the language in which they were presented but, rather, with the entire idea of whether a national core curriculum was necessary. A Belgrade newspaper summarized the basic attitude of all the speakers in one sentence: "We Slovenes will alone decide about our schools, and nobody should dictate to us."[42] Interestingly enough, Slovenes were also first to withdraw from the common textbooks written for the children of guest workers in Western Europe (*"Moja domovina SFRJ"*) at the beginning of the 1980s.[43]

This highly public and highly charged meeting was significant not only for its role in torpedoing a core curriculum in literature. It was the first such writers' manifestation in ex-Yugoslavia, and it anticipated the active role that writers' unions and other cultural institutions would play in creating and fanning nationalist political discourse through the rest of the decade. The most notorious such incident, of course, would be the famous draft Memorandum of the Serbian Academy of Sciences that was leaked to the public a year later. Also significant was the fact that the nationalist-larded discourse of Slovene writers was backed by republic-level political officials in both republic and federal institutions. This support was variously articulated in different political bodies, sometimes mitigated by a few "critical" remarks. The Council for Culture of the Slovene SSRN on September 22 endorsed the writers' stance, though admitting that Slovene writers failed to propose well-founded objections to the proposed solutions. A week later, the Slovenian Parliament took a more moderate stand, supporting the common core curriculum insofar as it respected the specific traits of each nation and determined only basic aims and characteristics in order to ensure that all Yugoslav citizens possessed some common level of knowledge.

Republic-level figures, however, took an even harder line than they had a week earlier. The president of the Slovene SSRN, France Šetinc, went so far as to call the idea of a core curriculum perverted (*izopačena*), although he simultaneously claimed to reject "expressions of impatient nationalism."[44] At the session of the federal SSRN (November 3, 1983), he made a sort of ultimatum: "If people want to insist on the cores as they are proposed, then we will prepare our own model of a core, focusing on realizing completely and in depth the spirit of the statutes of the twelfth congress of the SKJ. This goes specifically for language. And we won't allow anyone to call us nationalists."[45] This statement is one of the first open challenges to federal decisions from the Slovene side. It contains the seed of all later Slovene remarks: a concern for the fate of the Slovene language and a tacit hint at the republic's 'own path' if Slovene demands fail to be fulfilled.

The first official defense of the cores came from Croatia, where common educational cores were accepted in both intellectual and official circles. Predrag Matvejević, a pro-Yugoslav writer and essayist, wrote an article of tacit support for the core curriculum in the Belgrade magazine *NIN*. The Croatian educational authorities (*Prosvjetni savet Hrvatske*) accepted the idea as well. Their expectation was that all issues relating to them should be settled by October 15, 1984. Stipe Šuvar, the chief Croatian ideologist who had come to power as an antinationalist alternative to the leaders of the Croatian Spring movement in the early 1970s, asserted that the common Yugoslav economic and political system should "naturally give birth to a common educational system in which there would be sufficient place for the national essence and national culture of all our nations and nationalities." He defended the core curriculum proposal, noting that it had not been made up only in Belgrade but jointly in all the republics and provinces. He characterized the Slovene writers protesting the core proposal as "narrow-minded nationalists" (*uskogrudi nacionalisti*) who "took an arrogant pose and sent a pathetic message."[46] Šuvar's pro-Yugoslav faction combined a certain political dogmatism with Yugoslavism. During the second half of 1980s this faction was being defeated, assaulted both from Belgrade and from Zagreb. Serbian intellectuals criticized Šuvar as neo-Stalinist. In Croatia he was criticized essentially from a national point of view.[47] Ironically, he was perhaps the last outstanding non-Serbian politician who seriously tried to create a common Yugoslav political and cultural space. Šuvar's statement was an implicit challenge to the Slovene Central Committee itself, which had failed to condemn the writers' position. At a session held on October 7–8, the Slovene minister of culture, Matjaž Kmecl, hinted almost directly that Šuvar was a troublemaker: "What kind of sense or nonsense could lead an otherwise tested, intelligent, and often very farsighted politician from a neighboring republic to enter this discussion with an unbelievable statement against Slovene literature, claiming that the Slovene writers and politicians want to put the entire Slovene Writers' Union into the common Cores and that is why there is insufficient space in the Cores."[48] At roughly the same time, the educational leadership of Vojvodina and Macedonia joined their Croatian counterparts in supporting the core curriculum. A Macedonian representative at a meeting of all republic educational authorities (Skopje, October 21) accused some of fearing "to become too close to others" and asserted that the demand for full autonomy in textbook creation was unacceptable.[49]

The Slovenes pressed on, however. At a meeting of the federal working group on October 5, 1983, Slovene representatives (Boris Paternu and Breda Pogorelec) described the core proposal as "overly unifying" and "lacking respect for the specifics of every nation." They even hinted that the proposal provoked suspicions about a desire to "liquidate nations." Support for their point of view came from Kosovo: Albanian writers from Kosovo claimed that even Turkish and Kosovo Serb literatures were underrepresented in the core curriculum. In addition, the core contained only post-1945 Kosovar Albanian writers, which in their view gave an incorrect impression about the continuity of Kosovo Albanian literature (Isak Šama, Azem Škrelji, Enver Đerđeku). Fazli Sulja considered the core proposal "the biggest possible provocation."[50]

In April 1984 representatives of all Yugoslav writers unions met in Kruševo (Macedonia). Zlobec repeated his position that the core curriculum ideas were an "unfortunate invention of the bureaucracy" and demanded that the Communist Party stop interfering with cultural issues.[51] In the end, the Serbian writers union criticized the core curriculum as too hastily made. They demanded that literary value be the basic criteria for inclusion into the cores. They also raised their own complaints about some overlooked authors: Cyril and Methodius, Saint Sava, Dositej Obradović, and Vuk Karadžić should all have been in the core in the opinion of Serbian writers union.[52]

In June 1984, the agenda of the Joint Republican and Provincial Commission for Educational Reform contained mostly Kosovar Albanian complaints. They complained about the lack of time continuity in the treatment of Albanian literature, demanding a greater number of older authors and more authors from Albania itself. Both complaints were refused, with the explanation that only "world celebrities" from other countries should be in the common core curriculum. The argument against the time continuity issue was that it would require full coverage of all minority literatures, something that was seen to be "unfeasible."[53]

Despite myriad and growing objections from practically all quarters, a consortium of leading textbook and educational republic-level institutions concluded in November 1984 that work should be continued, and it was optimistically planned that the new core curriculum should be implemented by the 1985–86 academic year. However, Kosovar educational authorities refused to implement the proposal on the grounds that there were not enough Albanian authors in it, whereas Slovenes now demanded the inclusion of Slovene authors from Italy and Austria.[54]

Finally, in March 1986 a new compromise was proposed. The novelty was a reduction of the common cores to cover only 25 percent of literature curriculums (in other subject areas the percent covered by the core ranged from 50 to 90). Kosovar Albanians remained dissatisfied, however, despite the fact that there were as many Albanian as Macedonian authors in the final version of the cores. The president of the Macedonian writers' union, Kole Čašule, called this fifth version of the core curriculum an "intellectual catastrophe." For his part, the president of the Slovene committee for culture said that the whole proposal only "provoked unnecessary emotions." And Serbian and Croatian educational authorities objected to the primacy of political rather than literary criteria in choosing authors for the core.[55] By this point it had become obvious that the entire idea would have to be abandoned. With little fanfare the core curriculum proposal was dropped from the educational agenda, never to reappear.

Ultimately, the failure of the attempt to introduce a core curriculum for literature courses in Yugoslav schools is significant for several reasons. First, it offers an alternative timing concerning the national mobilization of writers. It has been widely accepted that the Memorandum and Kosovo Serb movements initiated such actions. This debate indicates, however, that Slovene writers were the first to use their writers union as an agent of national mobilization and that this happened as early as 1983. Slovene writers were to remain at the forefront of the national movement, and their successful opposition to the core curriculum project undoubtedly gave them a great degree of confidence in their ability to play a leading role in national mobilization. Second, in the debates about the core curriculum, the balance of republican actors was unusual. In her book *Nationalism and Federalism in Yugoslavia*, Sabrina Ramet shows that alliances among republic- and province-level actors were fairly fluid and ad hoc. The particular alignment that obtained in this debate was, however, somewhat surprising. The most unequivocal support for a core curriculum came from Croatia, with tacit backing from Serbia, whereas the fiercest assaults on the project were launched from Slovenia and Kosovo. Presumably, in this instance the Serbo-Croatian speaking republics did not feel threatened by a proposal in which the lion's share of writers and texts in the core came from what was at least linguistically still perceived to be a single literature. Kosovar and Slovene (and to a lesser extent Macedonian) writers, as well as some political figures, saw the issue as one that could be used to galvanize support for national mobilization through culture, the main area in which local autonomy had always been expressed. Finally, the core curriculum project was a final attempt at the integration of Yugoslav culture. The collapse of the project was not merely an omen for the disintegration of the state but perhaps as well for any bureaucratic attempts at cultural integration in multinational systems.

Notes

1. Branko Tkalčić, "Srednja škola kao rasadište jugoslavenske misli," *Jugoslavenska njiva*, Year 3, No. 17, April 26, 1919, pp. 263–64.
2. Charles Jelavich, "South Slav Education: Was There Yugoslavism?" in Norman Naimark and Holly Case (eds.), *Yugoslavia and Its Historians: Understanding the Balkan Wars of the 1990s* (Stanford: Stanford University Press, 2003), p. 100.
3. Dimić, Lj., *Kulturna politika Kraljevine Jugoslavije,* Vol. 2 (Beograd: Stubovi kulture, 1997), pp. 210f; Vol. 1, pp. 248–62.
4. *Čitanka za srednje škole*, comp. Asa Prodanović, 4 vols. (Belgrade, 1928).
5. In volume two, for example, we find thirty-three authors identified as coming from Serbia, fifteen from Croatia, seven from Slovenia, nine from Bosnia or Herzegovina, and two from Montenegro. In addition, there are seven from Dalmatia, and fifteen from Old Serbia (i.e., Kosovo region), Slavonia, Srem, Bačka, and Banat.
6. At the same time, the kinds of blatantly chauvinistic (i.e., Serbian, Croatian, or Slovenian nationalistic) texts that Jelavich found so prominently represented in the prewar readers are absent here.
7. *Nastavni plan i program za osnovne škole u narodnoj republici Hrvatskoj* (Zagreb: Ministarstvo prosvjete NRH, 1947), p.35.
8. *Nastavni plan i program za osnovne škole narodne republike Bosne i Hercegovine* (Sarajevo, 1947), p. 6.
9. *Nastavni plan i program za osnovne škole* (Belgrade, 1947), p. 13.
10. Ivan Božić, Sima Ćirković, Milorad Ekmečić, and Vladimir Dedijer, *Istorija Jugoslavije* (Beograd: Prosveta, 1972).
11. Predrag Marković, "Istoričari i jugoslovenstvo u socijalističkoj Jugoslaviji, "*Jugoslovenski istorijski časopis* 1–2 (2001), pp. 151–65; Kosta Nikolić, *Prošlost bez istorije* (Beograd: Institut za savremenu istoriju, 2003).
12. Goran Babić, *Jugoslavija u Hrvatskoj* (Beograd: Adeona, 2000).
13. Wolfgang Hoepken, "History Education and Yugoslav (Dis) Integration," in Melissa K. Bokovoy, Jill A. Irvine, and Carol S. Lilly (eds.), *State-Society Relations in Yugoslavia, 1945–1992* (New York: St. Martin's Press, 1997), pp. 79–104.

14. These were Napoleon, knez Mihailo Obrenović, Miloš Obrenović, Karadjordje, France Prešeren, and Dimitrije Tucović.

15. A session of the conference Marxism Historiography and Education was devoted to the common core problem. See contributions by Drago Roksandić, Hrvoje Matković, Nikša Stančić, and Marijan Maticka, in Lj Vujošević (ed.), *Marxism Historiography and Education* (Belgrade: Izdavački centar Komunist, 1987), pp. 193–258.

16. Božo Repe, "Jugoslovanska historiografija po drugi svetovni vojni," *Tokovi istorije*, 1–4 (1999), pp. 213–25.

17. Jasna Dragović-Soso, *"Saviours of the Nation": Serbia's Intellectual Opposition and the Revival of Nationalism* (London: Hurst & Company, 2002), pp. 65–114; Kosta Nikolić, *Prošlost bez istorije*; see also S. Dautović, *Krleža, Albanci i Srbi (u Enciklopediji Jugoslavije)* (Beograd: Narodna knjiga, 2000).

18. Jasna Dragović-Soso, ibid.

19. Wolfgang Hoepken, "History Education and Yugoslav (Dis) Integration."

20. Discussions of musical education cores, equally disputed by specialists as those for literature, failed to attract broader social attention, although the elements of disagreement were similar to those mentioned for literary cores and the disaffected also were again primarily Slovenes and Albanians. See "Bez konačnog rešenja," *Politika ekspres*, October 22, 1983.

21. On average, there were 1,700 lessons of literature and maternal language during twelve years of primary and secondary education in Yugoslavia. In this time, half were reserved for language and grammar and half for literature. Fewer than 340 lessons were reserved for common cores (Č. Nedeljković, "Jezgro nije aritmetika," *Prosvetni Pregled*, October 18, 1983, and "Program zajedničkog jezgra jezičko-umetničkog područja," *Književna reč*, October 25, 1983).

22. Dušan Petrović, "Pisce nismo brojali!" *Večernje Novosti*, September 25, 1983, p. 9.

23. "Program zajedničkog jezgra jezičko-umetničkog područja," *Književna reč*, October 25, 1983.

24. "Nacionalno i jugoslovensko," *Politika*, September 22, 1983, p. 9.

25. *13 Kongres SKJ-dokumenti,* Belgrade: Komunist, 1986, p. 196.

26. "Polako zatvaram dućan," *Večernje novosti,* October 17, 1983, p. 5.

27. Dragan Biskupović, "Osatičani ostaju Osatičani," *Mladost,* June 22, 1981, p. 6. Disputes over the question of "whose writer" Andrić is remain salient to the present day. Suffice it to note that the monument to Andrić in Višegrad was blown up in 1992, presumably by Bosnian Muslims who have criticized Andrić for his allegedly anti-Muslim stance while at the same time he was being canonized in Sarajevo as a great Bosnian writer and in Belgrade as a Serbian writer.

28. Ibid.; "Oko zajedničkokg minimuma: problemi nastave književnosti," *Književna reč,* June 10, 1981, p. 6.

29. The members of the working group were Zoran Gluščević, Zoran Gavrilović, Jovan Deretić, Vaso Milinčević, Vuk Milatović, Dragan Nedeljković, and Marko Nedić.

30. "Istorija, granice i merila," *Politika,* May 30, 1981, p. 11.

31. "Sporne biografije," *Književna reč,* March 25, 1983, p. 46.

32. "Brana samodovoljnosti," *Politika,* March 2, 1983, p. 15.

33. "Prošlost se ne može menjati," *Ilustrovana politika,* June 23, 1981, p. 31.

34. "Zajedništvo naših književnosti ili integralnost," *Pobjeda,* June 20, 1981, p. 6; Momir Marković, "O projektovanju i presuđivanju," *Pobjeda,* August 1, 1981, p. 10; "Zajedništvo naših književnosti ili integralnost," *Oslobođenje,* July 11, 1981, p. 7.

35. The series of articles began with an attack on Mujagić by Miroslav Egerić, a professor from Novi Sad on November 23, 1984 (p. 5), and continued with a long and sometimes

rambling response by Mujagić on January 4, 1985 (pp. 16–18). It was followed a week later by another attack on Mujagić by Milorad Vučelić (p. 36), and concluded with a group of four letters to the editor on January 18 (p. 4). The quotations here are from Mujagić's response of January 4, p. 18. Thanks to Dejan Jović for bringing this material to our attention.

36. The exception was for minority language speakers inside one of the non-Serbo-Croatian speaking republics. Thus, Kosovar Albanian children were required to learn Serbo-Croatian in their schools, but Albanian speakers in Macedonia who attended Albanian-language schools learned Macedonian rather than Serbo-Croatian.

37. "Korektnije o slovenačkim stavovima," *Borba,* November 3 (Matevž Krivic); "Izbeći uskogrudost" (Šetinc statement), *Politika,* November 6.

38. "Bez konačnog stava," *Politika Ekspres,* February 21, 1984, p. 7; "O zajedničkim 'jezgrima' ponovo," *Politika,* February 21, 1984, p. 9; *Borba,* February 26, 1984, p. 6.

39. "Jezgra nisu kraj posla," *Politika,* June 30, 1983, p. 5; "Smišljena podvajanja," *Borba,* August 23, 1983, p. 15.

40. "Ogledalo pesnika Janeza Menarta," *Borba,* September 10–11, 1983, p. 11.

41. R. Lazarević, "Strah od 'tuđih' pisaca," *Politika,* September 18, 1983, p. 7.

42. "Sporna jezgra," *Večernje Novosti,* September 21, 1983, p. 8; Aleksandra Plavevski, "Sami ćemo odlučivati," *Politika Ekspres,* September 21, 1983, p. 7.

43. From an interview with Petar Pjanović, deputy director of Serbia's biggest (until 2000 only) textbook publisher, Zavod za udžbenike i nastavna sredstva, held on May 20, 2004.

44. "Predlozi su neprihvatljivi," *Politika,* September 23, 1983, p. 7; "Kampanja ne doprinosi boljem razumevanju," *Politika,* September 29, 1983, p. 9; "Mirno o jezgrima," *Večernje novosti* September 30, 1983, p. 8.

45. "Izbeći uskogrudost," *Večernje Novosti,* November 4, 1983, p. 6.

46. "Oglasili su se kao uskogrudi nacionalisti," *Večernje novosti,* September 29, 1983, p. 9

47. Jasna Dragović-Soso, pp. 61–62, 232–33.

48. *NIN,* September 25, 1983, pp. 4–5; "Prihvaćene zajedničke programske jezgre," *Vjesnik,* September 28, 1983; "Oglasili su se kao uskogrudi nacionalisti," *Politika,* September 29, p. 9.; "Kako približiti gledišta?" *Vjesnik,* October 20, 1983.

49. "Kvalitet, a ne paritet," *Borba,* October, 23, 1983.

50. "Sve u ime—znaja," *Večernje Novosti,* October 6, 1983, pp. 6–8; "Posao od početka," *Politika,* October 6, 1983, p. 7; Slobodanka Ast, "Fuzija ili fisija?" *NIN,* October 9, 1983, p. 10.

51. "Stvari književnosti,stvari politike," *Borba,* April 2, 1983, p. 7.

52. "Osporena načela," *Vjesnik,* April 11, p. 4.

53. "Književna i druga odmeravanja," *Politika,* June 8, 1984, p. 8.

54. "Jezgra još nisu klasala," *Borba,* November 12, 1984, p. 3; "Opet se ista pesma peva," *Politika Ekspres,* November 23, 1985, p. 7.

55. Radovan Lazarević, "Štivo sazdano do kompromisa," *Politika,* March 3, 1986, p. 5; Slobodanka Ast, "O jezgru i konopcu," *NIN,* March 9, 1986, p. 29; "Jezgro ili haos," *NIN,* March 16, 1986, p. 34; "Pisci predstavnici," *Komunist,* March 21, 1986, p. 6; "Književnost pod ključem," *Vjesnik,* March 29, 1986, p. 3.

The Inter–Regional Struggle for Resources and the Fall of Yugoslavia

❖ Michael Palairet ❖

There were three components to the fall of Yugoslavia: the collapse of its authoritarian socialist economic system; the dissolution of the Titoist Yugoslav state; and the determination of Belgrade, the army, and the Serbs to resort to force to prevent this happening. The first of these components lies squarely in the economic historian's domain. The socialist economic system of Tito's Yugoslavia delivered high economic growth between 1954 and 1972 but performed disastrously during the period 1978–89, bringing the system increasingly into question. With the lifting of the Brezhnev doctrine under Gorbachev, there was no longer any external guarantee of its preservation. Yugoslavia was not unique: similar patterns developed throughout Eastern Europe. Nor was the fragmentation of Yugoslavia remarkable: only the nation states in Eastern Europe remained intact. The federalised supranational states, Czechoslovakia and the USSR, fragmented into nation states. The key explanatory issues for Yugoslavia's fragmentation are to be sought in the political domain, but economic linkage also mattered for Yugoslavia because there was no consensus among the ruling groups over abandoning the socialist economic system: Serbia, or more precisely the Milošević faction, did not assent to the aspiration of the northern republics and of the federation to abandon the socialist planned economy, at least not in Serbia itself. Consequently, in the course of 1990, Belgrade wrecked the reform process. This destroyed the hopes of premier Ante Marković that the federation might somehow hang together if reform could be made to work.

What made the Yugoslav case unique was that only in Yugoslavia did the new nation states have to fight for separation. Again, alongside the political struggle, an understanding of economic factors throws further light on why this happened. It is argued in this essay that in order to maintain its (corrupted) socialist system, Serbia needed to hold together the rest of Yugoslavia to be able to tap the resources of the breakaway republics. This essay looks at each of these three issues, and endeavours to provide the linkages.

Financing the Economy

Ever since 1945, the economic ambitions of the Yugoslav regime had consistently outrun the resources that its socialised sector could generate. Therefore, this sector continually had to draw upon resources external to it, mainly resources external to Yugoslavia. As a rapidly industrialising country in the 1950s, there was some justification for its dependence on foreign capital inflows, but because the regime rejected all but the most limited role for foreign business investment, the capital flows it attracted came in the form of aid or borrowing. Immediately after the war, recovery had depended heavily on assistance from UNRRA. The regime expected its first Five-Year Plan to receive substantial assistance from the Soviets, little of which it in fact received because of the breach with Stalin. This did not deter it from pressing on with the plan, but it tried to compensate by plunder economy on the country's natural resources[1] in order to pay for the plan's capital imports from the Soviets.[2] Beginning in 1949, Yugoslavia started to receive covert U.S. aid, and during the 1950s, PL480 food supplies, which compensated for the failure of its farming policies.[3] Financial aid also flowed in, and with state department encouragement, the commercial banks took a relaxed attitude to covering Yugoslav financial deficits. In the 1950s, external funding had been applied to securing growth through maximal investment, but for about seven years following the economic reforms of the mid-1960s, high growth was maintained with less investment by improving efficiency in resource allocation. The strain was taken off the balance of payments by two sources of invisible earnings, neither of which owed much to the enterprise of the state sector, namely the boom in international tourism and an inflow of emigrant remittances. This was a period of liberalisation, during which the managers of the enterprises were accorded wider powers. However, liberalisation inexorably led to the reopening of the hitherto suppressed nationality question, especially in Croatia, and in the early 1970s, Tito cracked down on liberal and nationalistic tendencies and on the powers of management.[4] This presaged a new wave of enterprise reforms identified with the work of the Slovenian Marxist ideologue, Edvard Kardelj. Kardelj's system was not a simple reversion to central planning, for power had shifted inexorably to the republics, whose own objectives, rather than those of the federation, would determine the allocation of resources. Rather, what Kardelj's reforms did was to harness the enterprises closely to (regional) party politics and to force them into a complex of planning agreements. The arrangements adopted were confusing and self-contradictory, and the economic system became decreasingly efficient and increasingly bureaucratic.[5] This weakened its capacity to secure growth through technological change and the more rational disposal of resources, so productivity growth fell away sharply. The Kardelj system was applied in tandem with a surge of investment spending in 1973–79 from an already high 32.2 percent of total stated output to 37.7 percent. Yugoslavia was no longer eligible for development assistance but was able—far too easily—to fund the mounting annual deficits caused by this investment drive by borrowing from the international banks. In consequence, foreign debt rose from $5.1 billion in 1974 to $14.6 billion in 1979.[6] Because this debt was contracted at floating rates, the leap in international interest rates at the end of the decade drove the interest cost of foreign debt up from 5.8 percent (1979) to 15.1 percent (1980).[7] By 1980 the debt stood at $18.5 billion, and because Yugoslavia was no longer able to service it, the country could no longer finance capital accumulation by adding to foreign borrowing.

After 1979, the output of the economy promptly declined, and with it real wages and consumption. The full extent of economic shrinkage was disguised in the official statistics. Under high inflation, the system of historic cost accounting created large illusory inventory gains. When converting aggregates from current to constant prices, the gains in nominal inventories were corrected for inflation, not the absolute value of inventories. If, say, between two accounting dates, the real volume of inventories was unchanged at 100 but there had been 50 percent price inflation, then the current value of inventories would rise to 150. Deflating the inventory gain of 50 to 33 would create illusory growth of 33 percent. This was explained by Harold Lydall,[8] who used quantitative research by Ljubomir Madžar.[9] At the per capita level, the erroneous official procedure purported to show (in 1972 dinars) that between 1979 and 1989, output stagnated at 16,800 dinars, whereas when recalculated using Madžar's tables and applying his method to later data, it declined from 15,387 dinars in 1979 to 13,887 dinars in 1989, a fall of 9.7 percent. From the point of view of the population, the experience of the same period was considerably worse. Social sector annual real earnings per employee declined by 25.4 percent from 15,424 dinars of 1972 value to 11,494, reflecting a productivity decline of 18.0 percent. Retail sales per capita declined from 7,319 dinars to 5,204, or by 28.9 percent.

De facto bankrupt after 1979, Yugoslavia could no longer look for substantial foreign funds apart from emergency assistance from IMF and consortia such as the Friends of Yugoslavia. Yet in the 1980s, the demand for enterprise funding remained intense. Between 1979 and 1984, investment subsided rapidly. But so, too, did enterprise surpluses, which fell and in 1984 subsided to zero. Between then and 1990, the social sector was to trade at a massive net deficit. This deficit was disguised by the inventory accounting distortion. Figure 1 shows stated and adjusted social sector profit and loss between 1979 and 1989. By the latter year, the aggregate net loss of the social sector reached a grotesque 120 billion dinars of 1972 value, compared with Yugoslavia's total output of 329 billion. No change was made to the accounting system because it suited the authorities to maintain an illusory presentation, but they were quite aware of the reality. In 1987, at a meeting between management of the "3. maj" shipyard and Ivo Vrandečić, president of the Yugoslav parliament, the question was asked whether it was true that losses in the federal budget transferred to the banks on the basis of exchange differences in 1986 amounted to 15 percent of national income (*dohodak*). The reply was that they amounted to 400 billion dinars, or 26 percent of social product.[10] But the authorities never displayed the figures so as to make the absurdity of the inventory revaluations obvious. The Yugoslav

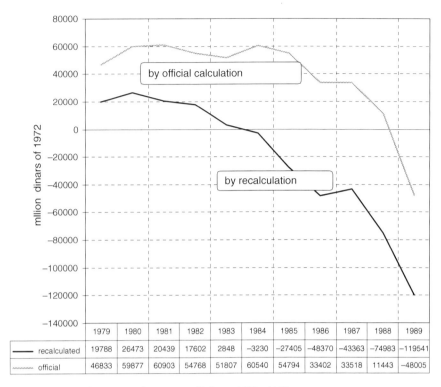

	1979	1980	1981	1982	1983	1984	1985	1986	1987	1988	1989
recalculated	19788	26473	20439	17602	2848	−3230	−27405	−48370	−43363	−74983	−119541
official	46833	59877	60903	54768	51807	60540	54794	33402	33518	11443	−48005

Figure 1. Yugoslavia: social sector profit/loss, 1979–1989.

statistical yearbooks continued resolutely to show a spurious social sector surplus right up to 1989, when their compilers resorted to creating a surplus out of a deficit by omitting the minus sign that, on the basis of their own presentation, should have preceded the figure.[11]

The causes of these enterprise losses were manifold. The 1970s investment drive, as was to become evident when the credits dried up in the 1980s, resulted in serious resource misallocation, and it was later officially admitted that less than half the debt incurred in the 1970s was invested in worthwhile projects.[12] Some of the projects, for example, the later notorious FENI and Ferronikl nickel mining schemes in Macedonia and Kosovo and the DINA petrochemicals project in Croatia, resulted largely in write-offs.[13] In each of the major enterprises I have researched, costly investment projects were launched that merely dissipated capital. At the MKS steel complex at Smederevo, a Soviet-built blast furnace was ordered in 1975 and had to be paid for but was never assembled, and the equipment was left to deteriorate in the open air.[14] Moreover, resources continued to be wasted on a grand scale in the 1980s. The Crvena Zastava vehicle factory at Kragujevac undertook a project to supply most of its car output to a U.S. partner. In 1987, production costs per unit appear to have exceeded the export price of $1,993 by around $1,800, and the enterprise compounded this error by developing a 1,400 cc saloon model (Florida) at a cost of over $400 million, then failed to produce the car save in petty quantities.[15] MKS, uninjured by the blast furnace fiasco, invested $363 million in a state-of-the-art British designed rolling mill, which was obsolescent by the time they completed it and was so defective that it had to be run at far below capacity.[16] The Trepča lead-zinc mining complex in Kosovo invested $86.4 million in a lead refinery, no more than half of whose capacity could ever have been employed, failed to complete it, and had to write it off.[17] These are only examples drawn from my own research on these enterprises. It would not surprise me to find that every major enterprise if carefully researched dissipated investment funds similarly. These financial disasters were, in the first instance, the fault of defective planning external to the enterprises themselves, but the enterprises were also mismanaged. Zastava was hopelessly slow in getting its new models into production and was forever plagued with production stoppages.[18] In part these difficulties were "subjective," that is the result of its own management, in part "objective" and the result of supplier incompetence. For example, Zastava was obliged to take supplies from the Ramiz Sadiku factory at Peć in Kosovo, whose quality and delivery dates were so variable as to cause Zastava continually to default on its own delivery commitments.[19] MKS found it impossible to manage its spare parts inventories.[20] Trepča mine and smelter productivity declined between 1965 and the late 1980s.[21] And, as MKS management reluctantly concluded, its workforce was totally unmotivated and nobody really cared.[22] To this we should add the consequences of pressures on these enterprises to export at a loss, to take on labour whether or not they needed it, the effects of price controls, and outright fraud, which in the 1980s became commonplace.

For want of foreign funds to finance enterprise borrowing, the domestic banking system had to carry the enterprises, their diminishing investment outlays, and their soaring losses. The banks in turn had to finance the demand for credits by borrowing from the central bank, and this intensified already serious inflation. Put another way, the strain on corporate funding was borne from the proceeds of seigniorage, at the cost of inflation tax borne by the public at large. For the 1980s, therefore, inflation tax replaced the earlier exploited external resources of foreign aid and foreign borrowing. Yet it could not regenerate growth because the mounting current losses of the enterprises crowded out investment to such an extent that by the later 1980s the enterprise sector could no longer meet its (artificially low) depreciation provisions, and became a net disinvestor.

Inter-Regional Resource Flows in the 1980s

Economic decline was a new situation for Yugoslavia. It gave rise—as elsewhere in communist controlled Europe—to increasingly searching questions as to why the much vaunted Yugoslav economic system was failing to deliver prosperity. It caused increasing criticism and resentment toward the regime and a mounting interest in market-based mechanisms for restructuring and rationalisation. However, there seemed to be an alternative, if illusory, means of making the existing system work better. This was to induce a "renewal of the investment cycle." In 1987 the issue gained momentum from the rise to power of Slobodan Milošević in Serbia. Serbia had suffered as much as the other republics from the economic downturn since 1979, but the Belgrade apparatchiks and the influential group of socialist economists associated with the regime were deeply wed to the old established mechanisms for inducing planned, capital-driven growth. They were also suspicious of economic reformers, whom they regarded as being in conspiracy to damage Serbian interests. Milošević's most high-profile project was to subordinate Serbia's autonomous regions of Vojvodina and Kosovo to tight Serbian control. Discussion of his domestic economic policies was eclipsed by the Kosovo drama, but these economic policies were also highly relevant to his role in the dissolution of the Yugoslav federation. A convinced communist, Milošević opposed all attempts to rationalise and remarketize the system. He was aware that it no longer delivered growth but attributed its failure to ill-defined "bureaucratic deformations" that had distorted a machine that once delivered high investment driven economic growth. True, the system had lost efficiency in the aftermath of the Kardelj reforms, but as a disciple of Kardelj, his reforms were far from being Milošević's target. What his circle of economists wanted was to "restart the investment cycle" in Serbia and to secure renewed growth by pushing up the rate of investment in Serbia within an unchanged economic system. Milošević's "anti-bureaucratic" revolution was not accompanied by measures that would enhance efficiency. Rather, interventions in Serbia were designed to maximise employment and to protect jobs in the loss-making "big systems" enterprises, particularly in heavy industry. Proponents of the investment cycle idea were, at best, hazy as to where the resources for such a renewal were to come from. They did not think that way. What they saw was unemployed labour and enterprises producing far below capacity for want of the foreign exchange to provide their raw materials: they construed this situation in a naive Keynesian manner, deducing that a restart of the "cycle" could be induced by the remobilisation of these idle resources.

At the Yugoslav level, it was impossible to "restart the investment cycle" for want of capital inflows and the propensity of enterprises throughout the country to consume most available credits to cover current deficits. By this time, however, preoccupations had shifted away from seeking "Yugoslav" solutions to seeking alternatives in which policy was to be made by the republics in their own interest without regard to the interests of the others. From the point of view of Serbia, therefore, the external resources that had sustained investment growth during the lifetime of Tito would have to be replaced by the transfer of resources from the other Yugoslav republics (and, if need be, from Serbia's autonomous regions). It is not clear whether the Serbian leadership pursued a conscious policy of extracting resources from other republics and regions, for their understanding of economics was primitive, but this was the ineluctable consequence of what it was trying to do. Anyway, no such policy could be made explicit because the other republics would not countenance yielding their own substance to support a spending boom in Serbia. Secondly, Serbian publicists twisted the issue round: Serbia's growth ambitions were being frustrated by economic exploitation by the other republics, so Serbia should take such defensive measures as she could to end this exploitation and release resources for Serbia's own development.

Not only in Serbia, but in all the republics, politicians saw conditions deteriorate and inflation mount, and they blamed the misfortunes of their own republics on exploitation by all the others. Ljubomir Madžar surveyed the inter-republican economic grievances of the period to try to sort out "who exploited whom?" It was far from easy to determine.[23] For example, an overt subsidy to the less developed territories was provided through the Federal Fund for Crediting the Economic Growth of the Insufficiently Developed Republics and Autonomous Regions. This provided investment funds for the underdeveloped, which were financed from general taxation. The sums involved were modest. The fund was budgeted to spend 1.97 percent of social sector social product in 1976–80 and spent "usually just over 1.5 percent of national revenue."[24] It absorbed 1.4 percent of social product in 1982.[25] This gave rise to resentment especially in Slovenia because so much of this money was blatantly wasted on prestige projects, especially in Kosovo, which received 39.4 percent of the total in 1982. Of this funding, it was reported that between 1966 and 1988 one single enterprise, RMHK Trepča, received "more than $4 billion" in dinar equivalent,[26] representing upwards of 82 percent of the fund's investment in Kosovo. Most of the funding covered Trepča's deficits. Kosovo's money was administered by the Republic of Serbia, and the Slovenes probably suspected that funds were misappropriated before they reached Kosovo because in 1989 they announced that they would no longer pass the funding on through Serbia but would transfer it directly to Priština.[27] If so, their suppositions were correct. Substantial sums were taken from enterprises in Kosovo to be "invested" in enterprises in Serbia.[28] The underdeveloped republics and Kosovo argued that any benefit they derived from the federal funds was offset by the suppression of raw materials and food prices relative to the price of manufactures, which caused them as primary producers and net importers of finished goods to face artificially unfavourable domestic terms of trade. Likewise, Serbia reckoned it was similarly disadvantaged by the policy of suppressing the price of electricity because Serbia had invested heavily in a complex of large thermal power stations that exported energy to Croatia.

Moreover, subsidies were created that ostensibly benefited the more advanced republics. Around the year 1970, 76 percent of the inter-regional flows through the development fund were offset, according to Madžar, citing K. Mijovski, by subsidies disguised as credits that were paid mainly to northern enterprises on exports by them of capital goods, mainly ships.[29] True, most of these ships were built in Croatian yards, but the shipbuilders needed their subsidies to offset the requirement to draw supplies from high-cost domestic suppliers. Around the year 1983, domestic supplies amounted to 46–49 percent of the cost of a ship[30] and were charged at between

40 percent and 90 percent over international prices.[31] In particular the yards had to take low-grade shipbuilding sheet (which accounted for 20 percent of all domestic inputs) from the hopelessly inefficient steel mill at Skopje, Macedonia.[32] In a free market, nobody would have bought steel from Macedonia and still less would have paid a premium for it because Skopje was incapable of keeping to its delivery dates or of producing to consistent quality standards. So in large measure, shipbuilding subsidies subsidised the Macedonian steel mill, as well as the numerous firms throughout Yugoslavia that supplied high-priced inputs for Croatian ship construction.

Madžar also instanced other alleged and real transfers between republics, including the post-1945 policies of moving industries out of Serbia proper into the north and later to less developed regions. He was reluctant to answer definitively the "who exploited whom" question with firm conclusions about the net gains and losses of individual republics and regions, but he thought that Serbia lay in a broadly neutral position between the losers and gainers. However, as he attached importance to Croatia's capital export subsidy in reaching this conclusion while ignoring the gains to central Serbia from its diversion of Kosovo funds to itself, it may be fairer to conclude that the forces he analysed created a net flow of funds in which narrower Serbia derived a small gain.

However, the Madžar analysis omitted one potentially important mechanism of inter-republic cross-subsidisation. For this purpose it may be useful to treat Yugoslavia in this period as a currency union with a common central bank and currency system. Of the various strains to which currency unions are exposed, the free-rider problem can be peculiarly damaging. Republic-level economic interests could, and did, establish claims on the resources of the currency union in disproportion to their contributions to them and therefore at the expense of the other republics by drawing disproportionately on the weakly managed credits created by the central bank. So we have here a textbook model of one kind of strain to which a currency union is susceptible, where one member determines on expansionist monetary policies that bid to extract resources from the rest. The question therefore arises: was Serbia in a position to significantly exploit and abuse the common currency as a means of sustaining its "anti-bureaucratic revolution"?

In normal times and circumstances, the federation could have survived a certain amount of cheating in the struggle for resources, and in any case, it is not the job of a central bank to prevent capital from flowing from areas where its marginal efficiency is relatively low to those where it is higher. But Yugoslavia disposed of no mechanisms to make capital markets behave rationally, and the circumstances of the later 1980s were anything but normal. Most glaringly, the corporate economy of Yugoslavia traded at a thinly camouflaged deficit, which was largely socialised by inflation.

The extent to which enterprises needed external financing was therefore the extent to which they ran cash flow deficits, plus the amounts they spent on investment. In a market economy, the enterprises most persistently in deficit would have been bankrupted and closed, but in Yugoslavia there was no mechanism to close the loss makers or even to curtail the "soft-budget" credits on which they depended.

Therefore it was the least efficient enterprises that created the biggest demand for funding, and this caused finance to flow perversely from the more efficient enterprises to the less efficient. Because there was a strong regional component in the distribution of corporate efficiency, this would cause finance to flow from republics with relatively efficient enterprises toward those whose enterprises were relatively inefficient, provided there were no barriers to these flows.

The banking system provided the mechanism by which finance flowed to meet the corporate deficits. The commercial banks were controlled by their largest corporate clients, whose nominees on the bank boards saw to it that the enterprises they represented were especially favoured in the provision of finance, no matter that the banks were already stuffed with the nonperforming debt of these same enterprises. To create the requisite credits, the commercial banks had to borrow from the central banking system, which included not only the National Bank of Yugoslavia, but also their own republic's central banks. These banks in turn secured "fresh money" through the credit creating powers of the National Bank of Yugoslavia. This was the main engine of inflation because the public authorities appear not to have run serious deficits on their own budgets. Indirectly however, the public authorities were important creators of the enterprise deficits because their revenues were raised by taxing enterprises that were themselves in deficit, and they could only pay these taxes by obtaining new credits from the banks.

If they were to secure substantial inter-republican and regional transfers for Serbia, the Belgrade commercial banks, which supported enterprise funding in narrower Serbia, would need better access to "fresh money" created by the central bank than was enjoyed by the commercial banks of the other republics and the autonomous regions. This we can test. For want of appropriate statistical information, our analysis has to be limited to two years, 1989 and 1990. Because a major economic reform divides the two years, we will examine whether in 1989, the banking mechanism did, in fact, enable Serbia to extract resources to sustain economic activity and to "restart the investment cycle" at the expense of Yugoslavia's other republics.

Bank credits met the cash flow deficits of the enterprises required by their investment programmes, their inventory changes, and their trading losses. Regionally disaggregated inventory change data are not available for 1989 in a usable form and have had to be excluded from the calculation. Table 1 shows the distribution of net enterprise losses and net investment, divided regionally in 1989.

The table shows that social sector enterprises in narrower Serbia ran current deficits equal to 14.7 percent of social product, which was the largest deficit of any territory in Yugoslavia. Despite the need to finance deficits that were abnormally large even by Yugoslav standards, narrower Serbia's enterprises were nevertheless able to secure net investment funding equal to 2.6 percent of social product during a year in which Yugoslavia as a whole experienced net disinvestment.

Table 2 illustrates the inter-republic financial flows that would have been needed to bring about the outcome displayed in Table 1.

Table 1: Enterprise losses and net investment, 1989. (Million dinars of 1990 denomination)

Territory	Social product	Net losses	Losses, percent of SP	Net investment	Losses + net inv. – percent of SP
Yugoslavia	221,862	20,411	9.2	–29	9.2
Bosnia	27,084	2,529	9.3	–13	9.3
Croatia	56,057	4,061	7.2	445	8.0
Macedonia	12,549	485	3.9	–335	1.2
Slovenia	41,577	2,103	5.1	–436	4.0
Narrower Serbia	*51,971*	*7,659*	*14.7*	*1356*	*17.3*
Serbia & Mont.	84,595	11233	13.3	318	13.6

Sources: Losses from *Ekonomska politika*, April 30, 1990, table 1, col. 4, p. 21; Social product, gross investment, and depreciation are taken from *Statisti ki Godišnjak Jugoslavije* (SGJ), 1991. This source does not give depreciation figures directly, but they are easily calculable as the difference between social product and Yugoslav concept national income, which does not take external flows into account.

Table 2: Yugoslavia—regional funding gain and loss in 1989

Territory	Losses + net investment	Fair share funding	Regional funding gain	Fair share net investment	Actual net investment
Yugoslavia	20,382	20,832	–	421	–29
Bosnia	2,516	2,543	–27	–49	–13
Croatia	4,506	5,264	–758	1203	445
Macedonia	150	1,178	–1028	693	–335
Slovenia	1,667	3,904	–2237	1801	–436
Narrower Serbia	9,015	4,880	4135	–2779	1356
Serbia + Mont	11,551	7,943	3608	–3290	318

Note: Regional funding gain = losses + net investment – fair share funding. Fair share net investment = fair share funding – actual losses.

If narrower Serbia had been allocated only its "fair share" of funding for these purposes (based on its proportionate contribution to Yugoslavia's social product), it would have received only 4,880 million dinars, which would have caused it to disinvest to the extent of 2,779 million dinars, rather than invest 1,356 million net. In other words, narrower Serbia secured flows from the rest of Yugoslavia of 4,135 million dinars, a sum equal to 8.0 percent of its social product. Conversely, the biggest loser in absolute terms was Slovenia, whose more moderate enterprise losses amounted to 5.1 percent of its social product. Under a "fair shares" regime, Slovenia would have had 3,820 million dinars to cover its losses and net investment, and therefore surrendered 2,153 million dinars, or 5.2 percent, of its social product. Relative to its social product, Macedonia, the poorest of the republics, was still more heavily the loser from this redistribution. It lost 1,003 million dinars, or 8 percent, of its social product. Croatia's loss was relatively slight, at 644 million dinars, or 1 percent, of its social product.

We can infer from these figures that Yugoslavia's inflation regime awarded enterprises in narrower Serbia a massive volume of transfers at the expense mainly of Slovenia and Macedonia. This indicates that the political power of the Belgrade banks in extracting "fresh money" from the central banking system was such as to force significant funding from the less influential peripheral republics. It should also be noted that similar ease of funding access did not extend to Montenegro and Serbia's associated provinces, Vojvodina and Kosovo, which were heavy net losers, and transferors of funds to narrower Serbia. There can be no suggestion that investment flowed between republics and regions in response to investment opportunities because the flows went in the reverse direction. Investment funding was allocated away from regions associated with relatively solvent and successful enterprises toward narrower Serbia, whose enterprises were the least successful and the heaviest loss makers. Nor could these flows be justified on regional solidarity lines—despite the operation of the Federal Fund, they were redistributed by the banking system away from the least developed territories (Kosovo and Macedonia) toward relatively developed narrower Serbia. In other words, they represented a tribute paid to narrower Serbia by the rest of Yugoslavia, which was the only means by which Milošević's counterreformist "anti-bureaucratic revolution" could be funded.

Even this gain at the expense of the other republics and regions was insufficient to satisfy the investment hunger of the Serbian authorities in Belgrade because narrower Serbia's net investment at 2.6 percent of social product still fell far short of the level needed to induce a renewal of economic growth. This was because Milošević's own policies caused most of the bank credits to be dissipated in financing enterprise losses. Therefore, to raise new investment funding, which could be used for the "economic rebirth" of Serbia, Milošević launched a public loan in 1989 of about $1.4 billion, targeted at Serbian citizens and the Serb Diaspora. Despite enormous publicity and a fair amount of coercion, only about

$162 million in hard currency and dinars was actually raised, of which about $50 million vanished through fraudulent exchange rate accounting. About $43 million was transferred through Cyprus to form an offshore reserve. On this basis, only about $70 million was made available to the enterprises, and because these were themselves interested mainly in transferring the money abroad, the investment boost given by the loan was negligible.[33] But Serbia was drifting into an era when virtually all high-level financial operations involved large-scale peculation by the Milošević *garnitura,* so its capacity to add to its capital stock and to renew the investment cycle became negligible.

Reform and Resistance, 1990

In the wake of the Agrocomerc scandal of 1987, Federal Premier Branko Mikulić, who had been heavily implicated in it, was dismissed in December 1988. After a hiatus, the federal premiership passed on March 15, 1989, to an outspoken reformer from Croatia, Ante Marković. Marković was not a Croatian nationalist. Far from it, he saw his remit as saving the federation. The threat to its integrity was all too real. By late 1989, the Soviet guarantee of Yugoslavia's integrity as a single socialist state had been kicked from under it. Survival would have to depend on a measure of popular assent, reinforced by military repression, for the military threatened Slovenia that it would not countenance secession. Marković was a cautious liberaliser who wanted to reduce the stifling thicket of government controls that had accumulated in response to the foreign exchange and unemployment problems. In the short run, Marković's policies aggravated inflation because he extended the ambit for free price formation, releasing repressed inflation. The authorities also engaged in currency dumping operations to buy back current account debt from the western commercial banks at a deep discount and to bolster the exchange reserves prior to stabilisation. This also speeded inflation.[34] By the end of 1989, however, Marković was ready to attempt a far-reaching economic *perestroika* to restore monetary stability and to renew hope for future prosperity—and consequently cohesion.

Price rises had broken through in the late autumn to hyperinflationary levels, and sound money was regarded by the federal authorities as prerequisite to deeper economic restructuring. Structural reform was considered to be a prerequisite to the survival of the federation and to obtaining western assistance. Above all, the reform needed to impress the IMF and the commercial bankers because Yugoslavia urgently needed to attract hard currency. To gain credibility internationally, Marković and Federal President Janez Drnovšek invited Jeffrey Sachs to visit Yugoslavia for a fortnight to provide advice on the impending reform. Sachs had already acquired a massive international reputation as a money doctor. At the time he was engaged in stabilising the Polish zloty. Any reform that received Sachs' imprimatur would be favourably received by the international financial community.

Sachs' advice to his Yugoslav client was confidential, and he appears not to have written about it, but he let himself be quizzed by a round table of Yugoslav economists during his visit. A report of his answers to their questions provides information on the advice he offered.[35] The central issue was the causes and control of inflation. Sachs' key point was that the Yugoslav state had not been running serious overt fiscal deficits. There is no reason to doubt the rightness of this conclusion. There were, however, off-budget deficits. The most serious of these arose through exchange losses in the central banking system. When a Yugoslav commercial bank purchased foreign exchange from a central bank on behalf of a client enterprise, the debt created was translated into dinars at the going rate. It then carried a net negative rate of interest. On repaying the credit, the borrower would sell the central bank sufficient foreign exchange to cover its outstanding dinar commitment. The sum returned would be reduced because the exchange rate would have fallen during the currency of the credit.[36] There were also other off-budget leakages, notably arising from Yugoslavia's difficulty in obtaining counterpart goods to offset her clearing surpluses with the Soviet Union. However, taking all off-budget financial deficits into account, Sachs reckoned the true government deficit to be "about five percent of GDP—much less relative to total output than the deficit of Italy."

Sachs was surprised by his own findings. Never had he encountered a case where "the causes of inflation were of so little significance, but economic policy was so inflationary." Inflation was therefore "mainly accidental." Responding to a critic who asked if there really was no explanation for the inflation, he admitted that its real causes were "very hard to understand." In this he was broadly at one with the OECD economists, who had accepted Yugoslavia's economic statistics at face value. He shared their conviction that monetary discipline would be essential to stabilisation. A monetary shock was needed to change expectations. "The key thing is to shut the wide open window of the central bank, through which the commercial banks and the economy are saturated with worthless pieces of paper called dinars."

Controlling inflation in Yugoslavia was, according to Sachs, "for the most part a simple matter" depending on "a few sensible measures." Yugoslavia should mobilise its $6 billion to which the reserves had been built up by Marković's financial operations in order to make the dinar convertible with the deutsche mark at a parity that would remain fixed for at least six months. Stabilisation would not set up serious strains. Bankruptcies and increased unemployment would follow, but he stressed that everything he proposed was "unfrightening" because the causes of inflation were so insubstantial. He denigrated World Bank stabilisation programmes for demanding "fifty heroic measures all simultaneously and at once." International finance would be supportive. He suggested Yugoslavia inform the Paris Club bankers that it would be unable to meet its interest payments. They would happily sacrifice their interest receipts, regarding the sacrifice as money invested in preserving the integrity of Yugoslavia. Additionally, the country would need about $500 million a year of help from the IMF.

In the report of Sachs's round table discussions, there is no mention of the concealed enterprise deficits and the massive structural problem they presented. This fundamental issue should have been given due prominence. Professor Harold Lydall's brilliant book *Yugoslavia in Crisis* (1989) had discussed the problem of inventory accounting at length. Lydall realised that the fictitious element in social product was reflected by social sector deficits. According to his information these deficits began to appear in 1977 or earlier and reached a very large magnitude by 1985.[37] Sachs did, of course, emphasise the need to use the monetary reform as a springboard for structural changes, but he wanted restructuring to be secured through the play of market forces. This was too optimistic. Yugoslav firms were political enterprises, not simply inefficient businesses. They were used to losing money and trading in de facto bankruptcy. Especially in Miloševic's Serbia, they assumed that the state would continue to look after them, and they could carry on as before.

The reform of December 1989 came into effect at the beginning of 1990. It provided for the dinar to be redenominated, fixed for six months at seven to the mark, and made convertible on current account transactions. There was also to be a credit squeeze and an increase in taxation. Wages were frozen for six months, a measure Sachs considered unnecessary. He thought it better if wages were stabilised by market driven discipline. Foreign currency loans from the central bank now had to be repaid in the currency originally contracted, closing off the exchange losses. Holders of inconvertible ruble claims were obliged to wait longer for settlement in dinars.

Apart from the wage freeze, the measures approximated so closely to Sachs's suggested programme that it is likely the stabilisation measures had, in fact, been planned by the Yugoslav authorities but needed Sachs's endorsement to ensure success with the IMF. It is open to question whether the authorities understood the reality behind their accounting figures. There is evidence that they did. If the statisticians, and the politicians they advised, knew how fragile the stabilisation really was, their aim was merely to restore a semblance of stability for long enough to secure new foreign funds. This crucial issue was not discussed, however. Analysis by Pitić and Dimitrijević at the Economics Institute acknowledges the existence of enterprise losses but only at "about 6 percent of GDP." So they attributed the severity of the inflation to dependence "on incomes policy without fiscal adjustment."[38] On this analysis, the reform probably should have worked.

The stabilisation therefore depended primarily on the implementation of restrictive monetary policy, so the National Bank of Yugoslavia set a high domestic short-term interest rate. The commercial banks, aware that "fresh money" would no longer be forthcoming to sustain their lending to the corporate sector, were supposed to impose financial discipline on the enterprises they supported. The enterprises would accordingly have to rein in their appetites for financial assistance. A relaxed import régime also made it more difficult for them to raise their prices. But because the programme was based on a gross underestimate of the deficits Yugoslavia needed to close, it soon proved incapable of effective implementation.

In the short run, the confidence in the currency for which Sachs had hoped did indeed revive. Citizens changed marks into dinars. A reflux of their savings returned to the banks, attracted by interest rates much higher than those offered on accounts expressed in deutsche marks. This inflow of funds enabled the banks to resume lending to the enterprises. Even so, the demand for credit was massive because of the rapid rate at which the enterprises continued to lose money. Immediately after the reform the commercial banks lent at 21 percent p.a., a penal rate on a currency supposedly locked to the mark but understandable as "shock therapy." However, instead of subsiding as firms minimized their demand for advances, interest rates rose in February to 34 percent. By April they settled at a plateau of 43–46 percent.[39] Clearly, penal interest rates were not deterring the big borrowers. They did not borrow the money for new capital formation because in 1990 net social sector productive investment turned sharply negative as gross investment fell far short of depreciation.[40] Instead, they spent it in covering losses. In the first quarter of 1990, the corporate deficit (net of profits) under Yugoslavia's unreformed accounting system amounted to 10,730 million dinars ($909 million). The true out-turn was even less favourable. Real losses had diminished from the monstrous proportions of 1989 but were still unsustainable in magnitude. However, the losses had been rendered sharply visible by the return to stable money values rather than being socialised via inflation financing.

The objective of monetary stability was not identified ex-ante as an inter-republic issue. This was an error because unsound money was only a symptom of Yugoslavia's malaise, not its cause, so price and exchange rate stability could not be maintained without structural change. In the northern republics, it seems that the monetary reform was allowed to work in the way intended, though at a cost greater than Sachs and Marković had anticipated. Financial distress started to take its toll upon the loss-makers. At Maribor (Slovenia) and Rijeka (Croatia) bankruptcies and reorganisations gave rise to heavy layoffs, which affected even powerful enterprises such as TAM (heavy goods vehicles) and Rade Končar (Croatia's electrical engineering giant).[41] The shipyards too, fell into acute financial distress. In June, 3. maj of Rijeka warned of impending bankruptcy and layoffs.

A by-product of this distress was a bout of ethnic discrimination in the selection of people to be made redundant. The 3. maj yard already seethed with "antipathy towards people of different opinions, nationality and faith."[42] Serb employees were forced out,[43] and at Uljanik (Pula) too they lost their job security.[44] Ethnic discrimination in redundancy was an unfortunate by-product of the Marković program, and it worsened the alienation felt by the Serbs of Croatia. Unintentionally, Marković had aggravated the ethnic jealousies that helped tear the country apart.

The financial disciplines imposed during 1990 should have curtailed the extent to which any enterprise and any Republic could meet its deficits and investment programmes by drawing on the central bank for "fresh" money. Therefore, reform-resistant Serbia, whose financial disequilibrium was more acute than elsewhere, should have been inhibited in continuing to enjoy a free ride at the expense of the rest of the federation.

Despite Milošević's non-co-operation with the Marković reform, industrial production in narrower Serbia slumped 11.1 percent in the first half of the year.[45] The investment collapse particularly hit the Serbian metals sector, the output of metal fabrication falling by 14 percent and machine building by 26 percent.[46] But hopes that monetary discipline would force structural change in Serbia were unfounded because "shutting the wide open discount window of the central bank" (Sachs's objective) was bound to make it impossible for enterprises both to maintain employment and to finance the resumption of the investment cycle. The Milošević régime blamed all the misery on the federation, demonized Marković as the author of the "anti-Serb" reform policy, and connived at its ruination. So redundancies were discouraged. Serbia's economically illiterate socialists (i.e., former Communists) demanded that money be poured into heavy industry investment programmes, which would supposedly restart the "investment cycle." Milošević regime "monetary expert" Branko Čolanović insisted that "we cannot permit the mass discharge of workers. . . . Yugoslav socialism, whatever weaknesses it has displayed . . . is inspired by the human relationship towards man and towards the employed person. We simply cannot delete that." He called for a programme of "revitalisation," which would "easily" overcome the labour surplus problem.[47]

It was not only in Serbia that massive enterprise losses continued, for they extended to all republics and regions, though in none more so that in narrower Serbia. Their regional breakdown is displayed as Table 3.

Yugoslavia's social product, 941,770 million dinars, amounted to 134,540 million marks at the official exchange rate of 7:1. On a population of 23.8 million, this amounted to 5,651 deutsche marks per capita.

As in 1989, these losses continued to be understated because of the unreformed inventory accounting system on which they were based. We do, however, have some inventory change figures for this period. Inventory values, which must have been revalued in dinars of the new 1990 denomination, are supposed to have changed, as shown in Table 4.

Table 3: 1990 social product and corporate losses in Yugoslavia, regional distribution (million dinars of 1990 denomination)

Territory	Social product	Net losses	Losses, percent of SP
Yugoslavia	941,770	67,037	7.12
Bosnia	118,300	7,457	6.30
Croatia	242,400	14,165	5.84
Macedonia	55,100	2,365	4.29
Slovenia	164,900	12,010	7.28
Narrower Serbia	224,060	21,539	9.61
Serbia & Mont.	361,070	31,040	8.60

Sources: *Ekonomska politika*, April 15, 1991, pp. 26–28; *SGJ*, 1992.

Table 4: Enterprise inventories in Yugoslavia, 1989 and 1990

Territory	1989 inventories	1989–90 inventory growth	1990 inventories	Actual 1989 inventories	True inventory growth
Yugoslavia	251,393	88,466	339,859	331,376	8,483
Bosnia	29,718	7,853	37,571	39,173	–1,602
Croatia	57,217	22,513	79,730	75,421	439
Macedonia	18,587	7,730	26,317	24,500	1,817
Slovenia	39,446	10,128	49,574	51,996	–2,422
Narrower Serbia	71,915	21,842	93,757	94,795	–1,038
Serb & Mont.	108,423	38,243	146,666	142,919	3,747

Sources: 1990 inventories: *Ekonomska politika*, April 15, 1990, table 6, p. 27; increase in inventories, ibid., table 1, p. 26.

Ostensibly, Yugoslav enterprise inventories rose by 35.2 percent. In current price terms this outcome was improbable because producers' prices rose by 434 percent between 1989 and 1990, so the figures must have been corrected to (ostensibly) stable prices. Our source[48] admits that this 35 percent increase exaggerates and suggests that this figure concealed around 15 billion dinars of inventory losses, lowering the true inventory increase to about 74 billion, though this would still be a very large sum, equal to a 29 percent increase on 1989 and 7.9 percent of total output.

In fact the overstatement has to be far greater. The published monthly index of inventories of finished goods (but not of raw materials) in the official journal *Indeks* rose in 1990 by 1.9 percent compared to 1989 for Yugoslavia as a whole. This did not include inventories of raw materials; however, imports of raw materials, intermediates and fuels in constant dinars rose by 3.4 percent. These figures suggest that inventories as a whole rose not by 35 percent but by between 1.9 and 3.4 percent. Let us take the mean of these figures (2.65 percent) in order to make a rough adjustment of true inventory change and assume that the 1990 inventory figure reflected reality. As shown in Table 4, col. 5, this makes 1989 inventories total 331,376 million dinars. In this column, 1989 inventories are proportioned territorially as in the original. In Table 5, the difference between the official inventory change (Table 4, col. 3) and the recalculated (col. 6) becomes the volume of spurious inventory change (Table 5, col. 2), which is then added in each case to the nominal loss sustained by each region (col. 4) and the federation as a whole.

This indicates that narrower Serbia's corporate losses continued to exceed the Yugoslav average in 1990. It did not automatically follow that they would continue to be financed to the same extent as hitherto externally by the diversion of funds from other republics, but Table 6, showing inter-regional funding flows, indicates that this was indeed the case.

Again, in Table 7, we can set up the fair shares comparison.

In a situation where Yugoslavia disinvested slightly (by 0.13 percent of its social product), narrower Serbia (now redesignated central Serbia) continued to achieve net

Table 5: Adjustment of current enterprise losses through eliminating spurious inventory changes, 1990 (million dinars)

Territory	Spurious inventory change	Nominal losses	Actual losses	Percent of social product
Yugoslavia	79,983	67,037	147,020	15.6
Bosnia	9,455	7,457	16,912	14.3
Croatia	18,204	14,165	32,369	13.3
Macedonia	5,913	2,365	8,278	15.0
Slovenia	12,550	12,010	24,560	14.9
Narrower Serbia	22,880	21,539	44,419	19.8
Serb + Mont	34,496	31,040	65,536	18.2

Table 6: Net investment and losses in 1990 (billion current dinars)

Territory	Social product	Losses	Net investment	Losses + net investment
Yugoslavia	942	147.0	−1.2	145.8
Bosnia	118	16.9	−3.3	13.6
Croatia	242	32.4	2.5	34.9
Macedonia	55	8.3	−1.1	7.2
Slovenia	165	24.6	1.1	25.7
Narrower Serbia	224	44.4	5.1	49.5
Serb + Mont	361	65.5	−0.3	65.2

Note: Net investment is calculated as created gross investment minus depreciation (social product – Yugoslav concept national income). Investment figures are from Savezni zavod za statistiku, *Statistički bilten (SB)* 1944, p. 14; social product and national income, *SB* 1942, pp. 19, 21.

Table 7: Regional funding gains and losses in 1990

Territory	Losses and investment	Fair share funding	Regional funding gain/loss	– as percent of net social product
Yugoslavia	145.8	145.8	—	—
Bosnia	13.6	18.3	−4.7	−4.0
Croatia	34.9	37.5	−2.6	−1.1
Macedonia	7.2	8.5	−1.3	−2.3
Slovenia	25.7	25.5	0.2	−0.1
Narrower Serbia	49.5	34.7	14.8	+6.6
Serbia + Mont	65.2	55.9	9.3	+2.6

Source: Table 6. "Fair share funding" is the total of losses plus net investment proportioned according to regional or republican social product.

fixed investment of 5.1 billion dinars, or 1.3 percent of social product despite sustaining disproportionately large enterprise losses. Had it only received its fair share of funding, its disproportionate enterprise losses would have resulted in disinvestment of 9.7 billion dinars (or 4.3 percent of its social product). As it was, in 1990 narrower Serbia extracted the equivalent of 6.6 percent of its social product through financial flows from the other republics and the autonomous regions. So, whence did it now draw its resources? To the extent of 8.4 billion they were drawn from the subsequently separated republics, and 5.2 billion was extracted from Serbia's satellites. It is notable, however, that Slovenia managed to distance itself from the payment of tribute, a wry outcome during a period throughout which Serbia mounted a trade embargo against it. Indeed, the loss of the Slovenian "tribute" to Serbia may well have been in part an undesired outcome of Serbia's economic blockade of that republic. Croatia still had to contribute, but the biggest tributary was Bosnia, which passed to Serbia some 4 percent of its social product, and in general, it was the least developed territories that assumed the heaviest burden of supporting Serbia relative to their own resources. It is, however, worth noting that central Serbia's net fixed investment had fallen by half since 1989 from 2.6 percent of social product to 1.3 percent, further frustrating the performance of the "anti-bureaucratic revolution." To that extent, the December 1989 reform mildly inhibited (central) Serbia's capacity to draw on the resources of other republics and regions. Unreformed Serbia still could not "restart the investment cycle" without external funds, which the northern republics were unprepared to release in significant volume. The fall in investment in Serbia and the increasing illiquidity of Serbia's "big systems" made it easy in Serbia to demonize Markovic's reform policy as a Croat-Slovene conspiracy, though it was conveniently overlooked that the investment cycle policy was predicated not on a return to profitability but on Serbia's ability to lose money and invest simultaneously at the expense of the other republics and regions.

The Deficits and the Breakup

In response to the distress of the enterprises, Yugoslav financial policy was already being loosened in the summer of 1990. Remarkably, deposits continued to flow into the financial system for a while yet, so the banks were still able to sustain economic activity with fresh credits. But by September, Serbia's net corporate loss had more than doubled from 3,984 million to 8,490 million dinars. It was claimed to have "engaged 43 percent of created value added."[49] Not surprisingly, the credits did not flow back to the banks when they fell due, so the banks could only go on lending while they enjoyed an inflow of deposits. Depositors became nervous in September and October 1990 when they withdrew $2,200 million from their hard currency accounts.[50] The economy of Yugoslavia lurched into recession. By November, the banks were foundering in the morass of corporate bad debt, so they lost their capacity to recycle new deposits to cover the enterprise deficits. The inability of the banks to create new credits except for the most privileged enterprises created unprecedented strains. The enterprises were stricken by the illiquidity caused by their losses. When enterprises became illiquid, they stopped paying their suppliers, and when this expedient was exhausted, they slipped into arrears on taxes and wages. By the beginning of 1991, in Serbia alone 310 enterprises had fallen seriously into arrears on pay.[51] They were not bankrupted. They continued to trade in a twilight world to the extent that a trickle of soft loans and supplies of materials allowed, and they ignored their bills for utilities.

The authorities were therefore confronted by ever more urgent demands from firms, banks, pension funds, and the social services for financial assistance and monetary relaxation. The demands were nowhere shriller than those emanating from Slobodan Milošević's Serbia. It appears that from mid-September to December 1990 Milošević arranged with his ally Borissav Atanacković, governor of the National Bank of Serbia, to create about 12.7 billion dinars in secret credits.[52] Theoretically this Serbian bank of issue should have been under control of the National Bank of Yugoslavia, but the National Bank of Serbia was acting as a source of emission independently and probably without the knowledge of the National Bank of Yugoslavia. Milošević was facing his first election, and he wanted to extinguish the arrears in Serbia in pay and pensions. The credits already created were inadequate, and in December 1990, Milošević reportedly asked federal premier Marković for a primary emission credit of 8,000 million dinars (1,100 million marks) from the Yugoslav central bank at half its regular discount rate with which to assist favoured enterprises and the Republic pension fund. Marković refused, fearing that a concession to Serbia would invite similar demands from the other republics. But—according to the account given in Mladjan Dinkić's remarkable study of the financial malversions of the Milošević regime—"Marković underestimated the famous Serbian *inat* [spite]." Milošević arranged for the National Bank of Serbia secretly to create further credits not of 8,000 million but of 18,300 million dinars.

Slovenia was also carrying out this type of operation but was doing it on a trivial scale so as not to draw attention to itself.[53] The same seems to have been the case with Croatia. However, Montenegro, which was then under the rule of Momir Bulatović, Milošević's faithful sidekick, created "grey emissions" which, proportionately to the small size of this republic, were double those even of Serbia.

The breakdown of the "grey" emissions is shown in Table 8. Serbia and Montenegro were responsible for 93.2 percent of the "grey" emissions. They represent $3.3 billion and 10.3 percent of the combined 1990 officially calculated social product of Serbia and Montenegro.

Most of the proceeds of the issue of "grey emissions" were transferred to the largest Belgrade banks, Beogradska Banka and Jugobanka. They passed big credits on to a few powerful Serbian enterprises, whose directors were strong supporters of the

Table 8: The "grey emissions" (million dinars)

Republic central bank	"Grey" emissions, 1990
Bosnia	Nil
Croatia	1,700
Macedonia	Nil
Montenegro	2600
Serbia	34,400
Slovenia	1,000
Total	39,700

Source: Dinkić, *Ekonomija destrukcija*, pp. 68–69; to Dinkić's original figure for Serbia of 21.7 billion, we have added the subsequently disclosed 12.7 billion noted in *Ekonomist magazin*, July 23, 2001, p. 20.

régime. Part of the proceeds was used on preelection pay disbursements. However, the object of the exercise was not merely to secure dinars for Serbia's economic élite but as far as possible to convert them into foreign exchange, so the greater part of the money was spent by privileged enterprises and banks in buying foreign exchange at the fixed official rate from the National Bank of Yugoslavia. Most of its exchange reserve originated from citizens' hard currency savings accounts in the commercial banks, whose total was dwindling as a result of mounting withdrawals. Once these resources had been released to the recipients of "grey emission" largesse, the asset cover for the savings accounts fell so heavily that the savings deposits could no longer be honoured. Therefore, on December 21, the central bank suspended any semblance of dinar convertibility, though it did not devalue. Soon afterward, citizens' hard currency savings (already virtually impossible to withdraw, except by bribing the right bank officials) were formally blocked.[54] This effectively wiped out $13.6 billion, the life savings of a generation.[55] The banks knew that the dinar was about to be devalued (by 29 percent) and could therefore repay their dinar credits by reselling part of the hard currency, either officially or at the still higher black market rate. It may be surmised that a large part of the windfall found its way into the hands of the "deserving" servants of the Milošević regime.

A copy of a secret document that disclosed the creation of Serbia's "grey emissions" was sent anonymously to Ante Marković, who convened an extraordinary meeting of the federal assembly (SIV). On January 8, 1991, the story was reported in the press. It did enormous damage. $3.6 billion of previously agreed United States credits were withdrawn. Because the proceeds of the "grey emissions" operation were largely exported, their spending did little to revitalise Serbia's enterprise sector. The infusion of new money to pay pensions and salary arrears may have helped Milošević to win his election, but the shock to the credit system deepened the existing depression.

The "grey emissions" operation, otherwise referred to as "Milošević's theft," deepened the rupture between Belgrade and the northern republics. In December 1990, Slovenia had held an independence referendum, which furnished the expected result, and made its plans for implementing it by the summer. For Slovenia, already subject since late 1989 to Serbia's trade boycott against it, Milošević's theft was the last straw. Its government vehemently protested to Ante Marković at Serbia's "coarse and unheard of attack on the monetary system," and announced the intention of taking over the customs posts, and tax offices in Slovenia to protect the republic's economic independence.[56] At the behest of the European Union, it was not till June that Slovenia finally declared its independence, but it was around this precise issue of seizing financial sovereignty that Slovenia's brief independence war was to be fought.

In discussing the lack of success of Marković's stabilisation programme, writers on the Yugoslav economy seem both to have missed the point of what Sachs and Marković were trying to do and to have overlooked the problem of the inter-republican financial flows. Pitić and Dimitrijević ascribe the failure "largely" to political reasons, including "resistance to privatisation and transition,"[57] rather than to its intrinsic shortcomings, which themselves aggravated these political tensions. Other writers, Štiblar and Žižmond, have, however, pointed to Sachs' association with structural "shock therapy" (i.e., the abrupt removal of protection and subsidy from state enterprises needed to make private sector expansion possible). These authors understood shock therapy to imply ruthless cutbacks, which would set up intolerable strains on the fragile Yugoslav system.[58] However, for Sachs "the policy of monetary shock" had only meant engineering a reversal of inflation expectations, preliminary to a relatively painless outcome. True, he designed his monetary reform to create more stable conditions for privatising the inefficient self-managed enterprises, but this task lay beyond his remit. He did not expect the monetary reform to set up acute strains on the economic system. Still, in view of the realities behind the Yugoslav financial crisis, he was perhaps incautious to claim that the task of stabilising the economy was going in any way to be simple. Moreover, his failure to produce a viable plan (or to reject the plan proposed to him) illustrates the danger arising in setting up programs in countries into which the adviser has, as it were, been parachuted and is dependent for his information on the presentations of the incumbent authorities.

Currency Fragmentation, 1991–92

The unfolding of subsequent events led, at least in the financial sphere, to a rather predictable sequence of dissolution. Already in the early part of 1991, with the whole country plunged into depression because of the foreign exchange crisis, financial relations between the republics began to dissolve. Belgrade controlled most of the foreign exchange and the printing press as well. When Slovenia and Croatia formally declared themselves independent on June 25, 1991, Belgrade moved rapidly to prohibit all financial dealings with them.

The Yugoslav currency union did not long survive the breakup of the Yugoslav state. The European Union did not yet write off its hopes that the seceded republics might be returned to Yugoslavia, presumably through amicable compromises rather than through victory by the Yugoslav People's Army, though this was what in fact was expected. So its own federalist agenda impelled it to put pressure on Slovenia and Croatia to retain the dinar even though they were being financially blockaded by rump Yugoslavia. Under the Brioni agreement of July 8, 1991, which got the Yugoslav People's Army out of Slovenia and gave a de facto basis to Slovenia's previously declared independence, the European Union officials who brokered the agreement compelled Slovenia for the time being to retain the dinar. This agreement was, like most European Union interventions in Yugoslav affairs, founded on sublime disregard for reality. The breakup had largely destroyed the fiscal basis of the federation because the federation was financed from the customs duties and a slice of the turnover tax, which was collected by the republics. After the secessions of Slovenia and Croatia, these revenues largely disappeared, leaving the federation in control of the national bank and the printing press and very little else with which to finance its army. It therefore increased the tempo of money printing to make good its deficits. This of course was hugely inflationary, especially because the banking system had to continue to finance the deficits of the enterprises. In 1991, the Yugoslav budget deficit jumped from 3 percent to 24 percent of GDP.[59] So Slovenia and Croatia were left in an absurd situation in which they were forced to use a currency whose sole raison d'être was the creation of seigniorage to finance their enemy, the Yugoslav People's Army. Therefore, their continued circulation of the dinar in effect contributed to the financing of this army, as well as financing the forces they assembled to counter it. Put another way, the Croatian public was financing the army against which it was fighting by holding its hand-to-hand money, on which it was paying inflation tax. True, both new countries disposed stocks of dinars, but they were not replaceable by the output of the Belgrade printing press, as they were in rump Yugoslavia. Therefore, on October 8, as soon as it was free to do so, Slovenia introduced its own currency, the tolar. In the early stages of the war in Croatia, the Croatian government financed its deficits from credits supported by hoarded stocks of dinars. Following the successful introduction of the tolar in Slovenia, Croatia followed suit and created a differentiated Croatian dinar in December. It is surprising it waited so long, because its stocks of dinars must have suffered rapid attrition through inflation. Yugoslavia lost out badly from the separation of currencies. It still had to finance the army, largely from the proceeds of the printing press. With the two richest republics, accounting for 43 percent of the national market, removed as sources of seigniorage, the tax base for inflation tax was diminished by at least a similar amount. Roughly double the former rate of emission would be needed to raise a given sum in seigniorage, so by March 1992, at the beginning of the war in Bosnia, prices in Serbia began rising at a hyperinflationary rate. The effect of this was to cause Macedonia to depart from the dinar area in July and to create its own currency, the denar. Bosnia was slow to dissociate itself from the dinar probably because Serb top officials controlled its central bank, but in due course it was to issue a differentiated (overstamped) Bosnian dinar, followed by a welter of inflationary local moneys. None of the new currencies was established as a vainglorious symbol of national prestige but rather as the response to emergency and as a means by which the breakaway governments could harness their new national banks to use inflation financing to support their own republics rather than support the Yugoslav Peoples Army.

Conclusions

From 1984 onward, enterprises throughout Yugoslavia ran large financial deficits. These deficits, as well as new investment, were funded through the banking system. Their distribution was regionally asymmetric. In 1989, Serbia, now under the rule of Slobodan Milošević, implemented expansionary policies that were supposed to boost investment but served to finance the bloated deficits of the enterprises rather than provide them with funding for investment. This created a flow of funds from the other republics (and Serbia's own autonomous regions) into narrower Serbia. Because all Yugoslavia was plagued by corporate deficits, the flow of funds could only be sustained through the inflationary creation of credit through the central banking system. Narrower Serbia's tactic was remarkably successful, because via its disproportionate receipt of central bank credits, it extracted the equivalent of 8 percent of its own social product at the expense largely of Slovenia, which bore 52 percent of this burden (5.1 percent of its social product) and Macedonia, poorest of the republics, which bore 24 percent of the burden, or 8 percent of its social product. This did not bring about the desired revival of the investment cycle in Serbia because most of these funds were devoted to financing corporate losses. Even so, narrower Serbia managed to achieve a small net investment, whereas Yugoslavia as a whole was depleting its assets. An attempt by the Milošević regime in Serbia in 1989 to mobilise the savings of its own citizens and émigrés through a state loan failed, and the funds that were raised were largely dissipated. The Marković-Sachs financial reform of December 1989 should have impeded the use of other republics' funds for the purpose of covering narrower Serbia's corporate deficits, but in 1990 central Serbia extracted the equivalent of 6.6 percent of its social product for this purpose. It was enough to cover its losses and to maintain small positive net investment. Serbia's need to keep drawing heavily on the funds of the other republics and regions was made overt in December 1990 through Milošević's theft, the creation for his own purposes of 18.3 billion dinars of "fresh money." Slovenia correctly interpreted this move as indicating that it would have to pay tribute to Serbia for as long as it remained within the federation.

In its early stages of the war, the Yugoslav Peoples Army was financed by imposing inflation tax on all the republics, so Slovenia demonetised the dinar as soon as the EU allowed it and established its own currency. So, too, did Croatia and Macedonia, then Bosnia. Hard experience had taught that under Milošević the incurably inflationary dinar currency system was a device for financing Serbia's deficits at the expense of others.

The consequences for Serbia of losing its financial support from the rest of former Yugoslavia were catastrophic. Not only did the 1990s witness an unparalleled contraction of total output, but the economy also disinvested with increasing rapidity. But that is another story.[60]

Notes

1. Susan L. Woodward, *Socialist Unemployment: The Political Economy of Yugoslavia, 1945–1990* (Princeton: Princeton University Press 1995), p. 124, citing Svetozar Vukmanovic-Tempo, *Revoljukoja Teče.*

2. Joseph T. Bombelles, *Economic Development of Communist Yugoslavia* (Palo Alto: Stanford University Press, 1968), p. 41.

3. John R. Lampe, *Yugoslavia as History* (New York: Cambridge University Press, 1996), pp. 247–248, 254; John R. Lampe, Russell O. Prickett, and Ljubiša S. Adamović,

Yugoslav-American Economic Relations since World War II (Durham, NC: Duke University Press, 1990), pp. 21–22, 56.

4. Discussed in Harold Lydall, *Yugoslav Socialism: Theory and Practice* (Oxford: Oxford University Press, 1974), p. 113.

5. See evaluation in Nora Beloff, *Tito's Flawed Legacy* (London: Gollancz, 1985), pp. 218–245.

6. David A. Dyker, *Yugoslavia: Socialism, Development, and Debt* (London: Routledge, 1990), p. 120.

7. Dyker, *Yugoslavia*, p. 121.

8. Harold Lydall, *Yugoslavia in Crisis* (Oxford: Clarendon, 1989), pp. 130–134.

9. Lj. Madžar, "Revalorizacija zaliha, fiktivna akumulacija i iluzija rasta," *Ekonomist* 38, Belgrade (1985), pp. 328–349.

10. *Informacije* [3. maj] March 6, 1987, p. 3.

11. *Statistički godišnjak Jugoslavije*, (SGJ) 1991, p. 174. In line 3, totals for 1989, surplus for accumulation (col. 5) should equal total surplus (col. 4) less items in cols. 6–10. The col. 5 figure, 25.4 billion dinars, should read –25.4 billion.

12. Branko Mikulić, "A Programme towards Significant Changes," *Yugoslav Information Bulletin*, No. 7–8 (1987), p. 17.

13. Lydall, *Yugoslavia in Crisis*, p. 84, and Dyker, *Yugoslavia*, p. 108.

14. M. Palairet, "Metallurgical Kombinat Smederevo, 1960–1990: A Case Study in the Economic Decline of Yugoslavia," *Europe-Asia Studies,* Vol. 49 (1997), pp. 1074–1075.

15. Palairet, "Mismanaging Innovation: The Yugo Car Enterprise (1962–1992)," *Technovation*, Vol. 13, (1993), pp. 125, 121, 123.

16. Palairet, "Metallurgical Kombinat Smederevo," pp. 1075–1077.

17. Palairet, "Trepča, 1965–2000: A Report to European Stability Initiative," p. 5.

18. Palairet, "Mismanaging Innovation," pp. 122, 120.

19. Palairet, "Ramiz Sadiku: A Case Study in the Industrialisation of Kosovo," *Soviet Studies*, Vol. 44 (1992), p. 905.

20. Palairet, "Metallurgical Kombinat Smederevo," pp. 1086–1089.

21. Palairet, "Trepča, 1965–2000," p. 10.

22. Palairet, "Metallurgical Kombinat Smederevo," p. 1096.

23. Ljubomir Madžar, "Who Exploited Whom?" in Nebojsa Popov (ed.), *The Road to War in Serbia: Trauma and Catharsis* (Budapest: Central European University Press, 2000), pp. 160–188.

24. Madžar, "Who Exploited Whom?" p. 164.

25. Fred Singleton and Bernard Carter, *The Economy of Yugoslavia* (London: St. Martin's Press, 1982), p. 223; Madžar, "Who Exploited Whom?" p. 164; *SGJ*, p. 497; *Jugoslavija, 1918–88. Statistički godišnjak*, p. 99.

26. *Politika*, March 7, 1989, copied in "Trepča," March 20, 1989, p. 11.

27. John R. Lampe, *Yugoslavia as History: Twice There Was a Country* (New York: Cambridge University Press, 1996), p. 346.

28. *Ekonomska Politika*, January 23, 1984, pp. 35–36; November 3, 1986, p. 33.

29. Madžar, "Who Exploited Whom?" p. 168.

30. Ilija Marjanović, "Neke karakteristike stanja u brodogradnji," *Brodogradnja*, Vol. 32 (1984), p. 138.

31. Marjanović, "U svjetlu rezultata kretanja izvoza i uvoza," *Brodogradnja,* Vol. 32 (1984), p. 336.

32. B. Ostojić, "Stimulans konkurenciji," *Ekonomska politika*, November 5, 1990, p. 29; M. Rajher, "Povećanjem udjela domaćeg čelika u proizvodnji brodova ka zajedničkom dohotku," *Brodogradnja* 299 (1981), pp. 87–89.

33. Mladjan Dinkić, *Ekonomija destrukcija. Velika pljačka naroda*, 2nd ed. (Belgrade: Stubovi Kulture, 1995), p. 84.
34. *Ekonomska politika*, August 23, 1989, p. 46; September 18. 1989.
35. The only account of which I am aware concerning Jeffrey Sachs's visit to Yugoslavia in 1989 and his recommendations is in V. Gligorov, 'Džefri Saks u Jugoslaviji: uklanjanje inflacije u Jugoslaviji je uglavnom jednostavan zadatak,' *Ekonomska politika*, November 20, 1989, pp. 12–14.
36. A. K. Lahiri, "Money and Inflation in Yugoslavia," *IMF Staff Papers* 38 (1991), pp. 751–788.
37. Lydall, *Yugoslavia in Crisis*, p. 131.
38. G. Pitić and B. Dimitrijević, "Two Yugoslav Hyperinflations: A Comparative Analysis," *Industrija XXII* (Belgrade 1995), p. 60.
39. *Ekonomska politika.*, June 11, 1990, p. 34.
40. *Statistički bilten SFRJ*, No. 1942 and 1944.
41. "Krah giganata socialističke privrede," *Novi list* (Rijeka) June 19, 1990, p. 9.
42. *Informacije* [3. maj] April 20, 1990, p. 2.
43. Three Bells Shipping Corp. (Gothenburg)—Trygg Hansen Holding AB, September 20, 1990.
44. N. Brkljača, "Društvena stratifikacija u funkciji razvoja brodogradjevne industrije Uljanik u Puli," master's thesis, Zagreb, Faculty of Political Science, 1993, pp. 115–16.
45. V. Dukanac, "Srbija: pred finansijskim kolapsom," *E.P.*, September 3, 1990, p. 14.
46. *SGJ*, 1991, p. 532.
47. B. Čolanović, interview in *Duga*, March 17, 1990, p. 17.
48. *Ekonomska politika*, April 15, 1991.
49. Dukanac, "Srbija," p.14.
50. *Ekonomska politika*, November, 26, 1990, p. 19.
51. *Ekonomska politika*, February 11,1991.
52. Given as DM 1.81 billion, *Ekonomist Magazin*, July 23, 2001.
53. Dinkić, *Ekonomija destrukcija*, p. 61
54. Dinkić, *Ekonomija destrukcija*, p. 71.
55. *SGJ*, 1991, pp. 215, 219.
56. Dinkić, *Ekonomija destrukcija*, pp. 67–68.
57. Pitić and Dimitrijević, "Two Yugoslav Hyperinflations," pp. 62–63.
58. E. Žižmond, "Collapse of the Yugoslav Economy," *Soviet Studies*, Vol. 44 (1992), p. 107; F. Štiblar, "The Rise and Fall of Yugoslavia: An Economic History View," in Alice Teichova (ed.), *Central Europe in the Twentieth Century: An Economic History Perspective* (Aldershot, Hants, England: Scholar Press, 1997), pp. 73–74. Sachs explained his use of the "shock therapy" concept in his "Reforms in Eastern Europe and the Former Soviet Union in Light of the East Asian Experience," *Journal of the Japanese and International Economies*, Vol. 9 (1995), p. 463.
59. Pitić and Dimitrijević, "Two Yugoslav Hyperinflations," p. 64.
60. This story is taken up in Michael Palairet, "The Economic Consequences of Slobodan Milošević," *Europe-Asia Studies*, Vol. 53 (2001), pp. 903–919.

The Slovenian-Croatian Confederal Proposal: A Tactical Move or an Ultimate Solution?

❖ Dejan Jović ❖

On October 2, 1990, the political leaderships of both Slovenia and Croatia officially proposed a new confederal agreement to the four other republics of the Yugoslav federation. If it had been accepted, the proposed Yugoslav confederation (or the Union of Yugoslav States that the proposal suggested as an alternative), would have turned Yugoslavia into a loose association of independent states, each of which would be recognized as a sovereign state—both by other members of the confederation and in the sense of international law.

Croatian scholar of international law Vladimir Djuro Degan was the main author of the draft of both the document titled *Model of Yugoslav Confederation* and the actual *Confederal Treaty* that accompanied it.[1] He has noted that the documents were based upon the assumption of contractual mutual recognition of full state sovereignty and international subjectivity of all post-Yugoslav states. The confederation plan called for a "union of states," not a "state union." In a structural sense the proposed confederation was to be modelled almost as a copy of the European Community, only marginally adapted to specific post-Yugoslav circumstances. Although the proposal and the contract offered many alternative solutions for practical issues—such as, for example, three options regarding the monetary issues, two on the issue of transport, three on the structure of defence forces, three on coordination of foreign policy, and many more on the structure (and existence) of the institutions of confederation— it offered no alternative to the proposal for statehood. According to the draft confederal agreement, all Yugoslav republics would recognize each other's right to unrestricted self-determination at any time. Some functions could still be delegated to joint institutions. However, each member-state would have the inalienable right to revoke any authority delegated to the confederation.

The Yugoslav confederation would, therefore, have discontinued the existence of Yugoslavia as sovereign state. A commonwealth of six internationally recognized sovereign states willing to cooperate with each other would have been established in its place. At least from the Slovenian perspective, the proposed confederation was to be à la carte, one that would allow its member-states to chose freely which (if any) elements of their sovereignty they wished to delegate to confederative bodies and which they wished to keep exclusively for themselves. The Croatian political elite viewed the confederation in somewhat more formal and more legally binding terms—with more precise rules and obligations—as long as full sovereignty of all the new states was recognized, including the unlimited right to withdrawal.[2] In their initial proposal, Slovenia and Croatia suggested that the confederal treaty should be time-limited to either five or ten years, with the possibility remaining open for any republic to leave at any time, even within this limited period.

Two weeks following the formal joint proposal, the Yugoslav state presidency rejected the plan. The representatives of the other four republics, as well as both autonomous provinces of Serbia, were also against. This left Slovenia and Croatia with no official support from any of the federal units.[3] While Bosnia-Herzegovina and Macedonia later accepted some elements of this proposal (but not before May 1991), Serbia (and to some degree Montenegro) remained hostile to the very end. At the same time the international community and its main representatives were opposed to the initial proposal because they still favored the formula of a "democratic and united" Yugoslavia and supported the federal government of Ante Marković. It was only later, not before September 1991, that they, too, agreed that the confederal agreement might perhaps be the last chance to save some form of institutionalized cooperation between the Yugoslav republics and (more importantly) to prevent an all-out war between them. However, by then it seemed it was already too late for a compromise. A confederation is, after all, an association of friendly states who are willing to cooperate, not a union of hostile and highly nationalistic states, most of which did not hesitate to use violence to achieve their strategic objectives.

With hindsight, one could indeed conclude that the confederation proposal was a missed opportunity for compromise between two bitterly divided sides: those who insisted on as much sovereignty as possible for all Yugoslav republics and those who preferred a recentralized Yugoslav state. An attempt to create a similar union of independent states on the constitutional ruins of the USSR did, indeed, offer some breathing space to the countries of the former Soviet Union, although it did not survive much beyond the immediate crises. Furthermore, it is one of the paradoxes of the Yugoslav tragedy that certain elements of a confederalist structure appeared in the postwar arrangements in many parts of former Yugoslavia. For example, the Washington agreement concluded in 1994 between Croatia and the government of Bosnia-Herzegovina was based on a promise of a postwar confederation between Croatia and Bosnia-Herzegovina. The structure of post-Dayton Bosnia-Herzegovina is also rather loose. There, the institutional and constitutional relationship between Republika Srpska and the Federation of Bosnia-Herzegovina effectively resembles some of the original Slovenian-Croatian confederal proposal. The relationship between Serbia and Montenegro, the two units of the Serbia-Montenegro state union (as defined by the Belgrade agreement of 2003) was equally loose. There were two currencies, few joint institutions and clear recognition of the sovereignty (i.e., the right of secession) of both republics. Unfortunately these arrangements were put in place only in the aftermath of several bloody conflicts that the initial confederal proposal had aimed at avoiding.

So, why did the Slovenian and Croatian confederal proposal of October 1990 fail? Was it a viable option at the time, or just a tactical move, an attempt to buy time and to prepare for the war that followed? What were the intentions of the political leaders of the two republics who proposed the confederation? Did they see it as a permanent solution, the one that could prevent violent disintegration—or as a temporary (and basically tactical) arrangement that would help them to achieve full independence for their two countries?

In this chapter I argue that the confederalist proposal was a genuine attempt to achieve first a de facto and then a de jure independence without violence. The ultimate objective was not a confederation but the international recognition of sovereignty and thus, ultimately, the full state independence of Slovenia and Croatia. The confederation was seen as a vehicle for this objective and as a good initial compromise that might prevent the violence that would inevitably characterize any open conflict with Serbia and/or the Yugoslav federal institutions (primarily, the Yugoslav People's Army, JNA).

This argument is based not only on analysis of political statements and decisions made at the time when the events were unfolding (i.e., during 1990), but also on analysis of recently published memoirs by the main participants in Croatian and Slovenian politics of the 1990s. With no exception, both Croatian and Slovenian politicians involved in decision-making processes in 1990 today admit that these two republics were only half-heartedly promoting their own project. The most explicit is perhaps Mario Nobilo, who in the early 1990s was the chief foreign policy advisor to Croatian President Tudjman. In his political memoirs published in 2000, Nobilo concludes that the "Croatian-Slovenian confederation project was little more than an attempt to buy time until our government was consolidated, until the issue of state-making was internationalized, thus ultimately—[it was] only an intermediate phase toward the full independence."[4] According to Nobilo, the main strategy of the Croatian and Slovenian leaderships in the final months of Yugoslavia was "to paralyse federal institutions as much as we could, so that their reaction to the ever widening independence of certain parts of Yugoslavia was weaker and more confused."[5] In addition, the confederation proposal was an attempt to convince international factors, that is, other states and international institutions involved in the Yugoslav crisis, that Croatia and Slovenia wanted a peaceful solution and a compromise. It served as an alibi to Slovenian and Croatian elites, who needed to demonstrate clearly that it was Serbia, not they, who destroyed Yugoslavia beyond possible repair. As France Bučar, the chairman of the Slovenian parliament said while the confederal proposal was still being drafted (September 1, 1990), "In no case we should take upon ourselves a burden of accusation that we [the Slovenes] undermined Yugoslavia from within. Let those who have indeed undermined it take full responsibility."[6] Sources presented in this chapter—including statements and articles published by leading Slovenian and Croatian politicians during the events of fall 1990—are largely consistent with Nobilo's later interpretation.

However, one could also conclude that although Slovenia and Croatia did not whole-heartedly believe that the confederal arrangement had a realistic chance of succeeding, they did genuinely hope that it could prevent a war by facilitating a peaceful route to the disintegration of Yugoslavia.[7] As Nobilo points out, the confederal model offered by Slovenia and Croatia was not intended as a blueprint for an ideal (or even desirable) institutional and political framework for post-Yugoslav space. Nevertheless, it did indeed represent "an attempt on the part of the weaker [republics] to avoid conflict, the aggression of the Yugoslav Army, and Serbian domination."[8] The driving forces behind the Slovenian and Croatian independence movements would not have sacrificed their ultimate objective—full independence—for peace. However, they did initially endeavour to achieve independence peacefully. It was only as a result of the failure of this attempt that they resorted to violence, which was in their view a form of self-defence and, therefore, a legitimate means of achieving independence.

The failure of the confederal proposal, however, cannot be fully attributed to its tactical character, that is, to the fact that neither the Slovenes nor the Croats seemed to be fully committed to their own concept. There were at least four other equally important factors at work.

Firstly, no other republic in Yugoslavia supported the confederal proposal at the time it was presented. In fact, they became supportive of it only once it was too late, namely after the first serious military conflict had come to a close (the one in Slovenia, June 26–July 7, 1991), and when Croatia faced an all-out attack by the joint forces of Krajina Serbs, the Serbian "volunteers," and the Yugoslav People's Army (JNA) in Summer 1991. Back in October 1990, when discussed by the Yugoslav state presidency, the confederalist proposal was rejected by a majority of 6 votes to 2.[9]

Secondly, although Slovenia and Croatia appeared to be united behind their joint confederalist proposal, there were still significant (and often visible) differences between them, both in terms of tactics (such as the dynamics of political change) and to some extent in terms of the desirable outcome, too. By the time of the first democratic elections in the two republics (in April and May 1990), Slovenia was already much more advanced on its road to full independence. While it cooperated with Croatia in their joint attempt to prevent the recentralisation of Yugoslavia, it also viewed Croatia as an anchor that was slowing down its own progress toward full independence. This was especially the case after August 17, 1990, when Croatia faced a rebellion by the Krajina Serbs within its own borders. Ethnically homogenous and with no major territorial disputes with its only Yugoslav neighbor, Slovenia was much more impatient to get on with its project of full independence. In order to achieve independence as soon as possible, the Slovenian government (even more than President Kučan) kept all options open, including one of direct negotiations with the Serbs. A permanent threat of a Slovenian unilateral secession by separate agreement with Serbia made Croatia suspicious of Slovenia's real intentions. At one moment, the Croatian strategic interest was to slow down Slovenia in its road to independence. This was because Slovenia's early achievement of independence would almost certainly leave Croatia in a more unfavorable and isolated position, in an ever more Serb-dominated "rump Yugoslavia." At the same time, Croatian president Tudjman's bilateral meetings with Serbian president Milošević in the last months of 1990 made the Slovenes equally suspicious of Croatia's real intentions, primarily over Bosnia. Although publicly they continued to cooperate, both republics left the doors open for bilateral negotiations with Serbia. The Slovenian-Croatian alliance appeared, in this light, to be a marriage of convenience, where both partners were aware of the existence of a third partner—always present as an alternative, and potentially harmful. This impacted negatively upon the further joint promotion of the confederal agreement.

Thirdly, there were very significant differences on strategic and tactical issues between the major political forces within both republics. In Croatia these differences were confined to fractional struggles between radical secessionists and moderate confederalists within the ruling Croatian Democratic Community (HDZ). In Slovenia they took a more open form of a political conflict between the government (the proindependence *Demos* coalition) and the opposition (the reformed communists, who favored confederation). These differences were also manifest in occasional disputes between the government, led by Christian Democrat Lojze Peterle, and the more proconfederationist Slovenian state presidency, led by Milan Kučan, the former leader of the Slovenian League of Communists. As will be explained later in this chapter, some crucial decisions—including, for example, the hasty organization of a plebiscite in December 1990—were the direct result of internal party competition in Slovenia. The confederalist proposal was never unanimously supported by all major forces, either in Slovenia or in Croatia. Divisions between those who argued for full independence and those who were prepared to compromise through a confederalist proposal disappeared only after national unity in favor of independence had been forged as a result of the wars.

Finally, failure of the confederalist proposal in October 1990 could also be attributed, at least to some extent, to the lack of support from influential international factors. All key international factors that had had a lengthy involvement in the Yugoslav crisis favored the preservation of a democratised Yugoslav state. This policy was best articulated according to the formula of "a democratic and united Yugoslavia" promoted by the U.S. Ambassador to Yugoslavia Warren Zimmermann,[10] and shared by others. When it appeared, the confederalist proposal was an outright challenge to this policy. To international observers it was clear that its authors saw it as only an interim arrangement for Yugoslavia that would eventually serve to facilitate the full independence of its republics. As such the confederalist proposal was in a sharp contrast with the international support for a united and democratic Yugoslav state. A good example of the difference between the dominant views of the key international factors and those of Slovenian President Kučan is offered in Warren Zimmermann's description of Kučan's meeting with U.S. Secretary of State James Baker on June 21, 1990, in Belgrade:

> [For Kučan] the question of secession is not whether, but how. . . . Kučan said it would be prepared to seek a future community of sovereign Yugoslav nations, along the lines of the European Community. I was struck by this reference to the EC; it showed that by "confederation," a term Kučan had used with me just the week before, the Slovenes were thinking about themselves as a fully independent country rather than as part of a Balkan Switzerland.[11]

The position of the key international players in the Yugoslav crisis altered only in the aftermath of the Slovenian war with the JNA—and only after the Yugoslav state presidency (on July 18, 1991) decided to withdraw the JNA troops from Slovenia. Thus, the international policy with regard to Yugoslav unity changed largely in response to the concept of a united and democratic Yugoslavia's being de facto abandoned by the informal agreement between the Slovenes and Serbs, making a unilateral secession of Slovenia possible. The final attempt to reintroduce the concept of confederation was initiated by Croatia through a "five-point plan" conceptualised by the Croatian minister of foreign affairs, Davorin Rudolf, in direct response to what seemed to be a Slovene-Serb agreement on unilateral secession of Slovenia.[12] But at this moment, it seemed that the international factors were much more interested in the proposal than both Slovenia and (especially) Serbia. In September 1991, a *confederation a la carte* was proposed officially by the International Peace Conference on Yugoslavia (via its chairman, Lord Carrington)—but was refused by Serbian President Slobodan Milošević.[13] As memoirs of the main participants from the Slovenian and Croatian sides now confirm, Slovenia only reluctantly agreed—perhaps also because it was convinced that Serbia never would. In conclusion, the international community supported the confederal proposal only when it became unrealistic to expect the various Yugoslav participants to agree to it.

In the sections that follow I will describe briefly the historical context in which the proposal for a confederation was made, discussed, and ultimately rejected. This context largely influenced political debates, which were often about the "real meaning" of the concepts, such as "federation" and "confederation." In addition, historical arguments were used by relevant political actors in the confederalist-federalist debate in 1990, which made them an integral part of the debate we follow in this chapter. Consistent with the main argument presented here—that the best (if not the only) chance the confederalist proposal had was before the beginning of the use of weapons in the Yugoslav crisis (thus, before fall 1990)—the chapter will focus on 1990, not 1991 when tensions were already so high that no compromise of this sort seemed to be possible.

Confederation Enters

The de facto end of socialist Yugoslavia was signalled on January 22, 1990, when in protest the Slovenian delegation walked out of the Fourteenth (Extraordinary) Congress of the League of Communists of Yugoslavia (SKJ). Because socialist Yugoslavia was—especially in its last phase, that is, after its last Constitution was enacted in 1974—built around its specific ideology, such a prominent display of the failure of this ideology meant that the foundations of the Yugoslav state were now badly shaken. The SKJ had been the real locus of sovereignty in Yugoslavia. Without the SKJ and its ideology of socialist self-management, this highly ideocratic state had little chance of surviving.

The question that the Yugoslav political elites now faced was, could Yugoslavia survive as a state under some alternative arrangement? Could it successfully accommodate to a change of ideology? Or would it instead inevitably disintegrate into its constituent parts—six republics, or even further—into many more territories?

The first incentives for a fundamental restructuring of the Yugoslav state had already emerged by the mid-1980s, when political elites in Serbia launched several initiatives for at first smaller but then more substantial amendments to the 1974 Constitution. Under the leadership of Ivan Stambolić (1982–87), Serbia became the leading force of the "reformers of the Constitution."[14] While the need for smaller reforms was accepted by others in Yugoslavia, the majority resisted any attempts to reject the main principles of the 1974 Constitution, which further decentralized the Yugoslav state and which it described as "neither a federation nor confederation but a new form of socio-political community."[15] Slovenian and Croatian political elites in the 1980s—together with those of the two provinces of Serbia, Vojvodina, and Kosovo—formed an informal block of "the defenders of the Constitution" and successfully blocked most of Serbia's reformist initiatives in the political sphere. Serbia soon found itself politically isolated in Yugoslavia. This significantly contributed to the failure of Stambolić's policy of gradual and institutional reforms of the political system. At the same time, this also contributed to the rise of Slobodan Milošević and his policy of combined institutional and extrainstitutional pressure for constitutional changes. As of 1987, Serbian demands for constitutional and political changes became not only more vocal but also more aggressive. Milošević interpreted the 1974 Constitution as being too confederalist and thus becoming the main generator of the disintegrative trends in Yugoslav politics. The "antibureaucratic revolution" he launched in 1988 demanded a new constitution that would have abandoned all elements of confederalism while promoting unity. In his public discourse, Milošević still used the concept of federalism to describe this new, recentralized, Yugoslavia. At the same time, however, the concept he used more than any other in his speeches between 1984 and 1989 was unity.[16]

Other republics, then still largely committed to the rhetoric of Yugoslav socialism (that identified "unitarism" as one of its main political enemies) viewed Milošević as a unitarist and thus as a serious danger for the fragile compromise of the 1974 political and constitutional arrangement. The political elites of Slovenia, Croatia, Kosovo, and Vojvodina now argued that Milošević's politics meant a return to the old days of statist socialism or even Stalinism. They argued that the "federalism" of Milošević was not really federalism but in fact was a mask for unitarism. On March 28, 1989, Milošević promulgated the new constitution of Serbia. The Slovenian and Croatian elites viewed this as a victory for his unitarist concept because it significantly reduced the autonomy of the two Serbian autonomous provinces—Vojvodina and Kosovo. Furthermore, in April 1989, Milošević made clear that he did not intend to stop at the borders of his own republic; he was prepared to try to "unite" Yugoslavia, too.

> Those who expect that now, when she has finally become a Republic, that Serbia would join the defenders of the *status quo* and oppose changes to the 1974 Constitution, are deluding themselves. They will soon have a chance to see how wrong they are. Serbia did not become a state to sleep on the wreath of glory, but—now strong and open towards others—to forcefully initiate democratic changes in order to make Yugoslavia a strong community of equal nations and nationalities. . . . Of course, those who do not care for Yugoslavia claim that our intentions and plans are "unitarist" and "hegemonistic." But they should be under no illusion that we would . . . abandon Yugoslavia and socialism.[17]

The Slovenian and Croatian political elites in particular understood this as an open threat. In response, they now moved toward one single objective: to defend (and if possible to expand further) the level of autonomy of their republics within Yugoslavia. The arrangements of the 1974 Constitution now became a "bottom line," a line past which the Slovenian and Croatian elites were not prepared to negotiate. Because the 1974 Constitution could only be changed by a consensus of all Yugoslav republics and provinces, the defenders of the constitution had, at least for the time being, the upper hand.

However, Milošević's antibureaucratic revolution in Serbia had already de facto changed the status quo—first through a combination of public protests and intrainstitutional pressure against the "defenders of the constitution" in Vojvodina (in October 1988) and then in Montenegro (in January 1989). In February 1989 the federal state introduced a state of emergency in Kosovo. These acts—as well as the announcement that the antibureaucratic revolution might soon be "exported" to Slovenia and Croatia—were seen by these two northern republics as illegal. This was because they fundamentally sought to undermine the constitutional arrangements for republican and provincial autonomy.

In spring 1989 Serbia announced trade sanctions against Slovenia (in response to Slovenian criticism of Serbia's policy toward Kosovo). The Slovenian political elite concluded that the 1974 Constitution had de facto ceased to exist. Subsequently, the Slovenian elite abandoned the policy of status quo as no longer realistic. The situation in which this happened is described by Janez Drnovšek, who was the first non-Communist president of Yugoslavia's state presidency, elected by the Slovenian electorate to represent the republic in this body as of May 1989:

> The actual situation had already moved forward so much that it was impossible to deal with it within the framework of the existing constitution, as this constitution was now completely lagging behind reality of the day. . . . It now became impossible to respect the law in the strict sense, as the new political and economic realities were now completely different from the self-managed, socialist, party state. At the same time, the argument that no law should be obeyed any more, that nothing was worth preserving, was also unacceptable—as it would lead to a complete chaos and would thus open the floodgate to this or that form of violence.[18]

Once Slovenia agreed that the old constitution was no longer viable, the Yugoslav presidency initiated, in January 1990, a debate on the new constitution. As Janez Drnovšek admits in his political memoirs, hopes that the Yugoslav republics would ever agree on a meaningful text of the new constitution were very weak.[19] It was obvious that the Slovenian and Serbian political objectives were worlds apart. Slovenia's main objective was to preserve—and, if possible, to extend—the level of autonomy that had been instituted by the 1974 Constitution. According to the letter of the 1974 Constitution, all republics were recognized as "sovereign states"—but due to the nature of Communist ideology and politics this phrase had little substance. In the new, post-Communist circumstances, the Slovenian elite sought to give substance to the phrase.

Having little hope for an agreement with other republics, the Slovenian politicians were now increasingly looking toward their own republic. The reforms launched within Slovenia included a series of constitutional amendments to the constitution of the republic, all of them aiming to further expand on Slovenian sovereignty.[20] Although the concept of sovereignty was not yet defined as full state independence, that is, as creation of a separate Slovenian state outside of Yugoslavia, this option was no longer unthinkable. The right to self-determination—on which Slovenian politicians insisted—clearly meant also the right to secede from Yugoslavia should the Slovenes so wish.

As the Yugoslav constitutional debate wore on, the Slovenes' position was to insist that Yugoslavia would remain acceptable to Slovenia only if further decentralization was carried out. On this basis, Slovenian politicians in 1989–90 objected not only to Milošević's attempt to recentralize Yugoslavia but also to large extent to proposals for political reforms promoted by Ante Marković, the new federal Prime Minister.[21] Marković (a Bosnian-born Croat representing Croatia) was a Yugoslav federalist and thus more popular in Bosnia-Herzegovina and Macedonia and among minorities (for example, Croatian Serbs) than among "sovereignists," such as Milošević and Kučan. Ljubljana supported Marković's economic reforms but was much more sceptical about his program of political reforms, which included federal-wide elections and thus the creation of a Yugoslav *demos* to supplement (and perhaps supplant) the republican demos.[22] As both Milošević and Marković used the concept of federalism to describe their program of reforms, the Slovenian political establishment now gradually moved away from this concept and introduced confederalism into the debate in order to emphasize the difference.

The introduction of the confederalist concept was a last-minute attempt of Slovenian reformed Communists to endear themselves to the Slovenian electorate. At one of its last sessions (on March 7–8, 1990), only a month before the first democratic elections, the outgoing Slovenian parliament (still controlled by reformed Communists) requested from its executive council (i.e., Slovenian government) to prepare a draft of a confederal treaty that would be offered to other Yugoslav republics instead of a new Yugoslav constitution. By the end of April the draft that emerged as a result of this initiative was discussed at the very last session of the outgoing government. The *Šinigoj proposal*—as the document was named after the outgoing prime minister, Dušan Šinigoj—went almost unnoticed by the general public. Soon after the change of government, the *Šinigoj proposal* was (at least temporarily) placed *ad acta*.[23]

Although fairly noncommittal when it came to political solutions, the *Šinigoj proposal* was very useful for its cost-benefit analysis of economic implications of Slovenian eventual secession from Yugoslavia.[24] The document prepared by the Slovenian Institute for social planning analyzed the structure of Slovenian trade and discovered that in 1988, 51.9 percent of all goods and services produced in Slovenia were sold within the republic, 30.1 percent in other Yugoslav republics, and 18 percent of total trade was realized through export to the international market. The main area of trade for Slovenian goods in Yugoslavia was Croatia (9.8 percent of the total), followed by Serbia in its territory outside of the two provinces (6.1 percent), and Bosnia-Herzegovina (3.3 percent). The figures on import to Slovenia showed that 57 percent of it originated from Croatia and Bosnia-Herzegovina. Thus, more than half of Slovenian trade with other Yugoslav republics was with Croatia and Bosnia-Herzegovina. Because Slovenia did not expect these two republics to join Serbia in its trade boycott (even in the case of Slovenia's secession), the damage to Slovenian economic interests would be limited.

The estimation presented to the Slovenian government indicated that in the worst case scenario—that is, if all other Yugoslav republics cut off their trade with Slovenia for political reasons—Slovenian GDP would immediately shrink by 37.3 percent. But if Serbia remained the only republic whose market would be lost, the Slovenian GDP would decrease by not more than 15.3 percent of the total. In short, experts offered an analysis that looked less bleak than politicians were led to believe by their own instinct or international warnings. Slovenia's strategic interest was to deter any other republic in Yugoslavia from joining Serbia in its trade boycott. For this reason, Slovenia had to be seen to be doing its best to contribute to a peaceful resolution of the Yugoslav crisis rather than acting in what could be perceived to be an extremist and unilateral manner. If seen as reasonable

and cooperative, Slovenia could perhaps even reverse negative trends by reorient-
ing some other republics from being linked with Serbia to itself in an economic
and political sense.[25]

Analysis prepared for Šinigoj's government predicted that the most difficult
aspect of confederalization would be in the sphere of military reforms—not least
because of deep animosities developed within the Yugoslav People's Army (JNA) for
Slovenian political reforms. These animosities began in the mid-1980s when Slovenian liberalized media protested against the JNA policy of treating only Serbo-Croat
as its de facto official language—and thus ignoring the constitutional status of the
Slovenian (and Macedonian) language as official in Yugoslavia. They further deepened
when the Slovenian weekly *Mladina* published articles on corruption within the JNA
and criticized the army for its close links with dictatorial regimes in Africa. In 1988
the JNA arrested and tried three Slovenian journalists (including Janez Janša) and
one noncommissioned officer in Ljubljana. The relationship with the JNA worsened
when in the last months of 1989 Slovenia refused to agree on the federal budget for
1990—of which the JNA was the main beneficiary. In a document submitted to
the government by the Slovenian Territorial Defence Headquarters (RŠTO), military experts proposed three alternatives for organization of the defence forces in an
eventual confederation. First, the Yugoslav army might remain the only armed force
in confederation but must be restructured in such a way that most of its units were
territorial, that is, clearly associated with a particular republic. The second option
allowed for a combination of a professional (thus, not conscript-based) Yugoslav
army and a separate armed forces of the republics. This proposal was in line with the
dual structure of the existing Yugoslav defence system, which consisted of the JNA
and territorial defence forces. However, in practice the JNA remained overwhelmingly the more important of the two components. In addition, the federal secretary
of defence, General Veljko Kadijević, launched an initiative in spring 1990 to abol-
ish territorial defence units, which he saw as potentially too nationalistic and thus
dangerous for Yugoslav unity.[26] Just before the elections in Slovenia and Croatia,
the Yugoslav Army removed much of the weaponry from the depots of territorial
defence units and transferred them to the JNA depots—especially in Croatia.[27] The
reforms proposed by the JNA were in direct conflict with those now considered by
the Slovenian government. This was especially the case with the third option of the
Šinigoj confederal proposal: that the defence forces of the confederation should consist of separate armies of the republics without the confederal army. In practice, this
would have meant the end of the JNA as an institution.

As events would soon demonstrate, the JNA did not forget this proposal—which
would, if accepted, have made it "an army without a state," as the federal secretary
of defence, Veljko Kadijević, described it.[28] As these options were proposed by the
Slovenian Communist government, the JNA became convinced that no political
party in Slovenia could be its potential ally. Thus, any attempt to negotiate with the
Slovenes would probably be futile. The conflict between the JNA and the Slovenes

continued throughout 1990 and 1991—escalating during the brief but violent "Ten Days War" between the JNA and Slovenia in June and July 1991.

Slovenia after the 1990 elections

Slovenia was the first republic in Yugoslavia to hold democratic, multiparty elections. A decision to open up political competition to non-Communist groups and parties was a direct consequence of five major influences that Slovenian reformed Communists could no longer ignore. First, by January 1990 the SKJ had de facto ceased to exist. Therefore, the Slovenian elite was no longer obliged by the principle of democratic centralism to support policy decisions over which it no longer had any decisive influence. Second, it was now recognized that the Yugoslav constitution was de facto suspended (the Slovenes argued that this was brought on by unilateral changes introduced by Serbia) and that the political system of self-management had come to an end. Third, the Slovenian political elite sought to demonstrate its popular legitimacy, which was contested by Serbia. The "anti-bureaucratic revolutionaries" claimed that—unlike Milošević, who obviously had a large number of active followers willing to organize massive rallies in his support—the Slovenian leaders spoke only for themselves and not for the people. Fourth, by being the first Yugoslav republic to organize multiparty elections, Slovenia hoped it would be seen as the most progressive and most democratic in the eyes of the Western world. This would enable the Slovenes to claim that the conflict in Yugoslavia was primarily fought between the forces of democratization (i.e., Slovenia and Croatia) and the forces of dogmatic antidemocratic neo-Stalinism (in Serbia and perhaps other republics). Slovenia (and Croatia) now portrayed themselves as the "Yugoslav west" and thus the main potential ally of the West.[29] Finally, the Slovenian reformed Communists were facing (by 1990) already very strong and growing unofficial opposition in Slovenia.

The first opposition groups in Slovenia emerged in 1986 and were largely organized around two institutions. The former Socialist Youth Organization (ZSMS) offered its institutional protection to various liberal, anarchist, pacifist, and other alternative groups, whereas the Slovenian Writers' Association and its journal *Nova Revija* became the main institutional locus for anti-Communist intellectuals of different political orientations, from liberals to separatists.[30] These two institutions—especially the latter—became vocal critics of Communist policy in the second half of the 1980s, whether it was Yugoslav, Serbian, or Slovenian.

In what is today recognized as a landmark event for Slovenian politics, in January 1987, the editors of *Nova Revija* (Niko Grafenauer and Dimitrij Rupel) published a special issue (No. 57) of this journal titled *Contributions to the Slovene National Program*. In one article after another, the leading anti-Communist intellectuals argued that Yugoslavia had become a burden on weak Slovenian shoulders and that the Slovenes should consider making their own, independent state. "Yugoslavism" and "Yugoslavianism" (the former referring to an attempt to create a Yugoslav ethnic, the latter to the Yugoslav civil nation) were identified as the main dangers facing the existence of Slovenian national identity.[31] Most authors in the special issue argued in favor of a fully independent Slovenian state and defined their role as one of convincing the Slovenian public that independence was a viable option and should be the primary aim, ranked higher than either socialism or Yugoslavia. In their subsequent writings, the *Nova Revija* authors became the main promoters of Slovenian independence. By 1989, one of them, Ivan Urbančič, concluded: "Yugoslavia as a state is a historical accident; it is without any indigenous imperative, without any idea of itself. Yugoslavia cannot exist, because she does not have any interior necessity."[32]

Faced with the uncertainties and offered an alternative to the long-standing crisis of Yugoslavia, Slovenian public opinion was now rapidly moving in support of independence. Already in 1987, 53 percent of the respondents in a survey conducted by the University of Ljubljana claimed that outside Yugoslavia, as an independent state, "Slovenia would increase its chances to develop in an economic sense," whereas only 18.9 percent claimed the contrary. More respondents than ever before (43.2 percent) claimed that Slovenian politics was "not sufficiently independent."[33] In addition, the LCY was rapidly losing its appeal with the Slovenian electorate. In 1986, only 18 percent of Slovenes agreed that "the LCY needs to exist no longer." By May 1989, 53.3 percent of the population shared this view. The May 1989 survey discovered that 75.1 percent of the Slovenian population favored multiparty democracy to a single-party state.[34]

In response to this change, several newly created opposition parties formed in December 1989 a forum-style coalition Demos. At the elections for three chambers of the Slovenian parliament, the parties of the Demos had won 54 percent of the votes, that is, 123 of 240 seats. Lojze Peterle, the leader of the Slovenian Christian Democrats (SKD), became the first non-Communist prime minister, and the editor-in-chief of *Nova Revija*, Dimitrij Rupel became the foreign minister. At the same time, however, the reformed Communists were more successful at the elections for the Slovenian state presidency—the collective head of the state. Milan Kučan was elected its president (having won 58.3 percent of the vote, to 41.7 percent for the Demos representative, Jože Pučnik), while the reformed Communists had two more members—thus a majority of 3 votes to 2. This created grounds for a cohabitation between the reformed Communists and the Demos.

These two main political forces in the new Slovenian politics had, however, very different views on the future of Slovenian relationship with other Yugoslav republics. Milan Kučan was at that time still a confederalist who claimed to be an opponent of Slovenian separatism.[35] But he was under heavy pressure from many quarters (public opinion, federal institutions, opposition in Slovenia, the JNA, the Serbian leadership, the international community) at a time when his political world was falling apart. Describing his feelings immediately after he decided to lead the Slovenian Communists out of the Fourteenth SKJ Congress in January 1990, Kučan revealed some of the dilemmas he was facing at the time:

All my life, and especially my youth, was linked with the Party. I have been influenced by these ideas through my family, and even if the Party is now clearly not what it once was, it is still not easy to say goodbye. . . . I can hardly even think about the possibility of Slovenia leaving Yugoslavia. Personally, I have never been for it. I cannot come to terms with this possibility. But, Yugoslavia as it is now is good for no one. If the Helsinki Declaration and the way of thinking in Europe, which is now hostile to any amendments of the borders, change—and I am not sure that Europe will remain committed to this view after all that has happened in Germany and in the countries of the East—then we Slovenian non-separatists would face a very difficult situation. Of course, it all depends on what Yugoslavia would look like.[36]

From this perspective, the new Slovenian president viewed the confederal proposal primarily as a means of preserving the Yugoslav name in some form—while the new government understood it as the first step toward full independence. These differences caused permanent tensions between Milan Kučan and the government of Lojze Peterle, with Kučan remaining skeptical about the feasibility of the quick and often impatient moves initiated by the majority in the Slovenian parliament. For Kučan, who was to some extent a political offspring of Edvard Kardelj and his vision of an ever more decentralized Yugoslavia, confederation was perhaps also a further step toward this permanent decentralization in new, changed circumstances.[37] For the Demos, however, confederation was possible only as a radical turnabout from Communism and various political and social experiments that came with it.

From a distance, primarily from Belgrade, Slovenia looked united behind the nationalist program. To Milošević and the JNA, there seemed to be little difference between Kučan and the Demos. This view was, however, a gross misinterpretation of reality. A new, postelectoral political system in Slovenia was truly pluralistic—to such an extent that it was sometimes very difficult to reconcile differences. Tensions between the government and the president continued over the whole period of transition from Yugoslavia to an independent Slovenian state. These tensions largely determined the dynamics of the key decisions in Slovenian politics in 1990 and 1991. Due to his previous role in the liberalization of Slovenian politics and to his resistance to the forces of centralism in Yugoslavia, President Kučan remained personally popular and influential. However, Slovenia was a parliamentary, not a presidential, democracy, and the Demos had full control over the first democratic parliament. The Demos used this institutional advantage to impose laws and enforce decisions that would lead to full independence. The Slovenian government practically ignored the president's confederalist approach and opted for full independence. In this, the government was supported by circumstances, which made a compromise in Yugoslavia very difficult or, perhaps, completely impossible.

Croatia Following the Elections of April 1990

Yugoslav politics during the late 1980s was characterized by a polarization between the Slovenian and Serbian visions of the future of Yugoslavia. Although more supportive of the Slovenes than of the Serbs, Croatian political leaders tried to promote a compromise rather than to place themselves openly in support of the Slovenes, against the Serbs. The Communist elite was aware that a strong anti-Serb position could result in a worsening of interethnic (Croat-Serb) relations in Croatia. However, such a reserved policy gave the impression of a weakness in Croatian politics. Croatian nationalism grew in response both to this perceived weakness of the Croatian Communists in the 1980s and to the expansionist character of Serbian nationalism. An increasing number of Croats saw the expansionist Serbs as serious and realistic threat. The Croatian Democratic Community (HDZ)—a radical nationalist party lead by Franjo Tudjman—emerged in February 1989 in direct response to the "policy of appeasement with Serbia," as Tudjman characterized the line taken by the Croatian reformed Communists. In criticizing Croatia's political elite, Tudjman often pointed out that the Croatian Communists should follow the example of their Slovenian comrades (if not that of the Demos), who strongly resisted attempts to recentralize Yugoslavia.

The Slovenian position on decentralizing Yugoslavia was popular in Croatia. In a series of public opinion surveys that I conducted for the leading Croatian political weekly *Danas* on March 19–21, 1990 (thus only three weeks before the elections), it was revealed that a large number of Croats were in favor of Yugoslavia being transformed into a confederation. The confederation was supported by 52 percent of the respondents in Zagreb, 48 percent in Rijeka, and 47 percent in Split. At the same time, 25 percent of the electorate in Zagreb, 26 percent in Split, and 13 percent in Rijeka favored full independence—with no confederal or any other formal links with other Yugoslav republics. The "reformed federation" (which for the Croats was mostly associated with Ante Marković, not Slobodan Milošević) was supported by 24 percent in Zagreb, 27 percent in Split, and 37 percent in Rijeka. The same survey, however, revealed that 54 percent of the HDZ voters preferred secession to any other option. The HDZ voters preferred to define Croatia in constitutional terms as "the nation-state of the Croats" (61 percent), thus omitting any reference to other ethnic groups. Unlike them, the voters for the centrist political parties preferred confederation to secession, whereas the supporters of the reformed Communists preferred federation (64 percent) to confederation. Therefore, at the moment of the first Croatian multiparty elections in 1990, the HDZ had yet to secure a majority for its preferred option: the full independence of Croatia.

It is within this context that one should understand Tudjman's hesitation to openly promote secessionist ideas prior to the first Croatian elections. As the project of a confederation had already been a part of the public debate in Slovenia, the Croatian and Yugoslav authorities could not blame the HDZ for being too extreme. The HDZ voters—more radical than the majority of the Croats—accepted the concept of confederation as a "public talk" in a situation in which it was illegal and politically damaging to promote secessionism. But it is fair to say that by confederation they did not understand an attempt to reform or save Yugoslavia in any form but an important further step on the road to independence. While the reformed Communists opted for "modern federation" as their main political program in 1990, the HDZ was now offering something new, more clearly distinguishable from the Serbs and federal government, and closer to the Slovenes—confederation. The party's position was expressed succinctly by Tudjman thus: "On the whole, there is no major difference between the program promoted by Slovenian politicians and that which is favored by the HDZ. . . . I am not saying that this is the end of any Yugoslavia. I am only saying that this is the end of Yugoslavism as a form of compulsory *brotherhood*, to which we would no longer be slaves. I am also saying that this is the end of the policy of preservation of Yugoslavia at any cost."[38]

The HDZ emerged as the sole winner of the 1990 elections. Although it did not receive more than 42 percent of all votes cast, due to the nature of the Croatian electoral system ("first past the post"), the HDZ received 58 percent of seats in all three chambers of Croatian parliament, the Sabor.[39] Unlike Slovenia, there was no cohabitation—the HDZ majority in the Sabor elected Franjo Tudjman president of the Croatian state presidency. In the euphoria that followed the historic (and, to many, the unexpected)[40] victory of the Croatian nationalists, Tudjman (and even more—members and supporters of his party) now saw the electoral victory as giving them carte blanche. They proceeded to exclude all other political groups from decision-making. In a way similar to that of the Slovenian intellectuals in the mid-1980s, the HDZ now wanted to increase public support for independence.

In one of its first foreign-policy steps after the elections, the new Croatian government officially approached the Slovenian government (and President Kučan) in order to coordinate further actions against their common opponent: centralizing forces in Serbia and in Yugoslav federal politics. In his inaugural speech in the Sabor made on May 30, 1990, Franjo Tudjman announced the new policy:

> Because of the fact that Croatia is a part of Yugoslavia, which is a recognized member of international order, we are prepared to enter negotiations with representatives of other nations of the SFR Yugoslavia and its federal bodies, in order to draft a new contractual settlement for our mutual relationships. Based on historical experience, we believe that the state sovereignty of Croatia—together with sovereignty of other nations of the current Socialist Federal Republic of Yugoslavia—can be secured only on the basis of confederation as a contractual association of sovereign states.[41]

According to Mario Nobilo, the Croatian side began working on the confederal proposal on July 20, 1990, only a month and a half into the mandate of the first Croatian post-Communist government, led by Stjepan Mesić. The initial idea was to create a long strategic document on the future of Croatia and its possible links with other republics, as well as the actual confederal contract.[42] But the Croats soon discovered that there was no time for such a megaproject. The paradox of the new Croatian politics was that at the same time that Croatia began to coordinate its politics with Slovenia it also wanted to slow down Slovenia's secession from Yugoslavia because it was aware that Slovenia's unilateral secession would reduce Croatia's chances to achieve independence on its own. Croatia feared that a Slovenian secession would turn the remaining "Yugoslavia" into a Serb-dominated country. Croatia was supportive of Slovenia's independence only if it was the result of the complete disintegration of Yugoslavia, which would then pave the way for Croatia's complete independence. Otherwise, the secession of Slovenia would be a part of the problem, not a solution.[43]

In addition, the now increasingly nationalistic (anti-Serb) Croatian elite feared that Slovenia would conclude a political pact with Serbia based on mutual recognition of the right to self-determination. This pact would allow Slovenia to leave Yugoslavia but would in turn also recognize the rights of the Serbs in other former Yugoslav republics to remain united with Serbia in one country. In several public speeches, Serbian politicians hinted that they would not object to such a deal. For example, in his inaugural speech on May 15, 1990, Borisav Jović, the new president of Yugoslavia's state presidency, announced his intention to enact the law on secession. As his political diary (published in 1995) testifies, at one of his private discussions with Slobodan Milošević (on June 28, 1990), Milošević proposed to "cut Croatia down the middle," with areas where the ethnic Serbs formed a majority remaining "on our side." Jović was then instructed to come up with developed proposals at the forthcoming sessions of the Yugoslav state presidency—"within a week, at most."[44] On July 23, 1990, while visiting Slovenia, Jović confirmed that "it would be possible for some republics to secede." In his memoirs, Janez Drnovšek also states that in "informal conversations we had in August 1990, Jović and Milošević said they had absolutely nothing against Slovenian independence—on the contrary, they thought Slovenes should organize a referendum and make a decision."[45] According to Drnovšek, occasionally even General Kadijević was not entirely hostile to Slovenia's leaving Yugoslavia but "only by agreement with others in Yugoslav federation." "He believed that the federation could survive the secession of Slovenia, but Croatia was a different thing. Independence of Croatia would mean a civil war—because of Serb minorities in Croatia. In that case, Bosnia-Herzegovina would become a problem too. He said that the Yugoslav Army would not allow this to happen."[46]

In later interpretations of the reasons why Slovenia did not accept such a "generous" Serbian offer (at least not prior to July 1991), four possible reasons were stated. First, Slovenia did not trust Milošević and thought his offer was only a tactical manoeuvre that—if accepted—would only reveal the secessionist nature of Slovenian politics. Second, Slovenia was not ready for independence. Not only was public opinion still divided over the issue,[47] but some Slovenian leaders (for example, Milan Kučan) were still genuinely sentimental about Yugoslavia. Others believed Slovenia was not yet in a position to implement policies leading to full independence.[48] Third, there was no international support for Slovenian independence at that time. On the contrary, at all official talks the Slovenian leaders had with foreign officials before July 1991, they were warned clearly that no European state would recognize a secessionist republic.[49] Finally, by accepting the Serbian offer of unilateral secession, the Slovenes would disturb bilateral relationship with all other Yugoslav republics, including the only ally they had at the time—Croatia. They feared Milošević would use Slovenian secession to consolidate his gains and defeat Croatia—but only to proceed further by trying to force a quasi-independent (but unrecognized) Slovenia into submission.[50]

In addition, the Slovenes did not want to take responsibility for the destruction of Yugoslavia. Through cooperation with Croatia they could successfully reject accusations that it was only they who were dissatisfied with federalism in Yugoslavia. At the same time, the confederalist proposal would portray Slovenia as a constructive and cooperative republic. As Milan Kučan explained in a speech to the Slovenian parliament on July 18, 1990: "If all these democratic attempts for an adequate solution come to nothing, and if we are left with no other option but to secede, then we must justify it in such a clear way that the outside world is completely convinced that we have had no other option."[51]

It was for these—primarily tactical—reasons that Slovenia agreed to the Croatian initiative for a joint confederal proposal. But it is important to note two key factors that subsequently influenced the destiny of the proposal. First, that this acceptance was given hesitantly, and second, that for Slovenia (and to a lesser extent also for Croatia[52]) there always was an alternative—a separate deal with Serbia. A part of the problem in the relationship between the two partners in this marriage of convenience was the almost incompatible personal characters of two (or possibly, with Lojze Peterle, three) leaders: Milan Kučan and Franjo Tudjman. While Kučan had a long and distinguished career in Slovenian and federal institutions, Tudjman was expelled from the SKJ in 1967 and even sentenced to prison on two occasions in the 1970s and 1980s. Kučan was a pragmatic leader, whereas Tudjman was inclined to "historicise" at official meetings—to the irritation of his visitors.[53] More importantly, Tudjman believed that the Serbs and Croats (not the Slovenes) held the key to the solution of the Yugoslav crisis. He criticized the Croatian Communists for allowing an "unnatural" situation in which the main conflict was between Slovenia and Serbia—with Croatia being entirely absent. Once in power, he "did not hide ambitions to become the *leader* of all endangered Yugoslav nations in their joint defence against the Greater-Serbian menace," as his intentions were described by Peter Potočnik, the chief Zagreb correspondent of the Slovenian daily newspapers, *Delo*:

> Dr Franjo Tudjman, who in his book *Wastelands of Historical Reality* criticised Slovenes for their history of *plotting* with Serbs against Croats and for not relying on Croats in Yugoslavia, said a month ago that for the democratic world Croatia was much more important than Slovenia, and that Slovenia lost its leading role in democratization of Yugoslavia after Croatian elections. When they mention a phrase "Croatia and Slovenia," the Croats assume that Slovenia is only *an appendix* to Croatia . . .[54]

The Slovenes were by now becoming increasingly alarmed by Tudjman's initiatives. They could not agree to become junior partners to the Croats—especially because they had rejected the status of junior partners to Serbs in Yugoslavia. The more Tudjman insisted on his leadership in the confederalist project, the more reserved the Slovenian government was about it.

One more element of Croatian politics alarmed Slovenian politicians: its ambition to change borders—especially in Bosnia-Herzegovina. Franjo Tudjman opened the issue of Croatia's borders in his main preelection TV interview when he pointed at the map on the wall behind him saying that "as everyone can see," these borders were "clearly unnatural." In his interview with *Danas* he went further:

> The borders were first contested by those who have led the *anti-bureaucratic revolution*. These people brought the country into the stage of disintegration. It was only then that the HDZ said: gentlemen in the country and in the world, the Croat nation cannot be reduced within such unnatural borders, because these borders had been created in the times of the Turkish expansion, and have remained the same until today, regardless of the fact that all colonial empires in the world have long disappeared. We have, therefore, placed the issue of the borders on the agenda only when we were threatened by the idea of their reshaping in Yugoslavia, and for us this question exists only in this context.[55]

In a later interview with *Der Spiegel* in June 1990, Tudjman linked the confederation proposal with his notion of a need for changed borders. He said that if Yugoslavia was to be transformed into a confederation, Croatia would seek to establish its "natural and historical borders."[56] According to a public opinion survey of March 19–21, 1990, the large majority of the Croatian electorate wanted the border of Croatia to remain unchanged: 66 percent of respondents in Split, 69 percent in Zagreb, and 78 percent in Rijeka. In favor of the change of the borders were 15 percent of respondents in Rijeka, 27 percent in Zagreb, and 31 percent in Split. However, the HDZ voters were again much more radical—54 percent of them wanted the borders to be changed so that they would include parts of Bosnia-Herzegovina and possibly Herceg Novi and Boka Kotorska in Montenegro.[57] In addition, Croats from Herzegovina simply could not imagine a proper state border between them and the Republic of Croatia.[58] To many of them, confederation was possible only if the borders would change because they would not agree to remain a part of Bosnia-Herzegovina, in which the Croats were the smallest of three constituent ethnic groups.

Slovenian politicians believed that Tudjman's attempt to open the issue of borders was playing with fire.[59] Not only did they have no interest in this, but they openly opposed it. Tudjman's nationalism strengthened secessionist forces in Slovenia, who on July 2, 1990, successfully rushed the declaration on sovereignty through the Slovenian parliament. Without any previous announcement the Slovenian parliament withdrew its representatives from Federal Parliament (with 131 votes for, 49 against, and 21 abstentions) and declared that federal laws and directives would be valid in Slovenia only if confirmed by Slovenian institutions.[60] In response to this, Croatia practically abandoned its original idea of drafting a long strategic document on Croatia's relationship with others, presenting instead on July 20 a shorter, nine-point proposal that in fact stated Croatia's expectations of the confederal agreement. For Croatia to agree to it, a confederal arrangement should include:

> a) recognition of its sovereignty and its borders; b) reciprocal treatment of minorities; c) balanced approached to issue of financial contributions to the costs of confederation; d) republics should give guarantees that they would accept servicing the existing external debt of Yugoslavia; e) fair division of property of federal institutions whose existence would not continue; f) the institutions of confederations should be dispersed throughout the "union of the states"; g) republics should have their own national guards, while recruits should be posted to units in their own republics only. Only elite units of the armed forces should be joint at the level of the union, and NATO structure should be mirrored in terms of joint command over them; h) obligatory financing of under-developed republics and provinces should be stopped; i) the budget for the army should be drastically reduced, and the army should be de-politicized.[61]

In addition, Croatian leadership, as Mario Nobilo confirms, sent a message to Serbia that Croatia "was ready not to insist on the preservation of the autonomy for Kosovo and Vojvodina, so that it could avoid a reciprocal demand for the same minority rights in Croatia."[62] Such a proposal, however, had little positive and much negative effect. First of all, its economic side—expressed in points c), d), and e)—meant less solidarity with underdeveloped republics, such as Macedonia, Bosnia-Herzegovina, and Montenegro and with the province of Kosovo. As expected, this was not welcomed by these regions—which could be potential allies and partners in Croatian and Slovenian efforts to create a confederation. Second, the proposal for army reforms went against everything the army wanted. Finally, the statement on Kosovo was not received well by Kosovo's Albanians. In a letter sent to Tudjman and Kučan on October 13, 1990, "500 Albanian journalists from Kosovo" complained about what they saw as backstabbing: "If in your model of confederal agreement there is no space for the Republic of Kosovo, then the Albanian nation will accept the third possibility, i.e. the full secession from Yugoslavia, based on the same principle you allegedly advocate: right to self-determination. . . . There can be no confederal Yugoslavia without recognition of the Albanian Republic of Kosovo as the second Albanian state in the Balkans. What can happen, however, is disintegration and war."[63]

Croatia's promise not to interfere in Serbia's internal affairs did not impress Serbian politicians much either. They believed Croatia could not—even if it wanted to—interfere in Serbian politics. In addition, any coalition between Croatia and Kosovo would only help them to galvanize Serbs in their opposition to Croatia. Croatia's nine-points proposal was entirely unacceptable to Serbia in almost all aspects because it ran entirely against Serbia's own proposals for the recentralization of Yugoslavia.

Confederation was the least desirable option, which—as Borisav Jović and Slobodan Milošević concluded even before the Croatian elections—"nobody could impose on Serbia." Serbia believed that by this proposal Yugoslavia would cease to exist, and Serbs would remain unprotected in other republics, especially in Croatia: "Even if we all accept such a contract, the Serbs would still be outsmarted in other areas—so we have no reason to accept a confederation."[64]

Instead, Serbian leadership supported a quid pro quo policy and now increasingly instrumentalized the Serb ethnic group in Croatia in order to undermine Tudjman's government from within. Any further steps on Croatia's part toward confederation or secession would now be met with equal steps by Croatian Serbs (primarily those in the Krajina region). As Jovan Rašković, the leader of the Serb Democratic Party (SDS) in Croatia explained in his interview for the *New York Times*: "If Croats want their own state, then the Serbs too want to decide for themselves whether they want to stay in Croatia or to separate from it."[65]

Based on this approach, municipalities with ethnic Serb majorities in Croatia enacted their own declaration of sovereignty and autonomy of the Serbs in Croatia on the same day (July 25, 1990) that the Croatian parliament enacted twelve amendments to the Croatian constitution.[66] Finally, tensions in Croatia escalated by mid August—in part as a direct consequence of Serbia's policy of "cutting Croatia down the middle" but also in response to ever more radical Croatian nationalism.[67] On August 17, the self-declared Krajina region physically separated from the rest of Croatia by setting up roadblocks and barriers and issuing political declarations that the Croats saw as threats and provocations. This was the beginning of what would a year later escalate into a war in Croatia, only to then spread to Bosnia-Herzegovina in April 1992.

Retrospectively, one may conclude that the events of August 17 and those that followed made any attempts for a workable confederation almost impossible. In part, the Serb rebellion in Krajina was directed against any coalition between Slovenia and Croatia.[68] And indeed, after August 17, Slovenia found itself exactly in the position that it had most wanted to avoid—by becoming a side in a violent Serb-Croat conflict. Logically, this led many Slovenes to ask themselves: would it not be better to accept Milošević's offer to secede and leave the Croats behind?

As a consequence, the Demos line, which promoted full independence more openly, was now prevailing in Slovenia. This was also what Serbian nationalists in Belgrade wanted. This line did not exclude the possibility of a confederation, but it did not want to commit Slovenia to only one option either. The argument was most clearly presented by the leading pro-Demos commentator, Janko Lorenci, in his article published by *Delo* only five days after the "events in Knin," as he called the rebellion in Krajina region of which Knin was the administrative centre:

> The chances for a *gentlemen's agreement* between the republics, for a workable confederation treaty, now seem to be slim. Even if talks on confederation continue, they would still be held under a deep shadow of complete chaos. . . . What does

that mean for Slovenia? More than anything else it means that Slovenia must return to a multiple options strategy, which has been abandoned of late for a policy of one single option—the confederation. This happened for a great many reasons: because of economic weakness, dependence on the Yugoslav market, because of a lack of support from abroad, because of many—not least military—threats and risks that would accompany our road to full independence. However, now—i.e. after the events in Knin—it is clear more than ever that confederation could be, if not entirely impossible, then certainly a much too distant aim. It certainly is so uncertain, that it should not be the only aim we have. To us, Knin should be a shock which would re-introduce the aim of Slovenian full independence to our political life again—not only as an equally desirable, but perhaps as the most desirable alternative to the confederalist tendencies. The politics of "one only option" (confederative) takes us to at least as equally uncertain a future as the politics of full independence . . .[69]

The Road to Independence

By October 2, 1990, when the two republics officially proposed the confederation, Slovenia was only partly interested in the success of this project. Events that followed in the next month—largely in response to the confederalist proposal—saw Slovenia more disengaged with each day that passed. On the same day that the confederalist proposal was agreed upon, the Krajina Serbs declared autonomy from Croatia. The first direct conflict between Croatian police forces and local militias of the "Serb Autonomous Region of Krajina" also happened that same day in the town of Dvor. At the same time, Borisav Jović (then the president of the Yugoslav state presidency) received a delegation of the Krajina Serbs in Belgrade in what was a clear demonstration of support. The next day, the Yugoslav presidency concluded that Yugoslavia was "on the verge of a civil war."[70] Subsequently, the presidency authorized the JNA to intervene, with only the Slovenian representative, Janez Drnovšek, voting against.[71] The Serbian opposition leader, Vuk Drašković, called for a general mobilization in Serbia and announced that his armed "volunteers" would be willing to defend Krajina Serbs. Only three days before (September 29, 1990), in an interview with *Delo*, Drašković said:

> What the Kingdom of Serbia held when Yugoslavia was created, on 2 December 1918, must be returned. In addition, in the case of the confederalization of Yugoslavia, Serbia must obtain all territories in what is today Herzegovina, Bosnia, Slavonia, Dalmatia, in these parts of Croatia where the Serbs made a majority of the population until 6 April 1941, when the Ustasha genocide against them began. . . . Wherever the Serb blood was shed by the Ustashas' knives, wherever there are our graves—there are our borders. Tudjman, or whoever else would want to trespass, cannot do that at a negotiating table—but only at the battlefield![72]

While issuing an open threat to Croats, Drašković issued a very reconciliatory statement about the Slovenes: "Slovenes have never tried to exterminate the Serbs, so why would we want now to be an obstacle in [the] Slovenian road to independence, towards full statehood?"

Drašković's radical speeches and open invitations at arms, showed to the Slovenes that confederation would be even less likely if Drašković won the forthcoming Serbian elections. At the same time, however, Drašković seemed to be even more explicit than Milošević in his support for a separate Serb-Slovene deal on Slovenia's secession from Yugoslavia.[73]

In addition, the panicked reaction of the Yugoslav presidency and the JNA to the Slovenian-Croatian confederal proposal further helped to shift Slovenian public opinion toward supporting independence. Once the presidency had concluded that Yugoslavia was on the verge of a civil war, the federal military police occupied the headquarters of the Slovenian Territorial Defence units on October 5, 1990. Slovenes saw this as showing straightforward contempt for the decisions of their democratically elected parliament. A public opinion survey conducted the next day revealed that 88.4 percent of Slovenes believed that the Slovenian political leadership (not the federal presidency) was the legitimate commander of the Slovenian Territorial Defense units. More importantly, when asked, "If confederation proves to be impossible, would you be in favor of Slovenia remaining a part of a Yugoslav federation, or in favor of secession from Yugoslavia?" 79.9 percent of the Slovenes said they wanted secession and only 5.3 percent federation (with 14.8 percent undecided).[74]

This was a signal to Slovene secessionists that a failure of a confederal proposal would play in their favor. In another public opinion survey, published in *Delo* on October 20, 1990, 43.2 percent of Slovenian respondents said they would be prepared to defend Slovenian sovereignty "by taking up weapons, if it was endangered," and a further 36 percent gave a conditionally positive answer to this question ("yes, but only if absolutely necessary").

Thus, by the beginning of November 1990, it had become clear that "in their minds, the Slovenes have already left Yugoslavia behind" as Tudjman's foreign policy advisor, Darko Bekić, said in his interview to *Journal de Geneve*.[75] Bekić argued that "only the Croats are serious about it, only they want to save Yugoslavia in this moment." And indeed, very soon afterward, on November 9, the Demos coalition officially proposed a plebiscite on Slovenian sovereignty. The initiative for the plebiscite was launched after the meeting between the Demos and the Serbian opposition parties—thus, further deepening the gap between the Slovenian and Croatian politicians. Jože Pučnik explained the motives:

> For more than two months already, confederation seems to be an impossible solution for the problems of Yugoslavia. Perhaps we could agree on it with Croatia and Bosnia-Herzegovina—although, after the events in Knin this became rather impossible too. It is therefore now the case that we will have to act on our own. Our confederal proposal was given as a matter of principle—but it seems that there is no realistic chance for its implementation. Therefore, our support for confederation is more of a tactical nature. The point we are making is that we would be

ready to accept a confederation too, in order to negotiate about the best solution to this problem. But, the others are not ready to accept this offer.[76]

Although he did not explicitly admit it, there was another internal reason for Demos to speed up with independence—and that was the growing unpopularity of Demos among the Slovenian electorate. In a public opinion survey conducted by *Delo* at the beginning of November, Demos was now significantly behind the reformed communists in electoral support—with 36.9 percent to 42.5 percent.[77] Its leader, Jože Pučnik, was one of the least popular politicians in Slovenia—ranked only sixteenth out of twenty leading Slovenian politicians. For Demos and Pučnik, thus, the plebiscite was a vote-catching initiative too—an attempt to promote Demos as the "most Slovene" of all Slovenian political groups.

Apart from this internal factor, two external factors also helped—although unintentionally—the Slovenian secessionists' cause. The first one was the unification of Germany, on October 3, 1990 (the day after the confederal proposal was agreed upon). Germany's unification challenged the Helsinki principle on the status quo of the borders in Europe. In addition, the unification was a result of the implementation of the principle of self-determination, thus of the same principle the Slovenian (and Croatian) secessionists claimed for themselves. This all created "a very difficult situation for us non-separatists in Slovenia," as admitted by Milan Kučan.[78]

The second unlikely source of support was the European Community. In 1990, the EC was fully supportive of the policy of "unity and democracy"[79] and in this vein supported the government of Ante Marković. It also warned Slovenia that it would not be recognized if it seceded unilaterally.[80] In order to demonstrate its full support for the federal government, on November 1, 1990, the EC decided to include Yugoslavia in the PHARE program.[81] Furthermore, the German minister of foreign affairs, Hans-Dietrich Genscher, expressed Germany's full support for Yugoslavia's prospective membership in the European Community after his meeting with Yugoslavia's Foreign Secretary, Budimir Lončar on September 2, 1990.[82]

The prospect of Yugoslavia (united and democratic) joining the EC made Slovenian and Croatian secessionists nervous. As Darko Bekić said in an interview with the foreign press on November 6, 1990, "Croatia did not want to enter Europe as an anonymous province of Greater Serbia."[83] In his strategic paper presented to Slovenian state presidency, Dimitrij Rupel was even more explicit, saying that "Slovenia must approach the restructuring of Europe as a nation-state, not as a subordinated unit of Yugoslavia." The EC offer to include Yugoslavia in some of its programs thus had an unintentional consequence: it encouraged the secessionists to speed up. What also encouraged them was a prospect of losing the "democracy argument." Before the Serbian elections in December 1990, Slovenia and Croatia argued that in its essence the conflict they had with Serbia was a conflict between "democratic western republics" and "unreformed Serbia, led by [the] neo-Stalinist Milošević." With the elections in Serbia approaching, this argument was no longer valid. With the elections in all Yugoslav republics nearly completed, secessionists expected more direct pressure for federal elections, which they wanted to avoid because such elections would democratically legitimize Yugoslav state institutions. In order to prevent federal elections, the Slovenian parliament concluded on November 13, 1990, that the Yugoslav state "no longer functioned" and that Slovenia therefore "had no future in Yugoslavia" because "economic and national death awaits us in it."[84] A declaration by the Demos representatives in Slovenian parliament stated: "International politics is not inclined or supportive of us, but—no state can be recognized before it becomes a state. Therefore, we first must establish the state, i.e., we must become independent from Yugoslavia. Taking into account that the great powers and European states are not supportive of us, we can expect great resistance and crisis to follow the plebiscite. People should be aware of this when they vote."[85]

Not everybody in Slovenia—and even less in Croatia—was supportive of this decision. The Slovenian reformed communists argued that the timing was inappropriate and that there was no certainty that independence was favored by a majority.[86] However, the opinion polls conducted at the time showed that independence was taking roots among the Slovenian electorate. On November 17, 1990, 64 percent of the Slovenes said they would vote for independence, whereas 16.1 percent would be against (and 19.6 percent undecided). People were less optimistic when asked whether Slovenia would be able to survive as an independent state: 49.7 percent said it would, and 15.6 percent said it would not.[87] But, one can safely assume that the Slovenes were even more pessimistic about Slovenia's prospects in Yugoslavia, which now increasingly appeared to be sinking into chaos, anarchy, and bloodshed. In this context, uncertainties and fears were still the prevailing sentiments among the Slovenes. During the brief war with the JNA in June and July 1991, these sentiments would be successfully manipulated by political elites and the media with the objective of achieving the unity of the nation faced with a realistic and serious threat.

Once the Demos agreed that the plebiscite question should also include a possibility that a sovereign state of Slovenia might enter into confederalist agreement with other Yugoslav states, a compromise was reached. Under the chairmanship of Milan Kučan, Slovenian political parties agreed on November 14, 1990, to call up a plebiscite for December 23, 1990.[88]

Croatian politicians were not amused by this decision, especially because it looked to them as if the immediate incentive for the rush came from the meeting between the Demos and Serbian opposition parties, which was held in Belgrade on October 24, 1990. President Tudjman made his contempt explicit in his statement to *Delo*: "When it comes to solutions to current problems in Yugoslavia, you in Slovenia are a bit impatient, while we in Croatia have some other problems to solve too. A large number of Croats live beyond the borders of Croatia, and as we all know—the Knin has happened too. . . . Croatia therefore thinks it should not get itself into a position in which it takes steps which cannot bring it any concrete results."[89]

Behind closed doors, Croatian politicians were even more direct in their criticism of Slovenian "selfishness." They feared that Slovenia might build up border-posts on its border with Croatia, which might deter some Croats from supporting Croatian independence.[90] In addition, the Slovenian example encouraged radical secessionists in Croatia (including those within the HDZ) to pressure the moderate confederalists, and—to some extent—Tudjman himself. In November 1990, one of the leading Croatian separatists, Vladimir Veselica, received a standing ovation from the HDZ representatives in the Sabor when he said that "a nation without a state is like a turtle without a shell."[91] At the same time, Croatian public opinion also moved toward supporting full independence, at least as a feasible option. In a public opinion survey that I conducted for *Danas* in the last days of November 1990, 54 percent of the Croatian electorate said that Croatia, too, should organize a plebiscite if Slovenes decided at their plebiscite to leave Yugoslavia. Against were 31 percent, and 15 percent of respondents were undecided. However, the split between ethnic Croats and ethnic Serbs—as well as between supporters of the HDZ and those who voted for opposition parties—now became almost complete. Among ethnic Croats, support for a plebiscite on independence was as high as 64 percent, whereas among the ethnic Serbs it was as low as 8 percent. In a sign of clear support for a more radical line within the party, the HDZ-voters were overwhelmingly (85 percent) supportive of the idea.[92]

Tudjman's chief domestic policy advisor, Slaven Letica, admitted in December that "Kučan's and Tudjman's vision of Yugoslavia is now also somewhat outdated."[93] The road to independence was now opened wide. In public discourse of the time, confederation was not yet entirely abandoned. However, neither of its two original promoters now perceived it as a desirable or even a feasible solution to the Yugoslav problem. At best, they thought of it as a tactic by means of which they could buy time. This time would be used to secure an alibi against accusations that they had destroyed Yugoslavia and to prepare new institutions, as well domestic and international public opinion, for a full declaration of independence. In the Croatian case in particular, the time would be used to prepare for a war that now looked almost inevitable in the aftermath of Slovenia's decision to leave Yugoslavia.

Conclusions

The Slovenian plebiscite on December 23, 1990, confirmed overwhelming (88.2 percent of those who voted, with 93.2 percent turnout) support for Slovenian de facto independence, although the actual question included an option that, once independent, Slovenia could enter into an association of Yugoslav states, should they wish to form a confederation.[94] By *lex specialis* enacted prior to the plebiscite, the implementation of the plebiscite's decision should take no longer than six months. In these six months, Slovenia negotiated with others nothing else but the models of becoming independent. To this effect, its leadership engaged in a series of bilateral meetings with other republics. On January 24, 1991, bilateral talks with Serbian leadership were held in Belgrade—ending in mutual recognition of the right to self-determination. In the next two weeks, meetings with Bosnian, Montenegrin, and Macedonian leaders followed. Between March 27 and April 29, five multilateral meetings of six presidents of Yugoslav republics took place with no positive results. On the negative side, they worsened the general political situation in Yugoslavia because they demonstrated a complete disunity and the scale of the tensions between political leaders. This tended to galvanize the population at large in support of their leaders and against the others. They also offered another good alibi to Slovenia—which claimed that no solution was possible within the existing framework. By May 1991, the Yugoslav federal presidency was blocked, first by a permanent stalemate in voting (with four votes against four) and then by a temporary resignation of its president, Borisav Jović, on March 15, 1991. An attempt by the JNA Headquarters to introduce a state of emergency failed in March 1991. On May 15, 1991, the Serbian and Montenegrin members of the presidency blocked (until July 1, 1991) election of Stjepan Mesić, the Croatian representative, as its next president.

On May 19, 1991, Croatia, which feared that it would be left in a "rump Yugoslavia" once Slovenia formally seceded, held a referendum on its own future. As Vladimir Đuro Degan concludes, the Croatian referendum was formally a choice between a confederation and a federation—but everyone knew it was a "plebiscite on independence."[95] Turnout at the referendum was 83.6 percent. The results showed that 93.2 percent were supportive of the proposal "that the Republic of Croatia, as a sovereign and independent state, which guarantees cultural autonomy and all civic rights to Serbs and members of other nationalities in Croatia, can enter into a union of sovereign states with other republics (as proposed by the Republic of Croatia and the Republic of Slovenia)." The other proposal—"that the Republic of Croatia remains in Yugoslavia as a united federal state, as proposed by the Republic of Serbia and the Socialist Republic of Montenegro"—was supported by 5.4 percent of the electorate. The Serbs from Krajina boycotted this referendum because they had already (on April 1, 1991) declared the Republic of Serb Krajina independent from Croatia.

Despite warnings that no republic would be recognized if it seceded unilaterally,[96] Slovenia and Croatia declared full state independence on the same day, June 25, 1991.[97] The next day, a conflict between the units of JNA stationed in Slovenia and the newly created Slovenian army and police began. Once it ended on July 7, Slovenia and Croatia agreed to suspend implementation of their declarations of independence for three months in order to enable negotiations on a peaceful resolution of the Yugoslav crisis. To this end, the EC organized a conference on Yugoslavia chaired by Lord Carrington. The conference proposed a confederal solution to Yugoslavia's problems. Slovenia and Croatia formally agreed, not out of any enthusiasm for the confederal proposal, but primarily for two other reasons: they needed international support and protection (and thus had to be seen as cooperative with international efforts to resolve the Yugoslav problem), and they correctly assumed that Serbia would never accept a confederation along the lines proposed by Carrington. The Carrington proposal had many elements of the original Slovenian and Croatian *confederation a la carte*, and it also meant international recognition of independence for all Yugoslav republics who applied for independence. For Serbia this was unacceptable because it meant—as Slobodan Milošević stated on November 5, 1990—"the abolition of Yugoslavia by the stroke of a pen."

In the meantime, the Yugoslav state presidency agreed (on July 18) to withdraw all JNA troops from Slovenia in a decision supported by Serbian representatives, to the complete surprise of the Yugoslav Army, of international factors, and even of Slovenian and Croatian leadership. The only member of the Yugoslav presidency who voted against this decision was Stjepan Mesić, the Croatian representative. This decision—more than any other—contributed to a change of policy of some key European states (especially Germany) toward the issue of Yugoslavia's unity. After all, once the Yugoslav state presidency decided to withdraw its own army from Slovenia (not only to barracks, as agreed on by the Brioni Declaration of July 7, 1991), how could one expect other states to insist for much longer on their policy of a democratic and united Yugoslavia? If Serbia agreed to support Slovenian de facto independence, how could one expect Germany or Austria to oppose it? With Slovenia becoming de facto independent following the withdrawal of the JNA troops in October 1991,[98] the de jure independence was now only a step away. But so was also a combined assault of the Krajina forces, JNA and Serbian "volunteers" first on the units of the Croatia's National Guard and then in an all-out assault on the civilian population in general. When the war in Croatia intensified in August 1991, for a large majority of the Croats—but also for a growing number of Macedonians and Bosnians—independence became the only possible option. The confederation proposal now lay under the ruins of Dubrovnik and Vukovar, which were both attacked in fall 1991. International recognition of Slovenia and Croatia followed on January 15, 1992.

Notes

1. For the full text of these documents see Vladimir Đuro Degan, *Hrvatska država u medunarodnoj zajednici* (Zagreb: Globus, 2002), pp. 281–306.
2. Degan, ibid., p. 229.
3. See Janez Drnovšek, *Moja resnica* (Zagreb: Mladinska knjiga, 2002).
4. Mario Nobilo, *Hrvatski Feniks* (Zagreb: Globus, 2000), p. 27.
5. Nobilo, ibid., p. 40.
6. France Bučar, interview, *Delo*, September 1, 1990.
7. Nobilo, op. cit., p. 65.
8. Nobilo, op. cit., p. 71.
9. See Janez Drnovšek, *Moja resnica* (Ljubljana: Mladinska knjiga, 1996).
10. Warren Zimmermann, *Origins of a Catastrophe* (New York: Times Books, 1996).
11. Zimmermann, ibid., p. 136.
12. For the full text of Rudolf's proposal, see Davorin Rudolf, *Rat koji nismo htjeli* (Zagreb: Globus, 1999), pp. 306–321.

13. See Laura Silber and Allan Little, *The Death of Yugoslavia* (London: Penguin Books, 1995), pp. 209–225.

14. For Stambolić's political program in these years see Ivan Stambolić, *Rasprave o SR Srbiji,* (Zagreb: Globus, 1988) and Ivan Stambolić (1995): "Put u bespuće," Radio B 92, Belgrade.

15. Edvard Kardelj, "Yugoslavia: The Socialist Self-Managing Community of Equal Peoples, 1969," in Edvard Kardelj, *The Nations and Socialism* (Belgrade: STP, 1980), pp. 190–216.

16. For Milošević's political program in 1984–1989 see Slobodan Milošević, *Godine raspleta,* (Belgrade: BIGZ, 1989).

17. *Informativni bilten CK SK Srbije,* No. 4 (1989), pp. 10–11.

18. Drnovšek, op. cit., p. 171.

19. Drnovšek, op. cit., p. 170.

20. The most important amendments were enacted on September 27, 1989—in defiance of warnings issued by federal institutions that they were unconstitutional (from the point of view of the existing Yugoslav Constitution of 1974). For the chronology of these changes see Božo Repe, *Jutri je nov dan* (Ljubljana: Modrijan, 2002), pp. 177–194.

21. In his diary, Borisav Jović, Serbia's representative in the Yugoslav state presidency wrote on October 31, 1989: "Slovenia attacks Marković even more than we do in Serbia." See Borisav Jović, *Poslednji dani SFRJ* (Belgrade: Politika, 1995), p. 64.

22. A survey conducted in May and June 1990 showed that Marković's program of political reforms was supported by only 26 percent of the Slovenes, which made the Slovenes least supportive of all Yugoslav nations. While in Yugoslavia on the whole Marković's program of reforms was approved by 66 percent, in Slovenia the rate of approval was only 32 percent. *Yugoslav Survey,* No 3 (1990), pp. 3–26.

23. In his book, Slovenian historian Božo Repe writes that on June 18, 2001 (thus, two years since the *Šinigoj proposal* appeared), the then Slovenian foreign minister, Dimitrij Rupel, was not aware of its existence. The first post-Communist prime minister, Lojze Peterle, knew about the proposal but did not pay close attention to it. See Repe, op. cit., p. 55.

24. For the *Šinigoj proposal* see Repe, op. cit. pp. 52–55.

25. The original analysis was titled "Vpetost slovenskega gospodarstva v jugoslovanski trg, strukturna analiza" (May 4, 1990). See Repe, op. cit., pp. 52–53.

26. For General Kadijević's views see Veljko Kadijević, *Moje viđenje raspada* (Belgrade: Politika, 1993). For an informed insider's view into the JNA thinking in these years, see also Branko Mamula, *Slučaj Jugoslavija* (Podgorica: CID, 2000).

27. For reaction of Slovenian political elite to this action, see Drnovšek, op. cit., pp. 167–175.

28. See the subtitle of his book—Kadijević, op. cit.

29. This rhetoric was successful and helped Croatia and Slovenia to receive some support from otherwise rather unlikely quarters—for example, from Margaret Thatcher. The most obvious example of this rhetoric is Franjo Tuđman's letter to the U.S. President George H. W. Bush on January 24, 1991. In this letter, Tuđman emphasizes that Western republics are fighting against "the Marxist communist Slobodan Milošević." See *Večernji list,* January 25,1991.

30. For Slovenian intellectual opposition to the regime, see Jasna Dragović-Soso, *Saviours of the Nation* (London: Hurst & Company, 2002), chapter 4, and Danica Fink-Hafner, *Nova družbena gibanja—subjekti politične inovacije* (Ljubljana: FDV, 1992).

31. See Tine Hribar, "Slovenska državnost," *Nova Revija* 57, pp. 3–29.

32. Ivan Urbančič, "Sedamdeset let Jugoslavije," *Nova Revija* 85/86 (1989), pp. 789–817.

33. Niko Toš (ed.), *Slovensko Javno Mnenje 1987* (Ljubljana: Delavska enotnost, 1987), p. 58.

34. Niko Toš (ed.), *Slovensko javno mnenje 1988–1989* (Ljubljana: Delavska enotnost, 1989), p. 265.

35. Warren Zimmermann confirms that Kučan had indeed made a transition from an opponent to (by mid-1991) a supporter of independence. See Zimmermann, op. cit., 136.

36. Milan Kučan's interview with *Danas*, January 30, 1990.

37. The link between Kardelj's previous project and the new proposal for confederation was also established by Dušan Bilandžić, Croatian historian who participated in the writing of the 1974 Croatian Constitution and was then (in 1991) one of seven Croatian vice-presidents. At a press conference in Zagreb on September 10, 1990, Bilandžić said that the Croatian confederalist proposal was similar to what Kardelj proposed in 1965 (*Delo*, September 11, 1990).

38. Interview with *Danas*, May 1, 1990.

39. See Nenad Zakošek, "The Croatian Parliament during the Period of Democratic Transition: Constitutional and Policy Aspects," in Atilla Agh (ed.), *The First Steps* (Budapest: Hungarian Centre of Democracy Studies, 1994), p. 89.

40. Among those surprised with Tuđman's victory was Slobodan Milošević, who expected the elections to be won by the moderate nationalists of the National Agreement Coalition (led by Savka Dabčević-Kučar). See Borisav Jović, op. cit., p. 125.

41. Cited in Nobilo, op. cit., p. 294.

42. Nobilo, op. cit., pp. 59–60.

43. Nobilo, op. cit.

44. Borisav Jović, op. cit., p. 161.

45. Drnovšek, op. cit., p. 209.

46. Drnovšek, op. cit., p. 219.

47. According to an opinion poll published in *Delo* on September 22, 1990, 47.8 percent of the Slovenes supported confederation, whereas 34.9 percent were in favor of complete independence. Some political leaders doubted the success of a plebiscite as late as in December 1990. See Janez Janša, *Pomaci* (Zagreb: Mladinska knjiga, 1993), pp. 72–80.

48. Janša, op. cit., p. 74. A similar cautious position was stated by the Slovenian minister of foreign affairs, Dimitrij Rupel, in his statement of October 11, 1990. See *Delo*, October 12, 1990.

49. For this see Janša, op. cit., pp. 82–84.

50. For this argument, see Boris Jež's column in *Delo*, September 15, 1990.

51. *Delo*, July 19, 1990.

52. For example, in direct talks between Tuđman and Milošević over Bosnia-Herzegovina, as attempted on several occasions in 1990 and 1991.

53. See Nobilo, op. cit., p. 109.

54. *Delo*, October 12, 1990. For Slovenian fears of Croatian domination in this partnership, see also Marinko Čulić's analysis in *Danas*, October 16, 1990.

55. Danas, May 1, 1990.

56. Quoted from *Večernji list*, June 18, 1990.

57. *Danas*, April 3, 1990.

58. For the political importance of the Croat Diaspora and its support for the HDZ, see Paul Hockenos, *Homeland Calling* (Ithaca, New York: Cornell University Press, 2004).

59. Some of these disputes between Slovenia and Croatia continued well after the war and are, indeed, still sources of tensions between two states. For example, despite the initial announcement that the two presidents would hold regular meetings twice a year, there were only two official meetings between Milan Kučan and Franjo Tuđman in the whole period of 1992–99.

60. *Delo*, July 2, 1990.
61. Nobilo, op. cit., p. 60.
62. Nobilo, op. cit., p. 60. This was in line with Tudman's previous statement on Kosovo published in *Danas*, May 1, 1990: "For us, the problem of Kosovo exists only as a human rights issue. But that does not mean that we intend to neglect the real interests of the Croats for the sake of bringing a solution to Kosovo—such as it was, here and there, the case in the past."
63. *Delo*, October 13, 1990.
64. Borisav Jović, op. cit., 131 (entry on March 26, 1990).
65. Cited in *Delo*, August 9, 1990.
66. Degan, op. cit., p. 225.
67. A good example was the rushed change of the flag, which introduced a symbol that reminded many (not only Serbs) of the times of the Ustasha-led Second World War Croatian state. Some of Tudman's public statements and speeches—including the one in Sinj on August 7, 1990, were also seen as inflammatory and provocative.
68. This was recognized by Tudman, who made this point clear at his press conference on August 14, 1990. See *Delo*, August 15, 1990.
69. *Delo*, August 22, 1990.
70. *Delo*, October 2, 1990.
71. Croatia was at that time not represented by its own member in the federal presidency: Stjepan Mesić, who replaced Stipe Šuvar as the Croatian representative, was not yet confirmed by the federal assembly.
72. *Delo*, September 29, 1990.
73. This impression was confirmed at the meeting between the *Demos* coalition leaders (Pučnik, Rupel and Tine Hribar) with representatives of Serbian opposition on October 24, 1990, in Belgrade. After this meeting, Pučnik said that he was convinced that "we had to leave Yugoslavia as soon as possible." "Differences between our and their positions are unbridgeable. Serbian opposition would like to resolve a problem of their national minority in Bosnia-Herzegovina and Croatia, and would therefore not support a confederation. . . . We also established that they had nothing at all against secession of Slovenia from Yugoslavia. For them, the primary objective is solution of the Serb question in Yugoslavia" (*Delo*, October 25, 2005).
74. *Delo*, October 6, 1990.
75. Quoted from *Delo*, November 6, 1990.
76. *Delo*, July 6, 1990.
77. Quoted in *Danas*, November 20, 1990.
78. *Danas*, January 30, 1990.
79. Milan Kučan stated this as one of the main reasons why it was convenient to use the concept of Yugoslavism within the confederal proposal. "We all went to see the world—Slovenia, Croatia, Serbia; and the world told us that it was interested in Yugoslavia only. . . . Thus, it is politically productive to talk about Yugoslavia, and to present our concepts as pro-Yugoslav" (*Danas*, October 23, 1990).
80. For example, even a year later, on July 3–4, 1991, the Croatian delegation was not allowed to participate in the OSCE meeting in Prague, as explained in Rudolf, op. cit., 233.
81. *Delo*, July 18, 1990, and November 1, 1990. Yugoslavia was to receive US$47m through this program. Greece was the only country that opposed this decision.
82. *Delo*, September 3, 1990.
83. Interview with *Journal of Geneve*, quoted from *Delo*, November 6, 1990. See also Nobilo, op. cit., p. 68.

84. *Delo*, November 14, 1990.
85. *Delo*, November 13, 1990.
86. A leading Slovenian sociologist, Veljko Rus, warned Slovenian public that the plebiscite would be a dangerous gesture, with no real meaning, and that it thus should not have happened. *Delo*, November 24, 1990.
87. *Delo*, November 17, 1990.
88. *Delo*, November 14, 1990.
89. *Delo*, November 18, 1990.
90. Rudolf, op. cit.
91. *Danas*, November 27, 1990.
92. *Danas*, December 4, 1990.
93. *Danas*, December 4, 1990.
94. Repe, op. cit., p. 426.
95. Degan, op. cit., p. 240.
96. These warnings were most explicitly conveyed to Yugoslav leaders on the occasion of James Baker's visit to Belgrade on June 21, 1991. Baker presented his warnings on behalf of the OSCE, not only in his capacity as the U.S. secretary of state—but was largely ignored. See Nobilo, op. cit., p. 186.
97. In another display of his leadership ambitions, Tudman insisted that Croatia should declare its own declaration before Slovenia. Indeed, the Sabor declared independence one hour before the Slovenian parliament.
98. The JNA troops withdrew completely by October 26, 1991.

Destruction of the Yugoslav Federation: Policy or Confluence of Tactics?

❖ Eric Gordy ❖

Obviously much could be said, and much has already been said, on the reasons for the dissolution of the Yugoslav Federation. It would be possible to offer broad theoretical (or, perhaps, ideological) arguments that Yugoslavia was never a tenable political construction at all or structural arguments that the 1974 Constitution imposed a level of decentralized competition that was bound at some point to disintegrate. Broad analyses of the historical weakness of federal arrangements, of the unrealized necessity of overcoming the divisions of the Second World War, or of the chronic problems of legitimacy and functionality that faced Communist regimes are all possible. There would certainly be good reason to offer a comprehensive assessment of such macro-level arguments and their theoretical and empirical foundations, and this is a task that several authors have begun in earnest.

This paper has a far more modest goal, which is to contribute to an explanation of why the violent dissolution of Yugoslavia happened at the time that it did and why it took the shape that it did. These questions require answers derived from facts specific to the political environment of the late 1980s and early 1990s. Although much of what lies behind these events remains unknown and many of the decisions that influenced the outcome took place behind the scenes in a way that was neither documented nor visible to the public, some of the broad outlines can be derived, at least provisionally, from memoirs and analyses that have been published to date. So what follows is intended as a preliminary response, to be added to and revised by future research, to the following two questions:

1. When did the break come that made Yugoslavia no longer possible?
2. What was the role of Slobodan Milošević's political leadership in bringing about this break?

Although this list is not exhaustive, seven moments might be suggested as marking the break at which the continued existence of Yugoslavia as a federal state of six republics and two autonomous provinces (or some other arrangement within the territory of the former SFRJ) was impossible or extremely improbable. These possibilities would be:

1. The Eighth Congress of the League of Communists of Serbia in 1987
2. The placement of Serbia's autonomous provinces under republican control in 1989
3. The failed Fourteenth Congress of the League of Communists of Yugoslavia in January 1990
4. The attempt by JNA to declare a state of emergency in March 1991
5. The crisis over the succession of Stjepan Mesić to the SFRJ presidency in May 1991
6. The failure of the various efforts at reaching an agreement on confederation through the first half of 1991
7. The declarations of independence by Slovenia and Croatia in June 1991

It might be useful to regard some of these possibilities as different instances of the same historical moment. Whether the point of no return was reached in May or June of 1991 might be a matter of splitting hairs, but it seems as though the items on the above list could be regarded as falling into three broad groups: in the first two (or is it two and a half?), there is a concerted campaign by the Serbian party, headed by Milošević, to establish control first over Serbia and then over the federation in order to carry out a program of constitutional reform that would have imposed greater centralization. In the last two, it is clear that the goal of a centralized federation, and indeed the federation itself, has already been abandoned. It would make sense, then, to concentrate on the middle three events: the failed Fourteenth Congress of the SKJ, the failed attempt at military intervention in March 1991, and the implosion of the SFRJ presidency in May 1991. These stand out as the moments in which it became apparent, in one way or another, that the principal federal institutions were fatally incapable of functioning.[1]

Why did these moments come? Broadly speaking, there are two possibilities: either they came because somebody wanted them to, or they came because events as they developed made them inevitable. In terms of an analysis of Serbian policy during this period, the concrete question is whether at some point in 1991 Milošević abandoned his initial goal of preserving and strengthening (and, of course, dominating) the Yugoslav federation and shifted to the goal of creating a new state centered around Serbia that he hoped would include some or all of the disputed territories in Croatia and Bosnia-Hercegovina. As many observers have noted, if this shift was a matter of policy, then it was a policy that Milošević himself never articulated publicly and continued, in his arguments before the International Criminal Tribunal for the Former Yugoslavia (ICTY), to deny.[2]

A close reading of events in this period does not offer strong support for the thesis that there was a conscious and premeditated shift in policy on Milošević's part in 1991, though it does not completely negate this possibility either. What seems probable is that the abandonment of the goal of preserving the Yugoslav Federation and its replacement with the (never publicly stated) goal of building a state out of Serbia, Montenegro, and some combination of territory conquered from Croatia and Bosnia-Hercegovina resulted from a combination of (at least!) six factors that came together over 1990 and 1991:

1. The failure on Milošević's part to extend his control of Serbian political institutions to the federal level
2. The demise of the League of Communists of Yugoslavia, which eliminated both the framework for the legitimacy of the federation and the principal institution through which conflicts in the federation could be worked out
3. The insecurity of the Serbian political leadership, who feared a violent demise if they did not succeed in maintaining political power
4. The motivations of the military leadership, which faced narrowing options in terms of maintaining their privileged position as an autonomous political and ideological force
5. A structure of opportunity that encouraged political leadership to dismiss federal solutions and continue the momentum toward independence
6. Inattention and confusion on the part of powerful international actors, which encouraged contradictory interpretations of their goals on the part of domestic actors

The sections that follow seek to outline the major elements of these six factors.

Milošević's Political Ambitions

Although the name of Slobodan Milošević is closely associated with the demise of Yugoslavia in current political discourse, it seems clear that the dissolution of the federation and alteration of borders were not among his goals during the period of his political rise from 1987 to 1990. Dejan Jović details Milošević's initial political goals as: 1) "reintegrating" Serbia and Yugoslavia through constitutional and political reform, 2) assuring that political and economic reforms would be slow and limited so as not to threaten socialism, 3) avoiding confrontation with non-Communist opponents by developing a "positive program," and 4) reinforcing the power of state structures as part of a "struggle against anarchy."[3] As Jović points out, his policy "was, at least in this initial phase, primarily political and not ethnic. For that reason it succeeded in gaining sufficient support (but, in the first phase, not more than that) within the Serbian party itself."[4] Lenard Cohen observes that this policy was not markedly different from that pursued by Ivan Stambolić and other Serbian political leaders of the period, who regarded "creative constitutional engineering as the best strategy for deflecting anticommunist and anti-regime criticism in Serbia."[5] In this regard, Cohen notes, Milošević was perceived in this early phase as being possibly more moderate than Stambolić.[6]

As Milošević's political power increased, the object of his political ambition broadened so that he began to be promoted not only as a political leader who would unify control over Serbia, but as one who would restructure the federal party and federal government in the centralist direction he had advocated in Serbia. In this regard, and also because of his well-publicized identification with the political goals of Serbs in Kosovo, he began to appeal to non-Communist intellectuals on the political right in Serbia. As Louis Sell observes on the early genesis of this alliance, the alliance was primarily strategic, with Milošević hoping to broaden his base of support beyond Party conservatives, and the nationalists hoping to make use of Milošević and then either win him over or dispense with him:

> The alliance between Milošević and the Serb nationalist intellectuals, weighted with reservations on both sides, was destined to be only temporary. The intellectuals looked down on Milošević as a provincial and an apparatchik. They believed they could exploit Milošević's popularity and the organizational strength of his party, and then dump him when they had achieved their objective of a non-Communist Greater Serbia. After a four-hour meeting with Milošević in July [1990], Ćosić patronizingly described Milošević as a politician who had his own views, but was also prepared to change them—implicitly to those of Ćosić and the intellectuals.[7]

This relationship, together with Milošević's well-defined profile on the Kosovo issue and his refusal to join the criticism of the 1986 SANU Memorandum, forms the basis of his early identification with Serbian nationalism.

To the degree that Milošević also had ambitions to restructure and dominate all of Yugoslavia, emerging as some type of "new Tito," he faced severe limitations from the beginning. In the first place, it is clear that the 1974 Constitution had been designed precisely to make the emergence of a new Tito impossible, a goal that suited Tito well while he was still alive. In the second place, perhaps more importantly, any new Tito would be strongly limited to the extent that he or she was identified with a particular republic, region, or ethnic group. Dejan Jović observes:

> Tito was a figure who transcended national and political divisions, and who was not identified with any Yugoslavian ethnic community. He was (by birth) Croatian and Slovenian, but he was never identified with Croat or Slovene politics, nor did he come to the leadership of Yugoslavia as a representative of Slovenia or Croatia. In contrast with him, Milošević was identified as a Serbian politician and as such was perceived as potentially biased in relation to the most important political and ideological conflicts.[8]

Milošević's goals in turning his attention to the federal party and federal government could be interpreted generally as applying the efforts at centralization of control that he had undertaken in Serbia to all of Yugoslavia, a program that would certainly only serve to identify him further not only as a Serbian politician but as a politician associated with narrowly Serbian goals not shared in every republic. "His program now [after the Eighth Congress of SKS] seemed clear even to those at the lowest level of the social hierarchy, and he carried them out resolutely: first the unity of the Serbian party, then the unity of Serbia, then of the Yugoslav party, and then Yugoslavia. So the program had four phases—Milošević has just accomplished the first, he would be stopped at the third and defeated in the fourth."⁹ It would be sensible to surmise that the Serbian leadership had considered at this point the possibility that the second two phases might not succeed. Controversial to begin with, it was built on proposals that ran counter to the direction of federal politics since 1965 and that were energetically opposed by the Slovenian leadership. Louis Sell cites and interprets the memoirs of Borisav Jović to suggest that a reserve plan existed as early as March 1990, after the SKJ Fourteenth Congress: "If agreement could not be achieved on transforming Yugoslavia into what it called a more efficient federation, the committee decided that Serbia would seek to redraw Yugoslav borders to include Serbs living in Croatia and Bosnia in a new state. Since it was already obvious that Slovenia and Croatia wanted to move Yugoslavia in the opposite direction, the decision amounted to a covert Serb decision to attack Yugoslavia."¹⁰

More documentation than that offered by Borisav Jović would be needed to attach certainty to this claim. Sell's U.S. Embassy colleague Warren Zimmermann¹¹ offers a similar assessment of Milošević's motivations but attaches a somewhat later date to it. Regardless of the date, however, it is clear that once Milošević's program was not accepted by SKJ, space for political maneuver within the federation was extremely restricted. The following section considers the elements and consequences of Milošević's inability to assert control over SKJ.

The Demise of the League of Communists of Yugoslavia

The League of Communists of Yugoslavia was structured as a coalition of the leagues of Communists of each of the republics and autonomous regions, in addition to the military, formally uniting them into a federal-level party. Because Yugoslavia was a single-party state, the federal party also functioned as a vehicle for rotation through and promotion into a variety of positions of economic or political responsibility, and as a quasi-governmental consultative body below the level of the federal parliament. In the post-1974 structure of "democratic centralism," SKJ operated as the field in which competing proposals were adjudicated and the popularity of initiatives was tested before they became policy. It is, therefore, not surprising that SKJ would be the place where initiatives for reform of the federal constitution would compete for support before making their way to formal political institutions.

In the late 1980s, however, the balance of forces in SKJ made the emergence of a comprehensive constitutional reform unlikely. The Serbian party and the military advocated initiatives for greater concentration of power in the federal government, positions that were backed by the parties of Montenegro, Kosovo, and Vojvodina as Milošević established political control over their governments. Such initiatives were consistently opposed by the Slovenian party, and their resistance was at least tacitly supported by the parties of Croatia, Bosnia-Hercegovina, and Macedonia, probably more out of fear of domination by Serbia than out of those parties' support for greater decentralization of power. Compromise solutions were made less likely by the insistence of Slovenia and Serbia on incommensurable demands.

Milošević saw the solution to the deadlock in SKJ in a program to change the structure of the party. He came to the Fourteenth Congress prepared to propose a new party statute that would have replaced the federalistic organization of SKJ with an organization based on a "one-person–one-vote" system. Given Serbia's position as the most populous republic and the differing levels of party membership in different republics, the proposal would have nearly assured Milošević a permanent majority in SKJ: 40 percent of SKJ members were from Serbia and 7 percent from Montenegro, suggesting that any support for initiatives originating with the Serbian or Montenegrin leadership would be assured a majority if they received even minority support among delegates from other republics.[12]

Regarding the competing proposals for the future structure of the federation, neither the Serbian nor the Slovenian proposal had the support of a majority of SKJ members. According to surveys conducted in late 1989 by Ivan Šiber, the Serbian position was more popular than the Slovenian position among SKJ members by 38.9 percent to 18 percent, but it was not popular enough to dominate, especially over the clear objection of the Slovenian, Croatian, and Kosovar parties.[13] The outcome of the confrontation at the Fourteenth Congress is well known: after seeing all its proposals outvoted by large margins, the Slovenian delegation walked out of the Congress. Milošević's proposals may well have passed had the remaining delegates agreed that a quorum still existed, but the Croatian delegation followed suit, and the Congress congress was adjourned. The SKJ would never meet again.

Not only had Milošević not succeeded in forcing through his proposal for reform of the SKJ and revision of the federal constitution, but the Fourteenth Congress ended with the demise of the institution that had provided most of the legitimacy for the presidency and government of SFRJ. Any efforts to reach a new agreement on the federal structure of Yugoslavia would have required the Serbian leadership, which had built its program on reviving centralism, to reach a compromise with leaderships that advocated greater decentralization. General Veljko Kadijević, whose narrative shifts between marking the beginning of the crisis of federal arrangement in SFRJ in 1974, 1984, and 1988, expresses resignation over efforts to reach a consensus on constitutional reform, suggesting the existence of a conspiracy to prevent agreement from taking place: "All efforts at strengthening the federal state failed completely, and everything remained the way the Slovenians wanted."[14] At this point, maintains Kadijević, "[i]t was already clear then to any serious person that many of the constitutional proposals were the result of an intention to make possible the destruction of Yugoslavia."[15] Conspiratorial tones aside, Kadijević was probably correct in assessing that an agreement was not likely to be reached, at least through the mechanism of federal institutions and the federal party.

The demise of SKJ affected the range of available political options fundamentally. Since 1945, the basis of Yugoslavia's legitimacy had been in large measure ideological. As Dejan Jović puts it, "Once it was left without its ideology, without the belief that had been absolutely central to its identity, Yugoslavia was simply no longer possible."[16] Whether or not one accepts Dejan Jović's thesis about the centrality of Communist ideology to the existence of Yugoslavia, it is clear that in the absence of a single ruling party organized around the principle of Yugoslavia, Yugoslav proposals had to compete on an equal footing with proposals that rejected Yugoslavia.[17] Given the fear of Serbian domination in the western republics, this was a competition in which Yugoslav proposals were not favored, and it meant that Yugoslav proposals in Serbia were required to adopt a posture that recognized a border between those areas that were pro-Yugoslav and those that were not. In practice, this meant political actors were compelled to begin to think in terms of ethnic borders.

The Insecurity of the Political Leadership

Given the endemic problem of legitimacy and failure of its political project discussed in the preceding section, it may be fair to ask why Milošević did not choose either to change course in a way that adapted his policy to the changed political situation or to open up the political field in a genuine way to competitors who would put forward alternative solutions. Perhaps the suggestion seems absurd on its face, with all that is known in retrospect with regard to the tenacity of Milošević's hold on power. This tenacity, too, has to be explained—explanations that posit a psychological attachment to power on Milošević's part cannot account for the support he received in securing this attachment. In the conditions of degraded power that took hold from 1990 on, it seems that: 1) awareness on the part of political actors of the degradation of legitimacy brought on by the rapid fall of the Soviet empire, and 2) the objective threat posed both by separatist nationalists in the western republics and non-Communist nationalists in Serbia played a fundamental role in creating a perception in the Serbian political elite that it could only lose power through violence and that the loss of power would lead to greater violence.

Ana Dević[18] offers a powerful argument on the construction of nationalist politics by Communist elites as a strategic effort to recapture legitimacy by synthesizing plebiscitary support. As Lino Veljak observes:

> It is important to mention that the "anti-bureaucratic revolution" took place from 1986 to 1989, that is during the time when the crisis of legitimacy in the countries under communist dictatorship had reached its peak and when the process of rapid collapse of the Soviet empire had begun. It should be added that the legitimacy in many of these countries, had never been established in the true sense of the word, especially in the countries in Eastern Europe, where communist power had been imposed thanks exclusively to the Soviet victory in the Second World War. To that

extent the populist movement organised by the Serbian communist leadership may be regarded as a preventive mass mobilization intended to supply the old power structures with a new legitimacy.[19]

Other observers, notably Zoran Slavujević,[20] have also noted that it often appeared as though Milošević's primary political strategy was to preempt the rhetoric of nationalist non-Communist intellectuals by adopting it and presenting it as his own.

Was this the "positive program" of which Milošević spoke in the late 1980s? More likely it is a sign that the Serbian leadership recognized that the greatest competition for popular legitimacy in the period was more likely to come from the nationalist right than from the democratic center. As Dejan Jović observes: "They seemed to be powerful, all-powerful, but really they were afraid that the departure of the Communists from the political scene could only lead to worse nationalism. They accepted nationalism in order to prevent it; they were compelled to make that decision not only by the general mood in the country and criticism from without . . . but also by their own fear of the consequences—not only for the idea and the country, but for themselves personally."[21] Considering the continued power of the image of fascism and its local domestic collaborators in the Yugoslav Communist worldview and the continued association of contemporary nationalist movements with the World War II–era *Četnik* and *Ustaša* movements, the belief that the way to prevent the enemy's return to power was to co-opt his or her beliefs may be explainable.

It is in the context of the all-encompassing fear of losing power that the panicked reaction of the Serbian leadership and military to the domestic events of the first half of 1991 makes sense. To General Veljko Kadijević, the political conflicts at the federal level, the skirmishes between JNA and reserve police units in Croatia and the Belgrade protests of March 9, 1991, were all of a piece:

> Similar processes [like the confrontation with police reserves in Croatia] had increased in Slovenia, and to a lesser degree in Bosnia-Hercegovina and Macedonia. The opposition in Serbia, having lost convincingly in the multiparty elections, tried in several ways to bring the electoral results into question. The complete condition in the country was such that the Military General Staff regarded it as the beginning of a civil war. That is why it requested the meeting of the High Command—the SFRJ Presidency and the Military General Staff—which was held on 12, 14 and 15 March 1991.[22]

At this meeting the military commanders requested that a state of emergency be declared and that the military be empowered to confront and disarm police, territorial defense units, and paramilitaries, a proposal that failed by a single vote. Borisav Jović expresses the fear of the leadership as being that "the ninth of March of 1991 could easily have been Slobodan Milošević's judgment day. The fate of Nicolae Ceausescu had been prepared for him."[23]

The Motivations of the Military Leadership

As suggested in the previous section, the JNA command had a concrete political interest in maintaining the Yugoslav Federation and in advancing centralist projects, on which its status, which was not only military but also political, ideological, and economic, depended. As Miroslav Hadžić points out, "from the death of Josip Broz to the period leading to the war, the generals' corps acted as a very powerful and relatively autonomous political subject."[24] In its political capacity, the JNA appears, at least through the lens offered by the memoirs of General Veljko Kadijević, to have been creative in interpreting the degree of its subordination to civilian control. Kadijević expresses deep suspicion and personal dislike for the federal prime minister, Ante Marković, who was named to the post despite Kadijević's personal intervention in 1989 to have Slobodan Milošević named prime minister. At one point he refers to Marković as a "destroyer" of Yugoslavia,[25] while at another he describes how JNA refused all contact both with Ante Marković and the Federal Executive Council.[26]

In Kadijević's memoirs, the JNA exercised similar selectivity in terms of its subordination to the command of the SFRJ presidency. At the beginning of his narrative the degree of free interpretation of this subordination is merely suggested:

> The High Command of the Armed Forces of SFRJ regularly followed and assessed all factors—external and internal—on which the security of the country depended, and all major decisions, from development plans to plans for the use of the armed forces, which grew out of those assessments, it recommended to the Presidency of SFRJ as the Commander in Chief of the Armed Forces. The High Defence Command did this constantly, while I was head of the General Staff, regardless of whether the Presidency was operating in its full, or, for various reasons, a reduced contingent.[27]

Already it seems apparent that JNA saw its role of subordination as applying more to some members of the presidency than to others. While it is not clear to what degree Kadijević's understanding of the political context is representative of all high JNA officers, he sees conspiracies to destroy Yugoslavia involving a wide range of both foreign actors, including the United States, Germany, and the Vatican,[28] as well as a long list of domestic actors from Edvard Kardelj on, whom he regards as "destroyers of Yugoslavia."[29] Among these was the last federal president, Stjepan Mesić. Kadijević describes the military's relationship with Mesić:

> The first phase [in the activity of the European Union] were the activities to bring Mesić to the office of president of the Presidency of SFRJ with the goal, among other things, of establishing the sort of control over the military which would make impossible any use of the Army for the defense of Serbian interests, or any autonomous role for the Army. . . . That phase, however, ended quickly, because they came to see, like Mesić too, in a very drastic way, that he could not realize any personal influence as the president of the Presidency, among other reasons because he had already become so compromised as a destroyer of Yugoslavia. All of his efforts in

that regard resulted comically, even. His efforts to give orders to the military through the information media are well known, and we in the High Defense Command simply ignored them, treating them as if they did not exist.[30]

The purely formal character of the military's consultations with the presidency becomes even clearer in Kadijević's description of the JNA response to Slovenia's declaration of independence, at which time, "we brought a part of our proposal to the whole Presidency, and a part of it only to those members of it who were working for Yugoslavia."[31]

Probably the key moment at which the JNA reached the point of no return in its alignment with the Serbian political leadership was in March 1991, with the failed effort to force a declaration of a state of emergency. At this point, Kadijević describes the assessment reached by the military commanders, which includes an abdication of the defense of the federation: "the military, relying on those political forces in the federation and the republics which represent those peoples who want to live in Yugoslavia, with a peaceful separation from those who want to exit from it, would continue to secure that policy."[32] In deciding on this political coalition, the JNA altered its essential mission. As Miroslav Hadžić describes the moment, "The fiasco with the state of emergency [in March 1991] was the last opportunity for the Serbian and military leaderships to reassess their relationship to Yugoslavia. At this time, a fateful decision came for Yugoslavia and the JNA—the generals retreated from the defense of the state at all costs and abandoned themselves to the command of the Serbian political leadership."[33]

At this moment, the JNA ceased to function as the defense forces of the Yugoslav federation, and transformed itself into the military wing of a political faction.

As it became increasingly clear that the armed forces had chosen a side in the confrontation between republican governments, there was an intensified tendency on the part of the Serbian political leadership to assert its overwhelming power, interacting with federal institutions only in a formal manner, or ignoring them altogether. Borisav Jović expresses this understanding as it was shared in the Serbian political leadership in March 1991:

> Regardless of all of the criticisms on the part of the opposition, the elections [of December 1990] represented the actual balance of forces and opinion in the electoral body of the Republic. The institutions of power, above all the police and the judiciary, were not the least threatened in their orientation to defend constitutionality and legality, and that means to defend the legally elected government against attacks of any kind. The same can be said for the Yugoslav Peoples' Army, which was, formally, under the command of the federal organs but was also inclined to the defence of the constitutional order of the country and prepared to carry out any command which would be issued in that interest.[34]

As if to dramatically represent this certainty in the support of the armed forces, on March 9, 1991, Borisav Jović, in the capacity of president of the SFRJ presidency, issued just such a command, ordering the JNA to send tanks to the streets of Belgrade in order to stop antiregime demonstrations in the city. This was the first of the official uses of JNA to intervene militarily in the political conflicts in the federation, and in deciding to issue the order, Jović recalls, he did not consult with the Slovenian member of the presidency, Janez Drnovšek, or with the Croatian member, Stjepan Mesić, because "it was not necessary."[35]

Although the effort to impose a state of emergency failed in March 1991, the Serbian political leadership nevertheless had an opportunity to demonstrate that it was capable of independently relying on the support of the military, even with a questionable legal foundation and even in an operation directed against civilians. At this point it may well have become impossible for the governments of the other republics to envision a future for themselves inside a Yugoslav Federation in which they would not have legal control over the forces of security. It may have also become impossible for the Serbian political leadership and the JNA to retreat once they had provided evidence of the strength of the Serbian-military alliance and of the willingness of this alliance to bypass the institutions of the federal state. The definitive alignment of the military might have given Milošević the opportunity to demonstrate that force was on his side, but it probably also eliminated the possibility that the federation could be preserved or renegotiated by means of agreements built on mutual interest and trust.

Increasing Momentum toward Independence

Before March 1991, there may have been a desire for independence in Slovenia and Croatia. This desire probably did not become a majority current of public opinion strong enough to encourage political leaders to act upon it until it became clear that the balance of forces in the Yugoslav Federation made a federal arrangement impossible except under conditions equivalent to surrender on the part of the western republics.[36] After this point, crisis meetings of the SFRJ presidency and EU-sponsored negotiations aside, there was no genuine will on the part of any of the republican political leaderships to reach an agreement that would prevent the violent dissolution of the country. The momentum toward independence became irresistible in Slovenia, which encouraged an emergent movement in Croatia, which forced Bosnia-Hercegovina and Macedonia to follow suit. Even Borisav Jović considered that "there was no political force which was able to stop the wave of feeling in Croatia and Slovenia for independence, which for certain national reasons was joined by Muslims in Bosnia-Hercegovina and Macedonians."[37] The quotation suggests that the Serbian leadership had come to the conclusion that the dissolution of Yugoslavia could not be avoided. What is less certain from the available documentary record is how Milošević planned to navigate the dissolution.

There can be little doubt by now that Milošević never intended to seriously resist the independence of Slovenia. American ambassador Warren Zimmermann cabled the U.S. State Department in May 1991 with the analysis that "he [Milošević] was trying to drive the Slovenes out of Yugoslavia so he could deal with a Croatia shorn of allies."[38] Zimmerman's political attaché, Louis Sell, went further in his analysis, surmising an alliance between Serbia and Slovenia by which Slovenia would receive a clear path to independence in exchange for Serbia's receiving political cover to try to establish new borders for Yugoslavia in Croatia:

> On 24 January [1991], the tacit Serb-Slovene alliance became explicit. After Kučan met Milošević in Belgrade, the two republics issued a joint statement asserting that self-determination should be respected for all nations in Yugoslavia. Serbia acknowledged the right of the Slovene people to follow their own path. Slovenia conceded that Yugoslavia should respect the right of the Serbian nation to live in one state. The import of the agreement was clear. Milošević announced his readiness to let Slovenia leave Yugoslavia, while the Slovenes gave Milošević carte blanche to create a Greater Serbia out of the wreckage.[39]

As Dejan Jović argues, at this point Milošević had decided not to oppose Slovenian independence with force, perceiving instead that "it was necessary to establish a border between Serbs and others, and to do that in Croatia."[40] Sell shares this assessment, arguing that in June 1991, after Slovenia's declaration of independence, Milošević and the Serbian leadership advocated that the JNA "conduct a redeployment of the military along the new Serbian borders of Yugoslavia."[41] It is also clear the Serbian leadership took no action by way of trying to prevent the independence of Macedonia.

At this point it is not entirely clear from the documentary record whether, as Sell and others argue, Milošević had decided to let Yugoslavia dissolve and try to "create a Greater Serbia out of the wreckage,"[42] or whether, as Dejan Jović and others argue, a plan had developed to form a third Yugoslavia without Slovenia and Croatia.[43] The key to determining which view is correct might lie in determining how Milošević envisioned the future of Bosnia-Hercegovina. If the policy was to assemble a new federation including Serbia, Montenegro, and whatever parts of Croatia could be conquered, this federation would have to include Bosnia-Hercegovina. If the plan was to abandon projects of federation in favor of a Greater Serbia, the project would have to involve some type of partition of Bosnia-Hercegovina, without which Greater Serbia could not be territorially contiguous.

On this point the available evidence seems contradictory, and no authoritative source has been published that would allow the contradictions to be resolved. At the same time, the possibility has to be entertained that there was no plan and that independent actors were instead actively creating facts on the ground that would make any plans for a smaller Yugoslav federation untenable. It would be possible to interpret the 1990 elections in Bosnia-Hercegovina, in which the three main nationalist parties—HDZ, SDS, and SDA—on the basis of a preelection power-sharing agreement engaged in vote sharing and held joint campaign events[44] as preparation for a patronage-based distribution of power in a new federation. At the same time, Adil Zulfikarpašić claims to have had knowledge as early as 1991 regarding military and police preparations for war, including the selective distribution of arms to villages, plans for the division of territory, and plans for local police forces to come under the command of the military.[45]

Zulfikarpašić offers the perception that just as it was in Serbia's interest to allow the independence of Slovenia in order to have a free hand in Croatia, it was in Croatia's interest to encourage the expansion of the war to Bosnia-Hercegovina so as to spread Serbia's forces along another front: "When the war began in Croatia, Croatian policy and Croatian politicians wanted to bring Bosnia into the conflict by any means, so as to ease their fight with the Serbs and so as to gain an ally . . ."[46] There is also ample evidence that Serbia had been preparing for war in Bosnia-Hercegovina, arranging military equipment and personnel to be ready to move when the time came. This would seem to indicate that as far as Milošević was concerned, no new federations including Bosnia-Hercegovina were being considered. Slobodan Antonić argues that in 1990 and 1991 Milošević expressly rejected the various confederation plans that had been proposed and that this was also the consensus in Serbian public opinion, as was expressed by both SPO and UJDI.[47]

On the other hand, there has been widespread speculation that at a secret meeting at Karadjordjevo in March 1991, Presidents Milošević and Tudjman had agreed on a partition of Bosnia-Hercegovina by which some territorial aspirations of Serbia would be satisfied; Croatia would realize its claim to western Hercegovina; and presumably some kind of concession might be made to accommodate Bosnian Muslims. Louis Sell seems certain that he has knowledge of such an arrangement: "By reiterating that Yugoslavia's republican borders were purely administrative and subject to change, Milošević made it clear that he still intended to carve up Croatia. Milošević also noted expansively that he would have no objection if the Croatian population in the Bosnian region of Hercegovina joined Croatia, revealing that the division of Bosnia, which he and Tudjman had already discussed on at least two occasions, remained very much on his mind."[48] Some potential indirect confirmation of the thesis has also come through testimony before ICTY on the part of former Yugoslav Prime Minister Ante Marković[49] and former Croatian Defense Minister Petar Kriste,[50] both of whom testified that they had knowledge of the meeting. Assertions of secondhand knowledge as a part of witness testimony hardly offer a basis for firm conclusions, however. If the war in Bosnia-Hercegovina was the result of an agreement on territorial division that was reached in advance, some documentary evidence should be expected, whether this evidence is in the form of notes, protocols, or maps. Although it might be said projectively that the "Karadjordjevo agreement" is probable, the existence of this agreement has yet to be established as fact.

All the same, it is evident that none of the efforts to produce a federal or confederal agreement to prevent the dissolution of Yugoslavia in 1991 made any serious headway. Although some of the actors in the final rounds of negotiations, such as Adil Zulfikarpašić, continued to express the belief that such proposals represented a final hope, most contemporary observers consider that such plans were never taken seriously, neither by political and military actors nor in public opinion. Zulfikarpašić himself notes that Alija Izetbegović was compelled by hostile public opinion to abandon his federation proposal almost immediately upon presenting it.[51] The last effort at negotiating a smaller Yugoslav confederation was led by Zulfikarpašić, but perhaps the best summary of its fate was offered by Nadežda Gaće, who interviewed Zulfikarpašić for his memoir:

> The process around this agreement lasted, or rather was kicked around, for two months. There will be an agreement—there will not be one. And at the end all that was really left of it was a document which you [Zulfikarpašić] prepared. It could be said that the responsibility for the failure to sign the agreement rests, after all, with Alija Izetbegović. You were then simply, in a way, lynched. Again you were accused of working against the interest of Muslims. I must say that the Belgrade opposition did not welcome that agreement either, because they thought, or at least the opposition leaders stated as much, that you were helping Milošević to survive. You were not well received by the Croatian government or the Croatian opposition either . . .[52]

By the middle of 1991, it seems clear that no powerful political actor in Yugoslavia saw a tenable future in any federal or confederal arrangement. For the republics that had by then set independence as a goal, any retreat from independence seemed to carry unbearable risks of domination by Serbia. Meanwhile the Serbian political leadership appeared certain enough of its ability to call on overwhelming military force to achieve its goals that negotiated agreements offered lesser potential gains than imposed resolutions might.

Inattention and Confusion of International Powers

In the context created by the demise of the Soviet empire in 1989, there does not seem to have existed a consensus on the part of the United States and the countries of the European Union with regard to how new crises in Europe ought to have been approached. It may well have been the case that these international political actors did not anticipate the dissolution of Yugoslavia and that domestic actors put excessive stock in the importance and prestige of Yugoslavia. The Croatian General Janko Bobetko suggests as much in wondering why Milošević did not act earlier than he did against the political rise of Tudjman in Croatia:

> Now the question might be asked: why did the Greater Serbian oligarchy not react immediately to the program and founding of the Croatian Democratic Union, since it had the power and all of the means to use it had already been worked out in their plans? I think that they were overconfident, since they had at their disposal all of the military and economic potential of the former Yugoslavia. They had inherited considerable political prestige, which Josip Broz had affirmed earlier through the nonaligned movement, and that combined with the tolerance of both blocs—the North Atlantic Alliance with America, and the Warsaw Pact led by the

Soviet Union. In that system the territory of Yugoslavia was treated as a buffer zone, which was in the interest of both blocs, and even now many countries have not diplomatically abandoned the idea of restoration, in some way, of some kind of Yugoslavia, maybe in a smaller form.[53]

This overconfidence related particularly to the anticipated engagement of the United States. Cohen argues that Milošević perceived that the United States was not likely to intervene to prevent the imposition of central control and that therefore "he could ignore with impunity criticism of his meddling in the affairs of the Yugoslav federation and its various republics."[54] Such a perception appears to have been confirmed by the visit of U.S. Secretary of State James Baker in 1991.[55]

To the degree that the Serbian leadership was confident of having a free hand to impose a solution, they may have not taken seriously the state of public opinion in the United States and Europe in the immediate aftermath of the Cold War. Susan Woodward notes "the general euphoria and self-confidence in the West, based on the belief that the peace dividend and economic interests would define the next period of global order."[56] In this context

> The judgment of most Western observers, including members of the US Congress . . . was still under the influence of Cold War anti-Communism: anyone who opposed the Communist Party and Communist leaders was, by definition, to be supported. The revolutionary transition in Eastern Europe during 1990–91 was being driven by alliances of longtime Western and relatively new Eastern anti-Communist crusaders who created an atmosphere of revenge and retribution against anyone with connections to the former regimes. On the basis of the stated objective of ridding Eastern Europe of the last remnants of Soviet influence, they in fact displayed a cavalier attitude toward human rights and due process. In the Yugoslav case, this was manifest in a tendency to judge events as described by the new Slovene and Croatian governments, whose ex-Communist leaders skillfully portrayed their election results as a victory for democrats in reaction to Communist dictators in Belgrade . . .[57]

Countering the inclination of international powers to resist border changes and the formation of new states, the environment immediately after the end of the Cold War produced an incipient inclination toward wary treatment of claims based on the status quo, on which the Serbian political leadership relied.[58]

In retrospect it appears that Milošević's confidence that outside actors would offer him a free hand was in fact overconfidence and that he did not consider the degree to which anti-Communist sentiment, public response to the violence of the wars, and lack of support for war in Serbian public opinion would stand in the way of his plans. In the analysis of Slobodan Antonić:

> Milošević, however, wrongly assessed not only the power of the Yugoslav People's Army and the willingness of Serbian citizens to participate in war, but also the position of various foreign factors (above all the US and the European Community) toward a military resolution of the Yugoslav problem. He was convinced that the

army was so strong and that Serbs were so eager to fight, that Slovenia's and Croatia's secession would be crushed within two or three days. He was also sure that the US and Europe would grumble at first, but in the end, would nevertheless accept a military solution, since they strongly supported a united Yugoslavia. That is why his attitude was so self-confident and arrogant, and that is why he threatened and was uncompromising in negotiations, practically rushing into war.[59]

Such an argument is indirectly supported by Kadijević, who cites "the failure of mobilization and desertion"[60] as reasons for the failure of the JNA's strategy in Croatia.

It appears that Milošević's anticipation that international powers and organizations would acquiesce in his efforts to impose new borders for a state centered on Serbia was not shared by the military leadership. Kadijević, in his memoir, details a belief that an international conspiracy led by Germany and the United States had a long-term interest in the dissolution of Yugoslavia, by means of which Germany would be positioned to take on the role of global power that had been abdicated by the Soviet Union.[61] A similar geopolitical assessment appears incidentally in the memoirs of Borisav Jović,[62] although he does not concern himself extensively with international actors. It is difficult to assess the degree to which the global conspiracy view actually directed policy, as opposed to being produced primarily for public consumption. The theory is so riddled with internal contradictions (for example, if U.S. policy-makers were genuinely sympathetic to Germany, why would they be trying to make Germany their principal rival?) that it is difficult to imagine it as a serious foundation for policy. On the other hand, much might be accounted for by Hadžić's observation that "[u]ninterrupted engagement in ideological and security policy resulted in a military ignorance of reality."[63] At the same time, it would probably not be possible to overestimate the publicity value of conspiracy theories in the sense that they operate to displace responsibility for failure from concrete actors and onto forces that are by definition unknown.

Conclusions

One of the key questions with regard to the development of Milošević's policy is whether at some point in the period 1990–91 he abandoned the goal of reorganizing Yugoslavia along the lines of a strengthened federation and opted instead to apply military power in order to achieve a larger state centered on Serbia. Although there is no room for doubt that he acted from 1991 onward in ways that appeared altogether consistent with this second goal, there is little definitive evidence to suggest that the goal was ever articulated or that the steps along the way were planned. This is of course not definitive; in the memorable words of the U.S. defense secretary Donald Rumsfeld, "absence of evidence is not evidence of absence."[64] The sorts of plans that would have been necessary in order to create a new state out of the territory of existing states would have to have been developed in secret, and it remains possible that documentary evidence of such plans could become available in the future.

Nonetheless, at this point it seems more probable that the Serbian leadership found itself at a loss with the failure of its project to reorganize the Yugoslav federation and that its efforts to force the issue had fundamental consequences for the legitimacy and the continued existence of the federation. Simply put, the tactics Milošević employed to try to force a resolution got out of his control. When this state was reached, the Serbian leadership's fear of the consequences of losing power combined with their confidence in the support of the armed forces to push them toward increasingly drastic violence. Though he is often portrayed as a rider of the Apocalypse, Milošević may have been an immobile Trojan horse. This could account for what appears to be the incoherence of Serbian policy from 1991 on. As Lenard Cohen observes, although his "plans were similar to historical goals advanced by earlier Serbian politicians of creating an expansive 'Greater Serbia,' Milošević's political calculations appeared to have little basis in any particular historical scheme."[65]

Milošević came to power on a program that was, by the standards of Serbian politics in the 1980s, fairly conventional—the controversial element mostly involved the use of police violence to suppress demonstrations in Kosovo. A marked incapacity to reach agreements led to a spiraling crisis of legitimacy that insecurity about power and security about the loyalty of the armed forces carried to the point of violent dissolution of the country. There was no long-term political vision, nationalistic or otherwise. He was carried by events. He was sure of his ability to use force. And he did not know what he was getting into.

Notes

1. Formally, the Federal Executive Council (SIV) continued to exist after the events listed here, and Ante Marković continued to hold the post of prime minister until he resigned on December 20, 1991. The reason for Marković's relatively long tenure in office after the dissolution of the federation might simply be that the federal parliament, the only body that would have the authority to remove him from office, was not able to do so.
2. This point is made clearly by Dejan Jović in *Jugoslavija: Država koja je odumrla: Uspon, kriza i pad četvrte Jugoslavije* (Zagreb: Prometej and Beograd: Samizdat B92, 2003). However, in his memoirs on his negotiations with Milošević, Hrvoje Šarinić, *Svi moji tajni pregovori sa Slobodanom Miloševićem: Izmedju rata i diplomacije 1993–95 (98)* (Zagreb: Globus, 1999) claims that the goal of partitioning Bosnia-Hercegovina between Serbia and Croatia was raised many times privately.
3. Dejan Jović, pp. 370–376.
4. Dejan Jović, p. 376. All translations are by the author.
5. Lenard J. Cohen, *Serpent in the Bosom: The Rise and Fall of Slobodan Milošević* (Boulder, CO: Westview, 2001), pp. 53, 65.
6. Cohen, 2001, p. 67.
7. Louis Sell, *Slobodan Milošević and the Destruction of Yugoslavia* (Durham: Duke University Press, 2002), p. 112.
8. Dejan Jović, 2003, p. 76.
9. Dejan Jović, 2003, p. 396.
10. Sell, 2002, p. 108.
11. Warren Zimmermann, *Origins of a Catastrophe* (New York: Times Books, 1995), p. 125.

12. Dejan Jović, 2003, p. 458.
13. Cited in Dejan Jović, 2003, pp. 463, 464.
14. Veljko Kadijević, *Moje vidjenje raspada: Vojska bez države* (Belgrade: Politika, 1993), p. 104.
15. Kadijević, 1993, pp. 104–105.
16. Dejan Jović, 2003, p. 481.
17. On the question of legitimacy in post-1945 Yugoslavia generally, see the succinct presentation by John B. Allcock, *Explaining Yugoslavia* (New York: Columbia University Press, 2000), pp. 417–431.
18. Ana Dević, "Anti-War Initiatives and the Un-Making of Civic Identities in the Former Yugoslav Republics," *The Journal of Historical* Sociology, Vol. 10, No. 2 (June 1997), pp. 127–157.
19. Lino Veljak, "The Collapse and Reconstruction of Legitimacy: An Introductory Remark," in Aleksandar Pavković (ed.), *The Disintegration of Yugoslavia: Inevitable or Avoidable?* Special issue of *Nationalities Papers*, Vol. 25, No. 3 (1997), pp. 443–454 and 447–448.
20. Zoran Slavujević, "Borba za vlast u Srbiji kroz prizmu izbornih kampanja," in Vladimir Goati, Zoran Slavujević, and Ognjen Pribićević (eds.), *Izborne borbe u Jugoslaviji 1990–1992* (Belgrade: Radnička stampa, 1993), p. 73.
21. Dejan Jović, 2003, p. 466.
22. Kadijević, 1993, p. 113.
23. Borisav Jović, *Knjiga o Miloševiću* (Belgrade: IKP "Nikola Pašić," 2001), p. 62.
24. Miroslav Hadžić, "Armijska upotreba trauma," in Nebojša Popov (ed.) *Srpska strana rata: Trauma i katarza u istorijskom pamćenju* (Belgrade: Republika, 1996), pp. 558–580, 559.
25. Kadijević, 1993, pp. 106–107.
26. Kadijević, 1993, p. 38. As federal minister of defence, Kadijević was himself a member of the Federal Executive Council.
27. Kadijević, 1993, p. 6.
28. Kadijević, 1993, pp. 10–34.
29. Kadijević, 1993, pp. 57–58, 108.
30. Kadijević, 1993, p. 37.
31. Kadijević, 1993, p. 120, fn7.
32. Kadijević, 1993, p. 114.
33. Hadžić, 1996, p. 579.
34. Borisav Jović, 2001, p. 63.
35. Borisav Jović, 2001, pp. 66–69.
36. Ivan Šiber, "The Impact of Nationalism, Values, and Ideological Orientations on Multi-Party Elections in Croatia," in Jim Seroka and Vukašin Pavlović (eds.), *The Tragedy of Yugoslavia: The Failure of Democratic Transformation* (London: ME Sharpe, 1992), pp. 141–172, presents survey evidence from the time of the Croatian elections of 1990 indicating that Croatian autonomy was not among the top concerns of voters in the elections and that independence from Yugoslavia was not the dominant preference of the supporters of any major political party, including HDZ (1992, p. 154). Any change in the subsequent state of public opinion had to be the result of subsequent events.
37. Borisav Jović, 2001, p. 71.
38. Zimmerman, 1995, p. 125.
39. Sell, 2002, p. 128.
40. Dejan Jović, 2003, p. 478.
41. Sell, 2002, p. 145.
42. Sell, 2002, p. 128.

43. Dejan Jović, 2003, p. 478.
44. Described in Nadežda Gaće and Milovan Djilas, *Bošnjak: Adil Zulfikarpašić* (2nd edition) (Zurich: Bosnjački Institut, 1995), pp. 165–167.
45. Gaće and Djilas, 1995, pp. 156–58.
46. Gaće and Djilas, 1995, p. 183.
47. Slobodan Antonić, "Could a Confederation Have Saved Yugoslavia?" in Aleksandar Pavković (ed.), *The Disintegration of Yugoslavia: Inevitable or Avoidable?* Special issue of *Nationalities Papers*, Vol. 25, No. 3 (1997), pp. 469–479, 472.
48. Sell, 2002, p. 146.
49. Ante Marković gave his testimony on October 23, 2003. The portions of his testimony that were given in public session are available at the ICTY web site at: http://www.un.org/icty/transe54/031023ED.htm.
50. Petar Kriste gave his testimony on January 27, 2003. The transcript is available at the ICTY web site at http://www.un.org/icty/transe54/030127ED.htm.
51. Zulfikarpašić, 1995, p. 184.
52. Gaće and Djilas, 1995, p. 197.
53. Janko Bobetko, *Sve moje bitke* (Zagreb: self-published, 1996), p. 183.
54. Cohen, 2001, p. 143.
55. Susan L. Woodward, "International Aspects of the Wars in Former Yugoslavia," in Jasminka Udovički and James Ridgeway (eds.), *Burn This House: The Making and Unmaking of Yugoslavia* (Durham: Duke University Press, 1997), pp. 220–221.
56. Woodward, 1997, p. 216.
57. Woodward, 1997, pp. 217–18.
58. Borisav Jović, 2001, pp. 70–81.
59. Antonić, 1997, pp. 474–75. The characterization of Milošević's policy by Antonić is drawn from Milošević's address to municipal assembly presidents on March 16, 1991.
60. Kadijević, 1993, p. 142.
61. Kadijević, 1993, pp. 6–17, 10, 17, 25, 26, 30, 34, 35–36.
62. Borisav Jović, 2001, pp. 70–81.
63. Hadžić, 1996, p. 567.
64. Press conference at NATO Headquarters, Brussels (Belgium), June 6, 2002. The statement is quoted in Chalmers A. Johnson, *The Sorrows of Empire: Militarism, Secrecy and the End of the Republic* (New York: Owl Books, 2005), p. 230. Rumsfeld was referring to the lack of evidence to support the contention that Iraq had been developing large stocks of weapons of mass destruction, which was the principal pretext for the U.S. invasion of Iraq in 2003.
65. Cohen, 2001, p. 142.

The Role of the Yugoslav People's Army in the Dissolution of Yugoslavia: The Army without a State?

❖ Florian Bieber ❖

*The Yugoslav Army defeated Yugoslavia more heavily than all
the national leaders, their militia, their volunteers and their national guards put together. It could not, however, have brought
victory to anyone, least of all to itself.*
—Stojan Cerović, 1991

*. . . [the] JNA . . . became an army without a state, which is a
unique case in the world.*
—Veljko Kadijević, 1993

Introduction

Looking back on the dissolution of Yugoslavia and the failure of the army to preserve the country, Yugoslavia's last minister of defense,[1] Veljko Kadijević, noted that
"[n]o purely military measures can be successful against a policy, unless they are
means in the hands of another policy. The other, Yugoslav policy did not exist, it
was confused, contradictory and paralyzed."[2] Indeed, the Yugoslav People's Army
(*Jugoslovenska Narodna Armija*, JNA) in the last years of Yugoslavia's existence suffered from inherent contradictions between viewing its primary role as preserving
Yugoslavia and at the same time seeking radical unilateral changes to the system that
were incompatible with the reform debates that shaped the late 1980s. The alliance
that eventually transformed the JNA into a partner, albeit never fully in line, of the
Milošević government, was neither a foregone conclusion nor based primarily on
any "ethnic" ties.

This chapter follows the transformation of the JNA in the years preceding the
dissolution of Yugoslavia and seeks to explore why and how it became associated
with the Serbian side in the dissolution process. It will seek to challenge simplistic

explanations for the army's support for the Serbian side in the conflict, such as the disproportionately high share of Serbs in the army. Instead, it will examine the institutional interests of the army and its loss of ideological orientation. Here in particular, a comparison with other federal institutions and their position during the dissolution process is necessary. Additional attention will be paid to the problem of the army's disintegration in terms of the recruitment crisis prior to and during the early phases of the war. In understanding the relationship between the army and Milošević, it is also crucial to address the clear distrust displayed by the regime toward the army, as exemplified by frequent purges in the army and the militarization of the police force during the 1990s. The key argument of the chapter is that it was the weakness of the army, both ideologically and structurally within the late Yugoslav system, that facilitated its support for Serbia during the conflict.

The Structure and Role of the Army after Tito's Death

The Yugoslav People's Army emerged together with the Communist Party of Yugoslavia as the key victorious force from World War II. The Partisan victory constituted a founding myth that bestowed upon the army a degree of legitimacy that none of the armies of other Communist countries enjoyed, with the exception of the Soviet Red Army. Although originally not highly professionalized and with little continuity to the prewar Yugoslav army, the Partisan forces rapidly transformed into a regular army modeled on that of the other socialist armies in Eastern Europe.[3]

During the Titoist era, the army was formally highly independent but in fact closely associated with the League of Communists and controlled by the Party. The Yugoslav army had been inherently political, shaped by the development of the League of Communists and being both a powerful symbol and key domestic actor. This symbolic importance of the army, based on the Partisan war, was carefully cultivated by official and popular culture. The symbolic foundation empowered the lobby of former Partisan generals within the armed forces and advanced the militarization of society in the educational system and other spheres.[4]

While generally tasked with the defense of the country from outside, important in the face of tensions with Italy in the immediate postwar period and after 1948 with the Soviet Union, the army constituted a key support to the regime domestically.[5] Generally, the army exercised this role on behalf of the Party and state and not as independent actor. However, considering that most of the key conflicts in Socialist Yugoslavia took place within the Party, it often took sides within the Party. Due to the dominant role of Josip Broz Tito, the army's key alliance was with the life-time President and Marshal of Yugoslavia. The army thus came to act with greater autonomy in times of crisis when its support for Tito helped stabilize the regime. The army played a decisive role in supporting Tito during three key episodes in postwar Yugoslavia: during the break with the Soviet Union (1948), over the removal of Aleksandar Ranković (1966), and in the purge of the Croatian party leadership

(1971).[6] The support in the removal of Ranković had been particularly significant because the minister of defense, Ivan Gošnjak (1953–1967), had been a key ally of Ranković, with whom he had opposed political reforms.[7] By 1971, a majority of officers perceived the main threat to originate from nationalism rather than from external aggression. When Tito opted for the suppression of the Croatian Spring and the dismissal of the leadership of the Croatian League of Communists, the army allied itself with the suppression of the both liberal and nationalist movement in Croatia, which had begun to challenge the party's dominance. For the first time, the veterans' organizations had also become a key tool to reassert control in Croatia. Following the purges in Croatia, Tito invoked in several speeches the domestic role of the armed forces, emphasizing that "our army must not merely watch vigilantly over our borders but must also be present inside the country."[8] At the same time, the influence of the army came to be seen as being too great.

Later on, Tito would note that "the chief guardian of the achievements of our revolution should be the League of Communists, not our army."[9] The army did not use its force to assert its influence autonomously but, rather, stabilized Tito in crucial moments by leaving no doubt about its loyalty. This domestic support was recognized by Tito, who pointed to the internal importance of the JNA: "our army is also called upon to defend the achievements of our revolution within the country, should that become necessary."[10]

The combination of the domestic use of the armed forces and the absence of an autonomous political identity would come back to shape the behavior of the JNA in the late 1980s. Anticipating the inability of the army to play the role of "savior" from the collapse of the country in the late 1980s and early 1990s, the leading Croat Communist functionary Vladimir Bakarić noted in an interview with a German newspaper in the early 1970s that Tito's authority was so great that nobody in Yugoslavia could inherit it, not even the army.[11]

A specificity of the Yugoslav army was its high degree of formal autonomy. The JNA had elements of sovereignty and its own legal system. Until the 1980s, the budget was linked to the national income, not the GDP. In addition to its source of budgetary funding, the army controlled a large sector of the economy through the armament industry and ran its own foreign trade.[12] In addition, it set the command language and sent its own deputies to party congresses and assemblies of the republics and the federation. In educational and social terms, the army also maintained a distinct health and educational system apart from the rest of society. The control of the army on the other hand was formally limited. The minister of defense was always a career officer, formally a member of the government, and an ex-officio nonvoting member of the presidency, proposed by the prime minister[13] to parliament but in reality chosen by a collegium of senior generals. The ministry of defense was thus under control of the army, and not the army under civilian control.[14] There is little doubt, however, that the formal autonomy of the army was held in check by the League of Communists, who effectively constituted the only source of political authority for the army. The choice of the minister of defense and high-ranking personnel decisions in the army would not be made without Party consent. In addition, the minister of defense would traditionally be a member of the Central Committee of the League of Communists. Nevertheless, the army operated largely separately from civilian structures and institutions. This considerable autonomy, in the words of the political scientist Miroslav Hadžić, gave rise to "autarchic tendencies as shown by the top generals' strivings to become functionally detached from society."[15]

The increased decentralization of the state starting in the mid-1960s affected the army despite its high degree of autonomy. In response to the Soviet invasion of Czechoslovakia in 1968, Yugoslavia established republic- and province-based territorial defense (*Teritorijalna odbrana*, TO). Formally, these units together with the JNA constituted the defense system of Yugoslavia, but factually they remained weak in terms of equipment and manpower. The territorial defense units were not only following the boundaries of the republics and provinces but operated in the language of the respective republic (or province) and had commanders from the same republic or province. The leadership of the JNA held a critical view of the territorial defense units, seeing them as a competition to the army's established dominance and as embryonic republican armies that might undermine the state. As such, the JNA sought to curb the independence of these units in the 1980s, well before the conflict between the republics and provinces escalated, with the army attempting to disarm the territorial defense in 1990–91. The Kosovo TO was already disarmed in the aftermath of the March 1981 riots, and by the mid-1980s, Secretary of Defense Branko Mamula established greater control over the units throughout the country. The 1974 Constitution also complicated the command structure of the JNA itself and gave rise to the operational organization of the armed forces following republican lines, as will be discussed later. The decentralization enhanced the importance of the army's intelligence agency, the Counterintelligence Service (*Kontraobaveštajna služba*, KOS) because the State Security Service (*Služba državne bezbednosti*, SDB) had been decentralized along republican and provincial lines.[16]

In addition to the structural impact of decentralization that shaped the JNA, the political and ideological consequences were probably even more significant. In general, the army, especially the higher ranks, was more Yugoslav in orientation with more dogmatic understanding of socialism than the rest of the party. This is due to structural reasons, such as extraterritorial stationing, greater mobility within Yugoslavia, as well as due to historical reasons that linked the army to the Partisan forces and the conservative and authoritarian structure of armies in general. The JNA did not have political officers who ensured the ideological dogma of the armed forces, but the League of Communists of Yugoslavia maintained a separate Organization of the League of Communists in the JNA (*Organizacija SKJ-a u JNA*, OSKJ), which was for obvious reasons influential in the army. The separate army organization was not established to ensure party control but, rather, as a consequence of the decentralization of the party that saw the establishment of separate organizations for each republic. Because the League of Communists of Yugoslavia thus became the association of the republican parties and the republican parties did not provide for an adequate structural home for party members in the army who were not necessarily linked to any particular republic, the army organization of the League of Communists was established. The OSKJ generally constituted part of the conservative grouping of party organizations during the reform debates of the 1980s. Within the overall party, the army organization was not particularly important numerically. In 1977 some 6 percent (97,424) of the total party membership was active in the army or police,[17] whereas in 1988 the OSKJ had some 76,000 members. However, this arrangement enabled the army to participate in all party structures and enabled members of OSKJ to formulate and express the army's position. In fact, the creation of the separate army organization resulted in a process that occurred as a consequence of the decentralization of the League of Communists from a Yugoslav party that expressed countrywide policies with some regional variations to a "transmission belt" between republics (and provinces) and the federal structures, and ultimately to an eventual "voice" of the republics. As such, the OSKJ was less and less the reflection of the Party's voice within the army but the army's voice in the Party. Nevertheless, the influence of the Party in the army, in turn, is obvious when considering the number of Party members at different levels in the army hierarchy. While only 12 percent of soldiers and cadets and 24 percent of the young officers belonged to the Party, 31 percent of the overall officers and 33 percent of the civilian staff were Party members.[18]

Other key political and social channels of communication of the army were the veterans' organization, the Federal League of World War II Veterans (SUBNOR), and other civilian organizations with close links to the JNA, such as the Alliance of Reserve Army Officers (SRVS), the newspapers and magazines it published (e.g., *Narodna armija*), and the representation it enjoyed in parliament and government at all levels.[19]

The Numbers Game: Ethnicity in the Army

A core controversy during the late 1980s, as well as in the ensuing literature on the role of the army in the dissolution of Yugoslavia, has been the ethnic composition of the officer corps of the army and its implications for the JNA support for Milošević. Although originally composed of the Partisan forces, the new Yugoslavia soon strove to build up a representative army. The multiethnic nature of the army was not only key in the general effort to structure Yugoslavia as an inclusive state but also based on the experience of the Royal Yugoslav army, which lacked legitimacy because it was viewed by non-Serbs as being dominated by Serb officers.[20]

The 1974 Constitution enshrined the principle of proportional representation in the high army ranks, drawing on earlier attempts to ensure the army's representativeness of Yugoslavia's population. Article 242 of the constitution required that "the composition of the strategic staff and the employment in the high command and leadership functions in the Yugoslav People's Army has to ensure the proportional representation of republics and autonomous provinces."[21] While this regulation did not stipulate strict proportional representation, it followed the concept of the "ethnic key" that pertained at other levels of state and party offices, in particular in Bosnia-Herzegovina. Measures taken to ensure the representativeness of the army included the introduction of national and republican quotas in military schools. In addition, within the republican quotas, the respective majorities had priority over minorities, which in effect confirmed the "national" nature of the republics and sought to counter the overrepresentation of Serbs from Bosnia and Croatia in the army in particular.[22]

Despite these measures to broaden the army's base, Serbs, Montenegrins, and Yugoslavs continued to be grossly overrepresented in the officer corps, whereas officers from most other nations made up a part smaller to their share of the population (see Table 1). At the time of Tito's death in 1980, the command of the JNA was dominated by Serbs, including the minister of defense, chief of the armed forces, and the secretary of the LCY committee in the JNA.[23] The mismatch is further visible when comparing the distribution of officers and recruits. Among recruits, nations with a relatively young population structure (Albanians, Muslims) constituted a share exceeding their overall percentage in the population. This meant that two of the most underrepresented nations among officers constituted a disproportionately large share of the total number of recruits, pointing to a source of tension that increased during the 1990s and also impaired the use of the army during a domestic conflict. The disproportional distribution among officers in general has to be further differentiated, particularly in light of the constitutional requirement of proportional-

Table 1: Representation of the main nations and nationalities of Yugoslavia in the general population and the armed forces (in percentages)[24]

Nations	In Yugoslavia (1981)	In Active Army Staff (1985)	Among Officers (1981)	Among Recruits (1989)
Serbs	39.7	57.17	60.0	31
Croats	22.1	12.51	12.6	18.52
Yugoslavs	1.3	n.a.	6.7	7
Macedonians	5.81	6.74	6.3	6.11
Montenegrins	2.5	5.82	6.2	2.48
Slovenes	8.2	2.64	2.8	7
Muslims	8.4	3.65	2.4	12.00
Hungarians	2.3	n.a.	0.7	1
Albanians	6.4	1.09	0.6	9
Others	3.3	n.a.	1.6	6

ity that clearly does not refer to all officers but only to the highest ranks. As a result, the representation of different nations in the highest ranks followed more closely the population census than in the officer corps in general. For example, generals from Slovenia fully reflected the population share, whereas Slovenes remained considerably underrepresented in other ranks, as can be seen in Table 2.

The overrepresentation of some nations in the army has a multitude of causes but was the consequence of structural reasons rather than deliberate policy. Only with the imminent outbreak of the war could a pattern of discrimination of staff along national lines be noted. The national composition of the army can be explained by a variety of factors, often with different emphasis dependent on the perspective. Socioeconomic explanations suggest that families from regions with higher unemployment and lower salary levels were more likely to encourage men to choose a career in the army than did those from more prosperous regions in the country. Individual reasons for choosing military careers, including the social and economic origin of the particular family, are particularly important.[26] As Moris Janowitz argues in his study of army recruitment patterns in the developing world, the "military establishment has its social origins among the rural middle and lower middle classes."[27] The socio-economic bias of army recruitment is thus a phenomenon at work with professional militaries elsewhere around the world.[28] Here, the goal of proportionality conflicted with the army's policy to favor career soldiers from modest origins and with a workers' and farmers' background.[29] Reducing the discrepancies in the army composition through socioeconomic factors might be satisfactory to explain the variation between Slovenes, Croats, and Serbs from Croatia. However, it fails to explain the overrepresentation of Serbs over Muslims, Macedonians, or Albanians, equally prone to hail from the lower strata of society. Here other reasons need to be

Table 2: Ethnic distribution among higher ranks of the JNA[25]

Nations	Generals	in %	Colonels	in %	Lieutenant-Colonels	in %	Majors	in %
Montenegrins	19	12.4	257	11.0	411	6.7	225	6.4
Croats	22	14.4	219	9.4	661	10.8	364	10.4
Macedonians	12	7.8	103	4.4	394	6.4	236	6.7
Muslims	3	2.0	28	1.2	109	1.8	82	2.3
Slovenes	12	7.8	72	3.1	142	2.3	68	1.9
Serbs	77	50.3	1,511	64.5	3,896	63.5	2,102	60.0
Albanians	1	0.7	5	0.2	15	0.2	8	0.2
Hungarians	—	—	6	0.3	15	0.2	14	0.4
Yugoslavs	7	4.6	123	5.3	422	6.9	360	10.3
Others	—	—	18	0.8	73	1.3	46	1.3
Total	153		2,342		6,138		3,505	

considered. Other arguments place greater emphasis on cultural reasons, including higher respect for and prestige of the armed forces and military service and careers in some parts of Yugoslavia, such as in the Krajina region of Croatia and in rural Serbia. Arguments include less credible cultural and historical references, such as the legacy of the *vojna krajina*, which brought with it a history of militarization in the regions of Croatia along the Bosnia border. More relevant is the Partisan legacy of the armed forces and the fact that a disproportionately large number of Serbs from Croatia and Bosnia partook in the Partisan forces, which reflected itself in the officer corps during the period of Socialist Yugoslavia. Thus, the number of Serb generals oscillated between 38.1 percent (1953–54) and 46.6 percent (1969) in Socialist Yugoslavia, but Serbia as a republic remained underrepresented among generals with only 13.98 percent being from Serbia in 1970, increasing to 28.47 percent by 1980. On the other hand, the republics that saw most Partisan warfare during World War II, Croatia, Montenegro, and Bosnia, accounted for the overwhelming number of generals: in 1970, 39.07 percent (1980: 30.56 percent) of generals came from Croatia, 17.2 percent (1980: 11.11 percent) from Montenegro, and 17.56 percent (1980: 15.28 percent) from Bosnia.[30] The national distribution thus needs to be viewed in connection with the republican distribution. Efforts to make the army more representative thus focused not exclusively on the national background of the officers but also on the republic of origin.

By the 1980s, the unwillingness of the army to reform itself had also become an increasing reason for the reluctance of many to join the armed forces, in particular in Slovenia, where the army became increasingly subject to criticism by the vibrant civil society.[31] The overrepresentation of Serbs, in particular from Croatia, cannot be reduced to a single explanation but is instead the result of a complex set of reasons, including socioeconomic factors, social prestige, and association with Yugoslavia, as well as the legacy of the Partisan war. Unlike in other spheres of public authority, the principle of proportionality is more difficult to implement in the armed forces. The hierarchical nature of the institution and it reliance on long-term ascent through the ranks rendered any attempt to construct a representative army leadership a long-term project at best.

Generally speaking, the ethnic distribution should not lead to conclusions about the behavior or political orientation of the army. The party did not perceive itself as being biased toward one particular nation, and most of its staff, especially among its higher echelons, identified more strongly with Yugoslavia as a whole than with particular nations or republics. Only once the dissolution began, as will be discussed later, did the national composition manifest itself as a considerable factor in the development of the JNA. Although the generals of the army were not fully representative of the population structure, they were nevertheless more so than lower ranking officers. As Mile Bjelajac discusses in his study of the Yugoslav army, the distribution of the highest army offices, such as the head of the party organization, the commanders of army, navy, air force, and intelligence services, as well as ministers and deputies in the ministry of defense did not favor Serbs, suggesting that the greatest distortions could be found in the officer corps but not among the highest officials, nor among recruits.[32] It would thus be misleading to attribute the strategic choice of the army to the distortion in the officer corps.

However, with the escalation of the Yugoslav crisis, the army had become more heavily dominated by Serbs. As the former commander of the fifth army in Zagreb and later Croatia's first minister of defense, Martin Špegelj, details, all key positions in the fifth army in Zagreb on the eve of the war were held by Serbs, whereas only a few years earlier some 50 percent of the command positions were held by Croats.[33] The transformation of the JNA at this late stage, however, was linked with the erosion of the army and the increasing alienation from the northern republics. The ethnic bias thus followed the political conflict, rather than vice versa.

The Army and the Reform Debates

The weakness of the army became apparent in the 1980s as Yugoslavia at large came under increasing pressure to reform itself. Although the army was an autonomous institution predestined to become a key actor in the post-Titoist period, it lacked a coherent political vision. Being a "system" rather than a single institution, the army, with its military, industry, and Party structure, was more dependent on the political and economic climate and interlinked with the larger society than it had often thought itself to be.

As Miroslav Hadžić suggests, the army was hardly a single unified actor.[34] The leadership of the army including the minister of defense, the chief of staff, and the top commanders of the different army units found themselves increasingly drifting apart in the late 1980s. Furthermore, the leadership of the JNA was constrained by the draft and a large officer corps and finally the economic component of the army's activities. As a result, the army should be viewed as a system that became increasingly unmanageable in the second half of the 1990s. Although the ministers of defense, especially Branko Mamula and his successor Veljko Kadijević, projected the image of representing the army as a whole, the political decisions of both could hardly reflect the entire JNA.

By the early 1980s, the army was torn between its role to maintain the status-quo and the self-perceived need to reform the decision-making process in the country. The president of the OSKJ, General Georgije Jovičić, noted the army's priorities in reforming the Yugoslav system: "Generally speaking, Communists in the army believe that our political system is complicated, and in some aspects incomplete and inefficient. The army . . . can only realize its function . . . if the political system . . . is stable, efficient and capable of action."[35] Jovičić openly identified the key causes for these difficulties to lie in the federalization of the SKJ and the disintegration of the Yugoslav market.[36] This and other pleas for the reintroduction of "democratic centralism" in the League of Communists and opposition to "federalization" of the

party and the strengthening of the "all-Yugoslav" character of the JNA were reoc-
curring themes in the public discourse of party officials in the army and the army
leadership in the first half of the 1980s.[37] These calls for changes stood in conflict
with the army's emphasis on "preserving the system ('the constitutional order') in
Yugoslavia" as being the army's "prime concern." The protection of the existing order
justified opposition to domestic challenges to the status quo in some republics and
provinces but was difficult to combine with the JNA's call for fundamental changes
to the same order it was charged to uphold.[38]

In the first half of the 1980s, the army lacked a partner at the republican level
who would support increased centralization while maintaining the overall status quo
and the role of the army therein. On the contrary, the army was confronted with
civil unrest in Kosovo in 1981—demonstrations turning to riots demanding the status of republic for the province—pressure from Slovenia for greater liberalism and
autonomy of the republics, and the ever-growing economic crisis. The continued
army presence in Kosovo not only incurred high financial costs but also undermined
its legitimacy and popularity among Kosovo Albanians, who constituted one of the
larger groups of army recruits.[39] The JNA further faced reductions in its financial
support from the federal budget and had to accept criticism of its autonomous position while seeing the federalist order of Yugoslavia further challenged. Kadijević, who
became secretary of defense in 1988, justified the contradiction between recentralization and preserving the existing order by saying that the JNA had "constitutionally
[been] given the task of defending the constitutional order [while being] abused by
that same Constitution."[40]

The challenge of decentralization did not only affect the state but also the
army directly.[41] Kadijević would later note that since the mid-1960s the state was
being deliberately dismantled, including the army. The 1974 Constitution was thus
viewed by him as a step toward breaking up the JNA.[42] Similar calls against the
decentralization of the army came from the Belgrade media. The well-known journalist Aleksandar Tijanić, for example, attacked the decentralization of the army
and noted that the "defense of a federal state is the function of the federal state,"
not the republics.[43]

The targets of criticism were the aforementioned Territorial Defenses of the
republics and the territorial organization of the JNA itself, which followed largely
republican borders.[44] As Martin Špegelj later noted, these features constituted a
"guardian of the essentially confederal elements of the 1974 Constitution."[45] Whereas
the army had few successes in advancing the centralization of Yugoslavia as a whole,
the reorganization of the armed forces in 1988 significantly reduced the autonomy
of the republics and reintroduced the dominance of the JNA. The restructuring
rested on two pillars: one was related to the internal structure of the JNA, the other
affected the relationship of TOs and the JNA. The first measure reduced the number
of armies (the term used for military districts), which had followed mostly republican boundaries. The six armies (Belgrade, Niš, Skopje, Zagreb, Ljubljana, Sarajevo),

one corps (Titograd), and the navy (Split) and air force (Zemun/Belgrade) were reduced to five forces, including three armies (Zagreb, Belgrade, Niš), the navy, and air force.[46] As Veljko Kadijević points out, the new "territorial divisions completely ignored the administrative borders of the republics and provinces."[47] According to Martin Špegelj, Lieutenant-General Milan Daljević, who worked on the changes, pursued the abolition of the armies along republican lines because the armies had come to be too close to the republican leaderships.[48] The army also abandoned the policy of appointing generals to the armies from the respective republics.[49]

The second component of changes affected the TOs. While still formally separate, they were subordinated to the theatre commands of the JNA, and thus the JNA reestablished stronger control over these units.[50] However, this degree of control was not as complete as the JNA had desired, leading to the 1990–91 JNA campaign to disarm the TOs. Already in 1988, during the changes to the structure of the armed forces, the TO in Kosovo was formally abolished after it had been de facto disarmed in 1981.[51]

The Looming Crisis

Amidst the crisis of Yugoslavia and the outspoken criticism of the status quo by the army leadership, fear or hope for a coup d'etat by the armed forces become common by 1987. Mamula, despite his political outspokenness, rejected the "Jaruzelski scenario"[52] and consistently noted the army's reluctance to directly intervene in politics. Branko Mikulić, the Yugoslav prime minister in 1987, explicitly noted that if the Yugoslav constitutional order were threatened, he would use all means necessary to protect it, "and that includes the army."[53] Even this threat, however, did not foresee an independent role of the JNA.

The crisis of the Yugoslav system expressed itself economically, as well as by increased calls for liberalization in Slovenia and ongoing tensions in Kosovo. Furthermore, the previously unchallenged authority of the army also eroded in the 1980s. In 1985 a number of incidents occurred against officers, especially in Kosovo, as well as in Split, where students of the naval academy were beaten up after a soccer game.[54] These incidents by what the army considered "irridentists, various separatists and unitarists"[55] furthered the sense of self-isolation of the army.[56] The "Paraćin massacre" when the Albanian recruit Aziz Kelmendi killed four fellow soldiers in army barracks in 1987 in Central Serbia particularly polarized the army. While it remained unclear whether it was mental illness or nationalism that motivated Kelmendi, media reporting and the army response considered it to be "a shot against Yugoslavia."[57] Subsequently, nine Albanian soldiers were sentenced to prison terms of twenty to twenty-two years for forming a "hostile group and spreading hostile propaganda."[58] *Tanjug* described the motivation to be "fanatical hatred towards Serbs and Montenegrins from Kosovo and support for his [Kelmendi's] proposals for actions under the slogan of Albanian chauvinists of ethnically pure Kosovo and the breaking off of the province from Yugoslavia."[59]

The incident was not only instrumentalized by the Serbian media during Milošević's rise to power but also by the army. Leading generals and Mamula invoked the incident to demonstrate the problems of the state, including "Albanian terrorism," and to call for a stronger role for the army.[60]

As mentioned above, the economic crisis directly affected the army. In real terms, the budget for the armed forces had declined in the 1980s, and the reform efforts of the Branko Mikulić government reduced the JNA's financial autonomy. The shortening of the military service from eighteen to twelve months in 1985 was justified as reflecting a better level of education of the youth but was in fact mostly the result of the costs of the longer military service.[61]

The crises also strengthened calls in Slovenia for greater liberalization. The support for the JNA dropped, with many recruits from Slovenia not reporting to duty.[62] France Popit, the president of Slovenia in 1987, laid most of the blame on the army itself: "If, today, there is no interest in the military profession, either among the Slovenes or among the Croats, Kosovars, the citizens of Vojvodina, and so forth, then the blame for such a situation must be honestly shared by all of us, from the JNA, as the most responsible factor, to the last communal administrative agency."[63] The army responded sharply to this criticism and appeared further convinced of the organized nature of the attacks against the JNA.[64]

"Special War" and the Crisis in Slovenia

Nineteen eighty-eight was a decisive year in the evolution of the JNA's relationship to reform in Yugoslavia. Because the army had earlier formulated its opposition to multiparty elections and signaled its support for a higher degree of centralization of Yugoslavia, the critique of the army in Slovenia and its responses set the scene for placing the army against the emerging pluralism in the western republics. The mounting critique of the army was described by high-ranking army officials as a "special war," reflecting the isolated view of society within the JNA in the mid-1980s. By grouping together different types of critiques, ranging from demands to financial cuts, greater openness to decentralization of the army, to even the dissolution of the state, the army closed itself to substantial engagement with the reform discourse and considered any critique of the army an attack on the state and thus a crime. As a result, the army's doctrine of total people's self-defense was defended by Admiral Stane Brovet, deputy minister of defense, in 1988, and he described its opponents as being "aggressive and constituting part of a special war."[65] The term *special war* was particularly popular in the language used by Mamula.[66] Hinting at a large conspiracy, Mamula took up a theme that would dominate the army's and its top leadership's explanation of developments in Yugoslavia in subsequent years: "[I]t is clear that this is a special war as it is clear that its creators are not the editors of single papers or magazines, but that these are just the implementers."[67]

The concept of the special war—a conflict against domestic and external enemies—had been part of the army's training and preparation for decades. It is no surprise that changes that Yugoslavia encountered in the 1980s were perceived by the army leadership not from the point of view of a domestic crisis but of an army trained on the basis of strategic plans against foreign threats and domestic collaborators.[68]

The siege mentality of the JNA was reinforced by a series of articles in the Slovenian student magazine *Mladina*, which had been on the forefront of challenging the remaining taboos. In an article entitled "Mamula, Go Home" published in February 1988, the paper sharply attacked Mamula for supplying weapons to Ethiopia during its famine. The Slovenian media that took up the issue suggested that Yugoslavia got its priorities wrong: it was the eleventh-largest weapon exporter but only the 112th-largest economic power.[69] Following the attacks on the weapons exports, Mamula defended himself by suggesting that the arms exports are normal around the world and that the armament industry is a key employer.[70] In addition, the army leadership stepped up the attacks against its critics. The paper of the armed forces, *Narodna armija*, singled out the youth publications in Slovenia (and to a lesser degree elsewhere) as the primary source of the attacks against the JNA and linked the style to similar attacks in the Diaspora media.[71] The conflict between *Mladina* and the army escalated in May 1988 when the army arrested journalists from the magazine for the possession of secret documents on army plans in Slovenia. Both the documents and the arrest of journalists polarized public opinion in Slovenia against the army and the federal state and effectively pushed the Slovene party leadership eventually in opposition to the army.[72]

As the media critique and the counterattacks by the army leadership and party officials continued, the funding of the armed forces indeed constituted a key source of contention in the federal institutions, with the army arguing for increases and Slovenia advocating cuts.[73] Mamula spoke openly about the problems of the army for the first time in parliament in late 1987. There he noted that 12,000 soldiers and staff of the JNA did not have apartments and that the response to recruitment drives had been declining by 15.5 percent between 1986 and 1987 and by 37 percent the previous year.[74] Similarly, *Večernje novosti* defended the need of the army to receive additional funding by pointing out that according to the amount of money spent per solider Yugoslavia found itself well below its neighbors.[75] With two-thirds of the federal budget allocated to defense, the presidency decided in 1988 to cut the personnel of the army by 12 percent in peace and 10 percent in wartime. Delays in the payment of the budget to the army and high inflation further reduced the funding of the JNA, increasing its financial crisis and causing continuous tensions between the army and republics that sought to curb army financing.[76]

Although the Slovenian critique of the armed forces had been nearly unilaterally rejected by the party, in 1988 Mamula had become untenable as secretary of national defense due to his virulent response to criticism. Furthermore, the army had threatened the Slovene leadership with direct intervention against "counterrevolutionary activities" with the consent of the presidency.[77] The increased tension between his leadership and the party and republican leadership from Slovenia and Croatia coincided with mounting opposition in the two republics against the government of Branko Mikulić as a whole. Mamula's retirement in May 1988 was thus an apparent attempt to salvage the overall government that would resign only half a year later. During the session in which Mamula's resignation was announced, the Mikulić government could defeat a vote of no confidence by a wide margin. Mamula's replacement, Veljko Kadijević, was only three years younger (sixty-three) and had been his deputy. However, during the conflict between the Slovenian press and Mamula, Kadijević had been largely quiet and was thus perceived as being a less politicized choice.[78] In the aftermath of the 1988 conflict, the army and the Slovene leadership sought to address some of the conflicts, which included compromise on army funding, publishing the army paper *Narodna armija* in Slovene, and putting up signs at army installations in Slovene, but as James Gow notes, "it is hard to conclude that the publishing of *Narodna armija* in Slovene... was enough to combat the damage done by the trial" of the *Mladina* journalists.[79]

Kadijević as Minister

Although Kadijević appeared to be less outspoken than Mamula, his conservative and dogmatic world view largely coincided with Mamula's. Throughout the final years of Yugoslavia, Kadijević supported the recentralization of Yugoslavia and remained hostile to the introduction of multiparty elections. Nevertheless, his shift in support from Ante Marković toward Milošević between 1988 and 1991 is indicative of the larger transition made by the army and parts of its top leadership.

This continuity between Kadijević and Mamula was not only a consequence of the fact that they had been close associates. Similar views on the political engagement of the army could be found in the public statements of most army and ministry of defense officials. As noted earlier, the army had a vested interest in a strengthening of the central government. The fact that the party had become relatively weak as a cohesive force and the Yugoslav governments had been unable to either maintain the status quo or engage in successful reforms had deprived the army of a patron or clear ally well before the party formally broke up in 1990.

Kadijević, like his predecessor, noted in October 1988 that "Yugoslavia can exist only as a true federation or else not at all. That is why neither the unitary nor the confederal system can be alternatives to the Federal system."[80] Clearly, he viewed the organization of Yugoslavia at the time as being "the most complicated thing the world has seen . . ." and noted that "the 1974 Constitution inevitably led the country to disintegration."[81] Kadijević and Mamula also shared their view that the critique from Slovenia was part of an orchestrated campaign organized by the Slovenian leadership.[82] The Slovene member of the last Yugoslav presidency, Janez Drnovšek, reports in his memoirs that his repeated request for the release of the journalists of *Mladina* were rejected by Kadijević and the pro-Milošević presidency members

(Serbia, Vojvodina, Montenegro). During one of these discussions, the president of the Slovene presidency, Janez Stanovnik, poignantly told Kadijević that "[i]f you do not listen to us now, you will negotiate with separatists the next time."[83]

Despite the army's rejection of budgetary cuts and attempts to link it to a plot against the JNA, the army was unable to confront the fundamental economic crisis. Although newly elected Slovene member of the presidency Janez Drnovšek was surprised by Kadijević's liberal economic views,[84] the army leadership neither endorsed economic reform nor had any answer to the economic crisis, resulting in an "apparent helplessness in the face of the country's fundamental problems [that] has served to reduce their influence on civilian institutions."[85]

The JNA and the Rise of Milošević

The rapid rise of Milošević to power in Serbia was the key transformative event in the second half of the 1980s. Not unlike the intellectuals who would ultimately find an ideological partner in Milošević, the army only gradually built up links with the Serbian president. As the events until 1991 and the repeated purges of the army after 1991 demonstrate, the alliance between the Serbian party and the army was never complete and often was motivated by different priorities.

During the crucial Eighth Session of the Central Committee of the Serbian League of Communists, when Milošević took full control of the party and sidelined his mentor Ivan Stambolić, support for Milošević came from Nikola Ljubičić, who had been minister of national defense before Mamula and continued to wield great influence within the party and the armed forces. He had already been a key actor in Tito's purges of the liberal party leaderships in the 1970s. Mamula suggests in his memoirs, however, that Ljubičić's support for Milošević did not reflect a broad position within the army, which at that point did not maintain direct contacts with Milošević. Despite the support Milošević received from the retired Generals Ljubičić, Gračanin, and Aleksandar Šimić, evidence does not suggest close ties between army and the new Serbian leadership in September 1988.[86] However, in December 1988, after the resignation of the Mikulić government, Kadijević proposed Milošević as prime minister to the president of the presidency, Raif Dizdarević.[87] Milošević himself, however, rejected the proposal, probably recognizing the weakness of the position of the prime minister.[88] From Kadijević's memoirs it clearly emerges that Milošević sought to focus on Serbia, whereas Kadijević, possibly naively, thought that his "political authority and proven abilities, especially his ability to find simple solutions (!) . . . could create a turning point."[89]

At the same time, Milošević's use of extrainstitutional means to consolidate his power, such as the support and organization of mass protest throughout Montenegro and Serbia in 1988, alarmed parts of army. In response, Mamula suggested that "[i]f the search for solutions for the crisis is being made outside the system, there will be the emergence of decision making centers, which incorporate even more chaos into the society and every organized measure to overcome the crisis will be impossible."[90]

Petar Šimić, head of the OSKJ, condemned even more explicitly the "happening of the people": "The mass protests can be a contribution to the system-destruction. Every mass protest . . . includes the possibility of manipulation, abuse and irrational behavior of human beings."[91] This critique suggests that although Milošević was enjoying the support from some senior military figures, such as the Generals Ljubičić and Gračanin, his tactics met with resistance among the high ranks of the JNA.

Kadijević's and the JNA leadership's support for Milošević was never entirely firm and fluctuated throughout the last years of Yugoslavia. Franc Setinc, a Slovenian representative in the Central Committee of the League of Communists, remembers being told by General Bunčić that "we in the Yugoslav Federal Army (JNA) are not for Milosevic!"; a position echoed by Kadijević and Mamula in a meeting with Milan Kućan and other members of the Slovene leadership during military maneuvers in Slovenia.[92] Although arguably the statements of the army toward the Slovenian leadership have to be evaluated with caution considering the strained relations since the *Mladina* affair, Prime Minister Ante Marković similarly suggested that Kadijević's support for Milošević was far from unwavering. Marković noted that the relations between him and Kadijević were at first often better than Kadijević's contacts with Milošević.[93]

The loyalty of the Serbian and army leadership was linked to the Milošević government's endorsement of the concept of centralization. The changes to the Yugoslav constitutions, driven by Serbia, satisfied the JNA, especially because they improved army financing.[94] Similarly, the army leadership broadly agreed with the Serbian leadership over Kosovo's being a key threat to Yugoslavia's stability.[95] The army had been concerned by what it termed nationalist "outbursts" among army recruits from Kosovo.[96] During the June 1989 commemoration of the 600th anniversary of the Kosovo battle, Kadijević expressed reservations to Drnovšek regarding Serbia's policies in Kosovo,[97] but the army supported the overall approach. However, it was only with the end of the League of Communists that the alliance between the JNA and Milošević intensified because the only other political patron had formally ceased to exist.

The End of the SKJ

Contrary to the retrospective claim by both Mamula and Kadijević[98] that the JNA was largely supportive of multiparty politics and democratization, the army opposed any liberalization of the political system for a remarkably long time.[99] The rejection of multiparty elections in 1988 by Major General Simeon Bunčić as "anti-Yugoslav and anti-Communist" was therefore unsurprising. He linked pluralism with the destruction of the armed forces and the state, a recurrent motif in the army's opposition to multiparty elections: "[C]ompromise and break up of the armed forces [are] a means of achieving their final goal, the destruction of Yugoslavia as a unified federal state."[100] The JNA continued to reject multiparty politics even in late 1989 because, in the words of Petar Šimić, head of the OSKJ, it would "further enhance a nationalist split within Yugoslavia."[101] Although the army grudgingly accepted the multiparty elections in 1990, its relationship with political pluralism continued to be uneasy. Thus, still in October 1990, the deputy secretary of national defense, Milan Čusić, noted that the army accepted pluralism despite resulting in more criticism of the JNA.[102]

In 1988 and 1989 the army leadership expressed its disappointment with the League of Communists increasingly openly. Petar Šimić attacked the party particularly strongly, accusing it of "opportunism, vacillation, insufficient ideology and action."[103] Warning that the army would not tolerate the feuding in the Central Committee, he noted that "in the postwar period we have never faced greater dangers to the integrity of the country," but "if someone has proclaimed the battle for Yugoslavia, this battle will not be fought without the JNA." The number of political statements by the army increased in the course of 1989 and took a more conservative line. Despite the forceful appearance of the army, the army recognized its own constraints in having an impact on the overall political situation. As Milan Andrejevich asked, "is [there] really a federal party left for the army to defend?"[104] or how could the army defend Yugoslavia in the absence of a federalally? With relations between Kadijević and Ante Marković increasingly strained, mostly over economic reforms and the unwillingness of Marković to reject the newly elected leaders in Slovenia and Croatia, the federal government no longer constituted a clear ally. The strength of the Marković government derived less from its limited formal powers than from the popularity of Marković himself and his reforms. The presidency, with members that were from the republics and provinces, had transformed itself in 1990 from including only high-ranking officials of the respective Leagues of Communists to including representatives of the newly elected governments, including Stjepan Mesić from Croatia and Janez Drnovšek from Slovenia. This left only the League of Communists as a political "forum" for the army. The party's fragmentation, the dissolution of the federal party following the "interruption" of the Fourteenth Congress, deprived the JNA of the only remaining means of pursuing its political agenda.

In October 1989, the army for the first time defined its political platform, bringing together the different elements that Kadijević, Mamula, and the army leadership, as well as the OSKJ, had formulated over the years. Largely, the political agenda combined strengthening of the federal state with limited economic reforms and a rejection of political pluralism.[105]

These views of the leadership largely coincided with the positions held by members of the OSKJ. Some 84.3 percent supported more powers for the federal state and democratic centralism in the party. There was also support for competition between candidates and some degree of market economy.[106] The ninth congress of the OSKJ, shortly before the last congress of the League of Communists of Yugoslavia, confirmed this platform. The congress also refused to accept any link between the end of socialism in Eastern Europe and the future of socialism in Yugoslavia.[107]

The last congress of the SKJ in January 1990 was a turning point for the JNA. The OSKJ together with the Serbian League of Communists favored centralizing state and party, or in the words of Stane Brovet, deputy minister of defense: "if the republics become states with all the attributes of statehood, then it will be impossible to talk of the statehood of Yugoslavia. . . . I think neither the LCY or any of its members should adhere to such stands."[108] Key links between the party organizations at the time were Nikola Ljubičić, who had been president of the Serbian presidency after Stambolić and later briefly Serbian member of the Yugoslav presidency (prior to Borisav Jović), and Petar Gračanin, minister of interior under Marković and president of the Serbian presidency after the dismissal of Ivan Stambolić. Both belonged to the Partisan generation and had been crucial in securing Milošević's legitimacy in the dogmatic and conservative wing of the party. Nevertheless, the OSKJ was hardly unified in its support of the Serbian party's tactics. Petar Šimić, for example, has been against the marginalizing of the Slovene party.[109] As a result, the army's delegates rejected a vote in favor of an economic blockade against Slovenia.[110]

The Slovenian delegation, on the other hand, favored the confederalization of the party, a position for which it found some support in Croatia. Many of the republican parties oscillated between the two positions and were more concerned with preserving the cohesion of the SKJ. While the OSKJ only accounted for 68 of the 1,457 delegates, it found itself in agreement in key issues with the Serbian delegation, which accounted for 38.7 percent of the total number of delegates. Together with some delegates from the other republics, the Serbian members could outvote the requests of the Slovenian delegation and find support for the agenda of a new, more centralist constitution.[111] The systematic outvoting of the Slovenian proposals triggered a walkout by the Slovenian delegates, followed soon after by most Croatian delegates. As a result the congress was adjourned, de facto breaking up the federal party. The congress was a display of the failure of crude majority rule in a complex and multinational environment. Although the party in the army and Serbia (and its allies) dominated, they were unable to impose their will on the rest of the country. In fact, the party congress was one of the few federal decision-making bodies that required neither consensus from all republics nor at least support from the majority of the republics. The dilemma between imposing a political solution and building a consensus between the republics would dictate the JNA's indecisiveness in the following year. Threatening the northern republics, the army sought to enforce its vision of Yugoslavia, while at the same time it shied away from enforcing its position without the formal consent of the key remaining institution, the presidency. After the congress of the party was adjourned, the political and ideological uncertainty of the army became increasingly pronounced.[112] As a consequence, the army leadership remained deeply ambivalent over calls for a depoliticization of the JNA.[113]

Borisav Jović, who had noted previously his concern with the strong ties between Marković and Kadijević, observed optimistically on February 22, 1990: "It is good that for once Veljko has 'seen through' Ante Marković. He has always been obsessed with the notion that Ante is fighting from Yugoslavia."[114] During the elections in 1990, the army clearly favored the League of Communists of Serbia (renamed Socialist Party of Serbia, SPS) and Montenegro by demonstratively welcoming the Parties' victory after the first round of elections, whereas the army papers attacked the winners in Croatia and Slovenia.[115] The increased polarization and the disappearance of a clear ideological roof for the army brought to the foreground the ideological differences in the army leadership, with Kadijevic and Stane Brovet appearing more moderate than the chief of staff, Blagoje Adžić.[116] The conflicts within the top leadership of the JNA focused on the alliance with Milošević and the possibility of a military takeover. According to Ivo Komšić, member of the presidency of the League of Communists of Bosnia, the army leadership, lead by Petar Šimić, approached the Bosnian party leadership in March 1990 informing them of the army's plan to carry out a coup. During discussions in Belgrade between army and party officials, divisions within the army leadership over a coup became apparent with eventually Šimić opposing it. The negotiations, according to Komšić, included Raif Dizdarević, whom the army proposed as prime minister to replace Ante Marković.[117] Although the discussions came to naught, they exposed the fragmentation of the army leadership, which in part explains the procrastination of the army when offered the possibility to take power in 1990 and 1991.

Generally speaking, the army had difficulties maintaining ideology cohesion, which was not only a consequence of the more dogmatic position of the army vis-à-vis society at large but also had structural causes. The information flow within the army was much slower and more hierarchical than in civilian structures, resulting in lower credibility and reduced responsiveness than the republics.[118]

The founding of the League of Communists—Movement for Yugoslavia (*Savez Komunista—Pokret za Jugoslaviju*, SK-PzJ) in November 1990 sought to fill the political void resulting from the disappearance of the federal party organization.[119] Although apparently the initiative of the army's top brass, it ended up becoming a tool of the Milošević regime. Because the party was only founded in November, that is, after the elections in all the republics except for the ones in Serbia and Montenegro, its ability to gain seats in any of the parliaments was constrained.[120] While running in subsequent elections in Serbia, the party never received more than marginal electoral support.[121] The new League of Communists carried over much of the structure of the OSKJ: the entire party organization formally joined the new party.[122] However, only 50 percent of the members joined the new party, which received hardly any support in Slovenia and Croatia, including among army staff.[123] For example, the head of the fifth army, Konrad Kolšek, noted that the "JNA leadership spent nearly a year with the party, the SKJ, which has already broken apart and which could not be brought back to life."[124] The new party also included dogmatic ideologues from Serbia, including Mira Marković, the wife of Slobodan Milošević. Despite this personal link between the SPS and the new League of Communists, the reception by the Serbian media of the new party was largely negative.[125] The party was to provide for a political home for "old-fashioned" supporters of Yugoslavia and dogmatic Communists, whereas the Socialist Party of Serbia opened itself more toward nationalism and a (limited) discourse of reform.[126]

Around the same time as the SKJ-PzJ was founded, the presidency moved toward banning party organizations within the JNA. The establishment of the SKJ-PzJ can be seen as a preemptive move to prevent the army from losing its party structure—Kadijević banned political party activities already in October 1990[127]—the ban also complicated the link between army and the Party. By January 1, 1991, no Party activities were permitted within the army. Considering the configuration of the conflict and the emerging party pluralism, the army leadership acted as if they were a party in the final months of Yugoslavia.[128]

The Failed Coup

During the final year of Yugoslavia, the conflicts between the republics increased, and the first local conflicts, in particular in the Krajina region and eastern Slavonia in Croatia, indicated the real risk of civil war. In 1990 and 1991 rumors of a direct army intervention had repeatedly circulated.[129] Although or perhaps because the army had been formally depoliticized and "its" party was not represented in any parliament in early 1991, the army de facto took a more explicit political role and sought to intervene in the conflict. The fundamental difficulty was the fact that the JNA had no coherent plan to respond to the challenges around it. As Veljko Kadijević correctly notes in his memoirs, a conventional coup would have had no chance of success because it would have been necessary to topple anything between two (Slovenia and Croatia) and seven governments (all republics and federal).[130] Recognizing the inability of the army to intervene at such a large scale created the inherent contradiction of the legal coup that the army strove to accomplish with support of Serbia in Spring 1991. After this failed in March 1991, the Serbian government abandoned centralizing Yugoslavia over the creation of an extended Serbia. The army followed but only reluctantly. By the time the first shots were fired, the army had equated protecting Serbs in Croatia with protecting supporters of Yugoslavia. That equation would see to the dissolution of the old JNA and its subordination to Serbia (from May 1992, Federal Republic of Yugoslavia) and the Serb statelets in Croatia and Bosnia.

In early 1991, the army leadership proposed four measures to the federal authorities, including the suspension of all republican laws and acts that contravened federal laws and constitution, reform of the constitution and economy, setting a date for a new constitution, and protecting Yugoslav independence from outside. Demonstrating the isolation of the army, the proposal received only limited support in the federal government and also did not find majority support in the presidency.[131] During presidency meetings on January 24 and 25, 1991, the unbridgeable differences between the republics and the army become visible. The topic of the debates was the refusal of the Croatian government to disarm special police units following a decision of the presidency on January 9 to disband all "unauthorized formations," as proposed by the Ministry of Defense already on December 11, 1990.[132] The formulation of the presidency's decision had been unclear because it did not define which units it considered paramilitary, and the army undertook no measure to forcefully disarm any unit. In effect, the army leadership itself remained undecided about which measures to undertake and against whom.[133] It was only clear against whom not to intervene. When Anton Tus, commander of the air force and from September chief of staff of the Croatian army, suggested the lifting of the blockades set up by Serbs in Krajina, Kadijević responded, according to Tus: "Do you really want the Serbs to say that the JNA is against them?"[134]

The fact that the army did not intervene more forcefully can be attributed not only to the ambivalent presidency's decision but also to the lack of clarity among the army leadership on how to confront democratically elected republican leaderships. During the well-known March 1991 sessions of the presidency, the JNA and Veljko Kadijević undertook a last attempt to obtain presidency support for a more forceful intervention.[135] Already a few days earlier, the army had intervened with presidency support against protesters in Belgrade.[136] In addition to setting a precedent for civilian intervention, it was the first time the army intervened on behalf of the Milošević regime[137] and was clearly a perceived threat to the other governments. As Miroslav Hadžić argues, the intervention could have been interpreted as a type of "ethnic neutrality" as the army signaled its readiness to intervene against Serbs.[138]

Already in late February the army leadership had prepared the key March presidency session together with Borisav Jović. Kadijević notes that although Serbs in Croatia and Bosnia, as well as Serbia and Montenegro supported Yugoslavia, Slovenia and Croatia were favoring independence, with Macedonia and Bosnia wavering yet leaning toward the northern republics. Kadijević proposed the presidency session, strengthening the Krajina Serbs and organizing mass rallies against the governments of Bosnia, Croatia, and Macedonia, and disarmament of illegal units. The plan, especially the organization of mass demonstrations, illustrates the loss of perspective in army leadership to which even Jović responded with skepticism.[139]

The meeting of the presidency[140] on March 12, 14, and 15, 1991, was held together with chiefs of staff and well orchestrated and filmed (on March 14 and 15) by the JNA in an attempt to put pressure on the presidency members.[141] The meeting was held in army barracks and was summoned by Borisav Jović, the Serb presidency member via television. While Jović in his memoirs notes that he was not clear what Kadijević would propose, the congruence of interests was clear.[142] During his introduction, Kadijević set the tone of the meeting: "the foreign factor is already here . . . we also have domestic quisling forces, fascists, Ustaša, Četnic, White Guards, Ballists, Bulgarophiles. . . . Once again we are clashing with them in a struggle for Yugoslavia."[143] In response to this threat, he proposed to the presidency that it would:

1. Impose a state of emergency
2. Mobilize the JNA
3. Bring the defense system within the framework of the law, disarming all paramilitary formation
4. Reach an agreement on the future of Yugoslavia
5. Propose a new constitution followed by Yugoslav-wide elections[144]

The central role of the army in implementing the plan was underlined by Adžić, who told the presidency: "I think that we are the only remaining element of society that is executing your decisions. . . . The JNA has no purpose without Yugoslavia. . . . Accordingly, no one should think that we are fighting for the army—we are fighting for Yugoslavia, and I hope you are too."[145] Because of the heavy-handed appearance of the army, most presidency members remained reluctant to give the army a free hand.

During a one-day break, Veljko Kadijević went to Moscow to receive support from the equally conservative Red Army and ministry of defense, including Minister of Defense General Dmitri T. Jazov. Kadijević had been suspicious of the West and believed that "the Yugoslav state depended directly on the fate of the Soviet state"[146] for the balance between the blocs. While Jazov was apparently sympathetic, he was unable to help. Vuk Obradović, a close aide to Kadijević later noted that Kadijević told him upon returning from Moscow that "the Russians are up to their necks in mud, and aren't even capable of helping themselves, let alone us . . ."[147] During the same time, Drnovšek and Mesić had been back in Ljubljana and Zagreb for consultations. During the one-day break, Blagoje Adžić, the chief of staff, suggested more openly than Kadijević to carry out a coup d'etat and depose the government and presidency if the presidency would fail to support the army's proposal.[148]

The proposal was watered down on March 14 from army mobilization to "combat readiness," but it become apparent that the army proposal would not receive the necessary support. Neither the Kosovo Albanian representative Riza Sapundziju nor the Bosnian representative Bogić Bogićević, who were considered possible allies in addition to the firm votes of Serbia (Borisav Jović), Vojvodina (Jugoslav Kostić), and Montenegro (Nenad Bućin), were ready to support the proposed army intervention. In response Jović developed the plan whereby he and his two allies in the presidency would resign to paralyze the presidency. This would provide the opportunity for the army to intervene in the absence of a functioning civil supreme command.[149] After the presidency failed to support the army proposal on March 15, Jović announced his resignation on TV, and Milošević subsequently declared Serbia's decision to not recognize the decisions of the presidency.[150]

Against the hopes of the Serbian leadership, the army decided not to intervene and stage a coup. This was in part due to the fact that Stipe Mesić, as deputy president of the presidency, reconvened a presidency meeting for March 21, thus sabotaging the attempt by Jović to render the presidency ineffective.[151] According to Ante Marković, Kadijević laid out to him a plan for a coup d'etat, following the failure to win support in the presidency. The plan was to arrest the Croatian and Slovene leadership. Kadijević had the plan ready but needed political support, which he hoped to receive from Marković. After Marković pointed out that the plan failed to arrest Milošević, Kadijević responded, "He is the only one who is fighting for Yugoslavia. Without him, we could not be proposing this."[152] After Marković refused to endorse the plan, the communication between Kadijević and Marković broke down.[153]

During a meeting between Milošević and Jović with the army leadership, including Kadijević, Stane Brovet, and Blagoje Adžić, the army backed away from the idea of a coup and instead proposed to raise combat readiness, mobilize, and declare an ultimatum by which the weapons would have to be collected. Only if this were to fail, Brovet suggested a blockade of the governments rejecting the measures, military administration, and even the use of force by the army.[154] Even these measures were not fully pursued by the army and Kadijević, who had become reluctant to act autonomously. This lack of army intervention brought about tensions with Jović, who noted in his diary on March 22, 1991: "All possibility of defending Yugoslavia has been lost. . . . Defending the Serb nation's right to self-determination is realistically impossible without the JNA, because the Serb nation is not armed."[155] Despite the tensions between the Serbian president and the minister of defense, Kadijević had come around to the Serbian position. In response to the failure at the presidency, Kadijević notes that he considered but rejected the collective resignation of the general staff.[156] Instead, he answered the concerns Jović expressed above: "[T]he army, relying on political forces in the federation and in the republics which wished to live in Yugoslavia, while peacefully parting with those which wished to leave it . . . this meant protecting the Serb nation outside of Serbia and assembling the JNA within the border of the future of Yugoslavia."[157] In this strategic shift, the army leadership chose to align itself with a particular vision of Yugoslavia at the cost of abandoning a consensual and possibly more decentralized Yugoslavia, as had been proposed by Macedonia and Bosnia. This shift, completed in March 1991, could be traced back at least to June 1990, when Kadijević agreed to a similar proposal made by Jović. In August 1990, he mentioned to Drnovšek the possibility of Slovene independence.[158] At the same time, he remained skeptical, as Jović notes in January 1991: "He [Kadijević] has not yet 'swallowed' the idea of defending Serb territory in Croatia. He still believes in the defense of Yugoslavia."[159]

The key conflict between the Serbian leadership and the army in the subsequent months thus focused less on the goals but more on the unwillingness of the army to intervene. Kadijević continued to support the Yugoslav constitutional framework, such as the election of Mesić to head the presidency in May 1991 while Jović and Milošević blocked his election. By May, Jović had given up on direct support from the army, exclaiming, "I have had enough of this empty talk by the military. I no longer have any confidence in them. They will neither undertake nor do anything, that is clear."[160]

In addition to Kadijević's indecisiveness, torn between the perceived need to intervene and the constraints of accepting the institutional framework, the question of the reliability of the army came to the fore. Although the leadership could be political actors, they required the whole machinery of the army to actually become active. Some of its staff, such as Stevan Mirković, were convinced that the army would remain coherent and that soldiers would follow orders, even among Albanians in Kosovo.[161] As the war would show, the ability to deploy would be considerably constrained by the mobilization crisis. During just the first weeks of the war in Croatia, according to Croatian army officials, some 1,000 soldiers deserted.[162] Not only did the JNA fall apart as a Yugoslav force by increasingly drawing on Serb recruits; it also failed to secure Serb recruits, as the continuous recruitment crisis demonstrates.[163] Later Kadijević would note that "mobilization became a key limiting factor in carrying out plans to deploy the JNA, more than all the other problems put together and much larger than the armed capacity of the enemy armed forces."[164]

Conclusion

The JNA found itself humiliated after the brief war in Slovenia and still uncertain of its role. The attempt to save Yugoslavia through military means clearly saved Slovenia. Although there is no space to discuss the reasons for the army's failure, it increased the army's dependency on Serbia in terms of manpower, financial support, and an ideological road map. It slowly became the force that would protect the Milošević regime and its military goals in Croatia, Bosnia, and later in Kosovo. This transformation was accompanied by numerous purges. First, most non-Serbs were removed or sent into early retirement in July–August 1991. In early 1992, the pro-Yugoslav army leadership was forced out, including Kadijević, who resigned over the shooting down of an EC helicopter by the JNA in January 1992 over Croatia. The new *Vojska Jugoslavije* (VJ) of the Federal Republic of Yugoslavia would continue to be subject to purges and never stood as loyally to the Milošević regime as the police forces did. Nevertheless, members of the army, trained in the Geneva Convention before Yugoslavia's dissolution, committed countless war crimes from Croatia to Kosovo.

The chapter has sought to address two key questions pertaining to the role of the JNA in the dissolution of Yugoslavia. First, how was this powerful and fiercely Yugoslav force unable to prevent the slide to war, and second, why did the army eventually align itself with the Milošević regime? A simplistic answer to these questions, such as reducing the complex role of the army to the ethnic affiliation of its leadership or officer corps, cannot explain the evolution of the army. Instead, this chapter explores the army as a complex institution that rarely spoke in one voice or was driven by exclusively one interest. During the crisis-shaken 1980s the army struggled to maintain the political order, that is, the Communist system and the state, while arguing for greater centralization in state, Party, and army (accomplishing only the latter to some degree). As the debates over change and reform in Yugoslavia wedded on the one side liberalization with decentralization and on the other conservativism and centralization, the army's allegiance fell with the latter, preventing it from being an effective arbiter.

The second key issue in this chapter has been the uneasy alliance between Kadijević, representing large parts of the army leadership, and Milošević. The cooperation between Milošević and Kadijević and other members of the army leadership was not automatic, nor was it due to the fact that "he and many of his colleagues were Serbs, but because Milosevic was defending socialism."[165] In fact it grew over the last years of Yugoslavia, based on the personal relationship between the two, Kadijević's ideological dogmatisms, and Milošević's pragmatic use of the army. Kadijević's indecisiveness and the inability of the army to fulfill Milošević's plan, in particular the March 1991 coup, constrained the relationship, as did the different degrees of commitment to Yugoslavia.

Examining the role of the army in the dissolution of Yugoslavia highlights the powerlessness of this army whose military might and social influence had been a myth within and beyond the JNA. As a multinational army, relying on recruits from throughout Yugoslavia, it could not intervene effectively in the emerging national conflicts. Furthermore, at the officer and leadership levels, the JNA incorporated different backgrounds and nationalities, irrespective of the misbalances. These divergent interests and allegiances expressed themselves not so much in open policy debates within the army but in the inability of the more dogmatic leadership to enforce its will. When studying the successors to the JNA, one cannot limit oneself to the Yugoslav army but has to include all armies in the successor states because they emerged largely from staff from the JNA. The personal continuity with armies that became the "enemy" of the JNA highlights the depth of the internal divisions of the army.

The army leadership itself was isolated from society and fell victim to its own myth about the external enemies of Yugoslavia. The army struggled since the 1980s with multiple contradictions: it supported centralization but defined its role in preserving the order it sought to change; it wanted to be politically active but not act independently; it wanted to preserve socialism and the state, even when the combination was no longer attainable. Its ideological alliance with Serbia prevented it from negotiating a confederal arrangement that might have preserved Yugoslavia.

In late 1990, the army leadership warned of the threat of a civil war, and Kadijević, invoking the civil war in Lebanon that was just winding down, suggested that he would use all means available to prevent Yugoslavia from turning "into a second Lebanon."[166] Although Kadijević, in a conversation with Drnovšek, according to the latter, noted that "if this [war] should occur, one would have to hang us [the generals] for failing to prevent it," the army not only did not prevent the war but let itself become a crucial element in its escalation.[167]

Notes

1. His formal title was secretary for national defense.
2. Kadijević, op cit., 1993, p. 102.
3. A. Ross Johnson, The Self-Destruction of the Yugoslav People's Army, unpublished paper prepared for a conference on "The Military in Democratic Societies," Sofia, November 16, 1991, on file with author.
4. Miroslav Hadžić, *The Yugoslav People's Agony: The Role of the Yugoslav People's Army* (Aldershot: Ashgate, 2002), pp. 209, 214.
5. Slobodan Stanković, "Tito and the Army: The Tito Era in Yugoslavia," *RFE Background Report*, 100 (May 5, 1980), p. 25.
6. Ibid., p. 23.
7. Ivo Paparela, "Die Jugoslawische Volksarmee als ein politischer Faktor," *Südosteuropa*, Vol. 39, No. 2 (1990), pp. 98–99.
8. *Vjesnik*, December 23, 1997, quoted from Slobodan Stankovic, "Yugoslav Army Adopts Wait-and-See-Attitude," RFE background report (January 13, 1986).
9. Adam Roberts, *Nations in Arms: The Theory and Practice of Territorial Defence* (New York: St. Martin's Press, 1986), p. 203.
10. December 24, 1971, quoted from Stanković, "Tito and the Army," p. 25.
11. *Frankfurter Rundschau*, December 17, 1971, quoted from ibid., p. 25.
12. In a sign of the limited accountability of the army, it first released detailed data on the military-industrial complex in June 1991. The army owned 56 large companies, 80 percent of which were in Bosnia and Serbia, with 70,000 employees and 100,000 suppliers. By 1991, many of the staff had been unemployed or on paid leave, and the factories worked only at 20 percent capacity (Ivo Jakovljević, "Bankrot vojne industrije," *Danas*, August 13, 1991.
13. Officially called the Chair of the Federal Executive Council (Savezno izvršno veće, SIV).
14. Paparela, op. cit., pp. 99–100.
15. Hadžić, *The Yugoslav People's Agony*, p. 211.
16. Marko Milivojević, "The Role of the Yugoslav Intelligence and Security Community," in John Allcock, John J. Horton, and Marko Milivojević (eds.), *Yugoslavia in Transition* (New York/Oxford: Berg, 1992), pp. 216–217.
17. Slobodan Stanković, "A Survey of the Yugoslav Party Membership," *RFE Background Report*, 152 (June 23, 1980).
18. Hadžić, *The Yugoslav People's Agony*, p. 69.
19. Hadžić, *Sudbina partijske vojske* (Belgrade: B92, 2001), p. 18.
20. Mile Bjelajac, *Die jugoslawische Erfahrung mit der multiet[h]nischen Armee 1918–1991* (Belgrade: UDI, 1999) Available at: http://www.udi.org.yu/dod_knj.asp?knj=6.
21. Ustav SFRJ, 1974, Art. 242.
22. Hadžić, *The Yugoslav People's Agony*, p. 215.
23. Podružbljanje varnosti in obrame, 1983–84, Ljubljana, p. 18, quoted from *Osteuropa*, 8/91, A482.; Anton Bebler, "Das Militär in Jugoslawiens Krise," *Europäische Rundschau*, Vol. 3 (1991), p. 10; Bjelajac, *op. cit.*, p. 12.
24. Stanković, "Tito and the Army," p. 23.
25. *Revija Obramba*, 4, 1991, pp. 56–61, quoted from Wolfgang Oschlies, "Wer hält Jugoslawiens Armee in der Hand," *BIOst, Aktuelle Analysen* (May 11, 1991). Due to rounding, the total percentages might not be 100.
26. Anton Bebler, "Political Pluralism and the Yugoslav Professional Military," in Jim Seroka, Vukasin Pavlović (eds.), *The Tragedy of Yugoslavia: The Failure of Democratic Transformation* (Armonk: M.E. Sharpe, 1992), p. 116; Vlatko Cvrtila, "Tko je što u armiji," *Danas*, February 5, 1991.

27. Morris Janowitz, *Military Institutions and Coercion in Developing Nations* (Chicago: University of Chicago Press, 1977), p. 104.
28. This phenomenon has been widely studied for the United States. Charles C. Mokos, "Making the All-Volunteer Force Work: A National Service Approach," *Foreign Affairs*, Vol. 60, No. 1 (1981), pp. 18–34; and in developing countries, for example, Morris Janowitz, *Military Institutions and Coercion in Developing Nations* (Chicago: University of Chicago Press, 1977), p. 104. For the case of Bulgaria see *Stephan E. Nikolov*, "A Gypsy Military Ahead? A Case Study from Bulgaria," Conference Paper, *Geneva Centre for the Democratic Control of Armed Forces* (2002).
29. Oschlies, *op. cit.*
30. Bjelajac, op. cit.
31. James Gow, *Legitimacy and the Military: The Yugoslav Crisis* (London: Pinter, 1992), pp. 70, 76–77.
32. Bjelajac, op. cit., pp. 15–17.
33. Spegelj, op. cit., p. 21.
34. Hadžić, *The Yugoslav People's Agony*, p. 13.
35. *Politika*, December 15, 1984, quoted from Slododan Stanković, "Warnings Against 'Hostile Elements' in Yugoslavia," *RFE Background Report*, December 27, 1984.
36. Ibid.
37. "O samupravljanju i jedinstvo," *Komunist*, June 7, 1985.
38. Mamula, quoted in Slobodan Stanković, "Yugoslavia Would Resist Any Foreign Aggressor," *RFE*, May 16, 1986.
39. Gow, op. cit., p. 70; Branko Mamula, *Slučaj Jugoslavija* (Podgorica: CID, 2000), pp. 35, 40.
40. Veljko Kadijević, p. 84; see Gow, op. cit., p. 72.
41. As James Gow argues, the federalization of the state in fact secured the autonomy of the army as the ninth unit of the Federation. Gow, op. cit., pp. 59–60.
42. Veljko Kadijević, pp. 72–73.
43. Aleksandar Tijanić, "Unutrašnje poreklo spoljne čvrstine," *NIN*, December 22, 1985, pp. 19–20.
44. Kadijević, op. cit., p. 76. As would become clear later on, the complex decision-making structures at the federal level and the strong role of republics in the presidency as the collective head of state constituted probably the greatest reason for immobilizing the army.
45. Martin Špegelj, "The First Phase, 1990–1992: The JNA Prepares for Aggression and Croatia for Defense," in Branka Magaš and Ivo Žanić (eds.), *The War in Croatia and Bosnia-Herzegovina, 1991–1995* (London: Frank Cass, 2001), p. 16.
46. The fifth army, based in Zagreb, covered Slovenia and Croatia without Slavonia and Dalmatia, the latter remaining under navy control. The areas of responsibility of the first army now included most of Bosnia (without Cazinska krajina), Slavonia, Serbia, and parts of Montenegro. The third army was responsible for Macedonia, most of Montenegro, Kosovo, and Southern Serbia.
47. Kadijević, op. cit., p. 77.
48. Špegelj, op. cit., p. 18
49. Bjelajac, op. cit., p. 17
50. Kadijević, op. cit., p. 78, "One of the most important steps taken . . . was the decision to disarm the territorial defense and place it under the control of the JNA."
51. Špegelj, op. cit., pp. 18–21.
52. Jens Reuter, "Der XIII. Kongress des BKJ," *Südosteuropa*, No. 10, 1986, pp. 552–553.

53. Slobodan Stanković compares the statement with Tito's speech in Rudo in 1971, which prepared the ground for the crackdown on the Croatian Spring. Slobodan Stanković, "Yugoslav Premier May Use Army in Defending System," *RFE Background Report*, March 24, 1987.

54. Stanković, "Yugoslav Army Adopts Wait and See Attitude," January 13, 1986.

55. Simeon Bunčić, "Refleksije nacionalizma u JNA," *Komunist*, March 7, 1986, p. 19, quoted from Slobodan Stanković, "Yugoslavia Would Resist Any Foreign Aggressor," *RFE Background Report*, May 16, 1986, p. 13.

56. *Borba*, February 18, 1986; January 4/5, 1986, quoted from *Osteuropa*, Vol. 36, No. 10 (1986), p. A491.

57. See Julie A. Mertus, *Kosovo: How Myths and Truths Started a War* (Berkeley: University of California Press, 1999), pp. 145–158.

58. "Strože kazne," *Večernje novosti*, May 8, 1988; Zdzislaw P. Gwozsdz, "Nationalitätenzwist in Jugoslawiens Kasernen. Albanische Soldaten vor Militärgerichten," *Die Presse*, January 21, 1988.

59. *Tanjug*, May 7, 1988.

60. Slobodan Stanković, "Yugoslav Military Leaders Warn the Opposition," *RFE Background Reports*, September 23, 1987.

61. *Narodna armija*, July 4, 1985, quoted from *Osteuropa*, Vol. 36, No. 10 (1986), p. A491.

62. *NIN*, July 7, 1985, quoted from *Osteuropa*, Vol. 36, No. 10 (1986), p. A491.

63. *Borba*, August 11, 1987, quoted from Stanković, "Yugoslav Military Leaders Warn the Opposition."

64. Stanković, "Yugoslav Military Leaders Warn the Opposition."

65. "Napadi poput kontrarevolucije," *Borba*, March 30, 1988.

66. "Jasni su ciljevi napada na JNA," *Politika*, March 6, 1988; see also Mamula, op. cit., p. 126.

67. Ibid.

68. Hadžić, *The Yugoslav People's Agony*, p. 10.

69. "In Belgrad wächst die Kritik an der Volksarmee wegen Waffenexporten in Krisengebiete," *Handelsblatt*, March 1, 1988.

70. Miroslav Lazanski, "Armija bez tabua," *Danas*, March 29, 1988; Mamula, op. cit., pp. 122–123.

71. As evidence for the fact that the attacks constituted a special war, the JNA issued a report on Mladina's reporting that noted that of 267 articles published on the army only one was objective (*Tanjug*, April 10,1988).

72. This case is discussed in detail in Gow, op. cit., pp. 79–85; Milan Andrejevich, "Yugoslav Military again Criticized by *Mladina*," *RFE Background Reports*, June 16, 1988.

73. In fact, funding for the army has been declining since 1976, ibid., p. 102.

74. Lazanski, "Armija bez tabua."

75. "Kosovo glavna bitka" *Večernje novosti*, November 11, 1988. The claim was later dismissed by defense analyst Gersak, who documents that among its neighbors only Greece spent a higher ratio of its GDP on defense; see Gow, op. cit., p. 105.

76. *Tanjug*, March 3, 1988; Zdzislaw P. Gwozdz, "Die Armee flirtet heftig mit der Politik," *Die Presse*, October 28, 1988.

77. Viktor Meier, "Militärs drohten der politischen Führung," *Frankfurter Allgemeine Zeitung*, May 16, 1988.

78. Milan Andrejevich, "Prime Minister Remains in Power; New Defense Minister Elected," *RFE Background Reports*, May 19, 1988. Mamula notes that he decided to

resign because he no longer had the support of the party and state leadership (Mamula, op. cit., p. 151).

79. Gow, op. cit., p. 87.
80. Comments at the Seventeenth Central Committee meeting of the League of Communists of Yugoslavia, October 17, 1988, quoted from Kadijević, op. cit., p. 60.
81. Ibid., pp. 61, 65.
82. Ibid., pp. 99–100.
83. Janez Drnovšek, *Meine Wahrheit* (Kilchberg: Smartbooks, 1998), p. 55.
84. Drnovsek, op. cit., p. 33.
85. Stanković, "The Role of the Army in Post-Tito Yugoslavia."
86. Mamula points out that General Djordjević opposed Milošević's methods during the session. At the same time Mamula's memoirs have to be viewed with some degree of suspicion because he goes to great lengths to present himself (improbably) as a democrat and opponent of Milošević (Mamula, op. cit., pp. 113, 116).
87. Dizdarević himself only mentions Milošević (and Kućan) as candidates but not as those who nominated him. He further notes that a number of presidency members supported the idea of Milošević or Kućan as prime minister because this would have removed them from the republics and focused their work on the federation (Raif Dizdarević, *Od smrta Tita do smrti Jugoslavije* [Sarajevo: Svjetlost, 2000], p. 321).
88. Ante Marković, "Moja istina o smrti Jugoslavije (6), Vojska van kontrole," *Danas*, November 11, 2003.
89. Kadijević, op. cit., p. 106. The personal links between Kadijević and Milošević became more apparent by the fact that their families spent their holidays in August 1989 together. During the holidays, Borisav Jović, a close ally of Milošević and the Serb member of presidency noted that Kadijević "has all the same positions as Serbia. That certainly puts us close to the Army" (Borisav Jović, *Poslednji dani SFRJ* [Kragujevac: Prizma, 1996], p. 45). Mamula notes that upon finding out about the close ties between Kadijević and Milošević, his relations with Kadijević cooled off (Mamula, op. cit., p. 158).
90. Gwozdz, "Die Armee flirtet heftig mit der Politik."
91. Ibid.
92. Svetlana Vasovic-Mekina, "Reactions on Stambolic's Book: Franc Setinc between a Genius and a Madman," *Vreme News Digest Agency*, No. 210 (October 9, 1995).
93. Ante Marković Evidence, Milosevic (IT-02–54) "Kosovo, Croatia and Bosnia" 23.10.2003, 28062–28062. Available at: http://www.un.org/icty/transe54/031023ED.htm; Ante Marković, "Mola istina o smrti Jugoslavije (6), Vojska van kontrole," *Danas*, November 20, 2003.
94. *Tanjug*, November 25, 1988.
95. "Kosovo glavna bitka."
96. Stanković, "The Role of the Army in Post-Tito Yugoslavia."
97. Drnovšek, op. cit., p. 62.
98. Kadijević, op. cit., p. 79.
99. Gow, op. cit., pp. 92–93.
100. *Tanjug*, December 16, 1988.
101. *AP*, November 23, 1989.
102. *Tanjug*, December 15, 1990.
103. *Tanjug*, June 21, 1988.
104. Milan Andrejevich, "Yugoslav Leaders Issue Stern Warnings to the LCY CC," *RFE Background Reports*, February 1, 1989.
105. *Politika*, October 19, 1989.

106. Hadžić, *The Yugoslav People's Agony*, pp. 61–63.
107. Ibid., pp. 56–57.
108. Milan Andrejevich, "What Future for the League of Communists of Yugoslavia," *RFE Background Reports*, January 22, 1990.
109. Mamula, op. cit., p. 167.
110. Konrad Kološek, 1991. *Prvi pucnji u SFRJ. Sećanja na početak oružanih sukoba* (Belgrade: Dan Graf, 2005), p. 28.
111. Jelena Lovrić, "Miting istine u Sava centru," *Danas*, 30.1.1990; Dejan Jović, *Jugoslavija-država koja je odumrla* (Belgrade: B92, 2003), pp. 470–471.
112. Borisav Jović notes that Kadijević became dispirited as a result of the failed congress. See Jović, op. cit., p. 94.
113. Milan Andrejevich, "The Military's Role in Current Yugoslav Developments," *RFE Background Reports*, October 16, 1990.
114. Jović, op. cit., p. 118.
115. Bebler, "Das Militär in Jugoslawiens Krise," pp. 3, 7; Hadžić, *The Yugoslav People's Agony*, p. 81. Some army leaders, such as Šimić, also criticized the Serbian and Montenegrin political elite (Paparela, op. cit., p. 104).
116. Viktor Meier, "Weshalb der Armee Jugoslawiens das Putschen scherfällt," *Frankfurter Allgemeine Zeitung*, October 17, 1990. At the same time, Jović reports a stinging attack on the Serbian leadership by Adžić in February 1990. He criticized Serbia for alienating the northern republic through its heavy-handed style and confirming their reservations toward Yugoslavia (Jović, op. cit., p. 119).
117. See "Debate on the Wars in Croatia and Bosnia, Part II," Bosnia Report, January–April 2005, available at: http://www.bosnia.org.uk/bosrep/report_format.cfm?articleid = 2966& reportid = 167.
118. Hadžić, *The Yugoslav People's Agony*, pp. 86–87.
119. See Mamula, op. cit., pp. 189–190.
120. The party president, Stevan Mirković called on its members to vote for the SPS (Robert Thomas, *The Politics of Serbia in the 1990s* [London: Hurst, 1999], p. 77). Kadijević mentioned the idea of founding a new socialist party already in April 1990 (Jović, op. cit., pp. 139–143).
121. The party later transformed itself into JUL, the Yugoslav Left, coalition partner of the SPS in Serbia until 2000.
122. Hadžić, *The Yugoslav People's Agony*, p. 80. The founding congress included prominent army leadership, Gračanin, Ljubičić, Kadijević, Mamula, and Adžić. Carl E. Buchalla, "Demokratische Erneuerung nicht mehr gefragt," *Süddeutsche Zeitung*, November 22, 1990; Cyrill Stieger, "Politische Ambitionen der Armee Jugoslawiens?" *Neue Zürcher Zeitung*, December 6, 1990.
123. Mamula, op. cit., pp. 189–193.
124. Kolšek, op. cit., p. 28
125. Viktor Meier, "'Armeepartei' in Jugoslawien," *Frankfurter Allgemeine Zeitung*, November 22, 1990.
126. Many army members, such as the first party president general, Stevan Mirković, left or became inactive in 1991 (Slavoljub Djukić, *Milošević und die Macht. Serbiens Weg in den Abgrund* [Bad Vilbel: Nidda Verlag, 2000], pp. 95–98).
127. Hadžić, *The Yugoslav People's Agony*, p. 89.
128. *Tanjug*, December 15, 1990.
129. Jelena Lovrić, "Scenarij državnog udara, *Danas*, October 16, 1990, pp. 15–17.
130. Kadijević, *op. cit.*, p. 114.

131. Ibid., pp. 108–109.
132. Drnovšek, op. cit., pp. 257–261.
133. Cyrill Stieger, "Jugoslawiens Armee im Zwielicht—Ablauf der Frist zur Entwaffnung der Milizen," *Neue Zürcher Zeitung*, January 24, 1991; Hadžić, *The Yugoslav People's Agony*, p. 118.
134. Anton Tus, "The War in Slovenia and Croatia up to the Sarajevo Ceasefire," Branka Magaš and Ivo Žanić (eds.), *The War in Croatia and Bosnia-Herzegovina, 1991–1995* (London: Frank Cass, 2001), p. 42.
135. The plan was coordinated with the different army units throughout Yugoslavia, although the commander of the fifth army notes in his memoirs that he received only minimal information on the plan of the army leadership (Kolšek, op. cit., pp. 100–101.)
136. Cyrill Stieger, "Jugoslawiens Armee zurückgebunden," *Neue Zürcher Zeitung*, March 15, 1991.
137. The JNA did, however, have 15,000 troops stationed in Kosovo since 1989 to suppress Kosovo Albanian opposition to the abolition of autonomy ("Jugoslawiens Armee warnt Kritiker," *Süddeutsche Zeitung*, April 1, 1989).
138. Hadžić, *The Yugoslav People's Agony*, p. 119.
139. Jović, op. cit., pp. 276–278.
140. Drnovšek did not attend the first meeting for fear of arrest but joined the meetings on March 14 and 15.
141. The best description of the circumstances can be found in Laura Silber, Allan Little, *The Death of Yugoslavia* (London: Penguin, 1995), pp. 135–139.
142. Jović, op. cit., pp. 286–295.
143. Ibid.
144. Kadijević, op. cit., p. 113.
145. Jović, op. cit., pp. 286–295.
146. Kadijević, op. cit., p. 31. Jović repeatedly notes Kadijević's hope of receiving support from Moscow, i.e., Jović (op. cit., p. 276).
147. Filip Svarm, "After the Battle: The Generals Write . . . ," *Vreme News Digest Agency* No. 299, June 28, 1997; see also "Vuk Obradović o tajnoj misiji V. Kadijevića u Moskvi," *Danas*, No. 11 (June 14, 1997).
148. Jović, op. cit., pp. 295–296; Drnovšek, op. cit., p. 272.
149. Jović, op. cit., pp. 296–297.
150. Ibid., pp. 297–306.
151. See Stipe Mesić, *The Demise of Yugoslavia* (Budapest: CEU Press, 2004), pp. 54–55.
152. Kadijević later noted that he considered the idea to topple Milošević a ploy to destroy Yugoslavia and notes that the two pillars of defense for Yugoslavia were "the Serb nation and the JNA," Kadijević, op. cit., p. 89.
153. Ante Marković, "Rupa u planu Kadijevića, Moja istina o smrti Jugoslavije (7)," *Danas*, November 21, 2003. This appears to be a change from 1989–90, when according to Martin Špegelj, the first minister of defense and general of the JNA, Kadijević contemplated to "get rid of both Milošević and the leading people in the Western republics . . . and to return Yugoslavia to the centralist model" (Špegelj, op. cit., p. 14).
154. Jović, op. cit., pp. 306–310.
155. Ibid., pp. 310–311.
156. A meeting of the entire army leadership took place on March 26 with the commanders from all the armies to discuss the failure of the presidency to make a decision. During the meeting Kadijević outlined the risk of a civil war and failure of federal institutions. Subsequently, the leadership decided to take a more active role in confronting the

conflict. During the meeting, Chief of Staff Adžić outlined steps for a higher state of alert on the basis of the S-2 plan for an attack from the West (Kolšek, pp. 114–117).

157. Kadijević, op. cit., p. 114.

158. Jović told Kadijević in June 1990 that he would prefer to "forcibly expel them [Slovenia and Croatia] from Yugoslavia, by simply drawing border . . . , but I do not know what we should do with the Serbs in Croatia. I am not for the use of force; rather I would like to present them with a fait accompli. Veljko agrees" (Jović, op. cit., p. 159; Drnovšek, op. cit,. p. 234).

159. Jović, op. cit., p. 264.

160. Ibid., pp. 337–338.

161. Stephen Engelberg, "In Tattered Yugoslavia, the Army's Loyalties Remain Unclear," *New York Times*, March 18, 1991.

162. *AP*, July 10, 1991.

163. Ofelija Backović, Miloš Vasić, and Aleksandar Vasović, "Who Wants to Be a Soldier? The Call-Up Crisis—An Analytical Overview over Media Reports," Branka Magaš and Ivo Žanić (eds.), *The War in Croatia and Bosnia-Herzegovina, 1991–1995* (London: Frank Cass, 2001), pp. 329–345.

164. Kadijević, op. cit., p. 97.

165. Vojin Dimitrijević, "Societal and Cultural Prerequisites for Promotion and Implementation of the Democratic Control of the Armed Forces," *DECAF, Working Paper*, No. 67 (2002), p. 6.

166. Carl E. Buchalla, "Konflikt in Jugoslawien verschärft sich, "*Süddeutsche Zeitung*, December 7, 1990.

167. Drnovsek, op. cit., p. 245.

THE DISINTEGRATION OF YUGOSLAVIA AND WESTERN FOREIGN POLICY IN THE 1980S

❖ Paul Shoup ❖

Introduction

In this chapter we shall reexamine the foreign policies of the United States and Europe toward Yugoslavia prior to the outbreak of war in June 1991. The subject is controversial; the so-called lessons learned, even more so. American foreign policy today, as we shall suggest at the end of this essay, is in some ways still trying to free itself from what many analysts (but not necessarily the author of this chapter) feel was a mistaken approach to Yugoslavia—one based on caution, on keeping one's distance, rather than in active engagement in the Yugoslav crisis, especially *before* the conflict began.

Our starting point will be the 1980s. For Yugoslavia, the decade was a turning point (or better said, a disaster). At the outset of the 1980s, Yugoslavia faced a number of challenges, the most important being the rapid deterioration of the economy. The prospect of the dissolution of Yugoslavia nevertheless seemed remote. By the end of the decade, Yugoslavia had, for all intents and purposes, disintegrated. Serbs, Croats, Slovenes, and Albanians were on the verge of civil war. The international community, for its part, was in the throes of uncertainty, distracted by events elsewhere (the collapse of Communism in Eastern Europe), and alternately hopeful and despairing that Yugoslavia could be saved.

As a consequence, the foreign policies of the United States and Europe were notable for their lack of engagement with Yugoslavia during the 1980s; one might call it a decade of "nonevents" on the foreign policy front. Only in the late 1980s, with the appointment of Warren Zimmermann as American ambassador to Belgrade in March 1989, did American policy show signs of interest in addressing the Yugoslav crisis. By then, many analysts and scholars have argued, it was too late. We shall take due note of these criticisms in the pages to follow. Indeed, the reader must bear in mind that the literature on the Yugoslav crisis is immense but seldom analyzed in its entirety. More regrettable, certainly, is the fact that primary sources have not yet been utilized to the extent possible in determining the motives of the actors in this tragedy. That task awaits future historians. This essay will take the second best approach and utilize as many secondary sources as can be mustered for the task.

Background

The achievements and the travails of the former Yugoslavia are an oft-told tale with which the reader of this essay is undoubtedly familiar. We shall not try the reader's patience by reviewing these events once again. Our special concern, to repeat, is the period 1980–June 1991.[1] But before turning to this period, we wish to comment briefly on certain issues that invariably arise in connection with the former Yugoslavia and its demise.

First, Yugoslavia was based upon, most historians would agree, and arose out of conflicting ideologies and principles. It was never clear whether the Kingdom of the Serbs, Croats, and Slovenes, as Yugoslavia was initially known, was founded upon the Yugoslav idea, that is, the union of the South Slav peoples, or alternatively, owed its legitimacy to either some form of social contract among its members or, as a third possibility, as a means for all Serbs to live in a common state. Both the strengths and weaknesses of the former Yugoslavia lay in this mixture of legitimizing principles. These principles might, on certain occasions, reinforce one another. Yet more often these very same principles were the source of endless controversy and misunderstanding, as other contributors to this volume have noted.

Second, several comments are in order concerning the nature of national and ethnic tensions in the former Yugoslavia. The existence of these tensions can hardly be disputed. Yet the literature on the Yugoslav conflict seems uncertain how to treat this fundamental fact of life in the former Yugoslavia. Did ethnic antagonisms make conflict inevitable? Or was it a convenient distortion that the Yugoslav conflict had its origins in "ancient hatreds"?[2] American and European policy makers, as the reader is aware, have been accused of taking this latter position and thus failing to exploit opportunities to head off the conflict or to intervene in a timely fashion once the conflict commenced.[3]

In the last analysis, one can hardly begin to understand the reasons for the demise of Yugoslavia without reference to ethnic and national tensions (primarily, it must be added, the latter). Unfortunately, the centrality of the national question in the history of Yugoslavia seems to have been passed over lightly by much of the recent literature on the Yugoslav crisis. The reasons for this would divert us from our primary task (is it because "ethnicity" has replaced "nationalism" in our discourse?), but the role played by the national question in mobilizing the ethnic communities of Yugoslavia behind their more radical leaders is beyond serious doubt.

We may now return to the 1980s. The death of Tito on May 4, 1980, brought the prospect of Yugoslavia's dissolution briefly to the forefront. Western policy makers had long speculated that Tito's death could be the occasion for Soviet intervention in Yugoslavia.[4] The immediate impact of Tito's passing was, however, slight. The Constitution of 1974 had already provided for a collective leadership in the party and state based upon consensual decision making among the six republics and two provinces.[5]

While the Yugoslav leadership maintained an outward consensus after Tito's death, it did so at the expense of badly needed reforms in the economy and revisions of the 1974 Constitution. Behind the deadlock in the leadership one could discern a changing dynamic in Yugoslav politics. First, any thought of a struggle for power—from which a more liberal leadership might have emerged—ceased following Tito's death.[6] Second, the growing power of the republics discouraged innovation. Slovenia, in particular, which had supported reforms in the 1960s, prevented any changes (for example, in the system of self-management introduced in the mid-1970s) that might threaten the autonomy it had won under the 1974 Constitution. Elsewhere, those advocating reforms found themselves blocked by conservatives placed in power before Tito's passing. Steven Burg, in an outstanding piece of analysis that appeared in *Soviet Studies* in 1986, concluded that in the mid-1980s "Yugoslavia is at the crossroads, between reaction and reform."[7] Burg described a leadership at odds over economic reform and uncertain of its future in the face of a growing loss of legitimacy, economic decline, and rising national tensions. The inability of the League of Communists to resolve the Kosovo question between 1981 (the year of student demonstrations in Priština for an independent Kosovo) and 1988 (when the Milošević regime in Serbia initiated its crackdown on the province) was a further symptom, as well as a cause, of this leadership deadlock.[8]

The latter half of the 1980s was marked by the emergence of the national question in Slovenia and Serbia as the result of the Memorandum of the Serbian Academy of Sciences and the Slovenian national plank published in the journal *Nova Revija*; the factional struggle within the League of Communists of Serbia between Slobodan Milošević and Ivan Stambolić; the mobilization of the Slovenes in their confrontation with the JNA; the adoption of amendments to the Slovene constitution in September 1989; and the declaration of martial law by the Serbian government (with the approval of the federal presidency) in Kosovo in the spring of the same year. It was during these tumultuous times that Western diplomacy toward Yugoslavia seemed frozen in place—distracted by events elsewhere, fearful of the collapse of Yugoslavia, yet guilty of placing an optimistic gloss over the crisis if only to facilitate emergency aid to Yugoslavia by the international community.

With these events in mind we can now consider the foreign policy dilemmas that the crisis in Yugoslavia posed for the United States and Europe. But first it is necessary to refer to Yugoslavia's position in the world, how that position underwent drastic change, and how American and European diplomacy tried to cope with the Yugoslav crisis at a time when events elsewhere were monopolizing the West's attention.

The United States, Europe, and Yugoslavia

Yugoslavia, as we know, enjoyed a privileged position during the years of the cold war. Its status as a maverick Communist country, the drama of the Partisan resistance movement during World War II, and the vitality of her peoples all contributed to this image. During the 1950s, the American military aid program was said to have equipped eight Yugoslav divisions at a cost of $750 million or more. As a spur to economic reform in the early 1960s, the United States and other Western governments made available $275 million in financial aid. Monetary reforms were introduced with the assistance of the IMF and other international agencies.

Sometimes overlooked in the West, if not by the Yugoslavs themselves, were the rocky moments in that relationship. Serbs, as many American visitors to Belgrade can testify, still talk angrily about the American air raid on Belgrade of April 16, 1944, when holiday strollers enjoying Orthodox Easter were caught in a rain of American bombs. Relations with Communist Yugoslavia were, by their very nature, subject to criticism from various quarters in the United States. In February 1957, Tito's first visit to the United States was put on hold in reaction to anti-Communist sentiment that was prevalent in the United States at the time. In June of 1962, the Senate barred aid to Communist countries, including Yugoslavia. George Kennan, who had been appointed ambassador to Yugoslavia the previous year, was quoted as saying that the actions of Congress "amount to the greatest windfall Soviet diplomacy could encounter in this area." In July 1975, Tito denounced the American ambassador, Laurence Silberman, for purportedly having a hostile attitude toward Yugoslavia.

Despite Yugoslavia's balancing act between East and West (as the reader is aware, Yugoslavia was one of the founders of the nonaligned movement and fought to keep the group from falling under the control of the socialist bloc), mutual suspicions between Yugoslavia and the United States could never be completely laid to rest. Zachary Irwin recounts how, in 1986, Admiral Branko Mamula picked up on the doctrine of "low intensity warfare," a product of the Reagan era, to warn of a threat from the West, especially in the case of "serious internal difficulties."[9] Mamula's warning was a sign that the JNA saw a threat to Yugoslavia coming not only from the Soviet Union but from the West as well. This fear grew as Yugoslavia disintegrated until the notion of "special warfare" being waged against Yugoslavia from the West became a virtual obsession with the JNA commanders. In the end, as we know, the JNA turned to Russia in the Spring of 1991 for aid in anticipation of Western interference in a war brought about by the secession of Slovenia and Croatia.

In the period of the cold war, Yugoslavia nevertheless retained its special status both as a maverick Communist country and because of concerns in the West that instability in Yugoslavia could lead to Soviet intervention and that a confrontation between NATO and Warsaw Pact forces might follow. (A common scenario for war gamers plotting the outbreak of war between the Soviet Union and the West was a Soviet invasion of Yugoslavia as a response to some form of instability in the country.)[10] Thus, Yugoslavs—and especially Tito—were accorded special treatment in Washington and the European capitals. In October 1963, Tito was a guest of President Kennedy (in the event, the last head of state to see Kennedy before his assassination). Other visits in both directions followed. In September 1970, Nixon visited Yugoslavia and pledged to uphold the country's independence. In October 1971, Tito paid a state visit to the United States and was received by President Nixon. In August 1975, President Ford briefly visited Yugoslavia upon his return from the Helsinki Conference; and in March 1978, Tito met with President Carter in Washington. Foreign dignitaries were a common sight in Belgrade in the 1960s and 1970s and continued to appear, if in somewhat lesser numbers, in the decade of the 1980s.[11]

Foreign aid continued to flow to Yugoslavia during the 1960s and 1970s even as the cold war eased. In 1980 Yugoslavia signed a cooperation agreement with the European Community (EC) opening European markets to Yugoslav exports.[12] Concern that instability in Yugoslavia could lead to Soviet intervention spurred the international community to continue to send aid to Yugoslavia while urging that it undertake economic reforms. In 1981 an IMF loan to Yugoslavia of 2.1 billion dollars was approved—the largest ever by the IMF, according to reports at the time.[13] When efforts by Milka Planinc to stem the growing foreign debt failed, the IMF and Yugoslavia reached a second accord in August 1988 to reduce debt servicing, which by this time had reached 45 percent of foreign currency earnings.[14] In December 1989 an agreement was reached with the IMF to provide a loan of 600 million dollars, and Yugoslav sources reported that they anticipated financial aid worth three billion dollars during the following two years (which, of course, did not materialize). Finally, on the eve of the civil war, in the spring of 1991, the EC held out the prospect of over four billion dollars in aid, contingent upon the Yugoslavs' finding a peaceful resolution of their differences.[15]

Although aid from the IMF was conditional upon the enactment of reforms and there was resistance within the EC (especially from the British) to European financial assistance to Yugoslavia, the overall commitment of Europe and the United States to aid Yugoslavia was impressive, given the sorry state of affairs in the country at the time.[16] The hope that the Yugoslavs would use this aid to carry out economic reforms (among which was the recentralization of economic authority in the hands of the federal government) proved illusory. One senses that Western governments were reduced to providing aid out of desperation rather than out of hope for real reforms, no other means of halting Yugoslavia's slide into chaos being at hand.

Yugoslavia also benefited in other ways from her engagement with the international community during the 1960s and 1970s, and these ties were not entirely broken during the 1980s. As we have seen, it was one of the founders of the nonaligned movement, a participant in the Helsinki process (the first review of the Helsinki Accords was held in Belgrade in 1978) as well as a member of the IMF, the World Bank, and GATT.[17] Thanks to the agreement of 1980 mentioned above,

Yugoslavia enjoyed a special relationship with the EC, and there was speculation that it might become a member of the EFTA (European Free Trade Agreement) as well.

U.S. relations with Yugoslavia—notwithstanding ups and downs in the 1960s and 1970s—remained strong throughout most of the period we are considering here. A dispatch from the *New York Times* of November 1, 1981, recounted the celebration in the United States and in Belgrade of the hundredth anniversary of relations between Serbia and the United States. "For the last several weeks," the *New York Times* reported, "a large number of Yugoslav and American scholars, artists, musicians and politicians have been meeting here [in Belgrade] and the United States to commemorate the centennial of the formal establishment of relations between the United States and Serbia. . . . To mark the centennial. Lawrence S. Eagleburger, Assistant Secretary of State for European affairs, flew here last week. . . . Mr. Eagleburger, who was Ambassador to Yugoslavia earlier this year, spoke warmly of the 'mutual trust and understanding' between the two countries and concluded, 'As Americans would say, we have a lot going for us.'" In conclusion, the *New York Times* noted that the American government contributed more than $200,000 to the sponsorship of the centennial exchanges.[18]

In part, as the *New York Times* dispatch suggests, this cordial, even enthusiastic relationship between the United States and Yugoslavia could be attributed to personal factors. Throughout the early and mid-1980s, Lawrence Eagleburger was a dedicated supporter of assistance to Yugoslavia, even as its economic crisis deepened.[19] John Scanlan, U.S. ambassador to Yugoslavia in the late 1980s, had the misfortune to be caught up in the pro-Milošević fervor that momentarily swept the diplomatic corps in Belgrade in the spring of 1988.[20] He was, as this author can testify from personal experience, a champion of Yugoslavia but at the expense of a deeper appreciation of the seriousness of the crisis the country was undergoing and the threat that Milošević represented to peace in the region as Yugoslavia dissolved.

In this, however, Ambassador Scanlan does not seem to have been alone. European diplomats also were guilty of a simplistic view of the situation in Yugoslavia as the crisis deepened. Although this was not uniformly the case, Viktor Meier's scathing criticism of the European and American diplomatic corps[21] seems borne out, as far as Germany was concerned, by Michael Libal in his volume *The Limits of Persuasion: Germany and the Yugoslav Crisis, 1991–1992,*[22] and by the criticisms of European indifference to the Yugoslav crisis when the issue was raised by the White House during the course of 1990 and 1991 (more on this below).

The pro-Milošević phase of American foreign policy—which was never fully embraced by the State Department—ended with the arrival of Warren Zimmermann in Belgrade.[23] According to Zimmermann, he and Eagleburger agreed that Yugoslavia and the Balkans remained important for the United States but not as before; that the country had lost its geostrategic significance; and that American policy should now pay attention to human rights issues, especially in Kosovo.[24] Following his arrival,

Zimmermann paid "numerous" visits to Kosovo—on occasion accompanied by U.S. senators and congressmen who were pressing for U.S. action against human rights abuses in the province. At the same time, the attention of European diplomacy, and of the United States as well, was directed elsewhere toward the dramatic events unfolding in Eastern Europe.

The upshot was that U.S. policy, in focusing on human rights issues, was giving priority to domestic (American) concerns and less directly to the crisis in republic relations, which, by 1990, following the adoption of the Slovenian constitutional amendments and revisions to the Serbian constitution ending the autonomy of Kosovo, threatened the very existence of the Yugoslav state. These actions (or better said nonactions) by Western diplomacy set the stage for subsequent attacks on the conduct of Western diplomacy toward Yugoslavia during the crucial years and months prior to June 1991.

Before we can adequately assess these criticisms we must, however, comment briefly on the seemingly contradictory strands in Western—and especially American—policy at the time.

The first strand was represented by the "old Yugoslav hands" in the State Department (Eagleburger, Brent Scowcroft, and others). The Yugoslavs appeared bent on self-destruction, and in the light of events in the rest of Eastern Europe—and the fact that the vibrant multinational Yugoslavia of the past was now a dream turned into a nightmare—there seemed no reason, or motivation, to have sympathy or concern for the country's plight. Eagleburger clearly became disillusioned; Zachary Irwin quotes the former ambassador to Yugoslavia saying that "If I know something about Yugoslavia, it's when you come at them not to do something that it is precisely the time they'll go ahead and do it."[25] Robert Hutchings notes how the visit of Prime Minister Ante Marković to Washington in October 1989 was "the sound of one hand clapping."[26] Warren Zimmermann added a poignant and painful observation to this last-minute effort of the Yugoslav prime minister for American aid to rescue Yugoslavia from its financial crisis. Marković, recounted Zimmerman, was compelled to pay for his own meals while in Washington even though he was on an official visit and received by President Bush and members of Congress.[27]

The chorus of irritation and despair could be heard on all sides. Christopher Cviić, a long-time observer of Yugoslavia for the *Economist*, warned the Yugoslavs that "Yugoslavia's many friends in the West simply cannot comprehend why it has made so little of the material aid and political support extended to it over the years."[28] David Anderson, at a conference held at the Institute of International Politics and Economics in Belgrade in 1990, was more than blunt with his Yugoslav audience: "The term used most often by people outside who look at this country," Anderson said, "is that it is not serious . . . you can go through Washington, New York, and the United States government and trade centers and you will be hard put to find anyone at all interested in Yugoslavia."[29] "At the heart of the problem for Western governments," Hutchings observed, "lay the judgment, reached early on in Washington and most European capitals, that Yugoslavia no longer mattered much because it was no longer likely to be an arena of East-West conflict."[30]

This disregard, mixed with irritation and perhaps a dose of contempt, was the basis for the charge that the United States lacked not only interest but also concern for the Yugoslav crisis. Hutchings, commenting on the attitude that "Yugoslavia no longer mattered," added "that from this flawed premise, flawed policy ensued."[31] In the literature on the Yugoslav crisis, there is hardly a study that fails to note and criticize this stance—and to argue, somewhat hastily in our view, that the West missed an opportunity to influence the outcome of the Yugoslav crisis if only it had acted earlier and with more determination.[32] It was a short step from these criticisms to the assertion that the United States, when the civil war began, suffered from a "frozen image" of the Balkans as a region steeped in primordial hatreds and that Yugoslavia should therefore be left to its own devices.[33]

But this harsh judgment of U.S. policy must be accepted cautiously. A second strand in American policy toward Yugoslavia was, as events were to prove, a quite realistic and accurate understanding of the depth of the Yugoslav crisis on the part of those with past experience in country and of the difficulty that outsiders would face in influencing the outcome. This was the other side of the coin, in fact, of the hesitation and frustration displayed by American diplomats in dealing with the Yugoslav question as the crisis deepened in 1989 and 1990. In this respect American diplomats in the State Department—although not always in the embassy in Belgrade[34]—appear to have been more realistic than their counterparts in Europe. Hutchings, in his account of the diplomacy of the period, notes that cables addressed to European capitals in the summer of 1990 and in January 1991 warning of the seriousness of the crisis met with little or no response.[35] The same charge of indifference by the Europeans to American warnings of a crisis in Yugoslavia has been voiced by David Gompert.[36]

Of all those involved with American foreign policy toward Yugoslavia during the Bush administration, Gompert has come forth with the most vigorous and convincing case that the United States was aware of the situation in Yugoslavia and acted appropriately. In Gompert's view, the Bush administration was well aware of the potential for violence in Yugoslavia but "simply knew no way to prevent this from occurring." "There was no intelligence failure"; no inattention due to preoccupation with the collapse of Communism or Iraq's invasion of Kuwait. "Rather," argued Gompert, "despite considerable deliberation and diplomatic activity, no good option emerged to arrest the accelerating awful logic of breakup and war."[37] This decision, we may assume, was not reached easily. The United States was keen to maintain stability and unity in the multinational states of Eastern Europe and the Soviet Union, above all, the latter.

It is in this context of pessimistic realism that one can best understand the report of the CIA of November 1990, leaked to the *New York Times*,[38] that Yugoslavia was on the verge of a violent civil war and that little or nothing could be done to prevent it. Hutchings writes that no one objected to its conclusions but "only with the smug finality with which they were rendered." He adds: "the estimate had little impact, for it was so unrelievedly deterministic that it suggested no possible avenue for American policy that might avert or at least contain the violence attending Yugoslavia's inevitable disintegration."[39]

The CIA report, in the form of a National Intelligence Estimate, was the result of a joint assessment made by American intelligence agencies including the CIA, the NSA, the Department of State, the Defense Intelligence Agency, and other government bodies. One suspects that far from catching the State Department "old hands" by surprise, the report largely reflected their views and had relied upon their input from the start.

For a first-time reader of National Intelligence Estimates, the document appears rather simplistic, as if afraid of taxing the attention span of the reader.[40] The conclusions of the report were as follows. First, "Yugoslavia will cease to function as a federal state within one year, and will probably dissolve within two. Economic reform will not stave off the breakup." Second, "Serbia will block Slovene and Croat attempts to form an all-Yugoslav confederation." Third, "There will be a protracted armed uprising by Albanians in Kosovo. A full-scale, inter-republic war is unlikely, but serious inter-communal conflicts will accompany the breakup and will continue afterward. The violence will be intractable and bitter." Finally, the report concluded, "There is little the United States and its European allies can do to preserve Yugoslav unity. Yugoslavs will see such efforts as contrary to advocacy of democracy and self-determination."

These conclusions were elaborated upon in a section titled "Key Judgments," which warned that the Serbs would attempt to foment armed uprisings in Bosnia-Herzegovina where "large scale ethnic violence is likely." The Soviet Union, the report continued, would have only an indirect influence on the outcome, and although the Europeans would have some leverage, "they are not going to use it to hold the old Yugoslavia together." The "Key Judgments" section also included a warning—prescient as events proved:

> Leaders from various republics will make claims on U.S. officials to advance their partisan objectives. Federal and Serb leaders will emphasize statements in support of territorial integrity. Slovenes, Croats and Kosovars, however, will play up U.S. pressure for improved performance on human rights and self-determination. Thus Washington will continue to be drawn into the heated arena of interethnic conflict and will be expected to respond in some manner to the contrary claims of all parties.[41]

With hindsight, one can see that the CIA report was in some ways not pessimistic enough. One could have argued at the time—and this is a key to the criticisms of Western policy that were to follow—that Yugoslavia had *already* dissolved. The consequences of a civil war in Bosnia were treated too lightly, especially in light of the fear among many Yugoslavs of the danger of what the collapse of Yugoslavia would mean for Bosnia.[42] On the other hand, the prediction of an insurrection in Kosovo reflected a notion that was current at the time (summer and fall of 1990) but demonstrated a poor knowledge of the Kosovo situation; in this case, the report was overly pessimistic. In assessing the Serbian threat to Croatia, the report showed signs of cold war concerns over external intervention by Yugoslavia's neighbors should violence break out. While the report rightly suggested that Serbia would try to reincorporate disputed territories in Croatia and might resort to "bloody shifts of population," it also suggested that Serbia would be constrained (1) by its own minority problems (presumably an uprising in Kosovo), and (2) by fear of external intervention by her neighbors, especially Bulgaria and Greece, in Macedonia.[43]

More important than these speculations—many of which were remarkably on target—was the pessimistic, "wash your hands" tone of the report spelled out briefly in the summary page:

> Any U.S. statements in support of the territorial integrity of the old federation will be used by federal leaders to strengthen their case against republic attempt [sic] to assert their independence. Statements by U.S. officials on behalf of national self-determination will be used out of context by republic leaders to rally support within their national constituencies against central controls. Albanian leaders in Kosovo will play up any attention by American officials to human rights issues. All parties are likely to press the United States for material support and will look askance at U.S. public pronouncements if such support is not forthcoming.[44]

If our hunch is correct that there was a large measure of input from the persons to whom the report was ostensibly directed—the officials in the State Department and those responsible for Yugoslav policy in the White House—then one cannot accuse American policy makers of being naive or ignorant about the Yugoslav crisis. On the other hand—and this was perhaps not what the intelligence agencies were tasked to do—there was no articulation of what vital interests, if any, the United States might have in the upcoming conflict and no specific warning of the need for the United States to prepare for a decision—the dilemma of Gladstone and Disraeli at the time of the "Eastern Question" in the nineteenth century[45]—on whether to intervene if the conflict led to massive violations of human rights. Thus a certain paradox hung over the assessment. The CIA was still viewing the conflict, which they felt was unavoidable, from a preconflict perspective. The agency did not warn the policy makers adequately of what—given the past of the region—might lie in store for them, and more to the point, the danger that they might be drawn into the conflict.

To sum up, the report did not go much beyond what was already the thinking of those responsible for Yugoslav policy in the State Department and White House. If one can generalize about the approach taken by the report, one might suggest that the intelligence analysts and those on whom they relied were adept at gaming—but poor historians. (Or alternatively, that history was not considered the kind of hard data that could go into a report of this kind.) This created a situation in which the United States was ill prepared to react to the deepening of the crisis in 1990 and 1991, as we shall now see.[46]

This takes us to the third strand in American policy prior to the breakup of Yugoslavia. It has been exhaustively treated by existing studies of American foreign policy and the Yugoslav crisis and can be summarized here.

In brief, we are alluding to the decision *not* to become directly involved in the Yugoslav crisis. Instead, American policy makers, when confronting the Yugoslavs, focused on the need for "unity and democracy." In doing so, American policy—and European policy as well—was simply repeating the now familiar hope that Yugoslavia would not disintegrate, while democratization was seen as a necessary step to fill the vacuum created by the collapse of the socialist system. Actions that might accelerate the disintegration of Yugoslavia—directly or indirectly—were hardly an option for American and European policy makers at the time. We have seen that Michael Libal, in his analysis of German foreign policy, criticized German diplomats for underestimating the crisis. Yet, as he pointed out, Germany had invested a great deal in its relationship with Yugoslavia. Given a history of excellent ties between the two countries, Libal suggested, "it was sheer lunacy" to advocate the breakup of the country.[47]

Yet, as critics were quick to point out, favoring democracy *and* the unity in Yugoslavia made little sense under the circumstances of the period we are considering. Saadia Touval comments as follows:

> Successful deterrence and dissuasion require the projection of clear goals and credible leverage. But instead of clarity, the West signaled ambiguity, leading the Yugoslav actors to varying interpretations of Western attitudes. The ambiguity stemmed from the West's definition of goals in terms of broad values, some of which, in context of the time and place, were contradictory. The main difficulty was inherent in the simultaneous advocacy of both unity and democracy. In the context of Yugoslavia in 1990–91, these two objectives were contradictory, undermining each other. Attempts to preserve unity were accompanied by the repression of nationalist and separatist tendencies, and with the violation of human rights. Democratization opened the way to the formation of nationalist parties, and to the victory in freely held elections in Slovenia and Croatia of leaders who were calling for the secession of these two republics from Yugoslavia. Thus attempts to preserve unity were anti-democratic, and the promotion of democracy encouraged disintegration.[48]

American diplomats were not unaware of these contradictions. In a demarche presented to the Yugoslavs in the second week of January 1991, Washington asserted that it would favor "democracy" over "unity."[49] Zimmermann, at the conference of the Institute for International Politics and Economics mentioned above, took note of criticism in the American press of Washington's advocacy of both unity and democracy but argued that the United States' support of unity, sovereignty, market reforms, and pluralism in meeting the crisis in Yugoslavia was still appropriate under the circumstances.[50] Eagleburger, addressing the conference, also attempted to clarify the American stand, suggesting that "It is stability through democratization that the United States seeks to support."[51]

One is forced to conclude that however laudable these goals were, and however distasteful the alternatives, the plea for "unity and democracy" was a way of avoiding the discussion of concrete issues, which, as the CIA report had warned, could only place the United States in an awkward position between the contending parties to the conflict. Thus, the content of the plea for "unity and democracy" was less important than the message that the United States, at least at the time, was not willing to mediate among the parties to the Yugoslav dispute. This in turn suggests—as does the evidence of the CIA report and the views of Gompert noted earlier—that no one on the American side was willing to consider the need to mediate *before* violence broke out, given that the chances of success were remote and the possibility of being accused of favoritism by one side or another, great.

Rather, the only option was to warn the parties of the disaster that confronted them if they continued on the collision course they had apparently set for themselves, at the same time stressing the territorial integrity of Yugoslavia in messages to the federal government of Ante Marković. In March 1991, President Bush addressed a letter to Marković, once more emphasizing the importance of the territorial integrity of Yugoslavia. The United States also requested that the EC issue a similar declaration, which was forthcoming the end of March.[52] (The EC declaration had been preceded by a statement of the Luxembourg foreign minister, Jacques Poos, on the occasion of his visit to Yugoslavia in August 1990, that the EC wanted Yugoslavia as a "strong federal state and had no interest whatsoever in a break-up of the country."[53])

As the crisis in Yugoslavia deepened in the spring of 1991, the tone of Western warnings to Yugoslavia underwent a change; in a May 28 note addressed to Marković, Helmut Kohl and François Mitterand stressed the need for a peaceful resolution of the crisis and omitted any explicit references to unity[54]; several days earlier, Eagleburger had said much the same, emphasizing the need to avoid the use of force (although, according to Wayne Bert, also omitting any reference to the inviolability of borders[55]). A meeting of the Commission on Security and Cooperation in Europe (CSCE) held in Berlin the third week in June repeated earlier warnings concerning resort to force and, for the first time, included reference to self-determination as a right that might be exercised by the peoples of Yugoslavia.[56] While these statements suggested a softening of the Western position toward the breakaway republics, they also, as reported by Bert and Libal, raised new issues. Was Eagleburger's failure to mention the inviolability of borders a way of condoning changes in republic boundaries? And the CSCE statement referring to the "peoples" of Yugoslavia raised the issue, referred to elsewhere in this essay, of exactly *who* had the right to secede (peoples or republics).

In the second week of June 1991, on the eve of the confrontation between Slovenia and the JNA, Ambassador Zimmermann made the rounds of the republics, warning Tudjman of the catastrophic effects for Croatia of a war that could lead to the loss of Krajina and repeating the refusal of the United States to provide military assistance to Croatia. In Slovenia he urged Kučan to remain in Yugoslavia.[57] These actions were preceded by pressure on Milošević and the JNA to avoid a military putsch and to permit Mesić to take up his position as president of the federal presidency (in both cases Zimmermann claims that U.S. intervention contributed to a favorable outcome).[58]

These initiatives, and others taken by the United States and the EC, culminated in the visit of Secretary of State Baker to Yugoslavia on June 21. Subsequent criticisms of the visit tended to confirm fears held by Washington that any direct American involvement at the highest level could only lead to misunderstandings and accusations that the United States had encouraged one side or the other to go to war. Indeed, the Baker visit has become a symbol of what many scholars and analysts view as a naive, confused, and ultimately disastrous American policy at the time.[59]

In retrospect, it appears that far too much importance has been attributed to Baker's visit. By June 13, the American position had been conveyed to all sides by Ambassador Zimmermann. Baker's utterances to the respective republic leaders appear to have been largely crafted by Zimmermann in any case. We know that General Kadijević was deeply suspicious of American intentions—indeed convinced that the United States was participating in a secret war to break up Yugoslavia. Given this fact, it hardly seems credible that the JNA concluded that Baker was tacitly giving them a green light to use force against Slovenia.[60] The Slovenians, for their part, had by this time turned their backs on Yugoslavia and were not to be dissuaded from acting on their intent to declare independence. Baker took the position with the Slovenians (according to Zimmermann) that "unity" was the best way of preserving human rights and achieving democracy, an argument that could not have made much of an impression on Milan Kučan, by then president of a democratic Slovenia confronted with an entrenched authoritarian regime in Serbia.

In substance, the American position was to admonish all parties to "behave," but to signal that the United States would not become involved if war broke out. Several aspects of the Baker visit nevertheless require comment. First, Baker committed the United States to a policy of nonrecognition by informing Kučan that the United States would not recognize the unilateral secession of Slovenia.[61] Baker felt he had received a pledge of restraint from Kučan (at a minimum, a delay in formally declaring independence), which the Slovenians then blatantly ignored, in Baker's view. Second, Baker warned Milošević in no uncertain terms—according to Baker's own account—that the United States would not accept Serbian claims to territories outside its own borders, although his message was made less palatable to Milošević by placing the blame largely on Serbia for the breakup of Yugoslavia.[62] Finally, Baker suggested to Marković that "if you force the United States to choose between unity and democracy, we will always choose democracy."[63]

These remarks were, in the event, a clue to American policy in the months ahead (that is, once the conflict began). On the one hand, the United States reacted with irritation bordering on anger when Slovenia (and then Croatia) declared their independence; on the other, American public opinion, and many in the foreign policy community, began to show sympathy for Slovenia and Croatia as underdogs in an unequal struggle against an aggressive Serbia. One might have wished that Baker's message that Europe and the United States would side with democracy over unity—which accurately foretold the American reaction to the conflict once it was underway—had been delivered more forcefully and to the right person (Milošević). And, perhaps more important still, one could have hoped that the secretary of state had been more concerned with the modalities of Slovenian secession than its postponement. But—to repeat—the importance of Baker's statements lay not in their impact on the actors in the Yugoslav drama at the time but in revealing ambivalence toward the Yugoslav crisis that was impossible to maintain, in the long run, after the war began.

What the West Could Have Done

In examining the events of the 1980s and early 1990s, one cannot help but speculate on whether the tragic civil war in Yugoslavia could have been avoided—if not by the peoples of Yugoslavia by themselves, then by the Yugoslavs with the assistance of the international community. Yugoslavia had played a more than honorable role in European affairs since its founding in 1918. Certainly, in the Titoist decades, there was no doubt that the average Croat, Serb, Slovene, or Macedonian was proud to be a Yugoslav and, more important still, harbored no deep-seated animosities (ethnic relations between Albanians and Serbs in Kosovo excepted) toward other ethnic communities in Yugoslavia.[64]

Beginning with this premise, it is easy to see why the actions (or nonactions) of Western diplomats subsequently came under attack. The aggression of Serbia against Croatia and the Serbian subjugation of the Kosovo Albanians—clearly in defiance of the international community—in addition to the vulnerability of Slovenia and Croatia to Western pressures (if the Western republics were to secede there was no guarantee they would be recognized)—all suggested that a more decisive stance by the West could have at least resulted in a peaceful divorce of the six republics; that is, that with Western assistance and Western pressure, the violent civil war could have been avoided.

Yet, as we can see from the above account, there are substantial difficulties with this position. Let us now look at these difficulties in greater detail. First, there was the question of *when and how* the United States and Europe were to take a more active role in the Yugoslav crisis. It has been frequently suggested that "the earlier the better." In practice, this should have meant some time in the period between 1985 (the moment when the economic crisis and other factors began to seriously delegitimize the Communist regime and thus undermine confidence in Yugoslavia) and the outbreak of violence between the JNA and Slovenia in the spring of 1991. But when, exactly? And how?

Ivo Daalder suggested that the moment for the West to act, using force if necessary, was in early 1991.[65] Robert Hutchings, for his part, proposed that the United States missed an opportunity to act in concert with Europe during the latter half of 1990. NATO, with CSCE backing, should have taken the initiative in resolving the crisis.[66] (What action NATO could have taken, and whether it should have threatened the use of force, is not explained by Hutchings.) Jasna Dragović-Soso suggested that the turning point for Yugoslavia came in mid-1988 when the Communists in Slovenia and Serbia adopted the national programs of the intellectuals. "When they did so," she writes, "the death of Yugoslavia became a virtual certainty."[67] Later in her account she notes the "fateful day" of February 27, 1989, the day of the Cankar Hall rally in Slovenia, the miners' strike in Kosovo, the first mass rally of Serbs in Knin, and the day of the founding assembly of the HDZ in Croatia.[68] If her appraisal of the situation is correct, the United States and Europe, if bent on intervening, should have acted much earlier than 1990. Christopher Bennett stated that "the decisive battle in Yugoslavia's disintegration was fought not in 1991, but in 1987,"[69] that is, at the Eighth Plenum of the LC Serbia. Viktor Meier, for his part, suggested that the turning point came in 1986–87, that at that time one could see most of the forces crystallize that would later tear Yugoslavia apart.[70] He added that if the West was truly concerned with preserving the unity of Yugoslavia, the time to act was late 1988 and early 1989, when, he suggested, the foundations of federal Yugoslavia were being destroyed in Kosovo and the army threatened a putsch in Slovenia.[71]

Nor does this exhaust the possibilities. One might wish to choose the spring of 1990 as the point at which Tito's Yugoslavia ceased to exist and Western policy could have perhaps dropped the themes of "unity and democracy," especially the former. The first free elections in Yugoslavia, held in Slovenia and Croatia in the Spring of 1990, spelled the end of the socialist myth of brotherhood and unity on which Tito's Yugoslavia was founded. This was the moment, as well, when Milošević appears to have given up the idea of a stronger federation and to have begun to focus on an enlarged, or "Greater," Serbia.[72] At this point, it could be argued, the United States and Europe could have begun to explore the modalities of either a Yugoslav confederation or a peaceful and total dissolution, knowing that, for the main actors in the Yugoslav drama, the country was already beyond saving. Finally, in a more speculative vein, there is the possibility that in the spring of 1991 the United States and Europe could have urged Bosnia, if and when Croatia declared her independence, to remain in a rump Yugoslavia. (We shall have more to say on this below.)

Yet, the very proliferation of recommendations for early intervention in the Yugoslav crisis leaves one in doubt. As Hutchings observed, when the crisis deepened "everyone inside and especially outside government seemed to know what should have been done *before*, but no one seemed to know what to do *next*."[73] The central fact was that the dissolution of Yugoslavia was a drawn-out and complex affair, beginning at least in the 1970s when it became obvious that Titoist Yugoslavia was an ideological construct meant to prevent, as much as to encourage, a lasting solution to the national question. Two contradictory, yet complementary, realities faced anyone who sought to intervene in this process.

On the one hand, one is repeatedly reminded of the underlying tension between the notion of Yugoslavia as a "compact" between her peoples (something the constitution of 1946 and subsequent socialist constitutions seemed to imply)[74] and the passionate (and sometimes ill-advised) search of the Serbs for unity. Arnold Suppan quotes Pašić as saying in November 1918: "Serbia wants to liberate and unite the Yugoslavs and does not want [to] drown in a sea of some kind of Yugoslavia, but to have Yugoslavia drown in her."[75]

Whether Milošević was ready to acknowledge that his proposal for a "modern federation" could not be based on this traditional Serbian view of Yugoslavia remained, to the end, unclear. One suspects that he never resolved the issue in his own mind; that is, that the Serbs' wish for unity was somehow seen—illogically—to be compatible with plans and proposals forthcoming at the time (1988–89) for the introduction of a federal system to replace the discredited constitution of 1974.[76] Given this stubborn confusion of ideas and principles, the ability of the United States or Europe to mediate on constitutional issues in the 1980s would appear slim.

At the same time, one can find many reasons to fault both the Croatians and the Slovenians: the former for their failure to make virtually *any* constructive moves to rescue Yugoslavia;[77] the latter because of the constitutional crisis initiated by the adoption of the amendments to the Slovenian constitution in September 1989 (which Robert Hayden has argued was the critical moment in the disintegration of Yugoslavia),[78] because Slovenia opposed reforms in the early 1980s, and because of the perverse, if not intentional, role of Slovenia as the weakest link in Tito's Yugoslavia. (Slovenia's move to assert her independence, as subsequent events proved, played the role of the first falling domino from which the wars in Croatia, Bosnia Herzegovina, and finally Kosovo, were to follow.)

The second hard fact that must be dealt with is that, when all is said and done, Yugoslavia was formed, sustained, and finally destroyed, to a large part, thanks to the actions of the great powers of the time and as a consequence of changes in the international environment. Although the formation of Yugoslavia had to have the consent of the peoples who would comprise the new state, the final decision on the fate of the Austro-Hungarian Empire and the nature of the state system in the Balkans that would follow World War I rested with the victorious Allied powers. After World War II, an almost certain breakup of Yugoslavia was avoided by the victory of the Communists and the support of the Americans and Russians for the new, socialist Yugoslavia. During the cold war that followed, international support for Yugoslavia was of significant, if perhaps not decisive importance (as long as Tito was alive) for the country's stability.[79] In turn, the death of Yugoslavia followed upon the demise of socialism, which, as we have seen, began in Yugoslavia a decade before the collapse of Communism elsewhere but was dramatically accelerated by the end of the cold war and events in 1989 and 1990 in the remainder of Eastern Europe.

The paradox, then, lies in taking as a foregone conclusion the fact that the victory of the West following the collapse of Communist Eastern Europe should have provided a hospitable—and peaceful—environment for the peoples of Yugoslavia rather than encouraging a descent into violence. The search for the perfect moment when the West could have intervened to save Yugoslavia must ultimately be seen as an expression of the belief that Yugoslavia should have benefited from, rather than been destroyed by, the transition to democracy following Communism's collapse. To state the case differently, criticisms of the West for allowing the civil war in Yugoslavia to take place seem to rest on the following argument: if the international system (that is, Europe and the United States) helped create Yugoslavia, certainly they should have been able to save her or at least guarantee a peaceful dissolution of the country into its constituent republics.

Ultimately, the conviction that a new democratic Europe was the essential underpinning for peace among the peoples of the former Yugoslavia was to be vindicated in a delayed and costly fashion. The wars of the Yugoslav succession discredited the nationalist government in Croatia, led to the ouster of Milošević in Serbia, and resulted in international protectorates under Western tutelage in Bosnia and Kosovo. The new states of the former Yugoslavia, in turn, pledged themselves to the principles of democracy, the peaceful settlement of disputes, and respect for (new) international boundaries. The international system, acting through (or at the behest of) the United States and Europe once more played a decisive role in determining the fate of the peoples of the former Yugoslavia.

But, given this fact, could not one have hoped for a different outcome from the start? To return to the central concern of this essay, could not the international community, having created and sustained Yugoslavia, have taken the initiative to save her before the carnage of the civil war began? Could not have things turned out differently even *if* the United States and Europe were only minimally concerned with Yugoslavia in the 1980s? What, for example, if the Stambolić faction had defeated the Milošević faction at the Eighth Plenum of the LC Serbia? Or, to return to the CIA report analyzed earlier, what if *the CIA had been right* and a rebellion had broken out among the Albanians of Kosovo? Would Belgrade have been so eager to foment a war on two or three fronts (that is, with the Croats in Krajina and against the Muslims and Croats in Bosnia), while at the same time dealing with the Albanians in Kosovo?

Here it is useful to remind ourselves that the factors contributing to Yugoslavia's downfall and the violence that followed could not be attributed solely to irresponsible leaders but were deeply structural. The crisis over Kosovo, which brought Milošević to power, was not imagined but very real and extremely complex. (After all, where could one find a situation such that the majority nationality—in this case the Serbs—was a "minority" within part of its own republic?) The domino effect that resulted when Slovenia left Yugoslavia was not created by opportunistic politicians but reflected the division between what *Mladina* called "Western" Yugoslavia and the remainder of the country (and, tragically, as events were to prove, Bosnia-Herzegovina's desire to be included in the former).

Finally, there was the problem of the "other" Yugoslavia that the diplomats and scholars knew only superficially; namely, rural Yugoslavia and especially rural Bosnia. Ironically, those who were most critical of the Western diplomatic corps for their ignorance of Yugoslavia outside Belgrade seemed to be little, if at all, concerned with the potential for violence in rural areas affected by World War II as Tito's Yugoslavia disintegrated.

One can acknowledge the danger that Milošević posed to Yugoslavia and legitimately ask why the West did not focus earlier on the problem of Serbian actions in Kosovo and of Serbian claims on Croatia and Bosnia. Yet one can have sympathy for the position attributed to German diplomats in the 1980s that it was "lunacy" to promote secession (if that, indeed, would be the effect of negotiating a peaceful restructuring of the country). One also forgets that, from the point of view of the Yugoslav actors, the demise of Yugoslavia raised a host of existential questions related to their own future—certainly not trivial or arbitrary issues, whether influenced by ancient hatreds or not. Finally, one is struck by the fact that virtually all the actors in this drama outside Kosovo *were ready to go to war to achieve their objectives*. This can be interpreted either as suicidal irrationality or a sign of how seriously they viewed their cause(s), but it was the rock on which all attempts to negotiate an end to the conflicts in the former Yugoslavia were to flounder.

Why did not the United States and Europe focus earlier, and with more skill, on the crisis? The question remains, especially if as we have suggested one could conclude that by 1990 the main actors in the drama had themselves given up on Yugoslavia and that the time had come to negotiate the modalities of a peaceful breakup. The CIA report and the fatalism of the Yugoslav experts who helped craft the report provide one answer. Only the threat of force might have altered the slide toward war, they believed, and this was not possible unless a commitment to use force—impossible at the time—lay behind the threat.[80]

Another factor at work, we have suggested earlier, was the inability of the CIA, and those behind its report, to take into account how American interests would be affected once the conflict, which they so confidently predicted, did break out. Neither the CIA nor the American diplomatic staff in Belgrade (as far as can be determined from published sources) showed a great interest in the "details" over which the war would be fought and which would preoccupy Western diplomats and international mediators in the months and years to come. What Western diplomats could not see at the time, in part because of their irritation with both camps (those preaching unity and those demanding the right to secede) was that American and European interests would eventually coalesce on the side of the victims of the war after the confrontation among the ethnic communities in Yugoslavia took a violent turn.

And it is here, perhaps, that we encounter an elusive, but important truth, namely, that a decision to intervene is, in the event, a matter of the heart rather than a calculation of cold national interest. In a word, and speaking realistically, it was unreasonable to expect the United States to intervene until it had an emotional involvement in the crisis. (The fact that a portion of the German public had already developed such a commitment to Croatia helps prove the point.) The war, ethnic cleansing, the image of the gallant Croats and then Bosnian Muslims under attack, provided a missing element in the equation. Yet even this was not enough. As Richard Ullman put it, "What determines whether the international community is moved to take decisive action, however, is less the magnitude of the crimes than the identity of the victims and the victims' friends."[81] And it was on this subjective plane that the advocates of preventive international intervention and American policy makers were in profound disagreement.[82] The former were focused on what they deemed was Serbian aggression, the latter on what they saw as the disintegration of the Yugoslav state.

One could nevertheless argue that far from exonerating the Americans and Europeans, the argument that preventive intervention must be from the heart only highlights the fact that Serbian aggression and the intention of creating a Greater Serbia was already clear—following the initial misguided enthusiasm for Milošević on the part of Western diplomats in the summer of 1988—almost three years before the war in Slovenia began. In brief, the argument runs, there were adequate grounds for threatening the use of force against Serbia before the conflict broke out. This in turn serves as a reminder that the only republic seeking a change in boundaries—and ready to pursue this goal by force if Yugoslavia dissolved—was Serbia.

At the same time, the Serbian demands for border changes should Yugoslavia dissolve had their origins, as we have seen, in the contradictions surrounding Yugoslavia's very formation. The emergence of Milošević was not accidental but a case of a failed transition anticipating other failed transitions further east with deep roots in the Serbs' emotional attachment to Kosovo and to the unity of all Serbs. Thus, the war in Croatia (and subsequently, Bosnia Herzegovina) was neither an accident nor easily avoided—or so it would seem, given the fact of an illiberal Serbia experiencing national homogenization (as had Croatia and Slovenia before her) in the late 1980s.

Yet there exist problems with what might be called a revisionist position, one that shows signs of gaining some acceptance, namely that the solution was, indeed, to accept border changes—if not necessarily those that Serbia demanded—as an obvious and historically justifiable approach to avoiding war. In the volume *Yugoslavia and its Historians* (cited earlier), John Fine, a passionate believer in Yugoslavia, suggests that the Serbian switch to a policy of a Greater Serbia emerged only in 1991 in response to Croatian secession. (As noted above, we suggest that the switch occurred earlier, in 1990, and largely in response to the victory of nationalist parties in Slovenia and Croatia.) Fine further suggests that the events leading up to the war were not a crisis but a gridlock in the state presidency that could have continued indefinitely until Milošević was ousted from power.[83] Gale Stokes, in the same volume, argues (as does

Arnold Suppan) that the breakup of Yugoslavia was not an anomaly but a late phase of a transformation that had already taken place elsewhere in Europe.[84] Stokes suggests that "stability will only come when state borders there are redrawn along ethnic lines, as they have been in the rest of Europe."[85]

One hesitates to embrace this position as an argument that border changes were the answer to avoiding the war in Yugoslavia.[86] And to be fair to the authors just cited, their comments were directed to the postwar, not the prewar, situation. Where does this leave us, then?

It is important in this connection to remember that focusing on the 1980s without reference to what happened once the conflict broke out can be misleading. The late 1980s saw the emergence of nationalist parties and movements, mass mobilizations in Serbia and to a lesser extent Slovenia, hunger strikes in Kosovo, and so on. In brief, it was a period of high emotions, including nationalist euphoria, which did not last once the realities of war set in. At least this was true in Serbia where, as events would prove, the Serbs of Serbia proper did not really have their hearts in the war in Croatia. Young Serb recruits were told that they were fighting in Croatia "for the Serbian borders of 1918" to no real effect—many defected.[87] Learning from this experience, Belgrade carefully avoided sending Serbs from Serbia to fight in Bosnia. In light of this fact, there is a certain irony—but not necessarily incorrectness—in the "inevitability of war" attitude that dominated American thinking in the late 1980s.

Yet the notion that the United States missed opportunities to intervene in the crisis—we have not fully examined the question of "how"—cannot escape its own questionable assumption that the United States (and Europe) could really make a case for going to war against Serbia for refusing to accept existing borders with Croatia as Yugoslavia dissolved. If Ullman is correct and what counts is not the magnitude of the crime but the identity of the victim and its friends, the threat to Croatia was not a sufficient rationale for American intervention in the Balkans—absent a pressing strategic threat to the United States—*prior* to the outbreak of the conflict.

Thus one can speculate that intervention in the Yugoslav crisis prior to June 1991 could not have been based on "unity and democracy" or on military intervention to save Slovenia and Croatia but on a solid grounding in the minutiae of the conflicting positions and how, realistically, they might have been reconciled.

Of course, this, too, seems unrealistic, given the uncompromising stands taken by all involved. But it should be noted that Serbia and Croatia did hold talks aimed, at the outset, at avoiding war as Yugoslavia disintegrated in the Spring of 1991. This occurred on several occasions when Tudjman and Milošević discussed the possibility of partitioning Bosnia as part of a deal that would have had the Serbs of Krajina remain in Croatia.[88] We know from Mario Nobilo's account of Croatian diplomacy that Tudjman, for one, was a firm believer that such a deal could have avoided war between Croatia and Serbia.[89] The idea that Bosnia could be partitioned is greeted with horror by almost all commentators, yet it held out advantages to all parties concerned if the Muslim population of Bosnia would have been willing to remain in a rump Yugoslavia and, further, if a rump Bosnia Herzegovina could have continued to enjoy the status of a republic as it had under Tito.[90] Why Milošević turned down (or did not implement) whatever was agreed to in March 1991 at Karadjordjevo remains unclear. One suspects that after fighting broke out in Croatia Milošević lost interest in negotiating a deal with Tudjman, convinced that the Serbs, with the aid of the JNA, could seize and hold Krajina (perhaps because Tudjman had done so little to prepare Croatia for war).

Would the United States and Europe have backed Tudjman and Milošević if a deal had been struck at the expense of the Bosnian Muslims? Much would have depended on the nature of agreement. The partitioning of Bosnia between Croatia and Serbia, accompanied by population transfers, was unequivocally rejected by Zimmermann when the matter was brought up in conversations with Tudjman.[91] But this did not rule out the possibility, however slim, that Bosnia might have remained in a rump Yugoslavia as part of a deal between Tudjman and Milošević to avoid a war between Croatia and Serbia.

What is perhaps more reasonable is to ask why the West did not, seeing a war in the offing, present the conflicting parties with one last chance to negotiate their differences under Western auspices while making it clear that the United States and Europe were firm in their support for existing republic borders and would assist the republics (with the possible exception of Bosnia Herzegovina), short of outright intervention, to maintain these boundaries.[92]

While this suggestion may seem far too speculative—and to remind the reader of those Robert Hutchings alluded to earlier who are always clever after the event—there is a larger point to be made here. The point is that there were steps short of actual intervention—in this case a pledge to help Croatia defend herself with arms and financial assistance—that might have persuaded Belgrade that it was in its best interest not to back the Krajina Serbs.[93] (Of course, removing the issue of the Krajina Serbs from the agenda could have precipitated an agreement between Tudjman and Milošević to partition Bosnia, as foreseen at Karadjordjevo, to the immense embarrassment of Europe and the United States.)

And this takes us back to the 1980s. The real choice was not, in this author's view, between active intervention and a hands-off policy. Rather the question was whether American and European policy could be based on a mastery of the Yugoslav situation in all its particulars. Perhaps, then, the United States and Europe would have felt ready to undertake the role of mediator rather than adopting the standoff policy that prevailed.[94] Unfortunately, from overoptimism and an idealized view of Yugoslavia in the 1970s and even early 1980s, American diplomats had become the ultimate skeptics, or perhaps worse, naive salesmen of Western democracy as the cure to Yugoslavia's problems. In so doing they opened themselves up, perhaps unfairly, to criticism. Yet they could better make their case that nothing would have helped had they focused at some point on the opportunity to head off the war between

Croatia and Serbia. It will be the task of future historians looking at primary documents (which we have not attempted to do in this essay) to determine whether such efforts might have stood some slight chance of success.[95]

The point could be restated as follows: the issue of what the West (primarily the United States) could have done to prevent war from breaking out should not be viewed solely as a choice between enforcing unity on the Yugoslav republics (which American policy makers rightly determined was impossible) or acknowledging and perhaps guiding the breakup of Yugoslavia at an early stage but tackling the more concrete (and doable) task of preventing a Serb-Croat war. In so doing, the United States, aided by Europe, might have been better positioned to head off the crises that followed.

Be that as it may, one is left with the feeling that the substantive issues could not be addressed by the international community until two conditions had been met: first, the absolute and unequivocal dissolution of Yugoslavia, and second, a breakdown of negotiations among the republics over the country's future. This takes us beyond the period 1980–June 1991. Yet it is not inappropriate to suggest that in the summer of 1991 these conditions had been fulfilled. If so, resolute (but limited) action by the West in defense of Croatia and her borders would have been appropriate. This, it should be added, need not have been anti-Serbian—or even anti-Milošević—in its intent. As we have seen, it was clear early on that the average Serb did not have his heart in the war in Croatia. (It need hardly be added that the West was in a position to insist on protection of the Serb minority in Krajina if Krajina was to remain in Croatia.)

And it is in this context that we can best judge American and European diplomacy of the 1980s. For a variety of reasons—cynicism, naivety, or ignorance—Western policy makers simply were not prepared to act decisively even after the war broke out. They then accepted responsibility for mediating the conflict in the former Yugoslavia—which they had refused to do earlier—but were not yet cognizant of the effect of the war on their own interests—and more important, their emotions, which would draw them willy-nilly into the war, if not at once, then only after the "old hands" had left following a change of administration in Washington.

We must add that while actions in support of the territorial integrity of Croatia might have prevented, or at least ended sooner, the war between Croatia and Serbia, such actions would not necessarily have halted the descent into civil war in Bosnia. Nor could the West have expected the Kosovo Albanians to abjure the use of force indefinitely. Indeed, the consequences of Western support for Croatia on developments in Bosnia could hardly be foreseen at the time and raise the question of whether it would have been possible or wise to extend the policy of recognition of Croatia and her borders to Bosnia-Herzegovina.

These speculations take us beyond the subject of this essay. But one must raise the issue, when all is said in done, whether "preventive diplomacy"—which has become a fashionable way of justifying activism in the cause of peace on the part of the United States—was really the answer to the dissolution of Yugoslavia. Judging from the suggestions made for early intervention in Yugoslavia, the doctrine is simply another way of simplifying complex international crises—often after the fact—as a substitute for mastering and understanding the limits of what can be done, and when, to deal with crises that challenge global stability. In the view of this author, the consequences of this urge to both simplify incipient crises and at the same time prevent them are now unfolding before us outside the Balkans with potentially disastrous consequences for all concerned.

Notes

1. The analysis to follow does not deal with the interrepublic negotiations to head off a war that took place in the spring of 1991, although these negotiations do fall within the time frame of the essay. The reader should be aware that these negotiations do bear on some of the concluding observations made in this essay.

2. For an analysis of this issue and of other explanations why Yugoslavia disintegrated, see Dejan Jović, *Jugoslavija—Država koja je odumrla: Uspon, Kriza i Pad Četvrte Jugoslavije* (Zagreb: Prometej and Belgrade: Samizdat B–92, 2003), chapter 1, pp. 23–101.

3. For example, see Noel Malcolm's foreword to Branka Magaš and Ivo Zanić (eds.), *The War in Croatia and Bosnia Herzegovina, 1991–1995* (London: Frank Case, 2001), p. xxvi.

4. See Stephen Clissold, "Yugoslavia and the Soviet Union," *Conflict Studies* No. 57 (April 1975), pp. 4–19.

5. For the decentralized decision-making system introduced at the time, see Steven L. Burg, *Conflict and Cohesion in Socialist Yugoslavia* (Princeton: Princeton University Press, 1983), and his contribution to Dennison Rusinow (ed.), *Yugoslavia: A Fractured Federalism* (Washington, D.C.: The Wilson Center Press, 1988), pp. 9–22.

6. Up to 1976, all trends seemed to favor the emergence of a powerful Executive Committee as the leading body in the LCY. This in turn favored Stane Dolanc, secretary of the Executive Committee and in control of the Party apparatus. Dolanc had ruthlessly purged republic nationalists and liberals after 1971. At the Eleventh Party Congress in June 1978 the Executive Committee was abolished, a blow to Dolanc. At the same time, the position of president of the LCY was strengthened somewhat; the unexpected move seemed to favor the person who would fill the post after Tito, more than Tito himself. Then in October and November 1978 new standing rules were adopted that introduced, under Tito's urging, the principle of collective leadership in the party. What prompted this move on Tito's part is unclear; it may have come about through the intercession of Edvard Kardelj, who, near death, might have persuaded Tito that Dolanc could not hope to fill the presidential post without an all-out power struggle. With this development and the death of Kardelj, the power struggle in the party was over before it began.

7. Steven L. Burg, "Elite Conflict in Post-Tito Yugoslavia," *Soviet Studies*, Vol. 37, No. 2 (April 1986), p. 170.

8. This essay will not deal at great length with the Kosovo question. It should be noted that Stambolić, not surprisingly and perhaps with some justification, points to efforts made to address the Kosovo question while he was head of the Serbian League of Communists. He makes particular note of the initiative taken by the Yugoslav presidency in October 1986 to change the 1974 Constitution, including those parts dealing with Kosovo; "Working groups simply flooded Kosovo," Stambolić reports. Ivan Stambolić,

Put u Becpuće (Belgrade: Radio B–92, 1995), p. 169. But the results were negligible—for example, banning the sale of land owned by Serbs to Albanians.

9. Zachary Irwin, "Yugoslavia's Foreign Policy and Southeastern Europe," in Paul S. Shoup and George W. Hoffman (eds.), *Problems of Balkan Security: Southeastern Europe in the 1990s* (Wilson Center Press: Washington D.C., 1990), p. 155.

10. See A. Ross Johnson, "Yugoslavia's Significance for the West," *Rand Paper* No. 6980 (July 1984), pp. 4–5. As late as 1984 Johnson could write, "The possibilities for miscalculation and accident, as well as for a fundamental test of will between the United States and the USSR, are great. It is surely no accident that most of the fictitious scenarios for East-West military conflict in Europe begin with a 'Yugoslav crisis' of some kind." See also Stephen Clissold, "Yugoslavia and the Soviet Union," where one can find an account of Russian contacts with Croat nationalists and Informburo sympathizers during the 1960s and 1970s. Clissold recounts the story of the Czech defector General Jan Sejna, who disclosed the existence of Operation Polarka, which posited an invasion of Austria and Yugoslavia by Russian, Hungarian, and Czech troops.

11. Tito's funeral was attended by Brezhnev, Thatcher, Indira Gandhi, Helmut Schmidt, and a bevy of other world leaders. President Carter was represented by Vice-President Mondale. See *Facts on File for 1980.*

12. But not all Yugoslav products were able to enter the EC duty free. Textiles, steel products, and ferrous metals were excluded. Quotas for agricultural products were reduced but not eliminated (*Economist,* March 1, 1980, p. 47).

13. *Facts on File for 1981.*

14. Viktor Meier, *Yugoslavia: A History of Her Demise* (London: Rutledge, 1999), p. 101. The accord was with Branko Mikulić, who had replaced Planinc in 1986.

15. See Saadia Touval, *Mediation in the Yugoslav Wars: The Critical Years, 1990–1995* (Palgrave: Basingstoke, 2002), p. 20, that between December 1990 and May 1991, through a variety of programs, the EC was ready to offer Yugoslavia 3.6 billion ECU (over 4.5 billion dollars).

16. In the early 1980s Lawrence Eagleburger, then under-secretary of state, was actively encouraging major banks in the United States to lend to Yugoslavia, over the objections of others in the administration (*New York Times,* May 10, 1982, Section D, p. 2). Aid from the United States faced resistance from Congress after 1988 and was under pressure from Senator Bob Dole and others concerned with violations of human rights in Kosovo. In November 1990, Congress adopted the so-called Nickles amendment that called for the suspension of aid to Yugoslavia. The Bush administration announced the cessation of aid in May 1991, as required by the amendment, but then lifted the ban two weeks later in a move aimed at strengthening the hand of the Marković government. See Touval, *Mediation in the Yugoslav Wars,* p. 25, and Wayne Bert, *The Reluctant Superpower, 1991–1995* (New York: St. Martin's Press, 1997), p. 136. Warren Zimmermann also recounts the refusal of Washington to negotiate a rollover of the Yugoslav debt, as the ambassador wished, at the time of the Marković visit to Washington (Warren Zimmermann, *Origins of a Catastrophe* [New York: Times Books, 1996], p. 51).

17. *Economist,* March 29, 1980, p. 76.

18. *New York Times,* November 1, 1981, p. 4. One is taken aback by the sum mentioned here, but correct or incorrect, it reflects the generous mood in the United States toward Serbia and Yugoslavia at the time.

19. Mark Almond, no friend of Eagleburger, claims that Eagleburger was known as "Lawrence of Serbia" in the corridors of the State Department (Mark Almond, *Europe's Backyard War* [London: Heinemann, 1994], p. 39). Viktor Meier notes, more correctly,

that Eagleburger was, according to Warren Zimmermann, "pro-Yugoslav" but not "pro-Serbian" at the time (Meier, *Yugoslavia*, p. 218).

20. Ibid., p. 41.

21. "The Western diplomats in Belgrade, most of whom went beyond the city limits of the capital only with great reluctance and whose usual conversation partners were above all Marković, Lončar, and their entourage, seemed practically without exception in the last two years of Yugoslavia's existence, to have misunderstood the realities of this country. In the last six months of Yugoslavia, their hostility to reality assumed grotesque dimensions. I must admit that the views which I heard from the circle of Western diplomats at this time made an almost traumatic impression and that I had never before encountered such a colossal jumble of political error, lazy thinking, and superficiality as I encountered then among the Western diplomatic corps in Belgrade" (ibid., p. 217).

22. Michael Libal, *The Limits of Persuasion: Germany and the Yugoslav Crisis, 1991–1992* (Westport: Praeger, 1997), pp. 4–5. He notes how the German diplomatic corps in Belgrade viewed the crisis in Yugoslavia as one of "modernization and democratization." Libal as much as admits that the German ambassador (at the time, Hansjorg von Eiff) and his staff did not appreciate the danger Milošević posed to Yugoslavia. Meanwhile, Meier points out that the German ambassador also slighted the Slovenian government (as did other EC diplomats) and adds that "there is, therefore, no evidence whatsoever that Germany supported the Slovenian and Croatian aspirations toward independence in any form" (Meier, *Yugoslavia*, p. 219).

23. Meier, p. 41, incorrectly dates Zimmermann's arrival as March 1987.

24. Zimmermann, *Origins of a Catastrophe*, p. 7.

25. Irwin, "Yugoslavia's Foreign Policy," p. 167.

26. Robert Hutchings, *American Diplomacy and the Cold War: An Insider's Account of U.S. Diplomacy in Europe, 1989–1992* (Washington, D.C.: Woodrow Wilson Center Press, 1997), p. 304.

27. Zimmermann, *Origins of a Catastrophe*, p. 47. The Council on Foreign Relations, to its credit, found the means to pay for Marković's lunch when he addressed the group. Zimmermann further comments that "Marković was a good sport about his rude experience of a no-frills official visit to the United States."

28. Christopher Cviić, "The Background and Implications of the Domestic Scene in Yugoslavia" in Shoup and Hoffman, *Problems of Balkan Security*, p. 89.

29. Predrag Simić, William Richey, and Mirko Stojanović (eds.), *American and Yugoslav Views in the 1990s* (Belgrade: Institute of International Politics and Economics-Center for North American Studies, 1990), p. 65.

30. Hutchings, *American Diplomacy and the Cold War,* pp. 304–305.

31. Ibid., p. 305.

32. For example, see Magaš and Žanić, *The War in Croatia and Bosnia Herzegovina,* passim.

33. See Lenard Cohen, *Serpent in the Bosom: The Rise and Fall of Slobodan Milošević,* rev. ed. (Boulder: Westview Press, 2002), p. 452.

34. We must rely exclusively on Zimmermann's account of the position of the American embassy at this time (1989–90). Zimmermann recounts that he was upset by the air of "inevitability" in the CIA report on the crisis in Yugoslavia (about which more below) and cabled Washington in November that "the game can be won. Dissolution is not inevitable." Yet the embassy, in Zimmermann's account, was fully aware of the seriousness of the crisis and informed Washington of its concerns (Zimmermann, *Origins of a Catastrophe,* p. 84).

35. Hutchings, *American Diplomacy and the Cold War*, p. 307. According to Hutchings, these cables warned that the United States believed that Yugoslavia was headed toward bloody disintegration and that common policies should be developed on such issues as recognition of breakaway states and international guarantees for minorities (especially the Serb minority in Croatia). Strenuous and concerted action would be needed by the international community, these cables continued, if a catastrophe was to be averted. The American position was that in reacting to the crisis in Yugoslavia, Europe should take the lead. Hutchings calls the European response "shockingly irresponsible," especially in the French case.

36. David C. Gompert, "The United States and Yugoslavia's Wars," in Richard H. Ullman (ed.), *The World and Yugoslavia's Wars* (New York: Council on Foreign Relations, 1996), p. 127.

37. Ibid., p. 122.

38. *New York Times,* November 28, 1990, p. 7.

39. Hutchings, *American Diplomacy and the Cold War*, p. 306.

40. "Yugoslavia Transformed," CIA National Intelligence Estimate NIE 15–90 (November 1990), Document ID No. 254259. The document is fifteen pages, including maps, charts and a cartoon.

41. Ibid., p. vi. The CIA blacked out parts of this section.

42. The report returned to the Bosnian question on p. 3. It suggested that "Bosnia Hercegovina represents the greatest threat of changing [word indistinct in the Xerox provided the author] the fundamental ethnic division in Yugoslavia—that between Serbs and Croats—into large scale communal violence. . . . Elections at the end of November will increase [word indistinct] the potential for intervention by Serbia and Croatia." This, in the author's opinion, does not go far enough. The undercurrent of deep disquiet and concern over what the breakup of Yugoslavia could mean for Bosnia could be detected before the war in Bosnia began in 1992 and should have been known to the intelligence agencies and the State Department. An example was Admiral Mamula's comment in London in November 1990, noted by Cohen, *Broken Bonds,* p. 186, that it was not secession per se that the JNA was against but the fact that any attempt to establish national states by either Serbia or Croatia would lead to protracted conflict in Bosnia.

43. Ibid., p. 9.

44. Ibid., p. 10.

45. For a summary account of the Eastern Question, see Almond, *Europe's Backyard War*, Part II.

46. The report lacks an historical overview of the region—perhaps this was felt to be too taxing on the recipients of the report—or the lessons to be learned thereby. One might also add that there are no in-depth psychological portraits of the Yugoslav leaders. Such analysis is of course a stock-in-trade of the intelligence community and presumably was made available to end users in other reports.

47. Libal, *The Limits of Persuasion*, p. 5.

48. Touval, *Mediation in the Yugoslav Wars*, p. 21.

49. According to Jović the demarche stated that "The United States will forcefully oppose any use of force, pressure or provocation to use force which would block democratic changes or result in non-democratic unity in Yugoslavia. In connection with this we shall oppose any effort to change borders in Yugoslavia, except by peaceful means" (Borisav Jović, *Poslednji Dani SFRJ,* 2nd ed. [Kragujevac: Prizma, 1996], p. 252; translated from Serbo-Croatian). Of course, one can see with hindsight that by making democracy a priority Washington was effectively ruling out any possibility of unity.

50. Simić, *American and Yugoslav Views on the 1990s,* p. 156.

51. Ibid., p. 9.

52. Norbert Both, *From Indifference to Entrapment: The Netherlands and the Yugoslav Crisis, 1990–1995* (Amsterdam: Amsterdam University Press, 2000), p. 95.

53. Ibid., p. 89.

54. Libal, *The Limits of Persuasion,* p. 8.

55. Wayne Bert, *The Reluctant Superpower,* p. 136.

56. Libal, *The Limits of Persuasion,* p. 8. The key passage of the CSCE resolution, according to Libal, read, "Ministers stressed that it is only for the peoples of Yugoslavia themselves to decide on their country's future."

57. Zimmermann, *Origins of a Catastrophe,* p. 132.

58. Ibid., p. 99.

59. See Cohen, *Serpent in the Bosom,* revised edition, p. 454, quoting Strobe Talbott, deputy secretary of state under Clinton, who rejected the notion of the area as a quagmire: "There was nothing predestined about the horror that has been raging in the Balkans for the past four years. It was foolish, demagogic, local politics, along with shortsighted international diplomacy, that helped trigger, in the late 1980s and early 1990s the third Balkan war of this century." See also Noel Malcolm's introduction to the Branka Magaš volume, *supra.;* Sabrina Ramet's introduction to the Meier volume; and the comments of Saadia Touval, *Mediation in the Yugoslav Wars,* p. 16, that American and European policy was "ridden with flaws" and was incoherent. For the pro-Slovenian critics of Western policies, see Christopher Bennett, *Yugoslavia's Bloody Collapse* (New York: New York University Press, 1995), p. 14, and Meier, *Yugoslavia,* chapter 7.

60. General Kadijević had already, in March, visited the Soviet Union in an effort to get military assistance for an anticipated conflict. It would seem that nothing that either Zimmermann or Baker could say to the Serbs would have changed the presumption that the United States was actively supporting the breakaway republics. Did Milošević nevertheless believe that there was little danger of American involvement once a war broke out? Evidence for this lies in a report, purportedly prepared by the JNA in the spring of 1990, that the United States was preoccupied with the Middle East and would not intervene in a conflict in Yugoslavia. The contents of the report are partially described in Cohen, *Serpent in the Bosom,* first edition, p. 143. The original source for this report, which has been mentioned in other sources as well, remains unclear, and its importance may be overrated. In fact, we know from Jović's diary that the JNA was already persuaded that the United States and Europe had ruled out the use of military force if Yugoslavia was to disintegrate—even as they were convinced that the United States was bent on destroying Yugoslavia by all other possible means. This may have pushed the JNA to intervene in the belief that the U.S. would not become involved militarily but was employing other means to undermine Yugoslavia; that is, that time was not on the side of those who waited and hoped that the West would on balance contribute to the unity of the country. In this connection, the JNA was convinced that the CIA was helping the Hungarians arm the Croatians. The irony here is that, as we have seen, on several occasions (according to Zimmermann) the United States had turned down requests by Tudjman for military assistance (Jović, *Poslednji Dani,* p. 237 and p. 276).

61. Zimmermann, *Origins of a Catastrophe,* p. 135.

62. In Baker's account, he told Milošević that "If you persist in promoting the breakup of Yugoslavia, Serbia will stand alone. The United States and the rest of the international community will reject any Serbian claim to territory beyond its borders. Serbia will become an international outcast within Europe for a generation or more" (James Baker

III, *The Politics of Diplomacy: Revolution, War and Peace, 1989–1992* [New York: G. P. Putnam and Sons, 1995], p. 481).

63. Ibid., p. 482.

64. Bennett, *Yugoslavia's Bloody Collapse*, pp. 113–14, makes the point for Yugoslavia on the basis of self-interest: "A single Yugoslav state enabled the vast majority of South Slavs to live within the same country and ensured that rival national claims to ethnically-mixed territories would not spill over into conflict." He suggests that if a genuine discussion of what was best for all Yugoslavs took place the Yugoslav idea would certainly have come out on top. In his words, "The Yugoslav ideal was not tried, tested and found wanting, it was not tried at all. The problem was not that different people could not live together, but that they were not given the chance."

65. Ivo Daalder, "Fear and Loathing in the Former Yugoslavia," in Michael Brown, ed., *The International Dimensions of Internal Conflict* (Cambridge, MA: The MIT Press, 1996), p. 63. In Daalder's words, "The most important and immediate consequence of not using force in the former Yugoslavia was unintended encouragement of the Serbs to continue with their aggressive behavior. . . . The best, although the most unlikely, moment to act was before the breakup of Yugoslavia in early 1991. At the time, the shared Western goal was to promote both unity and democracy, and the United States clearly told all parties concerned that it would oppose both unilateral secession and the use of force, a message that U.S. Secretary of State James Baker delivered personally in June. But the consequences of taking either action were never spelled out."

66. Hutchings, *American Diplomacy and the End of the Cold War*, p. 308. See also pp. 318–320, where he suggests that at the time the Slovenes and Croats were preparing independence declarations (late 1990), the United States should have focused not on preserving the federal state, but on the modalities of dissolution, backed by "massive engagement." In this way, he suggests, war might have been avoided; but only if the United States had decided that important U.S. interests were at stake. This suggestion seems more realistic than his recommendation that NATO be employed to ward off the crisis.

67. Jasna Dragović-Soso, *Saviors of the Nation: Serbia's Intellectual Opposition and the Revival of Nationalism* (Montreal: McGill-Queen's University Press, 2002), p. 205.

68. Ibid., p. 234. At the Cankar Hall rally the Slovene leadership sided with the Albanians of Kosovo, provoking an outburst of anti-Slovene emotion in Serbia.

69. Bennett, *Yugoslavia's Bloody Collapse*, p. 94.

70. Meier, *Yugoslavia*, p. 35. Nineteen eighty-six, it might be remembered, was the year of the Slovenian Tenth LC Congress when Kučan was chosen as president of the Slovenian Party. At the Tenth Congress of the Croatian Party in the same year, says Meier, the most conservative Croatian leaders were removed, thus paving the way for the subsequent choice of Racan as party president.

71. Ibid., pp. 220–221.

72. Note Milošević's speech to the Serbian assembly in June 1990, where, according to Marko Milivojević, Milošević first outlined a vision of Serbia going it alone—and raised the issue of Serbs outside Serbia—if Yugoslavia was to turn into a loose confederation. See Marko Milivojević, "The Armed Forces of Yugoslavia: Sliding into War," in Sabrina Ramet and Ljubisa S. Adamovich, eds., *Beyond Yugoslavia: Politics, Economics and Culture in a Shattered Community* (Boulder: Westview Press, 1995), p. 73.

73. Hutchings, *American Diplomacy and the End of the Cold War*, p. 318.

74. The 1946 Constitution, Article 1, stated that "The Federal Peoples Republic of Yugoslavia is a federal people's state republic in form, a community of people equal in rights, who, on the basis of the right to self-determination, including the right to separation,

have expressed the will to live together in a federal state" (Snežana Trifunovska [ed.], *Yugoslavia Through Documents: From its Creation to its Dissolution* [Dordrecht: Martinus Nijhoff, 1993], p. 212). The 1974 Constitution (in its preamble) stated that "The nations of Yugoslavia, proceeding from the right of every nation to self-determination, including the right to secession, on the basis of their will freely expressed . . . have together with the nationalities with which they live, united in a federal republic of free and equal nations" (ibid., p. 224). Neither document, it should be noted, ruled out the possibility of revoking this voluntarily expressed will to unite. Did the 1974 (and 1946) Constitution refer to the ethnic "narod" (as Milošević was later to claim), or to the republics? Vojin Dimitrijević in Payam Akhaven (ed.), *Yugoslavia: The Former and the Future, Reflections by Scholars from the Region* (Geneva: UN Research Institute for Social Development, 1995), p. 58, concludes that "it remained unclear whether the subjects of this right were ethnic nations, as opposed to peoples in the sense of inhabitants of a state or territory." Vojislav Koštunica, in his contribution to the Rusinow volume, *Yugoslavia: A Fractured Federalism,* p. 83, refers to the writings of Edvard Kardelj and concludes that Kardelj "reaches the conclusion that the Yugoslav federation is a contractual federation." But does a contractual federation allow republics to "contract out"? Koštunica suggests that the answer was no: "Since any contract is based on the consent of all the contracting parties, it is indispensable to have the consent of all the contractual parties when changing the contract."

75. Arnold Suppan, "Yugoslavism versus Serbian, Croatian, and Slovene Nationalism," in Norman Naimark and Holly Case, eds., *Yugoslavia and its Historians* (Palo Alto: Stanford University Press, 2003), p. 126.

76. For some clues on the kind of Yugoslavia Milošević had in mind, see Cohen, *Broken Bonds,* pp. 55–58, for the proposals of commissions set up by Milošević to recommend political and economic reforms. The political recommendations came out in July 1989 and proposed a half-socialist, half-democratic form of government that was clearly unworkable and soon given up in favor of free elections and political pluralism. The document is described in more detail in MarioNobilo, *Hrvatski Fenik: Diplomatski Procesa iza Zatvorenih Vrata 1990–1997* (Zagreb: Nakladni Zavod, 2000), pp. 36–39. According to Nobilo, it rejected both confederation and a centralized authoritarian state and proposed a modern federation of equal nations and national minorities in which there would be a national chamber (Viječe Naroda) that would operate with a mix of parity and majority voting.

77. Nobilo, *Hrvatski Feniks,* p. 35, describes a document produced by the presidency of Croatia, "Polaznim načelima za novi ustav Hrvatske i Jugoslavije," in 1989 (prior to the decision to hold free elections and the Slovene-Croat proposal for a confederal Yugoslavia). It spoke of the need for "authentic sovereignty" for Croatia; Nobilo adds that the party leadership in Croatia was willing, at this time, to accept the idea of an "asymmetric federation."

78. See Robert M. Hayden, *Blueprints for a House Divided: The Constitutional Logic of the Yugoslav Conflicts* (Ann Arbor: University of Michigan Press, 1999), chapter 2.

79. Ullman, *The World and Yugoslavia's Wars,* pp. 12–13: "When Cold War tensions ebbed, as they did during the period of détente between Washington and Moscow in the early 1970s, might the leaders of Slovenia and Croatia ever have felt they could get away with a unilateral push for independence without precipitating outside intervention?" Ullman's answer is no: "it seems unlikely that the leaders of either Slovenia or Croatia would have made a break for independence had they thought that one consequence of their doing so could well have been an East–West war. . . . Thus the international politics of the Cold War contributed significantly to holding Yugoslavia together."

80. One should keep in mind that early in 1991, the Serbs and the JNA were taking a hard line on the issue of foreign intervention. In a review of the crisis in Yugoslavia for the state presidency carried out in the second week in January 1991, Borisav Jović, in point five of his presentation, stated that "Every foreign intervention in resolving our international crisis, and especially foreign military involvement, from the point of view of our constitution, will be considered an act of aggression and must be met by armed force. No other choice is possible." It is reasonable to assume that Washington was aware of this hard line in the Serb-JNA camp (Borisav Jović, *Poslednji Dani*, p. 271). But see also footnote 93 for later modifications of this line.
81. Ullman, *The Wars in Yugoslavia*, p. 15.
82. See Gompert in Ullman, p. 124, for the Bush administration's distaste for both Slovenia and Tudjman's Croatia. For more on the motives for preventive intervention, see Michael Brown, "Internal Conflict and International Action," in Brown, *The International Dimension of Internal Conflict,* pp. 605–606. In his analysis of conflict prevention, Brown first focuses on palliatives such as autonomy for minorities, elections by proportional representation and other measures. But in the "Bad Neighbor" scenario, he suggests, preventive action is easier and a wide range of preventive actions, including coercion, is permissible. It is precisely in this context that the controversy between those who identified Milošević as an aggressor and those who claimed that the conflict was a civil war (and thus everyone was to blame), comes into focus as a crucial variable in any decision to intervene or to keep one's distance.
83. John Fine, "Heretical Thoughts about the Post-Communist Transition in the Once and Former Yugoslavia," in Norman Naimark, *Yugoslavia and its Historians*, p. 183.
84. In his words, "not an aberrant Balkan phenomenon or the striking out of backward peoples involved in tribal warfare. They are the final working out of a long European tradition of violent ethnic homogenization" (Gale Stokes, "Solving the Wars of Yugoslav Succession," ibid., p. 204).
85. Stokes is making this recommendation in the context of the situation that now prevails in the former Yugoslavia. It implies, of course, not only that Serbia might redraw her boundaries to include the Republika Srpska in Bosnia, but also that Kosovo should be permitted to secede, formally, from Serbia-Montenegro.
86. But see below our discussion of partitioning Bosnia, which would have involved changes in the republic borders of Croatia, Bosnia Herzegovina, and possibly Serbia.
87. See Steven L. Burg and Paul S. Shoup, *The War in Bosnia: Ethnic Conflict and International Intervention* (Armonk: M. E. Sharpe, 1999), p. 84.
88. See Burg and Shoup, *The War in Bosnia,* p. 82, for discussions between Milošević and Tudjman in March and September 1991. See also Smilja Avramov, *Postherojski Rat Zapada Protiv Jugoslavije* (Belgrade: Humanistika, 1997), p. 141, and Miloš Minić, *Dogovori u Karadjordjevu o Podeli Bosne i Hercegovine* (Sarajevo: Rabić, 1998), pp. 1–104.
89. Mario Nobilo, *Hrvatski Feniks*, p. 19.
90. This raises the issue of just what Milošević and Tudjman agreed to and how they intended to carry out their agreement if indeed an agreement had been reached. Burg and Shoup, *The War in Bosnia,* p. 82, suggest that Milošević did not agree at Karadjordjevo that the Krajina Serbs would remain in Croatia as part of a deal to partition Bosnia. On the other hand, Mesić testified at the Hague tribunal that he was told by Jović in February 1991 that Belgrade was not interested in Krajina but in obtaining 66 percent of Bosnia (ibid. and Minić, *Dogovori u Karadjordjevu,* pp. 85–86). It is indeed possible that in February–March 1991 Milošević was interested in avoiding a war with Croatia but that subsequent events led him to throw in his lot with the Krajina Serbs in Croatia.

Another possible scenario, based on anecdotal evidence and requiring further investiga-
tion, is that Tudjman broke off the talks about partitioning Bosnia after broaching the
idea with Warren Zimmermann, who was shocked by the proposal (see Warren Zimmermann, "Origins of a Catastrophe," *Foreign Affairs* 74, No. 2 [March–April 1995], p. 15).
Miloš Minić was convinced that an agreement had been reached at Karadjordjevo but
appears to argue that the real problem was not the fate of Krajina but how to divide up
Bosnia (Minić, *Dogovori u Karadjordjevu*, p. 22). That there was a problem of this nature
emerges from the Minić account and what is known about a commission made up of
Serbs and Croats, among whom (at various times) were Dušan Bilandžić on the Croatian
side and Smilja Avramov on the Serbian side. The commission was never able to agree
to a map on how Bosnia should be divided. Bilandžić is on record that the commission
spent its time arguing whether decisions taken by AVNOJ were still binding (by implication legalizing the present borders of Croatia). The Serbian members of the commission
argued that the borders of Croatia had been arbitrarily drawn by the Communists after
World War II (ibid., p. 32). Did any of this suggest an opening for the West? There
appear to have been at least three positions taken by the participants in the Karadjordjevo
talks: first, that of Mesić, who wished to bring in the international community from the
start; second, that of Tudjman, Milošević and Jović, who we know from various accounts
conceived of a plan to partition Bosnia and to carry out population exchanges (presumably of a peaceful nature, since the whole plan was conceived as a way of avoiding war
between Croatia and Serbia); and, third, the die-hard "Yugoslavs" on the Serbian side, led
by Avramov, who wished to redraw the borders of Croatia and Serbia on the basis of the
situation in 1918! (Avramov brought an ethnic map of Yugoslavia as it existed in 1918
to the meetings of the commission.) The variant that would have seen Bosnia remain in
a rump Yugoslavia (and thus save the Muslims from being partitioned) was, as far as we
can determine, not brought up in the negotiations between Croatia and Serbia in the
spring of 1991. One might at least speculate that this variant might have been considered
had the international community been informed from the beginning of the talks between
Belgrade and Zagreb to avoid war in the spring of 1991.

91. See footnote 90.
92. The United States in March 1991 considered the possibility of a third party's participating in the ongoing negotiations within Yugoslavia—while excluding the United States
from such a role. In the words of a U.S. note circulated to interested countries and
described by Jović, the United States welcomed input on how to resolve the Yugoslav
crisis but added, "We doubt that an offer of mediation from outside would be useful
except in certain concrete circumstances, for example, in case of the collapse and inability
to function of the Yugoslav federal government or if there was a consensus of the Yugoslav republics that mediation from without was necessary" (Jović, *Poslednji Dani,* p. 285,
translated from the Serbo-Croatian).
93. We know from Jović's diary, p. 311, that by the middle of March 1991, Jović and
Milošević were at odds with the JNA's plan to occupy Croatia and Slovenia, arguing that
this could lead to a strong reaction from Europe (military intervention is implied here)
and that it was therefore better to focus on protecting the Serb minority in the border
regions of Croatia. Could a similar fear have been generated by the United States and
Europe about the consequences of intervening militarily on behalf of the Serbs in Croatia, short of military intervention by the West? Jović's diary suggests that on the issue of
the Serbs in Croatia there could be no compromise. But see our discussion, above, of the
Milošević Tudjman talks. It should also be borne in mind that this new strategy appeared
to contradict Jović's statement to the state presidency in January, when he asserted that

any and all outside military interference in the affairs of Yugoslavia would be met by force.

94. As a corollary, one could at least speculate that a highly focused Western diplomatic effort begun several years earlier might have resulted in a decision to legitimize the notion that Yugoslavia no longer existed—and led to steps to uphold the integrity of Croatia and Slovenia earlier than was the actual case. (In March 1990, Jović held out the theoretical possibility that Serbia would accept a confederal system if Serbs outside Serbia received guarantees [not specified]—only to reject the idea as impractical [Jović, p. 131].) But apart from the fact that conditions at the time were not conducive to such an approach, such an action would have willy-nilly placed the burden of responsibility for the breakup of Yugoslavia on the West, something the Europeans and the Americans were determined to avoid.

95. Michael Libal, among those cited in this essay, makes the greatest effort to examine the terms under which the Europeans and Americans might have attempted to mediate the Serb-Croat conflict. He suggests that it was necessary to act in 1990–91 by proposing a confederal Yugoslavia to Slovenia and Croatia; in his words, "To conduct one's policies towards the non-Serb nations as if the preservation of Yugoslavia was an unquestionable duty, or possibly even a privilege or a pleasure, was to invite failure." In respect to the Serbs, Libal is less sure: "all efforts would have to be directed to at least trying to allay the fears of the Serbs of becoming a divided nation, which could be done only by preserving some sort of institutional unity of Yugoslavia and by securing a high degree of autonomy for those national and ethnic communities that would be minorities in different republics" (*Limits of Persuasion,* pp. 9–10).

DISINTEGRATIVE SYNERGIES AND THE DISSOLUTION OF SOCIALIST FEDERATIONS: YUGOSLAVIA IN COMPARATIVE PERSPECTIVE

❖ Lenard J. Cohen ❖

As nationalism grew, whether separatist or nationalist with a tendency to expansion, the [ministers] all started working more and more under instructions from their own republics and less and less as members of the [federal] government. . . . My competencies were so modest. But I did my best to prevent the worst from happening, and I failed, thanks in large part to [Slobodan Milošević].
> —Ante Marković, 2003

I understood quite well that the political struggle would develop mainly over the fate of the Union. . . . The leader of Russia [President Boris Yeltsin] was counter-posed to the idea of preserving the Union. . . . The President of Russia and his entourage in fact sacrificed the Union to his passionate desire to accede to the throne in the Kremlin.
> —Mikhail Gorbachev, 2000

It became clear that the country would be divided. . . . I could not put a brake on some kind of obvious momentum. . . . The notion that I caused the split is preposterous. . . . I was not the one to divide the state. For two years on end, I organized discussion among all Czech, Slovak, and federal constitutional officials. I invited them to various castles. . . . How could I have been the cause of the division Mr. Mečiar [the Slovak leader] sometimes speaks more quickly than he thinks.
> —Václav Havel, 2003

Introduction

The diverse character of all multinational states—whether large polyethnic empires or smaller ethnically plural states—endows them with a special vulnerability to centrifugal pressures and potential disintegration. The dramatic dissolution of three federal socialist states in Eastern Europe at the outset of the 1990s—Yugoslavia, the USSR, and Czechoslovakia—has stimulated considerable interest among both general observers and specialists regarding why that particular ideological and regional subset of multinational states unraveled in relatively rapid succession. For example, what accounts for the fact that prominent reform-oriented Communist and non-Communist leaders such as Mikhail Gorbachev, Václav Havel, and Ante Marković failed in their strenuous efforts to preserve the cohesion of the socialist federations? And how did various former colleagues or emergent rivals of those leaders, such as Boris Yeltsin, Vladimir Mečiar, and Slobodan Milošević, happen to emerge as the instigators and initial political beneficiaries of such disintegrative processes?

Of course, explanations for the disintegrated socialist federations in Eastern Europe are by no means limited to the saga of political leaders—either failed saviors or alleged villains—who endeavor to maintain or undermine state unity. A voluminous and expanding literature exists regarding the wide variety of historical and contemporary factors underlying the breakup of the socialist federations, including the political, economic, and social dimensions involved, the internal and external precipitants of state collapse, and the striking variability in the manner of the respective dissolutions. Questions concerning the avoidability or the inevitability of the collapse of the East European federations, along with the issue of the culpability of both domestic and foreign leaders in state dissolutions, also have been matters of considerable controversy. Indeed, studying the process of dissolution in Communist and post-Communist states has nearly acquired the status of a discrete subfield—perhaps what might be termed "disintegrationology"—as a branch of "transitology," that is, the area of study that emerged as a particular focus of research regarding the process of democratization and state transformation throughout Eurasia during the 1990s. The research studies reported in this volume have focused specifically on different aspects of socialist Yugoslavia's dissolution. But when considered together, such analytical efforts can be seen as part of a broader and continuing dialogue concerning the background, character, and consequences of state disintegration in multiethnic societies within and outside Eastern Europe.

The first section of this concluding chapter—a comparison of the dimensions of dissolution within the same regime species—will explore various analytical approaches or narratives that seek to identify the most salient factors responsible for the disintegrative process undergone by all the various former socialist federations. The second part of the chapter will examine why the former Yugoslavia followed such a distinctive path in contrast to the process of federal state breakdown in the two other East European Communist cases. Thus, although the dissolutions of the federalized Communist multinational states exhibit several common features, the major issue that analysts persistently focus upon, quite aptly, is why Yugoslavia experienced such a violent and sustained course of disintegration in comparison to the relatively peaceful, albeit certainly not conflict-free or bloodless meltdown of the USSR and also the rather benign "velvet divorce" of the Czechs and Slovaks. The final part of the chapter will briefly discuss current pressures relating to the further fragmentation of the states that emerged from the disintegration of the socialist federations. Thus today, the Western Balkans stand out as a region where a former federation is still undergoing dissolution and a reconfiguration into new states while elsewhere in Europe some postsocialist states are in the process of being integrated into an expanding supranational framework.

Narratives of Dissolution and the Collapse of the Socialist Federations

Four broad dimensions appear most prominently in the highly differentiated literature endeavoring to explain the process of disintegration experienced by the former Communist federations: 1) political-institutional legacies; 2) the ethnicization of politics and nationalist mobilization; 3) international political and economic factors; and 4) the politics of reform and democratic transition. Although most analysts emphasize one or two of these general dimensions, it is the interaction between or among the various factors, or what might be termed "disintegrative synergies," that best accounts for the dissolution of the Communist federations.

Historical Legacies and Formative Flaws: The Pre-Communist and Early Communist Periods

The collapse of the socialist federations can, in part, be traced to the persistence of political issues and conflicts that were associated with the policies and structures of the emergent Communist states and their pre-Communist predecessors. Thus, the political turbulence or warfare that immediately preceded the formation of the Communist systems often exacerbated societal cleavages in a manner that left a strong impact on subsequent Communist political development. The significance of such longstanding patterns for recent scenarios of state disintegration is usually stressed more by historians than by social scientists writing about the three East European federations. Historical perspectives focusing on political and institutional issues assume that problems arising from earlier patterns of political rule and interethnic coexistence, as well as past state-building experiences and episodes of state collapse, generate an accumulation of grievances and memories that have a long-term negative influence on the cohesion and legitimacy of multinational states.

For example, although both Russians and non-Russians in the Czarist empire suffered from a long history of autocratic and repressive rule, the official nationalism and Russian dominance characterizing the imperial system created a legacy of interethnic resentment. Strained interethnic relations may not have been the most critical factor in the Russian monarchy's collapse but were certainly one of its major weaknesses and a dimension that complicated subsequent efforts by the postimperial regime to find a genuine and lasting solution to the national question. Admittedly, governmental policy toward the non-Russian nationalities of the empire was a contradictory and unbalanced amalgam, including both paternalistic toleration and ethnic intermixture on the one hand, and Great Russian chauvinism, pan-Slavism and anti-Semitism on the other. However, as political concerns with regime maintenance and antirevolutionary prophylaxis assumed more importance at the end of the nineteenth and the early twentieth centuries—especially after the 1905 revolution—the persecution of minorities in the empire intensified, and a systematic policy of Russification was adopted. That trend underlined the description of the empire as a "prison of peoples." Interethnic relations worsened after the Czar abdicated, and despite some largely theoretical efforts of the powerless provisional government to address the problems of minorities, the national question became a central issue of political life throughout the disintegrating empire.[1]

The Russocentric character of the Bolsheviks' expanding power during the civil war (1917–21) and Lenin's decision to employ federalism in form but not in reality as part of the new state's architecture left a residue of suppressed aspirations among many non-Russians. Most pernicious was a Russian chauvinist mentality emanating from the center of political authority that, despite Lenin's best efforts, would affect early Bolshevik rule and influence the entire course of Soviet development. For most of the former empire's minorities and regions, the October revolution of 1917 was ethnically a *Russian* revolution. Thus, as Bolshevik troops reoccupied sections of the country that had broken away, a revolution that purportedly was to have delivered freedom to the minorities in fact gave impetus to a new pattern of Russian colonization.[2] As Alec Nove has pointed out, "the government lacked legitimacy vis-à-vis the Russian people as well as in relation to increasingly restive nationalities. It is most instructive to compare the increasingly strident claims from Ukrainians from 1917, first for autonomy, then for independence, with what happened in 1991."[3] Nove does not imply historical causation for the disintegration of the USSR but, rather, interesting parallels between the end of the Russian monarchy and the collapse of the Soviet Union. Such continuity is worth considering in an historically well-grounded consideration of the reasons for state dissolution, especially in the persistent "environment of weak political legitimation" that prevailed in many non-Russian areas of the USSR.

As is rather well known, Lenin showed tactical brilliance in developing a distinctive nationality policy that utilized ethnic and interregional tensions to assist the Bolshevik drive to consolidate power. But Lenin's decision to establish a new Bolshevik state as an ethnonational federation—the first in history where each constituent federal unit was alleged to represent the self-determination and sovereignty of the major nationality in that particular unit (nationalities that also gave the republics

Yugoslavia in Comparative Perspective ❖ 369

their names)—also would prove over the long run to be a fatal flaw undermining the adaptation and survival of federalism in the USSR. Thus, the legal-constitutional provisions regarding the technical sovereignty of federal units in the Soviet Union, features that were only symbolic and theoretical for almost the entire seven decades of Communist rule, would become a "legal boomerang" beginning in the late 1980s when secessionist and nationalist forces began their anti-Soviet state-building projects. The breakup of the Soviet Union is, in part, a dramatic case of "institutional path dependency," traceable to design features of the USSR's federal model adopted because of political exigencies in the period from 1917 to 1922.[4]

Both Czechoslovakia's and Yugoslavia's pre-Communist and early Communist political development also cast a shadow on later political life and the future prospects for the survival of these states. Leninist notions of ethnonational federalism and Stalinist practice would be a theoretical inheritance that the Communist Parties in Czechoslovakia and Yugoslavia would have difficulties assimilating, although in rather different ways and with important contrasts to the Soviet case. In Czechoslovakia after 1948, for example, Moscow and local Stalinists prevented the adoption of even a fictitious form of federalism, in view of the Communists' very weak legitimacy. Instead, a centralized form of one-party rule was imposed from Prague and aptly characterized as an "asymmetrical" model. This pattern of rule generated resentment among Slovak Communists and non-Communists alike. Paradoxically, the federalism that was advanced by Slovak reform Communists during the Prague Spring of 1968 was actually constitutionalized after the Soviet invasion. This "federalized totalitarianism" strangely satisfied some of the Slovak yearning for "national equity" and technical institutional equality but in no way really improved interethnic relations in the country.[5] Yugoslavia after World War II would also emphasize aspects of the Leninist and Stalinist legacy, but these were soon modified by the Tito-Stalin rift and Tito's "anti-Stalinist Stalinism." Soviet-style federalism would undergo considerable remodeling by Tito's theoreticians, but despite the introduction of a new self-governing model of socialism, Yugoslavia's federation would be largely spurious and subject to centralized one-party and police control until the mid-1960s.

The formative flaws of the pre-Communist period also help explain interethnic and interregional problems that would later afflict political life in the smaller multinational socialist federations. For example, in the case of Czechoslovakia, state founder Thomas Masaryk's "first republic" (1918–38) was a unitary system that provoked dissatisfaction on the part of many Slovaks and members of minority groups. Masaryk (although a democrat and part Slovak) embraced notions of "Czechoslovakianism" and regarded the country as the home of the "Czechoslovak" nation with "Czechoslovak" as its official language and in which all other groups were merely minorities. Masaryk regarded the more economically developed and westernized Czechs as the role model for the country's overall development. Decision making was centralized in Prague, and a heavy-handed policy of modernization was employed by the center in the less developed territories. Most Slovaks were relatively better off in the new interwar state than they had been under Hungarian rule in the Dual Monarchy,[6] but resentment ran deep in Slovakia regarding what many saw as a Czech model of political, cultural, linguistic, and economic imperialism. Thus, many Slovaks, as well as Hungarians and Germans, had anticipated that a federal or even confederal model would be institutionalized in the new state and consequently were deeply resentful. These problems bred extremism, which contributed to the Sudeten problem, and also assisted the rise of right-wing clericalism in Slovakia, both factors that helped external forces to destroy the state near the end of the 1930s. Each of the two principal ethnic groups in the country had self-perceptions, and perceptions of the other group, that fueled disagreements and that were made even more difficult by their separate experiences during World War II: the Czechs under a Reich protectorate and the Slovaks in the pro-Nazi puppet state. There were futile attempts to revive the idea of a federal model immediately after World War II, but the adoption of centralized Communist rule in 1948 and the brutal Stalinist suppression of any nationalist stirrings (in which the Slovaks suffered the brunt of the attack) simply drove the unresolved legacies of mutual resentment beneath a veneer of political uniformity.[7]

In the case of Yugoslavia there is little doubt, as some of the chapters in this volume illustrate, that the pre-Communist period of state development, especially in the first several decades of the twentieth century, left a negative legacy that had long-term implications. Thus, one might consider the important differences in political culture and levels of modernization among the peoples and regions that formed the first Yugoslavia and also the conceptual chasm between Serbian elites and non-Serb elites—from the Corfu Declaration of 1917 through the formation of the first Yugoslavia and on to the debates before and after the adoption of the 1921 constitution—over how power in the new state should be configured.[8] Serbian preferences for a more unitary state collided with Croat and Slovene elite expectations of living in a federalized country with considerable autonomy for regional units. The deficit of power for the unrecognized major minority groups in the "one nation-three tribes" formula (that was used in the new Kingdom of the Serbs, Croats, and Slovenes) was another major political factor causing resentment and fueling antiregime radicalization.[9] The royalist "integral Yugoslavism," which was advanced by the monarch, King Aleksandar, in 1929, supposedly to provide a more cohesive strategy, would prove just as deficient a formula for creating genuine interethnic and interregional harmony as the democratically imposed "Czechoslovakianism" of Masaryk or the formula of "proletarian internationalism" (or "nationalist in form, socialist in content") used in the authoritarian Bolshevik state. The territorial fragmentation and interethnic violence, which occurred in the mélange of occupied zones and pseudoindependent state units that followed the dismemberment of Yugoslavia in 1941—just as the experiences in the regions of the dismembered and occupied Czechoslovak and Soviet states during World War II—also left bitter legacies and serious cleavages for the Communist-Party state that was established after the war. The highly centralized structure of the initial

Titoist regime after World War II, albeit now technically federalized on a ethno-national basis, and the officially proclaimed view that the national question had been solved, simply masked problems and enhanced the persistence of earlier conflicts. The reemergence of such conflicts in the mid-1960s—as Yugoslavia tinkered with a model of "socialist pluralism"—together with new tensions and centrifugal forces, eventually converged in the 1980s and early 1990s to impede state cohesion.

The Politics of Ethnicization and Nationalist Mobilization

The specific role of politicized ethnicity is another major dimension in the literature concerning the dissolution of the Communist federations. Generally this approach explores the impact of nationality policies in the multinational Communist regimes and specifically the way deficiencies in the Communist management of multiethnicity generated ethnopolitical dissent and nationalist stirrings that eventually found expression in separatist and secessionist movements. The defects of Communist nationality policy, which provoked nationalism, are typically traced to a number of factors including: 1) Marxism's relative theoretical neglect of nationality as a potential political force in the projected socialist and Communist stages of development; 2) the inability of Communist federal systems to function as real mechanisms for representation and power distribution; 3) the overt suppression of nationalist beliefs in Communist regimes; 4) the predominance of "great" nation ethnic chauvinism over pan-ethnic or class-based values in the actual policies and politics of Communist federations; and 5) the failure of Communist modernization policies to both achieve a satisfactory standard of living and also prevent increasing economic disparities among groups and regions.[10] As a result of these factors, the ethnopolitical stratification that persisted in the Communist states many years after their establishment is alleged to have provoked feelings of relative deprivation and political discontent on the part of ethnic groups and regions who perceived their political position as subordinate.

The saga of Communist failure with regard to satisfying ethnic-based aspirations and dampening ethnic conflict is, of course, somewhat different in each particular party state and in each of the Communist federations discussed here.[11] But Richard Pipes is correct when he argues that because of the deficiencies of Communist regimes, "ethnic and territorial loyalties, when in conflict with class allegiances, everywhere and at all times, overwhelm them, dissolving communism and nationalism."[12] As the legitimacy of the multinational Communist regimes waned in the 1960s and 1970s—for a variety of reasons including a reaction to their earlier suppression of ethnic and religious identities—political solidarities based on such identities and overt nationalist convictions intensified. The emergence of nationalism as an autonomous political force during the twilight of Communist power found expression in various ways: as a generalized mindset in different groups opposed to the Communist system; as part of proposals to reform the federal system and overcome interregional and interethnic disparities; as forms of self-defense by specific national groups to alleviate their perceived suppression by the regime or other nations; and as a platform for specific groups and regions to escape, or exit from, the existing federal state. Together these dimensions converged to ethnicize the nature of political discourse in Communist states. The discernible "ethnicization of politics," which is very apparent in the last stages of the Communist regimes, becomes a critical factor in the dissolution of Communist federations and often continues, sometimes even more prominently, in both the turbulent and stabilized phases of post-Communism that follow.[13] "Nationalism is the last word of communism," Adam Michnik has observed, "a final attempt to find a social basis for dictatorship."[14] Indeed, nationalism usually is also the opening paragraph of post-Communism.

In its most pernicious form, the expressions of nationalism within the socialist states considered in this chapter became what Michnik correctly termed "a distorted form of national self-defense" in which nationalist leaders both represented and stimulated extreme views on the part of their own ethnic constituency.[15] Such extremist ethnic expressions in turn promoted negative national stereotypes of other ethnic groups and intolerance toward ethnic neighbors. It is elite-driven promotion of ethnonationalism, ethnocentrism, and "national homogenization," as well as the use of ethnicity as a political resource, that has the potential of transforming simply the ethnicization of politics into interethnic and interregional violence on a significant scale.

The former Sarajevo psychiatrist Dušan Kecmanović maintains that "ethnic identity was the key dimension of the wars in the second (former) Yugoslavia in the first half of the 1990s."[16] Exploring the roots of that war, Kecmanović focuses on the individual psychological factors that influence the existence and spread of ethnonationalist views and beliefs into civic populations. Kecmanović thoughtfully explores the basis for the growth of a "nationalist-like behavioral pattern," with its tendency toward intense feelings of group mentality or the "we-they syndrome" on the part of members of different groups. Potentially dangerous ethnocentric beliefs were advanced not only by opportunistic politicians but also by various intelligentsia elites, including members of the psychiatric profession in the former Yugoslav republics. For example, the alleged "ethnonationalist characteristics of the Serbs and Croats" described by psychiatrists in Croatia and Serbia during the 1990s helped promote the type of negative stereotypes that inflamed ethnic passions and created a situation that significantly expanded support for extreme nationalist appeals that went beyond a core of "endemic nationalists," thereby allowing ethnonationalism to reach epidemic proportions.[17] The most difficult task for the analyst, as Kecmanović concedes, is to explain the complex factors that account for the spread of ultranationalism throughout a population, and in a particular context, the reasons and mechanisms associated with the rise of ethnonationalism as a "desirable social pattern of behavior."[18]

Mark Beissinger has traced the dissolution of the USSR to the mobilization of nationalism. For Beissinger, "the disintegration of the Soviet Union was accompanied by an immense transformation in political discourse and public perceptions of politics . . . a population that could barely imagine the break-up of their country, came, within a compressed period of time to view the disintegration as inevitable."[19] Beissinger sees secessionist mobilization in the USSR as a "transnational tidal force," a "tsunami" of secessionist demands in different groups and regions that interact and stimulate one another. "In all," he determines, "210 demonstrations (in which more than 3.9 million people participated) occurred in the Soviet Union from late 1988 through the end of 1991 in which members of one nationality expressed solidarity with the secessionist demands of another." This interactive tidal wave of secessionist claims was promoted by the "mobilizational politics" of nationalists who "sought to mobilize their populations around secessionist frames." According to Beissinger, it is because of the "bandwaggoning" of secessionist sentiments throughout the Soviet Union and the institutionalization of secessionist sentiments in republics and local governments that "the Soviet state grew increasingly incoherent and more visibly on the brink of collapse."

Kecmanović links the violent "ethnic times" that overwhelmed the former Yugoslavia to the psychological triggers that helped spread ethnonationalist beliefs from a small group of "core endemic nationalists" to larger constituencies. Although both political and nonpolitical elites play an important role in spreading the virus of nationalism on an epidemic scale, the sources of ethnonationalism for Kecmanović lie more in a complex combination of the psychological predisposition of individuals and broad societal (including economic and political) factors. Similarly for Beissinger, the major factor responsible for the surge of nationalist secessionism is how Soviet "nomenklatura elites, seizing the current of history began their strategic appropriation of the independence agenda . . . in many cases simply refitting themselves as nationalists."[20] But for Beissinger, individual leaders or historical legacies are not the major elements in the dissolution of the USSR but rather "the sequence of connections between, and outcomes emerging from events" that are linked to the politics of "abnormal times." Kecmanović and Beissinger both demonstrate how nationalism can acquire a character of an autonomous political force in the demise of multinational states. Indeed, leaders are usually themselves transformed by the "epidemic of ethno-nationalism" and the secessionist mobilization they promote.[21]

The case of Czechoslovakia's dissolution alerts us to the fact that in some cases leaders may actually decide to dismantle a state without an underlying context of mass nationalism or may even rationalize the struggle for separation as a means to avoid promoting impassioned nationalist mobilization. Thus, the elite-level decision to dissolve Czechoslovakia was adopted despite the quite strong mass-level preferences on the part of citizens in both the Czech and Slovak republics to maintain a common state. Of course, mass preferences and mass mobilization were not totally absent in the case of Czechoslovakia's disintegration. Thus, the historically based Slovak quest for national sovereignty and the success of nationalist populist appeals by Vladimir Mečiar undoubtedly facilitated the elite-negotiated process of state dissolution. Václav Klaus, who was Czech prime minister at the time of the dissolution and who was highly averse to a compromise with the broad demands of the Slovak leadership, has observed that "Slovakia did not want to have an older, bigger, and stronger brother. It wanted emancipation, it wanted to be the master of its own fate . . . we did not enter the game with the interest of breaking away from Slovakia. It was Slovakia that entered it with the interest of breaking away from the Czech lands."[22] Of course, Klaus's own resistance to compromising with the Slovaks as a means to maintain a united state might be characterized as a form of Czech separatism.

International Political and Economic Factors

None of the socialist federations functioned in a vacuum, and there are various exogenous factors that help explain their respective dissolutions. For example, although analysts of nationalism, just as nationalists themselves, often emphasize the role of committed activists who mobilize the masses in the quest for sovereignty and nationhood, such accounts often suffer from a certain historical determinism, reductionism, or mythologizing that belies the full story. As Avial Roshwald has pointed out, in practice, "the trappings of political sovereignty often come within the reach of nationalists suddenly and unexpectedly, under extraordinary and short-lived circumstances arising from a regional or global crisis rather than from strictly internal developments."[23] For example, the multifaceted crisis of Communism in the latter stages and rapid conclusion of the Cold War had a profound impact on the internal course of development within the USSR and Eastern Europe. Such external aspects occurred during both the immediate prelude to the dissolution of Communist federations and also derived from earlier phases of Communist history.

The end of the Cold War and its bipolar pattern of confrontation between the western and Communist blocs is closely linked to diminished internal cohesion in all the Communist federations. Reduction in interbloc tension from the mid-1980s onward made it difficult for Communist elites to mobilize and demand internal consensus against the putative external "enemy" and also increase the space for antiregime centrifugal factors to operate internally. In the case of the USSR, the prolonged Cold War and its high expenditures on the arms race and competition for parity status with the United States in all areas, including space exploration, contributed to internal disintegrative trends by diverting resources that might have improved the standard of living and reduced the linkage between economic grievances and national sentiments in various republics. In the case of socialist Yugoslavia, the twilight of the Cold War reduced the importance of the post-Titoist system as a strategic zone that could have commanded more serious western attention and resources during the internal crises of the late 1980s and early 1990s.

Each of the socialist federations was also embedded in a network of international linkages that played a role in its respective dissolution process. For example, the Soviet Union was affected by the reduction in the price of oil on the world market, the debilitating quagmiric facets of the war in Afghanistan, the demonstration effect from the 1989 collapse of the East European Communist regimes, as well as China's success at economic reforms. All these factors exacerbated the USSR's problems of internal vitality and legitimacy, undermined the self-confidence of Soviet elites, and eventually contributed to state disintegration.[24]

In the case of Yugoslavia, the austerity measures imposed by the IMF and the general international financial environment in the 1980s proved highly disruptive to the economic plans of the Belgrade regime and impeded the country's ability to deal with the growing disparities between the more economically developed and less developed republics. For example, John Allcock views global anxiety concerning debt and the IMF's measures in the early 1980s as the "single most important blow to the integrity of Yugoslavia," developments made worse by the world depression in the later 1980s.[25] Moreover, as a result of the fall of the Berlin Wall in 1989, the end of the Cold War, and West European distractions with its own economic and political transformation, Yugoslavia lost its ability to evoke special treatment and attention. Indeed, when Yugoslavia was overwhelmed by internal turbulence and then warfare, European leaders were ill prepared to address the Balkan countries as a potential violent case of derailed post-Communism and internal fragmentation requiring a vigorous and thoughtful response. As Allcock puts it: "Yugoslavia can be seen to have been locked into a configuration of external events which either made for, or exacerbated the country's internal problems."[26]

Davorka Ljubisic has also argued that Yugoslavia's disintegration derived from a nexus between external and internal factors, a kind of "simultaneous suicide and homicide." But analyzing the case of Yugoslavia from a perspective far less nuanced and empirically grounded than Allcock, Ljubisic argues that a "foreign external dimension, particularly the role of the United States (US) and Germany, was decisive in the emergence of internal Balkanization or violent ethnic nationalism."[27] For Ljubisic, "the Yugoslav peoples were divided and turned against each other . . . by domestic nationalists sponsored by the US and Germany in accordance with the free market design of the New World Order for the Balkans." Conspiratorial theories aside, there is no question that external pressures of the major powers played a highly significant role in Yugoslavia's course of dissolution. For example, German nongovernmental support for Croatia's and Slovenia's self-determination prior to May–June 1991 and official support after that date encouraged elites in both Zagreb and Ljubljana to proceed with their respective policies of departing from the Yugoslav Federation.

Of course, the official German position throughout 1990 and the first part of 1991 was to support the unity of Yugoslavia. But as the German official in charge of the day-to-day conduct of German policy from 1991 to 1995 has argued, most German parliamentarians exhibited "more outspoken understanding for the positions taken in Ljubljana and Zagreb, and in consequence, were much less sanguine about the ability, or even desirability, of preserving Yugoslavia in its traditional form."[28] This mood in almost all German political parties foreshadowed the increased moral support extended to Slovenia and Croatia after the mid-1991 intervention of the Yugoslav military in those republics and finally Germany's urging of immediate recognition for those republics as independent states in the fall of 1991. The extent to which German espousal for international recognition of Slovenia and Croatia contributed to the violent scenario that unfolded in Bosnia remains a matter of debate.[29] In an interview in mid-January 2002, Croatian President Stipe Mesić put the situation of external intervention in the Yugoslav crisis into perspective from his point of view:

> To become independent was not just a decision. Croatia had to convince the world that Yugoslavia did not stand a chance, especially because many countries were very sentimental with regards to Yugoslavia and did not see that Yugoslavia had stopped being the Yugoslavia which used to be a sort of buffer zone between the opposed East and West. . . . We were aided by many in this. . . . I can say freely today that we were helped, above all, by the Holy See, with its resolute stand that all the former Yugoslav republics had the right to independence. Surely, Germany helped us, too. Both Chancellor Kohl and Genscher concluded that Croatia had to become independent and that it had the right to independence as all other republics.[30]

Meanwhile, Washington's fear that the virus of what George Bush called "suicidal nationalism" would spread to the USSR made the United States a rather reluctant cosponsor of socialist Yugoslavia's demise. As Slovenia and Croatia unilaterally seceded from Yugoslavia in June 1991, the Bush administration continued to be highly ambivalent regarding what to do about Yugoslavia. In the summer of 1991, U.S. Secretary of State James Baker III, commenting on Yugoslavia's impending collapse, famously claimed that the United States had "no dog in this fight," and by the summer of 1992, when Bosnia was beginning a slide into savage war, President Bush emphasized that the United States demurred from sending troops to the region: "We're not going to inject ourselves into a conflict in Yugoslavia."[31] Indeed, Mikhail Gorbachev claims that in the summer of 1991 President Bush told him: "Kohl is putting such a pressure on me so that Croatia and Slovenia would be recognized as quickly as possible. There was a competition. And this resulted in disintegration Yugoslav style with all the ensuing consequences. . . . Everything was started by the disintegration of Yugoslavia. That internal process was under the influence of outside forces."[32]

International factors were also operative in the case of Czechoslovakia's dissolution. Occurring in the aftermath of the dissolution of Yugoslavia and the USSR, and after Czechoslovakia was no longer a one-party monopoly, the major democratic countries took a more neutral position and chose not to put very strong pressure on the Czechs and Slovaks to stay united in a single state framework. For example, near the end of October 1991, when the Soviet Union was in the last stages of dissolution, President Bush emphasized the advantages, particularly economic, for the Czechs and Slovaks to maintain a federation. But Washington took no official position on the question.[33]

A particular exogenous factor in the case of Czechoslovakia's unique pattern of dissolution was the demonstration effect of what had taken place in the USSR and Yugoslavia. Such examples of disintegration illustrated for the Czechs and Slovaks the fragility and unworkability of Communist federal cohesion. For example, the centrifugal tendencies elsewhere gave heart to Slovaks arguing for autonomy and sovereignty. The Yugoslav case, and even the episodic conflicts in the USSR, also offered lessons—reinforcing aspects of political culture and history in Czechoslovakia itself—of the need to avoid violent dissolution. Indeed, in May 1992, Václav Havel warned his fellow citizens that "if they had to part ways, it would be better to do so in a constitutional and calm way" and avoid "a chaotic breakup of the state," which would involve a "price as high as in similar breakups in Yugoslavia or some parts of the former Soviet Union."[34]

One additional external influence in Czechoslovakia's dissolution was the role played by the existence and attractiveness of the European Union. Briefly, both Czechs and Slovaks not only yearned to jettison Communist control and their close association with the USSR but also to become full members of Europe. Thus, once the Communist system collapsed, there was a growing perception by the Czechs in particular that gaining entry into the new Europe was likely to proceed more expeditiously if the joint state was abandoned. Divergent outlooks regarding how to best "return to Europe" in other matters of foreign and defense policy tended to polarize Czech-Slovak relations within the federation.[35]

The Politics of Transition and Reform

A fourth perspective regarding the causes for the dissolution of the three socialist federations emphasizes pressures deriving from the reform and abandonment of authoritarian regimes. From this perspective, state dissolution is in large part a narrative of transition gone wrong, as difficulties related to the dismantling of party monism and nonmarket economies, create a disintegrative stimulus. Internal factors such as nationalism, and exogenous factors, are exacerbated when the imperatives of liberalization and democratization come into play. Reformist leaders and elites endeavoring to implement the restructuring of their societies play a central role in this narrative.

For example, Robert Strayer has pointed out that, although the failures of Soviet nationality policy had given rise to nationalist sentiment in a number of republics, and also to the emergence of nationalist elites who enjoyed relative autonomy from Moscow's control, such "nationalist explosion occurred only after glasnost and democratization had decisively weakened the center and permitted active mobilization along ethnic or nationalist lines."[36] Beissinger's discussion of nationalism and state collapse in the USSR also emphasizes how democratization becomes one of the "'autonomous vectors of mobilization,' at times intersecting with issues of nationalism and at times diverging from them."[37] Jack Snyder similarly explores the manner in which democratization produces nationalism. For Snyder, "popular nationalism typically arises during the earliest stage of democratization when elites use nationalist appeals to compete for popular support." Nationalist conflicts intensify not because of latent popular rivalries within a society, in Snyder's view, but are generally a "byproduct of the elites' efforts to persuade the people to accept divisive nationalist

ideas."[38] Thus, the pressures of liberalization, stimulated in part by ethnic sentiments within selected sections of civil society, generate the ethnicization of politics
and full-blown nationalist mobilization that helps to delegitimate the Communist
system and contributes to its eventual collapse. As Andranik Migrayan pointed out
in the early 1990s with respect to all three socialist federations: "these countries
began to disintegrate as soon as the democratic processes got underway . . . the anti-
communist unity that brings the nation together during the confrontation with the
communists often makes way for ethnic splits after the common enemy has been
eliminated . . . it is not accidental that Gorbachev was the idol of all democratic and
anti-communist forces in the Soviet republics during the first stages of perestroika
when he helped them stand on their own feet and demolish the CPSU's monopoly
of power. Later he became an obstacle to the same forces."[39]

The short-lived post-Communist democratization of Czechoslovakia as a federal
framework also illustrates how various elite perspectives regarding the transition to
pluralism can undermine the cohesion of a multinational composite state. Gil Eyal
argues that in the new environment of a nonauthoritarian system, Czech and Slovak
Communist elites found it impossible to bridge their differences and maintain a
unified country.[40] A "bi-polar elite constellation" emerged between two elites exhibiting "distinctive political rationalities." The Czech leaders in the new democracy had
emerged from the ranks of the dissident intelligentsia (within and outside the country), which had opposed the Soviet invasion and the termination of the 1968 Prague
Spring, whereas the post-Communist Slovak leaders were by and large characterized
by their relationship—collaborationist or reformist in nature—with the Communist regime. Democratic transition after 1989 only polarized the radically different
elite mindsets and set the stage for the break-up of Czechoslovakia. The two political
subelites adopted fundamentally opposed "discursive strategies," two different views
of the "mission" of the ruling class in a democratic state.

With the end of one of one-party rule in Czechoslovakia, the introduction of
democracy, and the "relative autonomy of the political game," political conflicts no
longer were ideological or bureaucratic struggles between two factions of a single
party. Very soon the new fault line of democratic political life became reduced to a
single dimension, the Czech "right" and the Slovak "left." By 1992, the fateful year
for negotiations concerning the maintenance of a unified state of Czechs and Slovaks,
the leaders of the two republics, whose mindset had been shaped by their "inherited
discursive strategies," had grown very far apart in terms of their world views about
further transition. Former Czech dissidents from the humanistic intelligentsia and
technical experts found common cause in rejecting the Communist past and facilitating democratic pluralism. The Slovak elite—Mečiar and his diverse allies—affirmed
the style of rule from the past and the need to put the defense of the nation above
continuation of the federal union. The Slovak elite, composed of many former "reform Communists," saw any radical break with the past, such as lustration, or shock
therapy in economic policy, as a threat. For the Czech leadership, compromise with

the Slovaks on issues relating to national sovereignty and constitutional change meant undermining democracy and the rule-of-law. Democratization, from the Czech leaders' point of view, meant fundamental elite turnover, and the new democratic and liberal Czech leadership had little in common with the nationalist and socialist Slovak leaders. Eyal demonstrates that for many Czech leaders "Czechoslovakia without Slovakia" was a "blessing." From this perspective, the story of Czechoslovakia's dissolution is essentially reduced to a crisis of democracy's "new class."

A convincing case can also be made that the process of liberalization (i.e., the pluralization of political life in a nondemocratic context) and democratization had a significant impact on the emergence of disintegrative factors that would eventually converge to destroy the Yugoslav socialist federation. For example, the decentralization of the party and the economy in the 1960s, the ferment and sharp termination of liberal tendencies and national expressions in both Croatia and Serbia during the late 1960s and early 1970s, and the pluralization of politics and growth of civil society in Slovenia during the 1980s, all were dimensions of Yugoslavia's political landscape that contributed to a spiraling centrifugal pattern that was a prelude to the state dissolution that followed. Indeed, Tito's crackdown on liberalizing factions of the League of Communists in both Croatia and Serbia short-circuited evolutionary reform and contributed to the rise of more anticentrist and illiberal elite policies following Tito's departure.[41] The results of the republican elections during the 1990s, which left some republics with a non-Communist and nationalist group of leaders ostensibly committed to pluralism and Serbia-Montenegro under the control of antipluralist nationalists who sought to maintain Titoist practices with a national face, also indicate how competition and the opening of the system actually contributed to the demise of the federal state.[42]

Yugoslavia's Exceptionality

Analysts have naturally devoted considerable attention to explaining why widespread violence and warfare became distinctive features of state dissolution in socialist Yugoslavia. Although armed conflict did arise within the "former Soviet-space" following the breakup of the USSR—including at least six regional wars—the toll of death and destruction relative to the size of the disintegrated polity did not approach the scale of violence in the former Yugoslavia. Episodic violence during the twilight of the Gorbachev regime (e.g., in the Baltic region) was also on a relatively small scale. The course of Czechoslovakia's "velvet" mode of dissolution did not involve any of the violent features that were so pronounced in the Balkans and, to a lesser extent, in the former USSR, such as the use of paramilitary militias, the use of heavy arms, or the notorious policy of "ethnic cleansing."

Four interrelated factors are generally advanced in the disparate literature in endeavoring to explain the different patterns of dissolution experienced by the three Communist federations during the early 1990s: 1) political-cultural factors, 2) the role of political leadership, 3) the role of military and paramilitary security forces, and 4) the duration and nature of liberalization and emergent pluralism.

Political-Cultural Values

Attempting to explain the differences in the levels of violence that accompanied the dissolution of Yugoslavia and the USSR, Veljko Vujačić points out that although a number of factors can be discussed (economic, institutional, etc.), it is the "autonomous importance of political culture" that is most significant.[43] "Despite the overall structural similarities in the positions of Russians and Serbs in the Soviet Union and Yugoslavia respectively," argues Vujačić, "there were important differences between the two nations' collective perceptions of 'what really matters' in the period of communism's terminal crisis." For Vujačić there were a number of political-cultural elements that account for the Serbs' "very strong reaction" to the prospect of socialist Yugoslavia's disintegration: 1) the strong identification of Serbs with the notion of Yugoslavia as "their, but not only their, national state," 2) the Serbs' collective memory of victimization in Croatia and Bosnia during World War II, and 3) the revivified myth of Kosovo as internal Serbian territory. Milošević was able, in Vujačić's argument, to anchor his nationalistic mobilization to a "symbolic reality" deriving from a foundation of such beliefs and myths. Moreover the legitimacy of using coercive state power against putative "enemies of the state" could rest upon such "symbolic pillars."

In contrast, in Russia, the state was historically perceived as an "alien" autocratic and oppressive force. The antistatist mentality—found in imperial Russia and reinforced during the Stalinist period—supported Yeltsin's argument that Russia should gradually disengage from the Soviet federation and that Russians need not rally around the center in order to preserve the USSR. Serbs felt they needed to support actions to preserve a state, whereas Russians, in Vujačić's view, saw the collapse of the Soviet Union as a way to achieve freedom. The fact that the dominant or core nation in the Soviet Union was not mobilized to quash secessionism within its own borders or in the other republics accounts for the relatively peaceful mode of dissolution. As Vujačić puts it: "the democratic movement led by Boris Yeltsin triumphed over the coalition of 'empire-saviours.' As the empire fell so too did its coercive state institutions, conservative party structures, and the military-industrial complex."[44]

Vujačić's argument regarding the basis for aggressive Serbian nationalism is quite convincing, although the factors that account for the absence of a more vigorous form of Russian national mobilization and the type of violent consequences that might have ensued certainly include factors beyond the antistatist aspects of Russian political culture. For example, Adrank Migranyan has argued that several reasons account for the fact that a "great power idea" or "ethnic dimension" did not become more pronounced within the Russian population during the late 1980s. First, ideas such as Russia's messianic role, anti-individualism, and similar concepts, were discredited because of their association with Communist rhetoric and practice. Second, the Russian people were "denationalized" throughout the Soviet period. Thus, although Russians constituted the core of the empire, Russian culture was suppressed, as was Russian national self-awareness. The fact that during perestroika the Soviet media and Gorbachev opposed manifestations of Russian nationalism also limited the appeal of the "Russian great power idea" and ultranationalistic extremism. Near the end of the USSR, the so-called empire-saviours launched the coup against Gorbachev and his proposed Union Treaty, but their attempt to use coercion from the center as an obstacle to secessionism and potential dissolution failed to garner substantial popular or military support.[45]

Summarizing the elements of uniqueness of Czechoslovakia's dissolution, Michael Kraus and Allison Stanger, also employing a political cultural approach, stress that a "tendency to resolve disputes by peaceful means" and a "noteworthy degree of moderation" help to account for the historical absence of conflict between Czechs and Slovaks, and the very tranquil character of "divorce Czecho-Slovak style."[46] The question of whether these specific habits derive from traits that are "embedded in the Czech and Slovak national characters by years of domination from without" or are aspects of an already formed democratic political culture is not explored by Kraus and Stanger. Perhaps their failure in this respect is due to the considerable difficulties of analyzing what Andrew Janos has called "the hoary concept of culture, the prism through which people see their every day life and construct ways of resolving conflicts within their narrower social sphere."[47] Janos is careful not to advance the idea of a correlation between ethnicity and violence, but he aptly points out that "the contrasts between the Balkans and Czechoslovakia are stark indeed." Representations of popular culture in the Balkans, such as literature and movies, Janos observes, exhibit considerable private and public violence (including violent sexuality or sexuality leading to violence). In the contrasting case of the Czechs and Slovaks, "stories of sly compromise to avoid physical confrontation" tend to be more prevalent.

The Role of Political Leadership

Perspectives on the importance of leadership as an explanation for the prevalence or absence of violence in the dissolution of Communist federations generally focus on the benign role played by principal actors such as Havel, Klaus, Gorbachev, and Yeltsin in contrast to the nationalist tactics of figures such as Milošević and Tudjman, among others. Valerie Bunce, for example, stresses the significant role played by the leaders of the core nations in the USSR and Czechoslovakia. For Bunce, Yeltsin and Klaus "defined nationalism in a manner that minimized resentments toward other nations."[48] By also focusing on a rejection of socialism, on capitalism and democratic transition and on either a continuation of the existing federal state or peaceful dismemberment of the existing federation along established "republican lines," Yeltsin and Klaus greatly reduced the propensity toward violence. Both of those leaders were also interested in gaining power and excluding the existing state leaders (Gorbachev and Havel) from power or any future dominant political role in the principal successor states, the Russian federation, and the Czech Republic.

Another perspective on the peaceful course of the Soviet and Czechoslovak dissolutions focuses on the apparently graceful manner in which Gorbachev and Havel stepped down from power during the dissolution of the federal states that they led. Both leaders may have failed to take measures that might have impeded the drift of their states toward dissolution, but they cannot be faulted for encouraging violent scenarios of state preservation. Looking back at his own role in the disintegration of the Soviet Union, Gorbachev, albeit self-servingly, reminds observers of his reluctance to employ violence. As he pointed out in a December 2001 interview: "I considered all possible options. . . . I could not have chosen any course of action that could have led to a division, to a civil war in the country, saturated with nuclear weapons. Besides, it would have looked as if I had tried to do this in order to keep my post."[49] Gorbachev also puts the blame for the collapse of the USSR squarely on Yeltsin working in association with the leaders of Ukraine and Belarus. A Gorbachev puts it: "there was a collusion of three leaders behind the president's back, behind the back of their national parliaments . . . this was premeditated long in advance, and in implementing this plan, advantage was taken of instability and disintegration. And in order to get rid of the old center they sacrificed the Union. I regard this as Yeltsin's strategic error of judgment."[50]

Why Gorbachev did not take more resolute action against the nationalist and secessionist leaders well before the August 1991 coup that weakened his authority remains an important and complex question. Vladislav Zubok has offered the interesting suggestion that it was Gorbachev's search for a new self-legitimation, his self-styled mission to humanize Communism that led to the Soviet leader's renunciation of violence and force. "The abstention from violence and blood was not a personal weakness," writes Zubok, "it was ironically the result of his extreme self-confidence and the exaggeration of his abilities to manage the cauldron of change." By the time Gorbachev had permitted Soviet republican elites to evolve into "ethnocracies" and to "rethink their legitimacy in nationalist and populist terms," Gorbachev had already "undercut the remnants of his own legitimacy."[51]

Václav Havel, who subscribed to an ethical conception of politics that went well beyond Gorbachev's pretensions of humanizing socialism, also eschewed a violent scenario to impede potential dissolution. In an interview in February 1992, Havel expressed his view on national unity: "I would not want to force our two peoples to live together in a single state. . . . Our situation is somewhat different from the Soviet Union. Our people voluntarily decided to live together. . . . This single state has a complex history, but there has never been a conflict between the two peoples. . . . I am against violence. If the peoples decide to live together independently, separately, they are fully entitled to do so."[52] In July 1992, when it was clear that the country was moving quickly toward a breakup, he observed: "I could have done many things differently. . . . On the other hand, if I'd done things different maybe everything would have been even worse."[53] In September 1992, Havel still described himself as a decided "federalist" but added that his personal idea of federalism did not go so far as to negate the right of another state to self-determination. "I think that if the Slovaks want to have their own state, they have every right to do so."[54]

The roles played by Havel and Gorbachev in preventing violence, and for that matter the influence of Yeltsin and Klaus, contrast sharply with the roles of Balkan leaders, most notably Serbia's Slobodan Milošević. Milošević's well-known comments on a number of occasions suggesting that force might become necessary to deal with the situation of impending disintegration (and especially the problems faced by Serbs outside of Serbia), his support for violent Serbian paramilitary groups, and his efforts to utilize Socialist Yugoslavia's military forces to advance his policies, not to mention his own nationalist-populist policies, which engendered Serbian radicalism and extreme forms of reactive nationalism, all contributed to the violent scenario of disintegration in the case of Yugoslavia.[55] Croatia's Franjo Tudjman was also not reluctant to make inflammatory statements and utilize Croatian security forces in a manner that provoked violence.[56] And in the case of the former Yugoslavia, the principal leader on the federal level, Ante Marković, was in a much weaker position—with respect to both the security forces and the political-governmental structure—to forestall the nationalist pressures in Serbia and Croatia.

Slovenia's former representative in socialist Yugoslavia's last collective presidency, Janos Drnovšek, claims that during the first half of 1991 his goal was the peaceful dissolution of the country. He absolves his own republic's leaders from responsibility for the chain of events leading to violent disintegration and claims that in hindsight he "can see that the Serbian regime was working on a military solution. . . . They blocked the federal presidency [and] the presidency ceased to function as the supreme commander of the army. When Slovenia and Croatia declared independence on June 25th, 1991, the Yugoslav army intervened in Slovenia. . . . The decision was the result of Serbian pressure and the mixed feeling of some naïve federal officials, including some generals and Prime Minister [Ante] Marković. This was the crucial step from political negotiation to war. . . . The Serbian regime opted for force at the moment when it appeared that they could achieve more with force than with negotiations."[57] Drnovšek does not mention the role of Slovene elites or the important role of territorial based militias—including Slovene forces—in the events that precipitated Yugoslavia's violent dissolution. Drnovšek also ignores the argument made by Slobodan Milošević, among others, that the Slovene decision to take over federal customs posts in June 1991, was the act that provoked action by the JNA and thus provoked the violent course of the former Yugoslavia's dissolution. For example, when Milan Kućan, the former president of Slovenia, testified against Milošević at The Hague in May 2003, Milošević asked him why Slovenia "opted for violence." Why did you not act like Slovakia did? Why didn't you take the issue to the federal bodies? Kućan replied that the course recommended by Milošević would have been impossible and that Slovenia, as a small nation in the former Yugoslavia, would have been out-voted. Milošević insisted that Slovenia could have left the federation peacefully.[58]

The Role of Military and Paramilitary Forces

The role of the armed forces—especially the higher ranks of the military establishment—and various security agencies within and outside the formal governmental structure also contributed to the violent nature of the former Yugoslavia. The close, albeit monolithic, alliance that formed between the Serbian political leadership on the one side and the JNA and paramilitary groups on the other is particularly important in this regard. In his testimony to the UN war crimes tribunal at The Hague in November 2003, Borisav Jović, one of Milošević's closest associates and a member of the SFRY presidency from 1989 to 1992, explained that strategic decisions at that time had been discussed at meetings of six individuals—Milošević; Jović; the Montenegrin political leaders, Branko Kostić and Momir Bulatović; and JNA generals Vjelko Kadijević and Blagoje Adžić. Jović claimed that by decision of the presidency, paramilitary forces were placed under JNA control and deployed in zones under JNA command. Paramilitary leaders, such as Arkan, Jović also maintained, had direct connections to the Serbian police and JNA and had become a "state within a state."[59] Of course, even before Jović testified at The Hague, the close relationship that existed between the JNA and the Serbian leadership, and also the military's role as a key factor in Yugoslavia's violent dissolution, had been extensively discussed (including in Jović's book-length study).[60] Indeed, military influences in Yugoslavia's politics had waxed and waned during the last decade of Tito's life and had become increasingly strong in the post-Tito period. The military establishment had come to perceive itself as playing a vital and essential role in the maintenance of domestic stability and state cohesion. As Žarko Puhovski observed in 2004 at a conference in Belgrade: "After Tito's death Yugoslavia was reduced to the Yugoslav People's Army since there was not any other Yugoslav institution, therefore the dissolution of Yugoslavia was predetermined to be—at the moment it happens—a violent one."[61]

It is also well established that during the period before and during the wars of the Yugoslav secession, a segment of the JNA leadership had come under the direct influence of the Serbian regime. For example, General Kadijević, in his book on the breakup of Yugoslavia, observes that the JNA decided in March 1991 to focus on "the protection and defence of the Serbian people outside Serbia and to regroup the JNA forces within the borders of a future Yugoslavia."[62] At the same point, Kadijević and his sympathizers, according to Jović's book, had even contemplated a military coup with the support of the USSR in order to implement a crackdown on secessionist elements in Croatia and Slovenia. The coup did not take place, partially because of a lack of support from Moscow and also because of the underlying mistrust between the activist generals and Milošević. Kadijević is also explicit in his memoir that the JNA provided the basis for three Serb armies: for the Federal Republic of Yugoslavia that was established in 1992 by Milošević; for the Republika Srpska; and for the Republic of the Serbian Krajina, which was controlled in part from Belgrade. Of course, the pro-Serb elements in the JNA were not the only military forces in the former Yugoslavia to take part in the country's violent dissolution. For example, the memoir of

Croatian General Janko Bobetko also details the manner in which regular Croatian troops took part in the Bosnian war, especially during 1992 and 1993, as well as in the establishment of the Bosnian-Croat statelet of Herzeg-Bosna.[63]

In the contrasting Czechoslovak and Soviet cases, the military establishments remained subject to far more civilian control than was the case in socialist Yugoslavia. In part, this is because the breakdown of central leadership began much earlier in Yugoslavia. As part of the Warsaw Pact military framework, the Soviet and Czechoslovak armies were also outward looking rather than primarily concerned with domestic priorities (although in the USSR, the military was a major "demand sector" in lobbying for resources from the country's budget). In Czechoslovakia Havel insisted that the military remain under strict civilian control. In March 1991, only one week after the Yugoslav military deployed tanks in the streets of Belgrade to assist Milošević in dampening antiregime demonstrations, Havel gave a speech in Slovakia to officers of the Czechoslovak army. He observed that his country's "young democracy is living through very traumatic moments. . . . Our army must not interfere or take part in this complicated process. . . . The image of tanks in the streets of towns is a terrifying image. To play with the idea that the army could influence internal events means to disdain all ideals of our democratic revolution and all the values in which we believe. I do not think that Czechoslovakia is in jeopardy of street unrest and clashes, but I proclaim that even if something like that happened to us, I will not permit our army to be called up to restore order."[64]

Larger and more complex than the Czechoslovak armed forces, the Soviet military could hardly be described as entirely passive and politically noninterventionist. Thus, within the Soviet military industrial complex, the military was an important "demand sector," seeking to influence budget allocations and political decisions that involved the military's corporate interests. But at crucial moments in the process of the USSR's disintegration, such as in August 1991 when the coup against Gorbachev took place and later when Yeltsin and his fellow leaders dismantled the federation, the Soviet military chose to follow the orders of the democratically elected authorities. Many of the Soviet generals may have been imbued with a "national-patriotic" ideology and also blamed the democratic authorities such as Yeltsin for assisting the collapse of the country. However, by and large the military establishment acquiesced in the dismemberment of the armed forces.[65]

The Duration of Liberalization and Electoral Sequencing

The unique features of the former Yugoslavia's transition away from Soviet-style socialism also helped to explain the anomalous nature of Yugoslavia's breakup in comparison to other socialist federations. For example, Omer Fisher has profitably directed attention to different modalities of transition and reform in attempting to compare the disintegration of Yugoslavia with Czechoslovakia and the USSR.[66] Fisher pays particular attention to the character and duration of regime liberalization and the degree of continuity in the transition process. Most of the socialist countries underwent some degree of liberalization before they collapsed, that is, an opening of the regime, but in an undemocratic context. But this was a relatively short phase in the case of the USSR—five years of actual perestroika (1986–91)—and even shorter (a few weeks at the end of 1989) in the case of Czechoslovakia. Even if we leave aside Fisher's manner of calculating "linear transition" (which does not include episodes such as the Prague Spring or Khrushchev-era reforms), the case of Yugoslavia stands out for its long period of liberalization under the one-party regime. Fisher's argument is that prolonged transition, or what he terms "liberalization by decay," provided the necessary gestation period for nationalist elites, both on the periphery and at the center in Belgrade, to accumulate power and gradually weaken the legitimacy of the federal state. The fact that socialist Yugoslavia was more open than any other liberalizing nondemocratic regime in Eastern Europe progressively weakened the fundamentally authoritarian regime and reduced its capability to manage economic crisis and elite tensions, especially after Tito's death in May 1980. The erratic nature of socialist Yugoslavia's reform trajectory, punctuated by both reform momentum and authoritarian relapses, also undermined the regime's legitimacy.

Fisher attributes the growing intervention of the Yugoslav military in political life and its subsequent alliance with Milošević to the country's long and legitimacy-eroding course of liberalization. Once Milošević had forged an alliance with the JNA, the way was paved for the federation's violent dissolution. "Possibly, armed conflict and violent mobilization were even more likely because in the pre-collapse phase of the Yugoslav crisis the army was the only institution capable of functioning, making an armed response virtually the only possible central response to centrifugal tendencies."[67] Valerie Bunce has also emphasized that because socialist Yugoslavia, in comparison with Czechoslovakia and the USSR, had an "unusually weak center" and a highly decentralized character, the regime was less institutionally capable of maintaining cohesion and fending off ethnoterritorial demands.[68]

The fact that after the advent of political pluralism of 1990 multiparty elections were never held at the federal level in the former Yugoslavia is also regarded as an aspect of the country's exceptionality that contributed to the federal government's inability to preserve legitimacy and maintain state cohesion. But the same problem regarding electoral sequencing and the delegitimization of the central authorities prevailed in the USSR, where the first really competitive elections were held at the republic level and where Gorbachev never was directly elected in a country-wide context (or the same problem that confronted Ante Marković in Yugoslavia).

In the case of Czechoslovakia, although federal- and republic-level elections were held simultaneously in June 1990, the enhanced democratic legitimacy of the federal authorities did not prove decisive in preventing state dissolution. The argument could be made, however, that Czechoslovakia's peaceful breakup was enhanced by the fact that both the federal and republican officials who were playing the "games of state dismemberment" enjoyed popular backing. But a systematic explanation of Czechoslovakia's nonconflictual path toward dissolution would have to include a number of unique factors, including the country's demographic landscape.[69] Thus, and very importantly, the absence of enclaves of minority ethnic communities within territories controlled by the two ethnic majorities proved to be a fortuitous feature of Czechoslovakia's ethnic configuration. In contrast, territorial claims by ethnic enclaves resulted in violent nationalist mobilization during the dissolution of the former Yugoslavia (e.g., the case of Serbs and Croats in Bosnia), and episodic violence (e.g., in the Baltics) during the USSR's disintegration.

Beyond Dissolution: The Integration-Disintegration Dialectic

For some fifteen years, the elites and citizens within the twenty-two successor states that emerged from the dissolution of the three multinational countries discussed in this chapter have been challenged by many of the same issues that they experienced as parts of the disintegrated socialist federations. Thus, the impact of political and institutional legacies, nationalist pressures, transitional dynamics, and the challenges of a rapidly evolving international environment—all dimensions explored in the first part of this chapter—have been significant factors influencing the stability and democratization of the successor states. Indeed, the nature of the state dissolution process has itself become one aspect of each successor state's political and institutional legacy, which, along with many other factors—including interethnic relations, economic conditions, leadership, political culture, and the security situation—has influenced postdissolution development.

Thus, many of the successor states to the three federations discussed in this chapter, to one extent or another, have had to deal with their own internal ethnoterritorial divisions after becoming independent units, and all of the states have had to confront internal issues relating to ethnic minorities. Many observers have pointed out that the dissolution of the former Yugoslavia did not conclude with the wars in Slovenia, Croatia, and Bosnia between 1991 and 1995. Thus, the 1999 war over Kosovo left the former province as an international protectorate that is de facto detached from Serbia and continues to have severe internal ethnic divisions. Meanwhile, Serbia and Montenegro are associated within a loose union that lacks settled legitimacy and cohesion. Speaking in April 2002, when the current Union agreement creating Serbia and Montenegro as a new state was negotiated, the then president of the Federal Republic of Yugoslavia, Vojislav Koštunica (who left that post in early 2003 and was elected prime minister of Serbia at the beginning of 2004), proclaimed: "The process of our state's disintegration and the process of disintegration in the Balkans has been halted. I am not saying that this will be forever, but for the time being it has been halted."[70] Koštunica was sensibly cautious in his prediction. Indeed, the future of Serbia and Montenegro as a united state remained a very tenuous proposition in early 2006 (the Montenegrin ruling coalition was preparing to hold a referendum on the question of independence in the spring of 2006). Ten years after the Dayton peace accord, ethnoterritorial segmentation within Bosnia and Herzegovina—among the three constituent peoples (Bosniaks, Serbs, and Croats), both between the Republika Srpska and the Muslim-Croat Federation and within the Federation itself—also remain substantial, as does the cleavage and ethnic distance between Albanians and Slavs in Macedonia.

The successor states to Czechoslovakia have also not been without their own interethnic problems, although those countries are not nearly as troubled as some of the Balkan cases. But in the current period of globalization of discourse regarding human rights, how the leaders of the Czech Republic and Slovakia deal with ethnic minority issues is no longer simply an internal problem for sovereign states. The difficulties of the Roma minority in the Czech Republic and of the Hungarian minority in Slovakia have challenged those two states, though on a level that has not proved threatening to their fundamental cohesion.[71] Indeed, some leaders in the two states now fear that the greatest threat they face today is how to preserve their national identity and attributes of statehood within an enlarged European Union. Czech President Klaus recently warned his fellow citizens that the most serious problem is how to defend "the national specifics of individual countries" in the EU. As he remarked in April 2004: "Our country—for the first time in its complicated and at times tortuous history—is voluntarily giving up parts of its sovereignty and handing them over to that large supra-national whole . . . in many respects the focal point for decision-making about the affairs of the Czech Republic will shift abroad. . . . Let us do everything we can to ensure that we do not get lost in the EU, to ensure that the unique thousand-year work of our ancestors does not get diffused and gradually lost entirely."[72] Euro-skeptic Klaus's worries about sovereignty shifting to Brussels resemble the earlier fear of some Slovak politicians about centralization of power in Prague. Meanwhile, in Slovakia, there is ambivalence in clerical-populist circles regarding potential threats to morality and sovereignty that may accompany membership in the EU.[73]

Each of the states seceding from the former Soviet Union has its own minority and territorial problems. In cases such as Moldova, Georgia, Armenia, Azerbaijan, Tajikistan, and especially Chechnya, these problems have been very destabilizing. However, despite the fact that the warfare, separation, and terrorism in the North Caucasus have been major factors of political instability and violence in the Russian federation, many analysts have pointed to that country's remarkable cohesion as a quite large and highly diverse state (which contains some thirty-two ethnically defined regions covering 53 percent of the country's territory). Some observers have suggested, for example, that the Russian federation's ability to cope with centrifugal forces has resulted from broad macrolevel factors that have been present in the post–1991 period including a substantial improvement in Russia's geopolitical conditions (e.g., an end to the drain of resources from the arms race and the military overextension that existed for the USSR, a shorter border to defend, etc.), improvement in the distribution of state power (constitutional strengthening of the executive, curtailing the power of regional elites and oligarchs, improved fiscal control, and economic strength), and improvement in demographic conditions (shrinking population growth, which reduced pressure on the economic and political subsystems).[74] Other observers believe that Russia, and indeed the entire post-Soviet region—with the exception of Chechnya—succeeded in avoiding the pressure of disintegrative synergies that afflicted the USSR because of more specific factors such as a shift in policy priorities by ruling elites toward state consolidation rather than national liberation; an end to disputes over borders (and the acceptance of internationally recognized borders); the integration of the Eurasian successor states into a network of international governmental and nongovernmental organizations that act to promote regional security and interethnic conciliation; and the growing number of Russians and non-Russians—both within the Russian federation and the other former Soviet republics—who have begun to identify with their new countries.[75]

Despite such factors, however, the highly diverse ethnic and regional landscape of the former "Soviet space," and particularly the internal complexity of the Russian federation and the struggle in Chechnya, creates strong anxiety concerning potential state dissolution. As President Putin remarked in December 2003 with regard to separatist claims in the Muslim-populated territories of Russia: "We don't want to see a disintegration of our state. If that happens it would be worse than in Yugoslavia, it will be the Yugoslavization of Russia at its worst and there will be a lot more victims."[76]

Midway through the first decade of the twenty-first century, the successor states of the three Communist federations that dissolved in the early 1990s are still grappling with various anxieties that derive from the pressures of two countertrends: one, the disintegration of states into smaller units (separatism, secessionism, peripheral nationalisms); and two, the integration of states into larger transnational and regional units of governance. Some states of the former socialist Yugoslavia, such as Serbia and Montenegro, Bosnia and Herzegovina, and Macedonia, exhibit both internal ethnoterritorial stresses and also anxiety about their current position outside of an enlarging European Union. For example, the Serbian leaders of the G17 Plus party (a former NGO of highly educated professionals that in early 2006 remained a part of the ruling coalition in Belgrade) have tried to reconcile devotion to a modern nonexpansive Serbian state (even without Montenegro or Kosovo) and a drive to secure Serbia's entry into a new European framework. As the G17 Plus national program proclaims: "In the past century the solution to Serbia's national question was called Yugoslavia. It proved to be short-lived. This cannot be replicated. . . . Times have changed. The solution to the national question in the 21st century will be Serbia—a European state. . . . European Serbia is in the best interests of all nations and minorities in Serbia's territory."[77]

Other countries, such as the three Baltic states, the Czech Republic, Slovakia, Slovenia, and Croatia, also have exhibited particular internal strains and minority problems, but by and large their elites are forward-looking and concerned with how to maintain their sense of nationhood and statehood after entering, or preparing to join, an enlarged EU. For example, on the eve of his country's entry into the EU, the president of Slovenia tried to appear magnanimous toward his former fellow citizens in disintegrated socialist Yugoslavia: "[We] remember today the nations with which we once shared a common state, and wish them every success in their development."[78] Such remarks—in this case a Slovene leader's way of trying to say goodbye to the Balkans—illustrate that all the successor states continue to be influenced to varying degrees by the nations and regions with whom they were previously united.

In the case of the Russian Federation, there is a certain ambivalence and fear regarding EU expansion and concerns that the former Soviet space has fallen under disproportionate foreign influence. Thus some Russians, both on the mass and elite levels, undoubtedly share a certain nostalgia for their lost imperial ambit. There also are in some circles revanchist political stirrings for renewed hegemony over the neighboring states of the former USSR. Still other Russians worry about the relatively weak position of their country in relation to the power and size of the EU, not to mention the United States. Many Russians simply hope that their country can remain a sovereign and powerful state that shares in European civilization but has its own model of democratic rule that is not subject to control by foreign decision-makers in Brussels or elsewhere. Such views may help explain President Putin's observation in 2005 that the collapse of the Soviet Union was "the greatest geo-political catastrophe of the [twentieth] century," and also his predilection for some sort of illiberal "sovereign democracy" or "managed democracy" in the Russian Federation.[79]

In all the successor states that previously were constituent units in the former socialist federations, various political issues relating to the challenges of maintaining identity and cohesion remain highly significant. A host of recent internal challenges and external pressures have naturally assumed priority in these successor states, but they cannot easily escape the legacy of the difficult dissolution processes they experienced only a relatively short time ago. In the case of the states that emerged from the former Yugoslavia, which were touched directly or indirectly by the violent process of state dissolution in the Balkans, the residual effects of that experience remain rather strong, and dissolution-related issues (e.g., forging new economic relations, mutual interstate and intergroup apologies, revamping historical accounts and textbooks, dealing with war crimes) remain parts of routine political life. Owing to that legacy, the imperative of avoiding renewed episodes of state collapse, and also the need to improve our understanding of recent history, the lessons and dimensions of the violent disintegration that befell the former Yugoslavia must continue to receive careful attention from both analysts and state-builders.

Notes

1. Richard Pipes, *The Formation of the Soviet Union: Communism and Nationalism, 1917–1923* (Cambridge: Harvard University Press, 1964), pp. 6–9, 41–51. See also George F. Kennan, "The Breakdown of the Tsarist Autocracy," in Richard Pipes, ed., *Revolutionary Russia: A Symposium* (Garden City: Doubleday, 1969), pp. 12–14.
2. Walter Kolarz, *Russia and the Colonies* (London: George Philip and Son, 1952), pp. 3–16. See also Tatiana Mastyugima and Lev Perepelkin, *An Ethnic History of Russia: Pre-Revolutionary Times to Present* (Westport: Greenwood Press, 1996), pp. 12–24.
3. Alec Nove, "The Fall of Empires: Russian and the Soviet Union," in Geir Lundestad, ed., *The Fall of Great Powers: Peace, Stability, and Legitimacy* (New York: Oxford University Press, 1994). "The Bolshevik dilemma," observes Sheila Fitzpatrick, "was that policies of proletarian internationalism in practice had a disconcerting similarity to the policies of old style Russian imperialism" (*The Russian Revolution, 1917–1932* [Oxford: Oxford University Press, 1982], p. 63).
4. Edward W. Walker, *Dissolution: Sovereignty and the Breakup of the Soviet Union* (Boulder: Rowman and Littlefield, 2003), pp. 21–30, 184–187. For a discussion of the way "segmental institutions" would have unintended consequences for the dissolution of all three Communist federations see Philip G. Roeder, "The Triumph of Nation States: Lessons from the Collapse of the Soviet Union, Yugoslavia, and Czechoslovakia," in Michael McFaul and Kathryn Stoner-Weiss, eds., *After the Collapse of Communism: Comparative Lessons of Transition* (Cambridge: Cambridge University Press, 2004), pp. 51–57.
5. See also Valdimir Kusin, *Political Groupings in the Czechoslovak Reform Movement* (New York: Columbia University Press, 1972), pp. 143–150; Minton F. Goldman, "Roots and Causes of the Division of Czechoslovakia," in John Morison, ed., *Ethnic and National Issues in Russian and East European History* (London: Macmillan Press, 2000), pp. 296–323; and Carol Skalnik Leff, "Inevitability, Probability, Possibility: The Legacies of the Czech-Slovak Relationship, 1918–1919, and the Disintegration of the State," in Michael Kraus and Allison K. Stanger, eds., *Irreconcilable Differences?: Explaining Czechoslovakia's Dissolution* (Lanham, MD: Rowman and Littlefield, 2000), pp. 29–48.
6. John W. Mason, *The Dissolution of the Austro-Hungarian Empire, 1867–1918,* 2nd ed. (London: Longman, 1997).
7. Maria Dowling, *Czechoslovakia* (New York: Oxford University Press, 2002).
8. Dimitrije Djordjević, ed., *The Creation of Yugoslavia, 1914–1918* (Santa Barbara, CA: CLIO Books, 1980). See also Ivo Banac, *Raspad Jugoslavije: Eseji o nacionalizmu i nacionalnim sukobima* (Zagreb: Durieux, 2001), pp. 115–119.
9. Zdravko Mlinar, "Transformation of Political and Ethno-National Identities in the Balkans," in Alberto Gasparini and Vladimir Yadov, eds., *Social Actors in Redesigning the Civil Society of Eastern Europe* (Greenwich, CT: JAI Press, 1995), pp. 225–241.
10. James Seroka, "The Demise of Socialist Federations: Developmental Effects and Institutional Flaws of the Soviet Union, Yugoslavia, and Czechoslovakia," in Andreas Heinemann-Gruder, ed., *Federalism Doomed?* (New York: Berghahn Books, 2002), pp. 103–115.
11. Walker Conner, *The National Question in Marxist-Leninist Theory and Practice* (Princeton: Princeton University Press, 1984).
12. Richard Pipes, *Communism: A History* (New York: Modern Library, 2001), p. 154.
13. Claus Offe, *Varieties of Transition: The East European and East German Experience* (Cambridge: MIT Press, 1997), pp. 53–73.
14. "Nationalism," *Social Research*, Vol. 58, No. 4 (Winter 1991), p. 759.
15. Ibid.

16. *Ethnic Times: Exploring Ethnonationalism in the Former Yugoslavia* (Westport: Praeger, 2002), p. 171, see also pp. 4–6, 67–70, 87–93, 139–154.

17. Mirko Pejanović has observed that Kecmanović may have himself, for a time, become caught up in the emotional tide of ethnic nationalism (*Through Bosnian Eyes: The Political Memoirs of a Bosnian Serb* [Sarajevo: TKD Sahinpašić, 2002]).

18. See also Vjekoslav Perica, *Balkan Idols: Religion and Nationalism in Yugoslav States* (Oxford: Oxford University Press, 2002). For another view, see Dragutin Babić, "Suživot Hrvata i Srba u prijeratom, ratom, i poslijeratom razdoblju," *Migracije i etničke teme*, Vol. 2–3 (2004), pp. 187–208.

19. *Nationalist Mobilization and the Collapse of the Soviet State* (Cambridge: Cambridge University Press, 2002), pp. 34–35, and also pp. 147–149, 159–160, 200–202, 441–442, and 448–459. See also Astrid Tuminez, "Nationalism, Ethnic Pressures, and the Break-Up of the Soviet Union," *Journal of Cold War Studies*, Vol. 5, No. 4 (Fall 2003), pp. 81–135.

20. Ibid., p. 416.

21. Nicholas Sambanis has aptly noted that "even where narratives of elite-driven mobilization seem entirely plausible, we still need to explain which groups are likely to be mobilized and why? What type of person chooses to commit violence and why? . . . If people are prone to be manipulated we must understand the root of their fear and distrust which allow them to be manipulated. . . . Therefore elite-driven explanation of wars such as the Bosnian war must be interpreted within the context of a history of ethnic violence and prior conflict" ("Conclusion: Using Case Studies to Refine and Expand the Theory of Civil War," in Paul Collier and Nicholas Sambanis, eds., *Understanding Civil War, Volume II: Europe, Central Asia, and Other Regions* [Washington, D.C.: The World Bank, 2005], p. 322).

22. *Bratislava Pravda*, December 31, 2002 as translated in FBIS-EEU-2002-1231. See also Zdenka Mansfeldova, "The Czech and Slovak Republics," in Sten Berglund, Tomas Heller, and Frank H. Aarebrot, eds., *The Handbook of Political Change in Eastern Europe* (Cheltenham: Edward Elgar, 1998), pp. 191–230.

23. Aviel Roshwald, *Ethnic Nationalism and the Fall of Empires: Central Europe, Russia, and the Middle East, 1914–1923* (London: Routledge, 2001), p. 2.

24. Robert Strayer, "Decolonialization, Democratization, and Communist Reform: The Soviet Collapse in Comparative Perspective," *Journal of World History*, Vol. 12, No. 2 (2001), pp. 375–406; http://muse.jhu.edu.proxy.lib.sfu.ca/journals/journal_of_world_history/V012/12.2strayer.html.

25. John B. Allcock, *Explaining Yugoslavia* (New York: Columbia University Press, 2000), pp. 424–425. See also David N. Gibbs, "The Origins of the Yugoslav Conflict," paper presented at the Forty-Third Annual International Studies Convention, New Orleans, March 24–27, 2002, and Susan Woodward, "Costly Disinterest: Missed Opportunities for Preventive Diplomacy in Croatia and Bosnia and Herzegovina, 1985–1991," in Bruce W. Jentleson, ed., *Opportunities Missed, Opportunities Seized: Preventive Diplomacy in the Post-Cold War World* (Lanham, MD: Rowman and Littlefield, 2000), pp. 133–173.

26. Vladimir Goati has argued that up until the war in Slovenia in June 1991, "which marks the turning point after which the process of disintegration of SFRY became irreversible—international factors had played a minor role compared to internal ones" ("The Disintegration of Yugoslavia: The Role of Political Elites," *Nationalities Papers*, Vol. 25, No. 3 [1997], p. 456).

27. Davorka Ljubisic, *The Politics of Sorrow: The Disintegration of Yugoslavia* (Montreal: Black Rose Press, 2004), pp. xiii, 97, 175.

28. Michael Libal, *Limits of Persuasion: Germany and the Yugoslav Crisis, 1991–1992* (Westport: Praeger, 1997), p. 6. See also Hans-Dietrich Genscher, *Rebuilding a House Divided* (New York: Broadway Books, 1997), pp. 491–492, 514–521.

29. Looking back in September 2000, German Foreign Minister Voschka Fischer observed that the international community had "committed a mistake . . . recognition must be the result of peaceful development" (*Mladina*, March 12, 2001). See also Wolfgang F. Scholer, "Germany and the Break-Up of Yugoslavia," in Raj U. G. C. Thomas and H. Richard Friman, eds., *The South Slav Conflict* (New York: Garland, 1996), pp. 315–330, and Richard Caplan, *Europe and the Recognition of New States in Yugoslavia* (Cambridge: Cambridge University Press, 2005).

30. *BBC Monitoring International Reports,* January 15, 2002.

31. *Federal News Service,* July 8, 1992. See also James Baker III, *The Politics of Diplomacy: Revolution, War, and Peace, 1989–1992* (New York: GP Putnam and Sons, 1995).

32. *Federal News Service, Official Kremlin International News Broadcast,* April 12, 1999.

33. *Federal News Service,* October 22, 1991.

34. *CTK National News Wire,* May 12, 1992.

35. Michael Kraus, "The End of Czechoslovakia: International Forces and Factors," in Michael Kraus and Allison Stanger, *Irreconcilable Differences?: Explaining Czechoslovakia's Dissolution* (Lanham, MD: Rowman and Littlefield, 2000), pp. 199–221.

36. Robert Strayer, "Decolonialization, Democratization, and Communist Reform: The Soviet Collapse in Comparative Perspective," *Journal of World History,* Vol. 12, No. 2 (2001), pp. 375–406; http://muse.jhu.edu.proxy.lib.sfu.ca/journals/journal_of_world_history/V012/12.2strayer.html.

37. *Nationalist Mobilization and the Collapse of the Soviet State* (Cambridge: Cambridge University Press, 2002), p. 49.

38. Jack Snyder, *From Voting to Violence: Democratization and Nationalist Conflict* (New York: W. W. Norton Co., 2000), pp. 31–32. Leonid Kravchuk, Independent Ukraine's first president, once commented that "The disintegration of the Soviet Union could be traced to the beginning of perestroika—and we know exactly who the author of this break-up was" (quoted in Ben Fowkes, *The Disintegration of the Soviet Union: A Study in the Rise and Triumph of Nationalism* [London: Macmillan Press, 1997], p. 196). On the democratic and nondemocratic aspects of the USSR's dissolution, see also Feoder Burlatsky, "Who or What Broke Up the Soviet Union?" in Meta Spencer, ed., *Separatism: Democracy and Disintegration* (Boulder: Rowman and Littlefield, 1998), pp. 139–160.

39. "Havel Goes, Who's Next," *Moscow News,* July 12, 1992.

40. *The Origins of Post-Communist Elites: From Prague Spring to the Breakup of Czechoslovakia* (Minnesota: University of Minnesota Press, 2003), pp. xx–xxi, 136–237, 140–143, 150–183, 194–196.

41. Dejan Guzina, drawing on the observations of the Croatian journalist Jelena Lovrić, has pointed out that the purge of liberal leader Marko Nikezić and his followers in Serbia in 1972 helped pave the way for the antiliberal and populist wave in the 1980s ("Why Yugoslavia Failed," *Federations,* Vol. 4, No. 1 [March 2004], p. 12).

42. On the critical role of the conceptual conflict over the reform of the political and economic system as a cause of Yugoslavia's disintegration, see Dejan Jović, *Jugoslavija: Država koja je odumrla: Uspon, Kriza i pad Kardeljeve Jugoslavije* (Zagreb: Prometej, 2003), and the interesting evaluation of that view in Aleksandar Pavković, "Why Did Yugoslavia Disintegrate? Is there a Conclusive Answer?" *Journal of Southeastern Europe and the Balkans,* Vol. 6, No. 3 (December 2004), pp. 299–306.

43. "One Hypothesis on the Different Outcomes of Soviet and Yugoslav Collapse," *East European Studies, Meeting Reports*, Woodrow Wilson International Center for Scholars (2002) http://wwics.si.edu/topics/pubs/mr274vujacic.doc. See also Vujačić's "Perceptions of the State in Russia and Serbia: The Role of Ideas in the Soviet and Yugoslav Collapse," *Post-Soviet Affairs*, Vol. 20, No. 2 (2004), pp. 164–194.

44. On the relationship between the Russian intelligentsia's traditional distrust of government and Gorbachev's failure to intellectually comprehend the complexities of regime transition or employ a more robust response to federal breakdown, see Jerry Hough, *Democratization and Revolution in the USSR, 1985–1991* (Washington, D.C.: Brookings Institution Press, 1997), pp. 491–492.

45. Andranik Migranyan, "Prospects for the Russian National Movement: The Former Empire after the Putsch," *Nezavisimaya gazeta* (November 14, 1991), p. 5, in *Current Digest of the Soviet Press*, Vol. XLIII, No. 47 (December 25, 1991), p. 9.

46. "Lessons from the Breakup of Czechoslovakia," in Michael Kraus and Allison Stanger, *Irreconcilable Differences: Explaining Czechoslovakia's Dissolution* (Lanman, MD.: Rowman and Littlefield, 2000), p. 300.

47. *Czechoslovakia and Yugoslavia: Ethnic Conflict and the Dissolution of Multinational States* (Berkeley: International and Area Studies, 1997), pp. 54–55.

48. *Subversive Institutions: The Design and the Destruction of Socialism and the State* (Cambridge: Cambridge University Press, 1999), pp. 122–124.

49. *On My Country and the World* (New York: Columbia University Press, 2000), pp. 63, 102–103, 119, 151, 157–159.

50. *Official Kremlin International Broadcast*, August 24, 1992.

51. "Collapse of the Soviet Union: Leadership, Elites, and Legitimacy," in Geir Lundestade, ed., *The Fall of Great Powers: Peace, Stability, and Legitimacy* (New York: Oxford University Press, 1994), p. 168. Gorbachev may have deliberately looked aside when hardliners planned and used limited force in Lithuania in early 1991. An elite unit of the KGB stormed a television station killing 14 persons. Jerry Hough suggests that rather than take direct action involving naked force, Gorbachev chose to send a "message" to the Lithuanians and other secessionists that if they did not cooperate, the conservatives at the center would act and he could not stop them. Instead, Gorbachev's tactic displeased all sides and only accelerated the drift toward dissolution (*Democratization and Revolution*, op. cit., pp. 398–400).

52. *BBC*, March 3, 1992.

53. *Washington Post*, July 21, 1992, p. A1.

54. *Guardian*, September 25, 1992.

55. Slavenka Drakulić points out that "Milošević would have us believe he would never hurt a fly, and very possibly it is true. The more I see of the individual cases of war criminals, the less I believe them to be monsters. As far as I know, Milošević never killed anybody himself. But he is on trial because he is a murderer. He is on trial because, even though he may never have lifted a finger in violence, his decade-long murderous nationalist politics created the conditions that produced hatred and killings and threw Yugoslavia, into a whirlpool of death and chaos" (*Los Angeles Times*, August 5, 2004). On the admixture of elite-driven factors and contextual factors related to historical ethnic antagonism in Yugoslavia's breakup, see also Lenard J. Cohen, *Serpent in the Bosom: The Rise and Fall of Slobodan Milošević* (Boulder: Westview Press, 2001).

56. In transcripts from a meeting held on July 31, 1995, planning Croatian military operations, Tudjman urged that the Serbs in Croatia "should be struck in such a way that they disappear from Croatia forever" (*Novi list* [October 12, 2004]). Tudjman's son

claims that his father's remarks are taken out of context and that the reference was to striking military formations, not the "Serbian people" (HRTVITV, Zagreb, October 12, 2004).

57. Janez Drnovšek, "Riding the Tiger: The Dissolution of Yugoslavia," *World Policy Journal*, Vol. HVII, No. 1 (Spring 2000), http://www.worldpolicy.org/journal/wpj00–1.html.

58. International Criminal Tribunal of the Former Yugoslavia, Transcript, May 21, 2003, pp. 20906–20918. Warren Zimmerman has felicitously described the Slovene role in the violent end of Yugoslavia: "In a lightening maneuver, the Slovenes had in a few hours moved the borders of Yugoslavia, stable for a half a century, a hundred miles to the east. It was the first act of war . . . even an army less primitive than the JNA would have reacted to a power play that annexed both the borders of Yugoslavia and its custom's revenues. . . . The Slovene defection set in motion the dynamics of a Serb-Croat confrontation that was also the lead to war in Bosnia" (*Origins of a Catastrophe* [New York: Random House, 1996], pp. 142–143, 146).

59. International Criminal Tribunal for the Former Yugoslavia, Transcript (November 18, 2003), pp. 29127–29159.

60. *Poslednji dani SFRJ: izvodi iz dnevnika* (Belgrade: Politika, 1995).

61. "Violent Dissolution of Yugoslavia: Causes, Dynamics, and Effects," (Belgrade, March 5–6, 2004); http://www.ccmr-bg-org/vesti/fromccmr0004.htm.

62. *Moje vidjenje raspada-Vojska bez države* (Belgrade: Politika, 1993).

63. *Sve moje bitke* (Zagreb: Vlastita naklada, 1996).

64. *BBC Summary of World Broadcasts*, March 16, 1991.

65. Indeed, the military would probably have followed orders to have preserved the USSR had Gorbachev ordered them to do so (Jerry Hough, *Democratization and Resolution in the USSR, 1985–1991* [Washington, D.C.: Brookings Institution Press, 1997], p. 488).

66. Omer Fisher, "Transition and Disruption: The Yugoslav Case in Comparative Perspective," in Dimitris Keridis and Charles M. Parry, eds., *New Approaches to Balkan Studies* (Dulles, VA: Brassey's, 2003), pp. 149–183.

67. Ibid.

68. Valerie Bunce, *Subversive Institutions: The Design and the Destruction of Socialism and the State* (Cambridge: Cambridge University Press, 1999), see chapter 6.

69. Michael Kraus and Allison Stanger, "Lessons from the Breakup," in Michael Kraus and Allison Stanger, *Irreconcilable Differences?: Explaining Czechoslovakia's Dissolution* (Lanham, MD: Rowman and Littlefield, 2000), p. 300.

70. *BBC Monitoring International Reports*, April 18, 2002.

71. Laura Laubeova, "The Fiction of Ethnic Homogeneity: Minorities in the Czech Republic," and Jan Bucek, "Responding to Diversity: Solutions at the Local Level in Slovakia," in Anna-Maria Biro and Petra Kovacs, eds., *Diversity in Action* (Budapest: Local Government and Public Service Reform Initiative, 2001), pp. 135–170, and 273–306.

72. *Mlada fronta DNS* (Prague) (April 22, 2004) as translated in FBIS-EEU-2004–0422.

73. Juraj Buzaka, "Is Rural Population on the Decline: Continuities and Changes in Twentieth Century Central Europe—The Case of Slovakia," *Sussex European Institute Working Paper*, No. 73, p. 31.

74. Rebecca S. K. Li, "Why Territorial Disintegration Has not Occurred in Russia: Applying State Breakdown Theories to Explain Stability," *Sociological Inquiry*, Vol. 73, No. 3 (August 2003), pp. 387–412.

75. Gail W. Lapidus, "Ethnicity and State-Building: Accommodating Ethnic Differences in Post-Soviet Eurasia," in Mark R. Beissinger, ed., *Beyond State Crisis?: Post-Colonial Africa*

and Post-Soviet Eurasia in Comparative Perspective (Washington, D.C.: Woodrow Wilson Center Press, 2002), pp. 323–358.

76. *Federal News Service*, Official Kremlin International News Broadcast, December 18, 2003.

77. http://www.gl7plus.org.yu as translated in FBIS-EEU-2003–0925.

78. Ljubljana STA, April 30, 2004, as translated in FBIS-EEU-2004–0430.

79. *BBC Worldwide Monitoring Service*, April 25, 2005. President Putin clarified his remarks regarding the USSR's breakup shortly afterward: "As for the tragedy I have referred to, it is obvious. . . . We have a current saying: those who do not regret the collapse of the Soviet Union have no heart, and those who regret it have no head. We do not regret it. We simply recognize the fact and we know that we should look forward and not backward. . . . But we should have a clear understanding of what happened" (*Official Kremlin International News Broadcast*, May 6, 2005).

CONTRIBUTORS

Dr. Florian Bieber is a lecturer in East European Politics at the University of Kent, Canterbury (UK). He received his M.A. in Political Science and History and his Ph.D. in Political Science from the University of Vienna, as well as an M.A. in Southeast European Studies from Central European University (Budapest). Between 2001 and 2006, he has been working in Belgrade (Serbia) and Sarajevo (Bosnia-Herzegovina) for the European Centre for Minority Issues. Dr. Bieber is also a visiting professor at the Nationalism Studies Program at Central European University; at the Regional Masters Program for Democracy and Human Rights at the University of Sarajevo; and the Interdisciplinary Master in East European Studies and Research (MIREES), University of Bologna. He has been an international policy fellow of the Open Society Institute. His research interests include institutional design in multiethnic states, nationalism and ethnic conflict, as well as the political systems of South-eastern Europe. He published articles on institutional design, nationalism, and politics in South-eastern Europe in *Nationalities Papers, Third World Quarterly, Current History, International Journal of Politics, Culture and Society, International Peacekeeping, Ethnopolitcs,* and other journals. He is the author of *Nationalism in Serbia: From the Death of Tito to the Fall of Miloševi* (Münster: Lit Verlag, 2005, in German) and *Post-War Bosnia: Ethnic Structure, Inequality and Governance of the Public Sector* (London: Palgrave, 2005), and he edited and co-edited four books on South-eastern Europe.

Dr. Mark Biondich is an analyst with the Crimes Against Humanity and War Crimes Section, Department of Justice Canada, and adjunct research professor at the Institute of European and Russian Studies, Carleton University in Ottawa, Canada. He obtained his Ph.D. in history from the University of Toronto (1997) and is the author of *Stjepan Radić, the Croat Peasant Party and the Politics of Mass Mobilization, 1904–1928* (2000), several articles on fascism and clericalism in Croatia, and Yugoslav history and politics. He is currently completing his second book, *A History of Croatian Fascism: The Ustaša Movement, 1929–1945.*

Audrey H. Budding received her Ph.D. in History from Harvard University, where she also held a post-doctoral fellowship at the Harvard Academy for International and Area Studies and served as a lecturer on Social Studies. Her articles have appeared in *Nationalities Papers, Harvard Ukrainian Studies,* and *Contemporary European History.*

Lenard J. Cohen is a professor in the School for International Studies at Simon Fraser University, Vancouver, British Columbia. His research has specialized on political change in Southeastern Europe, and his books include *Serpent in the Bosom: The Rise and Fall of Slobodan Milosevic* (Second edition, 2001); *Broken Bonds: Yugoslavia's Disintegration and Balkan Politics in Transition* (Second edition, 1995); and *The Socialist Pyramid: Elites and Power in Yugoslavia* (1990). He is currently working on a study of post-conflict state-building and democratization in the Western Balkans.

Jasna Dragović-Soso is lecturer in International Relations at Goldsmiths College, University of London, where she teaches courses on international relations, nationalist conflict and international intervention. She is the author of '*Saviours of the Nation*': *Serbia's Intellectual Opposition and the Revival of Nationalism* (Hurst & Co. and McGill-Queen's University Press, 2002) and a number of articles and book chapters on intellectuals, nationalism, and international intervention in the former Yugoslavia. Her current research is focused on international intervention, transitional justice, and confrontation with the recent past in the post-Yugoslav states.

Eric Gordy is senior lecturer in the Department of Social Sciences at the School of Slavonic and East European Studies of University College London. He is the author of *The Culture of Power in Serbia* (1999), in addition to articles on contemporary Balkan politics and culture, international law, and problems of "democracy assistance." He has been a fellow of the Collegium Budapest Institute for Advanced Study (Hungary), the Jefferson Institute (Serbia), the Center for European Studies at Harvard University (United States), and the Istituto per l'Europa Centro-Orientale e Balcanica (Italy).

Jill Irvine received her Ph.D. from Harvard University and is currently associate professor of Religious Studies and director of Women's Studies at the University of Oklahoma. She is author of *The Croat Question, Partisan Politics in the Formation of the Yugoslav Socialist State* (Westview, 1994) and co-editor of *State-Society Relations in Yugoslavia, 1945–1991* (St Martin's Press, 1997). She has written a number of articles, book chapters, and government reports about ethno-religious movements and ideologies as well as gender and democratization in the Balkans. She is currently working on a co-edited volume entitled *Gender and Democratization in Societies at War* forthcoming with Penn State University Press and a co-edited diary entitled *Natalija, Life in the Balkan Powderkeg, 1886–1956* forthcoming with Central European University Press.

Dejan Jović is director of the Centre for European Neighbourhood Studies (CENS) and lecturer in Politics at University of Stirling in Scotland, UK. He is author of a book on disintegration of Yugoslavia (*Jugoslavija—država koja je odumrla*) and holds a Ph.D. from London School of Economics and Political Science.

Predrag J. Marković is senior research fellow at the Institute for Contemporary History, Belgrade, where he works on social and cultural history. He is the author of *Beograd i Evropa, 1918–1941, (Belgrade and Europe)* (1992); *Beograd izmedju Istoka i Zapada 1948–1965, (Belgrade Between East and West)* (1996); *Ethnic Stereotypes: Ubiquitous, Local, or Migrating Phenomena? The Serbian-Albanian Case* (2003); and co-author of *Moderna srpska država 1804–2004: hronologija (The Modern Serbian State: A Chronology)* (2004).

Nick Miller is professor of history at Boise State University. He is the author of *Between Nation and State: Serbian Politics in Croatia Before the First World War* (Pittsburgh, 1997), *The Nonconformists: Culture, Politics, and Nationalism in a Serbian Intellectual Circle, 1944–1991* (Central European University Press, 2007), and numerous articles on Serbian and Yugoslav history.

Michael Palairet was reader in European Economic History at the University of Ediburgh until he retired in 2005. He is author of *The Balkan Economies c. 1800–1914: Evolution Without Development* (CUP, 1998), which has also been translated into Bulgarian and Turkish, and *The Four Ends of the Greek Hyperinflation of 1941–1946*. In addition, he has recently written many published articles, mainly on contemporary Yugoslav economic history. He lives part of the year in Edinburgh and part in Ohrid, where his new apartment gives a glorious view of the lake. Appropriately, he is now researching the history of Macedonia in the Byzantine era.

Stevan K. Pavlowitch is emeritus professor of History at the University of Southampton (UK). His latest book, *Hitler's New Disorder, The Second World War in Yugoslavia, 1941–1945,* is to be published at the end of 2007.

Dennison Rusinow, who was tragically killed while this book was in progress, received his B.A. from Duke University and his M.A. and D.Phil. from Oxford, where he was a Rhodes Scholar at New College and St. Antony's. His dissertation, under the supervision of Bill (later Sir William) Deakin, led to his interest in nationalism and later Yugoslavia where he reported for 23 years for the American Universities Field Staff from Zagreb, Belgrade, and Vienna. When the organization closed, he moved to the University of Pittsburgh as a research professor in the University Center for International Studies. Apart from more than 70 reports for the Field Staff, he was the author of *Italy's Austrian Heritage* (Oxford University Press, 1969) and *The Yugoslav Experiment* (C. Hurst, London, 1977).

Paul Shoup taught in the Department of Government and Foreign Affairs at the University of Virginia until his retirement in 1999. He has been the recipient of numerous fellowships and grants to carry out research on Eastern European politics and the national question in Yugoslavia. He served twice as the director of the

Center for Russian and East European Studies at the University of Virginia, and was president of the American Association for Southeast European Studies between 1985 and 1989. His dissertation, *Communism and the Yugoslav National Question*, was published by Columbia University Press (1968). He was editor of *Problems of Balkan Security: Southeastern Europe in the 1990s* (Woodrow Wilson Press, 1990); co-editor of *Bosna i Hercegovina izmedju rata i mira* (Belgrade: Institut drustvenih nauka, 1992); co-editor of *The Yugoslav War, Europe and the Balkans* (Ravenna: Longo, 1995); and co-editor of *Post Communist Transition as a European Problem* (Ravenna: Longo, 2002). With Steven Burg, he co-authored *The War in Bosnia Herzegovina: Ethnic Conflict and International Intervention* (M.E. Sharpe, 1999), which received the Ralph J. Bunche award of the American Political Science Association in 2000 for the best scholarly work appearing in 1999 dealing with the phenomenon of ethnic and cultural pluralism.

Andrew Wachtel is Bertha and Max Dressler Professor in the Humanities at Northwestern University, where he serves as dean of the graduate school and director of the Roberta Buffett Center for International and Comparative Studies. His interests range from Russian literature and culture to East European and Balkan culture, history, and politics. His most recent books are *Remaining Relevant After Communism: The Role of the Writer in Eastern Europe* (U. of Chicago Press, 2006) and *Plays of Expectations: Intertextual Relations in Russian 20th-Century Drama* (REECAS/U. of Washington Press, 2006). His book, *The Balkans in World History*, will be published by Oxford University Press in 2008.

INDEX

A

Adžić, Blagoje, 319, 322, 323, 384
Adriatic concept debate, 134
Agani, Fehmi, 194, 200
Aggressive nationalism, 2
Agreement of Socialist Republics and
    Autonomous Provinces (1981), 207
Agrocomerc scandal (1987), 233
Albanian
    intellectuals and, 192–194
    nationalism and, 140
    nationalist movement and, 193–194
Aleksandar, King
    dictatorship and, 45–46, 47
    National Parliament and, 45
    see also Interwar period; Political
    system
Alexander, Prince, 78
Allcock, John, 12, 375
Alliance of Reserve Army
    Officers (SRVS), 305
Allied Powers, 84
American foreign policy, 333, 338,
    340, 343
American neoliberal economic policies, 23
American Press, 343
Anderson, David, 339
Andrić, Ivo, 211
Anthropo-geography, 79
"Anti-bureaucratic" revolution, 232
Anti-Fascist Council of National Liberation
    of Yugoslavia (AVNOJ), 131
    Presidium, 99
    see also Partisan legacy
Antologija jugoslovenske misli i narodnog
    jedinstva, 205
Anzulović, Branimir, 18
Army structure, Yugoslavian, 302–305
Atanacković, Borisav, 241

Austro-Hungarian compromise (1867), 79
Autonomous province (pokrajina),
    102, 141
    see also Albanian nationalist
    movement; National question
Autonomous region (oblast), 97, 270
    see also Albanian nationalist
    movement; National question
AVNOJ. *See* Anti-Fascist Council of
    National Liberation of Yugoslavia
    (AVNOJ)
Axis Powers, 84

B

Badinter Commission. *See* European
    Community (EC) Arbitration
    Commission
Bakalli, Mahmut, 193
Bakarić, Vladimir, 154, 161, 162, 166
Baker, James, 345, 376
Balkan Tragedy (1995), 23
Balkan wars, 76, 97
    see also Longue durée
Balšić, Jelena, 210–211
Banac, Ivo, 5–6
Banking system, 229, 245
    see also Inter-regional resource
    flows (1980s)
Bankruptcy, 235, 236
Banovine, 61, 98
Barac, Antun, 205
Basanček, Djuro, 59, 60
Bekić, Darko, 271, 272
Belgrade
    agreement of 2003 and, 251
    air force and, 311
    American air raid and, 336
    army and, 310–311
    Croat Bloc and, 53

P

Pan-Serbian policy, 18
Paraćin massacre 311
Paris Club bankers, 234
Paris Peace Conference, 52
Paris peace settlement, 78
Parliamentary system, 45, 47
Partisan legacy, 153–155,
  163–164, 308
Pašić, Nikola, 50, 58, 59
Pašic-Pribicević (NRS-SDS) minority
  coalition government, 56
Pavček, Tone, 189
Pavelić, Ante, 62, 80
Pavković, Aleksandar, 7, 8, 18, 19
Peasant-Democratic Coalition (SDK),
  59–60
Perica, Vjekoslav, 171
Perović, Latinka, 139, 142, 143
Personal nationality, 101–104
Personal regime, 46
Peter II, King, 79
Peterle, Lojze, 253, 261
Petrović, Nastas, 58
Petrović, Veljko, 211
PHARE program, 272
Pirker, Pero, 141, 153
Planinc, Milka, 337
PNP. *See* Temporary National
  Representation (PNP)
Pobjeda (newspaper), 211
Political and intellectual agency, role of
  Croatian Spring political movement
    and, 17, 20, 22
  Croatian War of Independence
    (1991-1995) and, 19
  decentralization and, 17, 18
  disintegration and, 14, 15, 18
  ethnic cleansing policy and,
    15, 16, 19
  "Greater Serbia" and, 14, 16, 18, 19
  mobilization and, 21, 22–23
  pro-Yugoslav alternatives and, 17,
    19–20
  Serbian Academy's SANU draft
    Memorandum (1986) and, 14,
    18–19, 20
  see also Dissolution, scholarships of
Political-Cultural Values, 380–381

Political debates (1980s), 10
Political decentralization, 133
Political evolution, 58
Political factories, 133
Political homogeneity, 20
Political ideologies, 5, 9
Political leadership, 287–288
Political system
  Aleksandar, King and, 61, 63
  Bled Agreement and, 53
  centralism and, 50–51
  Constituent Assembly and, 52–55
  Croat Bloc and, 53
  federalism and, 51–52, 60–61
  Law for the Protection of the State
    against the HRSS and, 56
  Mehmed Spaho's Yugoslav Muslim
    Organization (JMO) and, 53,
    54, 56
  Sporazum Agreement and, 54, 62
  unitarists and, 50, 51, 55
  Vidovdan Constitution and, 53,
    56, 60
  Yugoslav unification and, 52–53
*The Politics of Ethnicization and Nationalist
  Mobilization,* 371–374
The Politics of Transition and Reform,
  377–379
Poos, Jacques, 344
Popit, France, 312
Popov, Stole, 209
Popović, Jovan, 209
Potočnik, Peter, 266
Pribićević, Svetozar, 46, 51, 60
Price systems, 136
"A Proposal for Reflection," 140
Protestant-Catholic watershed, 4
Protić, Stojan, 50, 58
Provincial committees (pokrajinski), 95
Pro-Yugoslav alternatives, 17, 19, 26, 48
Pučnik, Jože, 271

Q

Qosja, Rexhep, 194, 195

R

Račić, Puniša, 59
Racin, Kočo, 209

Milošević's political ambitions and,
283–285
political leadership and, insecurity of,
287–288
Yugoslavia and its Historians, 351
Yugoslavia in Crisis (1989), 235
Yugoslavism
defined, 101
dictatorship and, 45–46
Milošević and, perceptions of, 16
national ideology and, 7, 8
vs. particularist nationalisms concerns
and, 8–9
pro-Yugoslav alternatives and, 17
pro-Yugoslav faction and, 215
Yugoslavist project, 62
Yugoslav Muslim Organization (JMO), 48,
53, 54, 56, 59
Yugoslav National Army, 244, 245, 306
Yugoslav National Party (JNS), 61–62
Yugoslav People's Army (JNA), 245, 252,
254, 259
Yugoslav state (1918)
Axis Powers and, 84
CPY and, 94
Constituent Assembly and, 52
Croatina Sabor (diet) and, 52
founding fathers and, 75
history of, formation and the, 48–49
interwar Yugoslavia and, 45

KPJ and, 51–52
Muslim autonomist movement and, 54
national parliament and, 61
Paris peace settlement and, 78
political reformation and, 51
religious incompatibilities and, 4
restructuring and, fundamental, 255
Sporazum Agreement and, 62–63
Treaty of London and, 7
Western policy and, 26
Yugoslav People's Army (JNA) and,
17–18
Yugoslav system and, 12
Yugoslav unification and, 52
Yugoslav system, 11, 12, 22

Z

Zagreb army, 310–311
Zagreb University, 155
Žarković, Vidoje, 171
ZAVNOH council, 153, 155–158,
162–163
Zemun air force, 311
Zimmermann, Warren, 338–339, 343–345
Živković, General Petar, 61
Zlobec, Ciril, 213
ZSMS. *See* Socialist Youth Organization
(ZSMS)
Župančič, Oton, 209